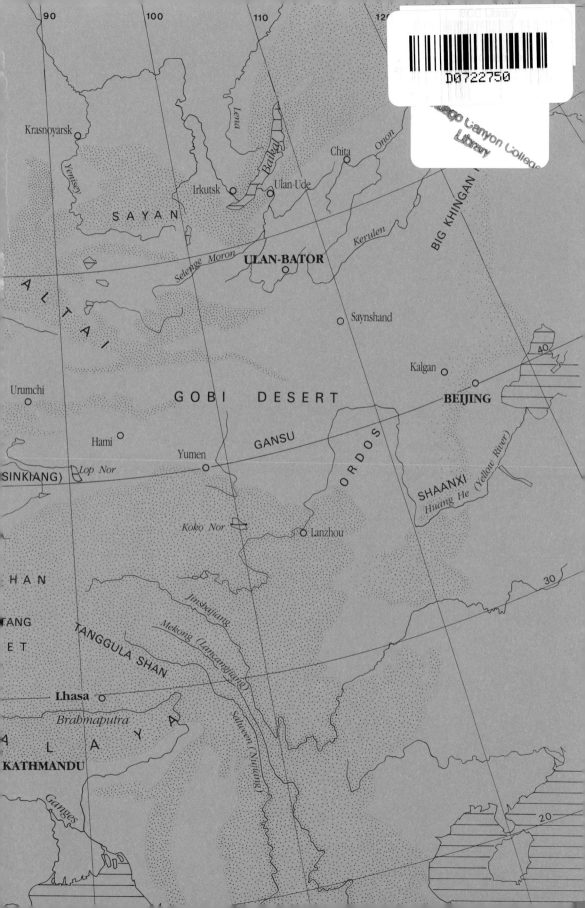

History of civilizations of Central Asia

Volume I
The dawn of civilization:
earliest times to 700 B.C.

Volume II
The development of sedentary and nomadic civilizations:
700 B.C. to A.D. 250

Volume III
The crossroads of civilizations:
A.D. 250 to 750

Volume IV
The age of achievement:
A.D. 750 to the end of the fifteenth century:
Part I:
The historical, social and economic setting
Part II:
The achievements

Volume V
Development in contrast:
from the sixteenth to the mid-nineteenth century

Volume VI
Towards contemporary civilization:
from the mid-nineteenth century
to the present time

History of civilizations of Central Asia

Volume III

The crossroads of civilizations:
A.D. 250 to 750

Editor: B. A. Litvinsky
Co-editors:
Zhang Guang-da
and R. Shabani Samghabadi

Multiple History Series

UNESCO Publishing

Published in 1996 by the United Nations Educational,
Scientific and Cultural Organization
7 place de Fontenoy, 75352 Paris 07 SP

Compiled by I. Iskender-Mochiri
Text revision by Dr D. W. MacDowall
English text edited by Jana Gough

Composed by Éditions du Mouflon, 94270 Le Kremlin-Bicêtre (France)
Printed by Imprimerie Darantiere, 21800 Quétigny (France)

ISBN 92-3-103211-9

PREFACE

Federico Mayor
Director-General of UNESCO

O NE of the purposes of UNESCO, as proclaimed in its Constitution, is 'to develop and to increase the means of communication between ... peoples and to employ these means for the purposes of mutual understanding and a truer and more perfect knowledge of each other's lives'. The *History of the Scientific and Cultural Development of Mankind*, published in 1968, was a major early response on the part of UNESCO to the task of enabling the peoples of the world to have a keener sense of their collective destiny by highlighting their individual contributions to the history of humanity. This universal history – itself now undergoing a fundamental revision – has been followed by a number of regional projects, including the *General History of Africa* and the planned volumes on Latin America, the Caribbean and on aspects of Islamic culture. The *History of Civilizations of Central Asia* is an integral part of this wider enterprise.

It is appropriate that the second of UNESCO's regional histories should be concerned with Central Asia. For, like Africa, Central Asia is a region whose cultural heritage has tended to be excluded from the main focus of historical attention. Yet from time immemorial the area has served as the generator of population movements within the Eurasian land-mass. The history of the ancient and medieval worlds, in particular, was shaped to an important extent by the succession of peoples that arose out of the steppe, desert, oases and mountain ranges of this vast area extending from the Caspian Sea to the high plateaux of Mongolia. From the Cimmerians mentioned in Homer's *Odyssey*, the Scythians described by Herodotus, the Hsiung-nu whose incursions led the emperors of China to build the Great Wall, the sixth-century Türks who extended their empire to the boundaries of Byzantium, the Khitans who gave their name to ancient Cathay, through to the Mongols who erupted into world history in the thirteenth century under Genghis Khan, the nomadic horsemen of Central Asia helped to define the limits and test the mettle of the great civilizations of Europe and Asia.

Nor is it sufficient to identify the peoples of Central Asia simply with nomadic cultures. This is to ignore the complex symbiosis within Central Asia itself between nomadism and settlement, between pastoralists and agriculturalists. It is to overlook above all the burgeoning of the great cities of Central Asia such as Samarkand, Bukhara and Khiva, which established themselves in the late Middle Ages as outstanding centres of intellectual inquiry and artistic creation. The seminal writings of the philosopher-scientist Avicenna (a native of Bukhara) and the timeless masterpieces of Timurid architecture epitomize the flowering of medieval culture in the steppes and deserts of Central Asia.

The civilizations of Central Asia did not, of course, develop in a vacuum. The impact of Islam was pervasive and fundamental. The great civilizations on the periphery of the Eurasian continent likewise exerted an important influence on these lands. For some 1,500 years this arid inland sea – far removed from the earth's true oceans – was crucial as the route along which merchandise (notably silk) and ideas flowed between China, India, Iran and Europe. The influence of Iran – although the core of its civilization lies in South-West Asia – was particularly strong, to the extent that it is sometimes difficult to establish a clear boundary between the civilization of the Iranian motherland and that of the outlying lands of Central Asia.

To the rich variety of peoples of Central Asia was thus added a multiplicity of external influences. For century after century, the region experienced the influx of foreign art and ideas, colliding and merging with the indigenous patterns of Central Asia. Migrations and the recurrent shock of military invasion, mingling and displacing peoples and cultures, combined to maintain the vast region in flux.

The systole and diastole of population movements down the ages add to the difficulty of delimiting a region whose topology alone does not prescribe clear boundaries. Thus, when, at the nineteenth session of its General Conference, UNESCO decided to embark on a *History of Civilizations of Central Asia* the first problem to be resolved was to define the scope of the region concerned. Subsequently, at a UNESCO meeting held in 1978, it was agreed that the study on Central Asia should deal with the civilizations of Afghanistan, north-eastern Iran, Pakistan, northern India, western China, Mongolia and the former Soviet Central Asian republics. The appellation 'Central Asia', as employed in this *History*, refers to this area, which corresponds to a clearly discernible cultural and historical reality.

UNESCO's call to specialists, and particularly to scholars native to the region, to participate in the undertaking met with a wide and generous response. The project was deemed by academics to be an excellent opportunity to draw back the curtain that had veiled Central Asia for so long. However, none were in any doubt as to the huge dimensions of the task.

An ad hoc International Scientific Committee was formed in 1980 to plan and prepare the work, which it was agreed should cover, in six volumes, the history of Central Asia from earliest times to the present day. The Committee's initial task was to decide where pre-eminence should be given in the very wide canvas before it. In due course, a proper balance was struck and teams of editors and authors were selected.

The preparation of the *History of Civilizations of Central Asia* is now well advanced. The best resources of research and archaeology have been used to make the work as thorough as possible, and countless annals consulted in major centres throughout the region. It is my sincere wish that this, the third volume, and those that follow will bring instruction and pleasure to readers all over the world.

It remains for me to thank the President, Rapporteur and members of the International Scientific Committee, and the editors, authors and teams of specialists who have collaborated to shed new light on Central Asia with this detailed account of its vital and stirring past. I am sure it will prove a notable contribution to the study and mutual appreciation of the cultures that are the common heritage of mankind.

CONTENTS

DESCRIPTION OF THE PROJECT

M. S. Asimov

T HE General Conference of UNESCO, at its nineteenth session (Nairobi, October, November 1976),adopted the resolution which authorized the Director-General to undertake, among other activities aimed at promoting appreciation and respect for cultural identity, a new project on the preparation of a *History of Civilizations of Central Asia.* This project was a natural consequence of a pilot project on the study of Central Asia which was approved during the fourteenth session of the UNESCO General Conference in November 1966.

The purpose of this pilot project, as it was formulated in the UNESCO programme, was to make better known the civilizations of the peoples living in the regions of Central Asia through studies of their archaeology, history, languages and literature. At its initial stage, the participating Member States included Afghanistan, India, Iran, Pakistan and the former Soviet Union. Later, Mongolia and China joined the UNESCO Central Asian project, thus enlarging the area to cover the cultures of Mongolia and the western regions of China.

In this work, Central Asia should be understood as a cultural entity developed in the course of the long history of civilizations of peoples of the region and the above delimitation should not be taken as rigid boundaries either now or in the future.

In the absence of any existing survey of such large scope which could have served as a model, UNESCO has had to proceed by stages in this difficult task of presenting an integrated narrative of complex historical events from earliest times to the present day.

The first stage was designed to obtain better knowledge of the civilizations of Central Asia by encouraging archaeological and historical research and the study of literature and the history of science. A new project was therefore launched to promote studies in five major domains: the archaeology and the history of the Kushan Empire, the history of the arts of Central Asia, the contribution of the peoples of Central Asia to the development of science, the history of ideas and philosophy, and the literatures of Central Asia.

An International Association for the Study of Cultures of Central Asia (IASCCA), a non-governmental scholarly organization, was founded on the initiative of the Tajik scholar B. Gafurov in 1973, assembling scholars of the area for the co-ordination of interdisciplinary studies of their own cultures and the promotion of regional and international co-operation.

Created under the auspices of UNESCO, the new Association became, from the very beginning of its activity, the principal consultative body of UNESCO in the implementation of its programme on the study of Central Asian cultures and the preparation of a *History of Civilizations of Central Asia.*

The second stage concentrated on the modern aspects of Central Asian civilizations and the eastward extension of the geographical boundaries of re-search in the new programme. A series of international scholarly conferences and symposia were organized in the countries of the area to promote studies on Central Asian cultures.

Two meetings of experts, held in 1978 and 1979 at UNESCO Headquar-ters, concluded that the project launched in 1967 for the study of cultures of Central Asia had led to considerable progress in research and contributed to strengthening existing institutions in the countries of the region. The experts consequently advised the Secretariat on the methodology and the preparation of the *History.* On the basis of its recommendations it was decided that this publication should consist of six volumes covering chronologically the whole history of Central Asian civilizations ranging from their very inception up to the present. Furthermore, the experts recommended that the experience ac-quired by UNESCO during the preparation of the *History of Scientific and Cultural Development of Mankind* and of the *General History of Africa* should also be taken into account by those responsible for the drafting of the *History.* As to its presentation, they supported the opinion expressed by the UNESCO Secretariat that the publication, while being a scholarly work, should be acces-sible to a general readership.

Since history constitutes an uninterrupted sequence of events, it was de-cided not to give undue emphasis to any specific date. Events preceding or subsequent to those indicated here are dealt with in each volume whenever their inclusion is justified by the requirements of scholarship.

The third and final stage consisted of setting up in August 1980 an Inter-national Scientific Committee of nineteen members, who sit in a personal ca-pacity, to take reponsibility for the preparation of the *History.* The Committee thus created included two scholars from each of the seven Central Asian coun-tries – Afghanistan, China, India, Islamic Republic of Iran, Pakistan, Mongolia and the former USSR – and five experts from other countries - Hungary, Japan, Turkey, the United Kingdom and the United States of America.

The Committee's first session was held at UNESCO Headquarters in December 1980. Real work on the preparation of the publication of the *His-tory of Civilizations of Central Asia* started, in fact, in 1981. It was decided that scholars selected by virtue of their qualifications and achievements relating to Central Asian history and culture should ensure the objective presentation, and also the high scientific and intellectual standard, of this *History*.

Members of the International Scientific Committee decided that the new project should correspond to the noble aims and principles of UNESCO and thereby should contribute to the promotion of mutual understanding and peace between nations. The Committee followed the recommendation of the experts delineating for the purpose of this work the geographical area of Central Asia to reflect the common historical and cultural experience.

The first session of the International Committee decided most of the principal matters concerning the implementation of this complex project, beginning with the drafting of plans and defining the objectives and methods of work of the Committee itself.

The Bureau of the International Scientific Committee consists of a president, four vice-presidents and a rapporteur. The Bureau's task is to supervise the execution of the project between the sessions of the International Scientific Committee. The reading committee, consisting of four members, was created in 1986 to revise and finalize the manuscripts after editing Volumes I and II. Another reading committee was constituted in 1989 for Volumes III and IV.

The authors and editors are scholars from the present twelve countries of Central Asia and experts from other regions. Thus, this work is the result of the regional and of the international collaboration of scholars within the framework of the programme of the United Nations Educational, Scientific and Cultural Organization (UNESCO).

The International Scientific Committee and myself express particular gratitude to Mrs Irene Iskender-Mochiri for her arduous and selfless work in preparing the first three volumes for the press.

It is our sincere hope that the publication of the third volume of the *History of Civilizations of Central Asia* will be a further step towards the promotion of the cultural identity of the peoples of Central Asia, strengthening their common cultural heritage and, consequently, will foster a better understanding among the peoples of the world.

MEMBERS OF THE INTERNATIONAL SCIENTIFIC COMMITTEE
(in alphabetical order)

Dr F. R. ALLCHIN (United Kingdom)

Professor M. S. ASIMOV (Tajikistan)
President
Editor of Volume IV (Parts I and II)

Dr N. A. BALOCH (Pakistan)

Professor M. BASTANI PARIZI (Islamic
Republic of Iran)

Professor S. BIRA (Mongolia)

Professor A. H. DANI (Pakistan)
Editor of Volume I

† Professor K. ENOKI (Japan)

Professor G. F. ETEMADI
(Afghanistan)
Co-editor of Volume II

Professor J. HARMATTA (Hungary)
Editor of Volume II

Professor LIU CUNKUAN
(People's Republic of China)

Dr L. I. MIROSHNIKOV (Russian
Federation)

Professor S. NATSAGDORJ (Mongolia)

Professor B. N. PURI (India)
Co-editor of Volume II

Professor M. H. Z. SAFI (Afghanistan)

Professor A. SAYILI (Turkey)

Dr R. SHABANI SAMGHABADI
(Islamic Republic of Iran)
Co-editor of Volume III

Professor D. SINOR (United States
of America)

† Professor B. K. THAPAR (India)

Professor ZHANG GUANG-DA
(People's Republic of China)
Co-editor of Volume III

15

MEMBERS OF THE INTERNATIONAL SCIENTIFIC COMMITTEE
(since 1993)

Professor C. ADLE
(Islamic Republic of Iran)
Editor of Volume V

Professor D. ALIMOVA
(Uzbekistan)

Professor M. ANNANEPESOV
(Turkmenistan)

Professor M. S. ASIMOV
(Tajikistan)
President and Editor of Volume IV
(Parts I and II)

Professor K. BAIPAKOV
(Kazakstan)
Co-editor of Volume V

Professor S. BIRA
(Mongolia)

Professor A. H. DANI
(Pakistan)
Editor of Volume I

Professor H.-P. FRANCFORT
(France)

Professor I. HABIB
(India)
Editor of Volume V

Dr L. MIROSHNIKOV
(Russian Federation)

Professor D. SINOR
(United States of America)

Dr A. TABYSHALIEVA
(Kyrgyz Republic)

Professor I. TOGAN
(Turkey)

Professor H. UMEMURA
(Japan)

Professor WU YUNGUI
(People's Republic of China)

MEMBERS OF THE READING COMMITTEE

Professor A. D. H. BIVAR
(United Kingdom)

Professor R. N. FRYE
(United States of America)

Professor J. HARMATTA
(Hungary)

Professor D. SINOR
(United States of America)

LIST OF CONTRIBUTORS

† P. G. BULGAKOV

K. CHAKRABARTI
Centre for Historical Studies
Jawaharlal Nehru University
New Delhi 110067, India

N. N. CHEGINI
Iran Bastan Museum
Khiaban-e Imam Khomeini
Tehran 11364/9364
Islamic Republic of Iran

A. H. DANI
Director
Centre for the Study of Civilizations of
    Central Asia
Quaid-i-Azam University
Islamabad, Pakistan

PH. GIGNOUX
École Pratique des Hautes Études
Section des Sciences religieuses
Sorbonne
45, rue des Écoles
75005 Paris, France

J. HARMATTA
Hattyu-u 2.V.1
Budapest 1015, Hungary

A. H. JALILOV
Tajik State University
Dushanbe, Tajikistan

† A. L. KHROMOV

S. G. KLYASHTORNY
Institute of Oriental Studies
Sector of Turco-Mongol Studies
Dvortsovaya Nab., 18
St Petersburg, Russian Federation

A. I. KOLESNIKOV
Institute of Oriental Studies
Dvortsovaya Nab., 18
St Petersburg, Russian Federation

L. R. KYZLASOV
Faculty of History
Moscow State University
Moscow, Russian Federation

B. A. LITVINSKY
Director
Institute of Oriental Studies
Rojdesvenko Street 12
Moscow 103753, Russian Federation

B. I. MARSHAK
State Hermitage Museum
St Petersburg, Russian Federation

MU SHUN-YING
Archaeological Institute of Xinjiang
Academy of Social Sciences
Urumqi, People's Republic of China

N. N. Negmatov
Institute of History
Tajik Academy of Sciences
Dushanbe, Tajikistan

E. E. Nerazik
Institute of Ethnology and Anthropology
Leninskiy prospekt, 32A
Moscow 117334, Russian Federation

A. V. Nikitin
The State Hermitage Museum
St Peterburg, Russian Federation

D. Sinor
Distinguished Professor Emeritus of
    Uralic and Altaic Studies
Indiana University
Goodbody Hall 157
Bloomington, Indiana 47405–2401
United States of America

A. Tafazzoli
Faculty of Letters and Human Sciences
Tehran, Islamic Republic of Iran

M. I. Vorobyova-Desyatovskaya
Institute of Oriental Studies
Dvortsovaya Nab., 18
St Petersburg, Russian Federation

Wang Yao
Central Institute for National Minorities
Department of Tibetan Studies
Beijing, People's Republic of China

M. H. Zamir Safi
Department of History
Faculty of Social Sciences
Kabul University
Kabul, Afghanistan

E. V. Zeimal
Oriental Department
State Hermitage Museum
St Petersburg, Russian Federation

Zhang Guang-da
Department of History
Beijing University
Beijing 100871
People's Republic of China

Other collaborating specialists

M. E. Bastani Parizi
Faculty of Letters and Human Sciences
University of Tehran
Tehran, Islamic Republic of Iran

G. S. Humayun
Faculty of Literature
Kabul University
Kabul, Afghanistan

M. Hussain Shah
Faculty of Social Sciences
Kabul University
Kabul, Afghanistan

M. A. Joyenda
Afghan Institute of Archaeology
International Centre for Kushan Studies
Kabul, Afghanistan

A. Khodadadian
Faculty of Letters and Human Sciences
Tehran, Islamic Republic of Iran

B. N. Puri
B-58, Sector A
Mahanagar
Lucknow 226006, India

A. Rahman
Department of Archaeology
University of Peshawar
Peshawar, Pakistan

Historical Introduction[*]

B. A. Litvinsky and Zhang Guang-da

The end of the period covered by Volume II of the *History of Civilizations of Central Asia* saw the weakening and collapse of the powerful Parthian, Han and Kushan empires. The present volume deals with the period *c.* A.D. 250–750, which witnessed the rise of mighty new empires (Sasanian, Gupta, Sui and T'ang; and the Arab caliphate) on the fringes of Central Asia. It also saw the successive movements of nomadic peoples (the Huns, Alan tribes, Chionites, Kidarites and Hephthalites, Türks, Türgesh, Karluks, Uighurs and other Turkic tribal confederations) that played a major and at times decisive role in the later ethnic and political history of the region.

The Sasanians

In Iran the entire period is covered by the Sasanian Empire (A.D. 224–651), the successor to the Parthian Empire (*c.* 250 B.C. – A.D. 224). The end of the first century and the beginning of the second were characterized by chronic internal disturbances in the Parthian state, which was also weakened by the constant wars with Rome. The Parthians were particularly unsuccessful in their struggle against the Roman emperor Trajan in the years 113–117. Although they later managed to regain their lost lands and achieve a certain degree of stability, the wars with Rome proved highly exhausting.[1] Entire provinces, including Hyrcania, were lost and Margiana became independent.

The beginning of the third century was marked by rivalry between the Parthian king Vologases V (207/8–221/2) and his brother Ardavan V (*c.* 213–224), who ruled independently, as well as by further battles against the Romans. It was at that time that a new dynasty emerged: the Sasanians. According to Lukonin:

[*] See Map 1.
1. Lepper, 1948.

The emergence of the Sasanians and the organization of a new state in Iran in the first quarter of the third century A.D. meant not only a change of dynasty. These developments were due to deep-seated economic and political factors. The growth of commodity production brought about mainly by the exploitation of the peasantry and slaves, the growth in demand for crafts and agricultural produce linked to the revival of trade routes running through Iran to China and India, and the general crisis in the system of slave-ownership which affected the Mediterranean in the third century and reached Iran were all expressions of a new stage in the history of that country which created an urgent need for new organizational and political forms. Ardashir [226–241], the son of Papak and scion of a local national dynasty, supported by a broad section of the increasingly feudal nobility both priestly and military, rapidly managed to unite scattered princedoms and domains around Persia (modern Fars province), an area associated from earliest times with the national unity of the entire country.[2]

As early as the third century the Sasanians destroyed the large Kushan Empire and annexed a part of its domains, including Bactria (Tokharistan). This region subsequently became part of the small Kushano-Sasanian kingdom and then, at times, part of the vast and mighty Sasanian Empire itself, which stretched from the southern regions of western Central Asia and Afghanistan to the Transcaucasus, Mesopotamia and part of Arabia. To the west, the Sasanians shared a border with the Roman Empire and subsequently with Byzantium, and this was the theatre of almost constant wars. Similar wars were waged on its eastern border with the Later Kushans, the Chionites, the Hephthalites and the Türks. Some of these tribes invaded the territory of Iran and their notables played a part in domestic Iranian political struggles.

The Sasanians had a developed bureaucratic and military system as well as a complex administrative, social and Zoroastrian priestly hierarchy. The reforms of Khusrau I Anushirvan (531–579) marked not only the establishment of a well-balanced, comprehensive and fairly centralized system of administration but also the completion of one stage in the feudalization of society.

A vigorous culture flourished in the Sasanian Empire. Many works of religious, artistic and scientific literature were produced and there was a large body of secular literature such as historical epics and poems, legal, geographic and other works, including some in poetic form. There were many translations from other languages, including Greek, Syriac and Indian languages. Majestic works of architecture have been preserved, which testify to the engineering and architectural genius of their creators. Among the arts represented were sculpture, bas-relief, painting, toreutics, glyptic and representations on medals and coins. It was a new and highly progressive stage in the development of the art of the East.

Art, crafts and architecture bear traces of previous Iranian, as well as Roman, Byzantine, Transcaucasian and Central Asian artistic creation. Sasanian spiritual and material life and culture also exerted a considerable influence on

2. Lukonin, 1961, p. 5.

those of many neighbouring and more distant peoples. Sasanian works of art and crafts were to be found from France to China and Japan and many examples have been discovered in the Urals and Siberia. The traditions, motifs and rites created under the Sasanians continued into the Islamic period.[3]

The Sasanian *shahanshah* (king of kings) of Iran was the bearer of kingly *khwarnah* (Avestan, *khvarenah*; Old Persian, *farnah*; New Persian, *farr*), in other words, he embodied the happiness and destiny of the royal dynasty and the entire state.[4] The Sasanian monarch was considered the earthly representative and counterpart both of the Zoroastrian religion and of its supreme creator deity, Ohrmazd (Avestan, Ahura Mazda). Consequently, the king in Zoroastrian belief, as sovereign of Iran and the entire corporeal world, was the divinely designated protector, religious and secular authority, and guide of the material creation. He served, in the corporeal, the same roles as does Ohrmazd as universal sovereign of both the material and spiritual worlds.[5] Identical or similar conceptions connected with sacral kingship were found in India and China, although both countries enjoyed a degree of religious tolerance that did not exist in Iran.

Zoroastrianism was the prevailing faith (and also the state religion) in Iran, with Christianity and Judaism existing alongside it. A syncretic Manichaean religion arose in the Mesopotamian part of the empire. From Iran, Zoroastrianism, Nestorianism, Judaism and Manichaeism spread east to western Central Asia, Afghanistan, East Turkestan, Mongolia and China.

Like the Parthian Empire, the Kushan Empire began to decline in the third century and severe blows were dealt to it by the Sasanians. The Indian part of the Kushan Empire also declined, losing its influence first in the Ganges valley. The Yaudheya Republic (*Yaudheyagana* on coin inscriptions) – situated on the plain between the Sutlej and the Jamuna and in northern Rajasthan – played a major part in the struggle against the Kushans. In the second century, western India was controlled by the dynasty of the Western Satraps, who extended their territories, but were eventually incorporated in the Gupta Empire by Chandragupta II at the end of the fourth century.

The Guptas

The region of Magadha rose to prominence during the third century largely because of its situation on the lower reaches of the Ganges close to the shores of the Bay of Bengal. At the beginning of the fourth century it became the political centre of the Gupta Empire, which rapidly united most of northern

---

3. *The Cambridge History of Iran*, 1983, Vol. 3, Parts 1 and 2; Christensen, 1944.
4. Bailey, 1971.
5. Choksy, 1988; see also Widengren, 1959; Frye, 1984.

India. Chandragupta I (*c.* 319–335 or 350) played a major role in this, and after his death he was given the splendid title of 'Great King of Kings'. His son, Samudragupta (*c.* 350–*c.* 375), was a skilful politician, a bold and successful military commander and a patron of the arts and sciences. It was during his rule that the Gupta Empire took shape in the valley of the Ganges. Its nucleus was surrounded by a belt of territories dependent to a greater or lesser extent on the Guptas and Samudragupta even led a campaign deep into southern India.

The territory of the Guptas reached its greatest extent under Chandragupta II (*c.* 375–*c.* 415) after he defeated the Western Satraps – a period known as the 'Gupta Golden Age'. There are even references to a campaign against Bactria. But the Gupta Empire weakened and eventually broke up under the attacks of new invaders, among whom the Hephthalites – the Hunas of Indian sources – played an important role. Many regions of northern India fell under the control of Turkic invaders, until Harsha of Kanauj (606–647), a powerful conqueror, rebuilt a strong empire in the north.

The Guptas played a major role in the history and culture of India and of the neighbouring countries. Although the empire had no standard administrative divisions or unified administrative system, there was a marked increase in the level of centralization. Record-keeping was highly developed and there was a complex system for the registration of land, donations, income and expenditure. Agriculture was developed, as were crafts, building, and foreign and domestic trade.[6] According to Rowland:

> Seldom in the history of peoples do we find a period in which the national genius is so fully and typically expressed in all the arts as in Gupta India. Here was florescence and fulfilment after a long period of gradual development, a like sophistication and complete assurance in expression in music, literature, the drama, the plastic arts and architecture. The Gupta period may well be described as 'classic' in the sense of the word describing a norm or degree of perfection never achieved before or since, and in the perfect balance and harmony of all elements, stylistic and iconographic elements inseparable in importance.
>
> Sanskrit became the official language of the Gupta court. The great Indian epic, the Mahābhārata, underwent a final recension as a document of a unified India under a godly Imperial race; the Rāmayāna enjoyed a renewed popularity . . . It was in this period that the Indian theatre, which, just like western drama, traced its origins to the performance of church spectacles or miracle plays, reached the extraordinary perfection of dramatic structure and richness of metaphor that characterize the 'Toy cart' and the famed Kālidāsa's rich and sensuous poetic drama 'Śakuntala'.[7]

Buddhism (Mahayana and Hinayana) flourished in Gupta India but external and internal factors gradually contributed to its decline. Hinduism was regen-

---

6. *The Age of Imperial Unity*, 1951; *The Classical Age*, 1954; Altekar and Majumdar (eds), 1946; Banerji, 1933; Dandekar, 1941; Mookerji, 1952; Bongard-Levin and Il'in, 1969*a*.
7. Rowland, 1970, pp. 215–16.

erated and absorbed many Buddhist beliefs. Gupta India contained many universally known centres of erudition, including the monastery at Nalanda. From Gupta India, ideas, teaching, scientific discoveries and also miscellaneous goods, works of art and literature, scientific and religious writings, preachers, merchants and craftsmen spread throughout Central Asia to the lands of the southern seas, the Mediterranean and East Asia.

The Sui dynasty

In China the end of the Han dynasty (206 B.C. – A.D. 220) was a dark period. Rebellions and internecine strife devastated the flourishing central regions of the Han Empire; towns lay in ruins, the fields were empty and trade routes ceased to operate. In 220 a new dynasty, the Wei, took power. During its rule the processes of disintegration continued apace and a mere 45 years later another dynasty, the Chin, was established. A short period of unity was followed by fresh rebellions, internecine wars and the movement of northern and north-western nomads, proto-Turkic, Tungusic and tribes of Tibetan-Chiang stock, who had been fighting among themselves for years. Separate states were formed in the north and south of China.

In 581 the Sui dynasty was founded: four centuries of rebellion and division gave way to a period of unity and centralization. Strong measures were taken to set up a bureaucratic type of government and major building works were initiated. The Sui emperors started wars on the borders of the empire but obtained few successes. In comparison with the advanced consolidation of the Han period, the state's territory during all the following periods (including that of the Sui) was significantly smaller. China's influence in Central Asia declined gradually, leaving few traces; trade routes also declined and cultural ties were weakened.

The T'ang dynasty

In 618 the T'ang dynasty came to power in China. Its real founder was the emperor T'ai-tsung (627–649), during whose 23-year reign many laws were codified and all aspects of life were carefully regulated. T'ang capitals and other cities flourished, as did trade. Although the empire reached its zenith under Hsüan-tsung (713–756), his reign also marked the start of the dynasty's decline.

China's consolidation and development during the Early T'ang period led to an expansion of its territory, especially to the west, where practically all East Turkestan was incorporated into the empire. T'ang troops advanced to the borders of western Central Asia, but were unable to consolidate their hold. In the last quarter of the seventh century, the T'ang Empire started to clash in

East Turkestan with the Tibetans, who had become very powerful. Tibetan expansion reached its zenith in the middle and the third quarter of the eighth century, when they held a large area of East Turkestan.

The T'ang maintained large military forces in the north to fight the Türks, who had united under the First (552–630) and the Second (682–744) Türk *Kaghanates*. The year 744 saw the establishment of the Uighur *Kaghanate*, which rapidly became very powerful. After an interlude, the Uighurs began to play a role in internal Chinese affairs at the invitation of the T'ang government.

The process of urbanization continued, accompanied by an expansion in crafts, and in domestic and foreign trade. In the area of spiritual life, Buddhism gained in importance. Outstanding works of literature, architecture and art were created. According to Schafer:

> How the Western Regions contributed to China and then T'ang China contributed her arts and manners to her neighbours of the medieval Far East, especially to Japan, Korea, Turkestan, Tibet and Annam, is a rather well-known story. To mention the arts of xylography, city planning, costume design, and versification is only to hint at the magnitude of the cultural debt which these peripheral countries owed to T'ang. We are also familiar with the material goods sought by foreigners in China or taken abroad by the Chinese themselves: luxuries like silk textiles, wine, ceramics, metal-work, and medicines, as well as such minor dainties as peaches, honey and pine nuts, and, of course, the instruments of civilization, great books and fine paintings.[8]

In summary, it is clear that the lands bordering on Central Asia (especially Iran and China) acted as mighty generators of military and political power. On their territories, great centralized states were established, mighty empires which played a crucial role in the fate of the various peoples of Central Asia and in diplomatic and economic history. The Indian, Iranian and Chinese civilizations also played an outstanding part in the development of the civilization of Central Asia as a whole, contributing to material culture, armaments and the design and construction of cities as well as to science, philosophy, literature and religion.

Oasis states

In the middle of Central Asia lay oasis states with settled agricultural (and also, to some extent, nomadic) populations and a developed urban life. They included Tokharistan (Bactria), Margiana, Sogdiana, Khwarizm, and many small kingdoms in the Tarim basin such as Kucha and Khotan, all of which enjoyed several common features – we shall mention just a few of them. The character of these states was monarchic in principle, but a theocratic monarchy (or some-

8. Schafer, 1963, p. 2; see also Wright, 1959; Kryukov et al., 1979; 1984.

thing resembling it in the case of Khotan, for example) had been established in some of them. There was a secular, hierarchical system in which vassalage was developing, and it is possible to speak of the growth of feudalism. In all these states, the period was characterized by the expansion of productive forces and by a complex system of trade. The Sogdians were especially renowned as traders from Byzantium to China – they not only travelled back and forth in caravans but founded entire cities[9] and acted as the transmitters of cultural values. The oasis states generated a very high level of urban culture, as testified by the creation of outstanding works of art which became part of the Eastern heritage.

Ecology, geography and climate

The ecological conditions prevailing in Central Asia are as follows. Although its territory lies on the same latitude as Spain and the southern half of France, the natural conditions are quite different. It is a land of boundless sandy deserts. There are mountains rising above the clouds, covered in eternal snows, and large mountain glaciers over alpine meadows. Swollen rivers flow from these glaciers and snowfields, rushing down into the plains with their cultivated lands, villages and towns. From the foot of the mountains, the deserts of western Central Asia – the Kyzyl Kum, the Kara Kum and the Ustyurt – stretch for more than 1,000 km to the Caspian Sea. Middle Asia (a region of the former Soviet Central Asia) lies in the internally drained part of Eurasia, that is in the Aral–Caspian (Turanian) plain, where the above-mentioned deserts and the T'ien Shan and Pamir-Alai (the highest mountain systems of this region) are located. Further east, regions with similar landscapes stretch all the way to Mongolia.

The main climatic features throughout most of western Central Asia are an abundance of heat and light, aridity and a continental pattern. The variations in daily and monthly temperatures can be as great as 40° C. On the plains, the frost-free period may last for up to 250 days. The summer is long, oppressive and dry. In the far south the temperature reaches 50° C in the shade. The lowlands are among the driest regions of Eurasia; thus the precipitation in the Taklamakan desert is insignificant – 10–15 mm per annum. In Dzungaria, the precipitation varies between 200 mm in the northern foothills and 400 mm in the northern plains. In the Alai and T'ien Shan mountains the climate is much more humid, and precipitation rises to 500–700 mm per annum. However, its volume does not automatically correspond to the relief and it is very low on some high mountain plateaux: for example, 60–80 mm per annum in the eastern Pamirs.

Types of vegetation associated with very arid conditions are typical of the deserts of Central Asia: ephemeral or fast-ripening, their rapid develop-

9. Chugevskiy, 1971; Pulleyblank, 1952.

ment mainly occurs during the humid spring. The nature of the desert vegetation depends on the ecological environment, such as the nature of the soil, its chemical composition, and humidity. There are several types of desert vegetation; thus a given region may be used only at a particular time of the year. Yet most desert pastureland can be used all the year round. Its productivity is low, and one sheep requires 5–10 ha of pasture.

The vegetation in the mountains and on the plains is much richer. Here there are separate spring, summer, autumn and winter pastures. On the plains, vegetation begins to grow in early spring and is already withering by the end of May. Livestock graze here in the spring. These pastures are also used later on, but mainly for the exploitation of dried grass. From 450 m to 1,500 m above sea level, mixed grasses and short-lived plants grow from April to the middle of June, after which they wither. These are good spring and early summer pastures. Higher up the humidity increases. The most productive summer pastures are to be found at that level, and also large areas of deciduous forest, including fruit-bearing trees. Higher still are sub-alpine and alpine meadows where climatic conditions permit livestock to graze for only three to three and a half summer months. These meadows are nevertheless held in particular esteem by herdsmen because of the high nutritive value of the vegetation.

Ecology requires pastures to be used in rotation, since there are both flatlands and mountains. The cattle 'follow the spring', grazing first in the valley and then being moved higher, until they eventually reach the alpine meadows. In the autumn the cattle gradually move down, lingering at spots where fodder is available. Since winter fodder contains only half the nutrition of spring fodder, winter is a critical period in the annual cycle.

Nomadic livestock-rearing also depends on the water supply, which differs from one area to another. In the mountains, humidity tends to be higher and there is sufficient water for animals. A completely different situation applies in desert areas and, to some extent, on the plains where there has always been a severe shortage of water. In both types of terrain, groundwater is widely used as well as water from rivers. In desert regions, water is obtained from wells 10–100 m deep.

Needless to say, the foregoing is an extremely general description. Every part of the vast region of Central Asia has its own particular, and often fundamentally different, features.

Nomadic societies

The nomads who occupied the vast deserts, steppes and mountains were a very important factor in the history of Central Asia. The *Han shu*, the official history of the Former Han dynasty, describes the Wu-sun people who lived in Central Asia in ancient times: 'The land is covered in vegetation and is flat . . .

[The people] do not work at cultivating the fields or planting trees, but in company with their stock animals they go in the same way as that of the Hsiung-nu.'[10] Independent reports from the most distant areas of the populated world all agree that these were nomadic peoples.[11]

The *Han shu*'s brief description conveys the essence of nomadism in Eurasia: its main ingredients were the migratory way of life and the operation of an economy in conditions which necessarily included vast expanses of pastureland. Nomadism implies the existence of a social entity developed for the operation of a specific economy, and a corresponding ecological niche where this entity can establish itself. It was only the combination of these two factors, ecological and social, that enabled nomadism to emerge and develop in various parts of Central Asia and of Eurasia as a whole.

There were several patterns of nomadism in Central Asia during the period from the third to the eighth century (as in the nineteenth and twentieth centuries). The most prevalent form was longitudinal, meaning migration from north to south and vice versa. Latitudinal migration involves movement to east or west, conditioned by climatic variations, whereas vertical migration exploits the differences in altitude. Radial movements are those distributed around a central area according to the availability of pasture. Depending on the terrain, the length of migratory routes varied between 5–10 and 1,000 km. Weakened by lack of fodder during the winter, livestock moved slowly. Possessions were loaded on camels, while horses and unburdened camels followed at a distance, with sheep and other livestock moving close to the migrating group. Such groups travelled 15–25 km in the course of a day.[12] In mountainous regions there was an intricate and well-developed system of horizontal and vertical movement.

The historical and archaeological evidence on nomads and their societies is supplemented by ethnographic material.[13] Pure nomadism was not encountered often, even in Antiquity; neither was livestock-breeding the sole form of economic activity. Alongside the nomadic way of life, several types of semi-nomadic existence were widespread in areas with various forms of (partial)

---

10. Hulsewé and Loewe, 1979, p. 144. Compare this with Strabo's description of European nomads in the Scythian orbit: 'As for the nomads, their tents, made of felt, are fastened on the wagons in which they spend their lives; and round about the tents are the herds which afford the milk, cheese, and meat on which they live; and they follow the grazing herds, from time to time moving to other places that have grass, living only in the march-meadows about Lake Macotis in winter, but also in the plains in summer' (Strabo, 7.3.17).

11. Chinese sources on the Hsiung-nu (Taskin, 1968; 1973); on the Türks (Chavannes, 1903; Liu, 1958).

12. Rudenko, 1961; Shakhmatov, 1963; Zhdanko, 1968; Tolybekov, 1971; Markov, 1976; *Khozyaystvo kazakhov*, 1980.

13. In addition to the sources listed, see also Vladimirtsov, 1948; Radloff, 1893; Barrou et al., 1973; *Pastoral Production and Society*, 1979; Khazanov, 1984; *Rol' kochevykh narodov v tsivilizatsii Tsentral'noy Azii*, 1974; Bongard-Levin and Il'in, 1969*b*.

settlement and a fairly developed, settled economy based on agriculture and crafts. Nomads started to adopt a settled and sometimes even an urban way of life.

Nomads were an important and integral part of the society of Eurasia. They established a characteristic economy, with highly developed techniques of livestock-rearing, the grazing of herds, nomadic movements and various forms of crafts and warfare. They also had a unique and highly developed social structure (based on the dual system of individual ownership of herds and communal ownership of pastureland), shamanistic religions and fine folk poetry, especially epics. Nomadic society is mobile in two senses: first, the internal mobility of the society itself; and, second, its external mobility, the capacity to execute rapid, far-reaching movements, both peaceful and military.

Nomads usually lived close to oases, with their settled, urban, agricultural way of life, and various types of relationship existed between the two civilizations. According to Lattimore:

> In the pre-industrial age, the advanced urban-agricultural civilizations produced a great many things which the nomads wanted, but the nomads produced not nearly so much of what the settled people wanted. When, therefore, the nomads were not rich enough to buy all that they wanted, but felt militarily strong, it was a great temptation to threaten, raid and even make deep invasions of the settled lands. (The 'imbalance' between the economies of China and the territories beyond the Great Wall was always very striking, but I believe that in the Indo-Iranian, Afghan and Arab lands, and the land of the Turkish-speaking peoples of Central Asia, both oasis dwellers and nomads . . . [there] may have been a much greater degree of integration.)[14]

The nomads often lived near settled oases or even within them, leading to a wide range of ethno-cultural and socio-economic contacts. Economic ties then became so close that at times it is possible to speak of the emergence of a common economic system with two intimately linked sectors, the settled and the nomadic.

The entire period between 250 and 750 was characterized by major movements of nomadic tribes and peoples. What was the cause of these movements? At present we are unable to supply anything like a satisfactory answer. Tempting preliminary explanations such as changes in the climate cannot explain why Mongolia and the adjacent regions released wave after wave of nomads from the end of the first century B.C. up to the time of Chinggis Khan. These waves spread south to China, south-west to western Central Asia and East Turkestan and west to the Volga, the Black Sea and beyond that to Italy and France.

14. Lattimore, 1974, pp. 172–3.

The Hsiung-nu and the Huns

The Hsiung-nu not only developed their society in Mongolia and the neighbouring regions of southern Siberia over the centuries but carried out raids and military expeditions in various directions. One of these directions was west: here they intervened in the struggle for East Turkestan and at the beginning of the second century B.C. the agricultural population of that region fell under their sway. The Hsiung-nu first engaged in a lengthy and critical struggle against other nomadic tribes, particularly the Wu-sun and the Yüeh-chih, and also with China and local settled agricultural princedoms.

In the year 22 B.C. a catastrophic drought occurred. Many nomads then moved south, recognizing the authority of the Han, while others, the Northern Hsiung-nu (or Huns), moved north-west. Nomads began to take a more active part in the affairs of East Turkestan and penetrated the north-eastern corner of western Central Asia. The Hsiung-nu became even more active in the first century A.D. Their westward movement towards the Volga and the Don appears to have started in the first or second century A.D., when they had to pass through territory densely populated by Sarmatians and other tribes. On the lower reaches of the Don they clashed with Alan tribes in the years 370–380. Referring to them as Huns, the Roman historian Ammianus Marcellinus (XXXI, 3.1) describes how 'the Huns killed and plundered [these tribes] and joined the survivors to themselves in a treaty of alliance'.

It is clear that the Huns – as these tribes were called in the west – mixed with the Alans, and before that with the Sarmatians and later with the Goths of Ermenrichus. Then they invaded Pannonia and moved on into western Europe. There followed the age of Attila (434–453) and the battle of the Catalaunian Plains.

The Huns were nomadic horsemen who played an important part in the 'great migration of peoples'.[15] According to Kryukov et al:

> A direct shock producing a kind of 'chain reaction': such was the westward migration of the branch of the Asiatic Hsiung-nu who left their original homeland in the second century and two and a half centuries later entered European history under the name of the Huns. But the 'great migration of peoples' embraced not only Europe in the third to the sixth century. In East Asia a process began in the third century which was extremely similar to the one observed at the same time on the borders of the Roman Empire. A branch of the Hsiung-nu, the Hsien-pi, the Ti, the Tibetan Chiang and other close neighbours of the ancient Chinese gradually began to move into the central Chinese plain. In the year 308, 100 years before Alaric took Rome and before the first Barbarian Empire (the Kingdom of Toulouse) was established on the territory of the Roman Empire, the Hsiung-nu general Liu Yüan proclaimed himself emperor and three years later his successor, Liu Tsing, captured the capital of the

15. Maenchen-Helfen, 1973; Tikhvinskiy and Litvinsky, 1988.

Chin Empire and took prisoner the Son of Heaven. What is referred to here is the emergence of a dynasty of Hsiung-nu origin: the Former Chao (304–325). The Hsiung-nu also founded the dynasties of the Northern Liang (397–439) and the Hsia (407–431). Historians have called Liu Tsing the 'Chinese Attila'.[16]

In the words of the ancient Chinese author, Chin-shu: 'The people is experiencing deprivation and is sad as a result; all have the same concern, all are waiting for peace and rest like dew and rain in a drought.'[17]

The history of western Central Asia is also marked by a series of large-scale nomadic movements from north and north-east to south. Of particular note is the movement of the Yüeh-chih in the second half of the second century B.C. which ultimately led to the formation of the powerful Kushan Empire, whose last days are described in this volume. The invasion of new ethnic groups led to the formation of the Chionite state, the Kidarites and subsequently the Empire of the Hephthalites, who moved into East Turkestan, Afghanistan and north-western India. Then came the invasion of the Türks, whose dominion was even more extensive than that of the Hephthalites.

These successive waves of nomadic invasions are usually considered in ethno-political terms – this is understandable since such movements did indeed play a major, and at times decisive, role in the ethnic and political history of Central Asia. Large nomadic populations appeared in the vicinity of the oases and then within them. This had fundamental consequences: the nomadic sector of the economy grew in importance, as did the interdependence – or even the intermeshing – of the economic contributions made by the nomadic and settled populations. Newly settled or former nomads appeared in settled rural and urban communities. Intensive inter-ethnic and linguistic processes developed alongside those of cultural synthesis and the mutual enrichment of cultures (see below). Members of nomadic clans were in overall charge of the state and of many domains; inter-ethnic marriages became common among the aristocracy.

The Silk Route

All these complex political and ethno-cultural processes developed with varying degrees of intensity, embracing part or all of the territory of Central Asia. Contacts between peoples grew with the development of commercial ties. In this connection, the Silk Route was of great importance. It is sometimes presented as something akin to a modern motorway linking different countries; but it was really a system of roads (and the principal direction in which they

16. Kryukov et al., 1979.
17. *Materialy po istorii kochevykh narodov v Kitae*, 1989, p. 158.

ran) rather than one specific road. There were also supplementary roads running close to the main road within each oasis and state. There were both land routes and sea routes. The entire network – running from China to the Mediterranean, over a vast expanse from the Yellow Sea to the central Mediterranean, from the southern Urals to the Indian Ocean – made up the Silk Route.

In the second and first centuries B.C., the Silk Route had two branches through East Turkestan, running into western Central Asia and thereafter south to India and west through Iran and Mesopotamia to Antioch. For political reasons and also because of climatic changes, the network of towns altered, and the direction of the routes shifted as a result. From the fifth to the seventh century A.D., three roads ran through East Turkestan. The northern road led to Lake Issyk-kül and then westward along the northern shores of the Caspian Sea, the Caucasus and the Black Sea to Asia Minor and Byzantium. The middle road crossed the Turfan depression and the northern rim of the Tarim basin in the direction of the Ferghana valley, Samarkand, Bukhara and Merv and then ran through Iran to the eastern Mediterranean. The southern road ran from the area of Lop Nor through Khotan and Wakhan to Tokharistan, Bamiyan, northwestern India and thence by the sea route across the Indian Ocean to the Mediterranean. As one ancient Chinese author noted, 'There are also roads running from each country which intersect in turn in the south and in the north. By following [these roads] it is possible to reach any point.'[18]

The path of many specific main and auxiliary roads has been established. At times they left unexpected traces: for example, stopping points for travellers have been discovered in the high mountains in Gilgit (Pakistan). There were also sanctuaries where they prayed. Here, too, the custom developed of carving a drawing or an inscription, a kind of *Gästebuch*, in one of the cliffs. More than 10,000 rock drawings (petroglyphs) have been discovered on the Karakorum road, as well as some 1,500 inscriptions in 17 languages and 24 scripts, the largest number of inscriptions being in the Middle Iranian languages, mainly Sogdian. There are also Chinese, Indian, Hebrew and other inscriptions dating from the second, third and ninth centuries.[19]

As mentioned above, the Sogdians played the most important role in trade in Central Asia. By the fourth to the third century B.C., they had already begun to penetrate the eastern part of Central Asia. There were many populous Sogdian colonies at various points in East Turkestan, in Dunhuang, in China and in Mongolia, and large numbers of Sogdian merchants lived in Ch'ang-an, the capital of T'ang China. According to the texts discovered in East Turkestan and known as the 'Ancient Sogdian Letters', the Sogdians of the diaspora did not lose their links with Samarkand.[20]

18. Herrmann, 1938; Raschke, 1978; Tikhvinskiy and Litvinsky, 1988.
19. Dani, 1983*a*; 1983*b*; Jettmar (ed.), 1989; Litvinsky, 1989.
20. Henning, 1977; Pulleyblank, 1952; Harmatta, 1979; Grenet and Sims-Williams, 1987.

Trade on the Silk Route was often closely interwoven with politics. One episode involving Türks, Sogdians, Iranians and Byzantines is typical. From the time of their arrival in western Central Asia, the Türks had shown an interest in the development of international trade and particularly in the colossal profits of the silk trade. This trade was conducted by the Sogdians through Iran but it was precisely in the Iranian sector of the route that the Central Asian (Sogdian) traders encountered the greatest difficulties. With the agreement of the Türks, the Sogdians themselves sent an embassy to Iran headed by the Sogdian, Maniakh (Menander fragment 18). The embassy proposed either that a through trade in silk to the Byzantine Empire should be permitted, or that the Persians themselves should purchase the silk from the Sogdians. These proposals were rejected.

A second embassy was then dispatched with the same mission, this time by the Türk *kaghan* (king). Only a few members returned; the others perished in Iran, an indication that the *shahanshah* was preparing to initiate military action rather than engage in trade. In order to reach an agreement with Byzantium directed against Iran, the Türks dispatched yet another embassy (again led by Maniakh), which travelled along the northern shore of the Caspian and through the Caucasus to Byzantium to pursue the question of the direct sale of silk to Byzantium. This embassy brought large quantities of silk and managed to conclude a Byzantine-Türk agreement directed against Iran. In 568 the delegation returned home, accompanied by a corresponding Byzantine embassy headed by Zemarkhos. Other embassies were then dispatched and the volume of trade increased considerably.[21]

The expression 'Silk Route' is perhaps a misnomer since much more than silk was traded along it. Lacquered ware, Chinese bronzes including (especially) mirrors, paper and much else from eastern Asia was sent to the West. It was in no sense a one-way road, as is often believed: a steady stream of goods was carried from the Mediterranean and Central Asia to the East and to China. The merchandise included cloth, silverware and coins, gold and gold artefacts, precious and semi-precious stones, glassware and livestock. There was also a considerable exchange of people.[22] An uninterrupted flow of Buddhist pilgrims from China and other regions travelled to and from India; in turn, Buddhist missionaries travelled from India to the most remote regions of Central Asia. A document found in Merv contains extracts from various Buddhist works compiled by a Buddhist missionary from Gilgit for his own use. Chinese merchants also transported their goods and a variety of books far to the west – traces of such activities have been found in the northern Caucasus. The Silk Route thus served for the movement not only of goods but also of ideas.[23]

21. Pigulevskaya, 1951; Moravcsik, 1958.
22. Schafer, 1963.
23. Litvinsky, 1986.

Cross-cultural influences

The discovery of written sources in East Turkestan provides clear evidence of the intensity of ethnic and cultural interaction. There are thousands of manuscripts in the Indian languages, Sanskrit and Prakrit, with the most varied content, both religious and secular; and there have been rich finds of literary texts in Chinese and Tibetan. Many manuscripts have been found in Iranian languages such as Middle Persian and Parthian, Sogdian, Khotanese Saka, Bactrian (Hephthalite) and also New Persian. Of great significance were documents in a previously unknown Indo-European language which has received the designation Tokharian. Mention should also be made of the literary texts in Turkic, Syriac and other languages.[24] The area was an ethnic melting-pot, sometimes simmering quietly and at other times erupting: the reciprocal influence and intermingling of cultures was equally intense.

A dominant role was played by the region's various religions, which did not spread in isolation but brought with them a religious and cultural structure or sets of structures. Thus the spread of Buddhism, together with the ideas and principles of Buddhist architecture and iconography, led to the diffusion of Indian languages, scripts, philosophy, artistic works, astronomy, medicine and other sciences in addition to related moral and ethical principles. (To this should be added the influence of Hinduism.) The same remarks apply to Zoroastrianism, Christianity and Manichaeism. The latter incorporated many principles from other religions, particularly Buddhism. Taoism also spread from China. The nomadic peoples brought much from the world of their societies, including elements of religion and culture in a broader sense. Certain Hellenistic traditions were maintained. All these elements intertwined with the equally varied local cultures and religions, producing clashes and interpenetration. Social structures also interacted in a parallel way.

This multi-stage and multi-tiered cultural synthesis, the multiplicity of forms of political and social life, together with the emergence and development of feudal structures, characterize the contradictory and dynamic history of an age which produced remarkable values and an imposing civilization.

Editors' Note

Middle Asia is the territory belonging to the Commonwealth of Independent States (former Soviet Central Asian republics).

---

24. For further details, see Litvinsky, 1984.

SASANIAN IRAN – ECONOMY, SOCIETY, ARTS AND CRAFTS*

N. N. Chegini and A. V. Nikitin

Part One

POLITICAL HISTORY, ECONOMY AND SOCIETY

(N. N. Chegini)

It is probable that Vologases IV died some time in A.D. 208/209, after which the throne of the Parthians was disputed between his sons, Ardavan V (Artabanus) and Vologases V.[1] Ardavan ruled in central Iran and Vologases in Mesopotamia, striking coins at Seleukia.[2] The conflict between the two brothers lasted until the end of Parthian rule. In Rome, Caracalla succeeded his father Septimius Severus in 211 and the weakness of the Parthians resulted in a Roman incursion into Parthia, during which a great part of Media was pillaged and the Parthian tombs at Arbela were stripped. Although Ardavan succeeded in defeating the heir to Caracalla, Macrinus, the war against Rome and internal struggles strained the Parthian Empire to its limits.[3] What is now known, following Simonetta's work, is that Ardavan did not issue tetradrachms because he did not control Seleukia.[4]

After the invasions of Alexander the Great in the early fourth century B.C., the region of Fars, the homeland of the Persians, had become one of the vassal kingdoms of first the Seleucids and then the Parthians, ruled by several local princes. The kingdom of Persia issued coins almost continuously between 280 B.C. and A.D. 200, using the title *prtrk'* (Frataraka, i.e. governor) and later *MLK'* (king). By the beginning of the third century, conflict within the Parthian royal family and war with the Romans had weakened central authority.[5]

One prominent king of Persia during the last years of the weakened Parthia was Gochihr of the Bazrangi family, although his name does not appear on coins.[6] Sasan, after whom the dynasty is named, may have been the

---

* See Map 2.
1. Simonetta, 1956, pp. 77–82.
2. Ibid., p. 77.
3. Ibid., pp. 77–8.
4. Ibid., pp. 78–9.
5. Frye, 1975, pp. 239–41; Sellwood, 1983, pp. 299–306; Frye, 1984, pp. 271–85.
6. Al-Tabari, 1879–89, Vol. 1, p. 815; Herzfeld, 1924, pp. 35–6.

chief priest of the Adur Anahid temple in Istakhr. Papak, his son or a descendant (as Sasan, although mentioned, does not appear in the family line of the Sasanians listed in Shapur's great inscription of the Ka'be of Zoroaster at Naqsh-i Rustam, near Persepolis), succeeded him and the family gained more authority by defeating the local governors and deposing Gochihr. Papak's name appears on coins using the title *MLK'*.[7] According to the Arab historian al-Tabari, Ardavan V asked Papak to submit to his authority and to send his son Ardashir to the court, but he refused. When Papak died he was succeeded by his eldest son Shapur to whom Ardashir, the younger brother, did not give allegiance. When Shapur died in an accident in Persepolis, however, Ardashir became the head of the local dynasty.[8]

According to the Bishapur inscription of Shapur I, Ardashir proclaimed himself king in 205. The series of coins showing him with a Parthian tiara probably commemorates this event.[9] Ardashir then campaigned in western Iran and conquered Susiana and Elymais in *c.* 222.[10] Characene (Meshan), the vassal kingdom of the Parthians, was captured and a new governor appointed. At the famous battle of Hormizdagan (whose site is not known),[11] which probably took place not later than 224,[12] Ardavan V was defeated and killed.

After their crushing defeat, the remaining forces of the Arsacids (i.e. Parthians) fled to the mountains and resisted for a while. On the basis of evidence in the *Mujmal al-tawārīkh*, Widengren suggests a second battle near Nihavend when Ardashir was marching towards the capital, Ctesiphon (Tespon).[13] According to al-Tabari, Ardashir advanced to Ecbatana (Hamadan) and then conquered Armenia and Adiabene (Mosul). In 226 he entered the capital and styled himself *shahanshah* (king of kings) and his official reign started. A commemorative bas-relief was ordered to be cut on the rock at Naqsh-i Rustam (Fig. 1) and coins showing him with a new crown were issued (Plate I, 3).[14]

It is now accepted that Ardashir I defeated Ardavan V several times, overthrew some of the minor local rulers who lived under the Parthians and replaced them with newly appointed governors from his own family.[15] If, however, al-Tabari's account[16] is correct, an eastern campaign must have taken place during the rule of Ardashir I, and Seistan (modern Sistan), Abarshahr

7. Frye, 1984, p. 271; 1975, p. 239.
8. Ghirshman, 1954, p. 290.
9. Frye, 1983, p. 117.
10. Al-Tabari, 1879–89, Vol. 1, p. 818; Hansman, 1978, p. 155.
11. Rawlinson, 1876, p. 37.
12. Bivar, 1969a, p. 50.
13. Rawlinson, 1876, p. 37; Widengren, 1971, p. 743; Frye, 1975, p. 242.
14. Henning, 1954, p. 44.
15. Bivar, 1969a, p. 50.
16. Ibid.

FIG. 1. Investiture relief of Ardashir I at Naqsh-i Rustam.
(Courtesy of M. I. Mochiri.)

(Nishapur), Merv, Balkh and Khwarizm were occupied. The overthrow of the
Great Kushans, at least in the western part of their realm, is now considered
the result of the rising power of the new dynasty in Iran.[17] According to al-
Tabari,[18] the king of the Kushans (perhaps Vasudeva I) sent a mission of surrender. Whatever the circumstances, the kingdom of the Kushans was divided
and the heartland of their empire in Bactria and the Kabul valley came under
the control of the Sasanians.[19] The Sasanian rulers of the captured territory are
known today as the Kushano-Sasanian governors, although the date when they
began to issue coins is not known.[20] It seems that during this period the Sasanian
kings regularly appointed governors of the principal provinces.[21]

The extent of Shapur I's empire in the east is known from the content of his
inscription on the face of the Kaʿbe of Zoroaster. This inscription is written in
three languages, Middle Persian, Parthian and Greek, and lists the provinces of
the Sasanian Empire in *c*. 260. It shows that Shapur was already victorious against
the Romans and in Transcaucasia, and under him Sasanian control in the east

17. Frye, 1975, p. 242.
18. Bivar, 1969*a*, p. 50.
19. Ibid.
20. Bivar, 1979, pp. 317–32.
21. Ibid., pp. 320, 323–4.

was also expanded.[22] The second part of the inscription, which is a description of the empire, gives Shapur's possessions as Merv, Herat and all Abarshahr, Kerman, Seistan, Turan, Makran, Paradan, Hind (Sind) and Kushanshahr as far as *pshkbwr* (Peshawar) and up to the borders of Kash, Sughd and Chach (Kashgar, Sogdiana and Tashkent). This passage also lists all the provinces situated in the east of the empire.[23] In mentioning the Kushans, Shapur indicates the extent of his control to the east and north-east. It should be pointed out that the land of Khwarizm, although not appearing in the list of provinces, had already been captured by the Sasanians during the rule of Ardashir I. Al-Tabari mentions a campaign in which Ardashir conquered Khwarizm as well as Gurgan, Merv and so on. According to the *Chronicle of Arbela* (whose authenticity is open to doubt), the final assault on Khwarizm took place in 239/240 during Ardashir's rule.

The appearance of *Kushanshah* (king of the Kushans) as a Sasanian title shows that the Great Kushan kings had been defeated. Shapur I's success evidently ended the rule of the Great Kushans and split their kingdom into two parts, the northern and the southern. Branches of the Kushans ruled in the southern part, east of the River Indus, where they are known as Murundas.[24] The northern part, or core, of the Kushan territory became a province of the Sasanian Empire.

Struggles against the northern nomads

Shapur II (309–379) was forced to wage war for ten years against invaders whom Ammianus Marcellinus (XVII, 5) refers to as the Chionites. Shapur was clearly successful in his operation and managed to impose his authority on the invaders and stabilize his eastern frontiers.[25] The victorious return of Shapur must have taken place some time before 360; it was apparently at this time that the city of Abarshahr was founded and used as his headquarters.[26] His success in containing the Chionites resulted in the conclusion of an alliance under the terms of which the Chionites would help Shapur in his war against the Romans. In 360, when he laid siege to the fortress of Amida (the modern Diyarbekir in eastern Turkey), the Chionites with their king Grumbates supported him, according to the eyewitness account of Ammianus Marcellinus (XVIII, 7. 1-2).[27]

A few decades later, it appears that Kushanshahr was no longer under the control of the Sasanians and was subject to new invaders.[28] This new power,

22. Henning, 1937–39; 1954, pp. 40–54.
23. Herzfeld, 1947, p. 182; Henning, 1947–48, p. 54.
24. Bivar, 1969*a*, p. 51.
25. Ibid., pp. 53–4.
26. Ibid., p. 53.
27. Ibid., p. 54; 1979, p. 327.
28. Bivar, 1969*a*, p. 54.

known to us as the Kidarites (after their leader Kidara, probably himself a Chionite chief), had appeared on the eastern frontiers by the end of the fourth century. Coins of Kidara, together with those of Shapur II, Ardashir II and Shapur III, have been found in the treasure of Tepe Maranjan near Kabul[29] and in the archaeological site of Butkara, Swat (in Pakistan). The Kidarites (who dominated Tokharistan and Gandhara) adopted the Sasanian title of *Kushanshah*, which indicates that they were the chief heirs of the Sasanian *Kushanshah*s and their administration.[30] We know that the new wave of invaders from Iran came at the time of Bahram V shortly before 440. It is reasonable to suppose that this new disturbance was caused by the arrival of the Hephthalites and that early in the fifth century they drove the Kidarites south from Bactria to Panjab, where the name Kidara appears on many gold coins.[31]

It is clear that from early in the fifth century, the Hephthalites had become the main power in the east: it was to them that the Sasanian prince Peroz appealed for assistance in defeating his brother Hormizd III in 457. Although Peroz (459–484) succeeded in recovering his throne, he was later defeated and captured by his former allies. According to al-Tabari, the name of the Hephthalite king was Akhshunvar (a Sogdian title, *khsundar* meaning 'king'); or Khushnavaz according to the poet Firdausi. Peroz was freed in return for leaving his son Kavad as hostage; and when Kavad was ransomed, Peroz returned and attacked the Hephthalites. This resulted in his defeat and death, and the loss of his army.[32] After this defeat the Sasanians had to pay an annual tribute to the Hephthalites and some parts of the eastern region fell into the hands of the enemy. Kavad even asked the Romans to lend him money to pay the tribute.[33] In 498 or 499, however, it was through Hephthalite support that Kavad I regained his throne.[34]

During the rule of Khusrau I Anushirvan (531–579) the Türks arrived on the Jaxartes steppes from Mongolia. In order to crush the Hephthalites, Khusrau allied himself with the Türk *kaghan* known in Arabic and Byzantine sources as Sinjibu or Silzibul. A fierce battle took place, the result of which was the defeat and dispersal of the Hephthalites and the division of their land. The southern part was taken by the Sasanians and the north by the Türks.[35] At the same time Khusrau I rebuilt the lines of fortification on the Gurgan plain of eastern Mazandaran. One such fortification was Sadd-i Iskandar ('Alexander's barrier'), or Sadd-i Anushirvan; a second was the wall of Tammisha, running

29. Bivar, 1979, p. 331; Curiel, 1953, pp. 107–9.
30. Göbl, 1976, p. 340; Bivar, 1979, p. 331.
31. Bivar, 1969*a*, p. 55.
32. Ibid.
33. Christensen, 1944, pp. 316–17.
34. Bivar, 1969*a*, p. 56.
35. Ibid.; 1975; 1983, p. 215.

from the mountains to the seashore and closing the eastern approach to Mazandaran. Khusrau is also supposed to have rebuilt the wall and defences of Darband in the Caucasus.[36]

The Sasanian administration

At the head of the Sasanian state stood the king. In official inscriptions the Sasanian kings called themselves 'Mazda – worshipping majesty, of the race of the gods'. According to Ammianus Marcellinus (XXIII, 6.5), the Sasanian king considered himself 'brother of the sun and moon'. On reliefs, 'in the language of transparent symbols, the King of Kings is shown as the earthly incarnation of the supreme deity'.[37]

During the Early Sasanian period the administration of the provinces and districts did not differ greatly from that under the Parthians. It was during this period that the royal cities, almost equivalent to semi-independent kingdoms, were built (see below).[38] In the early inscriptions we find mentions of *shahr*s (vassal kingdoms) such as Merv, Kerman, Sakastan, Adiabene, Iberia, Makran, Mesene, Kushanshahr and Armenia, which had submitted to Sasanian rule. In many cases the rulers of these kingdoms were the sons of the monarch himself.

In the Early Sasanian period, Shapur I was the ruler of the kingdoms listed, all of which had to pay tribute and submit in varying degrees.[39] It was in the later part of the Sasanian period that a greater centralization took place: in theory the empire was divided into four parts, each governed by an official appointed by the king, with both military and civil powers. The title of the commander was *spāhbad*.[40]

Royal cities

The Sasanian royal cities (under the administration of a *shahrab*) were the headquarters of the military garrison, centres of newly formed administrative districts and residences of the state officials.[41] Ardashir I himself founded many cities, one of which was Ardashir-Khvarreh ('Glory – or fortune – of Ardashir'). From a military outpost, it grew to become an administrative district with Gur

---

36. Frye, 1977, pp. 7–15; Bivar and Fehrevari, 1966, pp. 40–1, Pl. 11 (a–b) and Fig. 1 (map of the region); Kiani, 1982*a*, pp. 73–9; 1982*b*; Bivar, 1983, p. 215.
37. Frye, 1983, p. 160.
38. Lukonin, 1983, p. 735.
39. Ibid., pp. 731–2.
40. Ibid., pp. 723–5.
41. Ibid., pp. 120–1, 162, 751, 1056.

FIG. 2. Taq-i Kasra at Ctesiphon. (Photo: © Barbara Grunewald.)

as its centre. It was laid out on a circular urban plan. In the words of al-Tabari, 'Shapur I, like his father, founded or renamed cities and we can see an example of both in his inscription – Gundeshapur and Peroz-Shapur – while other towns mentioned by Arabic or Persian authors may be attributed to either Shapur I or II.'[42] According to Christensen, 'Other cities were Shad-Shapur, "Joyful is Shapur", or ʿUbulla in southern Iraq, Shapur-Khvast near Khurramabad, Vuzurg-Shapur or ʿUkbara in Iraq, as well as others, but none in the eastern part of the empire. These cities, like Darabgird and Gur in Fars, were surrounded by walls and were presumably well fortified, a feature of Sasanian city planning.'[43] The most famous city founded by Shapur I was Bishapur, with a Greek plan. It was probably built in A.D. 262, six years after his triumph over the Roman emperor Valerian.

The administrative capital of the Sasanians was Ctesiphon. It consisted of a group of towns known as the *madā'in* (meaning 'the cities' in Arabic), two of which were Veh-Ardashir and Veh-Antiokh-Khusrau; the district in which they were situated was called (at least during the sixth century) Shad-Kavad. Taq-i Kasra (Fig. 2), a building dating probably from the Early Sasanian epoch

42. Al-Tabari, 1879–89, Vol. 1, pp. 961–2.
43. Christensen, 1944, p. 361.

and extended or embellished during the rule of Khusrau I, was situated in the city. Ctesiphon was not only the seat of most Sasanian kings but also the most important of the Sasanian capitals in economic and strategic terms. Besides cities such as Ardashir-Khvarreh, Bishapur, Gundeshapur, Susa, Dastagird (held as a capital during the reign of Khusrau II and located east of Ctesiphon) and Ecbatana (a summer capital), the city of Istakhr in Fars also served as an administrative, religious and economic centre. It was the ideological heart of the empire, since the temple of the dynasty's fire – the coronation place of many Sasanian rulers – was situated there.

The reforms of Khusrau I

Khusrau's success in overcoming the religious movement of the Mazdakites (see Chapter 17) and managing to put the country's life in order gave him a great opportunity to start his reforms. One of these was the new policy on land taxation and the poll tax. According to al-Tabari, the change in the land tax had already begun during the reign of Kavad I.[44] The Arab historian reports that the farmers had had no right to harvest crops or gather fruit from their garden before the arrival of the tax collector; the long wait meant that their produce was frequently wasted. To avoid this, Khusrau introduced a new fiscal system. First, he ordered the lands to be measured. Next he fixed the amount of tax to be levied for each *griv* (Arabic *jarib*, one-tenth of a hectare) according to what was cultivated there; for example, 1 *griv* of wheat or barley = 1 drachm, and 1 *griv* of vineyard = 8 drachms. Under the new regulations, all persons between the ages of 20 and 50, except nobles, soldiers and priests, were compelled to pay the poll tax, whose amount ranged from 12 drachms (Arabic dirhams) to 4 drachms, according to wealth.

The taxes were collected according to the administrative sub-divisions of the country from village up to province, with the officer in charge of a province being responsible for overall supervision and the tax in each city being paid to the judge of that city. Al-Tabari reports that Khusrau ordered the list of the new tax rates to be kept in the royal treasury. With the implementation of these new measures and the appearance of organized tax collectors, Khusrau was able to maintain a regular income for the government. Supervision of the payment of taxes into the royal treasury was undertaken by the *hāmārkar* (accountant), who was also responsible for issuing documents on the right of ownership and possession.[45] The great tax reform of Khusrau I marked a turning point in the Sasanian state administration. For the first time, the power of the landed nobility was restricted and all the taxes were in the hands of the king.[46]

44. Al-Tabari, 1879–89, Vol. 1, pp. 961–2.
45. Lukonin, 1983, p. 726; Dennet, 1950, p. 15.
46. Al-Tabari, 1879–89, Vol. 1, p. 963; Christensen, 1944, p. 362; Lukonin, 1983, p. 746.

The economy

Since the vast majority of the population were peasants, the country's economy was based on land and agriculture. The archaeological survey of Khuzistan and the area north of Baghdad shows the great Sasanian interest in irrigation and cultivation. One of the great irrigation systems was the Nahravan canal, which supplied the water for a vast area of cultivation. The remains of Sasanian canals and dams can still be seen in various parts of Iran. These activities increased during the rule of Khusrau I, under whom large areas of land were brought under cultivation.[47]

Thus the national economy continued to be based on agriculture rather than trade. In commerce, Sasanian coinage of silver and copper, more rarely of gold, circulated over a wide area and the bill of exchange appeared.[48] More money was in circulation in the towns, as shown by the great number of silver drachms found in Iran and neighbouring countries. In the rural districts, however, the wages of the peasants, soldiers and officials, and even some of the taxes, were paid in kind. The levying of dues and taxes in kind enabled the government to build up large stocks of essential goods that could be called upon in time of famine.[49]

It is probable that silk was already being imported into Iran from China in Achaemenid times.[50] In the Sasanian era, two routes were used, one overland (still called the Silk Route) and the other the sea route around the coasts of South-East Asia, although this was less popular than the overland route.[51] Silk was woven mainly in Syro-Phoenician and Chinese workshops; besides the woven silk from China, large quantities of raw silk yarn were also imported for weaving to purely Sasanian designs, creating a rival industry. The workshops of Susa, Gundeshapur and Shushtar were later famous for their products.[52]

Luxury ceramics, glassware, textiles, amber and papyrus were imported and there was a transit trade in spices from China and Arabia.[53] However, Iran's position was as a middleman that benefited from the value of the traded items. The excavated finds from Begram, which can be ascribed to the Early Sasanian period, indicate commodities in transit such as decorated glassware and glass beads, ivories and manufactured metal. Although the Sasanian coin finds from China show the use of Iranian silver, this is not enough to prove

47. Frye, 1983, pp. 160–1; on Khuzistan, see Adams, 1961; on Iraq, see Adams, 1965.
48. Ghirshman, 1978, pp. 341–2.
49. Ibid.
50. Bivar, 1970, p. 1.
51. Ibid.
52. Ghirshman, 1954, p. 342; Bivar, 1970, p. 2.
53. Ghirshman, 1954, p. 342.

that Sasanian imports from China were substantially financed by a mass of silver coins.[54]

Sasanian coins

All the Sasanian rulers struck coins, and these are an invaluable source of historical, cultural and economic information. A constant denomination and weight standard were adopted, and the coins bore the ruler's effigy on the obverse and a fire-altar on the reverse. On the obverse the king's portrait faces right, in contrast to the practice under the Arsacids – except on commemorative issues, frontal portraiture is rare (Plate V, 29). The name of the king and his titles are inscribed close to the edge. Each ruler has his own personal crown, which is a reliable guide to the whole range of Sasanian art and its chronology. Only one queen's portrait, that of Boran, appears on the coins (Plate VI, 35).

On the reverse the fire-altar with flames always appears, with three principal variations: by itself (Plate I, 1, 2, 3), with two flanking figures, or with a bust in the flames (Plate III, 14, 15). The significance of the two attendant figures in the second type has not yet been clarified. At the beginning of the issues the figures carry long rods, and later barsom-bundles in their hands, facing towards or away from the altar. In the time of Khusrau I they appear frontally (Plate IV, 23), and from the time of Bahram II (275–293) onwards at least one of the attendant figures, judging from the crown, represents the ruler (Plate II, 7, 8). Special reverse designs allude to investitures (Mithra or Anahita); special issues under Khusrau II (590–628) show a bust in a nimbus of flames (Plate V, 29), or the king standing.

The Sasanians adopted the traditional silver drachm of Attic weight, the most common currency of the Parthian period. The weight (almost 4 g) and the fineness of the metal used were, with few exceptions, well maintained. Besides drachms there were half-drachms, obols and half-obols, and tetradrachms of a poor silver alloy (billon). The striking of gold was also revived, but only for prestige and display issues. Some rulers did not strike gold coins and after Khusrau II their issue ceases.[55] The formulation of Sasanian coin inscriptions was determined by the political and religious motives of the dynasty. They are written in Sasanian Pahlavi with the use of ideograms. On the obverse the royal name and titles appear, and on the reverse the name of the royal fire, with later the place of minting and regnal year.[56]

One of the chief characteristics of the Late Sasanian coinage is represented by the mint monograms that appear on the right side of the reverse and give

54. Bivar, 1970, pp. 2–4.
55. Göbl, 1983, pp. 322–8.
56. Ibid.

FIGS. 1, 2, 3. Ardashir I.

FIG. 4. Shapur I.   FIG. 5. Hormizd I.   FIG. 6. Bahram I.

PLATE I. (Courtesy of M. I. Mochiri.)

FIGS. 7, 8. Bahram II.   FIG. 9. Narseh.

FIG. 10. Narseh.   FIG. 11. Hormizd II.   FIG. 12. Shapur II
                                                    (gold dinar).

PLATE II. (Courtesy of M. I. Mochiri.)

FIG. 13. Ardashir II.   FIG. 14. Shapur III.   FIG. 15. Bahram IV.

FIG. 16. Yazdgird I.   FIG. 17. Bahram V.   FIG. 18. Yazdgird II.

PLATE III. (Courtesy of M. I. Mochiri.)

FIG. 19. Peroz.   FIG. 20. Valash.   FIG. 21. Kavad I.

FIG. 22. Jamasp.   FIG. 23. Khusrau I.   FIG. 24. Hormizd IV.

PLATE IV. (Courtesy of M. I. Mochiri.)

FIG. 25. Bahram VI.   FIG. 26. Vistahm.   FIG. 27. Hormizd V.

FIGS. 28, 29, 30. Khusrau II.

PLATE V. (Courtesy of M. I. Mochiri.)

FIG. 31. Kavad II.   FIGS. 32, 33. Ardashir III.

FIG. 34. Khusrau III.   FIG. 35. Queen Boran.   FIG. 36. Queen Azarmigdukht.

PLATE VI. (Courtesy of M. I. Mochiri.)

FIG. 37. Hormizd VI.   FIG. 38. Khusrau IV.

FIGS. 39, 40, 41. Yazdgird III.

PLATE VII. (Courtesy of M. I. Mochiri.)

51

the names of mint cities in abbreviated forms. These forms stand for the full Sasanian names of those cities authorized to possess mints. About 200 of these mint signs are known to us,[57] such as:

'W   for Hormizd Ardashir (present-day Ahvaz)
'PR   for Abarshahr (Nishapur)
'RT   for Ardashir-Khvarreh (Firuzabad)
'HM   for Hamadan
'YL'N   for Eran-Khvarreh-Shapur (Susa)
BYŠ   for Bishapur in Fars.

The army, warfare and armaments

Khusrau I's second most important reform was the reorganization of the army which, together with the implementation of the new taxation system, gave him a secure foundation from which to safeguard the empire. Previously, all nobles, great and small, had been obliged to equip themselves and their followers and serve in the army without pay, but Khusrau issued equipment to the poorer nobles and paid a salary for their services. Consequently, the power of the great nobles – who frequently had their own private armies – was reduced.[58] A permanent army of cavalry known as *aswārān* (Arabic, *asāwira*), designating a heavily armed and disciplined force, existed.[59] According to Ammianus Marcellinus (XXIII, 6.83): 'They rely especially on the valour of their cavalry, in which all the nobles and men of rank undergo hard service.'

The weaker part of the army was the infantry, consisting of peasants subject to military service. Ammianus Marcellinus reports (XXIII, 6.83; XXIV, 6.8), 'The infantry are armed like the *murmillones* [gladiators], and they obey orders like so many horse-boys.' According to Procopius, the Persian infantry were used to destroy town walls after a victory. There were also auxiliary troops from the various nations allied to the central government such as the Armenians, the Hephthalites and the Dailamites.[60] Al-Tabari tells how a group of Dailamites under the command of Vahriz were sent to capture the land of Yemen.[61] The command structure of the army was also changed under Khusrau I. Previously the entire army had been under the command of an officer known as the *spāhbad*. Now, four commanders were appointed, each in charge of the troops of one-quarter of the country.[62] Each of these newly created

---

57. Bivar, 1963, pp. 169 et seq.; Tyler-Smith, 1983, pp. 240–7 (review of Mochiri, 1977).
58. Frye, 1983, p. 155.
59. Al-Tabari, 1879–89, Vol. 1, p. 2562; Vol. 2, p. 1604.
60. Inostrantsev, 1926, pp. 23–4.
61. Al-Tabari, 1879–89, Vol. 1, pp. 948–88.
62. Ibid., p. 894; Christensen, 1944, p. 365.

commanders had a deputy called a *marzbān*. The soldiers were inspected every year in order to prevent them from escaping their duty, and to maintain their equipment. Conditions of service were arduous and all soldiers had to study and be familiar with a range of military instructions, information on which can be found in the Pahlavi book, the *Dēnkard*.[63]

A fragment of a military treatise found in the *ʿUyūn al-akhbār* (Ibn Qutaiba Dinawari) confirms the existence of a military book during the reign of Khusrau I, who himself may have written such a treatise. Al-Tabari[64] records the equipment that members of cavalry units were required to carry at muster parades of Khusrau I: mail, breastplate, helmet, leg guards, arm guards, horse armour, lance, buckler, sword, mace, battle axe, quiver of thirty arrows, bow case with two bows, and two spare bow strings. According to Frye:

> The reform of the army . . . was changed from the previous practice of the great feudal lords providing their own equipment and bringing their followers and retainers into the field to another system with a new force of *dihqāns* or 'knights' paid and equipped by the central government . . . Also, it should be remarked that the army reorganization under Chosroes [Khusrau I] was concentrated on organization and on training, rather than any new weapons or technical advances, and as previously the heavily armed cavalry remained the dominant force with archers less important. The masses, as usual, were still camp followers and little more than a rabble looking for booty, but a new nobility of service was created which became more influential than the landed nobility. Since payment in specie or even in kind did not suffice to recompense the 'knights', villages were granted to them in fief, and a large class of small landowners came into existence . . . Walls and forts also were built on the frontiers.[65]

The Sasanians expended great effort in fighting Rome, Byzantium and the eastern nomads who invaded the Iranian frontiers. They clearly had a strong and efficient military force.[66] There were changes in the conduct of warfare over time, however, one of which was the development of the bow as a primary weapon with the arrival of the Huns during the mid-fourth century.[67]

The relief frieze of Ardashir I at Firuzabad is a representation of cavalry warfare. It is known that the king personally took part in the battle.[68] Although the Ardashir relief does not depict the mace and battle axe, there is evidence of their use during the Late Parthian and Early Sasanian periods. The cavalry do not appear to have used shields in the Early Sasanian period.[69]

---

63. West, 1982, pp. 86–90.
64. Al-Tabari, 1879–89, Vol. 1, p. 964; Balʿami, 1874, p. 1048; Christensen, 1944, pp. 362–3; Bivar, 1972, pp. 276–91.
65. Frye, 1984, p. 326; on the military reforms, see Bivar, 1972, pp. 273–91.
66. Bivar, 1972, pp. 273–91.
67. Ibid., p. 281.
68. Ibid., p. 275.
69. Ibid., p. 276.

Part Two

Customs, Arts and Crafts

(A. V. Nikitin)

One of the best descriptions of Iranian customs and lifestyle in the Sasanian period is that given by Ammianus Marcellinus (XXIII, 6.75–80):

> Among these many men of differing tongues there are varieties of persons, as well as of places. But, to describe their bodily characteristics and their customs in general, they are almost all slender, somewhat dark, or of a leaden pallor, with eyes grim as goats', eyebrows joined and curved in the form of a half-circle, not uncomely beards, and long, shaggy hair. All of them without exception, even at banquets and on festal days, appear girt with swords; an old Greek custom which, according to the trustworthy testimony of Thucydides, the Athenians were the first to abandon. Most of them are extravagantly given to venery, and are hardly contented with a multitude of concubines; they are free from immoral relations with boys. Each man according to his means contracts many or few marriages, whence their affection, divided as it is among various objects, grows cold. They avoid as they would the plague splendid and luxurious banquets, and especially, excessive drinking. Except for the kings' tables, they have no fixed hours for meal-times, but every man's belly is, as it were, his sundial; when this gives the call, they eat whatever is at hand, and no one, after he is satisfied, loads himself with superfluous food. They are immensely moderate and cautious, so much so that they sometimes march through an enemy's gardens and vineyards without coveting or touching anything, through fear of poison or magic arts. Besides this, one seldom sees a Persian stop to pass water or step aside in response to a call of nature; so scrupulously do they avoid these and other unseemly actions. On the other hand, they are so free and easy, and stroll about with such a loose and unsteady gait, that one might think them effeminate; but, in fact, they are most gallant warriors, although rather crafty than courageous, and to be feared only at a long range. They are given to empty words, and talk madly and extravagantly. They are boastful, harsh and offensive, threatening in adversity and prosperity alike, crafty, haughty, cruel, claiming the power of life and death over slaves and commons. They flay men alive, either bit by bit or all at once, and no servant who waits upon them, or stands at table, is allowed to open his mouth, either to speak or to spit; to such a degree, after the skins are spread, are the mouths of all fettered.

This picture is supplemented by the surviving Sasanian works of art, most of which depict scenes from the lives of kings or noblemen. Life at the royal court was governed by a strict code of protocol: the Byzantine system of court etiquette borrowed much from the court of the Iranian *shahanshah* (king of kings).[70] Sasanian inscriptions enumerating the members of the royal family

---

70. Lukonin, 1983, p. 710.

FIG. 3. Sasanian silver dish showing a royal hunt. (Photo: © British Museum.)

and courtiers, and the positioning of the king and nobles on reliefs, are in a standard order. Arab and Byzantine sources provide descriptions of the ceremony for the reception of ambassadors to the court of the *shahanshahs*. One of the traditional pastimes of the king and nobles was the hunt, for which special preserves or game parks were built. Ammianus Marcellinus (XXIV, 5.2) describes one such park that Roman soldiers saw during the emperor Julian's campaign in Mesopotamia in the year 363. Scenes of the royal hunt were the most common theme used to ornament Sasanian silverware (Fig. 3).

Sasanian cities and fortifications

So far, there has been adequate archaeological investigation of only a small number of the cities of Sasanian Iran: consequently, there are few examples from which to assess the system of urban design. The layout of many of the ancient Parthian cities appears to have survived unchanged into Sasanian times. Late tradition ascribes the founding of a large number of cities to Ardashir I (226–241). The new capital of Ardashir-Khvarreh (modern Firuzabad) built by Ardashir in Fars was of archaic layout. Circular in ground plan, it was surrounded by a wall with four gateways placed at the points of the compass. The various districts were delineated by main streets radiating from the centre and dividing the city into 20 sectors.[71]

FIG. 4. Tureng-tepe. Sasanian fort.
(Photo: © Mission Archéologique Française en Iran.)

Bishapur, built by Shapur I (241–271) in the seventh decade of the third century, had a regular ground plan in keeping with the rules for city design elaborated by Hippodamus of Miletus. Two main streets intersecting at right angles divided the city into four main districts, which were also of a regular layout. The architecture of Bishapur reveals clear Roman and Iranian influences and the Greek and Syrian masters and artists whom Shapur invited also had a hand in its construction.[72] By contrast, the port city of Siraf on the coast

71. Huff, 1973, p. 193.
72. Ghirshman, 1956, p. 194.

FIG. 5. Takht-i Sulaiman. General view.
(Photo: © Deutsches Archäologisches Institut, Abteilung Teheran.)

of the Persian Gulf grew up without a master plan. Its districts, which occupied an area of around 1 sq. km, lay against the fortress that protected the port and were surrounded by a wall.[73] The irregular layout of some contemporary Iranian cities would appear to date back to Sasanian times.

Most Sasanian cities were fortified. A system of fortresses and forts protected the borders of Iran, the approaches to the cities and the caravan roads. Their walls were built of stone blocks, cemented cobbles or sunbaked brick. At the corners, and at regular intervals along the walls, there were round towers with narrow, vertical arrow-slots. The tower of the Sasanian fort at Turengtepe in northern Iran had eight arrow-slots on the lower tier, widening from their mouths (Fig. 4).[74] Studies have been undertaken of the fort in Siraf, probably built under Shapur II (309–379) to protect the port against Arab attacks: its stone walls with round towers form a square, each side measuring 50 m; and the entrance in the middle of the south wall is defended by a barbican.[75]

Some idea of fifth- and sixth-century fortifications is given by the walls and towers of Takht-i Sulaiman (formerly Shiz) in Iranian Azerbaijan (Fig. 5).

73. Whitehouse and Williamson, 1973, p. 35.
74. Deshayes, 1973, p. 144.
75. Whitehouse and Williamson, 1973.

Built of dressed stone embedded in cement, and crowned with battlements, the walls were about 4 m thick and reached a height of 12 or 15 m.[76] The remains of fortifications built in the Parthian period and rebuilt in the fifth and sixth centuries still stand near Gurgan: they once defended Iran's northern border against nomadic raids. A system of fortresses set every 3–6 km, and linked by an unbroken wall, stretched from the Caspian shore more than 180 km eastwards.[77]

The acme of Sasanian military construction is represented by the fortifications of Darband, which stood across the road along the west coast of the Caspian; their construction began under Yazdgird II (438–457). The defences include the city's northern and southern walls, the citadel and a wall strengthened by stone forts that stretched 40 km to the Caucasus mountains. The fortifications were originally built of sunbaked brick and later of raw stone, but in the mid-sixth century, under Khusrau I (531–579), new walls were built of large stone slabs on the old foundations. To this day, the walls of Darband stand 20 m high in places.[78]

According to tradition, Shapur I used Roman prisoners of war to build dams and bridges in Mesopotamia and Khuzistan. It appears to have been during his reign that the irrigation works were constructed on the banks of the Karun river near Shushtar; the most famous is the Valerian dam and bridge. Faced with stone slabs, this enabled the water level in one of the Karun's tributaries to be raised by 2 or 3 m. The length of the stone bridge, which is reminiscent of similar Roman structures, was over 500 m. Another bridge more than 400 m long has been preserved in Dezful, not far from Susa. There were several bridges across ravines and rivers on the ancient road that linked Ecbatana (modern Hamadan) and Susa.

Sasanian court architecture

Sasanian court architecture differed considerably from that of the Hellenistic and Parthian periods. From the outset it made use of a number of new principles that were then retained in later times. Some of them probably originate in the architectural tradition of Fars, which is as yet little known. In a number of cases a conscious imitation of Achaemenid models and Roman or Parthian influence are to be seen. The earliest monument of Sasanian court architecture is the palace of Ardashir I near Firuzabad.[79] Its design observes the principle of combining the *apadana* (official palace) and the *harem* (private residence).

76. Naumann, 1977, p. 34.
77. Kiani, 1982*b*, p. 12.
78. Kudryavtsev, 1982, p. 65.
79. Reuter, 1938, p. 534.

FIG. 6. Palace of Sarvestan. General view.
(Photo: © Deutsches Archäologisches Institut, Abteilung Teheran.)

Measuring 55 × 104 m, the palace is laid out along the north-south axis. The northern part contains the throne room and the large rooms alongside it, roofed with low cupolas on squinches. The anteroom to the throne room is of the open *aiwān* (hall) type. The southern part contains the inner courtyard onto which the private rooms look out. The plaster decoration of the niches imitates the stone ornamentation on the portals of Achaemenid palaces. The walls, which are up to 4 m thick, are made of stone cemented with lime mortar.

Shapur I's palace at Bishapur reflects Graeco-Roman architectural influence. A cruciform throne room is contained within a square of outer walls 50 × 50 m, with a narrow gallery around the perimeter. The plaster decor – the meander and the plant designs – imitates the typical motifs of the art of Imperial Rome. The mosaics adorning the floor of the Grand *Aiwān* are in the Syro-Roman style – the dancing girls, musicians and theatrical masks depicted scenes from the Dionysiac cycle.[80]

The combination of *aiwān* and domed premises was also used in later palaces. The same design was used for the palace at Sarvestan near Firuzabad (Figs. 6 and 7), which tradition ascribes to Bahram V (420–438). It has a more sophisticated roofing structure, however: the vaults of the two symmetrically located side rooms rest not on walls, but on a system of arches standing on square columns (Fig. 8).[81] The next development in this traditional design is

80. Ghirshman, 1956, p. 193.
81. Shepherd, 1983, p. 1065.

FIG. 7. Palace of Sarvestan. General view.
(Photo: © Deutsches Archäologisches Institut, Abteilung Teheran.)

FIG. 8. Roofing structure at the palace of Sarvestan.
(Photo: © Deutsches Archäologisches Institut, Abteilung Teheran.)

represented by the palace of Aiwan-i Karkha near Susa, built under Kavad I (488–531). Its central hall, roofed with a cupola, is an open pavilion, the walls being replaced by open arches.[82] Palace interiors were embellished with paintings (only small fragments of which have survived) and with plaster panels decorated with animal images or ornamentation. Palaces invariably had gardens and parks, for which special irrigation canals were dug.

The monumental architecture of the rule of Khusrau II (590–628) differs considerably from everything built earlier. The palace of Imarat-i Khusrau near Qasr-i Shirin, although laid out according to the traditional design, was built on an artificial terrace 8 m high.[83] The palace in Bisutun was built on a stone platform reminiscent of Persepolis. Colonnades came into use and elements of Achaemenid architectural decoration were copied. The Ctesiphon palace (which is of burnt brick) differs from the traditional Sasanian design; built probably in the Early Sasanian period on the site of an old palace of the Parthian kings, it largely followed its predecessor's layout, which resembles that of the Parthian palace discovered in Ashur. The façade is composed of six rows of blind arches and half-columns. The throne room is roofed with a parabolic vault spanning 26.5 m. The interior includes five large rectangular rooms, a corridor and a number of small rooms.[84]

Sasanian religious architecture

Zoroastrian religious structures of the Sasanian period are of two basic types: isolated square structures with circumambulatory corridors; and open-sided domed pavilions whose cupola stood on squinches resting on pillars at the corners that were linked by arches. Such shrines might serve as the centrepiece of a complex architectural ensemble. An Early Sasanian temple of the first type has been discovered at Bishapur. In ground plan it resembles the Parthian-period temple in Hatra. The square central building, each side of which was 14 m long, had four entrances. Another structure had a roof supported by Achaemenid-style imposts in the shape of the front part of bulls' protomes. The walls were built of rough-dressed blocks of sandstone without mortar.[85] *Chahār-tāq*s (simple domes set on four pillar-like walls) were common throughout Iran and images of them may be found on Sasanian vessels.[86] The ensemble of shrines near Firuzabad included both a *chahār-tāq* and an Achaemenid-type fire-temple.[87]

82. Shepherd, 1983, p. 1067.
83. Porada, 1965, p. 196.
84. Reuter, 1930; Shepherd, 1983, p. 1063.
85. Ghirshman, 1962a, p. 148.
86. Naumann, 1977, p. 43.
87. Vanden Berghe, 1961, p. 175.

At the site of Takht-i Sulaiman, a fire-temple has been discovered based on the same square plan with a domed roof, next to which were buildings for the priests, reception rooms and storehouses. A stone altar has been excavated similar to those shown on fifth- and sixth-century Sasanian coins. To the front of the temple complex, in the southern part of the site, there was a large lake. Together with the sacred fire, Anahita (the goddess of the heavenly waters) may well have been worshipped there. The ensemble dates from the fifth and sixth centuries.[88] There is an unusual temple, perhaps dedicated to Anahita, in Kangavar. It was probably raised on the site of an earlier temple to Artemis-Anahita that is mentioned by Isidore of Charax. The temple, which has not yet been fully excavated, stands on a stone platform 8 m high with a colonnade around the perimeter. Two gentle stone stairways lead to the platform. The structure has much in common with the architecture of the Achaemenid period but was probably built under Khusrau II.[89]

Sasanian art and crafts

Early Sasanian art is of the proclamatory type. Designed to assert the divine nature of kingship and to reinforce the state religion, Zoroastrianism, it has much that is reminiscent of official Achaemenid art. The origins of the Sasanian pictorial canon appear to lie in the culture of pre-Sasanian Fars. Much, too, was drawn from Parthian culture: both Parthian investiture reliefs and inscriptions and the relief of the Sasanian *shahanshahs* stress the concept of legitimacy. Graeco-Roman cultural influence is discernible in several genres of Iranian art at various times. In the third century the 'western style' became widespread due to Shapur I's victories over the Roman emperors, the seizure of cities in Rome's eastern provinces and the migration of Greek, Syrian and Roman artisans and artists to Iran. At the turn of the fifth and sixth centuries there was a second wave of western influence; themes relating to the cult of Dionysus became common on precious metalware and glyptic, while Dionysiac scenes appear to have been included in the Zoroastrian festivity cycles.[90]

The proclamatory nature of Early Sasanian art is best seen on cliff carvings. The choice of topics here is severely restricted: investitures, triumph and duel scenes or portraits of the *shahanshah* and his courtiers. The rules for the representation of the king and courtiers that emerged in the first years of Ardashir I's rule are much the same as those for the last kings of the local Persian dynasty that preceded the Sasanians, as illustrated on their coins.[91] The

88. Naumann, 1977, p. 48.
89. Lukonin, 1977*b*, p. 105.
90. Lukonin, 1977*a*, p. 160.
91. Lukonin, 1969, p. 23.

earliest known relief of Ardashir was carved in the ravine of Naqsh-i Rajab. Ardashir is shown standing before the god Ohrmazd (Ahura Mazda), who is crowning him king. Zoroastrianism personified its chief divinities at a relatively late period, and so Ohrmazd, the chief divinity, is portrayed in royal garb and crown. It was then, too, that the images of Anahita and Mithra were defined, as represented on coins of Hormizd I (271–272) and on reliefs of Narseh (293–303) and Ardashir II (379–383). A radiant crown was added to Mithra's kingly regalia while Anahita was shown dressed as the queen of queens.

FIG. 9. Bahram II's relief at Naqsh-i Rustam.
(Courtesy of M. I. Mochiri.)

In another investiture relief both monarch and divinity are depicted mounted, with the vanquished Parthian emperor Ardavan V lying beneath the hooves of Ardashir I's horse and the god of darkness, Ahriman, beneath those of Ohrmazd's steed (see Fig. 1). This graphic symbolism equates Ardashir's triumph with that of good over evil.[92] In the Firuzabad relief Ardashir I's victory over Ardavan V is shown in a series of mounted duels, with Ardashir unhorsing the Parthian emperor and his heir Shapur, a Parthian grandee.[93] The poses of the steeds of both the defeated and their adversaries are reminiscent of images on Parthian reliefs such as those at Bisutun or Tang-i Sarvak in Elymais

92. Porada, 1965, p. 203.
93. Ghirshman, 1962a, p. 125.

province.[94] The victories of Ardashir I and Shapur I over the Romans were reflected in reliefs showing scenes of triumph.[95] They were modelled on portrayals of the Roman emperors' triumphs: for all the differences in composition, many details are identical.

Under Shapur I and Bahram II (275–293) (Fig. 9), reliefs were carved that depicted the royal court, with the figures of the king, the crown prince, the queen of queens and the courtiers being positioned in a strictly defined order. The Zoroastrian *mōbad* (high priest) Kartir (Kirder) figures prominently in the reliefs of Bahram II. Four of Kartir's inscriptions are extant, containing his Creed and relating his activities. Alongside them, at Naqsh-i Rajab, there is a portrait of Kartir himself that is unique in Sasanian art (Fig. 10).[96] Also unusual is a relief showing Bahram II in single combat with lions at Sar Mashhad.[97]

FIG. 10. Portrait of Kartir at Naqsh-i Rajab. (Photo: © Barbara Grunewald.)

94. Lukonin, 1977*a*, p. 146.
95. Ghirshman, 1962*a*, p. 158.
96. Lukonin, 1977*a*, p. 208.
97. Ghirshman, 1962*a*, p. 173.

FIG. 11. Investiture relief of Narseh at Naqsh-i Rustam. (Courtesy of M. I. Mochiri.)

The *shahanshah*s who ruled after Bahram II have left only occasional reliefs, most of them investiture scenes. On the relief of Narseh at Naqsh-i Rustam he is crowned not by Ohrmazd but by Anahita, the patron of the Sasanian dynasty (Fig. 11). Apparently Narseh wished to stress the legitimacy of his claim to the throne he had seized and the end of Kartir's influence on the affairs of state. Ardashir II and Shapur III (383–388) each left one relief. The figures in fourth-century reliefs are more stylized and static; great attention was paid to decorative finish and to the representation of details of regal garb. Particularly interesting is Ardashir II's relief at Taq-i Bustan near Kermanshah (Fig. 12),[98] where the crown is given to the king by Ohrmazd who stands before him, while the god Mithra is shown standing on a lotus blossom behind Ardashir's back. Ohrmazd and Ardashir are trampling the figure of a fallen enemy (Fig. 13).[99]

98. Ghirshman, 1962*a*, p. 190.
99. Lukonin, 1969, p. 147.

FIG. 12. Investiture relief of Ardashir II at Taq-i Bustan.
(Photo: © Barbara Grunewald.)

FIG. 13. Detail of Ardashir II's relief at Taq-i Bustan.
(Photo: © Barbara Grunewald.)

FIG. 14. The 'great grotto' at Taq-i Bustan. (Photo: © Barbara Grunewald.)

We know of no fifth- or sixth-century reliefs: the revival of the genre dates from the time of Khusrau II (590–628). The reliefs carved in the 'great grotto' at Taq-i Bustan during his reign differ from the earlier examples in both technique and content (Fig. 14). The central scene depicts an investiture – the king is shown in the centre, larger than the figures of the divinities. Below is probably the image of the *shahanshah*, mounted and in military array, executed

67

FIG. 15. Detail of a royal hunting scene at Taq-i Bustan. (Photo: © Barbara Grunewald.)

FIG. 16. Detail of a royal hunting scene at Taq-i Bustan.
(Photo: © Barbara Grunewald.)

almost as a sculpture in the round.[100] To the left and right, on the side walls of the niche, the king is shown hunting boar in a reedy marsh or gazelle and ona-ger in a game park (Figs. 15 and 16). The scenes are executed in bas-relief with careful attention to detail. The image of the *shahanshah* is repeated several times. Taken together, the separate episodes make up a complete account that, in con-junction with the spatial aspect of the composition, is reminiscent of Assyrian reliefs. The arch-shaped façade of the niche is faced with stone blocks. In the centre are a crescent and ribbons towards which two winged Nikes are flying;

FIG. 17. Detail of ornamentation of the arch at
Taq-i Bustan. (Photo: © Barbara Grunewald.)

100. Porada, 1965, p. 207.

the figures of the goddesses and the ornamentation at the edge of the arch reveal a strong Byzantine influence (Fig. 17).[101]

The work of Iranian metalsmiths is represented by dozens of examples in the major museum collections, testifying to the wide spread of these artefacts in antiquity. They include gold and silver cups, vessels, pitchers and rhytons executed in various techniques. Casting, engraving, embossing and crusta technique might be combined in one and the same object. The earliest Sasanian metalwork was decorated chiefly with portraits of the *shahanshah*, members of his family, princes or grandees. This tradition may date back to the Parthian period, when a famous medallion bearing the portrait of a Parthian emperor was set into the centre of a vessel. Early metal artefacts include a cylix from Sargveshi (Georgia) bearing the portrait of Bahram II, Queen Shapurdukhtak and the *Sakanshah* (king of the Sakas) Bahram, and a cup bearing the portrait and inscription of the *bitakhsh* (prince) Papak.[102]

The subject that is most characteristic of Sasanian vessels, the *shahanshah* hunting on horseback, was only beginning to develop; it became widespread on fourth- and fifth-century artefacts. The king or crown prince is represented hunting lion, boar, ram or antelope. There are generally an even number of animals – two or four. The hunter attacks them with a bow or, more rarely, with a sword (Fig. 18). There are also images of kings hunting on foot; one example is a vessel bearing the portrait of Peroz (457–484) shooting caprid. The border around the edge of the vessel is a barricade of nets behind which the heads of beaters and dogs may be seen.[103] Other subjects relating to the image of the king include Yazdgird II feasting with the queen, or Bahram Gur (Bahram V) and Azada.

On sixth-century vessels, hunting scenes fade into the background – a vessel showing Khusrau I surrounded by his courtiers bears a royal hunting scene below the main composition.[104] Subjects from the Dionysiac cycle now became common – Sileni, maenads, theatrical masks and plant ornamentation – while scenes of the triumph of Dionysus that are typical of Roman and Byzantine metalwork were copied. Such vessels were probably used during Zoroastrian festivals.[105] A characteristic group is composed of rhytons in the shape of animal heads, a form common in Achaemenid times and known to the Parthians. Rhytons were used for ritual purposes while vessels bearing the king's portrait were traditional gifts from the *shahanshah* to his friends; many bore inscriptions showing the name of the owner and the weight.[106]

101. Lukonin, 1977*a*, p. 187; Fukai and Horiuchi, 1972, Pl. XXI et seq.
102. Lukonin, 1979, p. 35.
103. Trever, 1937, p. 6.
104. Porada, 1965, p. 217.
105. Lukonin, 1977*a*, p. 160.
106. Livshits and Lukonin, 1964, p. 155.

FIG. 18. Silver dish showing the king on a lion hunt.
(Photo: © British Museum.)

Little Sasanian jewellery is known. One of the most famous pieces is the so-called cup of Khusrau from the Abbey of Saint-Denis in France, which is decorated with coloured glass set in gold (Fig. 19). In its base is an inset disc of rock crystal carved in the image of an enthroned king.[107] In one hoard of coins in Iran an earring was found resembling those worn by Sasanian rulers as portrayed on coins. From Late Sasanian burials in Dailam come sword sheaths with gold and silver mountings decorated with filigree and granulation.

Sasanian gems are almost as common as coins and thousands have been described from various collections.[108] The bulk of the gems used were semi-

107. Shepherd, 1983, p. 1102.
108. Borisov and Lukonin, 1963; Bivar, 1969b; Gignoux, 1978.

FIG. 19. Cup of Khusrau.
(Photo: © Bibliothèque Nationale, Paris.)

FIG. 20. Amethyst ring. Hermitage Museum, St Petersburg.
(Photo: © Vladimir Terebenin.)

precious stones: chalcedony, amethyst, cornelian and lapis lazuli. These were either carved into ellipsoids and worn on laces or set into rings (Fig. 20). They were also used as seals. The most varied representations can be found on them – portraits of kings, grandees and private individuals, horsemen, scenes of sacrifice or feasting, fabulous creatures, animals, birds and symbols or devices. The image was frequently accompanied by an inscription giving the owner's name and title or an auspicious Zoroastrian phrase. The subjects reveal the influence both of ancient Iranian traditions and of Graeco-Roman culture. One group is of seals of officials which bear only inscriptions. Another group is of items that belonged to Iranian Christians, on which the symbol of the cross is sometimes combined with a subject from the Zoroastrian cycle. Each period had its own range of subjects and stylistic features. The images were executed either by careful working of the detail or in line technique. The chronological classification of Sasanian carved gems is still far from complete. The best-known early gems are the British Museum's stone bearing the portrait of Bahram, king of Kerman; the Hermitage Museum's amethyst showing the portrait of 'Queen of Queens' Denak (Fig. 21); and the Bibliothèque Nationale's gem representing a horseman. Stones of the later period are chiefly cut in line technique.

FIG. 21. Amethyst showing the portrait of 'Queen of Queens' Denak. Hermitage Museum, St Petersburg. (Photo: © Vladimir Terebenin.)

Sasanian ceramic vessels vary greatly in form and size. Each region had its own characteristic pottery linked with the previous period. The most common forms were various kinds of pitchers made on a quickly turning wheel. We know of vessels on which the potter's name was inscribed on the raw clay before firing.[109] The ornamentation was usually restricted to rows of straight or wavy horizontal lines, stamps or appliqué work. Throughout the Sasanian period, pottery was produced (rhytons and small, pear-shaped pitchers) that imitated metal artefacts.[110] Somewhat different are the Late Parthian and Early Sasanian vessels finished in green glaze that were common in Mesopotamia

109. Huff, 1978, p. 145.
110. Ettinghausen, 1938, pp. 664 et seq.

FIG. 22. Thick-walled spherical cups. (Photo: © Vladimir Terebenin.)

and Khuzistan.[111] Glassware is known from excavations in Kish, Ctesiphon and Susa and from Early Sasanian burials in northern Mesopotamia. The chief glass-making regions were Mesopotamia and north-western Iran. Sasanian glassware developed in isolation, although some forms are reminiscent of Syrian and Roman artefacts. Glass vessels were engraved; some extant examples are decorated with patterns cut from gold leaf and encased between two layers of glass. The most common forms were thick-walled spherical cups, with cut ornamentation made of slightly concave discs or oval facets (Fig. 22). Glass rhytons and amphorae were also produced.[112]

Weaving was a highly developed craft. Samples of Iranian silk cloth were kept in the church treasuries of Western Europe, and fragments have been found in Egyptian and Central Asian burials. Cloth was woven in the compound twill technique and was brightly coloured. The most common pattern was one of rhombic or round medallions with pictures of the *sēnmurw*s, winged horses, animals or birds, placed either in vertical rows or at random. An idea of the ornamentation and colouring of cloth and the cut of the clothing may be gained from Central Asian paintings or the Taq-i Bustan reliefs, which show the

111. Riccardi, 1967, p. 93.
112. Fukai, 1977.

costumes of the king and courtiers. A royal hunting costume designed for wearing on horseback, and consisting of trousers and a short tunic, is depicted on Sasanian vessels. Iranian clothing is described by Ammianus Marcellinus (XXIII, 6.84): 'Most of them are so covered with clothes gleaming with many shimmering colours, that although they leave their robes open in front and on the sides, and let them flutter in the wind, yet from their head to their shoes no part of the body is seen uncovered.' The products of Iranian weavers were in demand in many countries, where they were considered luxury items. The patterns on Sasanian textiles were long copied virtually unchanged in Byzantium and were imitated in Central Asia and China.[113] The artistic influence of Sasanian Iran may be detected in the cultures of many countries, from Western Europe to Eastern Asia. It made a major contribution to the subsequent development of the visual culture of the Muslim East.

113. Shepherd, 1983, p. 1107.

Table 1. The Sasanian Empire[1] (courtesy of M. I. Mochiri)

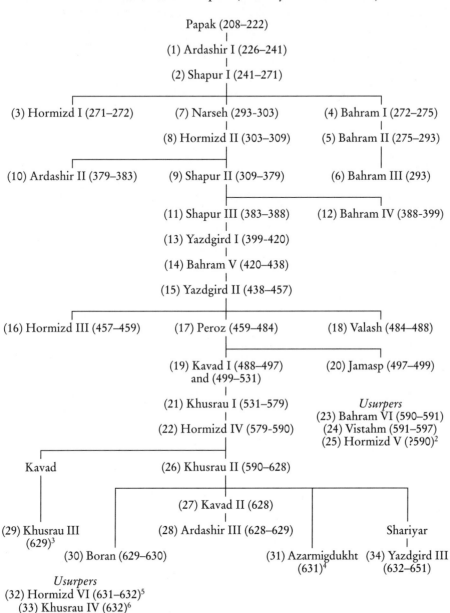

Papak (208–222)

(1) Ardashir I (226–241)

(2) Shapur I (241–271)

(3) Hormizd I (271–272) (7) Narseh (293-303) (4) Bahram I (272–275)

(8) Hormizd II (303–309) (5) Bahram II (275–293)

(10) Ardashir II (379–383) (9) Shapur II (309–379) (6) Bahram III (293)

(11) Shapur III (383–388) (12) Bahram IV (388-399)

(13) Yazdgird I (399-420)

(14) Bahram V (420–438)

(15) Yazdgird II (438–457)

(16) Hormizd III (457–459) (17) Peroz (459–484) (18) Valash (484–488)

(19) Kavad I (488–497) (20) Jamasp (497–499)
and (499–531)

(21) Khusrau I (531–579) *Usurpers*
(23) Bahram VI (590–591)
(22) Hormizd IV (579-590) (24) Vistahm (591–597)
(25) Hormizd V (?590)[2]

Kavad (26) Khusrau II (590–628)

(27) Kavad II (628)

(29) Khusrau III (28) Ardashir III (628–629) Shariyar
(629)[3]

(30) Boran (629–630) (31) Azarmigdukht (34) Yazdgird III
(631)[4] (632–651)

Usurpers
(32) Hormizd VI (631–632)[5]
(33) Khusrau IV (632)[6]

1. For some alternative dates, see Frye, 1984, p. 361. (Note, however, that some authors in this volume have their own datings.)
2. Mochiri, 1977, pp. 209–15.
3. Mochiri, 1972, pp. 17–18; 1977, p. 203; 1983, pp. 221–3.
4. Mochiri, 1972, pp. 11–16; 1977, pp. 203–5.
5. Mochiri, 1972, pp. 13–16; 1977, pp. 205–8.
6. Mochiri, 1977, pp. 174–202.

SASANIAN IRAN:
INTELLECTUAL LIFE*

A. Tafazzoli and A. L. Khromov

Part One

WRITTEN WORKS

(A. Tafazzoli)

Literary works extant from the Sasanian period may be divided into two groups, religious and secular. As the secular literature was written within the framework of Zoroastrian religious beliefs, however, it also manifests religious overtones. Translations of, and commentaries upon, the *Avesta* (the sacred book of the Zoroastrians) in Middle Persian (also known as Pahlavi), as well as books written on the basis of oral traditions of Avestan material, constitute the most important of the religious works. Literature of the Sasanian era bears the characteristics of oral literatures.

Secular literature

The interest in oral literature in pre-Islamic Iran[1] meant that, apart from state or commercial records and documents and, on rare occasions, religious works, nothing was written down until the Sasanian period. Secular literature was preserved orally by *gōsān* (poet-minstrels) or *khunyāgar*[2] (story-tellers). When Middle Persian had become obsolete and the religion, rituals and customs of the Iranians had undergone changes, the originals of many literary works of this type were lost. Thus our information, especially on the secular literature of this period, is based on secondary sources.

EPIC POETRY

The core of Iranian epic stories belonged to the Avestan people of eastern Iran. We find references in the *Avesta* to its heroes, especially the Kayanian princes who were the ancestors of Gushtasp (an Iranian king and the patron of

---

* See Map 2.
1. On the oral tradition, see Bailey, 1943, pp. 149 et seq; Boyce, 1968*b*, pp. 32 et seq.
2. Boyce, 1957, pp. 10–45; Tafazzoli, 1968, pp. 410–11.

Zoroaster). These stories, which recounted the deeds of military commanders and heroes of old, were gradually transformed in the minds of the people into marvellous feats, accumulated a wealth of detail, and were handed down orally – frequently in versified form – to later generations. There are three cycles of traditions concerning heroic tales in the Iranian national epic: the Kayanian, the Saka and the Parthian cycles.

Epic stories, frequently in verse, remained an oral form until the Sasanian period and some were used in the compilation of the *Khwādāy-nāmag* [Book of Lords] (see page 84) in Pahlavi. The only extant work of this type is the versified *Ayādgār-i Zarērān* [Memoirs of Zarer's Family]. This work was originally in the Parthian language and found its final redaction in a summarized, written form, probably towards the end of the Sasanian era. It concerns the wars between the Iranians and the Turanians after the conversion to Zoroastrianism of Gushtasp, the Iranian king. Zarer, the king's brother, was slain during these wars. The Parthian words appearing in the text betray its Parthian origin. Its poetic language is clear. A more detailed version of the story of Zarer appears in the tenth-century *Shāh-nāme* [Book of Kings] of Firdausi, who quotes it from Daqiqi.[3]

Titles of other epic stories, which probably existed independently of the *Khwādāy-nāmag* and were later translated into Arabic, are mentioned in Islamic sources. Examples are: *The Story of Rustam and Isfandiyār*;[4] the *Sagēsarān* [Leaders of the Sakas];[5] and the book of *Paykār* on the battles of Isfandiyar.[6] Short pieces of lyrical, panegyric or other types of poetry are also found in Persian and Arabic books from the early Islamic era.[7]

TALES AND LEGENDS

Towards the end of the Sasanian period, especially during the reign of Khusrau I (531–579) and later, increasing attention was paid to the task of collecting legends. The original versions in Pahlavi have been lost, but on the basis of their Arabic and Persian translations, as well as references made to them in Islamic sources, the books of stories of the Sasanians appear to fall into two groups: Iranian tales; and tales adapted or translated from other languages into Middle Persian.

The most important collection of Iranian tales was the *Hazār afsān* [The Thousand Tales], mentioned by both Ibn al-Nadim[8] and al-Masʿudi.[9] This work

---

3. Benveniste, 1932; Utas, 1975.
4. Ibn al-Nadim, 1973, p. 364.
5. Al-Masʿudi, 1965, Vol. 1, p. 267; Christensen, 1932, pp. 142 et seq.
6. Al-Masʿudi, 1965, Vol. 1, p. 229; Hamza, p. 94; Christensen, 1932, pp. 143 et seq.
7. Tafazzoli, 1974, pp. 338, 347–9.
8. Ibn al-Nadim, 1973, p. 363.
9. Al-Masʿudi, 1965, Vol. 2, p. 406.

was translated into Arabic, enjoyed widespread fame among Muslims, and was used as the basis for the compilation of *The Thousand and One Nights*. The present Arabic version, dating back to the fourteenth century, contains, in addition to Persian stories, others which were prevalent in Baghdad and Egypt at various periods. In addition to the *Hazār afsān*, Ibn al-Nadim mentions a book entitled the *Hazār dāstān*[10] [The Thousand Stories].

The most famous collection of tales translated into Pahlavi was the *Kalilag u Dimnag* [Kalila and Dimna], the original source for which was the Indian *Panchatantra*, probably its Prakrit version.[11] This work, which is now lost, was translated into Pahlavi in the middle of the sixth century by the physician Burzoe for Khusrau I (see also page 94). Ibn al-Muqaffaʿ and ʿAbdallah Ahwazi then translated it into Arabic. A Syriac translation of the Pahlavi text, dating from 570, is also extant. The *Kalilag u Dimnag* was also translated into Latin and Greek, and from Arabic into Persian on several occasions. The earliest of these Persian translations, dating back to the first half of the tenth century, has been lost; the most famous is the twelfth-century version by Abu al-Maʿali Nasrallah Munshi.

Another work of Indian origin which was compiled in Iran is the *Sindbād-nāmag* [Book of Sindbad], which probably dates back to the time of Khusrau I. Like the *Kalilag u Dimnag*, this work was also translated into Arabic, probably by the ninth-century translator Musa b. ʿIsa al-Kisrawi. According to Ibn al-Nadim,[12] two prose versions existed in Arabic. The *Sindbād-nāmag* was then translated into Persian in the tenth century and was later versified. Neither version has survived; the only available translation in Persian dates from the twelfth to the thirteenth century. It owes its fame in Europe to the Greek and Latin translations.

The *Bilauhar u Būdāsaf* is another story of Indian origin which was translated into Pahlavi during the Sasanian period, and thence into Arabic in the Islamic era. This work, which is basically an account of the Buddha's life, is not a translation of a specific Indian text but, rather, a collection of the legends surrounding the life of the Buddha. Its earliest translation into Arabic dates back to the eighth century; a tenth-century translation is also extant. Parts of the *Bilauhar u Būdāsaf* in classical Persian verse, written in Manichaean script, have been found amongst the Turfan fragments belonging to the followers of Mani.[13] The work was translated in the eleventh century into Georgian, Greek and Latin and, later, into other European languages. Many traces of the *Bilauhar u Būdāsaf* are found in Persian and Arabic books of manners and ethics.[14] The

10. Ibn al-Nadim, 1973, p. 364.
11. Mojtabayi, 1984.
12. Ibn al-Nadim, 1973, pp. 186, 364. On the *Sindbād-nāmag*, see Minovi, 1968, pp. 169 et seq.
13. Henning, 1962, pp. 91 et seq.
14. Gimaret, 1971; Sundermann, 1982, pp. 101 et seq.

Tūtī-nāmag, a translation of and adaptation from the Indian *Śukasaptati* [Seventy Tales of the Parrot], several Persian versions of which exist, was probably translated into Pahlavi in the Sasanian period.

Among the romantic tales in Pahlavi, the most important is the *Vīs u Rāmīn*, which is of Parthian origin and was translated into Pahlavi towards the end of the Sasanian period and into Persian in the Islamic era. (Both the Parthian original and the Pahlavi translation are lost.) Fakhr al-Din As'ad Gurgani turned it into Persian poetry early in the eleventh century. The work contains important information on the life, manners and customs of the Parthians.[15]

The *Vāmiq u 'Adhrā* is a romantic story of Greek origin which is said to have been translated into Pahlavi at the time of Khusrau I.[16] It was later translated from Pahlavi into Arabic (both these versions are lost). A Persian translation was made (probably from the Arabic) which was then turned by 'Unsuri (eleventh century) into poetry – some verses are extant. Part of it is also quoted in the *Dārāb-nāme*,[17] a Persian tale by the twelfth-century writer Tarsusi.

The *Alexander Romance* by pseudo-Callisthenes may have been translated into Pahlavi towards the end of the Sasanian period, probably from the Greek. It appears that a Syriac translation was later made by Christians living in Iran and using oral as well as written sources. Arabic translations were made from the Pahlavi and Syriac versions of the *Iskandar-nāme*. Versions of this romance also exist in Persian, the earliest belonging to some time between the twelfth and the fourteenth century[18] – in addition to the Arabic text, the authors used oral traditions.

The *Kārnāmag-i Ardašīr-i Pābagān* [Book of the Deeds of Ardashir Papakan], in Pahlavi, belongs to the epic genre (see also page 96). Its present version dates back to the Late Sasanian period and contains certain reworkings from Islamic times. The biography of Ardashir I (226–241) is narrated in this work through a mixture of legend and historical fact.

HANDBOOKS ON ETIQUETTE

There were several handbooks in Pahlavi dealing with institutions, court manners and ceremonies, the duties of the various social classes, the rules of battle, the arts of warfare (horsemanship and shooting), and games and entertainments (such as polo, chess and backgammon). The originals of these *Āyēn Ēwēn-nāmag* are lost, but some were translated into Arabic, parts of which, or references to them, are available in Islamic sources.[19]

---

15. Minorsky, 1964.
16. On the *Vāmiq u 'Adhrā*, see Shafi'°'s edition, 1967, Introduction.
17. Safa, 1965, Vol. 1, p. 209.
18. Afshar, 1964, Introduction, pp. 9–37.
19. Christensen, 1944, pp. 61–2; Tafazzoli, 1976, p. 266; 1985, p. 692.

LAW, EDUCATION AND GEOGRAPHY

The *Mādigān-i hazār dādestān* [Book of a Thousand Judicial Decisions] (see also pages 101–2), compiled by Farrukhmard, the son of Bahram, is the most important collection of legal texts of the Sasanian period. This work, which contains a number of legal cases concerning marriage, inheritance, ownership, endowments, and so on, was probably compiled at the time of Khusrau II, but its final redaction belongs to the ninth century.[20] Zoroastrian religious laws are also collected in other works.[21] In the field of education, a short extant treatise entitled the *Khwēškārih-i Rēdagān* [The Duties of Children] contains instructions concerning children's obligations towards their parents and teachers.[22]

The sole surviving Pahlavi work on geography is the *Šahrīhā-i Ērān*, a treatise containing a list of the major cities and fire-temples of Iran. Although it was written in the ninth century, its contents are mostly mythical and relate to ancient times.[23]

Royal *Res Gestae*

Important events of the reign of each of the Sasanian kings were written down and preserved in the imperial archives, a practice that probably dates from the very beginning of Sasanian rule. Shapur I (241–271) left a description of his deeds in a trilingual inscription on the wall of the Ka'be of Zoroaster. Narseh (293–303) left an account of his accession to the throne in a bilingual inscription at Paikuli (situated in the Zagros mountains in present-day Iraq). Copies of such works were probably preserved in the imperial archives. Through his learned Syrian friend Sergius, the sixth-century Greek historian Agathias gained access to the official written documents of the time of Khusrau I which were kept in the imperial archives. References in the *Shāh-nāme* of Firdausi suggest that when Hormizd IV (579–590) was imprisoned by his general Bahram Chobin and the nobility in *c.* 590, he expressed the desire for someone to come with a book and read the stories of the past kings to him.[24] Islamic sources mention the existence in the Sasanian period of official registers in which the events of each king's reign were registered along with his portrait.[25]

20. Perikhanyan, 1973; Macuch, 1981.
21. Tavadia, 1930; 1956; Kotwal, 1969; Safa-Isfehani, 1980; Anklesaria, 1960; Jamaspasa and Humbach, 1971.
22. Junker, 1912a; Freiman, 1918.
23. Markwart, 1931.
24. Nöldeke, 1920, §12.
25. Christensen, 1932, pp. 66–7.

THE *KHWĀDĀY-NĀMAG*

The idea of compiling a written national history for the Iranians appeared towards the end of the Sasanian period, especially at the time of Khusrau I, during whose reign books were either written in Pahlavi or translated from other languages, such as Syriac, the Indian languages and Greek. The *Khwādāy-nāmag* was probably completed during the reign of Yazdgird III, the last of the Sasanian kings, who assumed power towards the end of 631 or the early part of 632.[26] The work detailed events from the creation of the world up to the end of the reign of Khusrau II (590–628) and conformed to the viewpoint of the Zoroastrian clergy.

The Pahlavi original of this history was lost, but Arabic translations were made in Islamic times. The translators did not limit themselves to a literal translation of the original. The oldest translation is that of Ibn al-Muqaffaᶜ (c. 720–756).[27] Although none of these Arabic translations has survived intact, they served as the basis for the history of the pre-Islamic period in the works of the Muslim historiographers. The *Khwādāy-nāmag* was turned into Persian prose and verse in the tenth century. Among the prose versions, the most famous is the *Shāh-nāme* of Abu Mansur, completed in 957. Both the Arabic translations and the Pahlavi sources were used in the compilation of this *Shāh-nāme*, which, in turn, was used along with other oral and written sources by Firdausi in the creation of his epic.

Religious traditions as they existed in the *Avesta* of the Sasanian period, as well as its translations and the *zand* (commentaries upon it), naturally formed the basis of the *Khwādāy-nāmag*. According to Zoroastrian beliefs, the duration of the material world (*gumēkhtagīh*, or 'mixture') is 6,000 years, divided into 6 periods each lasting 1,000 years. All the events and reigns of the kings were placed within this framework. As may be seen in the case of the *Kārnāmag-i Ardašīr-i Pābagān*, the history of the fifth dynasty (i.e. the Sasanians), though partly based on court archives, was nevertheless influenced by legend.

POLITICAL TRACTS

Several works discussed government policies and ways and means of governing the kingdom. Among them is the *Nāme-i Tansar* [Letter of Tansar], written by Tansar (or, in the correct form, Tosar), the Zoroastrian *mōbad* (high priest) at the time of Ardashir I, in response to Gushnasp, king of Tabaristan. Although the original probably belonged to the time of Ardashir, changes were made to it in later periods, particularly during the reign of Khusrau I. The Arabic

---

26. Nöldeke, 1920, §13.
27. On the Arabic translations of the *Khwādāy-nāmag*, see Christensen, 1925, pp. 23 et seq.; 1934, pp. 81 et seq.; Osmanov, 1975, pp. 287 et seq.

translation by Ibn al-Muqaffaᶜ is also lost and what survives is an early thirteenth-century re-translation into Persian from Ibn al-Muqaffaᶜ's version. This version is by Ibn Isfandiyar, who includes it in his *History of Tabaristan*.[28]

The ᶜ*Ahd Ardašir* is another tract that bears a striking resemblance to the *Nāme-i Tansar*. The original in Pahlavi is lost and it survives in an Arabic translation.[29] The *Kārnāmag-i Anoširvān* [Book of the Deeds of Anushirvan, i.e. Khusrau I] (see also pages 96–7), an account of the work undertaken during Khusrau's reign together with methods of administering the affairs of state, is also extant only in an Arabic translation.[30]

Religious literature

AVESTAN TRANSLATIONS AND COMMENTARIES

The *Avesta* was preserved orally until towards the end of the Sasanian period, probably during the reign of Khusrau I, when it was compiled in 21 sections. To transcribe it, a script was invented from the Pahlavi script consisting of about 46 characters. An attempt was made to record the Avestan words exactly as they were pronounced at the time.[31] Although the *Avesta* was now written down, because of the importance attached to the oral tradition, manuscripts of the work were rare and the recorded text was consulted infrequently. The oldest extant manuscript of the *Avesta* dates back to 1258 or 1278. In the Sasanian period, Avestan was considered a dead language. So that the contents of the *Avesta* could be understood, it was translated into Pahlavi and the *zand* (commentaries) were written upon it. Oral traditions, as well as the sciences of the time – known to Iranians through the Greeks, Romans, Syrians and Indians – were also used in writing these commentaries. Today, translations of early works such as the *Gathas*, *Yasnas*, *Vendidād*, *Nērangestān*, *Niyāyish*, *Āfrinagān*, *Hērbadestān* and some parts of the *Yašts* are extant, but the translation of, and commentary upon, the complete *Avesta* certainly existed during the Sasanian period.

Based on the *Avesta* and its translations, many books and treatises were written on various subjects some of which, like the *Dēnkard*, constitute a religious encyclopaedia. The contents of this book, which is essentially a compilation, belong to different periods. The final redaction took place in the ninth century and we know the names of two of its compilers: Adurfarnbag, son of Farrukhzad, and Adurbad, son of Emed. Adurfarnbag was the *mōbad* of the

---

28. Minovi, 1975; Boyce, 1968c.
29. ᶜ*Ahd Ardašir*, 1967; Grignaschi, 1967.
30. Grignaschi, 1967, pp. 16–45.
31. Bailey, 1943, pp. 149–94.

Zoroastrians of Fars in this period. The *Dēnkard* was originally in nine books of which the first, second and part of the third were lost. The third book is nevertheless the largest; it deals with Zoroastrian religious principles, at times in a philosophical language, and at others in one mixed with mythical elements. The seventh book is a legendary biography of Zoroaster, based on a section of the *Avesta* called the *Spand nask*. The contents of the Sasanian *Avesta* in a condensed form constitute the eighth book. Since both the original and the Pahlavi translation of most of these parts are lost, these summaries are of great importance. The ninth book contains a commentary on three parts of the Sasanian *Avesta* which is particularly significant for its mythical contents.[32]

The *Bundahišn* [The Original Creation], an important work in Pahlavi, is also known as the *Zand-āgāhih*. Its subject-matter ranges from cosmology, astronomy and eschatology to lists of rivers, mountains and plants. Although the final redaction belongs to the ninth century, it was probably compiled in the Late Sasanian period. Two forms are available: the more detailed is called the *Great Bundahišn*; and the shorter, the *Indian Bundahišn*.[33]

The *Vizīdāgīhā-i Zādsparam* [The Selections of Zadsparam] is another important work that is similar to the *Bundahišn* in content and whose author has apparently used the same sources. Its compiler, Zadsparam, was a priest who lived in the ninth century. The book consists of four parts and deals with creation, cosmology and resurrection. It contains a section on the life of Zoroaster which is similar to the seventh book of the *Dēnkard* and uses the same sources.[34]

A book and three letters written by Manuchihr, leader of the Zoroastrians of Fars and Kerman, are extant. The book, entitled the *Dādestān-i dēnig* [Religious Judgments], contains 92 questions posed in written form by a Zoroastrian; it deals with a variety of topics such as the principles of Zoroastrian belief, cosmology, mythology and religious laws.[35]

The *Pahlavi Rivāyat* is a collection of miscellaneous material probably compiled by a tenth-century author. The work is particularly significant as it contains certain myths which are not mentioned elsewhere or are mentioned in passing, as well as providing information on religious rituals and ceremonies and popular beliefs. The practice of collecting *rivāyat* (traditions) continued among the Zoroastrians for many centuries, a collection also being extant in Persian.[36]

32. See Menasce, de, 1958; 1973, Introduction.
33. Anklesaria, 1908; West, 1880, Introduction.
34. Anklesaria, 1964, Introduction; Gignoux and Tafazzoli, 1993, Introduction.
35. West, 1882, Introduction; Dhabhar, 1912, Introduction.
36. Dhabhar, 1913, Introduction; Williams, 1990, Introduction.

Philosophy and theology

Iranians were familiar with Greek philosophy from the Achaemenid period. This acquaintance was deepened in Sasanian times, leading to the influence of Greek philosophy on Zoroastrian religious works. Although no philosophical works in Pahlavi are available from the Sasanian period, those written in the ninth and tenth centuries on philosophy and theology show that they are based on an older tradition. The third and fourth books of the *Dēnkard*, mentioned above, are among the principal philosophical and theological works. Another important example is the *Škand gumānik wizār* [The Doubt-crushing Explanation], written by Mardan Farrokh, son of Ohrmazd-dad, towards the end of the ninth or early tenth century.[37] The *Pus-i dānišn-kāmag*[38] is a short treatise containing arguments similar to those found in the *Škand gumānik wizār*. Another dialectical treatise is the *Gujastag Abāliš* [The Cursed Abalish]. It concerns a debate conducted in the presence of the ᶜAbbasid caliph al-Ma'mun (813–833) between Abalish, a Zoroastrian converted to Islam, and Adurfarnbag, one of the compilers of the *Dēnkard*. The treatise appears in question-and-answer form.[39]

Visionary and apocalyptic texts

Visionary and apocalyptic literature goes back to the *Avesta*, but the oldest extant Pahlavi text in this genre is the Kartir (Kirder) inscription at Sar Mashhad, in part of which Kartir describes his ascension to the other world. Unfortunately, this text is fragmentary and damaged. Several Pahlavi texts are extant in this field, the most important being the *Ardavirāz-nāmag* [Book of Ardawiraz]. It concerns the ascension of Viraz (Viraza in Avestan) who, according to some scholars, is identified in the work with Vehshapur, a famous priest of the time of Khusrau I. Having taken an intoxicating substance, he travels to the other world, sees paradise, hell, purgatory, the rewards accorded to the pious and the punishments meted out to evil-doers, all of which he describes upon his return. Though the essential core of the book's contents is very old, the extant version dates from the tenth century or even a little later.[40] Similar works in which the events of the world are foretold are the *Zand-i Vahman yašt*[41] and the *Jāmāsp-nāmag*, or *Ayādgār-i Jāmāspig*.[42]

---

37. Menasce, de, 1945.
38. Junker, 1959.
39. Tafazzoli, 1985, p. 58.
40. Gignoux, 1984; Vahman, 1986.
41. Anklesaria, 1957.
42. Modi, 1903; Messina, 1939.

Andarz (wisdom literature)

An important section of Pahlavi literature consists of the *andarz* (wisdom) collections, which are of two types: religious advice and pragmatic wisdom. The subject-matter of most of the *andarz* pieces of the second type may be found in the literature of other nations too, and translations of this group later found their way into the books of *adab* (literature) and ethics in Persian and Arabic. For those items which belong to the realm of oral literature, it is impossible to establish an author or a date. In Pahlavi, most such pieces are attributed to great and learned men in general – the *Andarz-i dānagān u Mazdaēsnān* is one example. However, some items are attributed to specific kings, dignitaries or religious personalities. In the third book of the *Dēnkard*, the mythical Jamshid, the Peshdadian king, is credited with the authorship of a number of these. A collection is also recorded in the name of Khusrau I. *Andarz* collections may also contain pieces of poetry; some items are in metrical prose while others are merely endowed with a poetic quality. The most extensive of the *andarz* collections is the sixth book of the *Dēnkard*.[43]

Languages and scripts

The most widespread languages during the Sasanian era were Middle Persian (or Pahlavi), Parthian, Sogdian, Khwarizmian, Khotanese Saka and Bactrian; various texts in these languages are extant.

Middle Persian (Pahlavi)

This is the development of Old Persian, or of one of its dialects, which used to be the language of the region of Fars. The evolution of Old Persian into Middle Persian probably began during the fourth century B.C., but the oldest extant documents in the latter language belong to the third century A.D. Middle Persian lacks gender and the dual form. With rare exceptions, the declensional forms of nouns and pronouns have disappeared. Among the items extant in Middle Persian are coins of the local kings of Persia (from about the middle of the third century B.C.), inscriptions by the Sasanian kings and dignitaries (mostly from the third and fourth centuries A.D.), Sasanian coins and seals, Zoroastrian Pahlavi texts, an excerpt from the Psalms and Manichaean writings. Except for the last-mentioned, they are all written in different variants of Pahlavi script.

Since the Pahlavi script was difficult, lists of words were prepared to be memorized by the scribes. The *Frahang-i Pahlawīg* is one such work in which words with different spellings, as well as heterograms (incorrect spellings), were

43. Shaked, 1987, pp. 11–16.

arranged systematically to make them easier to learn.[44] In this treatise, words are grouped under subject headings. An alphabetical version of the *Frahang-i Pahlawīg* is extant in an eighteenth-century copy.[45] A sheet from a Pahlavi glossary of the ninth or tenth century, containing seven Pahlavi verbs in the form of heterograms, was found amongst the Manichaean fragments discovered in Turfan.[46] An Avestan-Pahlavi glossary, entitled the *Frahang-i Ōim Ēwak*, is extant; it is of special importance as it contains Avestan words used in the Sasanian period but subsequently lost.[47]

The Pahlavi script is divided into two main forms, the lapidary and the cursive, both of which derive from the Aramaic. In these scripts, written from right to left like the Aramaic prototype, the vowels are not usually represented. The lapidary script is generally used in inscriptions, coins and seals – though a variant of the cursive called *kastaj* or *kashtaj* (from the Pahlavi *gaštag*) by writers of the Islamic era[48] is also sometimes used for these purposes. Unlike the cursive, the lapidary script includes 19 characters which cannot be joined. Middle Persian royal and private inscriptions of the Sasanian epoch are written in the lapidary script, the oldest being the short inscription of Ardashir I at Naqsh-i Rustam. Other important inscriptions are that of Shapur I on the wall of the Ka'be of Zoroaster (in Middle Persian, Parthian and Greek) and that of Narseh (dating from 293–294) at Paikuli.[49] Of the private inscriptions the most important are four by Kartir, all of which are located in Fars.[50] The latest inscription of this type is that of Mihrnarseh at Firuzabad in Fars, which belongs to the first half of the fifth century.[51]

The Pahlavi cursive or book script contains 13 characters and was mostly used in writing Zoroastrian works in Pahlavi. In this script, one character often represents several sounds; moreover, a ligature may be read in different ways, so that the script could be ambiguous. The oldest extant text in Pahlavi cursive was copied in 1323.[52] Cursive script was also used for writing on parchment, papyri, ostraca, stones and gems and it is found on tomb and funerary inscriptions like the Istanbul inscription.[53] Others of this type, and belonging to the Late Sasanian period, have been discovered in Fars.[54] The most recent funerary inscription, written vertically, is a ninth-century inscription found in

---

44. Junker, 1912*b*; Nyberg, 1988.
45. Nyberg, 1970, pp. 343 et seq.
46. Barr, 1936.
47. Kligenschmitt, 1968.
48. Ibn al-Nadim, 1973, p. 15; Hamza, 1967, p. 65.
49. Humbach and Skjaervø, 1978–83, p. 83.
50. For the inscriptions of Kartir, see Gignoux, 1973; 1991.
51. For the bibliography of the Pahlavi inscriptions, see Gignoux, 1972, Introduction, pp. 9–14.
52. Henning, 1958, pp. 46–7; Boyce, 1968*b*, p. 65.
53. Menasce, de, 1967; Harmatta, 1969, pp. 255–76.
54. Gignoux, 1972; Gropp, 1969; 1970; Harmatta, 1973, pp. 68–79; Tafazzoli, 1991.

China.[55] Commemorative inscriptions include those at Darband (in the Caucasus) from the sixth century,[56] the inscriptions on Shapur I's horse at Naqsh-i Rustam and Bishapur, as well as the two discovered at Maqsudabad and Tang-i Khushk and which include a statement explaining the ownership of the estate and its improvements. Finally, in cursive script, there are the tomb inscriptions of the rulers of Mazandaran (ninth–eleventh centuries).[57] A fragment of the translation of the Pahlavi Psalter, found in Central Asia, is in a variant of the cursive script. Its compilation dates back to the sixth century or earlier, but it was written down between the seventh and the eighth centuries or even later.[58]

THE MANICHAEAN SCRIPT

Manichaean works are written in a script which is a variant of the Syriac script and is peculiar to the Manichaeans (see also pages 99–101). Twenty-two letters were adopted from the Semitic alphabet and a newly evolved letter – *j* – was added to it. This script underwent little evolution from the third century until it was abandoned, probably in the thirteenth century.[59] Manichaean works in Iranian languages – Middle Persian, Parthian, Sogdian and, later, Persian – were generally written in this script. In contrast to other systems, each character in the Manichaean script represents a single sound, and there are almost no historical or pseudo-historical spellings, nor are there heterograms.

PARTHIAN (PAHLAVANĪG)

The Parthian language was spoken in the south-western areas of Central Asia and in Khurasan during the Arsacid period (third century B.C. – third century A.D.). It was a living language until some time in the Sasanian period. The main differences between Middle Persian and Parthian lie in their phonology and vocabulary, their verbal systems demonstrating remarkable similarity.

The principal remnants of the Parthian language include the ostraca (from between 100 and 29 B.C.) found at Nisa and other sites on the southern borders of Turkmenistan;[60] the first-century B.C. ostraca from Qumis in eastern Iran;[61] the first-century A.D. parchment from Awroman in Kurdistan; inscriptions on the coins of the Arsacid kings of the first half of the first century A.D.; the bilingual inscription of Seleukia (150–151);[62] the inscription of Ardavan V found

55. Harmatta, 1971, pp. 113–14; Humbach and Wang, 1988.
56. Gropp, 1975; Kasumova, 1987; Gignoux, 1992.
57. Henning, 1958, p. 50.
58. Ibid., p. 47.
59. Ibid., pp. 73 et seq.
60. Diakonoff and Livshits, 1976–79.
61. Bivar, 1970; 1972; 1981.
62. Morano, 1990.

in Susa (215); some third-century documents discovered in Dura-Europos; the inscriptions at Kal-i Jangal, near Birjand in eastern Khurasan (first half of the third century);[63] inscriptions of the Early Sasanian kings in Parthian; and the writings of the Manichaeans. The Parthian script and language began to be abandoned from the fourth century. With the exception of Manichaean literature, which appears in its own particular script (see above), all the above-mentioned items are in the Parthian script, which is an adaptation from the Aramaic with several variants. Harmatta has provided a table showing all of these.[64]

Part Two

LITERATURE, SCIENCE AND RELIGION

(A. L. Khromov)

Borrowings and influences

The fact of Persia's extensive literary borrowings from India in the Sasanian period has been established for some time. A substantial part of those borrowings subsequently passed from Pahlavi to Arabic literature and thence to the West.[65] Iranian interest in Indian philosophy and science during the Sasanian period is demonstrated by translations into Middle Persian of Indian works on mathematics, astronomy and medicine, and of belles-lettres and didactic texts (see above).

During the Sasanian period much effort was devoted to the translation of Indian works on astrology that predicted the future and described natural phenomena, such as the flight of birds and the cries of animals, in terms of good or bad omens. Some Arab sources report that the Sasanian court was visited by sages from India who advised on future events according to the position of the planets, the signs of the zodiac and the configuration of the stars. Their predictions were written down, conveyed to the king and subsequently preserved in a secret depository. Tradition has it that over 100 doctors, including several from India, were employed at the court of Khusrau I (531–579). It may thus be assumed that Indian medical works were translated in Sasanian Iran.[66]

The bulk of scientific literature in the Sasanian period, however, was translated from Syriac and Greek. To understand why this was so it is necessary to

---

63. Henning, 1958, p. 40.
64. Harmatta, 1958, p. 175.
65. Ol'denburg, 1907, pp. 49–50.
66. Inostrantsev, 1907, pp. 73–7.

explain the position of Christianity in the Sasanian Empire. In the western part of the empire (in Mesopotamia), Zoroastrianism coexisted with Christianity and Judaism and with the worship of ancient Babylonian, Greek and Syrian gods, but Christianity gradually became the main rival of the Zoroastrian clergy and the Iranian administration which it controlled. The new religion spread throughout the vast territory of Sasanian Iran, and by the seventh century Christian communities were to be found in nearly every province of both western and eastern Iran.

At the beginning of the third century there were still ethnic and linguistic differences between Zoroastrians and Christians in Iran: most Zoroastrians were Iranians while the majority of Christians belonged to other ethnic groups (Syrian, Greek, Armenian). Between the fifth and the seventh centuries, however, the Christian communities in central and eastern Iran underwent a process of 'Iranization' and the Iranian ethnic component became dominant. Relations between Zoroastrians and Christians can be summed up as follows. The Sasanian secular administration showed an extremely pragmatic attitude towards the Christians, harsh repression coexisting with the presence of Christians at court and even their acceptance as marriage partners. The Zoroastrian clergy, on the other hand, were fiercely intolerant of Christians at all periods, and were restrained only by the political and economic interests of the Sasanian rulers and their circle. Zoroastrians did not accept the alien Christian teachings, although they did not express open hostility towards the adherents of other faiths.[67] Each or all of these factors operated at some period during the Sasanian Empire and determined the extent to which literature in translation was able to circulate in Iranian society.

The Syriac-Nestorian literature of the pre-Islamic period developed to a considerable extent alongside the literature of the official Sasanian religion from roughly the fifth century onwards. Its authors were mainly Iranians.[68] The principal Nestorian schools in Sasanian Iran were in Nisibis (Mesopotamia), Ctesiphon, the Sasanian capital, and Gundeshapur (the Syriac Bet Lapat) in Khuzistan. The school in Nisibis was established following the closure in 489 of the Nestorian 'Persian school' in Edessa (founded in the fourth century by the Syrian, Ephraim), after which all the teachers and pupils moved to the territory of the Sasanian Empire. The Nisibis school, which was a theological academy enjoying special privileges, produced a number of Nestorian scholars who made an important contribution to the history of ideas in the East.[69] Its rector, Rabban, was also professor of biblical exegesis. His deputy, whose responsibilities included instruction in Bible reading and the liturgy, also taught

---

67. Kolesnikov, 1988, pp. 23–5.
68. Baumstark, 1968, p. 100.
69. Pigulevskaya, 1979, p. 67.

philosophy. The school had a tutor and a secretary. When Nisibis was taken by the Arabs in the seventh century, the school had some 800 students.[70]

The school of Gundeshapur was known less as a theological college than for its hospital (*bimāristān*) and the medical academy attached to it. The hospital was founded in the reign of Shapur I (241–271) but reached its maximum expansion in the sixth century under the patronage of Khusrau I. When the emperor Justinian closed the Academy in Athens in 529, the staff emigrated to Gundeshapur. The Nestorians who had been banished from Byzantium became energetic propagators of Greek education: it was to them that the school in Gundeshapur owed its world reputation. Students not only acquired a theoretical training based on the works of Galen but also participated in the medical work of the hospital.[71] The hospital survived until the beginning of the ʿAbbasid period in the eighth century. Many famous doctors from the school of Gundeshapur subsequently worked in Baghdad.[72]

Science and philosophy

Under the Sasanians, medicine was based on the spirit of the Zoroastrian religion but it was also influenced by Greek medicine. Great importance was attached to healing by the power of words, using magic formulae taken from sacred books. According to the *Dēnkard*, a doctor was required to have a good knowledge of anatomy, organic functions and the properties of medicine and also to be attentive to his patients. Since he was expected to visit the sick as many times a day as necessary, he had to be well fed, and provided with a good horse and a comfortable place to stay in the centre of the town. He should not be grasping: a good doctor was considered to be one who practised for religious reasons. There were, however, rules governing payment for medical care. The payment depended on the property and social position of the patient and on whether the whole body or only specific organs were treated. The doctor was required to provide the sick with regular and painstaking treatment; his refusal to examine a sick person was considered a crime. Doctors possessed a type of licence authorizing them to engage in medical practice. When an Iranian doctor was available, it was considered wrong to consult one of foreign origin; despite this, Sasanian kings often preferred to use Greek doctors or Syrian Christians.

The medical community had its own hierarchy. The first distinction was drawn between doctors who ministered to the spirit and doctors who ministered to the body. The former belonged to the same caste as the priests. Above

---

70. Fück, 1981, p. 276.
71. Ibid.
72. Siassi, 1963, p. 370; Endress, 1987, pp. 407–8.

the *drustbadh* (the state's chief doctor) stood the *mōbadān mōbad* (the state's leading religious dignitary). The autobiography of Burzoe (a famous physician during the reign of Khusrau I) was included by Ibn al-Muqaffaᶜ in his preface to the Arabic translation of the *Kalilag u Dimnag*. Burzoe gives a description of the medical literature of his day which testifies to the influence exerted by Indian medicine on that of the Sasanian period. The third book of the *Dēnkard* contains a medical treatise compiled from sources going back to the Sasanian era.[73] The tolerant attitude of the Sasanian court towards religions under Khusrau I, and the benevolent attitude of this ruler towards Christian scholars, did much to encourage the translation of works written in other languages. The Middle Persian translation of the Old Testament Psalms, fragments of which have been found in East Turkestan, was produced during this period. The basis for the translation was the Syriac text.[74]

It was Khusrau I, above all, who encouraged the development of the sciences in Iran and the use of Greek and Indian sources. Khusrau was extremely interested in philosophy and, in particular, the ideas of Aristotle and Plato. This interest was partly responsible for the appearance of a work by Paul of Persia, the *Prolegomena to Philosophy and Logic*, and the Commentaries on Aristotle's *De interpretatione* and *Analytica priore* which the same author dedicated to Khusrau I Anushirvan, 'Shahanshah, Benefactor of the People'.[75] At the court of Khusrau II (590–628), Ava of Kashgar was renowned for his knowledge of the Greek, Persian, Syriac and Hebrew languages and as a specialist in medicine and astronomy.[76]

Greek sources on astrology were reworked on the basis of Indian theories; parameters and astronomical calculations were taken over from Indian works. Works on astronomy and astrology by Greek authors were translated into Middle Persian as early as the reign of Shapur I. The Persian historian Maᶜna, the Catholicos of Seleukia under Yazdgird I (399–420), translated Greek works into Syriac and then from Syriac into Persian. Catholicos Akakios (484–496), also from Seleukia, translated the Syriac work *Discourse on Faith*[77] for Kavad I (488–531), who adopted a tolerant attitude towards Christians.

Our knowledge of Middle Persian scientific literature is predominantly based on Arabic translations and on information and quotations culled from Arab sources. The surviving Arabic versions of Middle Persian texts are based on late adaptations and exhibit the combination of Greek and Indian components that are typical of astrology in the Sasanian period. One example is the collection of tables for use in mathematical astronomy compiled during the

73. Christensen, 1944, pp. 414–20.
74. Ibid., p. 422.
75. Christensen, 1944, pp. 422–3; Pigulevskaya, 1979, p. 147; Endress, 1987, p. 408.
76. Endress, 1987, p. 408.
77. Krymskiy, 1905, p. 59.

reign of Khusrau I and re-edited under Yazdgird III (632–651). The later version was used by the Arab scientists Mashaʿllah and Abu Maʿshar, who compiled a work entitled the *Zig aš-Šahriyār* [Astrological Tables of Shahriyar], in which the combination of Greek and Indian astronomical theories can be clearly traced. In Arabic, the word *zig* became a term denoting a textbook on astronomy or astrology.[78]

A work entitled the *Varz-nāmag*, which contained an account of basic agricultural practice, was also translated into Middle Persian from Greek.[79] It is assumed that the Middle Persian text of the *Ain-nāmag*, which has come down to us in the Arabic translation and contains information on the military theory of the Sasanians, was composed under the influence of an anonymous Greek treatise and the *Strategikon* of Maurikios of Byzantium (*c.* 600).[80] The Syriac language was thus the link that enabled the Near and Middle East to assimilate the achievements of Greek science, which enjoyed a new period of creativity on Arab and Persian soil.[81] Literature translated into Middle Persian during the Sasanian period played an important part in this process.

Court chronicles and epic histories

The Sasanian period saw the revival of the ancient Iranian tradition of court chronicles, the essence of which was to interpret historical events in the light of the king's wishes. The content of historical chronicles was restricted to events which the king considered important for himself, his family and the state. They were composed under the king's supervision and were intended for his own personal use and that of his heirs.[82] The historical works of the Sasanian period focus less on contemporary events than on the past and on predictions of the future. Their purpose was to describe and extol the religious and national ideals propagated by the Sasanian élite.

There was no clear dividing line in historical works between fact on the one hand, and myth and legend on the other. Such works were not impartial accounts of events but included fantasy and emotional declarations. Hyperbole and metaphor were essential elements of their style. In the works of the Sasanian period, historical figures were endowed with the characteristics of contemporaries. For example, all the pre-Sasanian kings acquire Sasanian features and deliver speeches from the throne, as was done in the Sasanian period. References are made to sites of the Sasanian period and the historical circum-

---

78. Endress, 1987, pp. 413–14.
79. Ibid., p. 414.
80. Inostrantsev, 1909, p. 65; Pigulevskaya, 1946, p. 33.
81. Pigulevskaya, 1979, p. 31.
82. Klima, 1977, pp. 41–3.

stances described are also contemporary.[83] At the same time, these chronicles were sources of ethical guidance for all Iranians. They contained sage reflections and exhortations as well as examples of wise decisions by monarchs and their courtiers.

The *Kārnāmag-i Ardašīr-i Pābagān* [Book of the Deeds of Ardashir Papakan] belongs to the epic cycle on the Sasanian kings. Although the text was initially drafted in the sixth century, the version which has survived dates from a later period. The main character in the *Kārnāmag* is Ardashir I (226–241), the founder of the Sasanian Empire. The work describes the childhood and youth of Ardashir, his struggle for power and his ascension to the throne; it also tells of his son Shapur I and grandson Hormizd I (271–272) and of Ardashir's conflict with the Parthian king Ardavan V (c. 213–224). Although the account of Ardashir's life given in this work is largely based on legend, it reflects some historical events and facts: information is provided about Ardashir's campaigns against nomadic tribes, the history and geography of Iran and the social structure and religious conceptions of Sasanian society.

Various versions of the history of Ardashir I are to be found in works by Arab authors of the eighth to the tenth century and in Firdausi's *Shāh-nāme*. These variants, which differ from the text of the *Kārnāmag*, go back to the Late Sasanian collection of histories of the Iranian kings, the *Khwadāy-nāmag*, in which genuine historical facts are closely interwoven with legend. The royal chronicles were drawn on for descriptions of the events of the Late Sasanian period.[84]

The *Khwadāy-nāmag* and other historical works were translated into Arabic by Ibn al-Muqaffaʿ (757). The *Fihrist* of Ibn al-Nadim contains a lengthy list of Arabic translations of works of the Sasanian period. It is thanks to such translations and adaptations by authors of the Islamic period, and to references to them in the works of medieval Arabic- and Persian-speaking writers, that we have some idea of their content and nature. One of these works was the *Gāh-nāmag* which, according to the *Tanbīh* of al-Masʿudi, contained a description of the boundaries of the Sasanian Empire. Another work, entitled the *Ain-nāmag* [Book of Rules], describes the customs, morals and behaviour prescribed for kings, aristocrats and other high echelons of society. According to the information given in the Arabic and Persian sources, these works were of a rhetorical nature and were composed in the Iranian tradition. There were also a number of works on the administrative system and on individual kings and national heroes.

The *Kārnāmag-i Anōširvān* [Book of the Deeds of Anushirvan], a series of fragments presenting the thoughts and utterances of Khusrau I, is reproduced in full in the Arabic work the *Tajārib al-umam* by Maskawaih. It describes the hostile intentions of political and religious sectarians towards the

---

83. Yarshater, 1983*b*, pp. 402–3.
84. Chukanova, 1987, pp. 9, 11.

king and his efforts to preserve the traditional distinctions in society which divided warriors from peasants. The text contains information about the king's relations with other peoples, especially the Turkic Khazars to whom he extended his protection and dispatched Mazdakite missionaries. It also describes advances in legislation and cultural borrowings from Greece and India in spite of the religious differences.

The *Testament of Ardashir Papakan,* which has been preserved in the Istanbul manuscript,[85] belongs to the Late Sasanian period. It explains many aspects of royal power and touches on various questions involving the relationship between royal power and religion.[86]

The literature of the Sasanian period, particularly the historical chronicles and the *andarz* (wisdom) literature, devotes much space to the image of the ideal king, which was first conceived under the Achaemenids. The basis for the idealization of royal power is the notion that the Persian kings are called on to embody the 'national Iranian idea', the essence of which is that all world history is to be seen as a struggle between two primary principles: good and evil, light and darkness. In this struggle, it is the king's role to be the supreme commander of the army of Ohrmazd (i.e. the good principle) in the war against the forces of Ahriman (i.e. the evil principle).[87] This also determines the king's position in society and his personal qualities: he is the focus of absolute power and controls history; he surpasses all other men in physical strength, looks, intelligence and eloquence; he is the lawgiver and creator of order. All kings are not only great military leaders but also talented politicians and thinkers. They are heroes in battle, the fount of prosperity, builders of cities, creators of all that is useful in the administrative structure of the state and, most important, energetic defenders of the Zoroastrian faith.

According to the *mōbad* Kartir, the 'ideal king' should be religious above all: he must be completely subservient to his religious mentor and act and think in accordance with the dogmas of the Zoroastrian religion.[88] The king's main occupations were the administration of justice, in consultation with the *mōbadān mōbad,* courtiers of high rank and wise counsellors; the resolution of problems relating to peace and war, and the appointment of military commanders; the enactment of measures to ensure the country's prosperity; and the settlement of questions relating to hunting, banquets and weddings.[89] As the people's spiritual leader, the king was responsible not only for the country's administration but also for the regulation of its ethical and social life. He was answerable for his own conduct and for that of the government.

---

85. Grignaschi, 1967, pp. 1–2.
86. Menasce, de, 1983, p. 1,183.
87. Knauth and Nadjmabadi, 1975, p. 202.
88. Lukonin, 1969, p. 110.
89. Yarshater, 1983*b*, pp. 406–7.

The above qualities were reflected in the king's messages, testaments and pronouncements as well as in the messages of his ministers.[90] His first responsibility was to deliver a speech from the throne to his courtiers. Rendering thanks to God, he set out his plans, assuring the people of his desire to rule justly and asking for their support. The assembled courtiers approved the king's speech and his intentions and assured him of the people's obedience. The ceremony was conducted with great pomp. The king sent messages to regional governors, informing them of his ascension to the throne.

Among the Sasanians, Ardashir I, Shapur II (309–379) and Khusrau I were endowed with the traits of the ideal king. There are many written accounts in medieval Arab and Persian sources describing Khusrau I as a just and generous king. A typical story (based, in Christensen's view,[91] on a reliable source) is included in the work by Nizam al-Mulk entitled the *Siyāsat-nāme*.[92] In the story, Anushirvan the Just (i.e. Khusrau I) delivers one of his speeches from the throne in which, addressing his courtiers, he instructs them to deal generously with 'the people of God', to lighten the burden of the people, not to offend the weak, to respect the wise and to be attentive to good people. The king threatens to punish those who disregard these commandments.[93]

Religious life

ZOROASTRIANISM

In Sasanian Iran, religion played a central role in the life of society, regulating the entire spectrum of social and political life and official standards of behaviour. The Zoroastrian church was unified under the Sasanians and acquired considerable political power. Its privileged position greatly assisted the Sasanians' rise to power. The Sasanians and the Zoroastrian church were united by the idea of centralization – the power of the *shahanshah* and of the *mōbadān mōbad* were two expressions of the same view. The inscriptions of Kartir testify to his power and influence.[94] In spite of a degree of rivalry and occasionally strained relations, church and state shared the same world view and the same aims. The state usually supported the church and often helped to eradicate heresy. The church in turn supported the structure of the state, the privileges of the élite, the divine right of the *shahanshah* and the belief in complete obedience to him. Young people were nurtured in the ideals of the monarchy,

90. Yarshater, 1983*b*, p. 399.
91. Christensen, 1944, p. 369.
92. *Siyāsat-nāme*, 1949, pp. 34–42.
93. Ibid., pp. 35–6.
94. Yarshater, 1983*a*, p. xxxiv.

which was underpinned by and oriented towards the church.[95] Ardashir I issued the following admonition to his son Shapur I when the latter was preparing to ascend the throne:

> O my son, Religion and the State are sisters. They cannot survive without each other. Religion is the buttress of the State and the State is its protector. And whatever is deprived of support crashes down and whatever is not defended is lost.[96]

Zoroastrian temples in which the sacred flame was tended were to be found throughout the empire. One of the principal temples was located in Atropatene (in Azerbaijan), and in it was preserved the flame of the king and warriors. Another principal temple was situated in Fars (the flame of the priests) and a third in Khurasan (the flame of the farmers). A major role in the establishment of a unified state and church was played by the *mōbad* Kartir, whose career began under Shapur I and reached its zenith under Shapur's successors in the years 273–293 when he was *mōbadān mōbad* and spiritual director of the king.[97]

MANICHAEISM

In the course of the third century a new religion, Manichaeism, appeared in the Sasanian Empire (see Chapter 17). Its founder was Mani (216–276), who was descended from a notable of Iranian stock on his mother's side. Manichaeism, which expanded ancient Iranian conceptions of the eternal struggle between the kingdoms of light and darkness, also incorporated elements of Christianity, Gnosticism and Buddhism. According to the teaching of the Manichaeans, the world was a chaotic mixture of dark and light elements. In order to free themselves from the power of the devil, human beings had to cleanse themselves of evil and had therefore to escape from the power of the material principle.[98] Manichaeism, which spread widely throughout Mesopotamia, Iran, the Roman Empire and Central Asia, gradually came to resemble a kind of 'Protestantism', and to be an ideological weapon against evil in the world.[99] The Manichaeans (*Zandīks*) formed the principal heretical group in the Sasanian period and were frequently persecuted by the official church. Mani died a martyr's death on 20 March 276.[100]

Mani chose Middle Persian as the vehicle for the dissemination of his religion in the Sasanian Empire. Appearing at the court of Shapur I, he presented the king with a book entitled the *Shābuhragān* [Book of Shapur], which

95. Yarshater, 1983*a*, p. xviii.
96. Klima, 1957, pp. 40–1.
97. *Istoriya Irana*, 1977, p. 110.
98. Ibid.
99. Lukonin, 1969, p. 71.
100. Klima, 1957, p. 41.

contains a concise exposition of Manichaean doctrine. The work was originally written by Mani in Aramaic (his native tongue) and then translated into Middle Persian. Although all of Mani's canonical works were subsequently translated into Middle Persian, most of these translations have been lost.

One of Mani's most important works is the *Evangelion* [Gospel], which in the Middle Persian version has this Greek title. It comprises 22 chapters, each of which begins with a different letter of the Aramaic alphabet. A fragment of the introduction to this work has been preserved in which Mani refers to himself as *Yishōʿ Aryaman* (an apostle). The use of such an Iranian term indicates that the Manichaeans were concerned to make their teaching more accessible to Zoroastrians.[101]

The Middle Persian versions of Mani's other canonical works – the *Niyān-i zindagān* [Treasure of Life], the *Pragmateia* and the *Rāzān* [Mysteries] – have been lost. Fragments of the *Book of the Giants* exist in three languages: Middle Persian, Parthian and Sogdian. A collection entitled the *Epistles* has been preserved: it consists of letters written by Mani to various preachers of his community. In order to propagate their faith, the Manichaeans borrowed several stories and fables from India and China which subsequently reached the West. They thus played an active role as intermediaries in the transmission to Europe of Eastern fables.[102]

Most Iranian-language versions of Manichaean works have been preserved in Sogdian and only a small proportion in Middle Persian and Parthian. There are collections of prayers and two long psalms composed by Mani. The Parthian text of one of these psalms, entitled the *Vuzurgān Āfriwān* [The Blessing of the Great], has survived in good condition. A few Sogdian and Middle Persian fragments of this psalm have also been preserved. The second psalm, which is called the *Qšūdagān Āfriwān* [The Blessing of the Consecration] in Parthian, is similar to the first in structure and content.[103] Several Manichaean manuscripts possess good illustrations and it is believed that there was a text entitled the *Ārdhang* which contained commentaries on pictures. Iranian-language fragments of a text composed in the style of canonical tradition have also been preserved: it is known by the Greek title *Kephalaia*. The Middle Persian version of one text is a translation of a Christian apocryphal text entitled *The Shepherd of Hermes*, which was borrowed by the Manichaeans and used as an allegory of the life of man. There are also texts recounting Mani's last meeting with Bahram I (272–275)[104] and Mani's death[105] – both by eyewitnesses and dating from 274–276 or thereabouts. Middle Persian, Parthian and Sogdian frag-

---

101. Boyce, 1983*b*, p. 1198.
102. Henning, 1945.
103. Boyce, 1983*b*, p. 1200.
104. Henning, 1942.
105. Boyce, 1983*b*, p. 1201.

ments of texts have also been preserved which present the story of the Manichaean church and Mani's life, listing his works and recounting the early missions of his followers.[106]

Some Manichaean prose works contain the rules of the Manichaean faith, fragments of homilies and exhortations in the form of questions and answers (a type of oral didactic literature encountered in Zoroastrian works). Certain works (mostly in Middle Persian) have a cosmogonic content. The fragment of a creed, works on astronomy and calendars are also extant.[107] A large number of Manichaean texts are hymns, poetic works performed to music. Two long cycles of Manichaean hymns in Middle Persian entitled the *Gowišn īg Griw Zindag* and the *Gowišn īg Griw Rošn* are dedicated to the embodiment of the Manichaean deity: this is referred to as 'the living being itself' and, according to Manichaean beliefs, embodied all elements of light scattered throughout the world.

Middle Persian Manichaean literature is notable for the eclecticism of its content, structure and style. Manichaean hymns, which were influenced by the ancient Iranian tradition (especially the Parthian texts), may be considered as something akin to poetry.[108] Art, poetry and language developed in all the areas to which Manichaeism spread, particularly where it became the state religion, if only for a limited period of time. But Manichaeism was a blatant heresy from the Zoroastrian viewpoint. It was also perceived as such by the other religions which, although alien to each other, united in the struggle against the Manichaeans.[109]

Religion and the law

The history of religious struggles under the Sasanians throws light on the underlying causes of many events involving politics and ideology. The persecution of reformers and heretics – at times, intense; at others, less harsh – is an indication of the state religion's desire to maintain its supremacy. For Iranian Zoroastrians there was an intimate connection between law and religion. Evidence of this is provided by the *Mādigān-i hazār dādestān* [Book of a Thousand Judicial Decisions], which was written in Middle Persian in *c.* 620 and has survived in a single manuscript. Its author, Farrukhmard, from the town of Gur in the province of Ardashir-Khvarreh, was a contemporary of Khusrau II. As codified law did not exist in Sasanian Iran, the book cannot be considered a legal code. It is one of the collections that were compiled as manuals for the

---

106. Boyce, 1983*b*, pp. 1201–2; Sundermann, 1971*a*; 1971*b*; 1974.
107. Henning, 1947; Boyce, 1983*b*, p. 1202.
108. Boyce, 1983*b*, pp. 1203–4.
109. Bausani, 1965, pp. 50–1.

administration of justice. In addition to general information about the rights of specific state departments and officials, such manuals contained passages from official edicts and decrees. In the specialist literature, the *Mādigān* has become known as the 'Sasanian Legal Code'. It has been established that some of the sources of this and similar codes of laws of the Sasanian period reflect statutes recorded in the legal *nask*s (precepts) of the *Avesta* and in the commentaries on those *nask*s, the so-called *chaštaq*s. The Code contains references to certain edicts of Kavad I (488–531) and Khusrau I; it also contains a remarkable instruction concerning the appropriation by the royal treasury of the property of the Manichaeans and their followers. In compiling the Code, Farrukhmard made use of legal records from the town of Gur as well as private legal documents.

It is possible to reconstitute practically the entire system of Iranian law on the basis of the mass of information contained in the Code. Its content also contributes to an understanding of other Pahlavi texts including the *Dēnkard*, the *Dādestān-i dēnig*, the *andarz* and *rivāyat* and a number of Middle Persian and Parthian epigraphic texts. The text of the Code is also important for the study of the *Ishobokht* [Code of Laws], which has survived in a Syriac translation and contains legal norms of the Christian communities in Sasanian Iran; and for the study of the Babylonian Talmud, which describes the law of the Jewish communities of the Sasanian Empire.[110]

There were sizeable Jewish communities in the towns of Mesopotamia and Iran: that in Iran was self-governing and was generally not persecuted by the Sasanians.[111] The sage Samuel was a trusted adviser of Shapur I, and the mother of Shapur II lent her support to the Jewish rabbis. The only outbreak of persecution directed against the Jews occurred during the reign of Yazdgird II (438–457), particularly in Isfahan which was the centre of the Jewish community, but it was of short duration. Nevertheless some Jews subsequently emigrated to Arabia and India.[112]

110. Perikhanyan, 1973, pp. xiii–xxiv.
111. *Istoriya Irana*, 1977, p. 111.
112. Klima, 1957, p. 44.

THE KUSHANO-SASANIAN KINGDOM*

A. H. Dani and B. A. Litvinsky

In the early centuries of the Christian era the names of two great empires stand out boldly in the history of Central Asia. The first was Kushanshahr, named after the Great Kushan emperors, who held sway from the Amu Darya (Oxus) valley to the Indus and at times as far as the Ganges. Here flourished the traditions of the Kushans, who had brought together the political, economic, social and religious currents of the time from the countries with which they had dealings (see Chapter 7). The second great empire (which rose to challenge Kushan power) was Eranshahr, which expanded both westward and eastward under the new Sasanian dynasty. Its eastern advance shook Kushan power to its foundation.

State organization and administration

According to Cassius Dio (LXXX, 4) and Herodian (VI, 2.2), Ardashir I (226–241), who waged many wars, intended to reconquer those lands which had originally belonged to the Persians. He defeated the Parthian kings and conquered Mesopotamia – an event which led to his wars with the Romans. It is more difficult to judge his conquests in the east. According to the inscription of Shapur I (241–271) at Naqsh-i Rustam, 'under the rule of *shahanshah* [king of kings] Ardashir' were Satarop, king of Abrenak (i.e. Abarshahr, or Nishapur, in Khurasan), as well as the kings of Merv, of the Sakas and of Kerman, all of whom were called 'Ardashir'.[1] But al-Tabari's information is different. He describes the

---

* See Map 2.
1. The inscription text (Frye, 1984, p. 272). Earlier editions: Honigmann and Maricq, 1953; Sprengling, 1953. The first author pointed out the difference in the titles of Ardashir I and Shapur I in 1979. Nöldeke has expressed his opinion that information from other sources concerning Ardashir's conquests in the east (al-Tabari in particular) is much exaggerated (Nöldeke, Tabari, 1973, S.17–18).

conquest of Seistan (modern Sistan), Abarshahr, Merv, Balkh and Khwarizm 'up to the farthermost borders of countries of Khurasan'. Then he writes that envoys of the Kushans, of Turan and of Makran came to Ardashir and offered their submission.[2] Shapur's dominions in the east undoubtedly reached Merv and Seistan. To study the problem, Harmatta has used Greek, Latin and Armenian sources for the conquests of Ardashir I in the east against the background of all the wars that he waged; he has also taken into consideration the chronology of the Roman-Sasanian wars. His conclusions support al-Tabari's information. Ardashir's military activity in the west lasted from 224 to 232.[3]

Harmatta[4] has rightly argued that after the conquest by Ardashir I, the western part of the former Kushan Empire became a vassal kingdom under the Sasanians, and subsequently a province governed by the Sasanian prince-governors. These prince-governors issued coins as *Kushanshah*s (kings of the Kushans). At a later stage, the king of Kabul formed a marriage alliance with Hormizd II (303–309).

During the rule of Shapur I, Ardashir's son and heir, the power of the Sasanians in the east increased. This is demonstrated by the titles of Shapur I and the inscription on the Kaʿbe of Zoroaster, according to which:

> the state of Shapur I, '*shahanshah* of Iran and non-Iran', included Varkān [modern Gurgan], Merv, Harēv [Herat], the whole of Abarshahr, Kermān, Segistān [Sistan], Turān [near Kalat in Baluchistan], Makurān [Makran], Paradān [near Quetta], Hindustān [Sind], Kušānšahr up to Puškabūr [Peshawar] and up to the boundaries of Kaš [Kashghar or Kesh], Sughd and Šāš [Tashkent]' (ŠKZ, 2).[5]

Under Shapur I, the south-eastern provinces were united administratively and the country was called 'Sind, Segistān and Turistān as far as the sea shore'. Narseh (293–303), the son of Shapur I, was appointed ruler and he received the title of *sk'n MLK'* (the king of the Sakas). The main dynastic line of the Great Kushans from Kanishka I had come to an end, but another line of Eastern Kushans con-

2. Nöldeke, Tabari, 1973, S.17–18; Frye, 1984, p. 295. However, Nöldeke and Frye suppose that most of the events took place during the rule of Ardashir's successor, Shapur I.
3. According to Harmatta, 'the main target of Ardashir's eastern campaign was apparently the Kuṣāṇa Empire'. The king made his campaign to the east in 233–235 and the Sasanian invasion of Bactria occurred in 233 (Harmatta, 1965, pp. 186–94). But Maricq believes that the eastern campaign took place at the beginning of Ardashir's I reign (Honigmann and Maricq, 1953, p. 106). We cannot establish the matter with certainty, but Harmatta's interpretation seems the most convincing.
4. Harmatta, 1969, pp. 386–8.
5. Some scholars (Lukonin, 1969a, pp. 29–30; Zeimal, 1968, pp. 92–100) doubt the reliability of the inscription concerning the description of the territory controlled by the Sasanians. In their opinion the enumeration of provinces was only a pretence, and these lands were not really included in the state of Shapur. However, other scholars (Harmatta, 1969, pp. 420–9; Livshits, 1969, p. 56) consider that the inscription on the Kaʿbe of Zoroaster is a reliable historical source and all these lands, including Kushanshahr, were included in the Sasanian Empire.

tinued to rule (see Chapter 7) in Gandhara and the Indus valley. On this inter-pretation, only the northern part of the Kushan Empire came under the direct rule of the Sasanian prince-governors.

A great number of Kushano-Sasanian coins[6] connected with the Sasanian domains in the east have been found in Pakistan, Afghanistan and Central Asia. They may be divided into three groups.[7] The first group was minted according to the model of the Kushan coins of Vasudeva. They are represented by both bronze and gold coins. On the obverse there is a figure of a standing king, each with a distinctive crown on his head and a legend consisting of the name and the title *Şahano Şaho* (*shahanshah*) (Fig. 1) of the ruler. On the reverse there is a representation of Shiva and his vehicle, Nandi (the bull), with the legend, *borzaoando iazado* (the exalted deity) (Fig. 2). These coins were minted at Balkh and perhaps also at other centres (the mint name *Bahlo* for Balkh occurs on the obverse of some issues).

The second group, also struck in bronze and gold, follow the Sasanian pattern. On the obverse they have a portrait of the ruler with his own indi-vidual crown (there are at least eight types of crown). On the reverse a fire altar is represented. These coins were minted in Merv and Herat; the language of the inscription is Middle Persian, written in Pahlavi script.

The third group consists of bronze coins that are much thicker and often of irregular shape. Their portraits are similar to those of the second group. The language of the inscription is Middle Persian, in Pahlavi script on some issues, in the Bactrian alphabet on others. Many of these coins have been found in Pakistan and it has been suggested that they were issued and circulated there. However, they have also been found to the north of the Hindu Kush and in Tajikistan.

On the basis of the coinage, the following list of the Kushano-Sasanian kings can be established:[8]

Ardashir I *Kushanshah*
Ardashir II *Kushanshah*
Peroz I *Kushanshah*
Hormizd I *Kushanshah*
Peroz II *Kushanshah*
Hormizd II *Kushanshah*   (continued on page 108)

6. Cunningham, 1893; Bivar, 1956; 1979; Herzfeld, 1930; Lukonin, 1967; 1969a, pp. 39–40; Cribb, 1981; Zeimal, 1983, pp. 257–61; Göbl, 1984, pp. 70–86; Trever and Lukonin, 1987, pp. 64–9; Harmatta, 1969, pp. 385–7, 430; and others have contributed to their study.

7. Lukonin has suggested that the first group should be called 'Sasanian-Kushan', the second 'Kushano-Sasanian' and the third 'the Group of Kavādh' (Lukonin, 1967).

8. Some scholars have pointed out that the name of Hormizd on the coins corresponds to that of Hormizd II (302–309), *shahanshah* of Iran. This provides a number of synchronisms while typological analysis has made it possible to identify the context of other coins. The concept was developed in detail by Herzfeld, 1930, and Bivar, 1979.

FIG. 1. Kushano-Sasanian coins (obverse).
(Photo: © Bibliothèque Nationale, Paris.)

FIG. 2. Kushano-Sasanian coins (reverse).
(Photo: © Bibliothèque Nationale, Paris.)

Varahran I *Kushanshah*
Varahran II *Kushanshah.*

However, Lukonin and his followers have advanced a number of serious arguments against this sequence and its chronology. His outline agrees with that of Göbl.[9]

Economy, society and trade

Several excavations undertaken in Kushanshahr provide ample material to reconstruct different aspects of contemporary life. The economic base may be inferred from the currency. Although gold and silver coins are known for several Kushano-Sasanian prince-governors, it is the copper coinage that was widely current to meet the local demands of the population. Herzfeld has shown that gold continued to circulate in international markets, as it did in the time of the Great Kushans.[10] This must be due to the continuity of trade that followed the Silk Route as in the earlier period. The only change was that whereas the Kushans had earlier controlled this trade, it was now the Sasanians who, in spite of their wars with the Romans, were in charge of the principal flow of goods. Movements of the nomads in the east may have hampered the movement of caravans but the excavated materials suggest that goods were still freely exchanged from one country to another.

The best evidence for such international trade contacts comes from Begram, Taxila and Dalverzin-tepe, where imported goods from several countries have been found together. As Ghirshman rightly remarks:

> There was a transit trade in spices from China and Arabia, and nard and pepper were exported from India. International trade encouraged the growth of colonies of merchants, particularly Jews and Syrians, who established themselves as far afield as India, Turkestan, Brittany and the Black Sea. The exporting houses became more specialized, and confined their dealings to cor, cattle, and manufactured goods.[11]

Another indication of the extent of international contacts is provided by the free movement of missionaries, Christians, Manichaeans and Buddhists, who travelled long distances from the eastern Sasanian provinces across Transcaucasia to Xinjiang along the frequented routes and promulgated their faiths.

9. According to Lukonin, the conquest of the Kushan lands falls in the last decade of Shapur II (309–379) and the investiture relief of Ardashir II (379–383) at Taq-i Bustan represents the victory of the Sasanian *shahanshah* over the last Kushan king. Göbl comes to very similar conclusions but dates the beginning of the coinage to an earlier period – 356 – in his major work (1984). Other hypotheses refer the Kushano-Sasanian coinage to the fourth century. It is not possible to resolve the problem at present. However, the present author (Dani) supports Bivar's system and chronology.
10. Herzfeld, 1930.
11. Ghirshman, 1954, pp. 342–3.

The social picture of Kushanshahr is extremely complicated because of the movements of several nomadic tribes into the territories ruled by the Kushano-Sasanian governors. The picture will not be complete unless we start a little earlier and follow the process of migration until the coming of the Hephthalites.

Religious life

As the evidence of the coins clearly shows, the Zoroastrian faith, the traditional religion preserved in the province of Fars, enjoyed great popularity among the Kushano-Sasanians. Cults of Anahita and Ohrmazd (Ahura Mazda) continued to occupy a prominent place in Fars after the Sasanians came to power. In both south-western Iran and the north-east there were great sanctuaries served by priests. The influence of Zoroastrianism can be inferred from the representation of fire altars on the coins. The most important sanctuary of fire worship is that excavated at Surkh Kotal, which although originally built by the Kushan emperor Kanishka, was still in good repair during this period. The influence of Zoroastrianism can also be seen in Gandhara sculpture where fire worship is depicted; and fire temples have been excavated at Kara-tepe. The Zoroastrian religion in Bactria must have been reinforced by the expansion of the Sasanian Empire.

It was in this period that the cult of Mithra flourished. On the Kushano-Sasanian coins, we find the Bactrian legend, *borzaoando iazado* (Middle Persian: *bwld'wndy yzty*). Initially, this title was given to the Indian god Shiva but he soon received the nimbus with rays around his head like Mithra. Mithra was apparently regarded as a divine protector of the Kushano-Sasanian rulers and gave them their power.[12]

Ghirshman[13] mentions 'an imperial religion', the need for which he sees in the rise of Shapur I. The Sasanian emperor 'needed to mobilize all his national forces for the struggle with Rome'; hence 'the sympathetic interest shown by Shapur to the teachings of Mani' (for Manichaeism, see Chapters 3 and 17). But the real patron of Mani was the young Peroz, by whom he was probably introduced to Shapur. Mani was of noble birth and like other prophets he claimed to have been sent by God to fulfil the mission of earlier religions. 'He preached a universal religion' and 'derived his doctrines from the cults of Babylonia and Iran and also from Buddhism and Christianity.'[14]

According to Ghirshman, 'In the East, Buddhism [had been] at the height of [its] expansion' since the time of the Kushans. 'In the West, centres of

12. Lukonin, 1987, p. 138.
13. Ghirshman, 1954, pp. 309–10.
14. Lukonin, 1987, pp. 69–70.

Christianity had sprung up in northern Mesopotamia and Judaism was active in Babylonia.' Thus Zoroastrianism was squeezed by all these surrounding religions within its home province of Fars; and when Manichaeism challenged its position even here, there was a violent reaction. 'Mani was tried, condemned and put to death. His followers were persecuted and fled abroad, some to the East, where their teachings flourished in Central Asia.'[15]

How far was Zoroastrianism preserved in the Kushano-Sasanian kingdom? There is ample evidence to show the widespread popularity of the fire cult and some scholars even maintain that the followers of Zoroastrianism persecuted Buddhists. Ohrmazd was still worshipped, however, and the dogmas, with their emphasis on a single divinity, were upheld. The *mōbad*s (high priests) accepted the traditions of south-western Iran, and along with them continued the worship of Anahita and Mithra, although they were given a secondary place. The old sacred traditions were put in writing in the form of the *Avesta* in the fourth century. Strengthened by its religious organization, 'Zoroastrianism was able to drive out Manichaeism and hold Christianity in check on the line of the Euphrates and Buddhism on the Helmand.'[16]

Buddhist missionaries, on the other hand, continued to exert their influence throughout the whole of Afghanistan and Central Asia. Their famous centres at Ghazni, Kabul, Bamiyan, Balkh and Termez maintained continuous contact with the centres in Gandhara, and central and East Turkestan. It seems very likely that Buddhism itself was undergoing a great change in its practices, ideological concepts and rituals. With the acceptance of the image of the Buddha and the expansion of Buddhism and Buddhist monasteries, the educational character of the *saṅgha* (Buddhist community) had taken on a new shape. The place of the Bodhisattvas and several other local deities had greatly increased. But Buddhism was not alone in this new expansion. The evidence of coins suggests that the popularity of Shiva and Nandi had caught the popular imagination. At the same time, the seated goddess Ardokhsho had begun to be identified either with Lakshmi or with Hariti, the queen of the *yakshi*s. Other Hindu deities such as Karttikeya, Baladeva and Vasudeva were also prominent and the worship of the sun god remained important.

Funerary practices such as corpse position and the burial of bones stripped of flesh and soft tissue (which clearly refer to Bactrian Zoroastrian rites) provide important evidence for the religious beliefs of the local population. Burials took place in special structures (known as *naus*) as well as in ruins of old buildings. There were also burials in graves in the shape of pits. These are all a direct continuation of funerary rites of the Kushan period.[17]

15. Ghirshman, 1954, pp. 314–18.
16. Ibid., p. 318.
17. Litvinsky and Sedov, 1984, pp. 75–137.

Cities, architecture, art and crafts

Begram, Dalverzin-tepe, Kara-tepe and Surkh Kotal were among the principal foundations of the time of the Great Kushans. While Begram was the summer capital, Kara-tepe presents a group of caves, stupas and monasteries and Surkh Kotal preserved its character of a fire temple (probably built by Kanishka). As the excavations showed, Begram was sacked by Shapur I in *c.* 244 but the city continued to exist afterwards and to play a role. The Buddhist complex of Kara-tepe was also deserted at some moment when the Kushano-Sasanians occupied it, but the discovery of Kushano-Sasanian coins and later construction provides evidence of its subsequent continuity as a religious centre. Similarly, Surkh Kotal preserved its character.

Kara-tepe[18] presents a typical model of cultural material that is syncretistic in nature. In original concept, the Buddhist caves and monasteries copy the type that is so well known in Gandhara. Staviskiy sums up: 'The Kara-Tepe excavations brought to light wall paintings, stone and stucco (*ganch* in local terminology), sculpture, terracottas, and pottery, metal ware and coins, inscriptions on pottery and graffiti on the walls of the caves and their entrance niches.' The structures constitute a complex of caves, a courtyard and some grand buildings. The ensemble is divided into four groups, A, B, C and D. Groups A and B originally formed a single complex with three courtyards, placed next to one another on a terrace along the eastern slope. In the northern courtyard, the remains of a stupa have come to light, while the central and southern courtyards were bordered with porticoes. South of the southern courtyard was a Buddhist temple, consisting of a cella surrounded by three corridors. The cave temples consisted of a cella and a vaulted corridor that encircled it. The walls in most surface and cave premises of groups A and B were painted over the plaster.

A fire altar stood in an attached niche with a shell-shaped back wall: the existence of a fire altar in a Buddhist structure is most striking. It resembles those of the Kushan period found in Gyaur-kala in Khwarizm and Samarkand. Staviskiy remarks that 'altars of this kind were used by fire worshippers, and in temples of the local Mazdean cults, and also in early Buddhist structures'. They survived up to the period of the Arab conquest. Staviskiy notes:

> After the complex B was destroyed or had fallen into abandonment, a fire altar was built in the niche which had previously held a Buddhist statue. It was made hastily, out of materials that were at hand and symbolized the victory of some other cults (most likely Zoroastrianism) over Buddhism.[19]

Part of the wall-painting shows a figure of the Buddha seated under a tree with three standing monks, close in execution to the Indian style. Here the Buddha

18. Staviskiy, 1984, pp. 95–135.
19. Ibid., p. 114.

has a halo around the body, probably of local Bactrian origin. Numerous stone and stucco fragments have been found which originally formed part of the decoration. Staviskiy concludes:

> Stupas and cave premises (A and B complexes) were derived from India, along with Buddhism, whereas the planning of the cave temples is alien to the ancient Indian tradition and is rather to be traced to the religious architecture of the Middle East, where similar fire temples could be found consisting of a cella and the corridors encircling it. As to the temple courtyards of Kara-tepe, they go back to the Rhodian type east Hellenistic courtyards that had become common in Bactria and the neighbouring Parthia already in third–second centuries B.C.[20]

It may be noted that Buddhist temples of the type seen in Kara-tepe, particularly the planning and the representation of the Buddha with the nimbus and halo around the whole body, became common in East Turkestan and also in Eastern Asia during the post-Kushan period.

Many other cities and settlements are known where life developed in the Kushano-Sasanian period on the territory of Bactria (Tokharistan). At the Yavan site in southern Tajikistan, for example, a section of a small street was unearthed on the citadel. On each side there was a solid area of large house blocks with many rooms. These houses consisted of individual, interconnected premises. Walls were erected from *pakhsa* blocks (*pakhsa* is a local term for blocks of rammed clay mixed with finely chopped straw) and clay bricks. The structures probably had two storeys.[21] The structures at the site of Halkajar, on the hills of southern Tajikistan, are similar to those at Yavan. A good collection of terracottas was made from here.[22]

Dalverzin-tepe, in the Surkhan Darya region (southern Uzbekistan), was a large city under the Kushans; but towards the end of the period, the main parts of the city and its fortifications were neglected. However, buildings DT-6 and DT-7 and the temple in the northern part of the city continued to function, as did the potter's quarter with its kilns. The *naus* of Dalverzin continued to fill with funerary deposits, although burials were also found outside the *naus*. Kushano-Sasanian copper coins have been discovered at the site. Thus it is clear that the city continued to be inhabited in the traditional manner, although activity was not as intense as before.[23]

Zar-tepe, another large city in the Surkhan Darya region, is of considerable interest. Its heyday was in the Kushan period, but subsequently its fortifications fell into disrepair. In the centre of the city stood a palace-type complex with two halls: one was four-columned (13×9.3 m); the other was

---

20. Staviskiy, 1984, p. 133.
21. Zeimal, 1975, pp. 267–9; Litvinsky, 1973, pp. 14–17.
22. Sedov, 1987, pp. 80–4.
23. Pugachenkova et al., 1978.

twelve-columned (17.6 × 9.2 m), with an *aiwān* (hall) in front. During the last period, brick pedestal-supports for a fire altar were constructed between the columns. The halls adjoined other rooms where fragments of painted clay sculptures have been found. Zar-tepe had a Buddhist shrine, a large structure decorated with clay sculptures of which one head is preserved. Buddhism was not the only religion of the urban population, however.

A number of residential districts have been excavated. Blocks of adjoining houses were discovered on both sides of the street, each block consisting of 8–11 interconnected buildings. Every block was separated from its neighbour by a narrow street at right angles to the main road. In one of the house blocks a shrine was also found with, in its centre, a fire altar standing on a square platform. Similar shrines have been found at other sites. Here again, Kushano-Sasanian coins were discovered in the upper level.[24]

Kay Kobad Shah, the ancient capital of the Kobadian district, continued to exist under the Kushano-Sasanians, its fifth and last period of existence being separated from the previous occupation by a sterile layer.[25] Alongside the large cities a great number of villages and other settlements existed. In addition, cult buildings, burial monuments and other constructions have also been excavated. Even in the small Kobadian oasis many Kushano-Sasanian archaeological complexes have been recorded, in particular at the sites of Kay Kobad Shah, Ak-tepe II, Darakhsha-tepe, Klych-duval, Shodmon-kala and Munchak-tepe, where sanctuaries, burials, remains of irrigation works and other structures have been found.[26]

Among cult buildings, mention should be made of the monastery of Ushtur-Mulla, near the Amu Darya river. The monastery consisted of 26 buildings which surrounded a square courtyard. In the middle of the north side was a shrine with a Π-shaped circumbulatory corridor. There were small residential cells for individual monks and a large hall for *saṅgha* (congregational) meetings. The shrine was decorated with paintings and alabaster sculptures. Outside the complex was a stupa, the base of which was faced with stone reliefs.[27]

Another site of this period is Chaqalaq-tepe, in northern Afghanistan, which had an oval plan and was surrounded by two circles of city walls made of *pakhsa*. Its two lowest layers were dated by coins to the Kushan period. The 307 coins in the upper levels included 72 imitations of coins of Vasudeva and a coin of the Sasanian *Kushanshah*, Varahran II.[28] Village sites have also been excavated, such as Durman-tepe, where two small hoards of Kushano-Sasanian

---

24. Masson, 1976; Zavyalov, 1979.
25. Dyakonov, 1953, pp. 276, 289.
26. Sedov, 1987, pp. 11–48.
27. Zeimal, 1987.
28. Mizuno (ed.), 1970.

coins were discovered.[29] So, during the Kushano-Sasanian period life continued in the cities and villages to the north (that is to say, in 'right-bank' Bactria)
and south of the Amu Darya.

The number of sites in both northern and southern Bactria with settlements of the Kushano-Sasanian period is extremely large;[30] there were also some
in central Afghanistan, particularly in the Kabul region. Two Buddhist monasteries have been discovered at Tepe Maranjan (Kabul), in one of which a hoard
of 326 silver Sasanian coins and 12 gold Kushano-Sasanian coins was found.[31]

Some of the architectural features of the period have been mentioned
above. There were established categories of architectural structure: palaces,
common residential quarters and various types of cult buildings, including
Buddhist monasteries both in caves and on the ground. There were also buildings serving technical functions such as water-reservoirs and workshops. Monumental structures and ordinary everyday buildings existed side by side. They
differed greatly in the quality of their construction. *Pakhsa*, especially for wall
foundations, and square mud-bricks were the most common materials; baked
bricks and stone were used more rarely, mainly for paving and for the pedestals of column-bases. Roofs were usually flat, and in small buildings the beams
rested across the tops of the walls. In large buildings, however, columns were
also used. Vaults and domes were known. For the transition from the square
ground plan to the circular dome, squinches were adopted. All kinds of passages and niches had arches. The wall surface was covered with one or more
layers of plaster. The interiors both of monumental secular buildings and of
cult buildings were decorated with wall-paintings and sculpture.

There were two trends in the art of the time: Buddhist art developed from
traditions going back to the art of Gandhara with local features, whereas non-
Buddhist art displayed a complex fusion of local and Sasanian traditions. This
latter feature is well seen in the sculptures and wall-paintings from Dilberjin.[32]
Especially interesting are the wall-paintings from structure 12 of the north-
east cult complex. The largest fragment represents a figure on a yellow throne,
sitting frontally with knees apart. This pose is typical of representations of
Sasanian kings and gods enthroned. The arms also are kept apart and there is
an object, possibly a mirror, in one hand. The left hand is resting upon a shield.
The figure is dressed in a loose shirt and there is a belt around the waist. A
cloak is thrown over the shoulders and there is a golden helmet on the head.
Black plaits hang beneath the helmet and the head is surrounded by a yellow
nimbus. (The presence of the nimbus indicates that the figure represents a deity.) Two yellow horn-shaped objects project from behind the shoulders. On

29. Mizuno (ed.), 1968.
30. Sedov, 1987, pp. 11–48, 78–95; Ball and Gardin, 1982, especially p. 483, Map 67.
31. Curiel, 1953; Hackin, 1953; Fussman and Le Berre, 1976, pp. 95–9.
32. Kruglikova, 1976, pp. 96–100, Figs. 56–8.

each side there are two standing personages turning towards the deity and a number of smaller figures. The outermost personage of the right-hand group is only half as large as the other standing figures. The contours are traced with a thin black line. The painter understood the application of light and shade, and although frontal representation is a dominant feature of this style, profile figures are slightly inclined to the front.

This painting is a fusion of several traditions. The form of the helmet reflects that of Antiquity. There are strong connections with the subsequent paintings in Tokharistan at Balalyk-tepe and Kala-i Kafirnigan. This provides clear evidence that a local Bactrian art existed and was developed in Bactria during Kushano-Sasanian times, although it absorbed other traditions and was powerfully influenced by official Sasanian art.

Fine specimens of metal-working of the Kushano-Sasanian period are known. In Sasanian toreutics, Lukonin has singled out an 'East Iranian School' which he ascribes to masters at the court of the *Kushanshah*s. Among works of this school he lists five silver dishes, upon each of which an equestrian hunt is represented. The dish in the Hermitage Museum is remarkable (Fig. 3). It depicts a rider, hunting wild boar. One beast has already been struck by the rider's sword, the other is emerging from the undergrowth. On the rider's head there is a crown with spiral horns. The crown resembles in general terms that of Varahran II *Kushanshah*. The surface of the images is gilded and there is a Sogdian inscription of the fifth–sixth centuries on the dish, providing an upper limit for the date. Lukonin concludes that Kushano-Sasanian metal-work follows the general trends of Sasanian art, particularly in the choice of subjects such as heroic hunting scenes, but the composition differs in exercising more freedom.[33] The orientation of Kushano-Sasanian metal-work towards Sasanian art can be explained by its court character.

The minor arts are mostly represented by terracotta figurines. Only occasional examples follow the traditions of Sasanian art, especially those of Sasanian portraiture. Bactrian features emerge in the foreground in this rather popular art. Craft industry, especially pottery, was highly developed. There are examples of table-services, storage jars and kitchen ware. Some types were developed from those used in Kushan times, but new types continued to emerge. The ornament of vessels changed, and became more concentrated towards the top of the vessel.

Everyday utensils, ritual objects, mirrors of several types, buckles and ornaments were made of bronze. Tools and weapons were made of iron. Pins, combs and similar items were made of bone and there were beads, and vessels made of glass. A large quantity of jewellery was inlaid with a variety of precious stones. Armourers produced composite bows, arrowheads, daggers, swords, lances and plates of armour. The shape of certain types of weapon

33. Trever and Lukonin, 1987, pp. 61–73, 108, Pl. 14 (7), 15 (7).

changed, especially the triangular arrowheads, which developed a groove be-hind the point.[34]

Languages and scripts

It is only possible to judge the language of the Bactrians in ancient times by personal names. The situation changes, however, in the first centuries A.D. The discovery of the inscriptions at Surkh Kotal, and then other inscriptions, espe-cially in Central Asia, has allowed scholars[35] to determine the peculiarities of the Bactrian language. It belongs to the group of East Iranian languages, more precisely to the north-eastern group. There is a marked similarity with the modern Munji language, which is probably a continuation of one of the Bactrian dialects. Bactrian represents the Middle Iranian stage.

Written Bactrian used an adaptation of the Greek alphabet, with an addi-tional 25th letter, *san*, which reproduced the sound *s*. The Greek writing re-produced the Bactrian phonetics only approximately, although certain meth-ods of Greek orthography were transferred into Bactrian and Greek scribes apparently took part in creating the Bactrian writing-system. Initially its let-ters were of lapidary or 'monumental' style, but later a cursive form was devel-oped. In spite of the Sasanian conquest, Bactrian scribes continued to work in Balkh and other centres. By the third century the transition from a lapidary to a cursive style was completed. Round-shaped letters and the presence of liga-tures are characteristics of the cursive style. Kushano-Sasanian coin legends, as well as the inscriptions on wall-paintings from Dilberjin, are of this type. Some of them can be referred to the third–fourth centuries. The inscriptions include explanations of the content of the paintings.[36]

In the state of the *Kushanshahs*, apart from high officials and military personnel, there were inevitably natives of Iran, including both scribes and marginally literate persons. It is quite natural that they wrote their Middle Persian in Pahlavi script[37] (see Chapter 3), so that some issues of the Kushano-Sasanian coinage (see above) have Middle Persian inscriptions in Pahlavi script. At the Buddhist complex of Kara-tepe (Termez), Middle Persian inscriptions in Pahlavi script (written in the monumental style without ligatures) were found on the cave-walls. Specific palaeographic features suggest that these inscrip-tions go back to the fourth–fifth centuries rather than to the third. One

34. For details, see Sedov, 1987.
35. Maricq, 1958; 1960; Henning, 1958; 1960; Gershevitch, 1967; Humbach, 1966–67; Harmatta, 1964; 1965; 1969; Livshits, 1969; 1975; 1976; Fussman, 1974; Steblin-Kamenskiy, 1981; Lazard et al., 1984.
36. Livshits, 1976.
37. Saleman, 1900; Nyberg, 1964; 1974; Rastorgueva, 1966; MacKenzie, 1971; Gignoux, 1972; Rastorgueva and Molchanova, 1981.

FIG. 3. Silver dish. (Photo: © Hermitage Museum, St Petersburg.)

inscription originally had a date, but it is now destroyed. Another bore the one-line record, *zyk dpyr* (Zik, the scribe).[38] There are also inscriptions in Gandhārī Prakrit and Buddhist Hybrid Sanskrit.

Most inscriptions of the Kushan and Kushano-Sasanian periods come from Termez, in particular from the Buddhist monasteries of Kara-tepe and Fayaz-tepe. They are written in the Kharoṣṭhī and Brāhmī scripts, mostly on

38. Lukonin, 1969*b*.

potsherds. In Kara-tepe alone over 100 potsherds with inscriptions were discovered, besides 7 wall graffiti.[39] The use of both scripts was current at the same time.

The Brāhmī alphabet has indications for the vowels. The consonants with the inherent *a* are divided into twenty-five mutes, falling into five classes, four semi-vowels, three sibilants, one aspirate, one pure nasal and three voiceless spirants. The combination of vowels and consonants is represented by ligatures. According to Dani: 'This alphabetic system is maintained in India with minor additions or omissions down to the present day, though it is not phonetically suited to the various provincial languages in India.' The evolution of Brāhmī continued for many centuries. Considerable changes took place during the first–fourth centuries, among which the introduction of new forms of signs should be mentioned. Brāhmī is read from left to right, the same direction as that of European alphabets.[40]

As Dani explains: 'The whole system of Kharoṣṭhī follows the pattern of Aramaic. The resemblance is not so much in the identity of forms, though a few letters are the same, but in the way in which these forms are produced.'[41] The palaeography of Central Asian inscriptions in Kharoṣṭhī has its own peculiarities. There are two types of inscription, one following the tradition of stone inscriptions, with typical straight lines, the other resembling the manuscripts of Central Asia.[42]

As Vorobyova-Desyatovskaya observes:

> It is also important to point out the differences between the wording of the Kharoṣṭhī and Brāhmī inscriptions of Kara-tepe. Most of the Kharoṣṭhī inscriptions are based on a traditional formula indicating the donor, the gift, the recipient, almost resembling an incantation formula. However, the Brāhmī inscriptions, even though a dedication, mention a *saṅgha*, *vihāra* [monastery] or school. They are focused on the donor and his attributes. Others again serve as indications of the individual use of a vessel.[43]

The inscriptions from Fayaz-tepe are similar:[44]

> The comparison of Indian inscriptions on the territory of Central Asia with those from India and Afghanistan shows that as a rule they were worded according to a general pattern. The palaeography of the Kara-tepe and Fayaz-tepe inscriptions confirms the presence of a standard scribal tradition for the entire Kushan territory.[45]

---

39. Vertogradova, 1983, p. 3.
40. Dani, 1963, pp. 75–104.
41. Ibid., pp. 265–7.
42. Vertogradova, 1982, pp. 150–1.
43. Vorobyova-Desyatovskaya, 1983, p. 24.
44. Vertogradova, 1984, p. 167.
45. Vorobyova-Desyatovskaya, 1983, pp. 51–2.

The Kidarite kingdom in Central Asia*

E. V. Zeimal

Origin and rise of the Kidarites

The fourth century witnessed the appearance in Central Asia of a new wave of nomadic tribes known by a variety of names and recorded in numerous sources. By the Latin authors they were called Chionites, and by the Greek authors Kidarite Huns or 'Huns who are Kidarites'; in Indian chronicles they were known as Huna, in Armenian literature as both Honk' and Kushans, and in the Chinese annals as the Ta Yüeh-chih, or Lesser Yüeh-chih (i.e. the same name that denoted their forerunners in those lands, who founded the Kushan Empire). Their ruler was called Kidara or Chi-to-lo (Ancient Chinese, *kjie-tâ-lâ*). The use of different names sometimes makes it difficult to evaluate the information provided by the written sources[1] and to reconstruct a general historical picture. An important prerequisite is to make a clear distinction between the Kidarites and another tribal group known as the Hephthalites (Hua, I-ta, Hep'tal, Tetal, Hephtal, Abdel and Hayatila in the sources; see also Chapter 6).[2]

The terms Huns and Chionites seem to reflect the general ethnic appellation of this people,[3] whereas Kidarites should be understood as a dynastic designation derived from the name of their king, Kidara. Kushan (widely used in the Armenian sources to designate the tribes and state of the Huns) and Ta

---

* See Map 3.
1. Of the existing works, the most significant on Kidarite numismatics are Martin, 1937; Curiel, 1953; Göbl, 1967; and Enoki, 1969; 1970. See also Ter-Mkrtichyan, 1979.
2. Trever, 1954.
3. Neither here nor elsewhere does this term have any ethnolinguistic significance, since we know practically nothing definite about the language(s) of these peoples. Just as in the twelfth–thirteenth century the term 'Mongol' referred not only to those who spoke the Mongol language proper but also many other ethno-linguistic groups forming part of that society, so too could Huns and Chionites have apparently 'incorporated' ethnic groups speaking a variety of languages.

Yüeh-chih (used in the Chinese sources) refer to the country where they established their kingdom, and may reflect their claims to be successors to the Kushan kings. The primary basis for identifying the Huns or Chionites with the Kidarites is the fact that they are called Kidarite Huns (or 'Huns who are Kidarites') by the fifth-century Byzantine author and historian Priscus.[4] None of the other information we possess (including numismatic data) contradicts this identification.

The earliest report on these peoples dates from *c.* 350 when, according to Ammianus Marcellinus (XVI, 9.4), the Chionites (i.e. the Kidarites) fought in Syria as allies of the Sasanian king, Shapur II (309–379), at the siege of Amida (the modern Diyarbekir). They were led by Grumbates, 'the new king of the Chionites, a middle-aged man, his face already deeply lined, possessing an outstanding intellect and famous for the multitude of his victories. With him was his son, a fine young man, who fell in the battle' (Ammianus Marcellinus, XVIII, 6.20; XIX, 1.7–11). The Chionites (i.e. the Kidarites) assisted the Sasanians because of an alliance they had concluded with Shapur II (Ammianus Marcellinus, XVII, 5.1), who at that time was driven to war against the enemy on the eastern borders of his kingdom.

Early history of the Kidarites

Nothing is known about the history of the Kidarites before the second half of the fourth century. It has been suggested that they conquered K'ang-chü and Sogdiana in *c.* 300, but the literary sources have not yet been corroborated by the archaeological evidence. Attempts have been made[5] to link the appearance of the Kidarites in Central Asia with the Karshi steppe in southern Sogdiana and to date this event to *c.* 420, but this has not been supported by further archaeological investigations in the region.[6]

The only corroboration of the presence of the Kidarites in Sogdiana is provided by early Sogdian coins (see also pages 128 et seq.) with the image of an archer on the reverse and the word *kydr* (Kidara) in the obverse legend.[7] These coins were minted in Samarkand from the first to the fifth century. But out of some 2,000 such coins, only 7 bear the name of Kidara, indicating that Kidarite rule was short-lived. The chronology of early Sogdian coinage of the archer type helps to date the coins with the name of Kidara, which cannot be earlier than the middle of the fourth century – thus the conquest of Sogdiana by the Kidarites cannot have occurred prior to this time.

---

4. The accounts of the Kidarites in this source have been subjected to repeated scrutiny. They were examined and compared with the data from Chinese sources by Enoki, 1969.
5. Kabanov, 1953; 1977.
6. Isamiddinov and Suleimanov, 1984.
7. Zeimal, 1978, p. 208; 1983*b*, p. 251.

Foundation of the Kidarite state

The alliance between the Kidarites and Shapur II did not apparently last long. The nature of the relations between the Kidarites and Sasanian Iran is indicated by the Kidarite issues of silver drachms, copying coins of the Sasanian kings.[8] Martin[9] takes the Kidarite coins of the Sasanian type as evidence of the existence of a Kidarite state as early as the last quarter of the fourth century and dates these coins as close as possible to the time when their Sasanian prototypes were issued. He suggests that the Sasanians recognized the Kidarite state, while the Kidarites themselves accepted Sasanian suzerainty, and puts other events – the Kidarite invasion of the Kushano-Sasanian kingdom, the Sasanian invasion under Shapur II and the ousting of the Kushano-Sasanian princes – in the same historical context, *c.* 350. He suggests that the Sasanians recognized the Kidarite state, while the Kidarites themselves accepted Sasanian suzerainty.

Enoki[10] has shown that the establishment of the kingdom of Kidara took place somewhat later, and Göbl[11] has dated the prototypes of the Kidarite drachms to the period of Shapur II and Shapur III (383–388).

Kidara's conquest of Gandhara and Kashmir

The most detailed account of Kidara's reign is provided by the Chinese chronicle, the *Pei-shih* [Annals of the Wei Dynasty], written in 643 and covering events between 386 and 581.[12] The original nucleus of the Kidarite state was the territory of Tokharistan (now northern Afghanistan and southern Uzbekistan and Tajikistan), which was previously part of the Kushan Empire and subsequently of the Kushano-Sasanians. The capital of the Kidarites, the city of Ying-chien-shih,[13] was probably located at the ancient capital of

8. Cunningham, 1895, was the first to make this observation.
9. Martin, 1937.
10. Enoki 1969; 1970.
11. Göbl, 1967.
12. Information about Kidara in another Chinese dynastic history, the mid-sixth century *Wei-shu* [History of the Wei], was borrowed entirely (with a few divergences in the transcription of place names) from the *Pei-shih* and has no significance of its own.
13. In the *Wei-shu*, the Kidarites are said to have transferred their capital to another city called Liu-chien-shih. However, Enoki has clearly shown that both cities are in fact one and the same, because the accounts regarding the Kidarites' transfer of their capital were misunderstood by the author of the *Wei-shu*, who tried to explain why the capital of the Ta Yüeh-chih was called by a different name at the time of the Han and the Northern Wei (Enoki, 1969, pp. 8–10).

Bactria,[14] near Balkh. The lands of the Kidarites were known in Armenian sources as 'Kushan lands'.

The *Pei-shih* relates that Kidara, having mustered his troops, crossed the mountains and subjected Gandhara to his rule, as well as four other territories to the north of it.[15] Thus, during Kidara's reign, the Kidarite kingdom occupied vast territories to the north and south of the Hindu Kush. According to another passage from the *Pei-shih*, referring to the Lesser Yüeh-chih, the principal city of the Kidarites south of the Hindu Kush was situated near present-day Peshawar and called (in its Chinese transcription) Fu-lou-sha (Ancient Chinese, *pyəu-ləu-sa*, which probably represents Purushapura). Its ruler was Kidara's son, whose name is not mentioned.

Historians have found it difficult to determine the exact period of Kidara's reign, one reason being that, from the second half of the third century to the fifth century, news reaching China about events in the Western Regions was generally sporadic and patchy. Li Yen-nien, the author of the *Pei-shih*, writes that 'from the time of the Yan-wei (386–550/557) and Chin (265–480), the dynasties of the "Western Territories" swallowed each other up and it is not possible to obtain a clear idea of events that took place there at that time'. A painstaking textual analysis enabled Enoki (and Matsuda before him) to establish that information about Kidara in the *Pei-shih* was based on the report of Tung Wan sent to the West in 437.[16] From this we can infer that, although the Chinese sources do not provide any dates in connection with Kidara, the *Pei-shih* describes the situation as it existed in *c.* 437. On the other hand, Kidara's rise to power, the founding of his state and the annexation of the territories to the south of the Hindu Kush (including Gandhara) should be dated to an earlier period, that is to say, some time between 390 and 430, but probably before 410.

The Kidarites' advance to the south-east apparently continued even in the middle of the fifth century. This is indirectly proved by Indian inscriptions depicting the events which befell the Gupta king, Kumaragupta I (413–455), when a considerable portion of central and western Panjab was under Kidarite rule. Thus, it was in the first half of the fifth century that the greatest territorial expansion of the Kidarite state occurred.

14. The 'city of Balaam', referred to as the capital of the 'Kidarite Huns' by Priscus of Panium, evidently corresponds to Bactria-Balkh. For geographical details of events relating to the struggle between the Sasanians and the Kidarites and then the Hephthalites in the fifth century, see Marshak, 1971.
15. Zürcher, 1968, p. 373; Enoki, 1969, p. 8.
16. Enoki, 1969, pp. 8–9.

The decline of the Kidarites

Indian sources, which refer to all nomadic conquerors (Kidarites and Heph-thalites alike) as Hunas, cast little light on the final stage of the Kidarite state, during which it came into conflict with the Guptas. Having captured Gandhara, the Kidarites apparently tried to build on their success and extend their terri-tories eastwards into India. The only evidence of the war between the Kidarites and the Guptas is the mention of Huna invaders in Indian inscriptions refer-ring to the reign of Skandagupta (455–467).

The first encounter between the two rival powers apparently took place in the reign of Skandagupta's father and predecessor, Kumaragupta I. On the evidence of the Bhitari pillar inscription, towards the end of that king's reign the Gupta state was on the verge of extinction. In this critical situation, Kumaragupta I put his son and heir in command of the army with the task of restoring the country's power.[17] Before Skandagupta and his army had 'estab-lished his lineage that had been made to totter' (line 14), he suffered many hard-ships. According to the inscription, there were times when he had to 'spend a night sleeping on the bare earth' (line 10).

It seems that the enemies who threatened the very existence of the Gupta state included not only their feudatories, the Pushyamitras, but also the Kidarites. In the Junagadh inscription,[18] which dates from *c.* 457 and also refers to the reign of Skandagupta, it is obviously the Kidarites (or the Hephthalites; see pages 141–2) who are referred to under the name of the Mlecchas. Skanda-gupta's victories over them were described as the conquest 'of the whole world'. It is hard to establish what this claim implies in terms of geographical fact, but it appears that Skandagupta's armies repulsed the Kidarite invasion somewhere on the River Sutlej (or perhaps further east). Thus, even after Skandagupta's victories, central and western Panjab probably remained in the hands of the invaders,[19] although he had managed to stop their advance eastwards.

Yet another inscription – the Kahaum inscription (460–461)[20] – already describes Skandagupta's reign as 'peaceful' and calls him the 'commander of a hundred kings'. On some silver coins, Skandagupta is given the honorific title of *Vikramāditya* earlier bestowed on his famous grandfather, Chandragupta II (*c.* 375–413). Numismatic evidence shows, however, that war with the Kidarites and other enemies had exhausted the strength of the Guptas: considerably fewer gold coins were minted under Skandagupta than under his predecessors, and the quality of the metal was poorer. Despite the victories over the Hunas, the inscriptions show that the Gupta state had already lost a considerable area of

17. Fleet, 1888, No. 13, lines 10–14.
18. Ibid., No. 14.
19. Altekar, 1954, p. xxxiv.
20. Fleet, 1888, No. 15.

its Western Territories by the beginning of Skandagupta's reign. The most striking proof of this is the total absence of Gupta coins in the western regions of
India and in Pakistan.[21]

The war between the Guptas and the Hunas is reflected in a semi-
legendary form in other Indian sources, in particular in Book XVIII of
Somadeva's *Kathāsaritsāgara* (a collection of folk tales in Sanskrit literature in
the eleventh century), where these events are described from roughly the same
viewpoint as in the inscriptions of Skandagupta's reign. Despite the triumphant
tone of the inscriptions, the might of the Guptas declined after these encoun-
ters, while the Kidarite state continued to exist in western Panjab.

It was probably not Skandagupta's victories but a new wave of nomadic
invaders from the north – this time Hephthalites – that put an end to the Kidarite
state in Gandhara and Panjab. The surviving sources give no clues as to how
power passed from the Kidarites to the Hephthalites[22] – whether as the result
of a clash between opposing armies or of the overthrow of one dynasty by
another (in a 'palace revolution'). It is known, however, that the name Kidara
was kept, although now as an honorific title (meaning 'honoured', 'hero', 'valiant'), long after the Kidarite state had ceased to exist,[23] just as the original
Kidara used to style himself on coins *Kuṣaṇa Śahi* (king of Kushan) many years
after the fall of the Empire of the Kushans.

The new conquest of Bactria by the Sasanians (467)

During the second quarter of the fifth century the Kidarite state was again involved in serious fighting to the west with the Sasanian kings, who could not
accept the loss of the territories they had conquered earlier from the Kushan
Empire. Yazdgird II (438–457) took active measures to restore them to Sasanian
rule and several eastern campaigns were undertaken during his reign. The struggle continued under Hormizd III (457–459) and also under Peroz (459–484).

Western sources – Armenian,[24] Greek, Syriac and others – provide much
information about the deeds of Yazdgird II and subsequent Sasanian kings in
the east but, as mentioned above, give different names for Iran's enemies. Often
the 'land of the Kushans' or 'Kushan regions' are mentioned, which suggests

---

21. Allan, 1914, p. xlix.
22. This is probably not the event narrated in the 97th chapter of the *Pei-shih*, in the section
    dealing with the territory of the Lesser Yüeh-chih, whose capital was the city of Fu-lou-sha
    or Peshawar: 'Their king was originally a son of the Great Yüeh-chih king Chi-to-lo. When
    Chi-to-lo had moved westward under pressure of the Hsiung-nu, he ordered his son to hold
    this city' (Zürcher, 1968, p. 373).
23. Harmatta, 1984, pp. 188–9.
24. For a collection of references to the Sasanian wars in the east in Armenian sources, see Ter-
    Mkrtichyan, 1979, but bearing in mind their evaluation by Lukonin; 1969*a*; 1969*b*.

that the term 'Kushan' may be understood not so much in an ethnic sense as to mean the inhabitants of the 'land of the Kushans', that is the former territory of the Kushan Empire (or, more narrowly, the Kushano-Sasanians). The Hephthalites, who are mentioned from the second half of the fifth century, appear on the historical scene here, as in India, much later than the Kidarites and as a tribal group distinct from and apparently sometimes hostile to them.

Western, and especially Armenian, authors had a somewhat vague conception of the geography of the areas where the campaigns of Yazdgird II and Peroz took place, and this has led to conflicting readings and a confusion that is reflected in the conclusions of modern researchers.[25] The theory that these battles took place not only in the territory of northern Afghanistan but also near the Caspian Sea[26] has proved implausible.[27] There are no grounds for identifying two arenas of military action: all the fighting occurred mainly in, or in the immediate vicinity of, Tokharistan (one of Yazdgird II's battles was at Merv-i Rud), and the Sasanians' main stronghold in the east was Merv.

Yazdgird II's first eastern campaign was in 442. By 449 the advantage was on his side, and the *Kushanshah* (king of the Kushans) had been rendered powerless. The Sasanian army laid waste territories subject to the Kidarites and took fortresses. During the campaign of 450, Taliqan was captured. Nevertheless, the struggle continued, and sometimes the balance was in favour of the Kidarites. Their refusal to pay tribute to Yazdgird, mentioned by Priscus, prompted renewed military action by the Sasanians in 456. As a result, the Kidarites came close to losing all their territories in Tokharistan. This was prevented only by the outbreak of civil war (457–459) between Yazdgird II's sons – Hormizd III, who had succeeded his father on the throne of Iran in 457, and Peroz, who at that time ruled as governor in the 'Kushan regions'. The war between the brothers continued for two years and ended in victory for Peroz, who owed it to the help of the Hephthalites and handed Taliqan over to them.

When war with Iran broke out again in the 460s, Balkh (Po-ho or *b'âk-lâ* in the Ancient Chinese sources) was in the possession of the Kidarites, if we accept that the town of Balaam mentioned by Priscus is in fact Balkh.[28] At that time, the ruler of the Kidarites was Kunkhas, whose father (the source does not name him) had earlier refused to continue to pay tribute to the Sasanians. Peroz, however, no longer had the strength to continue the eastern campaign; in 464, according to Priscus, the envoys of Peroz turned to Byzantium for financial support to ward off invasion by the Kidarites but it was refused.

25. For example, there were two Chols (one in the region of Gurgan and one in that of Darband), two Taliqans (one in Khurasan and one in Tokharistan), etc. Some names have been found to be distorted. For further details, see Marshak, 1971.
26. Marquart, 1901, pp. 55, 211–12; Mandel'shtam, 1958, p. 72.
27. Marshak, 1971.
28. It has been suggested that the cities of Balaam and Bolo refer to the site of Er-kurgan in the Karshi steppe of southern Sogdiana (Kabanov, 1953; 1977).

In an attempt to put an end to the war, Peroz made peace overtures to King Kunkhas, offering him his sister's hand in marriage, but sent him a woman of lowly birth instead. The deception was soon discovered and Kunkhas decided to seek revenge. He asked Peroz to send him experienced Iranian officers to lead his troops. Peroz sent 300 of these 'military instructors', but when they arrived Kunkhas ordered a number of them to be killed and sent the others back mutilated to Iran, with the message that this was his revenge for Peroz's deception. The ensuing war against Kunkhas and the Kidarites ended in 467 with the capture of their capital city of 'Balaam'. It appears that the Hephthalites were again Peroz's allies, as they had been in his struggle with Hormizd for the throne of Iran. This put a final end to Kidarite rule in Tokharistan. After their defeat the Kidarites were probably forced to retreat to Gandhara, where, as previously mentioned, the Hephthalites again caught up with them at the end of the fifth century.

Economy, society and polity

The written sources give no details of the Kidarite conquest of Tokharistan, Gandhara and the other regions that came under their rule. However, archaeological data are available for the study of the Kidarite state, although only for certain areas and tentatively. In certain regions of the right bank of the Amu Darya (northern Tokharistan) many towns were largely destroyed and whole oases laid waste during the last quarter of the fourth century and the beginning of the fifth. It is probable that this was caused by military and political strife rather than by social and economic upheavals resulting from the natural development of society. The huge town of Shahr-i Nau (40 km west of the modern Dushanbe), which came into being in Kushan times under Vima Kadphises or Kanishka I and was surrounded by a strong defensive wall that was 7 km long and more than 8 m high, with towers every 25 m, was abandoned at the turn of the fifth century like many other settlements in the Hissar valley. Since the valley was beyond the reach of the Sasanian armies, the destruction and laying waste of the area is likely to have been connected with the Kidarite invasion. In Kobadian, on the other hand, the abandonment of the Bishkent valley and the Shah oasis[29] and the destruction of Kay Kobad Shah and a number of other towns and settlements can be attributed both to the Kidarite invasion and to the Sasanian occupation.

The picture is similar in the region of the Surkhan Darya, where the site of Dalverzin-tepe and other settlements were laid waste at this same time (in particular, in oases such as Band-i Khan on the right-bank tributaries of the Surkhan Darya). Here also, it can only be assumed that the destruction of

29. Litvinsky and Sedov, 1983.

economic life was connected with the Kidarites, but so far no positive traces of their presence have been found either in the Surkhan Darya valley or in southern Tajikistan.

The Buddhist religious centre in Old Termez, destroyed probably in the 360s–370s by the Sasanians, already lay in ruins; yet the mass burials of the victims of an epidemic, or some sort of catastrophe, in the abandoned buildings and caves of these monasteries date from the time of the Kidarites. More such examples can be given – the late fourth to the fifth century was obviously a violent time in northern Tokharistan. If such devastation and massacres were indeed the result of the arrival of the Kidarites (which is as yet only a hypothesis), then having passed through these regions 'with fire and the sword', they must very soon have moved south,[30] beyond the Amu Darya, where they were victorious over the Sasanian *Kushanshahs*.

The picture is rather different in the Karshi steppe, where archaeological evidence reveals a considerable change in the composition of the population in the fourth century. In particular, this can be seen from a sharp increase in modelled ceramics with characteristics typical of the Kaunchi-Dzhety-Asar archaeological sites (on the middle reaches of the Syr Darya, or Jaxartes). Further investigations should clarify whether this is connected with the arrival of large groups of nomads from the north (who might well have been Kidarites) in the Karshi oasis. It is clear, however, that the oasis did not suffer destruction and subsequent abandonment on the same scale as that noted in the regions of southern Tajikistan and the Surkhan Darya.[31] Archaeological investigations in other parts of the old Kidarite state will doubtless bring to light other patterns of interrelationships between the invaders and the local population.

Our knowledge of the organization of the Kidarite state and the way the conquered territories were governed is just as fragmentary. It is tempting to draw an analogy with the vast state of the Kushans. This is not only because the Kidarites claimed to be the successors to the glorious Empire of the Kushans; a no less important factor is that the former nomadic invaders came into possession of vast territories inhabited by settled agricultural peoples with a culture and traditions dating back many centuries, just as had been the case with the Tokharians (or Yüeh-chih), who created the Kushan Empire. It seems likely that the administrative and government structure created by the Kushans was left largely intact under the Kidarites.

---

30. On the right bank of the Amu Darya a large number of tombs (including tumuli) have now been investigated, but the vast majority of them belong to the Tokharo-Yüeh-chih and Kushan periods (Litvinsky and Sedov, 1984). So far, the right bank of the Amu Darya has yielded hardly any tumuli that can even tentatively be linked to the Kidarites.
31. Isamiddinov and Suleimanov, 1984.

FIG. 1. Kidarite coins with the inscription ᴑᴊᴕ.

Monetary system and trade

The *Pei-shih* (Chapter 7, 13) mentions that the Kidarites, whom it refers to as the Ta Yüeh-chih (Lesser Yüeh-chih), 'have money made of gold and silver'.[32] This information is confirmed by the evidence of their coins. The first comprehensive attempt to categorize and interpret Kidarite coins was undertaken by Cunningham.[33] Martin, Ghirshman and Curiel[34] subsequently made important contributions in the field, but the most detailed study of the Kidarite

---

32. Zürcher, 1968, p. 373.
33. Cunningham, 1895, pp. 55–73.
34. Martin, 1937; Ghirshman, 1948; Curiel, 1953.

FIG. 2. Kidarite coins.

coinage is that of Göbl[35] Gold, silver and copper Kidarite coins are now known (Figs 1–3). There are no grounds for maintaining that the Kidarites had a separate monetary system as in the case of Kujula Kadphises' early issues; their coinage was characterized by an adaptation to the local issues in each area they conquered. In Sogdiana small silver coins were issued (drachms reduced to 0.4–0.3 g). They followed the design of early Sogdian coins, with the ruler's head facing right on the obverse and a standing archer on the reverse, adding the word *kydr* (Kidara) written in Sogdian on the obverse.[36]

In Tokharistan gold dinars were issued in the name of Kidara, following the gold coins of the Kushano-Sasanians both iconographically and technically

35. Göbl, 1967; 1984.
36. Zeimal, 1978, p. 208, Pl. III, 11; 1983*b*, p. 251, Pl. 21, 10.

(on the obverse, a king, facing left, standing before an altar; on the reverse, Shiva with his bull, Nandi), which in their turn can be traced back to the last coins of the Kushan king, Vasudeva I.[37] The Tokharian issues of Kidarite coins bear an inscription in Bactrian (*Bago Kidara Vazurka Košano Šao*), with the title 'the great king of the Kushans'.

The silver coins of Sasanian type can be attributed to Gandhara and the area around. They have the ruler's bust facing right[38] or *en face* on the obverse;[39] and on the reverse, the traditional iconographic type for Sasanian coins – a fire altar between two standing figures and copper coins of the same type.[40]

In their Indian territories the Kidarites also issued gold coins[41] based on the model of the Late Kushan dinars with the name of Kanishka (III or, if one follows Göbl, II).[42] The Kidarite coins of this group bear the name of Kidara written in Brāhmī script, together with the names of dependent rulers or successors of Kidara, on the obverse. The earliest coins are the early Sogdian issues with the name of Kidara (not earlier than the mid-fourth century). As Göbl has convincingly shown, the Kidarite coins of Sasanian type follow the drachms of Shapur II and Shapur III, minted on former Kushan territory,[43] and should therefore be dated to the closing decades of the fourth century and the very beginning of the fifth.[44] The gold Kidarite coins issued in Tokharistan and in India can be dated more fully. Their issue probably began only in the fifth century (perhaps in its early years) and came to an end during the second half of that century.

As well as gold and silver coins, copper anepigraphic coins, minted on the model of the latest copper coins of the Kushan kings, Huvishka, Vasudeva I and Kanishka III (or II), were widespread throughout the entire territory of the Kidarite state. They were obviously used as small change, as can be seen from the quantities in which they were minted.[45] These copper coins show the same characteristics as the gold and silver Kidarite coins mentioned above – a

37. Göbl, 1967, Vol. III, Table 4 – XIII A, XIII B, XIV; 1984, Tables 67-9, Nos. 735–41.
38. Göbl, 1967, issues 14, 19–24.
39. Ibid., issues 11–13, 15–18.
40. Ibid., issues 25–8.
41. Göbl, 1984, Tables 46, 47, Nos. 612–15.
42. Ibid., Table 33, Nos. 538–53.
43. Göbl, 1967, issues 1–10.
44. There are no grounds for dating these Kidarite coins of Sasanian model to the time of Shapur II and Shapur III and concluding that the Kidarites were originally allies of the Sasanian *shahs* in their war against the kingdom of Kushan. Enoki (1970, pp. 34–5) put forward serious arguments against such a supposition: Kidara himself had nothing in common with Shapur II, although he used his coins as a model for his own.
45. For the many discoveries of 'copies' of coins of Vasudeva I and Kanishka III (or II) on the right bank of the Amu Darya, see Zeimal, 1983a, pp. 231–4, 241–56. Vast numbers of them have also been found on the territories of Afghanistan, Pakistan and the north-west of India (Wilson, 1841; Cunningham, 1895; Göbl, 1976; Cribb, 1981).

FIG. 3. Kidarite coins.

deliberate adaptation to the existing currency in the conquered territories, reproducing (with varying degrees of divergence from the model) the coinage that was customary in a particular market. As was the case during the reign of Kujula Kadphises, the Kidarites were clearly not yet aware of the political significance of coining money. This probably explains, first, why they followed alien iconographic models and, second, why certain gold and silver issues – and almost all the copper coins – had no name on them (with the exception of the copper coins of the Sasanian model mentioned above and issued in the name of Kidarite satraps).

Thus, the Kidarite monetary system did not disturb the economic life of the regions that came under their rule but, on the contrary, created favourable conditions for maintaining the established traditions in local trade. The numerous discoveries of imported articles in strata of the Kidarite period are proof of the existence of a flourishing international trade network and wide trading links between the various regions of the Kidarite state.

Life-style, culture and ideology

In the words of the *Pei-shih*, the Kidarites 'move around following their herds of cattle; they also [in this respect] resemble the Hsiung-nu'.[46] On the other hand, it is known that there were Kidarite capitals both in Gandhara and in Tokharistan, and thus that they lived in towns. This is only an apparent contradiction, as there have been many cases in history when nomads (or recently settled nomads), after establishing their rule over large groups of states, have, while wholly or partially preserving their traditional life-style, successfully adapted to the culture and life-style of the subordinate peoples.

It would therefore be more accurate to think of the Kidarite state not as a unified society but as one with a clear distinction between the conquerors – the ruling group – and their subject peoples, the latter preserving their own traditions. It appears that the most important elements in the overall organization and development of the state were the clan and tribal organizations traditional to all nomadic peoples; these were inevitably reflected in the administrative structure of the state and in the organization of its army – the main support of the ruling dynasty. It should be stressed, however, that in such conglomerate states, the rulers quickly assimilated the main achievements of the conquered peoples' cultures. The Kidarites were no exception, although the written sources mention only the unsuccessful attempt of the Kidarite ruler Kunkhas to marry into the Sasanian dynasty (see above).

The coins make it possible to follow this process of adaptation by the Kidarites in much greater detail. We do not know what language the Kidarites spoke, but the coinages they issued show inscriptions in Sogdian,[47] Bactrian,[48] Middle Persian[49] and Brāhmī.[50] Kidarite coins display a wide range of iconographic borrowings, reflecting the world of Sogdian artistic culture, and the official art of the Sasanians and the art of post-Kushan India. Yet it is hard to judge to what degree all these foreign elements penetrated the culture of the Kidarites themselves, and how deeply they were assimilated. It should be remembered that the elements of alien cultures reflected by the coins were the direct result of the Kidarites' adaptation to the conditions of the regions conquered by them, and of their intention that the coinage they issued should be

---

46. Zürcher, 1968, pp. 373–4.
47. Zeimal, 1978, p. 208, Pl. III, II; Zeimal, 1983*b*, p. 251, Pl. 21, 10.
48. Göbl, 1984, Tables 67–9, Nos. 735–41.
49. Göbl, 1967, issue 15.
50. Ibid., issues 11–28; 1984, Tables 46, 47, Nos. 612–15.

familiar to the local market. Moreover, just as there is no basis for assuming (on the evidence of the coins) that the Kidarites had a mastery of all the languages and scripts used in inscriptions on their coins, the iconography of Kidarite coins cannot be regarded as a reflection of their artistic tastes. We have hardly any knowledge of a specifically Kidarite art that is directly linked to the rulers of the state; it is possible to speak only of works of art of the Kidarite period, created by craftsmen and artists in the countries conquered by them but following standards and traditions that had no direct connection with the conquerors.

It appears that the Kidarites' beliefs had not yet developed into a rigid religious system, which must have encouraged (or at least not hindered) their receptiveness to the religious ideology they encountered in the lands they subdued – a local variety of Zoroastrianism (Mazdaism) in Tokharistan, various expressions of Buddhism and Hinduism in the territory of Gandhara and also, probably, the official Sasanian doctrine. There are no grounds for assuming that the Kidarites were Buddhists simply because the Chinese sources report the existence of famed Buddhist shrines in the Kidarite capital in Gandhara. At the same time, there is nothing to indicate active resistance to any of these religions on the part of the Kidarites. During the Kidarite period the Buddhist religious centre in Old Termez lay in ruins, like many other Buddhist sites in Tokharistan, but its destruction (as already mentioned) seems to be linked to the religious intolerance of the Sasanians. There are no traces of restoration work during the Kidarite period; the partial restoration of the monastery took place later, apparently during the second half of the sixth century.

The key to understanding the ideology of the Kidarite rulers probably lies in their tendency to consider themselves the heirs of the Kushan kings (many expressions of which have been mentioned above). Indeed, this is how they were seen by the neighbouring peoples. It is for future investigations (especially in the field of archaeology) to show how profoundly and consistently the Kushan heritage was assimilated by the Kidarites.

THE HEPHTHALITE EMPIRE*

B. A. Litvinsky

Origins

From the mid-fifth to the mid-sixth century Central Asia was ruled by the Hephthalite tribes. There are many gaps in our knowledge of the origin of the Hephthalites and the formation of their state, the first difficulty being that they are given different names in the various sources. In Chinese sources the name of the dynasty is I-ta (a variant of I-tien, ancient *iep-t'ien) and their king bears the name Yen-tai-i-li-t'o (ancient *Yeptalitha).[1] In Syriac sources they are called *eptalit̠, aβdel*; in Greek-language sources, *Αβδελαι, Εφθαλιται*; in Armenian sources, *hep't'al*; in Middle Persian sources, *ḥēftāl*, and also *ḥyōn*; in Arabic sources, *haiṭal*; and in New Persian sources, *ḥēṭāl*.[2] Another name for them is Chinese Hua. According to Balᶜami, the etymology of the word 'Hephthalites' is as follows: 'in the language of Bukhara', it means 'strong man'.[3] In Khotanese Saka a similar word exists, meaning 'brave, valiant'.

The legends on Hephthalite coins are in the Bactrian script. They feature a Bactrian title, *XOAΔHO*, for the ruler together with another Bactrian title, *šao*. One coin bears the title *bogo*, meaning 'lord' or 'ruler'. The names of Hephthalite rulers given in Firdausi's *Shāh-nāme* are Iranian. Gem inscriptions and other evidence[4] show that the official language of the ruling upper class of the Hephthalites in their Tokharistan territories was an East Iranian language.

Chinese sources do not agree on the origin of the Hephthalites. Some hold that they originated in Ch'e-shih, that is, from Turfan; others consider them to be 'descendants of K'ang-chü' in southern Kazakstan; still others

---

* See Map 3.
1. Enoki, 1959, p. 7.
2. Altheim, 1959, Vol. 1, pp. 41–3.
3. Balᶜami, 1869, p. 128.
4. Maenchen-Helfen, 1959, pp. 227–31; Livshits, 1969, pp. 64–75.

postulate that they were descended from the Great Yüeh-chih. The Chinese writer Wei Chieh, who personally conversed with some Hephthalites, deject-edly observed:

> However, the information has come from remote countries, and foreign languages are subject to corruption and misunderstanding. Moreover, it concerns matter of very ancient time. So we do not know what is certain. [In this way] it is impossible to decide [the origin of the Hephtalites].[5]

Information about the physical appearance and language of the Hephthalites also lacks precision. For example, Procopius of Caesarea (I, 3) writes:

> Although the Hephthalites are a Hunnish people and are so called, they do not mix and associate with those Huns whom we know, for they do not share any frontier region with them and do not live close to them . . . They are not nomadic like the other Hunnish peoples, but have long since settled on fertile land . . . They alone of the Huns are white-skinned and are not ugly. They do not have the same way of life and do not live such bestial lives as the other Huns, but are ruled by one king and possess a legal state structure, observing justice among themselves and with their neighbours in no lesser measure than the Byzantines and Persians.

With regard to language (see also pages 148–9), the Chinese chronicle the *Pei-shih* reports that 'Their language differs from that of the Juan-juan, Kao-ch'e and various Hu' and the account in the *Wei shu* is similar. The reference to the Hu language testifies to the fact that the language of the Hephthalites was distinct from that of those Iranian-speaking people of Central Asia who were called Hu by the Chinese.

In the seventh century, after the destruction of the Hephthalite state, Tokharistan was visited by a Chinese pilgrim, Hsüan-tsang, who wrote of the Hephthalite population:

> [Their] language and letters differ somewhat from those of other countries. The number of radical letters is twenty-five; by combining these they express all objects around them. Their writing is across the page, and they read left to right. Their liter-ary records have increased gradually, and exceed those of [the people of] Su-le or Sogdiana.[6]

This is a clear reference to a Greek-based script of Bactrian origin used in south-ern Central Asia and Afghanistan up to the eighth century.

In Middle Persian, Byzantine and Indian sources we find the designation 'Red' and 'White' Huns. This may reflect a division among the Hephthalites or a distinction between Hephthalites and Türks.[7] This is also reflected in the mural art: for example, some of the envoys in the scene of the Hephthalite embassy in the Afrasiab palace are ruddy-faced, while others are pale (Fig. 1).

5. Enoki, 1959, p. 7.
6. Ibid., p. 39.
7. Chavannes, 1903, pp. 229–33; Bailey, 1931, pp. 585–6; 1954, pp. 13–20.

FIG. 1. Afrasiab. Wall-painting. (Photo: © Vladimir Terebenin.)

These were possibly ethnolinguistic (less probably socio-economic) population groups. The total size of the Hephthalite population is unknown, but in Tokharistan alone there were 5–6,000 Hephthalite warriors – with their families, this suggests some 50,000 individuals, but there must have been considerable fluctuations during the period.

Political and military history

The political history of the Hephthalites can be deduced from Armenian, Arabic, Persian, Byzantine, Chinese and other sources. Under Yazdgird II (438–457) the north-eastern borders of the Sasanian Empire were under threat from Central Asian tribes. The fifth-century Armenian historian, Elishe Vardapet, who was a contemporary, reports that the emperor was obliged to do battle with the tribes of the Hephthalites from 442. The situation was so serious that Yazdgird even had to transfer his residence to the northern border. It has been suggested that this was also the time when the Hephthalites made their appearance.[8] As early as 456, an embassy from the Hephthalites arrived in China.[9]

According to the Arab historian al-Tabari, Peroz, while still a prince, fled to the 'country of the Haitals, or Hephthalites' and asked the king to provide him with troops to 'take possession of the kingdom of his father [Yazdgird II]'. Another source states that Peroz 'was supported by the inhabitants of Tokharistan and the neighbouring regions' and refers to 'the people which conquered Tokharistan called Haiṭal [that is Hephthalites]'.[10] In the mid-fifth century the Hephthalites increased greatly in strength and Tokharistan, with the surrounding regions, came under their rule. According to Harmatta, 'it is likely that the Hephthalites attacked the Transox[an]ian territory of the Kidarites in 466' and at the same time they 'took possession of the eastern part of Kušānšahr, and then very soon they occupied also Balx [Balkh] from the Persians'.[11]

In gratitude for their assistance, Peroz extended the power of the Hephthalites still further. In particular, he ceded to them the district of Taliqan.[12] But there were disagreements between the Central Asian tribes and the Sasanians, leading to conflict and wars. First, Peroz clashed with the Hephthalites, who are considered by some scholars to have taken advantage of the civil war in Mesopotamia to seize Balkh (Priscus of Panion, 35).[13] There is,

---

8. Trever, 1954, pp. 136–7; Gafurov, 1972, p. 198.
9. Enoki, 1955, p. 234, Table.
10. Shmidt, 1958, pp. 447–8; Nöldeke, Tabari, 1973, pp. 117–19.
11. Harmatta, 1969, p. 394.
12. Balʿami, 1869, pp. 127–8.
13. Marshak, 1971, pp. 63-4.

however, some doubt about this. What is known is that in the 460s or the 470s Peroz waged three wars against the Hephthalites. The first war ended in his being taken prisoner and later released for a ransom partly paid by the Byzantine emperor. The second war ended as ingloriously as the first: Peroz was defeated and was once more taken prisoner. He was forced to give assurances never again to oppose the Hephthalites and to send instructions that a huge ransom should be paid for him. Since the treasury was unable to send the ransom, Peroz left his son as hostage.

The Hephthalites had strong forces. Sources describe them as skilful warriors and their army as powerful. They were armed with clubs and the Chinese considered that they were excellent archers. According to other sources, their main weapon was the sword. Judging by their military operations, they probably possessed a strong cavalry force led by an *asbarobido* (cavalry commander).[14]

In Iran, according to Lazar of P'arp:

> Even in time of peace the mere sight or mention of a Hephthalite terrified everybody, and there was no question of going to war openly against one, for everybody remembered all too clearly the calamities and defeats inflicted by the Hephthalites on the king of the Aryans and on the Persians.

Not only the common soldiers but also the dignitaries and military chiefs feared the Hephthalites. When Peroz set off on campaign, 'his troops went forward more like men condemned to death than warriors marching to war'. When news of the third campaign reached the king of the Hephthalites, he sent his representative to Peroz with this message: 'You concluded peace with me in writing, under seal, and you promised not to make war against me. We defined common frontiers not to be crossed with hostile intent by either party.'[15] An important point to emerge from this text is that the Hephthalites appear not merely as a group of nomadic tribes but as a state formation, on an equal footing with Sasanian Iran and fully versed in statesmanship.

Al-Tabari's text is very similar in this respect, although he incorrectly calls these tribes Türks (instead of Hephthalites). According to his account (which, however, also contains some elements of legend), Peroz reached the tower which had been built by Bahram Gur (Bahram V, 420–438) on the border between the regions of Khurasan and the Hephthalites to prevent them crossing into Khurasan; this was in accordance with the pact concluded between the Hephthalites and the Persians (i.e. Sasanians) that neither party should violate the border. Peroz, for his part, had promised Akhshunvar, the king of the Hephthalites, that he would not go beyond their borders. Peroz had 50 elephants and 300 men harnessed to Bahram Gur's tower. They drew the tower

14. Altheim, 1960, Vol. 2, p. 269.
15. Ter-Mkrtichyan, 1979, pp. 55–6.

along in front of him while he marched behind, declaring that in that way he was not breaking his pact with Akhshunvar.

The Hephthalite troops retreated, but then Akhshunvar ordered deep pits to be dug, lightly timbered over and topped with soil. These booby traps, laid in the path of the pursuing Sasanian army, played a decisive part, breaking its battle formation and ensnaring many soldiers. Peroz was killed and many of his retinue, including his daughter, were taken prisoner by the Hephthalites, who seized his treasure. One of Peroz' followers, called Sukhra, subsequently managed to retaliate and forced the Hephthalites to withdraw.[16] A similar account is given by al-Dinawari.[17]

Following internecine conflict over the Sasanian throne, one of Peroz' sons, Kavad, fled to the Hephthalites. Having lived with great honour among them for four years, he married the daughter or sister of the Hephthalite king, who provided him with troops. Kavad seized the throne with these troops in 488, becoming king of Sasanian Iran.[18] As a result of political and kinship ties, the Hephthalites subsequently took part in Kavad I's military campaigns and Hephthalite troops armed with cudgels were present at the siege of Edessa.[19]

As a result of internal events in Iran – the Mazdakite movement (see Chapter 17, Part One) and the revolt of the nobility against the king – Kavad once more fled to the Hephthalites. The Hephthalite king agreed to provide him with 30,000 troops; in return, Kavad was obliged to make territorial concessions and in 498 he handed over Chaganiyan to his allies.[20] Iran had to pay tribute to the Hephthalites for many decades, from 484 until the middle of the sixth century. Part of the Sasanian coinage was countermarked with a Hephthalite sign, and these were the coins used for payment of the tribute.[21] This situation continued into the early years of the reign of Khusrau I (531–579).

In the second half of the fifth century and the first half of the sixth, silver coins of Peroz (and imitations with various overstrikes) circulated in northern Tokharistan. The genuine Peroz drachms belong mainly to the time when some of those regions, particularly Chaganiyan (Shi-han-na in the Chinese sources), were still under the Sasanians. Peroz drachms were subsequently minted in Chaganiyan with Bactrian and Sogdian overstrikes, together with imitations of Peroz coinage with Bactrian legends. Many coins were issued under Khusrau I, particularly from the 540s onward. Coins were subsequently minted which were imitations with overstruck names and portraits of local Hephthalite leaders.

16. Shmidt, 1958, p. 449; Nöldeke, Tabari, 1973, pp. 122–34.
17. See Altheim, 1960, Vol. 2, pp. 51–2.
18. Nöldeke, Tabari, 1973, pp. 135–7.
19. Pigulevskaya, 1941, p. 64.
20. Shmidt, 1958, pp. 476–7.
21. Göbl, 1967, pp. 193–4; 1971, p. 70.

This series is completed with the issue of a coin of the type of Khusrau I, but with the name of a local ruler.[22]

The Hephthalites thus entered the historical arena in the mid-fifth century, apparently in eastern Tokharistan. By the end of the century they had taken possession of the whole of Tokharistan, including the Pamirs, and a considerable part of Afghanistan. At the same time, they seized much of East Turkestan. In 479 they subjugated the region of Turfan, and between 497 and 509 the region of Karashahr and what is today Urumchi. In 522 P'o-lo-men, the leader of the Juan-juan in an area to the north of Dunhuang, fled to the Hephthalites to seek their protection. Earlier, probably in the late fifth century, Kashgar and Khotan had come under the power of the Hephthalites, who subjugated practically the whole of East Turkestan. As Enoki has correctly pointed out, the Hephthalites reached the zenith of their power with their seizure in 509 of Sughd (the capital of Sogdiana), which then ceased sending embassies to China.

Conquests in Gandhara and northern India

The late fifth and early sixth centuries saw the start of Hephthalite raids on Gandhara and subsequently on the whole of northern India. In 477 the Kidarites in Gandhara had sent an embassy to China,[23] but the Chinese pilgrim Sung Yün, who visited Gandhara in 520, noted that the Hephthalites had conquered the country and set up their own ruler. 'Two generations then passed.'[24] On this basis, Marshall assumes that the invasion took place earlier (reckoning one generation to be 30 years: 520 − 60 = 460).[25]

In the early second half of the fifth century the Hephthalites came into conflict with the Guptas, who had by then passed the zenith of their power and prosperity. According to the Junagadh rock inscription of c. 457, King Skandagupta won a victory over hostile kings and over tribes which seem to have been Hephthalites (or Kidarites; see pages 123–4). Another inscription proclaims that he bore the title, 'lord of a hundred kings'.[26] The initial attacks of the Hephthalites were thus repulsed, but at the price of stretching all the forces of the Gupta Empire.[27]

Skandagupta was the last great ruler of that dynasty, reigning from c. 454 to c. 467.[28] The central power of the Gupta state subsequently declined,

22. Rtveladze, 1983, pp. 74–5.
23. Enoki, 1955, pp. 234–5; 1959, pp. 25–7.
24. Yang Hsüan-chih, 1984, p. 235.
25. Marshall, 1951, p. 75.
26. Fleet, 1888, pp. 14–15.
27. Altekar and Majumdar, 1954, pp. 163–4; Majumdar, 1954, pp. 26–7. Concerning the Huns in Gupta inscriptions, see Sharma, 1978, pp. 133–4; Biswas, 1973.
28. Gupta, 1974, pp. 329–38; cf. Singh and Bannerji, 1954, p. 89.

particularly in the last quarter of the fifth century under King Budhagupta,[29] the time at which the penetration of the Hephthalites into the subcontinent began. In the late fifth and early sixth centuries the Hephthalites in India came under the leadership of Toramana (see also Chapter 7, Part One), described in one Indian inscription as the 'renowned Toramana, the boundlessly famed ruler of the earth'. Launching an offensive from Panjab, he conquered the whole of western India and even Eran (in modern Madhya Pradesh). Numismatic evidence indicates that he ruled in Uttar Pradesh, Rajputana, Panjab and Kashmir.[30] His conquests brought with them the destruction of towns, villages and Buddhist monasteries, and the monasteries never recovered. Many local rulers acknowledged themselves to be subjects of Toramana.[31]

In the time of Toramana, the Hephthalites in India began to operate independently of the Central Asian branch, though the link between them does not seem to have been broken.[32] According to the Gwalior inscription, Toramana's son was called Mihirakula (in Jain sources, Caturmukha-Kalkin or Kalkiraja). He intensified his father's efforts to conquer the whole of northern India, and in this he was highly successful.[33] Over a century later, the Chinese pilgrim Hsüan-tsang paid particular attention to this ruler's life and activities in the account of his travels. He writes of Mihirakula: 'He was of quick talent and naturally brave. He subdued all the neighbouring provinces without exception.'[34]

The account of Cosmas Indicopleustes (writing in the early sixth century) confirms that the Hephthalites in India reached the zenith of their power under Mihirakula, with their capital at Sakala (modern Sialkot). Hsüan-tsang recounts the fate of Mihirakula: he was ultimately opposed by the Gupta ruler Baladitya, who had previously been paying him tribute (this is assumed to have been Narasimhagupta I).[35] Baladitya's opposition stemmed from the atrocities perpetrated by the Hephthalite leader and the destruction of Buddhist buildings, which is also reported in the Kashmir chronicle the *Rājataraṅgiṇī* and in Jain sources.

According to Hsüan-tsang, Mihirakula was taken prisoner by Baladitya, but was subsequently released. Power over the Hephthalite tribes had meanwhile been seized by Mihirakula's brother and Mihirakula himself set off for Kashmir, where the king received him with honour. A few years later, Mihirakula incited the townspeople of Kashmir to revolt against their king and seized power there. He then went westwards and occupied Gandhara, where he killed many

29. Bongard-Levin and Il'in, 1969, p. 513.
30. Majumdar, 1954, p. 35.
31. Fleet, 1888, pp. 88, 159.
32. Harmatta, 1969, pp. 400–1.
33. Pathak, 1917, pp. 215–16; Gupta, 1974, pp. 372–7.
34. Beal, 1969, p. 167.
35. See Gupta, 1974, pp. 364–6.

of the inhabitants and destroyed the Buddhist shrines, only to die shortly afterwards.[36] While the details of this account by Hsüan-tsang may be unhistorical, the broad outline is worthy of note.

In assembling the events of Mihirakula's life, the *Rājataraṅgiṇī* asserts that he was a powerful king who ruled Kashmir and Gandhara and even (this is clearly an exaggeration) conquered southern India and Ceylon. Cosmas Indicopleustes calls him 'king of India', though he mentions that the possessions of the Huns in India (i.e. Hunas) were divided from the other Indian kingdoms by the mighty River Phison (Indus).

Persecution of the local population, combined with religious intolerance, set the local Indian population against the Hephthalites and deprived them of support. At the same time, the difficulties facing the Hephthalites of Central Asia in their struggle against the Türks, who utterly defeated them, deprived the Hephthalites in India of their Central Asian base, of the 'flow of fresh forces and support, and this led to their decline'.[37] Although small communities and even principalities of Hephthalites survived in India after the middle of the sixth century, they did not wield any significant political influence.

The Hephthalites of Central Asia

By the middle of the sixth century, the Hephthalites of Central Asia found themselves squeezed between Sasanian Iran, whose power had increased tremendously under Khusrau I, and the Türks, who had conquered much of the north-east of Central Asia. The opponents of the Hephthalites entered into diplomatic negotiations with one another, but when the *kaghan* of the Türks dispatched ambassadors to Iran, they were killed in Hephthalite territory at the command of the Hephthalite king. The *kaghan* moved his forces and seized Chach (modern Tashkent) and continued to the Syr Darya (Jaxartes). The forces of the Hephthalites gathered in the region of Bukhara, towards which Hephthalite detachments marched from Termez, southern Tajikistan and even the Pamirs. An eight-day battle was fought in the Bukhara area, in the course of which the Hephthalites were routed. Their troops fled south and there elected a new king, Faganish (or Afganish), but the south of Central Asia had been occupied by Sasanian troops and the new Hephthalite ruler acknowledged the supremacy of Khusrau I (see also Chapter 7). This marked the end of the Hephthalite state in Central Asia. (These events took place in the period 560–563.)[38]

---

36. Beal, 1969, pp. 169–72.
37. Gafurov, 1972, p. 201; see also Majumdar, 1954, p. 39.
38. Mohl, 1868, pp. 306–16; Shmidt, 1958, p. 453; Nöldeke, Tabari, 1973, pp. 158–9; Moravcsik, 1958, pp. 275–6; Grignaschi, 1980.

Central Asia was devastated as a result of this struggle, whereupon relations between the allies (Türks and Sasanians) became strained. This worked to the advantage of the Hephthalites: individual semi-independent Hephthalite principalities continued to exist in the Zerafshan valley, paying tribute to the Türks (Menander, fragment 18). The situation was similar in the south, except that here the Hephthalites paid tribute to the Sasanians. Khusrau I found a pretext to cross the Amu Darya (Oxus). Power over the littoral of the Amu Darya later passed to the Türks, who then occupied all the territory of Afghanistan. Small Hephthalite principalities continued to exist in southern Tajikistan and Afghanistan for a long time; some of them (in particular Kabul) remained independent.[39]

According to Gafurov:

> The Hephthalites thus established a huge state structure even greater in geographic extent than that of the Kushans, but at the same time it was more loosely-knit and more unstable. They succeeded both in halting the armies of Sasanian Iran in the east and in inflicting a shattering defeat on the Sasanian kings. Hephthalite rulers even settled succession claims to the title of *shahanshah* of Iran, while regular payment of tribute to them was a major concern for many Iranian governments. In conclusion, the Hephthalites played an important part in the ethnogenesis of the peoples of India, Afghanistan and, in particular, Central Asia.[40]

Social structure and administration

Although some evidence remains of the society of the Hephthalites, their customs and ways of living, the information is extremely contradictory. According to Procopius, the Hephthalites had 'since time immemorial' lived a settled life, 'were ruled by one king' and 'had a state system based on law'. A Türk mission reported to Byzantium that the Hephthalites were 'a tribe which dwelt in towns' (see also pages 149–50); indeed, after their victory over the Hephthalites, the Türks became 'the masters of their towns' (Menander, fragment 18). Theophanes Homologétés (fragment 3) states that after their victory over the Iranians, the Hephthalites became the masters of the towns and ports previously held by their enemy.[41] Chinese chronicles and travellers, however, provide a different picture. For example, according to the *Sui shu* [Dynastic Annals of the Sui], the *Pei-shih* and other sources, in the land of the Hephthalites there were 'neither cities and towns nor fixed residence of their king'.[42] Sung Yün reported in 518 that, in the land of the Hephthalites:

39. Harmatta, 1969, p. 402.
40. Gafurov, 1972, p. 202.
41. For a detailed analysis of Byzantine sources, see Moravcsik, 1958.
42. Enoki, 1959, p. 10.

there were no walled cities for residences; [the area] was kept in good order by a patrolling army. The people lived in felt [tents], moving from one place to another in pursuit of water and pasture lands: they moved to cooler areas in summer and warm regions in winter. The natives were simple rustic folk, unversed in writing the rites or moral precepts.[43]

Even the Chinese sources do not agree, however. Thus, according to the *Chou shu* [History of the Chou Dynasty] (15a), 'it [the land of the Hephthalites] has its capital in the walled city of Pa-ti-yen', a name meaning something like 'the walled city in which the king resides'.[44] Hsüan-tsang's report on the country of Hsi-mo-ta-lo (a Sanskritized form of the ethnonym, Heptal) helps to resolve these conflicting accounts. According to the Chinese pilgrim, after their ancestors had established a strong state and subjugated their neighbours, the Hephthalites 'migrated and scattered in foreign countries where they rule scores of strongly walled cities and towns with so many chiefs. They [also] live in tents of felt and remove from one place to another.'[45]

The following explanation may be advanced for all the differing accounts. The core of the Hephthalite population was originally nomadic or semi-nomadic but later, after seizing control of vast regions with towns and fortresses, the Hephthalite élite, like other conquering nomads (for example, the Karakhanids and the Seljuks), began to settle in towns and were followed by other groups from the newly arrived non-urban population. The sources simply mention isolated episodes in this complex story – hence the discrepancies.

One of the most difficult questions concerns the Hephthalites' social structure. From the description of their funeral rites in the Chinese chronicles (see pages 147–8), we learn that there were both rich and poor Hephthalites and that their rites were completely different.[46] Consequently, it was a class society with marked social and property differentiation. In his description of the luxurious dwelling of the Hephthalite king with his golden throne, and the magnificent clothes of the king and queen inlaid with gold and precious stones, Sung Yün notes that 'there were differences, it was observed, between the nobleman and commoners'. He continues: 'For the people's clothing and ornaments, there was nothing but felt.'[47]

At the apex of Hephthalite society was the king, whose residence was a fortified town.[48] According to Byzantine sources, the Hephthalites 'were ruled by one king'. The legends on coins sometimes contain the terms *XΔHO* and *XOAΔHO* (sovereign) and the expression 'great sovereign' is occasionally

---

43. The traveller, of course, meant Chinese writing, rites and moral precepts. See Yang Hsüan-chih, 1984, p. 225.
44. Miller, 1959, p. 12.
45. Enoki, 1959, p. 35.
46. Ibid., p. 49.
47. Yang Hsüan-chih, 1984, pp. 224–6.
48. Miller, 1959, p. 12.

encountered.[49] Names of individual monarchs are known (some from historical accounts). Thus, according to Firdausi, the Hephthalites were led by a king
called Gatfar during their struggle against the Türks, which ended in their defeat at the battle near Bukhara (see page 143 above). It is possible that the kings
were chosen in peacetime as well as in exceptional circumstances but it is not
known who chose them, perhaps the élite. One Chinese account states that the
throne of the Hephthalites 'was not transmitted by inheritance but awarded to
the most capable kinsman'.[50]

The Hephthalite state covered a huge territory and the regions forming it
were dependent upon the central authority to varying degrees. According to
Sung Yün, 'the state received tribute from a number of countries . . . altogether
delegates from more than forty countries came to pay tribute and offer con-
gratulations on appropriate occasions'.[51] According to another source, countries 'large and small, altogether more than twenty, are all subject to it [the
Hephthalite state]'.[52]

There was an administrative machinery at both central and regional levels. During the 550s the Hephthalite king had an adviser (minister?) by the
name of Katulf (Menander, fragment 10). Such titles as *oazorko*, *fromalaro*,
hazaroxto and *asbarobido* (commander of the cavalry) are known from inscriptions on gemstones.[53] The state system was a complex amalgam of institutions
originating in Hephthalite society and frequently going back to ancestral tribal
arrangements, as well as institutions which were native to the conquered regions. Money was minted and we know of many series of coins. Excellent
classificatory and typological works have been published,[54] but insufficient use
has been made of these coins as a historical source.

Central control in the Hephthalite state was weak and local dynasties
continued to rule in a number of regions. Such was the case in Chaganiyan, on
the upper and middle reaches of the Surkhan Darya. One of the rulers of this
dynasty was Faganish (see page 143 above), whose name is known from written sources; the names of other rulers appear on Chaganiyan-Hephthalite coins.
The name of another Chaganiyan ruler, Turantash, appears on a long inscription at Afrasiab. In the first quarter of the eighth century, Chaganiyan was
ruled by Tish, the 'One-Eyed' (in the Sogdian language, Tish is the name of the
star Sirius). The Manichaean religion was widespread in Chaganiyan together
with Buddhism.[55]

Another powerful domain, Khuttal (Kou-tou or Kou-tou-lo in the

49. Livshits, 1969, pp. 69–71.
50. Bichurin, 1950, p. 269.
51. Yang Hsüan-chih, 1984, p. 225.
52. Miller, 1959, p. 21.
53. Livshits, 1969, pp. 66–7.
54. Göbl, 1967.
55. Rtveladze, 1973; Bosworth, 1981.

Chinese sources), was also associated with the Hephthalites. It was located in the basin of the River Kyzyl-su, but at times also included the basin of the River Vakhsh. Khuttal also had a local dynasty with an established order of succession to the throne, according to Arabic sources. The rulers took the Iranian title of *Khuttal-shah* or *sher-i Khuttal*. The Arabs referred to them as *mulūk* (pl. of *mālik*, king).[56] In the southern part of Central Asia and northern Afghanistan, in the region known as Bactria under the Achaemenids and later as Tokharistan (T'ou-ho-lo or Tou-ho-lo in Chinese sources from 383), there were some 30 dominions in the sixth to the seventh century with their own rulers, some of whom were of Hephthalite extraction.

Religious life and polyandry

Information about the religion of the Hephthalites is provided by the Chinese sources. Sung Yün reports that in Tokharistan 'the majority of them do not believe in Buddhism. Most of them worship *wai-shên* or "foreign gods".' He makes almost identical remarks about the Hephthalites of Gandhara, saying that they honour *kui-shên* (demons). The manuscripts of the *Liang shu* (Book 54) contain important evidence: '[the Hephthalites] worship *T'ien-shên* or [the] heaven god and *Huo-shên* or [the] fire god. Every morning they first go outside [of their tents] and pray to [the] gods and then take breakfast.' For the Chinese observer, the heaven god and the fire god were evidently foreign gods. We have no evidence of the specific content of these religious beliefs but it is quite possible that they belonged to the Iranian (or Indo-Iranian) group.[57]

Although Sung Yün states that the Hephthalites did not believe in Buddhism, Buddhist religious establishments flourished in Tokharistan and other areas. In India, however, the Hephthalites showed intolerance towards Buddhist religious establishments. It may be supposed that the beliefs of the local subject populations – including Buddhism – gradually began to gain ground among the Hephthalites. Various forms of Zoroastrian beliefs were widespread in Central Asia and northern and western Afghanistan in competition with Buddhism. There were also many adherents of Hindu beliefs in Afghanistan and in Tokharistan. Lastly, Manichaeism had taken firm root and Christianity was spreading.

Chinese sources provide the following account of the funeral rites mentioned above: 'if a man dies, a wealthy family will pile up stones to form a house [to keep the corpse]; a poor family will dig the ground for burial. The articles of everyday use are buried with the dead.' Another source describes a third type of burial: 'In burying the dead, the coffin is laid in a wooden case.

56. Marquart, 1901, p. 30; Belenitskiy, 1950, p. 115.
57. Enoki, 1959, pp. 45–9.

When a parent dies, the child will cut off one of his ears.'[58] It is known, however, that various types of burial structure, including small, surface-level stone houses, pit graves and wooden coffins, were employed at the same period in Ferghana; hence the hypothesis that these Chinese accounts are actually descriptions of life in Ferghana.[59]

Polyandry was the Hephthalites' most noteworthy social custom. Brothers had one wife in common and the children were considered as belonging to the oldest brother. The number of 'horns' on a married woman's headdress corresponded to the number of her husbands. This custom was practised in ancient times among the Central Asian Saka people, the Massagetae (Herodotus, I, 216); in medieval Afghanistan (according to al-Biruni); and among present-day Tibetans.[60]

Language and scripts

Two accounts of the Hephthalite language have been quoted above, but they are not very informative. Some scholars believe that the Hephthalites spoke a Turkic language while others affirm that their language belonged to the East Iranian group. Although the reading of Hephthalite coins and gemstones is still the subject of much controversy, an interpretation of the names and titles appearing on them, and of the names of Hephthalite rulers in Firdausi's *Shāh-nāme*, is possible from East Iranian languages. This does not, however, constitute a conclusive argument. At present it can only be asserted that Bactrian enjoyed the status of an official language in the Hephthalite domains in Tokharistan.[61]

Late Bactrian script is a development of Bactrian script, which was itself an adapted form of the Greek alphabet. Hephthalite script is typically semi-cursive or cursive and much of it is difficult (or impossible) to read. Examples of the Hephthalite written language have been discovered in East Turkestan, Central Asia, Afghanistan and northern Pakistan. However, these are only insignificant vestiges of the large quantity of written material which, if we are to believe Hsüan-tsang, was to be found in the regions occupied by the Hephthalites and particularly in Tokharistan.[62]

In the vast region controlled by the Hephthalites, people spoke various languages, including Iranian (Middle Iranian, especially Bactrian, but also Sogdian and Middle Persian, or Pahlavi), Indian tongues and others of which

58. Enoki, 1959, pp. 49–50.
59. Litvinsky, 1976, p. 56.
60. For details, see Enoki, 1959, pp. 51–6.
61. Livshits, 1969, p. 67.
62. Steblin-Kamenskiy, 1981.

we have no written records. Various scripts were also in use, particularly Bactrian, Pahlavi, Kharoṣṭhī and Brāhmī.

Towns

The Hephthalite economy was composed of three sectors: urban, settled agricultural and nomadic. Urban settlements did not outnumber rural settlements, yet the economic, political, religious and cultural role of the towns was far more important than that of the villages. Although very little is known about the towns during the fifth and sixth centuries, it has been established that one of the largest towns was Balkh, where exploratory excavations have been undertaken. Hsüan-tsang (writing in 629) describes Po-ho (Balkh) as the Hephthalite capital, with a circumference of approximately 20 *li*. He continues: 'This city, though well [strongly] fortified, is thinly populated.' Balkh had about 100 Buddhist *vihāra*s (monasteries) and some 3,000 monks. Outside the town was a large Buddhist monastery, later known as Naubahar.[63] Some idea of what Balkh looked like in the fifth and sixth centuries may be obtained from the descriptions of Arab authors,[64] but their accounts all date from a later period. Unfortunately, little archaeological work has been carried out on Balkh.[65]

Of the same size as Balkh was the early medieval town of Termez which, according to Hsüan-tsang, lay on an east-west axis and had a circumference of about 20 *li*. Termez had some 10 *saṅghārāma*s (monasteries) and perhaps 1,000 monks.[66] Excavations have been conducted there but little evidence has been found of the town between the fifth and the seventh century. It consisted of a rectangular *shahristan*, or town (roughly 10 ha in area), and a large suburb enclosed by a wall. The total area was approximately 70 ha and the entire town was probably surrounded by a wall about 6 km long. It is likely that there was also a citadel.[67]

According to Hsüan-tsang, the capital of Chaganiyan was half the size of Termez and Balkh in terms of its circumference (10 *li*) and had five Buddhist monasteries.[68] It has been identified with the site of Budrach, which even in Kushan times had an area of 20 ha and at the period under consideration occupied a much greater area than the Kushan town. The expanded town had a rectangular citadel, a fortified *shahristan* with an area of over 50 ha and, beyond that, a large suburban area with farms, forts and religious edifices.[69]

63. Beal, 1969, pp. 43–6; cf. Hui-li, 1959, pp. 50–2.
64. Schwarz, 1933, pp. 434–43.
65. See Le Berre and Schlumberger, 1964; Young, 1955.
66. Beal, 1969, Vol. 1, pp. 38–9.
67. Shishkin, 1940, pp. 150–1; Belenitskiy et al., 1973, pp. 177–8.
68. Beal, 1969, Vol. 1, p. 39.
69. Rtveladze, 1983.

The capitals of other regional domains were roughly similar to or larger than the capital of Chaganiyan. The capital of the province of Hu-sha (or Vakhsh) had a circumference of 16–17 *li*[70] and is the site of Kafyr-kala in the Vakhsh valley. It has a walled citadel (measuring 360 × 360 m) in one corner of the rectangular town, which is, like the citadel, surrounded by a wall with towers. The citadel contained the palace of the ruler (see below). The town was divided in half by a central thoroughfare on which stood dwellings, and religious and commercial buildings. Outside the town fortifications lay extensive suburbs.[71] There were also medium- and small-sized towns such as Kala-i Kafirnigan.[72]

Architecture

An idea of the architecture of Tokharistan at the time of the Hephthalites is provided by the palace (KF-II period) in the citadel of Kafyr-kala (see Chapter 7). It had a square plan (70 × 70 m) and was encircled by two walls, a main inner wall and a secondary outer one (*proteikhos*). Strong rectangular towers were located at the corners, and in the centre of the wall stood semi-circular projecting towers. Between the corner towers and the projecting towers were recessed bays with arches containing false arrow slits. The passageways running along the protective walls had a defensive function.

In the courtyard of the citadel stood the palace buildings. The palace was laid out around a central rectangular hall with an area of 200 sq. m and was surrounded by smaller halls and domestic buildings. In the north-west corner stood a circular hall (8 m in diameter) with a corbelled cupola. This hall was entered from the east side. In the south-east corner was a Buddhist *vihāra*, a square sanctuary whose walls were decorated with polychrome murals depicting the Buddha and other Buddhist motifs. Buildings serving various purposes were located on the square of the *shahristan*. One complex has been excavated consisting of a central rectangular hall with a bay flanked by columns in the rear wall, and by subsidiary rooms.[73] Whereas the palace had only one storey, there were also two-storey buildings such as Kuëv-kurgan near Termez which, on the second floor, had a frieze of painted statues.

Some of the Buddhist buildings were extremely large, such as the 'New *Saṅghārāma*' near Balkh, which contained a magnificent statue of the Buddha in a spacious room. Both the statue and the room were decorated with rare and precious substances. There was also a renowned statue of the deity Vaishravana

---

70. Beal, 1969, Vol. 1, p. 40.
71. Litvinsky and Solov'ev, 1985.
72. Litvinsky, 1981.
73. Litvinsky and Solov'ev, 1985, pp. 8–95.

Deva. 'To the north of the convent is a stupa, in height about 200 feet [61 m], which is covered with a plaster hard as the diamond, and ornamented with a variety of precious substances.'[74] The tenth-century Arab geographer Ibn al-Faqih calls the main building *al-asbat*: the diameter and height of the stupa were said to be 100 cubits (about 35 m). It was surrounded by porticoes and contained 360 separate rooms.

The principal building materials were large, rectangular, unbaked bricks and large *pakhsa* blocks (made of clay mixed with finely chopped straw). The walls were often composite, consisting of *pakhsa* blocks with intervening layers of brick, or else the lower part was made of *pakhsa* and the upper part of brick. Little use was made of baked brick but wood (for columns, and so on) was often employed. The roofs were either flat (often supported by columns) or arched and domed. The arches were faced with sloping segments while the domes were either corbelled (and formed of a horizontal brick overhang) or supported by squinches.[75] In areas south of the Hindu Kush mountains such as Kapisa and Gandhara, the main building material was stone.

Art and crafts

Several murals at Dilberjin near Balkh date from the fifth to the seventh century. In the centre of one of these murals is a large female figure sitting on a throne with her knees wide apart. In her left hand she holds a shield, and on her head is an intricate headdress reminiscent of a helmet. Hornlike projections rise above her shoulders and behind her head is a halo. She has ornaments on her neck and hands; a cloak is thrown over one shoulder and she is wearing a belt round her clothing. Two smaller figures, one very small, are moving from the sides towards the central figure. Other murals feature a procession of men standing *en face*, some armed with daggers. They are dressed in narrow kaftans with turned-down flaps on the right-hand side. A distinctive feature of these figures is their position 'on tiptoes'. Another scene shows a feast with sitting or semi-reclining figures holding goblets in their hands. There are also elaborate compositions whose significance is not yet clear.[76] A comparison between some of the Dilberjin paintings and those at Kyzyl (see illustrations in Chapter 11), particularly 'the cave of the 16 swordsmen' and 'the cave with the picture of Maya', demonstrates the link between them and enables us to date these Dilberjin paintings to the fifth or early sixth century.[77]

The remarkable cycle of paintings at Balalyk-tepe depicting a feast dates

74. Beal, 1969, Vol. 1, pp. 44–8.
75. Litvinsky and Solov'ev, 1985, pp. 49–85; Pugachenkova, 1976, pp. 157–62.
76. Kruglikova, 1976; 1979; see also Buriy, 1979.
77. Litvinsky and Solov'ev, 1985, p. 139.

FIG. 2. Bamiyan. Panoramic view of the complex.
(Photo: © Andrea Bruno.)

to the end of the sixth or beginning of the seventh century. Great lords are seated with beautiful ladies, drinking wine from golden goblets while servants hold large umbrellas over them. The garments and ornaments of the figures at Balalyk-tepe are similar to those of the figures at Dilberjin.[78]

An enormous quantity of artistic and architectural remains have been preserved in central and south-eastern Afghanistan, amongst which are the objects found at the world-famous complex in Bamiyan (Figs. 2 and 3). There, in a mountain valley, lived a population whose customs, literature and coinage, according to Beal, 'are the same as those of the Tokharistan country. Their

78. Al'baum, 1960; on the dating, see Antonini, 1972, pp. 71–7; Belenitskiy and Marshak, 1979, p. 35.

FIG. 3. Bamiyan. View of the stone cliff.
(Photo: © Andrea Bruno.)

language is a little different, but in point of personal appearance they closely resemble each other.'[79]

It was at Bamiyan that Hsüan-tsang saw gigantic standing figures of the Buddha and 10 Buddhist establishments with 1,000 monks. They belonged to the Hinayana and the Lokottaravadin schools. The Chinese traveller was also struck by the size of the figure of the Buddha reclining in Nirvana. Two huge standing figures of the Buddha carved in the stone cliff have been preserved, one 38 m in height (Fig. 4), the other 53 m (Figs. 5–7). At a distance of some 1,800 m, the cliff is pierced at different levels by Buddhist cave edifices (of which some 750 remain) in which splendid paintings (Figs. 8–11), mainly with Buddhist

79. Beal, 1969, Vol. 1, p. 50.

FIG. 4. Bamiyan. Figure of the 38-m-high Buddha and cave edifices.

FIG. 5. Bamiyan. Figure of the 53-m-high Buddha.
(Photos: © Andrea Bruno.)

FIG. 6. Bamiyan. Close-up view of the highest Buddha.
(Photo: © UNESCO/A. Lézine.)

FIG. 7. Bamiyan. Close-up view of the drapery on the highest Buddha.
(Photo: © Andrea Bruno.)

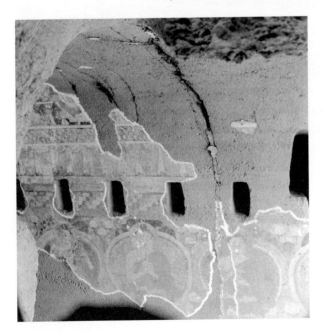

FIG. 8. Bamiyan. Detail
of the painted decoration
in the cave of the highest
Buddha.
(Photo:
© Andrea Bruno.)

FIG. 9. Bamiyan. Detail of the painted decoration in the cave of the highest Buddha.
(Photo: © Andrea Bruno.)

FIG. 10. Bamiyan. Detail of a wall-painting. Musée Guimet, Paris.
(Photo: © R.M.N. Paris.)

FIG. 11. Bamiyan. Wall-painting. Woman musician.
(Photo: © R.M.N. Paris.)

motifs, remarkable high reliefs, and so on (Figs. 12–14), have been preserved. The entire complex dates from between the third and the seventh century. The large figure of the Buddha is probably linked to the Hephthalite period.

Also dating from that period is an entire series of works of art, particularly from Balalyk-tepe and Kyzyl, in which Indian, Sasanian and Central Asian influences can be traced. Also worthy of mention are the complexes at nearby Kakrak (Figs. 15 and 16) and, much further off, at Dukhtar-i Nushirvan, and their paintings.[80] Huge sculptures of the seated Buddha and Buddha in Nirvana have been excavated at the vast Buddhist monastery of Tepe Sardar in Ghazni, where the central stupa and many surrounding votive stupas and places of worship have been unearthed.[81]

80. Godard and Hackin, 1928; Hackin and Carl, 1933; Rowland, 1946; Tarzi, 1977; Higuchi, 1983–4, Vols. 1–3; Kuwayama, 1987; Klimburg, 1987.
81. Taddei, 1968; 1974.

FIG. 12. Bamiyan. Detail of a relief *laternendeke* from cave 5. Musée Guimet, Paris.
(Photo: © R.M.N. Paris.)

FIG. 13. Bamiyan. Interior *laternendeke* decoration from a cave.
(Photo: © Andrea Bruno.)

FIG. 14. Bamiyan. Interior *laternendeke* decoration from a cave.
(Photo: © Andrea Bruno.)

Alongside monumental art, 'chamber arts' such as toreutics and the modelling of figurines were highly developed during the Hephthalite period. In India and Tokharistan, toreutic artists produced fine work, including silver (sometimes silver gilt) bowls depicting nude and semi-nude women: for example, dancers with scarves over their heads hanging down to their thighs at a royal feast, where the central element in the composition is the bust-length image of a king that resembles the portraits of kings on Hephthalite coins (see the Chilek bowl: Figs. 17 and 18). Episodes from the hunt are depicted on a bowl from Swat. The entire scene is executed with panache: horses race in a frenzied gallop; hunters and their prey are not only shown in movement but with complex foreshortening; and some episodes express the authentic drama of a real hunt.[82]

The modelling of figurines also achieved a high level. At the beginning of the Middle Ages, this art form was represented by appliqué work in the shape of human busts under the handles of vessels and, in later examples, under the spouts (Ak-tepe II, Tutkaul, and so on). It sometimes took the form of entire scenes pressed out of a mould and applied to the walls of large vessels or, at other times, separate ceramic tiles with impressed images.[83]

82. Dalton, 1964, pp. 53–5, 58–9, Pl. XXIX–XXXIII; Marshak, 1986, pp. 29–31, Figs. 11–13; Yakubov, 1985; Pugachenkova, 1987.
83. Litvinsky and Solov'ev, 1985; Sedov, 1987, pp. 103–5.

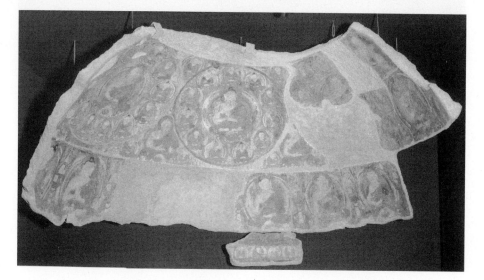

FIG. 15. Kakrak. Wall-painting from the ceiling of a cave. Musée Guimet, Paris.
(Photo: © R.M.N. Paris.)

FIG. 16. Kakrak. Statue of a Buddha.
(Photo: © Andrea Bruno.)

FIG. 17. Chilek. Decorated silver bowl. (Photo: © Vladimir Terebenin.)

FIG. 18. Chilek. Decorated silver bowl. (Photo: © Vladimir Terebenin.)

162

EASTERN KUSHANS, KIDARITES IN GANDHARA AND KASHMIR, AND LATER HEPHTHALITES*

A. H. Dani, B. A. Litvinsky and M. H. Zamir Safi

Part One
EASTERN KUSHANS AND KIDARITES IN GANDHARA AND KASHMIR

(A. H. Dani)

Eastern Kushans

The extensive empire of the Great Kushans lasted until the close of the reign of Vasudeva I in the early part of the third century,[1] but even during his rule there is little evidence of his continued control over the eastern parts of the Gangetic valley in northern India.[2] The campaigns of the Sasanian rulers Ardashir I and Shapur I (see Chapter 2) put an end to the prosperity of the Great Kushans.[3] On the evidence of the Begram excavations, this collapse was dated to 244; but the eminent Austrian and Russian numismatists, Göbl and Zeimal, put it much later. Neither date is generally accepted by Indian scholars,[4] who place the end of the Great Kushan Empire at c. 180. This date accords well with the contemporary rise of several tribal states in northern India.[5] These states ousted the Kushans and gradually usurped power right up to eastern Panjab, although in Gandhara and central and western Panjab the Later Kushans maintained their hold. Though weakened and hemmed in by the rise of new powers, the Kushans continued to exercise authority from Bactria to Panjab.

The names of only two Kushan kings of this period are known from coins. Many historians take them to be Kanishka III and Vasudeva II and distinguish them on numismatic grounds from earlier Kushan rulers bearing the same names. Numerous coins of Kanishka III have been found in Panjab, Seistan (modern Sistan) and Afghanistan, and also in southern Uzbekistan and southern

---

* See Maps 3 and 4.
1. The exact date depends upon fixing the beginning of the Kanishka era (for discussion, see Volume II).
2. Sastri, 1957, pp. 247–8.
3. Ghirshman, 1954, p. 291; but see Chattopadhyay, 1979, p. 92, where he maintains that the successors of Vasudeva I ruled in Bactria and Afghanistan.
4. Altekar and Majumdar, 1946, p. 12.
5. Ibid., Ch. 2.

Tajikistan. His coins bear other abbreviated names in Brāhmī which are taken to be those of his satraps, or governors.[6]

Altekar cites evidence from the *Purāṇas* (popular Hindu texts in epic form, containing some historical material; see Chapter 8),[7] which speak of 8 Yavana, 14 Tushara and 13 Murunda chiefs who probably ruled in Panjab in about the third and fourth centuries. These chiefs have been identified with names obtained from a series of coins found in Gandhara and Panjab. As all these coins follow the Ardokhsho type of Kanishka III, the names on them are thought to be the successors representing the Eastern Kushans, although not all of them may be ethnically related to the Kushans. In the excavation at Andan Dheri[8] four hoards of copper coins were found, all belonging to this period. On the obverse, they bear the name Saka in Brāhmī. Together with the tribal name, shortened names of the chiefs occur, such as Sayatha, Sita, Sena, Pra, Mi, Shri and Bha. These are understood to be the names of seven Saka rulers who had authority over Gandhara[9] after Vasudeva II or III, and probably ruled for nearly 100 years.

The Russian numismatist Zeimal, however, disagrees with the theory that there were several kings with the name of Vasudeva. He believes that there was only one king with this name who issued gold and bronze coins. Gold and bronze coins with the name of a later 'Kanishka' look like those of Vasudeva (though they are not identical). According to Zeimal, the comparison of gold coins of Kanishka in the Later Kushan series with those of Vasudeva, the last Great Kushan king, allows us to determine their relative chronology. The typological similarity of the earliest coins of the later Kanishka representing the king in armour allows us to classify them as gold coins of Vasudeva which formed the second stage in his minting. The similarity is so obvious that it allows us to regard them as issued at the same mint and probably by the same master, who then stopped making dies for the coins of Vasudeva. Thus the coins of the later Kanishka 'detach themselves' from the typological series of the gold coins of Vasudeva, and begin their own series. Rosenfield notes similar features in the gold coins of Vasudeva and those of the later Kanishka.[10]

Zeimal supposes that they reigned at the same period but in different territories, i.e. somewhere in the first half of Vasudeva's reign the kingdom of the Great Kushans was divided into two parts. A number of suppositions was made concerning the manner of the separation into western and eastern parts or north and south. As a rule, the starting point of the above discussions is a further development of the types of the enthroned Ardokhsho (= the

6. Banerji, 1908, p. 86; Altekar and Majumdar, 1946, p. 14.
7. Pargiter, 1913, p. 45.
8. Dani, 1968–69, pp. 42–6.
9. Altekar and Majumdar, 1946, pp. 28–9; Chattopadhyay, 1979, pp. 102–3.
10. Zeimal, 1983, p. 223.

later Kanishka) and Shiva in front of the bull (= Vasudeva). The Ardokhsho type was further developed in the Gupta and Kidarite coinage, while the Shiva type was used as a prototype for the Kushano-Sasanian coins. The circulation areas of coins of these kings were different, but their distribution is poorly investigated. That is why Zeimal considers that the boundaries of the territories they each controlled should be left open so far.[11]

The Kushan coin type of the standing king on the obverse and the seated Ardokhsho on the reverse is also seen in a series that has been given the tribal name of Shiladas. These coins, which are found in central Panjab, have, on the obverse, the names of Bhodva, Pasan and Baeharna, who appear to be rulers of the Shilada tribe holding sway over this area.

In the next series of coins we find the tribal name of Gadahara, who probably succeeded the Shilada rulers in central Panjab. These coins also show the names of Peraya, Kirada and Samudra. It is the name Kirada that has also been read in the coins of Kidara[12] (see below). Much controversy has been generated by the occurrence of the name Samudra: it is generally assumed that it refers to the great Gupta ruler Samudra (320–375) who, in his Allahabad pillar inscription,[13] claims to have allowed the *daivaputra-shāhi-shāhānushāhi* (obviously referring to the Kushan king) to rule in his kingdom and issue coinage in subordinate relation to him.[14] It attests to the autonomy of the Kushan king's rule over the territory. This statement may be judged against the background of the military successes of Samudragupta, who by this time had uprooted (see Chapter 8) the tribal states of the Yaudheyas and Madras, whose territories extended over eastern and central Panjab. Thus, although Samudragupta had gone to the very border of Gadahara territory, he did not uproot that tribe, but merely brought them under his suzerainty. It is equally possible that, being pressed by the Sasanians in the west, the Gadaharas established diplomatic ties with the Guptas and thus secured themselves a temporary reprieve.

Before discussing the consequences of this diplomacy, it is necessary to identify the Gadaharas. Cunningham[15] long ago suggested that they may be the same people who are today known as Gakkharas in western Panjab. Although there is a phonetic similarity in the names, the Gakkharas themselves trace their ancestry to the Kayanians in Iran and believe that they arrived in the area at the time of Sultan Mahmud of Ghazni (988–1030). On the other hand, the Allahabad inscription gives all the Kushan titles. They are taken to apply to the Gadaharas, who at this time were issuing Kushan types of coins in central Panjab. From this evidence the Gadaharas are taken to be the last of

---

11. Zeimal, 1983, p. 225.
12. Altekar and Majumdar, 1946, p. 105.
13. Sircar, 1939, p. 258.
14. Chhabra and Gai, 1981, p. 218.
15. Cunningham, 1893–94.

the Eastern Kushans ruling independently in Panjab. On the basis of the Allahabad inscription, they continued to rule well into the first half of the fourth century.

The economy of the kingdom can be judged from a variety of sources. First, the contraction of the empire considerably reduced the economic resources of the state. The international trade routes that had earlier supplied gold and other luxury items passed out of the hands of the Eastern Kushans, a loss that is clearly reflected in the currency of the time. The complete cessation of silver currency by the Eastern Kushans, and the debasement of the gold currency, show the adverse affect on the balance of trade. However, the abundance of copper currency proves the continuation of local demand. The Buddhist monasteries and Gandharan art flourished, there was no diminution in the production of works of art and urban life continued to be prosperous. The construction of the new city of Sirsukh at Taxila and the ruins of Rajar at Charsadda in Gandhara, together with the large number of urban settlements, speak of the prosperity of the people. This development must have been related to improved agricultural technology. Three types of irrigation project have been noted in Gandhara and Panjab. The local governors derived their power from control over this irrigation system. While it led to the strengthening of the local authority, it nevertheless increased the crops. There is evidence to show that iron mining was undertaken in the Kala Chitta range right up to Kalabagh on the Indus, whereas gold was extracted from the 'gold ant-hills' in Baltistan and Ladakh. Trade in precious stones continued with China.

In the land of the Eastern Kushans (i.e. Gandhara and Panjab), no contemporary royal inscriptions have been found but many private donations to Buddhist monasteries have been recorded in Gandhārī Prakrit in Kharoṣṭhī script. However, the use of Indian Brāhmī began to spread from this time. Simultaneously, as recorded in the later accounts of the Chinese pilgrims, the Buddhist monks in the famous Kanishka *vihāra* (monastery) at Peshawar used Sanskrit as their means of expression. The widespread popularity of Shiva and Nandi, and other deities such as Karttikeya and Durga, may point to the importance of the Hindu religion. On the other hand, Buddhism, which was widespread in this land, developed new monastic orders with lavish facilities. The role of the Mahayana, implying the cult of the Bodhisattvas, became increasingly prominent among the people. These developments in Buddhism may also show the impact of new ethnic elements upon the population of the area, although it is impossible to establish the resultant changes in the social system. The *smṛtis* (books of sacred law) present a picture of a society that is more applicable to mid-India, which was outside the territory of the Eastern Kushans, where Buddhist society continued to maintain its hold on the people. The social system is described by the law texts as that of *vrātya* (land holding), in other words, a system that fell outside the recognized rules of the orthodox Hindu system.

Kidarites in Gandhara and Kashmir

The earlier history of the Kidarites has been given above (see Chapter 5). The gold coins present the Kidarite king standing beside an altar on the obverse and an enthroned goddess on the reverse. Under the king's arm the legend *Kidāra* is written perpendicularly on the obverse while the reverse gives the names *Śrī Shāhi Kidāra, Kritavīrya, Sarvayaśa, Bhavan, Śilāditya, Prakaśa* and *Kuśala*. As the name *Kidāra* is attached to the term *Kushana* on the coins of Kidara, it is clear that Kidara must have conquered some parts of the Kushan territory and hence used the title *Kidāra Kushana Shāhi*. Other names that appear on the coins of Kidara may have been those of his governors posted in the different parts of his territory or even of those rulers who succeeded him. If this historical sequence is correct, Kidara must have established himself in Gandhara some time in the late fourth century. Altekar[16] assumes that Kidara extended his power eastward after the death of Samudragupta. Kidara was succeeded by his son, and then by Pira at a later date.

On the basis of his analysis of the evidence from Kalhana's *Rājataraṅgiṇī*, Harmatta concludes that Kimnara 'represents the Kidarite Hun king Kidara whose reign in Kashmir must have been presumed already on the basis of historical considerations and numismatic evidence but who could not be identified in the text of the *Rājataraṅgiṇī* hitherto'. He gives the approximate date of 400–410 for the beginning of Kidara's reign in Kashmir (see pages 123–4 above).[17]

It should be noted that the volume of gold coins circulated by the Kidarite rulers was considerably less than that of the Great Kushans, probably owing to the decline of commerce and the Kidarites' loss of control over the international trade routes.

With the coming of the Kidarites, Sasanian cultural penetration intensified, and we can note the influence of the Zoroastrian religion. This has been well documented by the presence of a fire altar on the coins and also by fire worship on the bases of many sculptures found in Gandhara. Persepolitan art motifs, such as the Persepolitan bell capital and winged animals, continued to be used in Gandhara art. Nevertheless, Buddhism was not eclipsed. It was during the rule of the Kidarites that the Chinese pilgrim Fa-hsien (*c.* 400) visited these lands and his account suggests the continuing influence of Buddhism.

Fa-hsien[18] reached the country of To-li (probably the Darel valley in Gilgit region), where he speaks of a society of priests all belonging to the Little Vehicle (the Hinayana school). He also describes a wooden image of Maitreya Buddha, 80 feet (24 m) high, to whom 'the kings of the countries round vie with

16. Altekar and Majumdar, 1946, p. 21.
17. Harmatta, 1984, pp. 185–9.
18. Beal, 1969, Vol. 1, Introduction, pp. xxix–xxxvii.

each other in their religious offerings'. He then proceeded towards Wu-Chang (Swat) via the Indus valley road and writes:

> The country of Wu-Chang commences North India. The language of mid-India is used by all. Mid-India is what they call the middle country. The dress of the people, their food and drink are also the same as in the middle country. The religion of Buddha is very flourishing. The places where the priests stop and lodge they call *saṅghārāmas*. In all there are 500 *saṅghārāmas*; they belong to the Little Vehicle without exception.

Fa-hsien also went to Gandhara, where he describes a great stupa, adorned with silver and gold. According to him, the people here also mostly followed the Little Vehicle. Then he came to Chu-Ch'a-Shi-lo (the modern Taxila), where great stupas had been built. He remarks: 'The kings, ministers and people of the neighbouring countries vie with one another in their offerings, scattering flowers and lighting lamps without intermission.'

The most important description that he provides, however, is of Fu-lou-sha (identified with Peshawar), where he speaks of Kanishka's *vihāra* and the great stupa. The last he calls 'Buddha tower', saying that it is 40 *chang* and more in height and adorned with all the precious substances. Of all the stupas and temples he has seen, none can compare with this for beauty of form and strength. This was the highest tower in Jambudvipa. Fa-hsien also refers to the alms-bowl of the Buddha (which was still in Peshawar at that time) and notes how a king of the Yuëh-chih wished to carry it away but, failing to do so, built a stupa and a *saṅghārāma* on the spot. There were 700 priests to look after the bowl and a daily ceremony was held in connection with it. At the approach of noon it was brought out by the priests and the *upasaka*s (laity) made all kinds of offerings to it before having their midday meal.

Next Fa-hsien went alone to the city of Hi-lo (modern Hadda near Jalalabad in Afghanistan), which contained the *vihāra* of the skull-bone of the Buddha. The ceremony is graphically described:

> The door being opened, using scented water they wash their hands and bring out the skull-bone of the Buddha. They place it outside the *vihāra* on a high throne; taking a circular stand of the seven precious substances, the stand is placed below it and a glass bell as a cover over it. All these are adorned with pearls and gems. . . . The offerings finished, each one in order puts it on his head (worships it) and departs. Entering by the east door and leaving by the west, the king every morning thus offers and worships, after which he attends to state affairs. Householders and elder-men also first offer worship and then attend to family affairs.[19]

Fa-hsien then travelled south into the Rohi country before crossing over to Bannu and then to Bhira in Panjab. On the way, he 'passed very many temples one after another, with some myriads of priests in them'. At last he arrived at

19. Beal, 1969, Vol. 1, Introduction, p. xxxiv.

the city of Mo-tu-li (present-day Mathura), beyond which lay the middle country (*Madhyadesha*). Without naming the ruler or ruling dynasty of this region,
Fa-hsien speaks of the social conditions, the laws of punishment, the habits of
the people and the position of the *chaṇḍālas* (outcasts of Indian society), who
are dubbed 'evil men' and hence 'dwell apart from others'. He provides a very
detailed account of Buddhism in this area and relates a number of traditional
stories about many cities in this country. From here he went on to Sri Lanka
and finally back to China by sea.

Later Hephthalites

Since the early history of the Hephthalites has been given already (see Chapter 6), we shall concentrate here on the later history, with particular reference
to Indian sources. In Indian works, the Hephthalites are known as *Śveta Huna*;
they are designated by these names in the *Bṛhatsaṃhitā* of Varahamihira and in
the *Mahābhārata*.[20] On the evidence of the *Avesta*, Bailey has identified *Śveta
Huna* with *Spēt Hyōn* (meaning White Huns), and *Hara Huna* with *Karmir
Hyōn* (meaning Red Huns).[21] Thus the Huns were split into two groups – Red
Huns and White Huns – in the Indian literature. The struggle of the White
Huns against the Gupta emperors, and their establishment of an independent
empire south of the Hindu Kush, has been discussed earlier (see Chapter 6).

Harmatta's view that there was a Khingil dynasty ruling over Kabul must
now be modified in the light of a fresh interpretation of the source material
from Kalhana's *Rājataraṅgiṇī*, coins and inscriptions.[22] The opinion given below follows the reconstruction made by Biswas,[23] who has listed a number of
Huna kings from the *Purāṇas* and from the *Rājataraṅgiṇī*. The most likely
person to have succeeded Mihirakula in Kashmir and Gandhara is
Pravarasena II, who is believed to be the son of Toramana. However, there was
an interregnum between these two rulers. Pravarasena came to the throne soon
after 530 and ruled for about 60 years. He founded a city with his own name,
Pravarasenapura (identified with modern Srinagar), and adorned it with markets. Here he also built the great temple of Pravaresha. Within the city he constructed a causeway or bridge. His coins bear, on the obverse, the figure of a
standing king and two figures seated below right and left, with his name
Pravarasena; and on the reverse, a goddess seated on a lion with the legend
Kidāra. The significance of this legend is not known. This king was followed
by Gokarna, some of whose coins have been discovered. He established the

---

20. Biswas, 1973, pp. 26–8, where quotations from the original are given.
21. Bailey, 1954, pp. 12–16; 1932, p. 945.
22. Harmatta, 1969, p. 404.
23. Biswas, 1973, Chs. 5 and 6.

shrine of Shiva, called *Gokarneśvara*. His son Narendraditya, who bore the second name of Khiṅkhila, also consecrated shrines to Shiva, called *Bhuteśvara*. His son was Yudhishthira, nicknamed Andha-Yudhishthira on account of his small eyes.[24]

Narendraditya Khiṅkhila is identified with a king whose name appears at the base of the stone image of Vinayaka (Ganesha), found in Kabul, but probably from Gardez. The king's name is recorded as *Parama-bhaṭṭāraka Mahārājadhirāja Shrī Shāhi Khiṅgala Odya (tya) na-Shāhi*. He also issued coins with the name either Deva Shahi Khingila or Shri Narendra. Some coins have the legend *Kidāra* under the king's arm. All these kings are identified as one and the same by Biswas, who maintains that Khiṅkhila ruled a domain stretching from Kashmir to Kabul. According to Kalhana, he ruled for some 30–36 years, that is roughly between 597 and 633. According to Biswas, the Chinese Buddhist pilgrim Hsüan-tsang came to Kashmir when Khiṅkhila was ruling here. Regarding the extent of his empire, Biswas concludes:

> The empire of Kashmir included the Kabul valley, the Swat valley and the mountain regions of Kashmir proper and in the south-east extended as far as Śākala on the Chenab river. If the king of Kashmir had a hold over Swat, the Kabul valley and Bannu, it is possible that his empire extended even to Gardez. The Gardez inscription of Khingala was probably thus of the Kashmir king Khiṅkhila, who was also the overlord of Udyāna.[25]

Khiṅkhila was succeeded by his son Yudhishthira who, according to the *Rājataraṅgiṇī*, ruled for 40 years (until *c.* 670), when he was dethroned by Pratapaditya, son of Durlabhavardhana, the ruler of the Karkota dynasty. According to another version Yudhishthira ruled for only 24 years, or until *c.* 657. Although Yudhishthira was the last great independent Huna (White Hun) ruler, Kalhana gives a further line of his successors who continued to rule in subordinate positions in Kashmir and other areas.

The end of the rule of Yudhishthira brought further changes in the Huna kingdom. One major consequence was the foundation of the so-called Türk Shahi dynasty in Kabul and Gandhara, whose history and origins have been reconstructed in great detail by Rahman:[26]

> The history of this Turkish family can be traced back to at least A.D. 666, when a Rutbil is for the first time mentioned in the Arabic chronicles. The date of Barhātigin who, according to Albiruni [al-Biruni], was the founder of the Turk Shāhi dynasty, must therefore fall about A.D. 666. It would seem that Barhātigin and the first Rutbil were brothers. The dynastic change mentioned by Huei Ch'ao [Huei-ch'ao] appears to have taken place long before his visit, but he came to know of it only when he was

---

24. Stein, 1900–1, Book 1, verses 346–50.
25. Biswas, 1973, p. 137.
26. Rahman, 1979, pp. 37–47 and Ch. 4.

in Gandhāra in A.D. 726 and at that time he mentioned it in the account of his journey. Thus the date of the beginning of the rule of the Turk Shāhis may be placed around A.D. 666 or slightly earlier[27] [i.e. immediately after the overthrow of Yudhishthira by the Karkota dynasty in Kashmir].

The Türk Shahis remained in power for nearly 177 years. The end of their rule in Kabul is dated to 843 on the basis of epigraphic evidence. But the western branch of the Türk Shahis (the Rutbils of Arabic sources, and generally known as rulers of Rukhkhaj) continued to rule a little longer until the rise of Ya'qub b. Laith, the amir of Seistan (modern Sistan), who captured Kabul in 870. The last of the Rutbils, a fugitive in Kabul or Zabulistan, was captured in 870 – a date which finally brought to a close the long history of the Turkic-speaking Hephthalites.

Rahman rightly points out that the political history of the Türk Shahis is inextricably linked with the history of the Muslim governors of Seistan. How Barhatakin came to power is wrapped in mystery, although it is probable that his base was in Gandhara. Sheltered behind the rugged hills of the Khyber Pass, he built up his strength slowly and waited for his chance when the kingdom of Kabul and Zabulistan were subject to repeated attacks by the Arab governors of Seistan. In the wake of two attacks by Ibn Samura, Barhatakin gathered his forces and attacked Kabul. We learn from Chinese sources that the ruler of Kapisa (probably Khinkhila) was killed and Barhatakin proclaimed himself king of Kabul. He extended his rule to Zabulistan and appointed his brother as Hindu governor with the title of Rutbil, i.e. 'war thruster'. This is sometimes corrected to *hitivira*,[28] but Harmatta takes it for *Zubil* and connects it with *yabghu*.[29]

From these sources[30] Harmatta builds up the following chronology of the Türk Shahi rulers:

Wu-san T'ê-chin Shai, 720–738 (*Shri Tagino Shaho* on the coins)
Fu-lin-chi-so, 738–745 (*Phromo Kesaro* on the coins)
Po-fu-chun, 745 onwards
Ju-lo-li in Gandhara, 759–764.

From a Tibetan source, Harmatta[31] quotes the name Phrom Ge-sar and identifies him with Fu-lin-chi-so, mentioned above. Further, on the basis of his interpretation of the Tochi valley inscriptions, Harmatta[32] concludes that the Sanskrit inscription there mentions the name of (Mihira) Bhoja of the Gurjara Pratihara dynasty who, in 860, extended his rule westward and helped Lalliya, the founder of the Hindu Shahi dynasty, to wrest Gandhara and Kabul from

27. Rahman, 1979, p. 47.
28. Ibid., p. 180.
29. Harmatta, 1969, p. 406.
30. Ibid., p. 409.
31. Ibid., pp. 409–11.
32. Ibid., p. 367.

the Türk Shahis and kept him there in opposition to Yaʿqub b. Laith. This inference of Harmatta brings the Gurjara dominion right beyond the Indus, for which we have no other evidence. However, the power of the Gurjaras certainly increased in eastern and central Panjab and the Karkota dynasty ruled supreme in Kashmir. As a result of their aggrandizement, Huna power collapsed in the third quarter of the ninth century; those Huna principalities that survived became assimilated to the local order and thereafter played an insignificant role.

Economic and cultural progress

The archaeological evidence from Taxila led Marshall[33] to speak of the great destruction caused by the Huns and the consequent disruption of the economic and cultural progress of the countries where they ruled. This conclusion has been contradicted by Dani,[34] who believes that urban life continued in Taxila and the monasteries were maintained, as attested by Hsüan-tsang during his visit in the seventh century. New evidence from along the Karakorum highway reveals a brisk trade and commercial relations between Gandhara, China and the trans-Pamir region. Although the Silk Route was disrupted because of new imperial alignments, trade was deflected southward.

One major change in this period relates to agricultural production and the administration of revenues. Up to the time of the Kidarites, there is evidence for the survival of the satrapal system of administration in the Kabul valley, Gandhara and Panjab; but during their rule this administrative system appears to have died out. In its place we note a large number of tribal chiefs who assumed the title of *rāja*. For the first time Bana (court poet from 606 to 647) in his *Harśa-Caritam* uses the title of *rājaputra*, from which is derived the modern term Rajput. The growth of the *rājas* and Rajputs (see Chapter 8, page 189) in the socio-economic life of the hilly regions and plains of Panjab is a new phenomenon that dates from the time of the Huns. The changing pattern of land tenure led to a new form of economic system, which has been loosely described as a feudal relation, although feudalism of the European pattern did not develop in this part of the world (see also Chapter 8, page 193). The Rajput system perpetuated the claim of the tribal heads to land which they possessed by right of their joint aggrandizement. Thus they became the real owners of the land, and also of the settlers upon it.

This new property system led to the development of a social order that has survived to the present time. Whether it also led to greater agricultural production is difficult to say. It undoubtedly led to new agricultural manage-

33. Marshall, 1951.
34. Dani, 1986, pp. 75–8.

ment by the officers of the state through the tribal heads who had a direct stake in the land. There are at least three pieces of archaeological evidence: from the Idak-Spinwam region in north Waziristan, from Gilgit proper and from Skardu. In all these places new irrigation channels were opened up. In other areas, natural springs were channelled to irrigate terraced fields. Consequently, there does not appear to have been any loss in agricultural production although the landless labourers undoubtedly suffered and slavery must have been rampant as a consequence. For example, the Türk Shahi ruler of Kabul had to pay an annual tribute of 2,000 slaves to the Arab governor of Khurasan.

On the other hand, the system led to relations of production in which the agricultural magnates enjoyed all the economic, social and even religious privileges whereas ordinary people struggled to survive and were at the mercy of the landlords. As amply demonstrated by the history of the rulers of Gilgit, there were continuous wars of succession between the sons of these chiefs, and a consequent wastage of property and manpower. The feudal Rajput system nevertheless established itself in the existing social milieu. Rather than destroying the caste system, it found its place within it, absorbing the caste groups within its own economic sphere and giving them a new function.

The Huns were fervent worshippers of the sun god and of Shiva and a number of Shiva temples were built in Kashmir. In the Gilgit region, Buddhism flourished and developed a new form. The most important piece of evidence comes from the Buddhist creations at Bamiyan, where tall Buddha figures, cave paintings and monasteries attest the progress of art in this region (see Chapter 6).

Hsüan-tsang has left a detailed description of the Buddhist centres and monastic life in the period of the Huns,[35] waxing lyrical when he visits Bamiyan. From a cultural point of view, his most valuable observation is the following:

> These people are remarkable, among all their neighbours, for a love of religion (*a heart of pure faith*); from the highest form of worship to the three jewels, down to the worship of the hundred (*i.e. different*) spirits, there is not the least absence (*decrease*) of earnestness and the utmost devotion of heart. The merchants, in arranging their prices as they come and go, fall in with the signs afforded by the spirits. If good, they act accordingly; if evil, they seek to propitiate the powers. There are ten convents and about 1000 priests. They belong to the Little Vehicle, and the school of the Lokottaravadins.[36]

The description of Kapisa is no less instructive in its picture of the economy and culture:

> It produces cereals of all sorts, and many kinds of fruit-trees. The *shen* horses are bred here, and there is also the scent (*scented root*) called *Yu-kin*. Here also are found

---

35. Beal, 1969, Vol. 1, p. 50.
36. Ibid.

objects of merchandise from all parts . . . In commerce they use gold and silver coins, and also little copper coins . . . The king is a Kshattriya by caste. He is of a shrewd character (*nature*), and being brave and determined, he has brought into subjection the neighbouring countries, some ten of which he rules.[37]

Hsüan-tsang's descriptions of the capital cities of Kapisa, Gandhara and Taxila leave no doubt that these centres continued to maintain their urban nature in this period, although some were no longer royal seats of government. On the other hand, the foundation of new cities in Kashmir by the later Huna kings, as noted by Kalhana, speaks highly of the patronage they exercised. Under their rule Shaivism and the worship of the sun god were encouraged (many images of the sun god have been found in Gandhara). But as far as the old cities such as Taxila and Purushapura are concerned, fresh archaeological evidence has not produced any new data. Only in the case of Taxila do new studies of the earlier finds suggest that the fortifications at the site of Giri belonged to the Huna period. On the other hand, Huei-ch'ao's visit to Purushapura in 726 and his description of the Kanishka *vihāra* there provide ample proof of the continued existence of the Buddhist centre.

Sanskrit references

The references in Sanskrit sources to the dynasty of Mihirakula are of great importance as they throw light on the character of the rulers. The largest number of references is found in Kalhana's *Rājataraṅgiṇī*.[38] In the *Purāṇas* the Hunas are equated with the Mlecchas and are said to rule over the *vrātya* countries (see above). The Prakrit work, the *Kuvalayamālā*, mentions the land of Uttara-patha through which flows the River Chandrabhaga (Chenab). On its bank lay the city of Pavvaiya, where lived Shri Toramana (the father of Mihirakula), enjoying the sovereignty of the world. In the Kura inscription,[39] which records the construction of a Buddhist monastery, the ruling king is thus recorded: *Rājadhirāja Mahārāja Toramāna Shāhi Jaula*. The Gwalior inscription[40] paints a memorable picture:

> [There was] a ruler of [the earth] of great merit, who was renowned by the name of Śri Toramāna, by whom, through his heroism [that was especially characterized by] truth-fulness, the earth was governed with justice. Of him, the fame of whose family has risen high, the son [is] of unequalled power, the lord of the earth, who is renowned under the name of Mihirakula [and] who [himself] unbroken [?] worships Paśupati.

37. Beal, 1969, Vol. 1, pp. 54–5.
38. On the basis of this, Biswas has reconstructed the political history of the Hunas in India; see Biswas, 1973.
39. Sircar, 1939, p. 56.
40. Ibid., p. 400.

These quotations show the nature of the Huna rulers who conquered this part of the world. Mihirakula was a devotee of Shiva. That he wielded great power is confirmed by the Mandasor inscription of Yashodharman, which says of Mihirakula: 'Through the embraces of whose arm Himālaya carries no longer the pride of the title of being [an inaccessible] fortress.' The Bhitari pillar inscription of Skandagupta describes the eventful scene of the Gupta king's terrible conflict with the Hunas in the following words: 'By whose two arms the earth was shaken, when he, the creator of a terrible whirlpool, joined in conflict with the Hunas.'

Bana, court poet of King Harsha, speaking of Harsha's father in the early seventh century, uses the phrase *Huna-Harina-Kesari* (lion to the Huna deer). In other words, from the great power that the Hunas wielded in their early career and so graphically described in Sanskrit literature, they lost their prestige after their defeat in *c.* 528 by Yashodharman (king of Malwa) and Baladitya (the Gupta king of Magadha), and were remembered as weak as deer before the lion king of Kanauj.

Coinage of the Hunas

The earliest Huna coins imitate those of Shapur II, except that the Pahlavi script is replaced by Bactrian. These coins also bear the Hephthalite symbol on the obverse. They do not bear mint marks, although a few coins show simple Brāhmī letters, such as *Thai, Sa,* or *Se, Je, Bra, Tu* or *Dhe*. These Huna coins are divided into three groups: (a) Early Huna coins; (b) Huna coins of Tunjina I, Toramana and Mihirakula; and (c) Later Huna coins of kings who ruled in Kashmir, Gandhara and parts of Panjab.

The Brāhmī legends of the second group of Huna coins establish their identity and also show more varieties. One coin of the earlier design has yielded the name *Thujana* (*Thuṃjina*) and is attributed to the first ruler, Tunjina. Then we find coins inscribed *Shahi Javukha* or *Shahi Javuvla*. The attribution of these coins to Toramana is doubtful. His coins are only in silver and copper: no gold coins of his time have so far been found. Toramana's silver coins are of three varieties: those showing the Sasanian bust and fire altar; those showing a horseman on the obverse; and those copying the Gupta coins from Gujarat. The reverse of the last series depicts a dancing peacock. The coins bear the Brāhmī legend meaning 'Shri Toramana Deva, the invincible, conquers'. His copper coins are of two categories: the first shows the Kushan type of standing king on the obverse with the king's name and a seated goddess on the reverse; the second variety has a Sasanian bust on the obverse, and a solar wheel on the reverse with *Tora* in bold letters.

Mihirakula struck coins in many styles. They are also of silver and copper. The silver coins show a bull on the obverse with the legend *Jayatu*

Mihirakula or *Jayatu Vṛṣadhvaja*. In examples where the bull is seated, the king has his face turned to the right; on the reverse is the fire altar. Mihirakula's copper coins are more common: they keep the bust type of the silver coins but omit the bull standard. On the reverse, however, the bull is shown in the upper register. Sometimes there is a trident before the bull with the legend *Jayatu Vṛṣa*. The second variety copies the Kushan example of standing king on the obverse with the legend *Shahi Mihirakula*. On the reverse again we find the bull.

The Later Huna coins of Pravarasena II (which are gold) continue the Kushan style of the standing king on the obverse and the seated goddess on the reverse, with the legend *Shri Pravarasena* on the obverse and *Kidāra* on the reverse. The coins of Narendraditya Khiṅkhila are struck with his name, *Deva Shahi Khiṅgila*. These coins have the beardless king's head to the right. Another type shows the standing king on the obverse with the legend *Kidāra*, and the seated goddess with the legend *Shri Narendra* on the reverse. We also find the coins of Lahkhana Udayaditya showing the bust of the king. Thus the coins of the Hunas, which begin by copying the Sasanian type, later show the Kushan type and then gradually become more localized with Brāhmī legends and symbols.[41]

Part Two

THE LATER HEPHTHALITES IN CENTRAL ASIA

(B. A. Litvinsky and M. H. Zamir Safi)

Between 560 and 563, the Türks inflicted a crushing blow on the Hephthalites. The fact that Sughd resumed its external political relations in 564, after a long interval, enables us to pinpoint this date more precisely: Sughd could no longer have been controlled by the Hephthalites, and the decisive battle against the Türks at Bukhara probably took place in 563. According to Firdausi's *Shāh-nāme*, troops from Balkh, Shughnan, Amol, Zamm, Khuttal, Termez and Washgird fought on the side of the Hephthalites in this battle and weapons and essential equipment were also obtained from those places,[42] that is chiefly from the right-bank regions of Tokharistan (ancient Bactria).

After the battle, the remnants of the Hephthalite levies fled to the south, where Faganish, the ruler of Chaganiyan, was chosen as king. Upon learning of these events, the *shahanshah* of Iran, Khusrau I (531–579), moved his troops,

---

41. For another classification, chronological consequences and an analysis of coins, inscriptions, symbols, etc. of Huna coins, see the very important work of Göbl, 1967, Vols. 1–4.
42. Mohl, 1868, pp. 308–16.

obliging Faganish to accept vassal status. The areas to the north of the Amu Darya (Oxus) were subsequently recognized as possessions of the Türk *kaghan*s while the areas to the south were acknowledged as belonging to Sasanian Iran. It is reported that the Türks exacted tribute from the Hephthalites (evidently, the Hephthalites of northern Tokharistan). It is also recorded that Khotan, Persia and the Hephthalites (i.e. the same Hephthalites of Tokharistan) rebelled against the Türks in 581.[43]

Al-Biruni writes in his *al-Qānūn al-Mas'ūdī* that Tokharistan 'in the days of old was the country of the al-Hayaṭila [Hephthalites]'.[44] According to modern researchers, the Islamic geographic term Haital (Hephthalite) 'was for long synonymous with the regions of Tuxāristān and Badaxšān to the south of the upper Oxus and those of Chāganiān, Qubādiyān, Xuttal and Waxš to the north of it'.[45]

Thus Hephthalite buffer principalities with vassal status were formed in the south of Central Asia. One of them, Chaganiyan, lies in the upper and central valley of the Surkhan Darya river. It is certain that a Hephthalite dynasty – which may have been descended from the Faganish mentioned above – ruled in Chaganiyan. The coinage in circulation was mainly that of Khusrau I Anushirvan: at first, this was the genuine currency of the *shahanshah*, but imitations later appeared with the name of the local rulers, '*σαρρο χδηο, ξαρινο χδηο*'. Finally, coins appeared stamped like those of Khusrau I but with the name of the local ruler, '*ποινοιο χδηο*', on the reverse, on either side of an altar; while the obverse bears no inscription.[46] The local ruling dynasty, whose representatives bore the title of *Chaghān khudāt*, continued to exist in the pre-Arab period.[47] Several of the rulers are known to us by name: an Afrasiab inscription states that emissaries arrived in Samarkand from the Chaganiyan ruler, Turantash. Later, in the first quarter of the eighth century, the ruler of Chaganiyan was Tish[48] the 'One-Eyed', who also ruled the whole of Tokharistan with the title of *yabghu*. There was also a developed system of administration. The above-mentioned emissaries from Chaganiyan were led by the *dapirpat*, the chief scribe or head of chancellery.

Another major Hephthalite possession was Khuttal, which lay within the territory of the present-day Kulyab region, that is, the basin of the River Kyzyl-su, and at times also included the Vakhsh valley. The local dynasty here also followed an established order of succession.[49] The local rulers bore the Iranian title of *khuttal-shah* or *sher-i khuttal* while the Arabs referred to them

43. For further details, see Mandel'shtam, 1964, pp. 42–3.
44. See al-Biruni, 1973, p. 467.
45. Bosworth and Clauson, 1965, p. 5.
46. Rtveladze, 1983, p. 75.
47. Bosworth, 1981, pp. 1–2.
48. 'Tish' was the Bactrian name for the star Sirius.
49. Nöldeke, Tabari, 1973, Vol. 2, p. 1618.

as *mulūk* (pl. of *mālik*, king).[50] There is as yet no evidence that specifically Khuttal coinage was minted, but the practice existed in several neighbouring territories. In particular, the territories of Termez and Kobadian minted their own copper coinage from the end of the fifth to the beginning of the seventh century. Pierced copper coins bearing cursive Hephthalite inscriptions circulated in Kobadian and Vakhsh from the second quarter of the seventh century.[51]

A further important Hephthalite possession was Balkh, the premier town in Tokharistan, which, at that time, had extensive territory. Written reports provide detailed descriptions of Balkh and its buildings, including the renowned Naubahar (Buddhist temple near Balkh) of the late sixth century. Its name derives from the Sanskrit *nōva vihāra* (new monastery). The Buddhist community was headed by the *barmak*, a title derived from the Sanskrit, *parmak* (superior or chief). At Balkh, too, coins were minted.

Important information about all these territories is given in the description of the journey made by the Chinese Buddhist pilgrim, Hsüan-tsang; although he travelled after Tokharistan had been conquered by the Türks, much remained unchanged at the time of his journey in 630. Tokharistan (Tou-ho-lo) comprised 27 territories 'divided by natural boundaries'. Of the local population he says: 'Their language differs somewhat from that of other countries.' His description of the written language corresponds to Bactrian Hephthalite writing, which was based on the Greek alphabet. Hsüan-tsang also mentions the wealth of literary works and remarks that 'most of the people use fine cotton for their dress; some use wool'. He refers to their coinage, which differs from that of other countries.

The territory of Termez (Ta-mi) lay on an east-west axis, as did its capital, which contained some 10 Buddhist *sangharāmas* (monasteries) with approximately 1,000 monks, and stupas and images of the Buddha. The territory of Chaganiyan (Shih-han-na) was somewhat smaller than Termez, its capital was only half the size and there were only some 500 *sangharāmas*. Similarly, the territory and capital of Kobadian (Kio-ho-yen-na) were half the size of those of Termez and the country contained 10 monasteries with hundreds of monks. Although the territory of Vakhsh was slightly smaller than that of Termez, their capitals were almost the same size. The capital of the territory of Khuttal (Kho-to-lo) was the same size as Termez.

The territory of Balkh (Po-ho) was larger than that of Termez and bordered on the River Amu Darya to the north. The capital was the same size as Termez, well fortified but with a small population. Agricultural produce was varied. There were roughly 100 *sangharāmas* with 3,000 Hinayana monks. Outside the town was the 'new *sangharāma*', 'which was built by a former

---

50. Marquart, 1901, p. 30; Belenitskiy, 1950, p. 115.
51. Davidovich and Zeimal, 1980, pp. 72–4.

king of this country'. There follows a description of this *saṅghārāma* and the buildings in the religious complex, including a giant stupa.[52]

The Hephthalites settled over a much wider area within the limits of modern Afghanistan than the area of Balkh, penetrating westwards as far as Herat and Badghis. In the struggle against the Arabs, the tribes of the Herat Hephthalites helped to resist the troops of ʿAbdallah b. Amir in Kuhistan (see Chapter 19, Part One).[53] The Hephthalites are mentioned in connection with the events of 704,[54] along with 'Tibetans' and 'Türks'. The leader of the Hephthalites of Herat and Badghis, Tarkhan Nizak (Figs. 1 and 2), played a major role in the struggle against the Arabs. Arab sources provide detailed information about this ruler and his role in the events connected with the fall of the last Sasanian king, Yazdgird III (632–651). According to the early thirteenth-century geographer Yakut (V, 461), Badghis was the 'headquarters of the Hayatila [Hephthalites]'. Other sources describe Tarkhan Nizak as 'king of the Hephthalites'. He also played an active part in the struggle against the Arabs in Tokharistan and twice attempted to capture Balkh. Taken together, this evidence indicates that a powerful confederation of Hephthalite tribes existed in north-western Afghanistan.[55]

The Khalaj, the successors of the Hephthalites

The Hephthalites were succeeded by the Khalaj, a people or tribes originally living in western Turkestan and then in Afghanistan during the ninth (eighth?) to the twelfth centuries. Arab geographers of the ninth and tenth centuries place them among the Türk tribes and frequently confuse the Khalaj with the Khallukh (i.e. Karluk) as only diacritical marks distinguish these two ethnonyms in Arabic script. Hence, information relating to the Khallukh is often included in descriptions of the Khalaj. For example, the Arab geographer Ibn Khurradadhbih includes the Khalaj among the Türk tribes and locates their winter quarters in the region of the River Talas adjoining the land of the Khallukh, but also states that they live 'on this side' of the Amu Darya, i.e. to its south and west. According to the tenth-century geographers al-Istakhri and Ibn Hauqal, the Khalaj lived in Zamin-Dawar. They are said to have moved in ancient times to that province situated between Hind and Seistan (modern Sistan) but to have retained 'Turkic appearance, dress and language'. The Persian geography, the *Hudūd al-ʿālam* [Regions of the World], provides the following information:

---

52. Beal, 1969, Vol. 1, pp. 37–46.
53. Nöldeke, Tabari, 1973, Vol. 1, p. 2886.
54. Ibid., Vol. 2, p. 1,153.
55. Marquart, 1901, pp. 76–8; Markwart, 1938, pp. 39–41; Bivar, 1971, p. 304.

FIG. 1. Coin of Tarkhan Nizak (obverse).   FIG. 2. Coin of Tarkhan Nizak (reverse).
(Photos: © Bibliothèque Nationale, Paris.)

> In Ghazni and in the limits of the boroughs which we have enumerated, live the Khalaj Turks who possess many sheep. They wander along climates, grazing grounds and pasture-lands. These Khalaj Turks [are] also numerous in the provinces of Balkh, Tukharistan, Bust and Guzganan.[56]

A later author (beginning of the thirteenth century), Muhammad b. Najib Bakran, writes in his *Jahān-nāme* that:

> the Khalaj are a tribe of Turks who from the Khallukh limits emigrated to Zābulistān. Among the districts of Ghazni there is a steppe where they reside. Then on account of the heat of [the] air their complexion has changed and tended towards blackness; the language, too, has undergone alterations and become a different dialect. A tribe of this group went to the limits of Bāvard and founded some settlements.[57]

The author notes acutely that the appearance and language of the Khalaj differ significantly from those of the Türks. Another source, the *Tārikh-e Sistān* [The History of Sistan], distinguishes the Khalaj from the Türks when describing the peoples conquered by Yaʿqub b. Laith.[58] They are also said to differ in Firdausi's *Shāh-nāme*.[59] The account by al-Khwarazmi in his *Mafātih al-ʿulūm* (composed shortly after 977) is conclusive with regard to the origin of the Khalaj. He writes that the Hayatila (Hephthalites) 'are a tribal group who were for-

56. *Hudūd al-ʿālam*, 1970, p. 111.
57. Ibid., p. 348.
58. *Tārikh-e Sistān*, 1976, p. 170.
59. Mohl, 1868, p. 682.

180

merly powerful and ruled over Tukhāristān; the Khaladj and Kandjīna. Turks are remnants of them.'[60] According to Minorsky, 'the early history of the Khalaj tribe is obscure'.[61]

Marquart[62] considers that the Khalaj belonged to the Hephthalite people or Hephthalite confederation and that they were a Turkic people.[63] He arrives at the conclusion that they belonged to the Hephthalites on the basis of al-Khwarazmi's *Mafātīh al-ʿulūm* and by analysing 'two names found in pre-Islamic sources'. The first name, *Xwls* (or *Khwls*) (Marquart suggests the reading: **Kholas*), occurs in a Syriac history known as the *Zaharias Rhetor* (554–5), which lists the names of the Northern Barbarians. The second name, Kholiatai or Choliatai, occurs three times in the account by Zemarkhos, the Byzantine envoy to the Turkic court in 568. For Minorsky, it is clear that the Kholiatai: '(1) lived to the east of the Jaxartes, (2) probably to the west of Talas, (3) that they had towns, and (4) that their ruler was an important vassal of Dizabul [king of the Türks]'.[64]

In his list of the 'lands of the Turks', Ibn Khurradadhbih mentions the Karluk and the Khalaj together 'and these [latter] are on this side of the River [Oxus]', that is, to the south and west of the Amu Darya. In another passage, he reports that the winter quarters of the Karluk were near Kasra-bash to the south of the Talas, 'and near them are the winter quarters of the Khalaj'. But the distance between the Amu Darya and the Talas is such that it would have been impossible for the tribes living beyond the Amu Darya to use the Talas pastures as winter quarters. The logical conclusion is: 'Either the text is mutilated or there were still (?) some Khalaj living near the Khallukh.'[65] Minorsky adds, 'The tempting point in Marquart's theory is that both Zemarkhos and Ibn Khurradadhbih have in view the region near Talas. However, the identity of the names *Xwls χολιαται* and Khalaj is still to be proved.'[66]

In spite of this and other objections, Marquart's view has become the prevailing one in the field. It may be taken as established that the Khalaj were the descendants of the Hephthalites who moved to the south of Afghanistan, although some of them remained in the north. Subsequently, they are frequently referred to in historical accounts as participating in various wars. Some of them moved to western Iran (Khalajistan) and even to Anatolia; they now speak a very archaic Turkic language. After a number of ethnic transformations, the

60. Bosworth and Clauson, 1965, p. 6.
61. Minorsky, 1940, p. 426.
62. Marquart, 1901, pp. 251–4.
63. Elsewhere he is inclined to believe that their language was Mongolic: see Marquart, 1914, p. 73; Markwart, 1938, p. 93.
64. Minorsky, 1940, p. 427.
65. Ibid., p. 428.
66. Ibid.

Afghan Khalaj became 'the Pashto-speaking Ghalzay or Ghilzay tribe of Afghans'.[67] This Pashto-speaking tribe is first referred to in connection with Babur's campaign against Ghalji near Ghazni, which means that this process was completed by the beginning of the sixteenth century.[68]

Urban life and art in Tokharistan

The sixth century was characterized by a degree of progress in urban life in Tokharistan. Old towns and settlements, including such major ones as Balkh, Dilberjin and Termez, continued to exist. There are over 100 early medieval monuments on the territory of the Surkhan Darya region of Uzbekistan alone, of which roughly 60 per cent date from the fifth to the eighth century. The network of urban settlements was reorganized, perhaps fundamentally, with the development of new social and economic conditions and the beginnings of feudal relationships. Many new settlements sprang up, including some which were medium-sized or large. As far as we can judge from the incomplete data, the internal structure of urban settlements underwent modification. Despite the far-reaching changes in all areas of urban life, material culture and art, however, links may be observed with the previous period.

Among the urban centres which finally took shape in the sixth century was Kafyr-kala, capital of the Vakhsh valley. The town and citadel formed a regular square with sides of 360 m. They were surrounded on all sides by a large ditch (50–60 m wide and 5 m deep) and by defensive walls reinforced with strong towers. The citadel (of 70 × 70 m) in the north-east corner of the town had exceptionally strong fortifications. It was surrounded by two walls. The inner, main wall had strong angle towers and projecting semi-circular towers. Between the towers were stepped arched niches containing false arrow-shaped loopholes. The fortifications were exceptionally strong. Passages running along the fortified walls were used for defensive purposes. The palace complex in the citadel was built around a rectangular hall with an area of 200 sq. m, surrounded by smaller halls and domestic offices. The southern part of the palace contained the Buddhist *vihāra* and a courtyard. The *vihāra* had a central sanctuary and ambulatory. The walls of the sanctuary were decorated with polychrome murals depicting the Buddha and other Buddhist figures.

There were also castles, one example being Kuëv-kurgan. This was a two-storey structure (18 × 20 m) erected on a 3-m platform of *pakhsa* (sun-baked brick). The rooms on the lower floor were built around a small, almost square hall. There were also several rectangular and passage-like rooms, some of which were very elongated. The layout of the upper floor is uncertain, although a

67. Minorsky, 1940; Bosworth and Doerfer, 1978; Rahman, 1979.
68. Frye, 1965, p. 1001.

richly decorated ceremonial room was apparently located on the upper floor above the hall. This room contained a frieze of some ten or twelve painted statues and the walls were covered by murals.[69]

Balalyk-tepe with its remarkable cycle of paintings, the later areas of Dilberjin with the corresponding paintings, Bamiyan and a number of other monuments in Afghanistan apparently belong to the sixth century, when architecture, painting and decorative metalwork achieved a high level of development. A detailed description of the surviving examples of the art of the period is provided in Chapter 6.

69. Litvinsky and Solov'ev, 1985.

THE GUPTA KINGDOM*

K. Chakrabarti

Origin and political history of the Guptas

The political disintegration which followed the dissolution of the Kushan Empire continued up to the beginning of the fourth century. The Kushans still ruled over western Panjab, but they had ceased to exercise any authority further east. The Sakas ruled over Gujarat and a part of Malwa, but their power was also on the decline. The rest of northern India was divided into a number of small kingdoms and autonomous states.

The origin of the Guptas is somewhat obscure. Many authorities on Gupta history believe that they came from Magadha or northern Bengal, which was the original nucleus of their empire. On the basis of the provenance of early Gupta coin hoards and the distribution of the important Gupta inscriptions, historians have now come to accept the lower Doab region as the original home of the Guptas.

From the Allahabad pillar inscription of Samudragupta we learn that while the first two kings of the Gupta dynasty were merely *mahārājas*, Chandragupta I (*c.* 319/320–*c.* 335 or *c.* 350), the son and successor of the second king, Ghatotkaca (*c.* 280–*c.* 319), assumed the title of *mahārājadhirāja*. This has led some historians to believe that the ancestors of Chandragupta I were petty landholders under the Later Kushans, the Bharashivas or the Murundas.

The Gupta era dates from the accession of Chandragupta I in *c.* 319/320, although the era itself was not introduced by him. Chandragupta I married a Licchavi princess early in his career. The Licchavis were an old-established clan who ruled over the Magadhan region during the first quarter of the fourth century. The Guptas were very proud of this alliance: they publicized it by issuing a class of gold coins known as the Chandragupta I–Kumaradevi type

---

* See Map 4.

and by describing Samudragupta, the son and successor of Chandragupta I, as *'Licchavi-dauhitra'* (son of the daughter of the Licchavis) in their inscriptions.

At the time of the death of Chandragupta I in *c.* 350, the Guptas, in alliance with the Licchavis, had become the greatest power of northern India. This alliance brought with it certain problems, however, since the nature and traditions of the two states were fundamentally different. The Guptas were monarchical and patrons of Brahmanism, whereas the Licchavis had strong Buddhist leanings. The Allahabad pillar inscription tells us that Chandragupta nominated Samudragupta as his successor. This choice was obviously resented by some members of the family, since Kacha, who is known to us from his Chakradhvaja and Garudadhvaja variety of coins, revolted against his brother Samudragupta. Kacha's reign was shortlived, however; he was easily overcome and Samudragupta ascended the throne in *c.* 350.

A lengthy eulogy to Samudragupta (who ruled until *c.* 375) was inscribed on an Aśokan pillar at Allahabad that provides detailed information about his military achievements and lists the names of the states and people conquered by him. Unsupported by other evidence, and coming from a eulogy, this information must be treated with caution. Nevertheless the list is impressive. In real terms, however, Samudragupta's direct political control was confined to the Ganges valley, since the kings of the south and the Deccan were not under his suzerainty, but merely paid him tribute. The position was similar with the tribes of Rajasthan and Panjab, although Samudragupta's campaigns broke the power of the already weakened tribal republics. In the west, the Sakas remained unconquered. The validity of Samudragupta's wider claims is questionable. *Daivaputra shāhi shāhānushāhi* is clearly a Kushan title, but the precise nature of the relationship with them remains uncertain (see Chapters 5 and 6). Nevertheless Samudragupta achieved the difficult task of bringing about the political unification of the Ganges valley.

Samudragupta was succeeded by his son, Chandragupta II, who ruled for 40 years (*c.* 375 – *c.* 415). There appears to have been trouble over his succession, just as in the case of his father. A play entitled the *Devi Chandraguptam*, written by Vishakhadatta some two centuries later and supposedly dealing with events on the death of Samudragupta, suggests that Ramagupta succeeded Samudragupta. The discovery of copper coins of Ramagupta in Vidisha-Airikina (in the eastern Malwa region), of the lion, garuda (a bird that was the vehicle of Vishnu and the badge of the Guptas), garudadhvaja (a garuda standard) and border legend types, lends credence to the possibility that Ramagupta was a governor of Malwa who assumed independence at the death of Samudragupta, but was eventually defeated by Chandragupta II.

The *Devi Chandraguptam*, however, points to the fact that Chandragupta II's major campaign was fought against the Sakas. The Udaygiri cave inscription of Virasena, Chandragupta II's minister of war and peace, records that Chandragupta came with him to that region to 'conquer the whole world', referring to the Saka wars. The last known date of the *kṣatrapa* coins is *c.* 388 and the earliest silver coins of Chandragupta II, struck in imitation of them, were of 409. Thus the annexation of western India to the Gupta kingdom must have taken place between these dates. This completed the Gupta conquest of northern India and gave them access to the western Indian ports.

It is generally believed that Chandragupta II gave his daughter Prabhavatigupta in marriage to the Vakataka crown prince Rudrasena II to secure an ally for his Saka campaigns. But the Vakatakas, who had risen to the position of major power in the Vidarbha and adjacent regions in the latter half of the third century, were then passing through a crisis and were thus unable to act as a safeguard for the Guptas against their Saka adversaries. The Guptas nevertheless put this marriage alliance to good use. Rudrasena II died five years after coming to the throne and as his sons were minors, his widow, the daughter of Chandragupta II, acted as regent from 390 to 410. This allowed the Guptas to secure virtual control of the Vidarbha region.

Gupta power reached its apogee under Chandragupta II. In the east the frontiers were preserved and in the west they were stretched beyond the Jamuna. The republican states to the west of Mathura were finally integrated with the kingdom; western India was added; and the Deccan was brought under its orbit of direct influence. Chandragupta II assumed the title of *Vikramāditya*. He developed fully the concept of kingship, in consonance with the religious ideal of the time, as attested by the discovery of his Chakravikrama type of coins. The reverse of the coin contains a *chakra* (wheel), inside which is a standing male handing three balls to a haloed royal figure. The entire symbol has been interpreted as the *chakrapuruṣa* of Vishnu, who is bestowing on the *chakrabarti* (sovereign) the three kingly virtues of authority, energy and counsel.

The reign of Kumaragupta I (*c.* 415 – *c.* 454), the son and successor of Chandragupta II, was one of peace and relative inactivity. Thirteen inscriptions of his reign that have come to light show that, like his father, he succeeded in keeping the kingdom intact. The discovery of his coins from as far as Ahmedabad, Valabhi, Junagadh and Morvi suggests that he kept the newly acquired western provinces in a firm grip. There was possibly no fresh conquest to his credit. Towards the end of his reign, peace was disturbed by the invasion of an enemy whose identity has not been definitely established. According to the Bhitari pillar inscription of Skandagupta (*c.* 454 – *c.* 467), the son and successor of Kumaragupta I, the hostile forces belonged to a tribe called Pushyamitra. Far more serious, however, was the threat of a Huna (Hephthalite) invasion and Skandagupta had to concentrate on defending the kingdom against external invasions throughout his reign. Although the Bhitari inscription leaves no doubt as to the severity of the struggle, the Hunas were finally repulsed.

After Skandagupta's death, the Guptas were unable to resist the repeated waves of Huna invasions (see Chapter 6) and central authority declined rapidly. The succession of the kings that followed is uncertain. A number of administrative seals have been discovered with the names of the same kings, but in a varied order of succession, which points to a confused close of the dynasty. A major blow came at the end of the fifth century, when the Hunas successfully broke through into northern India.

The Hunas who attacked northern India, and eventually ruled parts of it, were not entirely independent but functioned under a Huna overlord whose dominions extended from Persia to Khotan. The Huna king Toramana consolidated Huna power in Panjab, from where he invaded the Gupta kingdom. Toramana was succeeded by Mihirakula, who ruled at the same time as the Gupta king, Narasimhagupta II, *c.* 495. In his struggle against Mihirakula, Narasimhagupta II received support from some powerful feudatories, particularly the Maukhari chief Ishvaravarman and Yashodharman of Malwa, whose Mandasor inscription states that Mihirakula paid tribute to him. The political impact of the Hunas in India subsequently subsided. Acting as a catalyst in the political process of northern India, however, the Hunas saw the slow erosion and final dissolution of the Gupta kingdom by the middle of the sixth century.

With the disintegration of the Gupta kingdom, the notion of a pan-Indian Empire came to an end until the advent of the Türks, although it was briefly revived during the reign of Harshavardhana in the seventh century. The post-Gupta period in northern India saw the emergence of regional kingdoms, mostly derived from the feudatories of the Guptas. The more important among them were the Later Guptas, the Maukharis, the Pushyabhutis and the Maitrakas.

The Later Guptas had no connection with the Gupta main line. The Aphsad inscription gives a detailed history of the dynasty which shows that the Later Guptas were rulers of Magadha with suzerainty over Malwa. They were eventually ousted from Magadha by the Maukharis of Kanauj, who originally held the region of western Uttar Pradesh. The Pushyabhutis ruled in Thaneswar (modern Harvana). They had made a marriage alliance with the Maukharis and on the death of the last Maukhari king, the Maukhari nobles requested Harsha, the reigning king of the Pushyabhuti dynasty, to unite his kingdom with them and rule from Kanauj. The Maitrakas ruled in Gujarat, with Valabhi as their capital.

Of all these states which arose out of the ruins of the Gupta kingdom, that of Valabhi proved to be the most durable. The unusually large number of records of this family that have come to light help to reconstruct their political history with some degree of certainty. There were able rulers among them, such as Shiladitya, under whose leadership Valabhi became the most powerful kingdom of western India towards the close of the sixth century. The Maitrakas continued to rule until the middle of the eighth century, when they succumbed to outside attacks – probably from the Arabs, as mentioned by al-Biruni.

Of all the successor states to the Guptas, that which rose to greatest eminence, however, was ruled by the Pushyabhutis of Thaneswar. The

Pushyabhuti family came to the fore with the accession of Prabhakaravardhana, but it was during the reign of his son Harshavardhana (606–647) that they succeeded in establishing political authority over most parts of northern India. The early history of Harsha's reign is reconstructed from his biography, the *Harśā Caritaṃ*, written by his court poet Bana. This is supplemented by the account of the Chinese pilgrim Hsüan-tsang, who visited India during Harsha's reign. Harsha made Kanauj the seat of his power and it rose to political prominence from the late sixth century as a place of strategic importance. From there he extended his authority in all directions. Rajasthan, Panjab, Uttar Pradesh, Bihar and Orissa were all under his direct control and he exercised influence over a much wider area. The peripheral states acknowledged his suzerainty and thus Harsha, like the Guptas, ruled a large kingdom in northern India that was loosely connected by feudal ties.

The most important political development in western India from the seventh century was the rise of the Rajputs. Their origin is somewhat obscure, but it has been suggested that they came from Central Asia with the Hunas, displaced the original tribal inhabitants of Rajasthan and laid the foundation of the later Rajput families. The theory of indigenous origin has also been proposed. The most notable among the Rajput dynasties were the Gurjaras Pratiharas, the Guhilas and the Cahamanas, but they were to play their part in wider Indian politics only at a later date.

Social and economic conditions

For a reconstruction of social conditions under the Guptas, we depend heavily on the contemporary legal texts, or *smṛtis*. A number of such texts, most of which took the *Dharmaśāstra* of Manu as their basis, were written during this period, the best-known being the *Yājñavalkya*, the *Nārada*, the *Bṛhaspati* and the *Kātyāyana*. These *smṛtis* provide an ideal representation of society from the brahmanical point of view. Contemporary Sanskrit plays and prose literature, however, do not always corroborate this ideal and it may be safely assumed that the injunctions of the *smṛtis* were not necessarily strictly enforced. This conclusion is supported by the inscriptions of the period and by the accounts of the Chinese pilgrims Fa-hsien and Hsüan-tsang.

In the Gupta period, brahmanical reaction against Buddhism and Jainism became stronger. As a result, *varṇa-* (i.e. caste-)based social stratification and the supremacy of the brahmans (the highest caste) received much greater emphasis. It is difficult to ascertain the caste of the Guptas, but they were, in all probability, brahmans themselves and strongly supported the brahmanical social order. The brahmans were given land on a large scale and they claimed many privileges which are listed in the *Nārada*. For example, under no circumstances was capital punishment to be inflicted on them or their property

189

confiscated. The *kṣatriyas* (the second, or warrior, caste) continued to enjoy great prestige due to their political influence, and there was a tacit understanding between these two upper castes in sharing social and political power.

The degeneration of the *vaiśyas* (the third, or trader, caste), which had begun earlier, intensified during this period. Because of advanced agricultural techniques and developments in handicrafts, the condition of the *śūdras* (the fourth, or menial, caste) improved and there was no great difference between a poor *vaiśya* and a prosperous *śūdra*. The *vaiśyas*, however, retained their supremacy in industry and commerce and held important positions on the municipal boards. There are repeated references to the *śūdra* peasantry in the contemporary sources as opposed to their status as agricultural labourers in earlier times. The *smṛtis* of the Gupta period make a clear distinction between the *śūdras* and the slaves. This period saw the emergence of the untouchables, who were beyond the pale of the caste structure and lived outside the city boundaries.

From this cumulative evidence it appears that the significance of the traditional *varṇa* structure, based on colour and race, was being seriously undermined and the *jāti* structure, based on occupational status, was becoming increasingly important. Like the *varṇas*, the *jāti* system was hereditary and the number of *jātis* gradually proliferated. As a social institution the *jātis* were independent of the *varṇas*, although Hsüan-tsang describes occupations demarcated for each of the four *varṇas*. In this period the *jāti* system was not particularly strict and it was still possible for a person to move from one occupational status to another. That social mobility was not altogether restricted is demonstrated by examples of brahmans taking up the professions of merchant, architect or government official. Hsüan-tsang gives a comparative account of the political rights of the four *varṇas*. He had seen five brahman, five *kṣatriya*, two *vaiśya* and two *śūdra* kings. However, people increasingly came to be identified with the small occupational groups and the wider *varṇa* consciousness was replaced by a commitment to the *jātis*.

The brahmans had tried to explain the creation of the *jātis* in terms of the mixed castes, born out of intermarriage between the *varṇas*, which was prohibited but practised. The father of Bana married a *śūdra* woman. The *Yājñavalkya* prescribed that the son of a *śūdra* mother and a brahman father should inherit his father's property, although this right was not recognized in the *Bṛhaspati*, a text composed towards the end of the Gupta period. The contemporary *smṛtis* mention a number of mixed castes.

Although women were idealized in literature and art, in practice they had a distinctly subordinate social position. Education of a limited kind was permitted to upper-class women but they were not allowed to participate in public life. Early marriage was advocated and strict celibacy was recommended for widows. The attitude of the contemporary *smṛtis* towards women was one of contempt. Women were described as almost a consumer commodity, exclusively owned by their husbands. But there were exceptions to this norm in real life. For example, as mentioned earlier, Prabhavatigupta, the daughter of Chandragupta II, managed the affairs of state for some 20 years. On the whole, however, the only women to enjoy a measure of freedom were those who deliberately chose to opt out of the prevailing system of regulations by becoming a Buddhist nun or a courtesan.

The social supremacy of the brahmans is also reflected in the economy of the period, as attested by the frequency of tax-free land-grants made to them. This was a period of partial decline in trade and consequently a greater concentration on land. There were four categories of land – fallow and waste land, state-owned land and privately owned land. Agriculture expanded with the reclamation of new land for cultivation. Contemporary texts reveal a more liberal and practical attitude towards waste land, with the state encouraging the peasantry to bring uncultivated and forest land under the plough. Those who reclaimed land on their own initiative and made arrangements for its irrigation were exempted from paying taxes until they started earning an income of twice their original investment. Inscriptions of the Gupta period repeatedly mention the sale and purchase of waste land, which indicates that such transactions were financially profitable. The state actively patronized agricultural activity. This is suggested by the Junagadh inscription of Skandagupta, which records work on Lake Sudarsana at Girnar under state supervision, presumably for irrigational purposes. Kalidasa describes agriculture and animal husbandry as the mainstay of the royal exchequer, since the major portion of revenue came from the land, at one-sixth of the net produce.

Agricultural implements remained much the same, although iron was more widely used for their manufacture. Varhamihira, in his astrological work, the *Brhat-samhitā*, refers to an instrument for measuring rainfall. Crops were grown twice a year. According to Hsüan-tsang, sugar cane and wheat were grown in the north-west and rice in Magadha and further east. Southern India was known for black pepper and spices. The *Amarakoṣa*, the Sanskrit lexicon belonging to this period, also refers to a large variety of fruit and vegetables. Despite overall growth, however, brahmanical and Buddhist religious injunctions were not conducive to the expansion of agriculture. The *Brhaspati* was unwilling to respect the income derived from agriculture and cultivation was prohibited for the Buddhist monks.

The manufacture of textiles of various kinds was one of the more important industries at this time. There was a vast domestic market, since textiles were a prime item of trade between northern and southern India. There was also a considerable demand in foreign markets. Silk, muslin, calico, linen, wool and cotton were produced in great quantity. The production of silk decreased towards the end of the Gupta period since many members of an important guild of silver-weavers in western India abandoned their traditional occupation and took to other professions. This might have been due to the increasing

191

use of the Silk Route and the Sea Route to China, which brought a large amount of Chinese silk to India or, more generally, to the decline in trade with the West. Metalwork, particularly in copper, iron and lead, continued as one of the essential industries. The use of bronze increased and gold and silver ornaments were in constant demand. We have little clue as to the sources of the abundant supply of metals in the Gupta period and it seems that copper, lead and tin had to be imported from abroad. Gold may have been obtained from the Byzantine Empire in exchange for Indian products, although Hsüan-tsang mentions that it was also produced indigenously in huge quantities. The working of precious stones continued to maintain its high standard. Pottery remained a basic part of industrial production, although the elegant black polished ware of earlier times was now replaced by an ordinary red ware with a brownish slip.

The guild was the major institution in the manufacture of goods and in commercial enterprise. Some historians believe that the importance of the guilds declined in the Gupta period. India no longer participated in the long-distance trade in luxury goods. Instead a new kind of commercial network emerged on regional lines, based on the exchange of articles in daily use. In these changed circumstances, the powerful guilds of the earlier times disintegrated. Contemporary sources, particularly the seals found at Vaisali and Bhita, suggest nevertheless that both the activities and the significance of the guild remained during this period. Guilds sometimes acted as bankers and loaned money on interest, as did some of the Buddhist *sangha*s (communities). The rate of interest varied according to the purpose for which money was required. The lowering of the interest rate implies an increased confidence in overseas trade as well as a greater availability of goods and the consequent decrease in profit margins.

Trade between northern India and South-East Asia was conducted through the ports of the east coast. The west coast ports served as the link in India's trade contacts with the Mediterranean region and Western Asia. Several inland routes connected India with China through Central Asia and Tokharistan and across the Karakorum range and Kashmir. The most important event in the economic history of East and South-East Asia during this period was the development of an inter-oceanic trade, reaching from China through Indonesia and the east coast of India up to Simhala and extending from there along the west Indian coast to Persia, Arabia and Ethiopia. Despite commercial competition between China and India, the two countries maintained close links. Coins of the T'ang emperors of China have been discovered in southern India and Indian merchants resided in Canton. Still more far-reaching in their consequences were India's trade contacts with South-East Asia, leading to Indian settlements there and an Indian influence that permeated the local pattern of life, particularly in Thailand, Cambodia and Java.

The export of spices, pepper, sandalwood, pearls, precious stones, perfumes, indigo and herbs continued as before. Pepper was exported from the ports of the Malabar coast and sesame, copper and cotton garments from

Kalyana. The Pandya area had an important role to play in the pearl trade. The commodities that were now being imported to India, however, differed from those in earlier times. Chinese silk came in greater quantity, as did ivory from Ethiopia. Imports of horses from Arabia, Iran and Tokharistan also increased. Copper came from the western Mediterranean region and sapphire from Simhala. The Gupta king issued special charters to merchants' organizations which relieved them of government interference. Since this was the time when the law-makers declared it a great sin for a brahman to travel by sea, this may have resulted in reduced Indian participation in maritime trade.

Some historians have characterized the socio-economic developments of the Gupta period in terms of feudalism. They argue that although there had been a long tradition of donating land to the brahmans, the number of such donations greatly increased in the Gupta period. Villages along with their in-habitants, revenue due to the king, administrative and judicial rights, exemp-tion from the interference of government officials, and even the right to enjoy fines levied on cultivators, were all transferred to the religious beneficiaries. What began as grants to the priestly class were later extended to administrative officials. With the emergence of a local, self-sufficient economy, religious do-nations as well as land-grants to secular officials (either in lieu of salary or as a reward for services) became popular. The principal characteristics of this self-sufficient economy were the decline of trade and urban centres and a scarcity of coinage. Thus from the economic point of view, the central feature of Indian feudalism was the emergence of landed intermediaries. As a result, the freedom of the peasantry was curtailed, their mobility was restricted and they were forced to serve as unpaid labour.

Those historians who do not subscribe to this view have challenged the premises of Indian feudalism. They argue that during the Gupta period, trade did not decline and the scarcity of coins was at best marginal. Quantitative analyses of the coinage of this period have still to be made and the relative scarcity of coins is still merely an assumption. Some of the old-established towns did lose their importance, but new urban centres emerged to replace them. Finally, the two indispensable institutions of European feudalism, namely manor and serfdom, never developed in India. Historians who subscribe to this sec-ond view are therefore inclined to describe the practice of land-grants as noth-ing but India's traditional landlordism. The debate is still to be settled.

The literary records of this period suggest an overall economic prosper-ity at least among the upper classes. Fa-hsien describes the people of Madhyadesha (the 'middle country') as prosperous and happy towards the beginning of the fifth century. Evidence of material conditions obtained from excavations also points to a high standard of living. The prosperous urban-dwellers lived in luxury; and comfort, in the urban centres at least, was not confined to the upper classes. Yet it was a culture with wide variations. The untouchables lived on the outskirts of the opulent cities and the peasantry were being gradually impoverished. The maintenance of an imperial façade was a purposeless expense which must have been a drain on the economy. Indeed, the debased Later Gupta coinage indicates an economic crisis.

Administration

In many respects, the Gupta administration constitutes the watershed between India's past and future traditions of polity and government. The most noticeable feature of the post-Mauryan administrative development was the gradual erosion of the government's centralized power. First, the Satavahanas and the Kushans entered into feudatory relations with the smaller kingdoms. Second, land-grants, which began from this time, created administrative pockets in the countryside managed by the religious beneficiaries. A third factor which contributed to the process of decentralization was the existence of autonomous governments in several cities of northern India. Guilds of traders from these cities even issued coins, which was normally the prerogative of the sovereign power. At several points, however, the old centralized system of administration was continued and even strengthened by the accession of new elements.

The Guptas discarded the modest title of *rāja* and adopted the high-sounding ones brought into vogue by the Kushans. The most typical example is *mahārājadhirāja* which, along with its several variants, appears in Gupta inscriptions. The Gupta kings also claimed superhuman qualities for themselves. They continued the traditional machinery of bureaucratic administration with nomenclature that was mostly borrowed or adopted from earlier times. Thus the *mantri* (prime minister) stood at the head of the civil administration. Among other high officers were the *mahābalādhikṛta* (commander-in-chief), *mahādaṇḍanāyaka* (general) and *mahāpratihāra* (chief of the palace guards). A high-ranking officer, encountered for the first time in the Gupta records but destined to have a long career, was the *sandhivigrahika* (foreign minister). The *bhuktis* (provinces) were usually governed by princes of royal blood and sometimes by a class of officers called *uparikas*. The link between the central and provincial administration was furnished by *kumārāmātya*s and *āyukta*s who ruled over *viṣaya*s (districts). The district officers were nominated by the provincial governors.

For the first time, the inscriptions give us an idea of systematic local administration in the Gupta period, which assumed many new dimensions. The series of northern Bengal epigraphs mentions the *adhiṣṭhānādhikaraṇa* (municipal board), *viṣayādhikaraṇa* (district office) and *aṣṭakulādhikaraṇa* (possibly, rural board). The full *adhiṣṭhānādhikaraṇa* is said to consist of four members, the *nagaraśreṣṭhī* (guild president), the *sārthavāha* (chief merchant), the *prathamakulika* (chief artisan) and the *prathamakāyastha* (chief scribe). The precise significance of the *aṣṭakulādhikaraṇa* is unknown, but in one example it is said to be headed by the *mahāttaras* (village elders) and also includes the *grāmika* (village headman) and the *kuṭumbins* (householders).

Under the Guptas, the scope and functions of royal authority underwent a significant change. The Guptas left a number of conquered states in a position of subordinate independence. With the exception of Uttar Pradesh, Bihar and parts of Bengal, the kingdom was held by feudatories such as the Parivrajaka princes, who issued their own land-grants. The presence of these feudatories must have severely restricted the Guptas' royal authority. We do not have much information about military affairs, but can reasonably surmise that the troops supplied by the feudatories must have accounted for a good proportion of the Gupta army. The state no longer enjoyed a monopoly over the possession of horses and elephants. The significant aspect of Gupta bureaucracy was that, since it was less organized and elaborate than the Mauryan administration of the third century B.C. (seen in Kautilya's *Arthaśāstra*), it allowed several offices to be combined in the hands of the same person and posts tended to become hereditary. In the absence of close supervision by the state, village affairs were now managed by leading local elements who conducted land transactions without consulting the government.

Similarly in urban administration, organized professional bodies enjoyed considerable autonomy. The law-codes of the Gupta period, which provide detailed information about the functioning of the guilds, even entrusted these corporate bodies with an important share in the administration of justice. With the innumerable *jātis* (which were systematized and legalized during this period) governing a large part of the activities of their members, very little was left for central government. Finally, the Gupta kings had to take account of the brahman donees, who enjoyed absolute administrative privileges over the inhabitants of the donated villages. Thus in spite of the strength of the Gupta kings, institutional factors working for decentralization were far stronger during this period. This Gupta administration provided the model for the basic administrative structure, both in theory and in practice, throughout the early medieval period.

Religious life

The rise of the Guptas was analogous to the emergence of Puranic Hinduism. The vehicle for the propagation of this resurgent Hinduism was a set of texts called the *Purāṇas*, the earliest of which were composed in this period. The *Purāṇas*, which began as the historical tradition recording the creation of the universe and detailed the genealogies of each dynasty, were originally composed by bards. During this period, however, they were rewritten by the brahmans in classical Sanskrit to include information on Hindu sects, rites and customs. Before the coming of the Guptas, the ideal brahmanical social order had been disrupted to such an extent by rulers who patronized the heretical cults that we see an obsessive fear of the *Kali*, or Dark Age, in all the early *Purāṇa*s.

All the major aspects of brahmanical religion, by which Puranic Hinduism came to be identified in later centuries, crystallized in this period. The image of the deity emerged as the centre of worship and worship superceded sacrifice, although a sacrificial offering to the image remained central to the ritual. This in turn encouraged *bhakti* (devotionalism), which consisted of an intense personal attachment to the object of worship. As a result, worship of a god became an individual concern and the priest ceased to be so dominant a figure as in the sacrifice.

Hindus became divided into two main sects, Vaishnava and Shaiva, claiming Vishnu and Shiva respectively as the supreme deity, just as each *Purāṇa* extolled the superiority of one or the other. The worshippers of Vishnu were more prevalent in northern India, where they received active patronage from the Guptas; Chandragupta II called himself a *paramabhāgavata* (devotee of Vishnu). Shaivism took firm root in the south, although it was not confined to that region. The Huna king Mihirakula, Shashanka the ruler of Bengal, some kings of the Pushyabhutis of Kanauj and the Maitrakas of Valabhi were all followers of Shiva. Despite such sectarian preferences, at times expressed in acute rivalry, there was an underlying strain of monotheism in Puranic Hinduism which saw the various deities as manifestations of a unified whole. The social existence of a Hindu came to be defined in terms of a correct *dharma* (law), *artha* (economic well-being), *kama* (sensual pleasure) and *mokṣa* (salvation of the soul).

A notable feature of intellectual life in this period was provided by the lively philosophical disputations between the Buddhists and the brahmans, centring around six different schools of thought which came to be called the six systems of Hindu philosophy. Although their origin can be traced to the thinking of a much earlier period, some of their cardinal principles were enunciated at this time. *Vedānta* is the most influential of the six systems. The doctrines of *Vedānta* were based on the *Upaniṣada*s (books of the teaching of sages) and gave logical and organized form to their many mystical speculations. It postulated the existence of the 'Absolute Soul' and maintained that the final purpose of existence was the union of the individual and this 'Absolute Soul' after physical death. Together these six systems constitute the core of Hindu philosophy and all subsequent developments are its ramifications.

Although Buddhism was theoretically still a formidable rival of Hinduism, by the end of this period its influence was waning (see Chapter 18, Part Two).

Jainism was saved from a similar fate by its essentially conservative character. Unlike the other religious systems, it underwent little change in ideas or doctrines. The fact that it failed to adapt to new environments accounts for its restricted popularity but much longer life compared with Buddhism. Jainism continued to be supported by the merchant community of western India. In certain areas of the Deccan and the south it received patronage from local royalty, though much of this patronage ceased after the seventh century. The organizational split between the two principal Jaina sects, the *Śvetāmbaras* and the *Digambaras*, reached its culmination during this period. In the early sixth century, the second Jaina Council was held at Valabhi to recover and systematize the Jaina canonical instructions which were facing extinction. At this council, the Jaina canon was defined substantially as it exists today. The Jainas had by now evolved a series of icons: the images of the *tirthankaras* (Jaina teachers) in the Khandagiri cave at Bhubaneshwar are some of the best examples.

Literature

Sanskrit literature was given lavish encouragement during this period, mostly through royal patronage. It was a literature of the élite and those associated with the court circle. Classical Sanskrit poetry flourished with Kalidasa's works probably in the late fourth and early fifth centuries. Kalidasa reflects the court culture of the time. Though deeply imbued with tradition, all his works reveal his distinct personality. He wrote two long poems, the *Kumārasambhava* and the *Raghuvaṁśa*, and also the *Meghadūta*, a work of a little over 100 verses, which is one of the most popular Sanskrit poems; it has unity, balance and a sense of wholeness that is rare in early Indian literature. Kalidasa's long poem the *Kumārasambhava* has a religious theme, but is essentially secular in character and contains passages of great beauty.

Many poets after Kalidasa wrote courtly epics, but none so ably as he. The two best examples of such poems are Bharavi's *Kirātārjunīya* (mid-sixth century) and Magha's *Śiśupālavadha* (late seventh century). Magha had set the trend for the poetic style of the later period, which became progressively ornate and artificial. The finest poet in this genre was Bhartrhari, possibly of the seventh century, who left only 300 separate stanzas on the subjects of wordly wisdom, love and renunciation respectively, which are considered masterpieces of concise expression. Another important exponent of this style was Amaru, also of the seventh century.

As in poetry, the greatest exponent of Sanskrit drama in this period was Kalidasa, who was able to achieve the effects he wanted and to capture the conflicting emotions of his characters. The real value of his work, however, lies in his imagery, language and dialogue, which are fresh and vigorous. Shudraka, probably Kalidasa's contemporary, has left only one play, the *Mṛcchaktika*, which is the most realistic of Indian dramas. Vishakhadatta, who probably belonged to the sixth century, has only one complete surviving play, the *Mudrārākṣasa*; the plot is exceedingly complicated, but is worked out with great skill and leads to a breathtaking climax. One interesting convention of the Sanskrit theatre of this period is that it allows no tragedy. Tragic and pathetic scenes are common enough but the endings are almost invariably happy and melodramatic, often necessitating an unnatural forcing of plots. Another notable feature is that the characters of high social status speak Sanskrit while women and the 'lower orders' speak Prakrit: this defines the standing of Sanskrit and Prakrit in a social context. The best examples of Sanskrit prose literature of this period are provided by Dandin, Subandhu and Bana, all of whom lived in the late sixth and early seventh centuries.

The *Śvetāmbara* Jaina canon and its exegetic literature in Ardha-Magadhi Prakrit, the few religious texts of the *Digambara* Jainas in Shauraseni Prakrit and the commentaries of Buddhist texts written in Pali constitute the most important specimens of Prakrit and Pali literature of this period. The attempts of the Jaina monks to redefine their canon, following the second Jaina Council, resulted in the production of a vast literature, which is didactic in style, arid in content and deficient in literary value. Mention may also be made of independent religious narratives such as the *Vasudevahiṇḍi* by Dharmadasa and Sanghadasa and a religious romance called the *Taraṅgavartikathā* attributed to Padalipta. Among the Prakrit long narrative poems, the most noteworthy are the *Setubandha* by Pravarasena and the *Gauḍa-vaho* by Vakpatiraja.

The Gupta period is referred to as the 'classical age' of ancient India, mainly because of its cultural achievements. The description seems to be true for the upper classes, amongst whom material and intellectual culture reached a level never before attained. It has been suggested that every great literary form implies the unfolding of a new social grouping, headed by some new class. Those who hold this view argue that this great period of classical Sanskrit literature – which witnessed an unprecedented growth and development – was intimately connected with the rise of feudalism. Motivated by an entirely different set of reasons, the nationalist historians of the early twentieth century sought instead to locate the utopian 'golden age' in this period, again primarily because of its literary and artistic excellence. These divergent conclusions, however, agree on the common point of the cultural flowering during this period.

Science

There was a corresponding development in the field of science, though it was not comparable in scale or quality with the growth in literature, and the knowledge of metals had improved tremendously. The treatises of *Aṣṭāṅga-saṁgraha* and *Aṣṭāṅga-hṛdaya-saṁhitā* were mostly compilations from earlier texts. Books on the diseases of animals, particularly horses and elephants, now appeared for the first time.

It was an intensely active period in mathematics which encouraged the development of astronomy as a precise science. Aryabhata, who composed his famous work the *Āryabhaṭiyā* in 499, was an accomplished mathematician who knew the use of the decimal place-value system and dealt with area, volume, progressions, algebraic identities and indeterminate equations of the first degree. He was the first writer to hold that the earth was a sphere rotating on its axis and that eclipses were caused by the earth's shadow falling on the moon. With remarkable accuracy, Aryabhata calculated the length of the solar year to be 365.3586805 days. Varhamihira, who is more known for his astrological work the *Bṛhat-saṁhitā*, flourished in the sixth century.

Despite an accurate knowledge of the duration of the solar year, the basic unit in recording dates was the lunar day, approximately 30 of which formed the lunar month. Twelve lunar months make only 354 days and hence every 30 months an extra month was added to the year. The Hindu calendar, though quite accurate, was thus rather cumbrous. The solar calendar, imported with Western astronomy, was also known from the Gupta period, but it did not replace the lunar calendar. Hindu thinkers had evolved a cyclical theory of time.

Art and architecture

The Gupta period also represents a watershed in the history of Indian art. In one respect, it marks the culmination and ultimate exhaustion of earlier tendencies in architectural types and forms. In another, it marks the beginning of a new age, connected with the phenomenal growth and development of the temple. The material prosperity of the period is reflected in its town planning. Most cities were laid out in squares; wooden buildings were replaced by buildings of brick; houses were oriented to the cardinal points; and drains and wells were carefully planned.

Rock-cut cave architecture persisted in this period – mostly Buddhist but with a few brahmanical and Jaina examples. The rock-cut architecture of the Buddhists consisted of two conventional types, the *chaitya* (shrine containing a stupa) and the *vihāra* (monastery). The most notable groups are found at Ajanta, Ellora, Aurangabad and Bagh. Of the 23 caves at Ajanta which were excavated during this period, only caves XIX and XXVI were *chaitya* halls and the rest were *vihāras*. The most significant innovation here is the wealth of sculptures of the human figure.

The *vihāra* was planned in the form of rows of cells around a central court. Of the *vihāras* at Ajanta, the most important are caves XVI, XVII, I and II, remarkable for the beauty of their pillars. Of the stupas, which were built in large numbers, two deserve special mention – that at Mirpur Khas and the Dhamekh stupa at Sarnath. The rich, elegant patterns of the ornamental scheme constitute the chief beauty of the Sarnath monument and its cylindrical shape indicates a date of *c.* the sixth century.

FIG. 1. Deogarh. Dashavatara temple. General view.
(Photo: © Archaeological Survey of India, Janpatch, New Delhi.)

Unfortunately not much has survived of Gupta temple architecture, although the sources indicate that many temples were constructed. It has been suggested that such temples were on the whole unimpressive shrines which were either absorbed in domestic architecture or else built over in later centuries. Extant examples consist of three major groups – the flat-roofed square temple with a shallow porch in front or a squat tower above; the rectangular temple with an apsidal back and barrel-vaulted roof; and the circular temple with shallow projections at the four cardinal points. The Dashavatara temple (fifth century) at Deogarh (Figs. 1 and 2) is one of the best examples of an age of experiments in types and forms which was later elaborated and finally crystallized in the eighth-century Hindu temple in northern India.

The pivot of Gupta sculptural art was the human figure. By now all animal and vegetal patterns had been eliminated from the narrative and simply underlined the importance of the human form. The body was given perceptual form with the help of a full modelling that, in its naturalism, is almost unparalleled

200

FIG. 2. Deogarh. Dashavatara temple. Side view.
(Photo: © Archaeological Survey of India, Janpatch, New Delhi.)

in Indian art. The Buddhas and Bodhisattvas of the fifth and sixth centuries represent the final achievement of the highly subtle, mystical and fluid thought of the Mahayana school. The most important centres of sculpture were Mathura and Sarnath. One of the best examples is the seated Buddha in *dharma-chakra-pravarttana* (Fig. 3) attitude from Sarnath, where the body sheds its toughness and attains complete ease and serenity. All this is achieved with the help of delicate modelling, a smoothly flowing, melting line and an utmost economy of technique.

The Hindus, however, treated the image as a symbol. Although the god took a human form, he might well have several arms or the head of an animal. The Hindu gods, as represented in the sculpture of this period, were mainly incarnations of Vishnu, the most popular among them being those of *nṛsimha* (half man/half lion) and *varāha* (boar). The cult of Shiva was mostly confined to phallic worship, which did not offer much sculptural scope. The more significant brahmanical sculptures of the time were influenced by the Puranic vision

201

FIG. 3. Sarnath. Buddha in *dharma-chakra-pravarttana*.
(Photo: © Archaeological Survey of India, Janpatch, New Delhi.)

of the evolution of the universe from its material cause and its re-creation from the constituent elements into which it is merged. This explains the origin and meaning of the latent dynamic strength and power in the magnificent reliefs of the Udaygiri caves of eastern Malwa or of Badami, Ellora, Aurangabad and Elephanta. For example, the Great Boar (an incarnation of Vishnu who rescued the earth from the cosmic ocean) carved in relief near the entrance of a cave at Udaygiri conveys the impression of a great primordial power working for good against the forces of chaos and destruction, and bears a message of hope, strength and assurance.

While the quest for form in stone concerned itself with themes and expressions of a deeper and more fundamental significance, painting had a secular character and was presumably in more general demand. The *Viṣṇu-dharmottara*, a text of the Gupta period, devotes an entire chapter to the art of painting, laying down many of its theoretical canons. The best examples of painting can be found in the murals of caves I, II, XVI, XVII and XIX of Ajanta (Figs. 4–7), caves IV and III of Bagh and caves III and II of Badami. The Ajanta paintings do not show a progressively developing style, as in contemporary sculpture. The murals chiefly depict scenes from the life of the

FIG. 4. Ajanta. Mural painting in cave XVI. Dying princess.
(Photo: © Archaeological Survey of India, Janpatch, New Delhi.)

FIG. 5. Ajanta. Mural painting in cave XVII. Indra accompanied by his celestial musicians. (Photo: © Archaeological Survey of India, Janpatch, New Delhi.)

FIG. 6. Ajanta. Mural painting in cave XVII. Vessantara *jātaka*.
(Photo: © Archaeological Survey of India, Janpatch, New Delhi.)

FIG. 7. Ajanta. Mural painting in cave XVII. Rahul and his mother Yashodhara.
(Photo: © Archaeological Survey of India, Janpatch, New Delhi.)

Buddha and from the *jātaka*s (birth stories of the Buddha). There is no per-
spective, but an illusion of depth is given by placing the background figures
somewhat above those in the foreground. Although painted for religious purposes, the Ajanta murals bear a secular message. They depict the entire pano-
ply of life in ancient India: princes in their palaces, ladies in their apartments,
coolies, beggars, peasants and ascetics, together with the many Indian birds,
beasts and flowers.

Very different are the enormous number of terracotta reliefs from northern India and Bengal. Produced from sketchy moulds in large quantities, they
were carefully finished and often painted. Employed for various purposes, their
primary use was in decorating the exterior walls of Buddhist establishments
and residential houses.

A remarkable example of handicraft is the ivory Triratna (trident symbol
of the three jewels of Buddhism) in high relief representing a Buddha with

attendant Bodhisattvas. The central figure is like a miniature Mathura image of the period. The wealth of jewellery worn by women of this period is seen in the flying *apsarās* (nymphs of the sky) in the Ajanta murals (Fig. 8), which also show the variety of high-quality textiles such as embroidery, tie and dye work, brocade and muslin. A rare example of Gupta metalwork is an object that has been identified as an architect's plummet, made of iron coated with bronze. On its neck is a plaque with a representation of dancing figures framed in prongs terminating in lotus buds which is reminiscent of the decorative forms of Gupta stone sculpture. Among the most splendid examples of the minor arts of the period are the gold coins of the Gupta dynasty, executed with impeccable finesse.

Some authorities have depicted the Gupta kings as the liberators of India from foreign rule. But the invaders had become thoroughly Indianized by the Gupta period and this made the task of assimilating them into Indian society relatively simple by assigning them appropriate caste status. They continued to exert an influence on aspects of Gupta culture, however, and this is nowhere more pronounced than in Gupta art. Many characteristic architectural forms and motifs of the Guptas were inherited from Kushan Mathura and Gandhara. Gupta sculpture undeniably developed from an emphasis on massive power inherited from the Kushans, but gradually it evolved its own style, with graceful and more linear creations. Gupta culture, with all its inevitable borrowings from previous traditions, was essentially indigenous in character and set the norms for subsequent developments.

FIG. 8. Ajanta. Mural painting in cave XVI. Flying *apsarā*.
(Photo: © Archaeological Survey of India, Janpatch, New Delhi.)

KHWARIZM[*]

E. E. Nerazik and P. G. Bulgakov

Part One

HISTORY AND CULTURE OF KHWARIZM

(E. E. Nerazik)

Uncertain early history

The period from the late third to the eighth century was a very complex one in the history of Khwarizm (Chorasmia). It was marked initially by the decline and fall of the huge Kushan Empire, the rule of the Hephthalites in Central Asia and their conflict with the Sasanians, while the close of the period coincides with the Arab conquest of the entire region. The area's development over these centuries was determined by two basic factors: the growth of feudal relations and outside invasions.

There is as yet no irrefutable evidence that Khwarizm became part of the Kushan state. Opponents of this theory commonly cite as evidence of the country's independence the appearance of a local overstrike on Kushan coins in circulation in the territory of Khwarizm.[1] They further maintain that the wealth of archaeological material cannot properly be taken as reflecting close links between Khwarizm and the Kushans, mainly because of the almost complete lack of any tangible vestige of Buddhism, which had been propagated in the lands conquered by the Kushans, particularly Tokharistan (Bactria). It should be noted, however, that not all the Kushan coins found in Khwarizm are overstruck; and investigation of the material and spiritual culture of the population in the early centuries of the Christian era points to some Indo-Buddhist connections.[2] However, influence in the field of art is not necessarily determined by conquest; it may emerge and spread through cultural and historical contact. Only if fresh data are amassed will it be possible to settle this vexed question. It is noteworthy that Toprak-kala (see also pages 213–17), an outstanding architectural group and grandiose dynastic centre, was built in the

[*] See Map 5.
1. Masson, 1966, pp. 82–3; Vaynberg, 1977, pp. 87–9.
2. Tolstov, 1948*a*, p. 201.

second century of the Christian era. This was undoubtedly a very significant event, and Tolstov is perhaps correct in believing that the palace was built to mark the liberation of Khwarizm from dependence on the Kushans and in ascribing the appearance of a local overstrike on Kushan coins to that very period.[3]

In the early fourth century, Afrig came to power in Khwarizm after founding a new era, according to al-Biruni who lists 22 rulers of the dynasty founded by Afrig.[4] Numismatic evidence, third-century material from the archives of the Toprak-kala palace and inscriptions on the ossuaries from Tok-kala (seventh and eighth centuries) (Fig. 1), however, have significantly rectified this account. First, the notion of the Afrig era must be rejected, since it has been established beyond doubt that the Khwarizmian era, reflected in dates in the above-mentioned documentary material, began in the first century.[5] Furthermore, only certain names of rulers from al-Biruni's list tally with those found on coins,[6] a discrepancy believed to be the result of his lack of reliable information on the pre-Islamic Khwarizmian dynasty.[7] It is thought, however, that the discrepancy will prove to be less important as more numismatic evidence is accumulated.

Particular uncertainty surrounds the second half of the third century and the fourth century, a period which saw the appearance of many small copper coins and various seals. This seems to reflect a trend towards the political isolation of individual parts of Khwarizm.[8] Between the last third of the third century (which corresponds to the reign of King Vazamar, possibly a usurper of the Khwarizmian throne)[9] and the end of the seventh century there are no satisfactorily dated coin series; indeed, there is a gap in the coinage.[10] It is important to note that the period in question corresponds to the time of the Sasanians' eastward campaigns, Khwarizm being recorded as one of the countries they conquered. Thus, according to the Arab historian al-Tabari, Ardashir I seized Balkh, Merv and Khwarizm as far as the extreme limits of Khurasan.[11] However, the inscription of Shapur I on the Ka'be of Zoroaster at Naqsh-i Rustam, which lists the realms conquered by him, makes no mention of Khwarizm.[12] At the same time, numismatic and archaeological evidence suggests that Khwarizm was in some way dependent on the Sasanians. We may

3. Tolstov, 1984*b*, p. 16.
4. Biruni, 1957, p. 48.
5. Henning, 1965, p. 169; Livshits, 1968, p. 440; Vaynberg, 1977, pp. 77–80.
6. Livshits, 1968, pp. 442–4; Vaynberg, 1977, pp. 80–2.
7. Gudkova and Livshits, 1967, p. 10.
8. Tolstov, 1948*a*, p. 183.
9. See Tolstov, 1962, p. 225; Vaynberg, 1977, p. 97.
10. Henning, 1965, p. 170; Livshits, 1968, p. 443.
11. Nöldeke, Tabari, 1973, pp. 17–18.
12. Sprengling, 1953, pp. 7, 14; Lukonin, 1969, pp. 62, 126.

FIG. 1. Tok-kala. Painted ossuary. (Photo: © Vladimir Terebenin.)

nevertheless question Henning's view that the country was totally subjugated for a considerable period.[13] We cannot rule out the possibility that Khwarizm was part of the state of the Türks in the sixth and seventh centuries, though relations between the Khwarizmians and the Türks are as yet obscure.

The only events in Khwarizm about which the sources are comparatively clear are those that occurred at the time of the campaigns of conquest led by the Arab general Qutaiba b. Muslim (see pages 228 et seq.).

Social structure and administration

Between the fourth and the sixth century the cities of Khwarizm underwent a marked decline, with a cut-back in the irrigation network. This is usually blamed on a socio-economic depression, the scale of which is unclear, though it was more pronounced on the periphery of the country. It may have been at least

13. Henning, 1965, pp. 169–70.

FIG. 2. Coin from Khwarizm (sixth century?). Bronze.

partly the result of invasions by nomadic tribes at the time of the great migration of peoples, when the outlying areas were undoubtedly overrun. Furthermore, the country's internal situation must have been affected by the abovementioned events of political history. The seventh and eighth centuries, however, saw some stability and even a measure of economic and cultural progress.

We can only guess at the political and administrative organization of Khwarizm. There is some numismatic evidence of the existence of independent local rulers in the seventh and eighth centuries. For example, coins have come to light from the Kerder region of the lower valley of the Amu Darya (Oxus). That territory had been taken over by settlers from Khwarizm and by immigrants from the Syr Darya (Jaxartes) regions and its rulers succeeded in usurping the throne of the *Khwarizmshah* on several occasions. The 'king of Khamjird' seems to have ruled in northern Khwarizm. There is also a theory that Khamjird and Urgench were one and the same place.[14]

The monetary reform carried out in Khwarizm at some point in the fifth, sixth or seventh century led to the minting of new types of coins (Fig. 2) with a different value, and with the ideogram *MR'Y MLK'* (lord king) instead of the earlier *MLK'* (king).[15] What prompted the reform is unclear, but it may have reflected the desire of the *Khwarizmshah* to consolidate his power over the other rulers. Al-Tabari mentions them when referring, in connection with the events of 711–712 (see pages 229 et seq.), to kings and *dihqāns* (lords). Clearly some hierarchical order or rule may be indicated by the coinage of the seventh century, which bears the Khwarizmian inscription *ḫwt'w* (lord) accompanying the portrait of the ruler, with the ideogram *MR'Y MLK'* on the reverse. Some authorities believe that the terms *MLK'*, *MR'Y* and *γwβw* in narrative sources and on Sogdian coinage of the seventh and eighth centuries also indicate three degrees in the local hierarchy.[16] In the Sogdian documents from Mount Mug, however, *MR'Y* (equivalent to *γwβw* or *xwt'w*) is the title assumed both

14. Vaynberg, 1977, p. 99.
15. Ibid., pp. 59–65.
16. Smirnova, 1963, p. 31.

Fig. 3. Berkut-kala. Castle of fifth–seventh century (eastern Khwarizm). Aerial view.

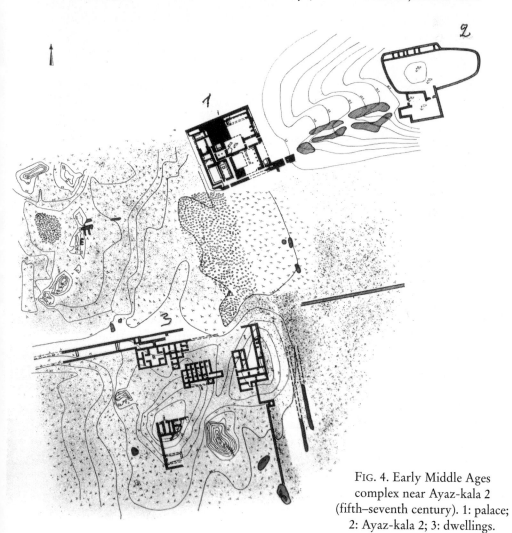

Fig. 4. Early Middle Ages
complex near Ayaz-kala 2
(fifth–seventh century). 1: palace;
2: Ayaz-kala 2; 3: dwellings.

FIG. 5. Ayaz-kala 2. Fortified complex.

by Divashtich (the ruler of Panjikent) himself and by his underlings.[17] At the same time, the entire nobility of Iran of lower rank than the king bore the title of 'lord'.[18] Nevertheless there can be little doubt about the general hierarchical structure of Khwarizmian society in the seventh and eighth centuries. Of particular significance is the archaeological evidence concerning Khwarizm's oasis settlements which sprang up along the major canals around the urban centres.

The structure of the towns varied: the old towns founded in antiquity on the major trading routes continued to exist, still with a rectangular grid layout and fortified walls and towers; but new towns often sprang up by the walls of the castles of powerful feudal lords, reflecting the prevalent trend in the development of medieval towns. One example was the small town of Berkut-kala (Fig. 3): it was composed of two parts, one containing buildings occupied by craftsmen, around a market square, and the other entirely taken up with housing.[19] Another example is the vast complex of buildings (Fig. 4) at the foot of the fortress Ayaz-kala 2 (Fig. 5): here, in the fifth to the seventh century (and

17. Livshits, 1962, p. 50.
18. Harmatta, 1957, p. 303; Lukonin, 1961, pp. 16–17.
19. Nerazik, 1966, p. 109.

probably even before), a beautiful palace of the *Khwarizmshah*s emerged and a town developed near by (Fig. 6). Little is known about the appearance of the old towns. According to Arab authors, Madinat al-Fir, the capital of Khwarizm, was the country's largest and most strongly fortified town, the historian al-Baladhuri even comparing it to Samarkand.[20] It consisted of three parts surrounded by a moat:[21] the al-Fir citadel, the old town and the new part. In the tenth century, when the old town and the citadel had been almost destroyed by the Amu Darya, the new part grew into a town known at the time as Kath.

Hazarasp was one of the country's main towns, according to Bal'ami.[22] Small-scale excavations there have revealed portions of strongly fortified walls and a large citadel may have existed in an angle of the town. It should be noted that Toprak-kala was a royal residence, a town specially built to serve a number of palaces, around which it lay (Figs. 7–9). The layout of the town, which covered 17.5 ha, was marked by great regularity throughout its existence (second to sixth century). The town of Kerder, the centre of an independent domain, was laid out just as regularly as Toprak-kala, a fact which appears to reflect centralized urbanization. The Kerder settlements cannot be called towns in the full sense of the word, however. Surrounded by a primitive outer enclosure in the form of an embankment, and sometimes lacking outer walls, they arose

FIG. 6. Ayaz-kala 2. Palace near the fortified complex.

20. Al-Baladhuri, 1924, p. 188.
21. Bolshakov, 1973, p. 171.
22. Bal'ami, 1874, p. 176.

FIG. 7. Toprak-kala. General view. (Photo: © Vladimir Terebenin.)

FIG. 8. Toprak-kala. Reconstruction of the palace by Y. A. Rapoport.

FIG. 9. Toprak-kala. Reconstruction of the interior of the palace by Y. A. Rapoport.

spontaneously as a result of the settlement of the nomadic and semi-nomadic population around a central fortification. The largest of them was Kuyuk-kala (41 ha), on whose territory have been found two ruined citadels belonging to different periods, vestiges of yurts and meagre traces of the handicrafts that were developed in the area, mainly by Khwarizmians.

In the agricultural oases of Khwarizm, groups of farmsteads lay along canals at whose outlets stood well-fortified castles. This reflects the hierarchical structure of a feudal society. The rural (and seemingly the urban) population lived in large patriarchal families spanning three generations. Well-to-do families of the third century (whose houses were the *BYT'* of the Toprak-kala documents) employed many slaves, slavery then being patriarchal in character in the opinion of Livshits (Fig. 10). The house records use the term *xrytk*, meaning 'purchased'.[23] Here also, as in Sogdiana, there may have been slaves in debt bondage.[24] In inscriptions on ossuaries of the seventh and eighth centuries, where we find the same large kinship groups, the term 'Hunnanik' (son of a Hun) occurs; it is an indication of yet another significant source of slaves – prisoners of war. These inscriptions include information on polygamy (which was common in wealthy families),[25] while the Toprak-kala documents also refer to concubines.[26] In the service of the wealthy there were also *kedivar*s (dependent persons or clients), who had become landless peasant members of the community.

Judging by excavations of dwelling-houses, ordinary farm labourers also lived in the large patriarchal families that made up rural communes. Some communities of this kind lived in the agricultural territory provided by an oasis, whose population may have attained 4–5,000. Indirect evidence of the communal way of life can be deduced from such names of Khwarizmians as *Xwānθačak* ('possessed of good share'), *βaγδārak* ('holding a share') or ('owning a garden').[27] Each commune was a fairly closed world, based on a natural economy. In the oases, cereals, vegetables, cultivated crops and fine-fibre cotton were grown. Home trades and crafts (potting, iron founding and smithery) almost satisfied the needs of the rural inhabitants.[28] After a short burst of activity in the third century, monetary circulation was not further developed until the seventh and eighth centuries, but the bulk of the coins still came from the castles. Silver and copper coins were in circulation; their face value and weight were approximately the same as other drachms of the time.

With the accumulation of written and archaeological evidence concerning Khwarizm in the seventh and eighth centuries, it is becoming increasingly

---

23. Livshits, 1984, p. 267.
24. Livshits, 1962, pp. 35–6.
25. Gudkova and Livshits, 1967, p. 14.
26. Livshits, 1984, p. 14.
27. Ibid., pp. 269, 272.
28. Nerazik, 1966, pp. 100–8.

FIG. 10. Toprak-kala palace. Written document on wood giving the list
of men living in the house of 'Harak'. (Room no. 90.)

clear that the Sogdian and Khwarizmian societies developed along similar lines.
It is important in this connection that the three Sogdian social groups (*ηβ*),
according to the documents from Mount Mug, included the tradespeople
(*γw'ky*) in addition to the nobility (*'rtkr*) and the workmen (*k'rykr*).[29] The
merchant class also seems to have played an important part in the socio-
economic life of Khwarizm. Indeed, the Chinese chronicle the *T'ang shu*
[Annals of the T'ang Dynasty] makes special reference to Khwarizmian merchants journeying afar in ox-drawn carts, which seem to have been a feature of
the country.[30]

Trading relations with the regions of the Aral Sea and the north-
west Caspian area, together with the Volga and Ural regions, were extremely

29. Livshits, 1962, p. 37.
30. Bichurin, 1950, pp. 315–16.

FIG. 11. Toprak-kala palace. Drawing from a mural painting. Woman with a thread.
(Room no. 85.)

FIG. 12. Toprak-kala palace.
Drawing from the head of a statue
in painted clay. (Room no. 36.)

important for Khwarizm's economy from the fourth to the eighth century. This trend in trading relations played a definite role in establishing Khwarizmian culture. Its influence was particularly marked in the periods of the political predominance of Kerder (see above), and was felt, for example, in the interior layout of dwellings and the forms and ornamentation of ceramics. Overall, the culture of Khwarizm was the product of a complex interaction between, on the one hand, dominant, profoundly traditional local elements and, on the other, those brought by an immigrant population and arising from the country's historical and cultural contacts. While possessing a distinctive character and identity, Khwarizmian culture followed the course of development common to all artistic canons and forms elsewhere in the Early Middle Ages in Central Asia.

Art, architecture, religion and language

In the second half of the third century the unique complex of Toprak-kala was still in existence, embodying the highest achievements of the architects, painters and sculptors of Khwarizm (Figs. 11 and 12). Dynastic ceremonies were held in its many sanctuaries, which were sumptuously adorned with numerous paintings, coloured bas-reliefs and alabaster and clay sculpture in the round. The artistic traditions and the construction and architectural methods of the builders of the palace date back to antiquity. In the period from the fourth to the eighth century, private fortifications became widespread, and the castles of the aristocracy, with their mighty walls and towers, drawbridges, secret staircases and other structures, studded the countryside. That period saw the beginnings of the major types of popular dwellings and a number of public buildings of the Khwarizmian Middle Ages. At the same time, in view of the spread of polychrome subject paintings in the seventh and eighth centuries in other regions of Central Asia, the absence of monumental pictorial art in Khwarizm of the Early Middle Ages is striking. Although we know of nothing so far except painted ossuaries, the situation may change as more towns are excavated.[31] The applied arts are best represented in the form of engraving, toreutics and so on.

On the brink of the Early Middle Ages in Khwarizm, traces of religious ideas that date back to remote antiquity, heathen agrarian cults and worship of the natural elements are frequently found. The kinds of deities which are apparent from the Khwarizmian names found in the Toprak-kala written documents – the water deity Vakhsh, the sun god Mithra, the fire deity and the god of the wind Vayu – could only have emerged in the context of ancient beliefs.[32]

31. In fact, many fragments of subject paintings have been discovered during excavations of the palace of Ayaz-kala 2, but it is only after restoration that their meaning will become clear.
32. Livshits, 1984, pp. 264–5, 272.

The traces of the Zoroastrian calendar in this material and the pantheon of deities that is constantly found in the art, together with the rituals of worship, make this system of beliefs comparable to the Avestan pantheon,[33] although there are marked differences. By the end of the third century, the earlier anthropomorphic representations of the deities had almost completely disappeared; fine plastic art was dying out, and statuary ossuaries were replaced by simple stone boxes. These changes are ascribed to the influence of orthodox Iranian Zoroastrianism, which banned idolatry. Finds of statuettes of idols, however, particularly in strata from the fourth to the sixth century, testify to the vitality of heathen cults among the ordinary people of Khwarizm. The isolated terracotta figurines are quite different in form, their features bearing a strong resemblance to those of the stone idols of the steppe. They were introduced by the nomads living on the periphery of Khwarizm, perhaps at the time of the Türk campaigns.

The ancient pantheon seems to have been preserved from the fourth to the eighth century, if sometimes in a barely perceptible symbolic form. For example, the four-armed goddess on seals and silver dishes (Fig. 13) is seen as the ancient goddess Anahita, the goddess of fertility and the aqueous element, which brings felicity,[34] while the statuettes of horses and riders symbolize Mithra, whose cult was closely linked to the figure of Siyavush. This legendary ancestor of the Khwarizmian dynasty was also represented in the form of a horseman on the reverse of coins and on seals, and was the hero of a variety of ceremonies which were part of the great ritual cycle of New Year (*Nowruz*) celebrations.[35]

A complex interlacing of different religious beliefs, principally ancestor worship, can be observed in the burial ceremonies of the people, who placed the cleaned bones of their dead in ossuaries, which were then deposited in burial chambers or interred. Images on the ossuaries depicted both a real scene of mourning for the dead person and a number of ritual scenes showing the passing of the deceased, which were also part of the New Year cycle (Fig. 14).[36]

A major role in the system of religious beliefs was played by fire worship, which is extensively attested archaeologically. Fire sanctuaries in the form of small, single-chambered cupola-shaped towers have been discovered in the oases of east-bank Khwarizm (Fig. 15). One of these, dating back to the fourth century, is the oldest domed structure in Central Asia. Toprak-kala boasted a fire temple; and, as Rapoport rightly observes, the social stratification of the population was reflected in religious differentiations, for the townspeople worshipped in a temple unlike that used by the lords of the citadel and the

33. Livshits, 1984, pp. 264–5, 272; Rapoport, 1971.
34. Tolstov, 1948a, p. 201.
35. Ibid., pp. 200–3.
36. Gudkova, 1964, pp. 95–100; Yagodin and Khojaiov, 1970, pp. 138–42.

FIG. 13. Silver dish. (Photo: © Vladimir Terebenin.)

FIG. 14. Tok-kala. Drawing from a painting on an ossuary in alabaster with a mourning scene (end seventh century).

FIG. 15. Oasis of Yakke-Parsan (eastern Khwarizm).
Single-chambered cupola-shaped room with remains of an altar.

palace.[37] The town's fire temple consisted of a small chain of chambers connected by a broad axial thoroughfare. The temple of Hvarna (*xvarenah* or *farn*, the personification of power and material prosperity) was similar to the fire temple; richly decorated rams' horns symbolizing Hvarna were worshipped in it.[38]

No significant traces have been found of foreign religions in Khwarizm at that time. There is no indisputable evidence that Buddhism was commonly practised in Khwarizm, as distinct from other regions of Central Asia. On the other hand, the presence of Christian communities in the country can be surmised.[39] A burial chamber apparently belonging to such a community has been discovered in the necropolis of Gyaur-kala.[40] An independent ruler portrayed on a coin with a Nestorian cross on the crown was evidently a Christian.[41]

37. Rapoport, 1984, p. 296.
38. Nerazik, 1982, pp. 52–4, 146.
39. Tolstov, 1948*a*, pp. 227–8.
40. Yagodin and Khojaiov, 1970, pp. 146–51.
41. See Vaynberg, 1977, Table XXIX, 4.

As archaeological work proceeds, increasing information is coming to light about the language of the people of Khwarizm in the period covering the third to the eighth century. Apart from inscriptions on coins and dishes, we now know of over 100 inscriptions on ossuaries, dozens of documents on skin and wood from Toprak-kala and 2 documents from Yakke-Parsan (eighth century). It has been established that the Khwarizmian language was related to the East Iranian group, while the writing was based on the Aramaic script. The inscriptions record dates of the Khwarizmian era, forms of greeting, proper names, terminology reflecting patrilineal kinship, and the names of the 12 months and of 18 days (out of 30), which may enable us to fill in some gaps in al-Biruni's data concerning the Khwarizmian calendar.

Part Two

AL-BIRUNI ON KHWARIZM

(P. G. Bulgakov)

The Khwarizmian calendar

Information on the history and culture of Khwarizm is given in the works of Abu Raihan al-Biruni, the learned Khwarizmian encyclopaedist who lived from 973 to 1048. His main source was the oral information of authorities on ancient traditions who were still alive when he was in Khwarizm, but he was also well versed in the historical literature which had been compiled by his time. In his work the *Kitāb al-āthār al-bāqiya* [Chronology of Ancient Nations], known to modern scholars as the *Chronology* and written *c.* 1000–1003, al-Biruni gives information about the Khwarizmian calendar which is still the most detailed and comprehensive account we possess.[42]

Analysis of this information has established that the calendar was based on the so-called New Avestan Calendar,[43] but in time had taken on certain characteristics of its own. The Khwarizmian solar calendar consisted of 12 months, each of which had its own name[44] and consisted of 30 days, each of which also had a name. Five extra days were added to the end of the last (i.e. the 12th) month. These extra days did not have their own names, but were called by the same names as the first 5 days of the month. In this way,

---

42. Biruni, 1957, pp. 62–3.
43. See Bickerman's study of the Zoroastrian calendar (Bickerman, 1967, pp. 197–207).
44. Al-Biruni gives two variations of the names of most months, one of which was the official name used by the Zoroastrian priesthood, and the other the name in everyday use.

the Khwarizmian calendar consisted of 365 days. The additional 6 hours were not taken into account, and there was no leap year to correct this. The official names of the months and days given below are taken from Livshits' study.[45]

MONTHS

I.	*r v r ǰ n'*	VII.	*'w m r y ('m r y)*
II.	*'r d w š t*	VIII.	*y'n'x n (y'b' x n)*
III.	*h r w d' d*	IX.	*'r w*
IV.	*ǰ y r y*	X.	*r y m z d*
V.	*h m d' d*	XI.	*'š m n ('h m n)*
VI.	*'x š r y w r y*	XII.	*x š w m*

DAYS

1.	*r y m ž d (r y m z d)*	16.	*f y γ*
2.	*'z m y n ('h m y n)*	17.	*'s r w f*
3.	*'r d w š t*	18.	*r š n*
4.	*'x š r y w r y*	19.	*r w r ǰ n*
5.	*'s b n d' r m ǰ y*	20.	*'r θ γ n*
6.	*h r w d' d*	21.	*r' m*
7.	*h m d' d*	22.	*w' δ*
8.	*δ d w*	23.	*= 8, 15*
9.	*'r w*	24.	*d y n y (δ y n or δ y y)*
10.	*y' n' x n (y' b' x n)*	25.	*'r ǰ w x y*
11.	*'x y r*	26.	*'š t' δ ('š t' d)*
12.	*m' h (m' x)*	27.	*'s m' n*
13.	*ǰ y r y*	28.	*z' t (= z ā t ?)*
14.	*γ w š t*	29.	*m r s b n d*
15.	*= 8*	30.	*'w n r γ*

As Livshits remarks, apart from occasional copyists' mistakes, al-Biruni's information is extremely accurate, and the names he gives for the months and days of the Khwarizmian calendar are in almost complete accordance with the inscriptions of the Tok-kala ossuaries.[46]

The Khwarizmian calendar came into being at the beginning of the Christian era and officially remained in use until Khwarizm was incorporated into the caliphate in the eighth century, when a system of chronology reckoning from the hegira was adopted at the time of the introduction of Islam. However, the people of Khwarizm continued to use the local calendar at least until the end of the tenth century. Its disadvantage was that, because there was no provision for the leap year, the beginning of the Khwarizmian months changed

45. Livshits, 1970, pp. 167–9. More exact forms suggested by Livshits are given in brackets.
46. Ibid., p. 167.

constantly from one time of the year to another. For this reason, according to al-Biruni, in 960 the *Khwarizmshah*, Abu Saʿid Ahmad b. Muhammad b. Iraq, introduced a reform to make the beginning of the Khwarizmian months coincide with the fixed days of the Julian calendar.[47]

Khwarizmian eras

In his *Chronology*, al-Biruni also mentions three Khwarizmian eras: the first beginning with the settlement of the country, which supposedly took place 980 years before the time of Alexander the Great (i.e. 1290 B.C.);[48] the second starting with the arrival of Siyavush in Khwarizm and the beginning of the reign of Kai Khusrau, 92 years after the settlement of the country; and the third beginning with the reign of the *Khwarizmshah* Afrig, who is said to have built a castle near Madinat al-Fir (Kath), the ancient capital of Khwarizm.[49] While it is generally agreed that the first two eras are legendary, certain scholars regard Afrig and his era as historical.[50] The genealogical list of the *Khwarizmshah*s of the 'Afrigid' dynasty given by al-Biruni would seem to support the authenticity of his information. For the period from 306 to the middle of the eighth century, this list is as follows:[51]

> Afrig. Bagra. Sahhasak. Askajamuk (I). Azkajwar (I). Sahr (I). Shaush. Hamgari or Hangari. Buzgar. Arsamuh. Sahr (II). Sabri. Azkajwar (II). Askajamuk (II). Sawashfan.[52]

So far, however, there is no confirmation of the use of a chronology based on the era of Afrig and attempts to read his name on Khwarizmian coins have proved unsuccessful.[53] The archaeological material discovered in the last few decades – in particular, the archive of Toprak-kala and the Tok-kala ossuary inscriptions – in conjunction with the time scale of the Tok-kala culture have allowed us to establish that an official chronology existed in Khwarizm, but it was based on another age, for which we have no written sources. According to

47. Biruni, 1957, pp. 262–3.
48. It should be borne in mind that al-Biruni takes the year 310 B.C., not 312, as the beginning of the Seleucid era ('the era of Alexander'). Thus he dates the second year of the reign of Justinian I as the year 838 of the era of Alexander; and he counts the year 1191 of the era of Alexander as the year 267 from the hegira, and the year 1194 of the era of Alexander as the year 270 from the hegira (Biruni, 1966, pp. 96, 128).
49. Biruni, 1957, pp. 47–8.
50. Tolstov, 1948*b*, pp. 10–11, 191–2.
51. Biruni, 1957, p. 48; Livshits, 1970, pp. 165–6, and his transliteration; Vaynberg, 1977, p. 83.
52. Continuing this list, al-Biruni names a further seven *Khwarizmshah*s, the last of whom, Abu ʿAbdallah Muhammad, was killed in 995.
53. Livshits, 1970, p. 167.

Henning and Livshits, it began in the 10s or 20s A.D., and according to Vaynberg in the 40s or early 50s.[54] Thus, as was noted by Bartold,[55] al-Biruni's information cannot be regarded as reliable in its totality.

The genealogical list of *Khwarizmshah*s given by al-Biruni is also unreliable for the period up to the beginning of the eighth century. Of the early rulers, only the names of Azkajwar and Sawashfan are confirmed by Khwarizmian coins. The name of Arsamuh is also confirmed, but coins struck in his reign (no later than the end of the third century) do not coincide chronologically with his reign as given by al-Biruni.[56] Moreover, the names of the 13 *Khwarizmshah*s who reigned before Azkajwar as given on coins of Khwarizm are completely different from those given by al-Biruni.[57] The presence on most coins of the traditional *tamgha* (symbol or mark) for the period between the middle of the first century and the end of the eighth, and also the image of a horseman, give grounds for belief that there was a firmly established dynasty in Khwarizm during that period. However, there is no justification for calling it the 'Afrigid' dynasty.

Religious beliefs

The religion of ancient Khwarizm was a local version of Zoroastrianism mixed with pagan beliefs. In his *Chronology*, al-Biruni mentions traditions concerning the time and place of Zarathustra's (Zoroaster's) activities.[58] Until recently little was known of al-Biruni's other work, the *Al-Qanūn al-Masᶜūdī* [Canon of Masᶜudi] (written over 30 years after the *Chronology*), because it had not been translated. In it al-Biruni reconsiders the date suggested in his *Chronology* for the beginning of the prophetic activities of Zarathustra – he now gives the year 276 before the Seleucid age ('the age of Alexander') or 1218 of the age of Yazdgird III, which was counted from the year A.D. 632.[59] Bearing in mind that al-Biruni believed that 310 B.C. was the beginning of the Seleucid age, not 312, and considering the dating according to the era of Yazdgird, we may conclude that, according to al-Biruni's latest information, Zarathustra began his activities not in 570 but in 586 B.C. If this is so, and if Zarathustra was then 42 years old, as tradition has it, then he was born 108 years before the reign of Darius I. Thus al-Biruni's data are evidence against (and not for) attributing the activities of Zarathustra to the time of Darius I and his father.

54. Henning, 1965, pp. 158–69; Livshits, 1970, pp. 163–5; Vaynberg, 1977, p. 79.
55. Bartold, 1965, p. 545.
56. The first third of the seventh century (Biruni, 1957, p. 48); Livshits, 1970, pp. 166–7; Vaynberg, 1977, p. 81.
57. Vaynberg, 1977, p. 81.
58. Biruni, 1957, pp. 24, 205–6.
59. Biruni, 1973, pp. 114, 148.

225

Al-Biruni informs us that certain Zoroastrian texts in the Khwarizmian language were destroyed as a result of the Arab conquest.[60] However, Zoroastrianism was not a legally established state religion in Khwarizm, as it was in Iran, and therefore did not follow strict canons. Both from al-Biruni's information and from archaeological evidence, it is clear that Zoroastrianism had a special character in Khwarizm, where it coexisted with survivals from earlier beliefs and local cults. Some of the manifestations of these were shared by pre-Islamic Sughd.

Animistic notions such as the belief in jinns and in good and evil spirits survived in Khwarizm right up to al-Biruni's time (tenth to eleventh century). The cult of Vakhsh – the tutelary spirit of the element of water, especially of the Amu Darya – was a survival of early animism. As al-Biruni tells us, the Khwarizmian feast of Vakhsh was celebrated on the tenth day of the last (i.e. the twelfth) month of the year.[61] The link between the name of this spirit and the Amu Darya still survives in the name of the River Vakhsh, a tributary of the Panj, the upper reaches of the Amu Darya. There was a widespread belief in spirits, which were no longer associated with the elements or with plants and animals. Most were regarded as hostile to human beings. Smoke, steam and the smell of food were used to ward them off, as were certain types of ritual food prepared on set days, for example bread baked with fat on the first day of the seventh month of each year.[62]

The feasts of the New Year (the first day of the first month) and Chiri-Ruj (the thirteenth day of the seventh month), which coincided with the days of the vernal and autumnal equinoxes, were linked with the cult of nature, its death and revival. The beginning of the year marked the awakening and development of life-giving forces, while the autumn feast was its antithesis, and marked the time after which these forces faded away and died.[63]

The cult of the dead or of ancestors was observed with great respect in Khwarizm. According to al-Biruni, it was the Khwarizmian custom to place food in the burial chambers on the last five days of the twelfth month and five additional days of the New Year.[64] This ritual of 'feeding' the ancestors was apparently linked with the belief that the fertility of the fields could be secured with the help of higher forces.[65]

In his *Chronology*, al-Biruni describes the rituals observed by the Sogdians in memory of Siyavush, a legendary divine king who supposedly died as a result of being slandered at the height of his prosperity. It can be

60. Biruni, 1957, pp. 48, 63.
61. Ibid., p. 258.
62. Ibid., p. 257.
63. Ibid., pp. 224, 234, 256, 257.
64. Ibid., p. 258.
65. Rapoport, 1971, p. 115.

assumed that the same customs also existed in Khwarizm, as one of the legendary Khwarizmian ages was dated from the arrival of Siyavush in the country.[66] The commemoration of Siyavush, which was accompanied by sacrifices, was closely linked to the cult of the dead and to hopes of obtaining prosperity both on earth and after death.[67] It is possible that all the dead were honoured collectively in the form of Siyavush.[68] In the opinion of Tolstov, Siyavush was also venerated as the Central Asian god of dying and reviving vegetation.[69] The day of the ritual commemoration of the legendary Khwarizmian Queen Mina (who froze to death in warm weather), which was observed on the fifteenth day of the tenth month, was apparently also connected with the cult of the dead.[70]

Khwarizmian Zoroastrianism differed substantially from the canonical Iranian form in its burial rites. Whereas in Iran the bones of the dead were entombed in niches carved in rock or in vaulted burial chambers,[71] the Khwarizmians used ossuaries. According to Rapoport, the sources of the ossuary ritual should be sought not in Zoroastrian dogma, but in earlier beliefs.[72] The earliest statuary ossuaries, which were anthropomorphic and unacceptable to orthodox Zoroastrianism, were clearly a survival of ancient idolatry. The Khwarizmians continued to use them from the second century B.C. or slightly earlier until the third century A.D., when they were superseded by stone boxes as a result of the growing influence of Zoroastrian dogma in Khwarizm.[73] Canonical Zoroastrianism forbade the mourning of the dead. In Khwarizm, however, as in Sogdiana, this ritual existed, as can be seen from the paintings on the Tok-kala ossuaries (see Fig. 1).[74]

As for other religions, Buddhism probably never reached Khwarizm since there is no evidence of its having left substantial traces in the region. There was a community of Melkite Christians, whose clergy were under the jurisdiction of the Metropolitan of Merv. Among the Melkite feast days celebrated in Khwarizm, al-Biruni mentions the feast of roses, which were brought to church on 4 May (*Ayyar*) every year.[75]

Al-Biruni's *Chronology* is the only source of information about the existence of certain secular holidays in pre-Islamic Khwarizm. In connection with the agricultural calendar, the first day of the third month was observed as the

66. Bartold, 1971, p. 83.
67. D'yakonov, 1951, pp. 34–43.
68. Rapoport, 1971, p. 83.
69. Tolstov, 1948*a*, pp. 202–4; 1948*b*, pp. 83–7; Gafurov, 1972, pp. 284–5.
70. Biruni, 1957, p. 257.
71. Herzfeld, 1935, p. 39; 1941, pp. 217–18.
72. Rapoport, 1971, pp. 5, 18, 32.
73. Ibid., pp. 120–1.
74. Gudkova, 1964, pp. 95–102.
75. Biruni, 1957, pp. 318, 326.

beginning of the sowing season for sesame and some other crops.[76] The fifth day of the fourth month was also kept as a feast; the Khwarizmians counted seventy days from that date, and then began sowing the winter wheat.[77] The feast celebrated on the first day of the sixth month had its roots in their former nomadic way of life: according to tradition, at that time (which in the past had coincided with the beginning of the cold season), the kings of Khwarizm used to leave their summer quarters and go out onto the steppe to protect their lands from nomadic raids.[78]

In ancient and early medieval Khwarizm, astronomical observations were made for both religious and practical purposes. Archaeological data give grounds for believing that as early as the second and third centuries B.C., a great temple stood on the site of the ruins of Koy-Krylgan-kala. It was built where an ancient mausoleum had stood, and was used both as a burial place and as a centre of the cult of the dead and of the stars.[79] Observations were concentrated mainly on the sun and the moon, both because they were the most highly venerated in Zoroastrianism and because of their role in measuring time. The ancient Khwarizmians were familiar with eclipses of the sun and moon (the 'houses' of the moon), and were therefore able to determine and correct the times of the seasons and thus the calendar system as a whole. In his *Chronology*, al-Biruni gives the Khwarizmian names for all the 12 signs of the Zodiac, the 28 'houses' of the moon (the groups of stars in which the moon 'stands' on each of the 28 days of the lunar month) and also the names of the Sun, Moon, Mars, Venus, Jupiter and Mercury.[80] He observes that the Khwarizmians knew more about many constellations than the pre-Islamic Arabs did, and gives a number of examples.[81]

The Arab conquest

The Arab conquest of Khwarizm and the country's subsequent conversion to Islam provoked a crisis in the indigenous culture. The first attempt by the Arabs to conquer Khwarizm came at the very end of the seventh century. Umayya b. ʿAbdallah, the Arab governor of Khurasan (693–697), after capturing the capital city of Kath (which he held for a time), forced the *Khwarizmshah* to sign a treaty recognizing the power of the caliphate. Immediately after the departure of the Arab forces, however, this treaty was abrogated.[82] The attempts of Yazid

76. Biruni, 1957, p. 256.
77. Ibid., pp. 256–7.
78. Ibid., p. 257.
79. 'Koy-Krylgan-Kala', 1967, pp. 235–6, 253–64.
80. Biruni, 1957, pp. 187–8, 261.
81. Ibid., p. 259.
82. Al-Baladhuri, 1866, p. 426.

b. al-Muhallab, another governor of Khurasan (702–705), to take possession of Khwarizm were equally unsuccessful[83] and it was not until 711–712 that his successor, Qutaiba b. Muslim, succeeded in doing so, by exploiting the civil war that was raging in the country.

According to al-Baladhuri, Khurrazad, the younger brother of the reigning *Khwarizmshah*, raised a revolt against his brother, became *de facto* ruler, took the law into his own hands and robbed the local nobles. As the *Khwarizmshah* could not withstand Khurrazad, he sent messengers secretly to Qutaiba b. Muslim, who was in Merv. The *Khwarizmshah* agreed to pay tribute to Qutaiba and to recognize the power of the caliphate on condition that he remained lord of Khwarizm and that Qutaiba deliver him from Khurrazad's oppression. Qutaiba agreed and sent his brother, ʿAbd al-Rahman b. Muslim, against Khurrazad. He was victorious in the battle and Khurrazad was killed. ʿAbd al-Rahman publicly executed the 4,000 prisoners he took.[84]

Al-Tabari, and later Balʿami and Ibn al-Athir, tell us that in addition to Khurrazad the *Khwarizmshah* had another sworn enemy, a certain King Khamjird.[85] According to the combined information provided by these historians, the sequence of events is as follows. In the year 93 A.H. (A.D. 712), a *Khwarizmshah* by the name of Jigan (or Chigan)[86] was faced with his younger brother Khurrazad's open flouting of his authority and with an even more powerful enemy, King Khamjird. Without informing anyone, he turned for help to Qutaiba b. Muslim, who was then in Merv. As a sign that he recognized the power of the caliphate, the *Khwarizmshah* sent Qutaiba the golden keys to the three main cities of Khwarizm. Qutaiba set out with his forces from Merv, ostensibly on a campaign against Sogdiana. Rumours to this effect were also spread by the *Khwarizmshah* to put those who favoured war with the Arabs off their guard. When Qutaiba unexpectedly appeared with his army in

---

83. Al-Baladhuri, 1866, p. 417; al-Tabari, 1881–89, pp. 1142–3.
84. Al-Baladhuri, 1866, pp. 420–1.
85. The term *malik Khamjird* is understood by some scholars (Tolstov, Vyazigin) as 'King Khamdzhird' (Khamdzhard) and by others (Bartold, Vaynberg) as 'the king of Khamjird'. The title *The Conquest of Khamjird* in Ibn al-Athir's *Chronicle* suggests that Khamjird was a toponym. Vaynberg, basing his opinion on one of the editions of Balʿami's work in which Gurganj appears instead of Khamjird, considers that it is the same town. The fact that Khamjird is not mentioned in other sources can be explained, according to Vaynberg's hypothesis, by the fact that the town's old name is replaced by its new one (Ibn al-Athir, 1301 A.H., p. 273; *Istorya Turkmenskoy SSR*, 1957, pp. 163–4; Tolstov, 1948*b*, p. 225; Bartold, 1965, p. 546; Vaynberg, 1977, pp. 98–9).
86. Only Balʿami gives this name and in the manuscripts of his work kept in the Institute of Oriental Studies of the Uzbek Academy of Sciences it is spelt in different ways. As well as the most common form, there are others which are graphically close to them (Balʿami, MS 33, p. 359 a; MS 4226, p. 371 b; MS 6095, pp. 368 b–369 a; MS 7466, pp. 273 b–274 b; MS 11273, p. 459 b).

Hazarasp, the *Khwarizmshah* advised his entourage not to resist, in view of the obvious superiority of the Arab forces. The *Khwarizmshah* concluded a treaty with Qutaiba according to which he gave him 10,000 head of livestock, money and other property, on condition that Qutaiba would advance against King Khamjird. Qutaiba accepted these conditions. His brother, ʿAbd al-Rahman b. Muslim, won a victory over the ruler of Khamjird, and the latter was killed. ʿAbd al-Rahman took 4,000 prisoners, whom Qutaiba ordered to be executed. Then Qutaiba captured Khurrazad and his henchmen and handed them over to the *Khwarizmshah*, who had them executed.[87]

Having achieved his aims in Khwarizm, Qutaiba besieged and took Samarkand in the same year, 93 A.H. (A.D. 712); during this campaign the people of Khwarizm revolted and killed the *Khwarizmshah*, who had betrayed their country. When Qutaiba returned from Sogdiana, he dismissed Ilyas b. ʿAbdallah b. ʿAmr, his commissioner in Khwarizm, for failing to take action and sent ʿAbdallah b. Muslim to replace him. Although the latter maintained his authority for a time, revolt soon broke out again and was not suppressed until al-Mughir b. ʿAbdallah, another of Qutaiba's generals, was sent there with his forces. It was then, according to al-Biruni, that Khwarizm was sacked by barbarians; as a result, many objects of cultural value were destroyed, including Khwarizmian manuscripts.[88]

It is reasonable to assume that there are considerable gaps in the medieval historians' account of the violent events which took place in Khwarizm in 712. Coins of the *Khwarizmshah* Azkajwar II have been found overstruck by the types of a certain Khusrau, who only reigned for a short time.[89] The most likely explanation is that Khusrau was put in power by the Khwarizmians when they revolted and overthrew Jigan. Then, after Qutaiba had suppressed the rising, he put a member of the old ruling dynasty, Askajamuk II, the son of Azkajwar II, on the throne.[90]

The absence of the name of Jigan (Chigan) on Khwarizmian coins and in the genealogical list of *Khwarizmshah*s given by al-Biruni has given rise to two hypotheses. According to the first, Jigan was a usurper, who unsuccessfully tried to consolidate his power with the help of the Arab conquerors,[91] but who ruled for such a short period that he did not have time to issue his own coinage. According to the second hypothesis, the one most widely held by scholars, Jigan is an etymologically obscure nickname of the *Khwarizmshah*

---

87. Al-Tabari, 1879–89, pp. 1236–9; Balʿami, MS 4226, pp. 371 b–372 a; Ibn al-Athir, 1301 A.H., pp. 273–4.
88. Biruni, 1957, pp. 48, 63.
89. Henning, 1965, pp. 168, 175; Vaynberg, 1977, pp. 78–9.
90. Biruni, 1957, p. 48; Gudkova and Livshits, 1967, p. 6; Livshits, 1970, p. 164.
91. Gudkova, 1964, pp. 120–1.

Azkajwar II, the father of Askajamuk II.[92] The available data do not yet allow the issue to be settled.

Early Arab rule in Khwarizm was unstable. In 110 A.H. (A.D. 728) a rising supported by neighbouring Türk tribes broke out in the north of the country, in the town of Kerder and the area around it, but it was suppressed in the same year.[93] From then on, the political situation was somewhat more stable. Members of the ancient dynasty continued to reign over Khwarizm as vassals of the caliphate with limited rights until 995, when the last of them was executed by the amir of Urgench, who united the entire country under his rule.

92. Gudkova and Livshits, 1967, p. 6; Vaynberg, 1977, pp. 81, 91–3. Rtveladze has given his reasons for objecting to Vaynberg's theory that there was a dynastic link between Jigan and Chaganiyan (Rtveladze, 1980, pp. 51–8).
93. Al-Tabari, 1881–89, p. 1525.

SOGDIANA*

B. I. Marshak and N. N. Negmatov

Part One

SUGHD AND ADJACENT REGIONS

(B. I. Marshak)

During the third to the eighth century Sughd (Sogdiana) included the basins of the rivers Zerafshan and Kashka Darya. The name 'Sughd' was frequently applied only to the area near Samarkand – Samarkandian Sughd – but sometimes it was extended to the whole area where the Sogdian language was predominant, which in the seventh century included regions to its north-east (Ustrushana, Chach – the modern Tashkent – and western Semirechye; see Part Two). From the third to the eighth century Sughd, which had originally lagged behind its neighbours to the south and west, became one of the most advanced countries and the leader of all Transoxania. It was neither a powerful state itself nor firmly subjected to any of the neighbouring empires. From the second or first century B.C. each district had developed independently, maintaining ancient community traditions. Private individuals such as merchants, missionaries and mercenary soldiers were extremely active and penetrated into distant lands. Thus political isolation did not entail cultural isolation.

Other peoples knew the Sogdians mainly as silk merchants, but the basis of the Sogdian economy was agriculture on artificially irrigated land. From the very beginning, the Silk Route was controlled by Sogdian merchants, but in the fifth century their domestic trade and monetary relations were still at the stage of 'Barbarian imitations'.[1] Century after century each of the main areas of Sughd minted coins that can be traced back to the coinage of various Hellenistic rulers of the third to the second century B.C. Moreover, the coins of Samarkandian Sughd had become extremely debased by the fifth century; the image of an archer had been reduced to a mere outline and the weight of the coin was considerably reduced. Although Sughd was a neighbour of the Kushan Empire and was invaded by Iranian forces during the third century, it was not incorporated into these states with highly developed administrative systems.

* See Map 5.
1. Zeimal, 1983, pp. 69–76, 269–76.

In the sixth century the minting of coins with the image of an archer, which had continued for many centuries, ceased; this marked the end of the stage of 'Barbarian imitations' and the beginning of a new stage in the development of trading and monetary relations.[2]

In ancient times large numbers of nomadic or semi-nomadic herdsmen lived around Sogdiana. Some of their burial places have been excavated near the borders of oases; the ceramics found in the graves are of Sogdian workmanship, showing the crosscultural influence. At some time between the third and the fifth century (the exact date has not yet been established) these burial places fell into disuse, settlements were destroyed and sometimes even deserted, and the craft traditions, as revealed by the forms of the wheel-turned pottery, changed. In the fifth-century strata in the Kashka Darya valley there are large quantities of handmade ceramic articles, together with turned pottery. People with a tradition of handmade pottery, characteristic only of settled peoples and found to this day among the Tajik hillsmen, migrated from the backward outskirts to the partially abandoned fertile land. Around the fourth century what is called the second wall, enclosing an area of 66 ha, was built inside the ancient wall of the capital city, Samarkand – there were clearly not enough people to defend the old wall, which was almost 6 km long.

Between the third and the seventh century there were no prolonged periods of decline. New settlements appeared in both the third and the fourth centuries, and during the fifth century whole towns were built, including Panjikent, 60 km east of Samarkand (Fig. 1). The evidence of local crises in the third and (especially) the fourth century can be explained by the migration of new groups of nomads who appeared on the borders of Iran in the middle of the fourth century, and in the following century began a long struggle with Iran for Tokharistan. It was probably the arrival of the Sasanians that drove the local semi-nomadic herdsmen away from the land on which they had settled.

Four generations before the beginning of relations between the Wei dynasty and foreigners from the West, i.e. in the second half of the fourth century, the Huns killed the ruler of Sogdiana and seized possession of his lands.[3] The Sogdians called this people *xwn*. Were these the same Huns who overran northern China in the fourth century or were they Chionites, whom the Indians called Hunas? There was a difference in the physical appearance of the two peoples, although some of the Huns were probably included among the Chionites.[4] The Huns who appeared in Sogdiana were probably not the same people as the Chionites, but even if they were, no Chionite Empire encompassing Sughd and Tokharistan existed in the fifth century. It is believed that the Chionites (the sources mention Türks) attacked Iran from the direction of

2. Zeimal, 1983, p. 234.
3. Enoki, 1955.
4. Czeglédy, 1980, pp. 213–17.

FIG. 1. Panjikent. Excavations of the palace on the citadel.
(Photo: © Vladimir Terebenin.)

Sughd.[5] This was probably not, however, a real historical event from the fifth century but an anachronistic episode from the *Romance of Bahram Gur* inspired by the later victory of the Sasanian general Bahram Chobin over the Türks. It is not impossible that in the fifth century Sughd was ruled by a dynasty of nomadic origin, although there is no evidence of the activities of nomads in the country. The increased strength of the nomads in Tokharistan in the fourth and fifth centuries may have been connected with their departure from Sughd.

Sughd came under the rule of the Hephthalites in *c.* 509, from which time Hephthalite 'embassies' from Samarkand (consisting essentially of trading caravans) to China were known.[6] The Hephthalites seem to have come to Sughd from the south after victory over Sasanian Iran. For the first time since the Seleucids, Sughd came under the power of an organized state with an army rather than the Sogdian rulers' retinues, and this army was considerably stronger than the local militia.

In Tokharistan, where tribes of Hephthalites lived, Chinese travellers report seeing nomads with archaic customs, but Byzantine authors describe the Hephthalites as an urban population with a highly organized state. Menander's information about the urban Hephthalites goes back to the conversation

5. Marquart, 1901, pp. 50–1.
6. Enoki, 1959.

of Sogdian envoys of the Türk *kaghan* with the Byzantine emperor and hence refers to the Hephthalites in Sughd. The town of Panjikent grew during the Hephthalite period, its fortifications were strengthened and temples were re-built, although the arrival of the Hephthalites is thought to have been accom-panied by ravages (Fig. 2).

At the end of the Hephthalite period or the beginning of the Turkic pe-riod (during the sixth century), a ruler by the name of Abrui held sway over the oasis of Bukhara. This tyrant drove the nobles and the rich to emigrate to Semirechye.[7] Contrary to Tolstov's opinion, there is no mention in the sources of the people's struggle against the aristocracy; on the contrary, the poor who remained under Abrui's rule begged the emigrants for help. Abrui was finally defeated by Türk forces who came at the request of the people of Bukhara. (Abrui himself was not of Türk origin: although he and the Bukharans are described as coming 'from Turkestan', this refers to the earliest days of the settlement of the oasis of Bukhara.) Legend tells of a prince's struggle against a community of citizens headed by nobles. Such a struggle might have been all the more bitter because of the rapid growth of the towns in the fifth to the seventh century, as revealed by the archaeological evidence. Paikent, the residence of Abrui, became a free 'merchant city' in the seventh to the eighth century.

Typically, in the legend of Abrui, justice is re-established due to the ar-rival of the Türks. When the inheritance of the Hephthalites was divided up between the Türks and the Sasanians (who had defeated the Hephthalites in the 560s), Sughd fell to the Türks, although their forces probably left the coun-try after the victory. They came again in the 580s, when the war with Iran be-gan.[8] After establishing the *kaghanate* over a vast territory stretching from the Black Sea to the Chinese border, the nomadic Türk *kaghan*s recruited Sogdian civil servants to run it. The Sogdian colonization of Semirechye and the Sogdian caravan trade were of benefit not only to the Sogdians but also to the Türks. The Türk state aspired to make the roads safe and gave its backing to the Sogdian diplomats' trade negotiations. The Sogdian language, which had become the *lingua franca* of the Silk Route long before the sixth century, became the offi-cial language of the *kaghans*' administration in the second half of the sixth century.[9] During the first third of the seventh century, after the division into Eastern and Western *Kaghanates*, Türk influence increased, but the *kaghan* and the king of Samarkand were now more like equal allies than sovereign and subject. The *kaghan*'s daughter married the king of Samarkand.

In the middle of the seventh century, after the fall of the Western *Kaghanate*, the Sogdian states gained *de facto* independence, although formally

7. Marquart, 1901, p. 309; Tolstov, 1948, pp. 248 et seq.; Gafurov, 1972, pp. 223 et seq.
8. Gafurov, 1972, pp. 217–21.
9. Klyashtorny and Livshits, 1971; 1972.

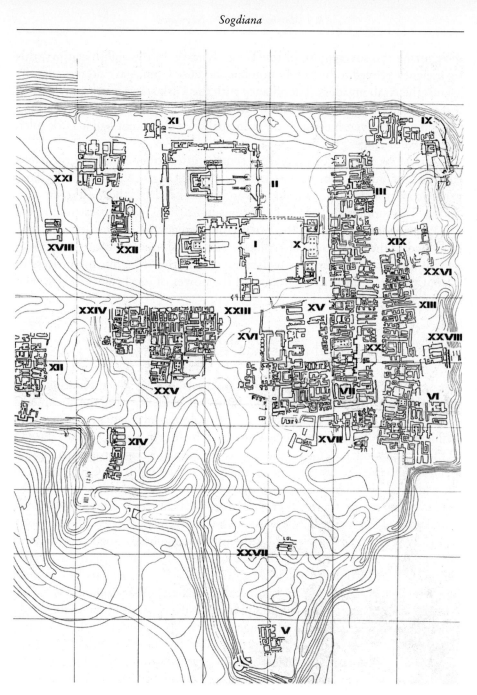

FIG. 2. Panjikent. Plan of the city (without the citadel).
(Drawing by B. I. Marshak.)

recognizing the sovereignty of the T'ang dynasty. In the eighth century, this sovereignty proved to be purely nominal, because China gave no real support against the Arab invaders. The alliance with the Türk states was unstable, with the Turkic nobles frequently looting or seizing Sogdian territories; as early as the end of the seventh century the principality of Panjikent had a Türk ruler, Chikin Chur Bilge.

In the second half of the seventh century, after conquering Iran, the Arabs advanced on Sughd. During the first few decades of the eighth century Arab garrisons were established in Bukhara and Samarkand and the local rulers submitted. The suppression of local uprisings in 720–730 led to mass emigration. In 739 the Arabs concluded a treaty with the Sogdians, many of whom returned home and, as the excavations in Panjikent show, tried to re-establish their former way of life. Mass conversions to Islam began in the 750s, but the process of Islamization and the gradual waning of the power of local rulers took several more decades.

Economic, cultural and social life

The seventh century and the first half of the eighth were the economic and cultural heyday of pre-Islamic Sughd. However, evidence from the documents of Dunhuang reveals the existence of large colonies of Sogdian merchants in Chinese towns[10] as early as the beginning of the fourth century (if not the end of the second) and, judging by the Karakorum rock inscriptions, Sogdian merchants predominated at that time on the southern routes from Central Asia to the Indus valley.[11] The general upsurge in the domestic economy allowed the profits from foreign trade to enrich not only the emigrant merchants but the population of Sughd itself. Silk weaving began in the country in the late sixth and early seventh centuries and by the following century Sogdian silks were already playing a major role on the Silk Route.[12] From the sixth to the seventh century the 'Fur Route' to north-west Europe was also in the hands of Sogdian and Khwarizmian merchants – as revealed in the Sogdian and Khwarizmian owners' inscriptions on Byzantine and Iranian silver vessels found in the north, where they were imported in exchange for furs.[13] In Sughd itself the comparatively primitive bowls of the sixth century had, by the seventh century, given way to magnificent artistic vessels and sculptures fashioned in silver.[14]

The changes in life-style were reflected even in such a 'democratic' craft

10. Henning, 1948; Harmatta, 1971.
11. Humbach, 1980.
12. Yerusalimskaya, 1972.
13. Livshits and Lukonin, 1964.
14. Marshak, 1971.

as ceramics. The second half of the seventh century and the beginning of the eighth saw a complete change in the design of table crockery, whose shapes and ornamentation began to copy those of the nobles' silver vessels.

The new stage in the development of trading and monetary relations was associated with the wide circulation in Sogdiana of a cast bronze coin with a square hole in the middle (Fig. 3).[15] The coins of Samarkand, Panjikent, Paikent and certain other centres are well known. Silver drachms were minted in imitation of the Iranian drachms of Bahram V (420–438). Their inscription normally included the title of the ruler of Bukhara, although in the eighth century they were issued in other centres as well.[16]

FIG. 3. Bronze coins from Panjikent.
(Photo: © Vladimir Terebenin.)

Art and architecture

There was architectural progress in towns and settlements such as Samarkand (the site of Afrasiab) (Fig. 4), Panjikent and Varakhsha (near Bukhara) (Figs. 5 and 6). In the seventh century Samarkand again covered the whole plateau of Afrasiab, an area of 219 ha. Other Sogdian towns were much smaller. The area of Bukhara (without the citadel) was 34 ha, and that of Panjikent (also without the citadel) 13.5 ha. The buildings within the city walls have been best studied in Panjikent.[17] In the fifth century the residential quarters were composed of detached houses, but over the sixth, seventh and early eighth centuries the whole town was built up with uninterrupted terraces in each quarter. The houses were

15. Smirnova, 1981.
16. Davidovich, 1979, pp. 105–6.
17. Belenitskiy et al., 1981.

FIG. 4. Afrasiab. View from the old city towards Samarkand.
(Photo: © Vladimir Terebenin.)

FIG. 5. Varakhsha. General view. (Photo: © Vladimir Terebenin.)

FIG. 6. Varakhsha. Corridor. (Photo: © Vladimir Terebenin.)

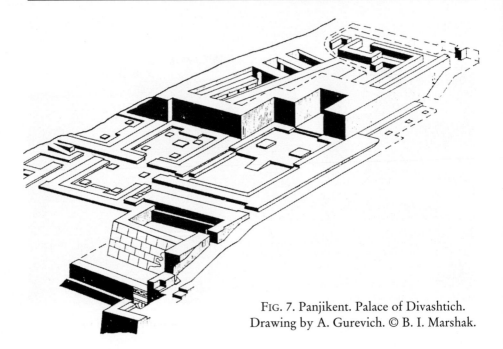

Fig. 7. Panjikent. Palace of Divashtich.
Drawing by A. Gurevich. © B. I. Marshak.

of compressed clay (loess) and mud-brick and roofed with mud-brick vaults or wooden structures, which were then plastered with clay. In the sixth century upper storeys began to appear, and by the eighth century some buildings even had three storeys. The houses of the late seventh century and the first half of the eighth were more spacious, taller and in every way superior to the earlier dwellings.

Panjikent reached the height of its prosperity during the first quarter of the eighth century, when its ruler Divashtich claimed power over all Sogdiana (Fig. 7). Private houses with murals had started to be built in Panjikent as early as the sixth century; in the early eighth century, one house in three had murals. In their ornate architecture and decoration, the rich town houses resemble the royal palaces discovered in Panjikent, Varakhsha[18] and, perhaps, Samarkand.[19] Although the palaces contain several large state apartments, they are basically very similar to the houses of wealthy townsfolk. This is because of the particular Sogdian social structure, in which an important role was played by urban communities with their own officials and revenues. During the seventh and eighth centuries, the rulers (who enjoyed no absolute or despotic powers over the city-states) were frequently elected by the notables.

The shopkeepers and craftsmen lived in two-storey houses with several

18. Shishkin, 1963.
19. Al'baum, 1975.

rooms, but mainly did business and worked in rented shops and workshops located in wealthier areas. Coins have often been discovered in these shops.

Fortified homes belonging to the country aristocracy had existed in Sughd since Hellenistic times, becoming particularly numerous in the Early Middle Ages. In the seventh and eighth centuries the chambers in castles were very similar to those in the town houses of the wealthy, whereas the peasants' homes were unlike those in towns and resembled nineteenth-century Tajik peasant houses.

Sogdian temples are known from the site of Er-kurgan in south Sogdiana (fourth–sixth century) and from two temples discovered in Panjikent. Of similar design and built at the same time in the fifth century, the Panjikent temples were rebuilt several times and continued in use until after 720; although they have been subjected to more detailed study than the temple at Er-kurgan, it is hard to know to which religion they belonged as the main images worshipped

FIG. 8. Panjikent. Ceremonial hall in a private house. Drawing by B. I. Marshak.

FIG. 9. Panjikent. Mural painting. Clay on plaster.
(Photo: © Vladimir Terebenin.)

FIG. 10. Panjikent. Mural painting. Clay on plaster.
(Photo: © Vladimir Terebenin.)

there have not survived. The architectural plan of both temples was based on a road leading east to west and passing through two rectangular courtyards with colonnaded entrance porticoes; from here a narrow ramp led up to the platform of the main building, which also had a portico. A four-columned hall without an east wall opened on to it. A door in the west wall of the hall led to a rectangular cell. A gallery ran round the hall and the cell on three sides. During the late fifth and early sixth centuries one of the temples had a special chamber for the sacred fire, but no such chambers of earlier or later date have been found. The temples were similar (but not identical) in plan to Kushan and even Graeco-Bactrian examples.

The murals in Sogdian towns – not so much those in the temples but, rather, in seventh- and eighth-century private houses – depict daily life. In the ceremonial hall of a house, opposite the entrance, there was usually a large image of a god (or a more elaborate composition on a sacred theme) and small figures of Sogdians before a fire altar (Fig. 8). Every house owner had his own divine patron (or patrons). Sometimes other gods were also depicted, but on less important parts of the walls. To the sides of the religious scene ran smaller friezes depicting a banquet (Figs. 9 and 10), a hunt (Fig. 11), a ceremonial rite or – quite frequently – episodes from an epic. At the bottom of the wall ran an

FIG. 11. Panjikent. Mural painting in location VI. Clay on plaster.
(Photo: © Vladimir Terebenin.)

FIG. 12. Panjikent. Mural painting
in location VI. Clay on plaster.
(Photo: © Vladimir Terebenin.)

FIG. 13. Panjikent. Statue of a dancer.
Wood.
(Photo: © Vladimir Terebenin.)

FIG. 14. Panjikent. Carved wood. (Photo: © Vladimir Terebenin.)

FIG. 15. Varakhsha. General view of a painted panel. (Photo: © Vladimir Terebenin.)

ornamental border or a frieze of small pictures: animals in motion or a series of small rectangular panels illustrating tales, parables, anecdotes, and so on (Fig. 12). The elaborate pictorial scheme was complemented by carved wooden statues and reliefs (Figs. 13 and 14), with figures of gods, hunting scenes, and so on, adorning the elaborate wooden ceiling.[20]

This hierarchy of subjects was typical of the main halls of Panjikent, but was not so rigidly followed in Varakhsha (Fig. 15) and in Afrasiab (nor, indeed,

20. Azarpay, 1981.

FIG. 16. Afrasiab. Mural painting. (Photo: © Vladimir Terebenin.)

FIG. 17. Afrasiab. Mural painting. (Photo: © Vladimir Terebenin.)

in some houses in Panjikent itself or its temples). Palace murals include subjects from Sogdian history, the reception of ambassadors (Afrasiab) (Figs. 16 and 17), a coronation and the Arab siege of the town (Panjikent). Particularly expressive are murals with figures picked out in ochre on an ultramarine blue background. A similar colour scheme is found in the murals of Iran and

FIG. 18. Sughd. Silver jug (end of seventh century).
(Photo: © Vladimir Terebenin.)

Fɪɢ. 19. Sughd. Silver dish (second half of eighth century).
(Photo: © Vladimir Terebenin.)

Tokharistan, which share certain other details, attitudes of figures and types of composition. There are many Indian traits in the depiction of gods. There are also pictures of Chinese people, drawn with a knowledge of Chinese iconography. Motifs of foreign origin (Byzantine, Iranian, Türk and Chinese) can also be traced in the metalwork (Figs. 18–20). These varied influences are explained by Sughd's role as intermediary. Sogdian artists were familiar with the achievements of other schools of art, but developed their own original style, distinguished by its narrative content, dynamism and love of contrast. Sogdian art had a strong influence on that of many countries, in particular on the toreutics of the steppe peoples (Türks, Khazars, nomadic Magyars) and of T'ang China.

Archaeological discoveries show that Sogdian artists had been faithful in their depictions of architecture, weapons and costume. Fifth-century Sogdian

FIG. 20. Sughd. Silver dish (second half of seventh century).
(Photo: © Vladimir Terebenin.)

costume was similar to that in the Kushan Empire; during the sixth century the influence of Hephthalite Tokharistan (and through it that of Sasanian fashions) was noticeable. In the seventh and eighth centuries similarities with Turkic costume appeared. Belts decorated with gold plaques were the mark of noble rank. Military clothing and equipment (Fig. 21) and, to some degree, vessels used in banquets also showed Turkic influence. Sogdian armour, which was elaborate and heavy and protected the warrior's whole body, showed advanced craftsmanship.

The mural paintings are a valuable source of information about feast-day customs and rituals, banquets, wrestling, dances and ritual bathing (Fig. 22). In connection with the harvest festival, an artist in Panjikent painted grain being conveyed from the threshing floor and a tutelary spirit of agriculture.

FIG. 21. Mount Mug. Shield with a warrior horseman (end of seventh century).
Painted wood.
(Photo: © Vladimir Terebenin.)

FIG. 22. Panjikent. Mural painting showing ritual bathing. Location VI.
(Photo: © Vladimir Terebenin.)

Religious life

Our knowledge of religions in Sogdiana comes from works of art, funerary monuments and writings – mainly Buddhist, Manichaean and Christian (Nestorian) discovered in East Turkestan.[21] A Christian text and Buddhist inscriptions on pottery have also been found in Panjikent. Buddhism, which came to Sughd from the south at an early period, flourished according to the *Sui shu* and the *T'ang shu*.[22] By the seventh century, however, it had almost disappeared from Sogdiana. In the eighth century T'ang Buddhism spread among Sogdian emigrants, as a result of which most Sogdian Buddhist works are translations from Chinese. An inscription in the Afrasiab murals shows that in the seventh century a Sogdian king received assurances from foreign envoys that they were acquainted with the local religion of Samarkand.[23] This is clearly linked to aspirations to cultural self-determination during the heyday of Sughd.

No correctly painted Buddhist images exist in Sogdian painting, but images of Hindu gods (of secondary importance from the Buddhist point of view) helped the Sogdians to create their own religious iconography in the sixth to the eighth century. As in Sogdian Buddhist and Manichaean texts,[24] Zurvan is depicted in the form of Brahma, Adbag (Ohrmazd) in that of Indra (Sakra) and Veshparkar (Vayu) in that of Shiva (Mahadeva). A four-armed Nana mounted on a lion (Fig. 23), a divine couple with symbols in the form of a camel and a mountain ram and other images of divinities are also known. The absence of highly developed forms of state organization explains the important role played by the worship of the divine patrons of individual families and communities. Although there were non-Zoroastrian divinities among these gods, the influence of Zoroastrianism was indubitable.[25] The Sogdians probably regarded themselves as Zoroastrians, as indeed they were considered by al-Biruni and other authors writing in Arabic. Those Sogdian customs that seem contrary to Zoroastrian doctrine (Hindu-style iconography, the mourning of the dead) also existed in Khwarizm, whose Zoroastrianism is not open to doubt and where the Avestan *gāhanbār*s (phases of creation) were celebrated as religious feasts. There is evidence from the fifth century onwards in Sughd of the custom of cleaning the flesh from bones and burying them in ossuaries, as in Khwarizm (Fig. 24).

21. Livshits, 1981, pp. 350–62.
22. Litvinsky, 1968.
23. Al'baum, 1975, pp. 52–6, translation and comments by V. A. Livshits.
24. Humbach, 1975.
25. Henning, 1965, p. 250.

FIG. 23. Panjikent. Four-armed Nana mounted on a lion (seventh century).
Drawing by B. I. Marshak.

Scripts, epics and literary sources

Sogdians used different types of script according to the religion to which they belonged. The Buddhists used a national script of Aramaic origin, with heterograms. This script is also known from secular writings and from what is probably the only Zoroastrian text in it.[26] The Manichaeans had their own alphabet and the Christians used Syriac script, but both sometimes wrote in the national Sogdian script. There was also what could be described as scientific literature in Sogdian, in particular a book about minerals, documents on medicine and on the calendar, and glossaries.

A fragment of the epic of Rustam, probably translated from Middle Persian, has been found near Dunhuang.[27] Among the Manichaean writings, tales and fables, including some from the Indian *Panchatantra* and the Greek fables of Aesop, have been discovered. There are also non-Manichaean fairy-tales. The paintings of Panjikent show a similar but wider repertoire of subjects from both translated and local literature: among the epic narratives, in addition to the story of Zohak, the tales of Rustam[28] and perhaps the *Mahābhārata*, there are also illustrations of several episodes of a previously unknown Sogdian

26. Sims-Williams, 1976, pp. 46–8; Gershevich, 1976; Livshits, 1981, p. 354.
27. Gershevich, 1969, p. 227.
28. Belenitskiy, 1980, pp. 103–5, 199–202, Abb. 25–33.

FIG. 24. Sughd. Ossuary (seventh century).
(Photo: © Vladimir Terebenin.)

FIG. 25. Panjikent. Wall painting showing a judgment scene. Location VI.
(Photo: © Vladimir Terebenin.)

epic. In one of the halls the pictures are accompanied by fragments of text.[29] The murals illustrate tales about the man who promised his daughter to a sea-spirit; a prince, a bear, a wolf and a jackal; a wise judge (Fig. 25) and a woman's wiles; fables about a dog barking at an elephant, and about a blacksmith and a monkey; Aesop's fables about the goose that laid the golden eggs, and about the father and his sons; parables from the *Panchatantra* about the jackal, the lion and the bull; the lion and the hare; the learned men who resuscitated a tiger; and the foresight of the king of the monkeys. In Iran – the home of the Parthian and Middle Persian authors of the Manichaean works translated by the Sogdians – literary and folkloric parables and tales similar to those known in Sughd and recorded by the artists of Panjikent were popular. Similar subjects can be found in many countries.

Direct and remarkably vivid evidence of the past is provided by the 'Ancient Sogdian Letters' from Dunhuang (probably written at the beginning of the fourth century) and the documents from Mount Mug on the upper reaches of the Zerafshan (Figs. 26 and 27). The 'Ancient Letters' describe the life of Sogdian settlers in China, while the Mug papers show Sughd at the time of the Arab conquest. These letters were found with legal and economic documents in a castle that served as the last refuge of Divashtich, the ruler of Panjikent,

29. Belenitskiy, 1980, pp. 116–18; Azarpay, 1981, Fig. 60.

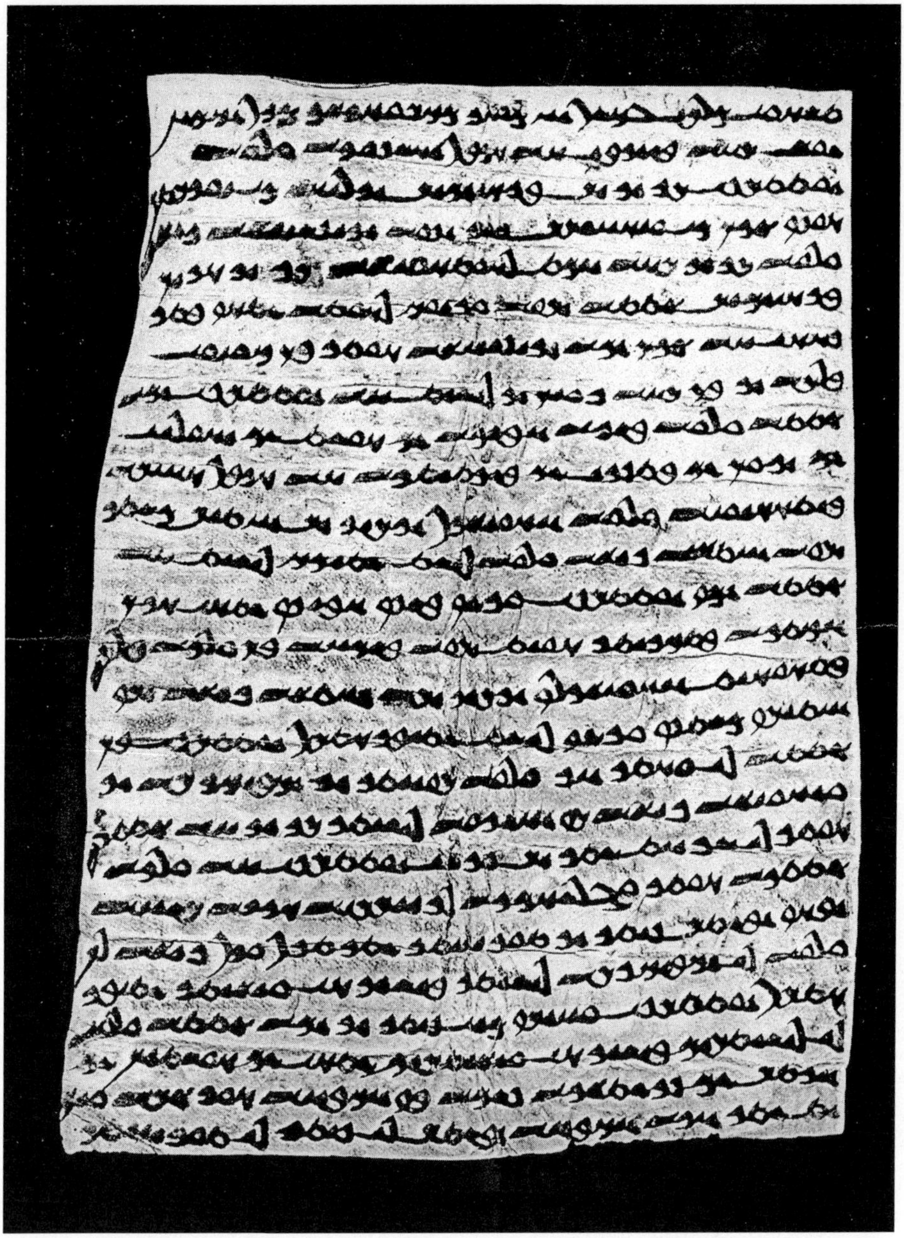

FIG. 26. Mount Mug. Sogdian document. Marriage contract. Leather.
(Photo: © Vladimir Terebenin.)

who was captured by the Arabs in 722.[30] Syriac, Bactrian, Indian (Brāhmī) and Arabic texts have been discovered in Sughd; and in Panjikent there is a Middle Persian wall inscription whose writer obviously came from Iran. The first evidence of the penetration into Sughd of the New Persian (Tajik) language, which supplanted Sogdian between the ninth and the eleventh century, dates to the eighth century.

FIG. 27. Mount Mug. Inscription affirming receipt of helmets and armour. Wood. (Photo: © Vladimir Terebenin.)

30. *Sogdiyskie dokumenty s gory Mug*, 1962–63.

Part Two

USTRUSHANA, FERGHANA, CHACH AND ILAK

(N. N. Negmatov)

Ustrushana

Ustrushana was closely linked to Sughd (Sogdiana) by its historical destiny and ethnic, linguistic and cultural history. It originally formed part of the territory of Sughd, but then developed its own historical and cultural identity as the area became more urbanized. Its rich agricultural and mineral resources, and its situation on the main trans-Asian route from the Near and Middle East to the heart of Central Asia, played a considerable role in this process.

Ustrushana occupied a large area of the valley and steppes on the left bank of the middle reaches of the Syr Darya (Jaxartes), the foothills and gorges of the western part of Turkestan's range, the headwaters of the Zerafshan river and its principal tributaries, the Matcha and Fan Darya. To the west and south-west it bordered on Sughd, to the east and north-east on Khujand and Ferghana and to the north on Ilak and Chach (present-day Tashkent). Ustrushana is mentioned in the *Wei shu* and the *Sui shu* and frequently appears in the history of the T'ang dynasty. In the *T'ang shu* the region is called Eastern Ch'ao (the ideogram for Cao without the sign for 'water'), and Su-du-li-she-na (in Hsüan-tsang, 629–630), and Cao (in Huei-ch'ao, 728). Early Arabic and Persian historical sources give this name variously as Ashrushana, Asrushana, Ustrushana, Usrushna, Surushana and Sutrushana. The discovery and deciphering of the Sogdian documents from Mount Mug on the upper Zerafshan established that the correct form of the name is Ustrushana.[31]

By the Early Middle Ages, new towns and settlements with the characteristics of the rising feudal system had replaced those of the ancient period. The old capital Kurukada (Ura-tyube) was replaced by the city of Bunjikat (Fig. 28), 20 km to the south of the modern town of Shahristan. According to archaeological evidence, the intensive growth of this city began in the seventh and eighth centuries.[32] A new historical map of Ustrushana[33] came into being, divided into a number of *rustaks* (regions), both on the plains and in the mountains, with towns such as Vagkat, Mink (in the valley of Dahkat), Shaukat (Nau), Kurkat, Havast, Savat and Zaamin (all of which still exist) and country settlements centred on castles and estates (Ak-tepe, Dungcha-tepe, Tashtemir-tepe, etc.). In the suburbs around the capital Bunjikat there were noblemen's castles

---

31. *Sogdiyskie dokumenty s gory Mug*, 1962, pp. 77–87.
32. Negmatov and Khmel'nitskiy, 1966.
33. Negmatov, 1957, pp. 34–49.

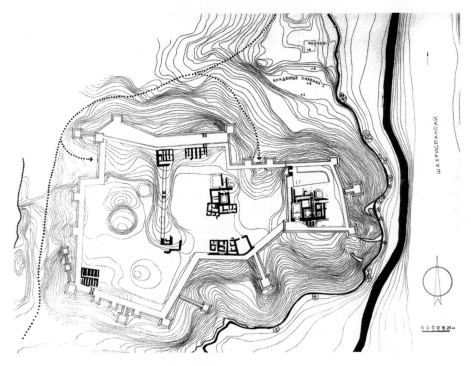

FIG. 28. Bunjikat. Kala-i Kahkaha I.
Plan of the city with the reconstruction of the city-walls.

with strong fortifications and elaborate architectural layouts, such as Chilhujra
and Urta-kurgan.[34]

The sources give little information about the political history of
Ustrushana during this period. The break-up of the great Central Asian states
of late antiquity led to the secession of Ustrushana from the Sogdian federation, as recorded in the *Pei-shih*. From the late fifth to the seventh century,
Ustrushana formed part of the Hephthalite and Western Türk states, although
it probably preserved its internal autonomy and was ruled by its own kings,
the *afshin*s of the Kavus dynasty, some of whose names are known from written sources and coins. In the late seventh to the eighth century, Ustrushana
was drawn into a long and dramatic struggle against the forces of the Arab
ʿAbbasid caliphate.[35]

34. Negmatov et al., 1973; Pulatov, 1975.
35. Smirnova, 1981, pp. 31–5, 324–35.

CULTURE, AGRICULTURE AND TRADE

The population of Ustrushana consisted of tribes and clans, speaking a dialect of Sogdian, with an economy based on settled agriculture and urban crafts. The Chinese Buddhist pilgrims Hsüan-tsang and Huei-ch'ao note a certain community of culture – language, mores and customs – between the people of Ustrushana and the Sogdians of the Zerafshan valley, Ferghana, Chach and the adjacent regions. Hsüan-tsang calls the whole land between Suyab and Kish by the name 'Su-le', and its population 'Sogdians'.[36] Archaeological excavations show common traits in the artefacts of the region's culture.

Agriculture, stockbreeding and mining provided a reliable threefold economic basis for the development of craft production, trade and urban life in Ustrushana.[37] With considerable use of artificial irrigation, its people grew a wide range of agricultural produce (cereals, cotton, garden crops and grapes), and bred livestock and riding and draught animals on the rich upland pastures. Mining output was considerable, with iron ore in the region of Mink, gold, silver, ammonium chloride and vitriol in the upper Zerafshan valley, lead in the Ura-tyube region and a number of other minerals. There was an extensive craft production of metal articles (such as weapons, agricultural implements, tools and household utensils), cotton, wool, silk and leather goods. Pottery manufacture was widespread, producing unglazed cooking pots, tableware and storage jars (for liquids and foodstuffs). There were potters' quarters with kilns at Bunjikat, Vagkat and Gala-tepe (fifth–sixth century). Building, fortification and woodwork were well developed, as were wood-carving and mural painting. During the sixth and seventh centuries, Ustrushana's own bronze coinage was current in trade.

ARCHITECTURE AND ARCHITECTURAL DECORATION

The architecture of Ustrushana is remarkable for its variety. From the early medieval period (sixth–eighth century), we find structures of varied purpose and type, each with a well-developed, characteristic layout – royal palaces, castles of the urban and rural aristocracy, barracks and temples. The palace of Kala-i Kahkaha II is a three-storey building, with middle and upper levels set on a stepped, beaten earth platform. The first level includes an entrance vestibule, a stateroom, and an *aiwān* (hall) opening on to a courtyard. The second level consists of a corridor, rooms for servants and kitchens. On the third level there is a suite of three staterooms, including a throne room with wide windows opening on to the courtyard, decorated with murals and carved woodwork.

---

36. Livshits and Khromov, 1981, pp. 347–9, 367.
37. Negmatov, 1957, pp. 82–112; Bilalov, 1980.

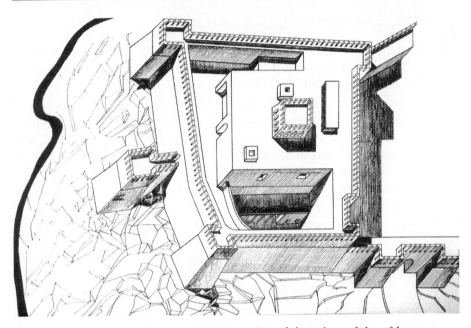

FIG. 29. Kala-i Kahkaha I. Reconstruction of the palace of the *afshīns*.
Drawing by S. Mamajanova.

The layout of the palace of Kala-i Kahkaha I is very complex, but clearly planned (Fig. 29).[38] It is also built on a high platform but has a small keep, or tower, in the middle of the building. Its entrance in the form of an *aiwān* looks out on the town's *rabad* (suburb). An axial corridor divides the palace into two unequal parts. To the west there is a two-level hall with a throne loggia (Fig. 30) opening out at its far end and an entrance area in front, a second parallel 'lesser' hall and the palace shrine. To the east are found a large living room, a small room for servants and a separate corridor with an 'arsenal' (a store of stones). To the north and south, the palace had walled courtyards with kitchen, bakery and domestic premises. The palace gates were in the west wall of the north courtyard.

There are two principal types of castle in the Shahristan depression. One has an elaborate individualized layout with staterooms, living quarters, shrines and domestic offices, and an extremely rich decor of mural paintings and wood-carvings. The building is either positioned on a mountain crest (as in Chilhujra) (Fig. 31) or on a high man-made platform (as at Urta-kurgan) (Fig. 32). The other type has a simple, 'corridor-ridge' layout, without ornamentation, and is either placed on a mountain ridge (as at Tirmizak-tepe) or in an arable valley with fortified courtyard walls and chicanes (as at Tashtemir-tepe).

38. Voronina and Negmatov, 1975, pp. 50–71.

FIG. 30. Kala-i Kahkaha I. Palace of the *afshin*s. Throne hall.
Drawing by V. L. Voronina.

FIG. 31. Chilhujra. Castle. Drawing by S. Mamajanova.

The dwellings of early medieval townspeople have long, wide interiors, usually divided by partition walls into a back room, middle room and front *aiwān* (the northern quarter of Kala-i Kahkaha I). At the south wall of Kala-i Kahkaha I there is a neighbourhood of small separate units, detached but built close to each other. Each has a common corridor leading to two or three rooms, and its own street entrance. The dwellings in the quarter near the city square of Kala-i Kahkaha I have a more individualized layout, which includes entrance *aiwān*s, reception rooms and rooms with rich interior decoration of benches, roofs supported on columns and mural paintings (Figs. 33 and 34).

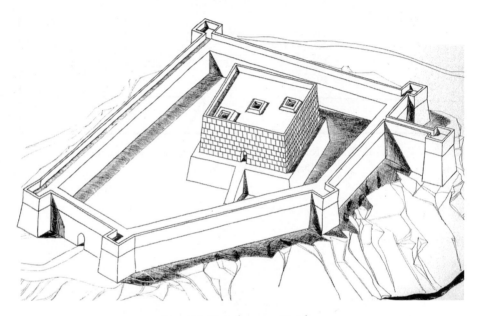

FIG. 32. Urta-kurgan. Castle.
Drawing by S. Mamajanova.

The architectural ornamentation and monumental art of Ustrushana are rich and varied. Murals of high artistic quality with floral and geometric patterns and depictions of secular, epic-heroic, mythological and cultural scenes were an important feature of the interior decoration of palaces, castles and other buildings (Figs. 35–39). Many examples of wood-carving and clay-moulding have survived: columns, beams, cornices, friezes, thresholds, door posts and door frames, lintels, window grilles, entrance screens, artistic clay mouldings and patterned fired bricks (Figs. 40–45). The capital, Bunjikat, was the main centre for the development of architecture and the applied arts.

FIG. 33. Kala-i Kahkaha I. Palace. Mural painting.
A she-wolf feeding two youngsters.

FIG. 34. Kala-i Kahkaha I. Palace. Drawing of a fragment
of mural painting showing musicians.

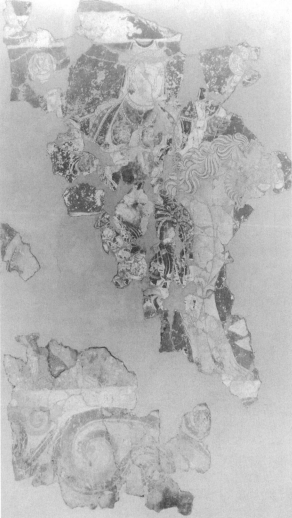

FIG. 35. Kala-i Kahkaha I. Palace.
Fragment of a mural painting representing
the goddess Nana on a lion.
(Photo: © Vladimir Terebenin.)

FIG. 36. Kala-i Kahkaha I. Palace.
Fragment of a mural painting representing the goddess Nana.
(Photo: © Vladimir Terebenin.)

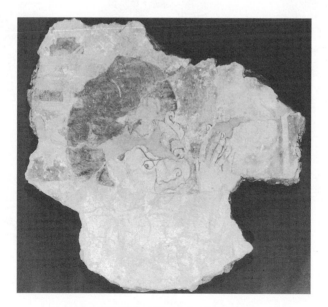

FIG. 37. Kala-i Kahkaha I. Palace.
Fragment of a mural painting representing a demon.
(Photo: © Vladimir Terebenin.)

FIG. 38. Kala-i Kahkaha I. Palace. Fragment of a mural painting representing demons. (Photo: © Vladimir Terebenin.)

FIG. 39. Kala-i Kahkaha I. Palace. Drawings of the fragments of mural paintings representing demons.

FIG. 40. Kala-i Kahkaha I. Palace.
Fragment of a wooden panel 'tympanum' showing the
legendary King Zohak (lower level).

FIG. 41. Kala-i Kahkaha I. Palace.
Fragment of a wooden panel 'tympanum'.

269

FIG. 42. Kala-i Kahkaha I. Palace.
Wooden panel 'tympanum'. Detail of the medallion.

FIG. 43. Kala-i Kahkaha I. Palace. Fragment of a wooden frieze.

FIG. 44. Kala-i Kahkaha I. Palace. Fragment of a wooden frieze.

FIG. 45. Kala-i Kahkaha I. Palace. Drawings of wooden friezes with floral
and geometrical designs.

FIG. 46. Chilhujra. Head of an idol.
Charred wood.

RELIGIOUS AND CULTURAL LIFE

Ustrushana also had a rich variety of spiritual and cultural traditions, for the most part purely local. According to written sources, the Ustrushanians practised the so-called 'white religion', in which carved wooden idols were adorned with precious stones. Idols of this type were kept in the palaces of Haidar (the Ustrushanian ruler) in Samarra, in Ustrushana itself and in Buttam, and they were also brought to Ustrushana by refugees from Khuttal. Many toponyms in this region included the word *mug* (fire-worshipper). So far archaeologists have discovered the castle and palace shrines mentioned above and an urban idol temple. Other finds include wooden idols in Chilhujra (Fig. 46), a house of fire at Ak-tepe near Nau, a *dakhma* at Chorsokha-tepe near Shahristan, rock burial vaults near Kurkat with human remains in *khum*s (large jars) and ossuaries, and a number of other burials in *khum*s and ossuaries in various regions of Ustrushana.

All these finds are evidence of a particular local form of Zoroastrianism that incorporated the worship of idols and various divinities and other religious practices, and is also reflected in the monumental art of Ustrushana. In particular, the paintings of the lesser hall of the palace of Kala-i Kahkaha I show a three-headed, four-armed divinity, which may be a specifically Ustrushanian interpretation of the Hindu Vishparkar. Also depicted is a four-armed goddess mounted on a lion, which has been interpreted as an image of the principal goddess of Ustrushana and the great warrior-mother, thus personifying the worship both of the productive forces of nature and of fertility, and identified with the Kushano-Sogdian great goddess Nana (see above, Fig. 35).[39]

The central figure of the huge composition painted on the west wall of the same lesser hall is of special interest. This is a large, richly dressed male seated on a zoomorphic horse's-head throne. A warrior-king in a chariot, identified with this first image, is depicted three times on the north and east walls of the hall. These paintings are generally considered to represent an ancestor of the ruling dynasty of Ustrushana. The male figure has no apparent divine attributes and his immediate entourage includes musicians, aristocrats seated under a canopy, and warriors in various situations. The worship of the ancestor of a family line and dynasty is known from written sources. It is also known that religious as well as secular power was concentrated in the hands of the *afshīns* of Ustrushana and that they were almost deified, as is clear from the formula by which they were addressed – 'To the lord of lords from his slave so-and-so the son of so-and-so'.[40]

Other important features of the spiritual life of Ustrushana were extra-religious, epic-mythological traditions concerning Good and Evil, Light and Dark, the struggle between these principles and the victory of the forces of Good and Light. They were personified in the well-known oriental images of Kava, Faridun, Surush and Zohak; abandoned infants nurtured by animals (a she-wolf feeding two babies) (see above, Fig. 33);[41] a 'celestial musician', the harpist Zuhra (Venus); the bird-woman, Shirin; and a number of other images recorded in monumental painting, wood-carving and ceramics.

Artefacts reveal the characteristics of Ustrushanian culture. First, it was very traditional, rich and complex. Second, it was in the forefront of Central Asian cultural traditions and those common to the entire Eastern world. Third, in its general features and content, it had a number of elements close to the related Sogdian culture seen in excavations at Panjikent and Samarkand. These fit in with the general ethnic and linguistic history of Sughd and Ustrushana, although Ustrushanian culture developed independently and had its own identity.

---

39. Negmatov, 1984, pp. 146–64.
40. Negmatov and Sokolovskiy, 1977, pp. 152–3.
41. Negmatov, 1977; Negmatov and Sokolovskiy, 1975.

Ferghana

Whereas the third to the eighth century was a time of economic, national and cultural upsurge in Ustrushana, Ferghana (Pa-khan-na in Chinese sources) was in a different position. After the fall of the state of Dawan, the trend was towards territorial disintegration into a series of small regions and domains that experienced markedly uneven development. The sources reveal Ferghana's troubled political history. Although it had its own ruling dynasty with the title of *ikhshid*, their rule was sometimes interrupted. The name Alutar or At-Tar, a powerful king during the first quarter of the eighth century, is known. In 726 Ferghana had two kings, one ruling over the north and subject to the Türks, the other ruling over the south and subject to the Arabs. From 739 onwards, all Ferghana was ruled by the Türk, Arslan Tarkhan.

Ferghana occupied the whole basin, surrounded on all sides by mountains; it was rich and fertile and especially abundant in fruit, the famous Ferghana horses and other livestock. Cotton and many types of cereal were grown, and leather goods and cotton cloth were made. Horses, cereals, medicine, paints, glass and other goods were exported to neighbouring countries.

The capital of Ferghana was first the city of Kasan, then Akhsikat on the bank of the Syr Darya.[42] The other towns included Urast, Kuba, Osh and Uzgend. During the seventh and eighth centuries, the total area of Uzgend was 20–30 ha and it consisted of a citadel (*kuhandiz*), the town itself (*shahristan*) and a commercial and craft quarter (*rabad*). It was particularly important as a trading post because of its proximity to the territories of the Türks. Osh, which consisted of a *shahristan* with a *kuhandiz* and a *rabad*, was regarded as a large and beautiful city. Rich and well supplied with water, it had markets at the foot of the hill. The towns of Bamkakhush and Tamakhush were situated in the valley of Isfara.

KHUJAND

In the western part of Ferghana, on the bank of the Syr Darya, the city of Khujand was going through a period of change. From the second to the fifth century, it had remained within the same territorial limits as during ancient times, its central nucleus occupying an area of approximately 20 ha. During the sixth to the eighth century, however, Khujand experienced a period of rapid growth and radical changes were made to its basic layout and fortifications, the eastern half of the old city being transformed into a new citadel approximately 8 ha in area. This was done using the east wall and parts of the north walls of the old city as foundations for the walls of the new citadel. Only the west wall was entirely new, as can be seen from excavations 31 and 32, from samples

42. For a review of the sources and literature, see Gafurov, 1972, pp. 292–3; Litvinsky, 1976.

taken from the outer surfaces of the wall and from the fragments of ancient pottery in the clay of the early medieval walls. Parts of the former city moat were left around the east and south walls of the new citadel, and at the foot of the west wall a new moat was dug. The ancient citadel was converted into the inner palace arc of the new citadel. This early medieval reconstruction transformed Khujand into a large city with three main areas – the citadel, the town itself, and the commercial and craft quarter equipped with a mighty system of fortifications.

Khujand is mentioned in written Arabic and Persian sources in the accounts of events in the second half of the seventh century and in the *T'ang shu*'s description of events of the second half of the eighth century (Chapter 221). According to the Arab encyclopaedist Yaqut, it was incorporated at an early date into the domains of the Haytal (the Hephthalites). During the 680s, it was first raided by a detachment of the forces of the caliphate (the invaders were routed near the town). Khujand was involved in the Sogdian campaign against the caliphate in 721–722, when military action took place at the gates of the commercial quarter, opposite whose strong walls the invaders' catapults were set up.

During the medieval period, the territory of Khujand had its own ruler, with the title of *malik* (king). The territory was not large: apart from the city of Khujand itself, it included Kand and the smaller town of Samghar. Kand, which is mentioned in the early eighth-century Sogdian documents from Mount Mug, subsequently came to be known as Kand-i Bodom (town of almonds) because of the large quantities of almonds it exported to various countries. According to al-Muqaddasi, a river or canal ran through the bazaars of Kand. Samghar was in the centre of a small agricultural oasis on the right bank of the Syr Darya and consisted of a citadel-castle, a town and outlying buildings. The territory of Khujand also included several small settlements in the cultivated areas along the Syr Darya and in the delta part of the Khujabakyrgan. Khujand was situated on the main trans-Asian trade route, Kand on its Ferghana branch and Samghar on its Chach branch. This fact, together with access to mineral and agricultural resources, promoted the growth of these cities' trade and economies and also their rise to political prominence.[43]

ARCHAEOLOGICAL EVIDENCE

Archaeological research has been carried out on several dozen early medieval Ferghanian urban and rural settlements. Varied and significant material has been obtained: (a) from the ruined fortifications of Kasan (a fortified citadel with chicanes in front of the gates, angle towers on the irregular outline of the city walls, and a castle with a mighty curtain wall and six towers built on a rock

43. Negmatov, 1956, pp. 103–9.

platform); (b) on the architecture and Buddhist religion from Kuba (a temple with two halls, each with its own entrance, with colossal figures of horses and a bearded deity with a human skull depicted on his forehead at the entrance to the *aiwān*, and with painted clay statues representing the Buddhist pantheon in the halls); (c) on the construction of the castle from Kala-i Bolo in the valley of Isfara (a high platform with sloping sides and vertical fortress walls with loopholes, and dwellings and domestic offices with sloping roofs); (d) from a number of inaccessible mountain castles in the Asht and Isfara regions forming the defences of their river valleys; and (e) in the rural settlements (the estate of Kairagach in the valley of the River Khujabakyrgan, which has a large complex of buildings and a private chapel decorated with murals and pedestals bearing carved alabaster idols in the form of human figures with distinctive attributes, possibly used in the worship of family and clan ancestors).

Interesting material has been obtained concerning the fortified settlement of Tudai-kalon, which is built on a high platform, with a reception room in the centre, side chambers and a flat roof supported on wooden columns. Among the finds is an ivory plaque depicting flying goddesses of victory (Nike-Victoria), half-turned towards each other and each holding a wreath in her hand.[44] In all, over 600 small sites (*tepes*, or mounds, with platform; and separate *tepes*) representing Ferghanian settlements and castles have been recorded, most of them belonging to the period from the third to the eighth century.[45] During the fourth century the culture of Ferghana's settled agricultural population reached its finest flowering and the characteristic thin-walled, red slip ceramic ware of excellent quality spread throughout the region. After a short period of cultural decline, the sixth to the eighth century saw an upsurge in the material culture of towns and settlements on the basis of new socio-economic conditions.

ETHNIC HISTORY

The ethnic history of Ferghana is quite complicated. First the K'ang-chü and Sogdian, then Hephthalite elements were grafted on to the ancient local Saka stock, and all these elements combined to form the fairly cohesive population of Ferghana with its own East Iranian Ferghanian language. During the sixth and seventh centuries, when Ferghana became subject to the Türks, there was increasing infiltration by Türk elements from the east and north, as can be seen from a group of inscriptions in runic script from Ferghana. In palaeo-anthropological terms, the population now belonged to the mesocranial and

44. Bernshtam, 1952, pp. 233–44; Bulatova-Levina, 1961, pp. 41–3; Davidovich, 1958; Brykina, 1971; Saltovskaya, 1971, pp. 12–14, 20.
45. Gorbunova, 1977, pp. 107–20; Filanovich, 1985, pp. 311–16.

brachycranial Europoid group, with only a small percentage of dolicranial Europoids very sparsely interspersed with Mongoloid admixtures.[46]

Chach and Ilak

The lands of Chach and Ilak gradually emerged as historical and geographical entities over the first half of the first millennium, although they were often given the same name of Chach (Shash in Arabic sources and Shi-Luo in Chinese sources). They were situated on the right bank of the middle reaches of the Syr Darya in the basins of its important tributaries, the Parak (Chirchik) and Ahangaran (Angren), and the neighbouring mountains of the western part of the T'ien Shan range. The economies of Chach (based on arable farming in the valleys and stockbreeding in the mountains) and Ilak (based on mining and stockbreeding), together with the local urban crafts of both regions, gave them an important role in the overall history of Central Asia.

Written sources give little information about Chach and Ilak in the third to the eighth century. After the break-up of the K'ang-chü state which was centred on this region, it appears that lesser domains with their own ruling dynasties sprang up. During the fifth century they came under the supreme power of the Hephthalite state. In 606, after the ruler of Chach was killed and the region was incorporated into the Western Türk *Kaghanate*, a Türk *tegin* (ruler) was put on the throne of Chach. Under the Hephthalites and the Türks, however, the local autonomy of the regions continued – their rulers bore the titles of *tudun* of Chach and *dihqān* of Ilak. In the 560s, Chach was the arena of the ruinous wars of the Türk *kaghan* and the Sasanian king Khusrau I against the Hephthalite king Gatfar. One episode of this war ended in the capture of Chach, the Parak (Chirchik) region and the bank of the Syr Darya by the Türk *kaghan*. In the seventh century, part of the nomadic Türgesh people settled in Chach. During the first half of the eighth century, according to Arab sources and a Sogdian document from the castle on Mount Mug (see above, Figs. 26 and 27), Chach, Ferghana and Sughd repeatedly formed military alliances to defend their territories against the Arab incursions, especially during the invasions of the forces of Qutaiba b. Muslim in 711, 712, 713 and 714 and of Nasr b. Sayyar in 737–738. In 739 the Kharijites, led by Harith b. Suraij, found refuge in Chach when harried by the forces of the same Nasr b. Sayyar.

46. Klyashtorny, 1964; Livshits, 1968; Litvinsky, 1960; 1976, pp. 49–65: these works give a complete bibliography of the question.

Religious culture and trade

According to Hsüan-tsang, the territory of Chach was one-third smaller than that of Ustrushana, but the produce of both regions was the same and their peoples shared the same customs. The inhabitants of Chach are included in the 'List of Nations and Tribes' known to the Sogdians, which was found among Sogdian Manichaean texts of the eighth–ninth century. The people of Chach mainly followed Zoroastrian-Mazdean teachings and practised burials in ossuaries (*astodan*s). Buddhist preachers came as far as the territories of Chach, where they erected Buddhist buildings. The epic genre was widespread in Chach; interestingly, Firdausi states that in the *Shāh-nāme* he used epic material collected for him by a *dihqān* from Chach. Chach, like Sughd, Ustrushana and Ferghana, was famed for its music. Dancing girls from Samarkand, Kumed, Kish, Maimurg and Chach were in high repute at the Chinese Imperial Court.

Chach and Ilak were situated on an important sector of the trans-Asian trade route: roads passed through them from the Near and Middle East via Samarkand, Jizak in Ustrushana and Khujand, and from Central Asia through Taraz and Isfijab. The region's economic prosperity owed much to the caravan trade, in which silver, lead, gold, iron and copper ware from Ilak were important, and also to commercial exchanges in basic necessities with the nomads of the nearby steppes.[47]

Archaeological evidence

Archaeological investigation of the sites of Kaunchi II (late second–early fourth century), Kaunchi III (second half of the fourth–eighth century) and Ming-uruk (second half of the sixth–eighth century) has shown them to be representative of the culture of their period. Kaunchi II and III are remarkable for their advanced fortifications, and also for the building of monumental houses, palaces and public and religious buildings, with characteristic methods of building domes, vaults and arched structures. At the Ming-uruk sites, citadels, castles and city walls were built on artificial mounds. Residential, public and religious buildings came to be decorated with large murals and carved clay reliefs. Burials in ossuaries began to be practised in addition to the previous custom of internment in tumuli. A wide variety of iron, non-ferrous and precious metalware and a variety of coinage have been found.

Many towns and large mining centres grew up in Chach and Ilak, with a sharp increase in the number of towns and their geographical spread during the Kaunchi II and III periods. These sites show two types of town layout: geometrical and amorphous. Towns of the first type were probably influenced by the ancient Central Asian urban cultures, while those of the second type

---

47. Summary of information from *Istoriya Uzbekskoy SSR*, 1967; Gafurov, 1972.

reflect the semi-nomadic life-style of agricultural and stockbreeding economies. On the archaeological evidence, some 100 settlements belong to this period. The progress of town building was accompanied by a general development of the region's settled agricultural life: a change to irrigated farming can
be observed, based on artificial irrigation and the building of protective dykes
and small reservoirs. Overall, the period was characterized by the development of crafts and trade, the exploitation of ore and raw materials and the growth
of commercial and monetary relations.

Thirty-two towns dating from the Ming-uruk period are known (two-
and-a-half times more than in the previous period), although few of them were
large. Greater attention was paid to fortification, and citadels were equipped
with round and rectangular towers and with covered walkways. Groups of
palace, religious, residential and workshop buildings have been studied. Most
of the citadels combine the defensive, residential and administrative functions
of a ruler's residence; some, however, were purely defensive. In the towns,
groups of smelters', metal workers' and potters' workshops have been found.
The towns were densely built up, with a network of streets and market places
and a water supply system. During this period the towns of Tunkat (the capital
of Ilak), Ulkai-toi-tepe, Ming-uruk, Kanka and many others expanded. There
was a chain of fortresses in the Chirchik basin. It was also during the fourth to
the seventh century that Chach grew up as a town, with a citadel, a ruler's
palace and a *shahristan*. Two hundred and twenty-five archaeologically identified settlements throw light on the rural environment. In the Chirchik valley
more than 30 large canals, with water-collecting installations supplying the
various branches of the local economy, have been recorded.[48]

ETHNIC HISTORY

The complex ethnic history of Chach and Ilak between the third and the eighth
century is similar to that of Ferghana. The oldest local ethnic group consisted
of Saka and K'ang-chü tribes from beyond the Syr Darya, who were joined by
large numbers of Hephthalite and Sogdian settlers. By the early medieval period the basic Iranian-speaking population of Chach and Ilak had been established. They probably spoke Iranian (Saka or Sogdian) dialects, which have left
considerable traces in local toponyms and early medieval onomastics, as recorded in medieval Arabic and Persian literature and in numismatic and other
material. The incorporation of Chach and Ilak into the sphere of Türk states in
the sixth and seventh centuries led to a marked intensification of the settling
and migration of the Turkic-speaking population. The following centuries saw

---

48. Classification and descriptions from Buryakov, 1975; 1982; see also Filanovich, 1983; 1985,
    pp. 297–303.

the formation in Chach and Ilak of a Tajik population (speaking the present-day archaic Brichmulla dialect of the Tajiks on the border of the Tashkent district and southern Kazakstan) and a local Turkic population, just as the same process led to the formation in Ferghana of the Ferghanian group of northern Tajik and Turkic dialects.[49]

49. Oranskiy, 1960, pp. 63–6, 147–8, 205–10; Livshits and Khromov, 1981, pp. 247–8; Klyashtorny, 1964.

THE CITY-STATES
OF THE TARIM BASIN*

Zhang Guang-da

Geography and climate

Between the third and the eighth century, a number of relatively large and powerful city-states, situated widely apart along the border of the Taklamakan desert in the Tarim basin, partitioned among themselves the region's oases. The Tarim basin stretches east for nearly 1,600 km from the foothills of the Pamirs to the westernmost end of the Hexi (Ho Hsi) corridor, the narrow passage along the peninsular territory of China's Gansu province through which ran the ancient Silk Route. With the vast expanse of the Taklamakan (337,000 sq. km) in the centre, the Tarim is surrounded by magnificent mountain ranges except towards the east where it ends in the depression of Lake Lop Nor. Along the southern edge of the Tarim lies the mighty Kunlun range. Farther to the south-east of the basin the Kunlun is continued by the Altyn-tagh, which extends eastward to the Tsaidam basin in Koko Nor province and forms the southern boundary of the corridor. To the north-east of the Pamirs lies the main range of the T'ien Shan, which follows an easterly course and separates Dzungaria to the north from the Tarim basin to the south.

The configuration of these ranges constitutes the most striking feature of the Tarim. The isolation from oceanic influences has had far-reaching effects on this enclosed region, producing extreme aridity and enormous temperature variations. In Central Asia, there are several striking instances of fluctuations in the water level of the great lakes. This led some explorers to believe that the climate there had also fluctuated widely. Ellsworth Huntington, the American geographer and a leading investigator of desiccation in the history of Central Asia, put forward this theory more systematically[1] to explain the terracing of lake shores and similar phenomena. The number of abandoned sites seemed to

---

* See Map 6.
1. Huntington, 1919, pp. 359–85.

provide further proof of progressive desiccation and fluctuating water supply under the impact of cyclical climatic changes. These then bore directly on the interaction of nomads and sedentary peoples in the impulses to migration, and the rise and fall of oasis populations.

Such an assumption is far from confirmed by the archaeological and geographic evidence, however, and there are alternative explanations. For example, Stein's careful on-the-spot observations of the marshy basin levels showed that large numbers of abandoned settlements were not the victims of drought. On the contrary, many failed to survive because of a surplus of water which damaged the irrigation systems. Others disappeared because of drifting sand which buried cultivation areas on the desert fringe. Nevertheless there had indisputably been a process of desiccation and the level of lakes and marshes had fluctuated in response to the varying annual snowfall. Given the present state of knowledge, it is difficult to demonstrate that the climate in the Tarim region underwent notable changes in historical times. Nor can a link be made between the climatic condition of the Tarim and the precipitation received by high ranges.[2]

Obviously, the desert could support no society: water is life in this area. Oases around the Tarim, such as Kashgar, Yarkand, Karghalik, Khotan, Keriya, Niya, Aksu and Kucha, owe their water – and with it their existence – to the snow-fed streams from the northern glacis of the Kunlun and the southern slopes of the T'ien Shan. These oases, in sharp contrast to the surrounding desert or semi-desert waste, are highly fertile and provide sites for human settlements. Because of the practice of irrigation agriculture, communities of great antiquity grew up and important city-states were formed.

Although the water carried by the streams usually reaches far beyond the irrigated areas, it does not cross the great expanse of the desert, where the streams soon dry up or become lost among the dunes and change into a subterranean flow. The extreme points reached by the rivers, however, are of archaeological interest. They constitute a type of ruined oasis termed 'terminal oasis' by Stein.[3] Owing to the sand, which preserves what it buries, ancient sites can be traced far more easily in these 'terminal oases' than in other cultivated sites. The most striking illustrations are the numerous sand-buried sites such as those of Dandan-oïlig, Niya, Endere and Uzun-tati. Located on the southern rim of the Taklamakan, they represent typical 'terminal oases' buried by moving sand during the first to the eighth century.

2. Stein, 1921, Vol. 2, pp. 664–5.
3. Stein, 1907, Vol. 1, pp. 95–6, 383, 419.

Peoples and languages

Archaeological and anthropological discoveries have shown that long before the gradual infiltration by Türks, this region was largely inhabited by Europoids and Indo-European-speaking peoples. From earliest times the nomadic peoples of Central Asia have constantly shifted their locations, some branches extending their tribal movements to the region of the Sita river, the modern Tarim.

People known to the Chinese as the Sai (archaic Chinese *sək*) sought a home in the west and south of the Tarim at an early date. Patient studies of the geographic, epigraphic and literary evidence have identified the Sai with the *Sakā* known to the Achaemenid Persians, Greek geographers and historians, and with the Sakas in Indian texts. This is an ethnic name like 'Yavana', 'Pahlava', 'Tukhara' and 'Cina'. The Sakas must have come to Khotan long before the second century B.C. and formed the kingdom of Khotan by combining with an indigenous people. According to the *Han shu* [History of the Former Han], the Sai tribes split and formed several states. To the north-west of Kashgar, states such as Hsiu-hsün and Chüan-du were all of the Saka race. The people of Tashkurgan in the Pamirs may perhaps have been a branch of the Sakas, since they could have spoken a language close to Khotanese and Tumshuqese. Excavations have revealed Saka cemeteries in this region. Another Saka group settled in Tumshuq – an important site located between Kashgar and Aksu – and probably formed the ruling class. Documents in Saka, written on wood or paper and dating from the seventh to the tenth century, have been found in Khotan and Tumshuq. They were written in Brāhmī script and represent several dialects: of those from Khotan and Tumshuq, the latter represents the more archaic.[4] The Tibetans called Kashgar 'Ga-hjag' and clearly the word is the same as Kanchaki, a language still spoken in villages near Kashgar in the eleventh century, as reported by Mahmud al-Kashgari in his *Dīwān lughāt al-Turk* (1076). It can thus be deduced that the population of the Kashgar area also spoke a dialect of their own which can be classified as a Saka language.[5]

More than one of the peoples who settled on the northern rim of the Tarim basin have been identified as speakers of the language known as Tokharian. According to the linguistic classification, Tokharian belongs to the *centum* type, or western branch of Indo-European languages. It shows no affinity to its immediate neighbours, belonging to one or another *satem* type of Indo-European. Manuscript fragments recovered from Kucha, Karashahr and Turfan, mostly Buddhist literary texts translated from Sanskrit or Central Asian languages, were written in the two dialects of Tokharian. Various proposals have been advanced to name these two dialects. They are commonly called Tokharian A and B or designated as Agnean and Kuchean. The former has

4. Bailey, 1958, p. 134.
5. Bailey, 1982, p. 56.

been identified as the eastern dialect, which spread throughout Karashahr (Argi or Agni in ancient times) and also the Turfan region, while the latter, the western dialect, spread mainly in Kucha and its environs.

Strong evidence for the existence of a third Tokharian dialect is provided by the documents of Lou-lan and Niya, recovered in the east and south-east of the Tarim. It is clear that the language of these documents in Kharoṣṭhī script was not pure Gandhārī or north-western Prakrit. It had borrowed some terms from the aboriginal dialect that was similar to Tokharian. It seems likely that the Krorainic of Lou-lan, Shan-shan and Niya district was a dialect closely akin to Agnean and Kuchean before the spread of Gandhārī as an official language.[6]

From the third century onwards several oasis city-states came to dominate the Tarim and overshadow their weaker neighbours. The oases in the south and west were separately united to the kingdoms of Kashgar and Khotan. Kucha, Karashahr and Kocho were consolidated into independent powers to the north while the kingdom of Lou-lan still held sway in the east towards Lop Nor. According to Chinese records, the name of the ruling family with the title of *A-mo-chih* (*Amača*) in Kashgar was P'ei. Khotan (Khotana in Kharoṣṭhī script, Hvatäna in Brāhmī and Hvamna or Hvam in the later Khotanese texts) was known throughout its 1,200 years as a kingdom (Hvatäna-kshīra). It was founded by the Saka royal lineage of Visha (Vijaya in Tibetan and Yüeh-chih in Chinese), which continued to the end of the kingdom in 1006. The hegemony of the Khotanese over the southern oasis states seems to have begun in the second half of the first century. In Kucha the ruling princes came from the House of Po ('white'), first mentioned for the year 91 and referred to in 787 in the Chinese sources. Agni was under the rule of a royal family called Lung (Dragon) by the Chinese.

Social life and the economy

Owing to the scant information available, our understanding of the social structure of these oasis city-states remains fragmentary. However, since their geographic setting and many other aspects were similar, the written sources and archaeological material allow us to draw a general picture of their socio-economic life.

The Chinese pilgrim Hsüan-tsang has left us a personal observation of Khotanese life and character in the fourth decade of the seventh century:

> The country [Khotan] is about 4,000 *li* [1 *li* = 0.274 of a mile, or 0.44 km, as given by the explorer Sven Hedin] in circuit, the greater part is nothing but sand and gravel, the arable portion of the land is very limited. It is suitable for the cultivation of cereals and produces an abundance of fruits. It manufactures carpets, felts of fine quality,

---

6. Burrow, 1937, pp. vii–ix. See also Tikhvinsky and Litvinsky (eds.), 1988; Litvinsky (ed.), 1992.

and fine-woven light silks. Moreover, it produces white and dark jade. The climate is soft and agreeable, but there are wind storms which bring with them clouds of dust. The manners and customs show a sense of propriety and justice. The inhabitants are mild by nature and respectful, they love to study literature, and distinguish themselves by their skill and industry. The people are easy-going, given to enjoyments, and live contented with their lot. Music is much practised in the country, and men love the song and the dance. Few of them wear garments of wool and fur, most dress in light silks and white clothes. Their appearance is full of urbanity and their customs are well regulated.[7]

Further information of a similar character is given in the special Notices concerning the Western Regions in the official Chinese dynastic histories. For example, there is additional (though fragmentary) material about life in Kucha. According to the *Chin shu* [History of the Chin] (Chapter 97):

They [the people of Kucha] have a walled city and suburbs. The walls are threefold. Within are Buddhist temples and stupas numbering a thousand. The people are engaged in agriculture and husbandry.

The *Chou shu* [History of the Chou] (Chapter 50) relates:

In the penal laws [of Kucha], a murderer is executed, and a robber has one arm and one leg cut off. For the military and civil administrative taxes, they measure the land in order to assess the levies. Those who hold no fields remit in silver coins. Marriage, funerals, customs and products are about the same as in Karashahr. It also produces delicate felt, deerskin rugs, cymbals, sal ammoniac, cosmetics, good horses, wild oxen and the like.

These descriptions are in full agreement with other early records. According to another report, the city walls of Kucha were indeed triple, equal in circumference to those of Ch'ang-an, the capital of the T'ang dynasty, and the number of stupas and temples within the city amounted to 1,000. We have similar descriptions of other cities. In Khotan, for example, Buddhist stupas were built in front of almost every house; the total number of stupas and temples was estimated at 1,000 and some 10,000 monks resided in the city.

The economy of these oasis city-states was based on irrigation agriculture combined with livestock breeding and crafts. Two wall paintings in Kyzyl cave no. 175 depict peasants ploughing with two oxen.[8] Other iron tools were in use besides the plough, showing that the local residents had mastered advanced agricultural techniques. As cultivation depended entirely on irrigation, and water constituted the mainstay of economic life, the maintenance and periodic distribution of canal water between the various villages and households were strictly regulated. This activity was the primary concern and occupation of the royal administration. People living along the great canals were permitted only shared use of water and were obliged to keep the canals clean and in

7. Hsüan-tsang, 1985, Ch. 12, Notice on Khotan.
8. Yan Wen-ru, 1962, Nos. 7–8, p. 45.

FIG. 1. Kyzyl. Wall painting.
(Photo: © Staatliche Museen zu Berlin –
Preussischer Kulturbesitz Museum für Indische Kunst.)

FIG. 2. Kyzyl. Wall painting. (Photo: © Staatliche Museen zu Berlin –
Preussischer Kulturbesitz Museum für Indische Kunst.)

good repair. The T'ang even had a special office, the *T'ao-t'o-suo*, in charge of
irrigation in Kucha.[9]

Wheat, barley, millet, peas, lucerne and cotton were the chief agricultural
products. According to the reports on the Western Regions in the *Liang shu*
[History of the Liang] and the *Pei-shih* [History of the Northern Dynasties],
rice was also planted here. Melons, peaches, apricots, almonds, chestnuts and
jujube were extensively grown. Grapes grow quickly and easily in this area
and many people in Kucha kept wine in their houses, some even as much as
1,000 *hu* (1 *hu* = approx. 13.25 litres) – this wine would keep for up to ten years.
In regions such as Shan-shan, people's livelihood depended on raising livestock,
but stock-breeding was also pursued in Kucha and other regions. Paintings in
the Kyzyl caves depict horses, cows, sheep and other domestic animals (Fig. 1).

9. Pelliot, 1967–88: Duldur-Aqur, Nos. 57, 80, 84, 86, 90, 98.

As mentioned above in Hsüan-tsang's report, the people were luxury-loving and given to enjoyment. The royal palace buildings in Kucha were splendidly decorated with gold and jade, shining like the dwellings of the gods. The garment and adornment of adult men and women conformed to the Western Barbarian style. The hair-styles so characteristic of the donors depicted in the Kuchaean frescoes must illustrate the coiffure referred to in the text of Hsüan-tsang (Fig. 2).

Shan-shan: administrative system

The literary evidence has been supplemented by archaeological material that provides new data on the social life and customs of the oasis city-states. Administrative documents on wood found in Lou-lan, Shan-shan and Niya, and which cover a span of 88 (or 96) years from the middle of the third century to the middle of the fourth, show that the state of Shan-shan was a monarchy. During this period, five kings – Pepiya, Tajaka, Amgoka, Mahiri (or Mayiri) and Vasmana – ruled in succession.[10] In the documents every king is designated by a lengthy title: 'Great King, King of Kings, Greatness, Victory, Right Law Staying at the Truth, His Majesty [*mahanuava*], Great King and Son of Heaven [*devaputra*]'. Later, in the seventeenth year of Amgoka, a new title for the king appears: *jiṭugha*, *jiṭumgha* or *ciṭumgha*. This seems to be a transcription of the Chinese title *Shih-chung*, transmitted to Shan-shan or conferred by Chinese emperors on the kings of several Western countries.

All official orders were issued in the name of the king; he was assisted by officials who attended to administrative, judicial and financial affairs at both central and local level. To judge by his position as described in the documents, the *ogu* was the highest official. Other high titles were *kitsaitsa* and *guśura* (both of a judicial nature), *kāla* (prince), *caṃkura* (protector), *chu-kuo* (pillar of the state) and *rājadarāga* (governor of the kingdom). The *cojhbo*, although inferior in rank to the dignitaries mentioned above, was an important and active functionary in the local administration. On a still lower level, the *soṭhaṃga* was charged with keeping the accounts of royal property and collected wine and other commodities, paid as taxes in kind. The *vasu* and *ageta* were the local judicial authorities. *Divira* (scribes) and *lekhaharaga* or *dutiyae* (letter-carriers) are among the subordinate designations that occur most frequently in the documents.

From the mid-third to the mid-fifth century the kingdom of Shan-shan maintained its control over the southern route of the Tarim, leading from Dunhuang to Khotan, and incorporated the smaller kingdoms and principalities of Ch'ieh-mo (Calmadana, Cherchen), Hsiao Yüan and Ching-chüeh (Niya,

---

10. Rapson and Noble, 1929.

Cad'ota). At the height of its power, Shan-shan seems to have been composed of a series of *rājas* or *rāyas* (districts) administered by *rājadarāgas* or *rājadareyas* nominated by the king. Ching-chüeh was listed, for example, among the *rājas*, retaining its original ruler. Each *rāja* was divided into *avanas* and *nagaras*. *Avana* might first have meant a local market, but later it took on the broader meaning of market-town, including the land around it. *Nagara* (town) was sometimes used as a synonym for *avana*. The *śata* or *śada* (100 house-holds) constituted the basic division of the *avana*, with a *śadavida* or *karśenava* at its head. It seems likely that taxes in kind (butter, wine, cereals, sheep, cam-els, carpets, felt and many other commodities) were levied by the *śata* and col-lected by the *soṭhaṃgas*. The year's tax was assessed both from the *kilme(ṃ)cis* and from the *rājya*. The *rājya* seems to have been the land directly owned by the king, while the *kilmes* were fiefs or estates granted to the nobility. Freemen owned farm land in the state and had the right to buy and sell their holdings. Monasteries apparently had independent economies and possessed their own lands.

Apart from wooden tablets conveying royal orders, official decisions and civil and penal judgements, most of the Kharoṣṭhī documents on wood and leather are contracts for marriage, purchases, sales and other domestic transac-tions. Contracts concerning slave-trading are evidence of the existence of slav-ery. From all these documents, it appears that the society of Shan-shan was composed of a nobility, officials, householders, Buddhist monks and *dajhas* or *dāsas* (slaves).[11]

Political upheavals

In 445 the kingdom of Shan-shan was definitively annexed by the Wei dynasty (386–534) of northern China and an administrative system similar to that of China proper was introduced. However, the Northern Wei soon lost the king-dom of Shan-shan to the Juan-juan, a tribal confederacy that made its appear-ance on the steppe around the beginning of the fifth century.

The rapid political upheavals experienced by the kingdom of Shan-shan were a common occurrence in the history of most city-states in the Tarim ba-sin. Owing to their strategic geographic position, these principalities have, since the mid-third century, been subject to the vicissitudes of the outside world. Contacts with the Kushans, for example, profoundly influenced the function-ing of government in some oasis states. The incessant interventions of the eques-trian steppe confederacies sometimes brought severe trouble. At best, the oasis cities maintained a precarious independence, or enjoyed local autonomy in exchange for the payment of tribute.

11. Cf. Boyer et al., 1920–29; Burrow, 1940; Litvinsky (ed.), 1992.

At the beginning of the fourth century, China underwent a north-south division. After more than two centuries of invasions and infiltration by the northern peoples, Barbarian dynasties were established in its northern and north-western provinces. Over a span of 135 years (304–439), 16 ephemeral kingdoms sprang up along the northern marches of China proper, ruled by 3 Chinese and 13 immigrant leaders of 5 different nationalities: 3 Hsiung-nu, 5 Hsien-pi, 3 Ti, 1 Chieh, and 1 Chiang. In 327 the Former Liang (313–376), one of the Sixteen Kingdoms founded by the Chinese, with the Hexi corridor as its principal domain, set up a prefecture in the Turfan area on the model of the commandery system used in China proper. Chinese was used here side by side with the local Hu language, and schools were established for Confucian doctrines.

During the fourth and fifth centuries the Former Liang and Former Chin (351–394) sent a number of punitive expeditions against Shan-shan, Karashahr, Kucha and Turfan. The mission of Yang Hsüan, general of the Former Liang, took place in 334. Four years later Lü Kwang, general of the Former Chin and subsequently founder of the Later Liang (386–403), was commissioned at the head of a force of 70,000 to conquer Kucha. In 441–442, with the extinction of the Northern Liang (397–439) by the Northern Wei, Wu Hui and his brother An Chou, scions of the former royal house, fled west and occupied Shan-shan and Kocho. Shortly afterwards, all or part of this region fell successively under the control of the Northern Wei (445), the Juan-juan (413–448), the Kao-chü (?–492) and the Hephthalites (484–558 or 567) (see also Chapters 6 and 13).

Between 560 and 563 the Western Türks inflicted crushing defeats on the Juan-juan and the Hephthalites. As a direct consequence of these victories, the Western Türks became the uncontested masters of the vast stretch of Eurasian steppe. The situation changed radically after the T'ang conquest of Kocho in 640. The decades that followed witnessed consistent efforts by the T'ang court to consolidate its position in the Western Regions by implementing a series of important administrative measures. Local institutions already established in China proper, such as the prefecture-county and canton-neighbourhood system, were introduced into the Qomul, Turfan and Beshbalyk districts and the Chinese equal-land system was put into practice in Turfan. Through a protracted and bitter struggle against the Tibetans (see Chapter 15), who made incursions into this area in alliance with the Türks, the Türgesh and the Karluks, the Chinese managed to regain control over the Tarim. Following the traditional suzerain-vassal pattern, the T'ang court granted autonomy to all the oasis city-states. The local kings, retained as rulers and governors, were left in charge of the local administration under the supervision of the Protector-General of An-hsi (Kucha). For almost 150 years Kucha, Kashgar, Khotan and Suyab (replaced by Karashahr after 719) were called the 'Four Garrisons of the An-hsi Protectorate-General'.

The presence of these military bases, established to maintain T'ang rule over the Western Regions, led to Chinese influence in many areas of life, as revealed by recent archaeological excavations. A number of Confucian classics, copied in duplicate, such as the *Lun-yü* [Analects of Confucius] with Cheng Hsüan's commentary, recently unearthed in the Turfan cemetery, show how deeply Chinese language and culture penetrated this region. It is no surprise to find that Qoshu Han, a Türgesh youth from Kucha who became a great general at the T'ang court in the mid-eighth century, was fond of reading the *Han shu* and other Chinese historical literature (*T'ang shu*, Chapter 104, Biographical Notice on Qoshu Han).

At about the time that the T'ang dynasty was engaged in consolidating its hegemony over the Tarim, a great new power arose in the west: the Arabs (known to the Chinese as Ta-shih), who had already penetrated Transoxania and were advancing eastward. Their presence in Central Asia led to a clash with the Chinese. In a battle fought in July 751 on the plains near the Talas river, Kao Hsien-chih, the T'ang deputy Protector-General, was defeated by the Arabs under the command of Ziyad b. Salih. This disaster marked the end of the T'ang advance into the Western Regions.

Trade

In spite of numerous vicissitudes, the period from the third to the eighth century saw the expansion of overland commerce and cultural exchange, together with the spread of Buddhism. The Silk Route created favourable conditions for an unprecedented increase in commercial and cultural activity. The most important merchandise traded along this caravan road was Chinese silk. Its market value greatly exceeded that of other goods and it brought a substantial income both to local rulers and to residents of the oasis states. Large amounts of Chinese silk were exported to the West by Sogdian merchants who, from very early times (and to a greater extent than the nomadic peoples), were instrumental in carrying on the Eurasian caravan trade. Specimens of Chinese and Sogdian silk products have been found in districts as far west as Moshchevaya Balka in the Caucasus.[12]

The technique of sericulture seems to have been introduced into Khotan very early (it is alluded to in the legend concerning a Chinese princess who smuggles silkworms into the region).[13] The domestic silk-weaving industry appears to have existed in other oasis states too, as the terms 'Kuchean brocade' and 'Kashgar brocade' both appear in Turfan documents. Persian brocade (or an imitation) has been discovered in ancient tombs of the Astana cemetery in Turfan that date from after the seventh century. The weave is a

12. Yerusalimskaya, 1972.
13. Stein, 1907, Vol. 1, pp. 229–30.

weft-patterned compound twill with a double yarn warp,[14] totally different from that of Chinese warp-patterned design. It appears that such Persian-style brocade was specially manufactured for export to China proper or even to Iran. Turfan was also famous for its cotton textiles and almost all the oasis states were widely known for their fine carpets, felt products and home-woven woollen fabrics.

Other articles transported along the Silk Route included jade from Khotan, turquoise from Iran, lapis lazuli from Afghanistan, tortoiseshell and ivory from India, coral and pearls from the Persian Gulf and the Red Sea, gold and silverware from Sasanian Iran, glassware from the eastern Mediterranean and bronze mirrors, tricoloured pottery and lacquerware from China. Other exotica, such as embroidered robes, tapestry, armour, swords, harness with gorgeous decorations, and metalwork, were also traded along the Silk Route. Byzantine gold coins and large amounts of Persian silver species have been found in many sites of the Tarim.[15]

Religion

Among those who used the Silk Route were Buddhist monks from the territory of the Kushans and north-west India travelling to the east, and itinerant Buddhists from Kucha, Khotan and China proper going to the west. The introduction of Buddhism into the Tarim basin and China is first connected with the missionary translators from Parthia and Sogdiana, and then with the expansion of the Kushan Empire, especially during the reign of the great ruler Kanishka I. In the earlier period of Buddhist expansion, most Buddhist scriptures were introduced to China through the Tarim, with the addition of many local cultural elements. One example is the Chinese translation of Buddha as *Fo* and *Fu-Tu*. This was simply a transliteration into Chinese of the term '*But*' that was used in the Tarim basin.[16]

The two major schools of Buddhism – Hinayana and Mahayana – coexisted in the Tarim region, each becoming predominant at certain periods, and it is not always possible to draw a sharp distinction between them.[17] The earliest Buddhist texts, written mostly in Gandhārī Prakrit, may be dated to the latter half of the second century. The discovery by Dutreuil de Rhins of a manuscript of a Prakrit version of the *Dharmapada* shows that the establishment of Buddhism in Khotan is of considerable antiquity. The Mahayana school had flourished there since the beginning of the fourth century, without arousing

---

14. Hsia Nai, 1979, pp. 89–97.
15. Hsia Nai, 1974.
16. Bailey, 1931, Vol. 6, Part 2, pp. 282–3; Ji Xianlin et al., 1982, p. 341.
17. Asmussen, 1965, pp. 144.

FIG. 3. Duldur-Aqur.
Wall painting.
Musée Guimet, Paris.
(Photo: © R.M.N. Paris.)

any appreciable hostility from the Sarvastivadins.[18] The Hinayana school was predominant in Kucha, where most of the wall paintings found in rock-cut *vihāras* (monasteries) are connected with the Hinayana, though, occasionally, themes belonging to the Mahayana also appear.[19]

Khotan played an important role in the propagation of Buddhism: to zealous Chinese Buddhists of the earlier period, it was the chief seat of Buddhist studies and the foremost source of original Buddhist texts. According to Hsüan-tsang, a large number of Sanskrit manuscripts of the Buddhist canons reached Khotan from Kashmir.[20] Sutras like the *Avaṃaṁśaka* appear to have been compiled in Khotan and huge quantities of Buddhist manuscripts were translated from Sanskrit and Gandhārī into Khotanese Saka. It should be noted that in the later period the extreme mysticism of the Vajrayana school is also found in Khotan.

The religious influence of Kucha was very strong and the region is dotted with many Buddhist sites (Kyzyl, Duldur-Aqur, Kyzyl-Qagha, Kumtura, Su-bashi, Simsim, Acigh-Iläk and Kirish) (Figs. 3–6). The site of Tumshuq was

18. For the *Dharmapada*, see Brough, 1962.
19. Gaulier et al., 1976, Vol. 1, p. 24.
20. Asmussen, 1965, p. 143; Litvinsky (ed.), 1992.

FIG. 4. Kyzyl. Wall painting (detail). (Photo: © Staatliche Museen zu Berlin.)

FIG. 5. Kyzyl. Painted dome. (Photo: © Staatliche Museen zu Berlin –
Preussischer Kulturbesitz Museum für Indische Kunst.)

FIG. 6. Kumtura. Terracotta figurine. Musée Guimet, Paris.
(Photo: © R.M.N. Paris.)

FIG. 7. Tumshuq. Buddhist decoration. Terracotta. Musée Guimet, Paris.
(Photo: © R.M.N. Paris.)

FIG. 8. Tumshuq. Buddhist decoration. Terracotta. Musée Guimet, Paris.
(Photo: © R.M.N. Paris.)

also a place of great importance in the spread of Buddhism (Figs. 7–9). Kumarajiva (344–413), one of the four great translators into Chinese of Buddhist scriptures, was of Kuchean origin. A monk of great attainments, he acquired a mastery of Chinese thought and literary style and his translations reached a high degree of accuracy.

Side by side with Buddhism, pre-Zoroastrian Old Iranian beliefs continued among the Khotan Saka population. Remnants of the old Indo-European religion were preserved among the Tokharian population, and Taoist beliefs among the local Chinese. The dominance of Buddhism was also challenged by other religions. Zoroastrianism and Manichaeism may have entered the Tarim region much earlier than Buddhism; their activity manifested itself in the T'ang period. According to T'ang sources, Hsien-shen ('the Zoroastrian god') was worshipped in Kashgar and Khotan. The term *Hu-t'ien* (Barbarian god) in the Chinese Turfan documents is sometimes interpreted as meaning Ohrmazd. Manichaeism did not prosper until the Uighurs established their supremacy in Kocho in the first half of the ninth century. Sogdian Manichaean merchants

FIG. 9. Tumshuq. Buddhist decoration. Terracotta. Musée Guimet, Paris.
(Photo: © R.M.N. Paris.)

must have brought their faith to Turfan and other states as they travelled along the Silk Route, as shown by the discovery of Manichaean texts in Tokharian B and by the Manichaean Sogdian *X^{u}āstvānīft* fragment. In 635 a Syrian missionary called Aloben (known to the Chinese as A-lo-pen) introduced Nestorian Christianity to Ch'ang-an and established a Nestorian Church there three years later. However, traces of Nestorianism in the Tarim region are lost in obscurity (Fig. 10) (see also Chapters 17 and 18).

Since the Tarim basin is located at a crossroads, its culture came to reflect a peculiar syncretism of various heterogeneous civilizations. This can be seen clearly in Buddhist art. The source of Buddhist iconography in the Tarim region is to be found in Gandhara. Its features include the huge statues of the Buddha in various poses, the treatment of his hair and the drapery of his clothes, and the representation of *arhat*s, Bodhisattvas, the various Buddhist divinities, ascetics, donors and other figures. The paintings of Turfan are characterized by an elongation of the images, a pronounced contrast of light and shade, and similar devices. These characteristics provide eloquent evidence that, during

FIG. 10. Kocho. Wall painting representing a Christian scene.
(Photo: © Staatliche Museen zu Berlin –
Preussischer Kulturbesitz Museum für Indische Kunst.)

the Kushan period, Gandharan styles were mixed with Iranian, Hellenistic and Bactrian elements and had a predominant influence upon Buddhist art, especially during its earlier phase. This can be observed in the paintings of Miran in particular. Later periods even reveal traces of the influence of Sogdian art.

The ruined complexes of Buddhist monastic buildings (examples include Rawak in the vicinity of Khotan, Duldur-Aqur and Su-bashi in Kucha, and Shorchuk near Karashahr) (Fig. 11) also bear silent witness to the inspiration derived from the planning of similar structures in India, Gandhara and Bactria. The hewing of caves or grottoes into the rocks seems to have been a practice borrowed from India via the Bamiyan valley and the Termez area (Kara-tepe). The layout of *vihāras* and stupas of various types around the Tarim basin also points to the close affinity of architectural styles.

Music, dance and the associated fine arts, especially the Buddhist arts,

299

FIG. 11. Shorchuk. Buddha. Painted clay.
(Photo: © Staatliche Museen zu Berlin –
Preussischer Kulturbesitz Museum für Indische Kunst.)

also flourished under the influence of both east and west. Many of the musical instruments shown on the wall paintings of Kucha had their origin in Central Asia, India and China. The dances of Kucha show strong Indian influence: the swaying of the hips, the frequent changes of gesture and the expression in the eyes shown in the paintings are all typical of Indian dance. The Hu-hsüan dance, which was very famous at the T'ang court, originated from Sogdiana, developed in Kucha and was later introduced into Ch'ang-an, the capital of the T'ang. Artists of the Tarim area – such as the famous painter Yü-ch'ih I-sen (Visha Irasangä) from Khotan, several of whose paintings of the *Devaraja* still survive – introduced new techniques to China proper.

Buddhist canons, religious plays and other kinds of performances were also known in these oasis states. Manuscripts dating from this period of the Buddhist sutra, such as the *Dharmapada* and the *Udānavarga*, and of the Buddhist play the *Maitreya-samitinataka*, both in Sanskrit and in their translation into Tokharian A, have been discovered.[21] Tibetan manuscripts of the *Li-yul lun-bstan-pa* report the performance of a Buddhist play in the temple of Khotan.[22]

---

21. Lüders, 1911; Sieg and Siegling, 1921.
22. Emmerick, 1967, pp. 41–5; Litvinsky (ed.), 1992.

KOCHO (KAO-CH'ANG)*

Zhang Guang-da

T he Turfan depression, located in the eastern T'ien Shan region, has an
area of 50,147 sq. km, of which 4,050 sq. km are below sea level. Lake
Ayding-köl lies at 156 m below sea level, the lowest point of Turfan,
which is bounded on the south by Mount Chol Tagh and on the north by
Mount Bogdo Ula. These steep, rugged mountains are covered with snow all
the year round, and the melting snows irrigate the oases of the depression's
north-central plain. Stone and pottery relics unearthed north of the village of
Astana and west of the moat of the ancient city of Yar (Chiao Ho) indicate that
there was already human activity in the area more than 4,000 years ago. Over
the centuries, the reputation of these fertile, lush and very habitable oases grew.

The area's favourable natural conditions and its strategic location attracted
many ethnic groups and it became a meeting point for various cultures. The
Chü-shih people were early settlers of the Turfan depression; like the Agni of
Karashahr, they presumably spoke an Indo-European dialect. According to
Ssu-ma Ch'ien's *Shih-chi* [Historical Records] and Pan Ku's *Han shu* [History
of the Former Han], the Chü-shih 'lived in felt tents, moved from place to
place in search of water and pasture, and applied themselves to agricultural
work to an appreciable extent'. In 200 B.C. Turfan was bordered on the north
by the territory of the Hsiung-nu tribe who had '3,000 trained bowmen' (*Shih-
chi*, Chapter 123, Notice on Ta-yüan, i.e. Ferghana), on the south by the oasis
city-states founded by the area's original inhabitants and on the east by the
Western (Former) Han dynasty (206 B.C.–A.D. 24), whose capital was on the
site where Xi-an stands today. In 108 B.C. the Han authorities sent a 700-strong
cavalry unit headed by Chao Po-nu to rout the Chü-shih.[1] However, the area
of Turfan inhabited by the Chü-shih was still ruled by the Hsiung-nu, leading
to a struggle for control between the Hsiung-nu and the Han. This period,

---

* See Map 6.
1. Hirth, 1917, p. 106.

which lasted from 99 to 60 B.C., is known in Chinese history as 'the five wars for the control of the Chü-shih' (*Han shu*, Chapter 96, Notice on the Western Regions). Finally, in 60 B.C., the Han seized the area and appointed Cheng Chi as the first Protector-General of the Western Regions (*Hsi-yü Tu-hu*).

For the next 70 years, the Han exercised firm control over the area and their culture was to leave a significant mark. The area was divided into the kingdoms of 'Anterior Chü-shih' and 'Posterior Chü-shih'. The former, which had Yar as its capital, was inside the depression itself. The latter was situated north of Bogdo Ula, a mountain of the eastern branch of the T'ien Shan range. In 48 B.C. the Han stationed a *wu-chi hsiao-wei* (colonel of Wu and Chi)[2] in the Anterior Chü-shih city of Kocho (Kao-ch'ang), 30 km south-east of Turfan in Xinjiang. The *wu-chi hsiao-wei*'s main responsibilities were, first, to command the Han troops from the central plains of China and, second, to make the soldiers work the agricultural colonies which provided food for the Han troops garrisoned in the Western Regions and for the Han diplomatic envoys passing through the area. During the period of Yüan-shih (A.D. 1–5), the *wu-chi hsiao-wei* Hsü P'u-yü opened the 'New Northern Route', which greatly shortened the journey from the Jade Gate in the Dunhuang limes to the territory of the Posterior Chü-shih.[3] With the opening of this direct route via Hami (Qomul), Turfan was destined to become even more important to the Chinese than before.

In the first century A.D., control of Turfan constantly changed hands between the Han and the Hsiung-nu. From 73 onwards, and especially after 89 when General Pan Ch'ao of the Eastern (Later) Han (24–220) brought the Tarim basin back under Han control, the Chü-shih were once again under Han jurisdiction. Following the conquest of Chü-shih, the Eastern Han re-established, after an interval of some 60 years, the offices of Protector-General and *wu-chi hsiao-wei*. Increasing numbers of Han garrison troops were stationed in the area and the newly opened up territory was expanded. Pan Chao's son Pan Yung, who was appointed *chang-shih* of the Western Regions in 123, stationed his troops at Lukchun (T'ien Ti), an important site located in the centre of Turfan, not far east of Kocho. Gradually, the Han Chinese from the central plains of China and the Ho Hsi corridor intermingled with the Chü-shih natives. During the Wei dynasty (220–265), founded by the House of Ts'ao, and the Western Chin dynasty (265–316), the kingdom of Chü-shih was basically loyal to China thanks to the implementation of a continuous policy of 'control by reconciliation' through the *wu-chi hsiao-wei*. The so-called 'Kocho soldiers' of the Wei and Chin dynasties may have been a local army made up of Chü-shih natives and immigrant Han Chinese.

---

2. For the title *wu-chi hsiao-wei* and its supposed origin, see Chavannes, 1907, p. 154, note 2; Hulsewé and Loewe, 1979, p. 79, note 63.
3. Stein, 1921, Vol. 2, pp. 705 et seq.; 1928, pp. 542, 571 et seq.

The Kocho Prefecture period (327–460)

The fall in 316 of the Western Chin led to the fragmentation and breakdown of Chinese power. In 327 Chang Chun of the local dynasty, the Former Liang (313–376), occupied Kocho and captured the *wu-chi hsiao-wei* Chao Chen, who had attempted to proclaim the independence of Turfan. The same year, Chang Chun established a prefecture in Kocho to administer the counties of Kocho and Lukchun. The Turfan depression and its agricultural colonies became a prefecture of the Former Liang. As power over the Ho Hsi area changed hands, so did the administration of the prefecture. Ephemeral dynasties followed and when in 439 the Northern Liang (397–439) were defeated by the Northern Wei (386–534), Wu Hui of the Northern Liang royal family led a retreat of some 10,000 families from Dunhuang west to Shan-shan. In 442 Wu Hui occupied Kocho, establishing himself the following year as king of Liang and creating a regional state that was independent of Ho Hsi district.

In 448 Wu Hui's younger brother An Chou took control of the city of Yar and finally destroyed the Anterior Chü-shih regime; the remaining Chü-shih forces moved westwards to Agni (Karashahr). Turfan's political, economic and cultural centre thus moved from Yar to Kocho. It was at this point that the Chü-shih people, who had been active in the Turfan depression since the Han dynasty, left the stage of history. In 460 An Chou[4] was killed in a Juan-juan invasion. As there were over 10,000 Han Chinese families living in Kocho, the Juan-juan – whose power base was in Mongolia – found it difficult to exercise direct rule and therefore placed a Chinese puppet king, K'an Po Chou,[5] on the throne. K'an Po Chou's reign marked the beginning of a period during which the Turfan depression was governed as a kingdom.

Despite its remote location to the west of the central plains, the Turfan depression was strongly influenced by Han Chinese culture during the Kocho Prefecture period when it was governed by the local Ho Hsi regime. Its political and military institutions were very similar to those of China proper. For example, at the time when family clans held sway over the central plains, rich and powerful families also ruled in Turfan. Moreover, under the long-term influence of the *wu-chi hsiao-wei* system, there was almost no difference in status between the military and civilian populations. Civilians and soldiers recruited or dispatched from the central plains joined with the native inhabitants to form Kocho's prefectural armies which guarded the borders and built roads and canals, enabling Turfan to develop and prosper.

4. The memory of An Chou is celebrated in the Chinese inscription of 469 acquired by Grünwedel from the ruins of a Buddhist shrine of Idikutshahri; this inscription has been edited and discussed by Franke, 1907, and Pelliot, 1912.
5. For the entire fifth century, some interesting notices concerning Turfan are extracted from Chinese historical sources, especially the *Pei-shih*, and lucidly discussed in Franke's important papers, 1907.

The Kocho kingdom period (460–640)

In 460 the Juan-juan established the House of K'an as puppet rulers. By 485 internal conflicts had undermined the Juan-juan and Kocho seized the opportunity to break away from their rule. However, various nomadic tribes, including the Juan-juan, the Kao-chü and the Hephthalites, competed for power over Kocho and the independence of the House of K'an was shortlived. In 491 the regime was brought down by the Kao-chü nation, a powerful force on the steppe. The Kao-chü king set up Chang Meng Ming, a native of Dunhuang, as the king of Kocho. A few years later, Chang was killed by his countrymen, who put Ma Ju on the throne. Ma Ju, constantly harrassed by the Kao-chü, sent an envoy to the Northern Wei in 497, asking for permission to move his people into the interior. This caused dissatisfaction among the native inhabitants. The Kao-chü killed Ma Ju, placed Ch'ü Chia on the throne and made Kocho the capital. Although constantly harassed by northern nomads and besieged by dissenters, the precarious Kocho kingdom founded by Ch'ü Chia was to survive for 138 years (502–640), making it the longest lived of the local regimes.

The Kocho kingdom ruled by the Ch'ü family measured 300 *li* from east to west and 500 *li* from north to south (*Chou shu*, Chapter 50, Notice on Kao-ch'ang, i.e. Kocho), with about 8,000 households and a total population of some 30,000. Kocho was the most powerful and most culturally advanced city-state of the western oases. Recent research by scholars into Turfan documents has revealed numerous reign titles (Yüan Ho, Ch'eng Ping, Lung Hsing, etc.) that are not recorded in China's historical annals. These findings help to clarify a series of political changes during the Kocho kingdom period. On the basis of detailed scholarly research, it is possible to plot a rough chronology of the Kocho kingdom under the House of Ch'ü.[6]

The kingdom was controlled by wealthy, influential local clans closely connected through intermarriage. Apart from the Ch'ü family, the most eminent clans were the Changs, the Fans, the Yins, the Mas, the Shihs and the Hsins. At the beginning of this period, the tiny kingdom of Kocho was threatened by the Kao-chü. In 552 the Türk *Kaghanate* became immensely powerful, conquering the Juan-juan and dominating the northern Gobi desert. The kingdom of Kocho submitted to Türk rule and several Türk princes married into the Kocho royal family. By the beginning of the seventh century, however, the Türk *Kaghanate* had begun to decline and the T'ieh-le tribe held suzerainty over Kocho.

During Ch'ü Po-ya's reign, the kingdom of Kocho developed close relations with the Sui dynasty (581–618) and actively pursued a policy of Sinicization. This caused dissatisfaction among the great families, resulting in a

6. Hou, 1984, p. 75.

coup d'état. The rebel's reign lasted 6 years, after which the Ch'ü were restored to the throne with the aid of the Chang clan, who were closely linked to the Ch'ü family by generations of intermarriage. The T'ang dynasty (618–907) won a succession of military victories against the nomads in the north and west, and in 630 they eliminated the powerful Eastern Türk *Kaghanate.* The 7 cities of Qomul (I-Wu), which had belonged to the Eastern Türks, were merged with the T'ang nation. Because his kingdom was adjacent to the Western Regions, the king of Kocho, Ch'ü Wen-t'ai, was fearful of T'ang ambitions to move westward and he reached an agreement with the Western Türks to resist the T'ang. When attacked by the T'ang, however, the Western Türks were the first to surrender; in 640 the Chü rulers of the Kocho kingdom also yielded. Having lasted for over 100 years and 10 reigns, the Ch'ü family's rule over Kocho now came to an end. The T'ang government established the Hsi-chou district and the An-hsi (An-xi) military Protectorate-General at Yar (Chiao Ho),[7] and for the next 152 years (640–792) Turfan was ruled directly by the T'ang.

Recently discovered documents at Kocho

Following the 1898 Turfan expedition by the Russian archaeologist D. Klementz, a succession of archaeological teams from Britain, Germany, Japan and Sweden came to this area to conduct excavations (Fig. 1). As the reports of these excavations were published long ago and are well known, we shall not dwell on them here.[8] Since 1959 other excavations have been conducted by Chinese archaeologists at the cemeteries of Astana and Karakhoja, north of the ancient city of Kocho. According to reports published between 1959 and 1975, 13 major excavations were conducted and 459 ancient graves were opened, including 354 at the Astana cemetery. Documents were found in 119 of the excavated graves. Of the 1,586 documents written in Chinese,[9] 403 dated from the period when the Ch'ü family ruled the Kocho kingdom and 1,020 from the T'ang period. Many of the 300 epitaphs excavated belong to the Ch'ü period. Because of Turfan's extremely dry climate, the documents are well preserved and the manuscripts appear quite new. Taken together, these documents provide a comprehensive record of contemporary social, political, economic and cultural life in the Turfan region.

7. Zhang, 1988, pp. 81–7.
8. Dabbs, 1963.
9. Tang, 1982.

FIG. 1. Kocho. Ruins of stupa 'Y'. (Photo: © R.M.N. Paris.)

Administrative system and socio-economic life under the House of Ch'ü

The Turfan documents provide a general picture of the capital, prefectures and territory of the Kocho kingdom, which probably derived its name from that of its capital, Kocho. The city was divided into at least four districts, and there were gates on all four sides of the surrounding city wall. The gates bore the same names as the gates of Lo-yang, the capital of the Han, Wei, Chin and Northern Wei dynasties; and of Gu Tsang (Wu-wei county), a city of the Sixteen Kingdoms. The names clearly reveal the cultural influence of China proper.

The Kocho kingdom under the House of Ch'ü established prefectures and counties modelled on the institutions that had existed in China proper during the Kocho Prefecture period. As a sop to those clans that had emigrated from China proper and from the Ho Hsi corridor, additional prefectures and counties were established. It is believed that the administrative system of this period was roughly based on a division into 4 prefectures and 22 counties and cities, with Kocho at their centre. The most important prefectures included Kheng-chieh Prefecture, the political and economic centre of north-eastern Kocho, and Yar Prefecture, the political and cultural centre of western Kocho and formerly the capital city of the Anterior Chü-shih kingdom.

During this period, the oases of the Turfan depression were fully exploited and great emphasis was placed on irrigation. The Kocho king had direct con-

308

trol over all lands, and every transaction involving land or vineyards required his approval. The king's permission was also needed when a lay person do- nated lands or vineyards to a temple (according to the documents: 'let the lay service turn into the divine one'). The king's permission was required even for bequests of land from father to son. These practices indicate that the system of land distribution in accordance with the number of people in a household – as implemented in the central plains of China proper – was not applied in the Kocho kingdom during the rule of the House of Ch'ü.

In early times, the system of calculating wealth was to assess a family's assets by converting the household's land acreage into the amount of grain it could produce. The taxes, corvées and horses due from each household were determined in accordance with this amount. During the period of the Kocho kingdom, the system of levying taxes and corvées drew a distinction between monks and lay citizens, the rates probably being more moderate for monks than for laymen. Taxes, payable in silver coins, were levied not only in accord- ance with acreage, but also in accordance with the fertility of the land. The same system was applied to determine the quota for each of the various types of corvée. A multitude of other rents, corvées and trade taxes were introduced over the years. Trade flourished in Kocho and silver coins were used as cur- rency. Tenancy was common during the rule of the House of Ch'ü. Discover- ies of land lease deeds and contracts show that land was rented by government bodies, temples and individuals.

The documents and epitaphs also reveal that a few influential families enjoyed a monopoly of power in Turfan. For example, 68 of the 300 epitaphs discovered belong to the powerful Chang family. Three successive generations of Changs were important officials at court; the Changs were linked with the Ch'ü clan through intermarriage and were powerful enough to help the Ch'ü family regain the throne.

The meeting and merging of cultures

In Turfan, local civilizations met and intermingled with those of China, India, Iran and the eastern Mediterranean. Because its very foundations were the Han Chinese garrison troops and their agricultural colonies under the *wu-chi hsiao- wei* system, the Kocho Prefecture was profoundly influenced by Han culture. Later, when the regional governments of the Ho Hsi (Hexi) corridor estab- lished their prefectures in Turfan, the Han and Wei cultures, mingled with lo- cal elements specific to the Ho Hsi area, were introduced. During the rule of the House of Ch'ü, the administrative system and official titles in the Kocho kingdom were nearly identical to those used in the Chinese government.[10] The

10. Hou, 1984, pp. 52–74.

grave patterns, sepulchral inscriptions and documents found all indicate the dominant role of Han culture;[11] for example, the names of the deceased and their official titles appear in Han style. Fragments of Mao Heng and Mao Ch'ang's version of the *Book of Odes*, dating from the Northern Liang dynasty, have been excavated at the ancient cemetery in Astana, an indication that the Confucian classics were in circulation there at an early time.

Han culture rose to even greater prominence during the period when the Kocho kingdom was ruled by the House of Ch'ü. Ch'ü Chia, the first Ch'ü king of Kocho, petitioned the Northern Wei for a loan of the Confucian *Five Classics* and the *Book of History* and invited a Chinese man of letters (*Pei-shih*, Chapter 97, Notice on Kao-ch'ang) to give instruction to students in Kocho. Ch'ü Jian, the third king of Kocho, had a picture of 'Ai Gong, the duke of Lu, asking advice from Confucius' (*Sui shu*, Chapter 83, Notice on Kao-ch'ang) painted in his home to illustrate his own policy of benevolence. The books recovered from the Astana tombs include not only Confucian classics, but also books on history, as well as some poems and children's readers in Chinese such as the *Ch'ien-tzu-wen* [Book of One Thousand Characters] and the *Chi-chiu-chang* [Elementary Book of Chinese Characters]. Under the Ch'ü, the ruling class actively encouraged the study of Confucian thought, with the aim of consolidating their own power. Confucianism thus became the dominant ideology of the ruling class.

The kingdom's official records were written in Chinese characters and were similar in form and wording to those used in China proper during the Han and Wei periods. The kingdom nevertheless had its own culture. The native inhabitants wrote in the so-called 'Barbarian script', which, judging from the existing evidence, was probably Tokharian A, although further study would be needed to confirm this. All in all, the influence of Chinese culture in Kocho was, at that time, far more profound and far-reaching than the influence of Buddhism from the west.

Taoism and metaphysics, which enjoyed great popularity in China during the Wei, Chin, Southern and Northern dynasties, also found their way to Kocho. Taoist talismans (vermilion characters written with cinnabar on yellow paper) have been unearthed from tomb no. 303 at the Astana cemetery, proving that the grave's occupant was a Taoist.[12]

Because of its location on the main artery of the Silk Route, Turfan was inevitably influenced by Buddhism from the Kushan Empire and Tokharistan, and many Buddhist scriptures in Sanskrit reached Kocho from these areas. In the early twentieth century, a large number of hand-copied Buddhist scriptures were found in the ancient cities of Kocho, Yarkhoto and Sengim-aghiz by Prussian and other foreign expeditions. In the early days of the Kocho

11. Stein, 1928, Vol. 2, Ch. 19, p. 668.
12. *Texts of the Documents Found in Turfan*, 1981–87, Vol. 2, p. 33.

Prefecture period, local Buddhist monks supervised the translation into Chinese of Sanskrit Buddhist scriptures. In an ancient catalogue concerning the translation of the Buddhist *Tripitaka (Ch'u San Tsang Chi Chi)*, several references are made to the translation of Sanskrit Buddhist scriptures by Buddhist monks from Kocho.

Under the Ch'ü, Buddhism developed rapidly. The first few kings, including Ch'ü Chia and Ch'ü Chian, considered themselves to be Confucians. Later monarchs, including the seventh king, Ch'ü Ch'ien-ku, and the ninth, Ch'ü Wen-t'ai, were pious Buddhists. Ch'ü Wen-t'ai was especially noted for his devoutness. When on his pilgrimage to India to find the Buddhist scriptures, the seventh-century Chinese monk Hsüan-tsang stopped at Kocho and gave lectures on Buddhism. Ch'ü Wen-t'ai knelt on the ground so that Hsüan-tsang could use his back as a step to mount the dais.[13]

In addition to the translation of Buddhist scriptures, religious activities included the building of temples and the carving of grottoes. The building of rock temples reached its peak during the period of the Sixteen Kingdoms (304–439). To this period also should be assigned the carving of the Thousand-Buddha grottoes in Toyoq and Bezeklyk (Fig. 2). Steles erected in commemoration of the completion of temples and statues bear witness to the religious fervour of the imperial families. Over 40 temples were named after prominent families, reflecting the growing power of the family clans. In a sense, Buddhist temples became family shrines, indicating a process by which Buddhist power was merged with that of the aristocratic families of Kocho.

The *Pei-shih* provides a description of the clothes worn in Kocho: 'the adult men attire themselves in conformity with Hu [Barbarian] style, women are in jackets and skirts and wear their hair in buns' (*Pei-shih*, Chapter 97, Notice on Kao-ch'ang). 'The adult men allowed their queues to fall to the back and wore long robes with narrow sleeves' (*Liang-shu*, Chapter 54, Notice on Kao-ch'ang). Recent excavations at the Astana cemetery have yielded women wearing right-buttoned silk jackets and skirts and men with queues coiled under their necks. Many of the faces are covered with face guards (face cloths) and the eyes are covered by metal eye shades called 'eye cages' in Turfan documents.[14] Similar objects have been discovered in tombs on the Eurasian steppes as far away as Hungary, indicating that the use of eye shades may have been a part of the burial customs of the steppe nomads.

Many of those with the surnames K'ang and Ts'ao had come from Samarkand, Bukhara and Gubdan of Zerafshan district. In Chinese historical literature, these surnames are generally applied to the 'Nine Hu' (Barbarians) of the Chao-wu in Sogdiana district. Their skill as traders made them well known

---

13. Hui, 1959, Ch. 1; see also Litvinsky (ed.), 1992 and Ch. 18.
14. Stein, 1928, Vol. 2, Ch. 19, p. 670; *Texts of the Documents Found in Turfan*, 1981–87, Vol. 2, pp. 61 et seq. See also Litvinsky (ed.), 1992.

FIG. 2. Bezeklyk. Buddhist grottoes.
(Photo: © R.M.N. Paris.)

on the Eurasian plains throughout the Middle Ages. As the intermediaries of inland trade between Europe and Asia, the Sogdians also played an important role in the dissemination of various religions. They were actively engaged in the translation of Buddhist texts and played a key role in the spread of Zoroastrianism and Manichaeism. Zoroastrianism was brought to Turfan during the Kocho Prefecture period and the god Hu T'ien of the local pantheon may, in fact, have been Ohrmazd. The title *sabu* which occurs in documents may well have indicated an administrator in charge of Zoroastrian affairs. Sogdians were also instrumental in the spread of Manichaeism. Manichaean texts written in Sogdian, Middle Persian, Parthian and Old Turkic have been discovered in Turfan (Figs. 3–5), in addition to a fragment in Bactrian and two fragments in Tokharian B.[15] However, most Manichaean texts are posterior to the influx into the Turfan region of the Uighurs, following the dissolution of their empire in Mongolia in 840.

15. Lin, 1987; Litvinsky (ed.), 1992.

312

FIG. 3. Kocho. Manichaean painted book.
(Photo: © Staatliche Museen zu Berlin –
Preussischer Kulturbesitz für Indische Kunst Museum.)

FIG. 4. Kocho. Manichaean painted book.
(Photo: © Staatliche Museen zu Berlin –
Preussischer Kulturbesitz für Indische Kunst Museum.)

FIG. 5. Kocho. Portrait of Mani engraved on a silver dish.
After: S. F. Ol'denburg, *Russkaya Turkestanskaya eskspeditsiya 1909–1910 goda,*
kratkiy predvoritel'niy otchët. St Petersburg, 1914.

In 840 the Uighur Empire of Mongolia was overthrown by another Turkic people, the Kyrgyz. Fifteen of the defeated Uighur tribes fled west to settle around Kucha, Karashahr and Kocho and, in *c.* 850, finally established themselves in the Turfan basin with Kocho as its capital. In their new land, the Uighurs abandoned nomadism for agriculture and adopted a sedentary way of life. They played a major role in the Turkicization of Chinese Turkestan.

The old religion, Manichaeism, continued to flourish but was progressively replaced by Buddhism. The Uighurs introduced a new cursive script adapted from the Sogdian Letters, which was later adopted by the Mongols. Archaeological discoveries at the beginning of the twentieth century have demonstrated the high level attained by Uighur culture in the Turfan region: a large number of the manuscripts (written in 24 different scripts) date from the late ninth century. Wang Yan-te, an envoy of the Sung court, visited Kocho between 981 and 984 and was impressed by its highly colourful and civilized way of life.

In 1209 the *idi-kut* Barchuk, ruler of the Uighur kingdom of Kocho, voluntarily submitted to Chinggis Khan as his vassal. As the first teachers of the Mongols, the Uighur scribes performed a valuable service in helping the Mongols organize their administration.

NORTHERN NOMADS*

L. R. Kyzlasov

In the first five centuries A.D. tribes of various origins, who were mostly herdsmen, inhabited the wide open spaces of the Eurasian steppes between the Caspian Sea in the west and the Great Wall of China in the east. Many of them were semi-nomadic, others were stock-breeders and farmers and some were agriculturalists who kept cattle. These economic differences resulted from the great variations in the geographical environment, ranging from the arid plateaux of the steppe to oases along great rivers and lakes.

Written sources, especially in Chinese, provide the most detailed information about the history of the people who lived in the steppes. Unfortunately, the tumuli in the steppes dating back to the first five centuries have not yet been subjected to detailed archaeological investigation, nor are there any local epigraphic sources.

K'ang-chü

The most extensive and stable state in the west of this region was K'ang (the ancient Kangha in the *Avesta* or K'ang-chü in the Chinese chronicles). Some scholars believe that the K'ang-chü state was centred on oases situated between the upper and lower reaches of the River Syr Darya (Jaxartes),[1] known in ancient times as the River Kanga. During the early period, the power of the rulers of K'ang-chü extended to the territories of Transoxania and the valley of the River Zerafshan, while in the north there were vassal states, the largest of which was Yen-ts'ai. According to the Chinese chronicles, by the second century it

---

* See Map 6.
1. Litvinsky, 1968, pp. 14–15; Groot, 1921, pp. 5–15. See also Zuev, 1957; Hulsewé and Loewe, 1979, pp. 123–31.

had been renamed Alania and was dependent on K'ang-chü.[2] Alania was situated between the Caspian Sea and the Aral Sea.

A military and political alliance between the Sarmatian and Alan tribes living between the lower reaches of the Volga and the Aral Sea was formed under the name of Yen-ts'ai–Alania. It consisted mainly of semi-nomadic herdsmen speaking Iranian languages. According to Chinese sources, their customs and costume were similar to those of the inhabitants of K'ang-chü and their forces were 100,000 strong. The climate of their country was temperate, and there were many pine trees and large areas of broom and feather-grass. According to sixth-century sources, the Alanian region of Yen-ts'ai was renamed Su-te or Su-i and the Hsiung-nu from Central Asia took possession of it (apparently in the second century). It is reported that large numbers of merchants from Su-te came to trade in the Chinese region of Lanzhou, and in 564 envoys from that land came to China bearing gifts.

In K'ang-chü itself, which lay north-west of Ta-yüan (Ferghana), although there were many semi-nomadic herdsmen, most of the Iranian-speaking population were reported to be farmers and craftsmen. The inhabitants of the region were said to lead a settled life, have towns, cultivate the land and breed livestock. Originally all the territories were dependent on the great Hsiung-nu power. The sources mention that in the first century B.C. dissent among the Hsiung-nu leaders weakened their power and Chih-chih (56–36 B.C.), a rebellious *shan-yü* (ruler) of the Hsiung-nu, sought refuge for a short time in K'ang-chü and was killed there. K'ang-chü is still mentioned in fifth-century sources, but in the sixth century instead of K'ang-chü we find five principalities which, as the chronicles stress, were situated in the 'former territories of K'ang-chü'.[3]

The Huns

During the middle and the second half of the second century, the Greek authors Dionysius and Ptolemy mention the presence of Huns on the Caspian coast among the 'Scythians and Caspians'. In the scholarly literature, the Huns appearing on the European horizon are often considered a branch of the Hsiung-nu which had migrated to the West when the united Hsiung-nu power disintegrated in the first century. This view has been seriously challenged and has been the subject of controversy since the eighteenth century. According to the Roman historian Ammianus Marcellinus, the Huns, 'this restless and untamed

---

2. Hulsewé and Loewe, 1979, p. 129, No. 316; see also Maenchen-Helfen, 1944–45, p. 230; Shiratori, 1956, p. 232.
3. Bichurin, 1950, pp. 149–275. K'ang-chü was divided into five principalities in antiquity; see Hulsewé and Loewe, 1979, pp. 130–1; McGovern, 1939, p. 400; Pulleyblank, 1966, p. 28; Enoki, 1956, p. 47, No. 25.

people, burning with uncontrolled passion to seize the property of others, as they advanced, robbing and slaughtering neighbouring peoples, came to the Alans'. The Alans were routed, and most of them fled from the Aral Sea region and the lower reaches of the Volga to the northern Caucasus. There also, however, they were subject to the Huns and Alanian detachments were incorporated into the Hun forces. The works of Armenian historians contain hints of a struggle between the peoples of the Caucasus and the Later Huns in the third and fourth centuries.

In the 370s a mass of nomadic tribes, united by the Huns in a powerful alliance, burst into Europe and, in 375, attacked the Eastern Goths.[4] Ammianus Marcellinus describes the Hun invasion in the following terms: 'This race of untamed men, without encumbrances, aflame with an inhuman desire for plundering others' property, made their violent way amid the rapine and slaughter of the neighbouring peoples . . . '.[5] The language of the Huns is unknown. According to Ammianus Marcellinus, they were a new tribe about which 'ancient works know little'. He was a bitter enemy of the Huns and extremely biased in his descriptions of them. Nevertheless, we can deduce from his information that the Hun army was well organized and presented a formidable threat. Their forces were generally victorious and nothing could stem their advance.

There are grounds for presuming that the Western Huns, like the Hsiungnu of Central Asia, had a clear-cut military and administrative system, with subdivisions into groups of tens, hundreds, thousands and tens of thousands. This warrior people had hereditary rulers.

> And when deliberation is called for about weighty matters [writes Ammianus Marcellinus], they all consult for a common object . . . No one in their country ever plows a field or touches a plow-handle. They are all without fixed abode, without hearth, or lax, or settled mode of life, and keep roaming from place to place, like fugitives, accompanied by the wagons in which they live; in wagons their wives weave for them their hideous garments, in wagons they cohabit with their husbands, bear children, and rear them to the age of puberty. None of their offspring, when asked, can tell you where he comes from, since he was conceived in one place, born far from there, and brought up still farther away . . . They dress in linen cloth or in the skins of field-mice sewn together, and they wear the same clothing indoors and out . . . They cover their heads with round caps and protect their hairy legs with goatskins; their shoes are formed upon no lasts, and so prevent their walking with free step.[6]

The Western Huns had lived in conditions of constant war and mass migration. When they reached central Europe, however, they settled in Pannonia.

In the early 350s peoples known as the White Huns or Chionites appeared in Central Asia. Several scholars believe that they spoke a language of

---

4. Maenchen-Helfen, 1973, pp. 18–168.
5. Rolfe, 1939, p. 387.
6. Ibid., pp. 383–7.

the Iranian group and had come south from the Aral Sea area. These warlike semi-nomadic herdsmen took part in raids on Sasanian Iran and even on the northern regions of India. They founded several principalities in Central Asia and India. Remains of their original towns and settlements have been found in the lower reaches of the Syr Darya (the sites of the Dzhety-Asar group) (for details, see Chapters 5 and 6).

The Hsien-pi

When the ruler of the Northern Hsiung-nu was beaten by Chinese forces in 91 and fled in an unknown direction, a new people,

> the Hsien-pi, took the opportunity to migrate, and settled on his territories. The remaining Hsiung-nu clans, which numbered more than 100,000 yurts, began to call themselves Hsien-pi, and from that time on the Hsien-pi began to gather strength.

According to the Chinese chronicles, the Hsien-pi originated in a land of forests and high mountains near the basin of the River Amur. Their language and customs are described as similar to those of the Wu-huan, except that before a wedding they first shaved their heads, then held a large assembly on the river during the last month of spring; they feasted, and once the feasting was over, celebrated the marriage. Wild birds and beasts not to be found in the Middle Kingdom of China lived in the territories of the Hsien-pi, who made bows out of horns. There were also sables, foxes and squirrels with soft fur, from which fur coats renowned for their beauty were made in the Celestial Kingdom. The breeding of cattle, sheep, goats and horses by the Hsien-pi is also mentioned and they are said frequently to rustle each other's herds of livestock and horses.

The Hsien-pi were described by one of the Chinese emperor's councillors in 117 as follows:

> After the Hsiung-nu fled, the Hsien-pi, who took over their former territories, grew in strength. They have hundreds of thousands of warriors, they are remarkable for their physical strength, and are more quick-witted than the Hsiung-nu. It should also be noted that, as a result of lack of discipline at the guard-posts on the line of fortifications, there are many ways of evading the embargo, which robbers use to obtain fine metal and iron of good quality. The Chinese get in [through these gaps] and become the main counsellors of the Hsien-pi, and so they acquire keener weapons and faster horses than the Huns.

During the reign of the Han emperor Huang-ti (146–168), an energetic leader named T'an-shih-huai appeared among the Hsien-pi. He subjected the elders to his authority, introduced laws, gathered large forces and defeated the Northern Hsiung-nu around 155.

> All the elders of the eastern and western nomadic communities submitted to him. As a result of this he looted the lands along the line of fortifications, repulsed the Ting-

ling in the north, made the Fu-yü kingdom retreat in the east, attacked the Wu-sun in the west, and took possession of all the former Hsiung-nu territories, which extended for more than 14,000 *li* to the east and the west, were intersected by mountains and rivers, and had large numbers of fresh and salt water lakes.

Thus the territories of the Hsien-pi extended as far as those settled by the Wu-sun in the Ili basin in the west, while in the north they adjoined those of the Ting-ling alliance of tribes which occupied the Altai mountains, the basins of the upper and middle Yenisey and the areas adjoining and to the west of Lake Baikal.

During the Hsien-pi period, culture in Central Asia declined and society regressed compared with the Hsiung-nu state which preceded it. Many towns and settlements which had flourished during Hsiung-nu rule appear to have died out, craft production declined and centres of agricultural activity vanished (or at least the written sources which describe the Hsien-pi make no mention of them).

During their heyday, the Hsiung-nu *shan-yüs* had been recognized as Sons of Heaven and the equals of the emperors of Han China, and Chinese historians considered their state to be comparable in strength and power with the Middle Kingdom. When the might of the Hsien-pi was at its greatest, the emperor Huang-ti is reported to have sent an envoy with a seal and cord granting T'an-shih-huai the title of *wang* (prince) and seeking to conclude a peace treaty with him on the basis of kinship. T'an-shih-huai unhesitatingly rejected these advances, refusing to accept a tributary relationship with the Han emperor.

The history of the Eastern (Later) Han dynasty (24–220) is full of information and complaints about the Hsien-pi raids on the frontier districts and territories of China. These areas suffered greatly from robbery, mass murders and the abduction of vast numbers of people into captivity. One of the sources gives the following explanation for these raids:

> The number of the Hsien-pi increased every day, and stock-breeding and hunting could no longer satisfy their needs for food. T'an-shih-huai therefore rode out to inspect his lands. He saw the River Wu-huo-ching, extending for several hundred *li*. There were large numbers of fish in the creeks, but the Hsien-pi did not know how to catch them. When he heard that the inhabitants of Vozhen were skilled in catching fish with nets, T'an-shih-huai attacked this land on the east, captured over 1,000 families and resettled them on the banks of the River Ukhotsin, ordering them to catch fish in order to make up the insufficiency of food.

It is clear that the Hsien-pi did not even consider engaging in agriculture or crafts.[7]

There is no evidence that the Hsien-pi expanded to the west or north. All their efforts appear to have been directed to the south, to the rich districts of

7. Taskin, 1984, pp. 70–80.

northern China. By the end of the rule of the Eastern Han in 220, the Hsien-pi, together with other nomad armies, had advanced as far as the basin of the River Liaohe and some of their tribes (A-zha in Tibetan literature) had even migrated to Gansu and Chinghai. Tens of thousands of Hsien-pi had settled over the Central Plain and other inner regions of China by the end of the third century. The largest ethnic groups among them were the Mu-jung, T'o-pa (Tabgach) and Yü-wen.

Nomad kingdoms of northern China

These nomadic settlers enjoyed great military strength and founded their own kingdoms in northern China. Of the various kingdoms established by the Hsien-pi in northern China, the Northern Wei (386–534), founded by the T'o-pa leader T'o-pa Kui, became particularly strong. T'o-pa Kui is said to have pacified the people and devoted his attention to agriculture. The Hsien-pi who settled in the Northern Wei kingdom rapidly made the transition from a patriarchal slave-owning society to the feudal system. They later assimilated with the Chinese.[8]

The Late Hsiung-nu realm of Yüeh-pan, described by the sources as situated 'to the north-west of Wu-sun' (in the present-day district of Tarbagatai), was one of the districts belonging to the *shan-yü* of the Northern Hsiung-nu. In 93, when the Northern *shan-yü* had migrated westwards over the mountains to K'ang-chü:

> the weaker nomads who were not up to following them remained in the north of Kucha. They occupy an area of several thousand *li*, and number up to 200,000 . . . Their customs and language are the same as those of the Kao-chü [i.e. Turkic-speaking tribes], but they are better groomed . . . They trim their hair and make their eyebrows even, applying a paste to them which makes them glossy. They wash three times a day before eating.

The Juan-juan

The inhabitants of Yüeh-pan waged war against the Juan-juan. In 449:

> their ruler sent an envoy to the court with gifts, and he also sent a remarkable physician . . . It was said that in their state there were sorcerers who could produce long periods of rain, great storms and even flooding during Juan-juan attacks. Two-tenths – or perhaps as many as three-tenths – of the Juan-juan drowned or died of cold . . . Afterwards the ruler always sent envoys with gifts.[9]

8. Shan, 1959, pp. 138–41.
9. Bichurin, 1950, Vol. 2, pp. 258–60.

The Juan-juan became known as a distinct ethnic group from the end of the third century. Constantly attacked by the Wei kingdom, the Juan-juan manoeuvred in the Gobi until, at the end of the fourth century, they overcame the Kao-chü (see pages 323 et seq.) who lived to the north of the desert. Their ruler, She-lun, settled on the River Khalkha.

> Here for the first time he established military laws, according to which 1,000 men formed a detachment under an appointed commander, and 100 men made up a 'banner' under an appointed leader. The prisoners and booty taken were granted to the man who first broke into the ranks of the enemy . . . They had no written alphabet, so that they could not keep written records, but later they learnt to make records well by making notches in wood . . . She-lun earned the epithet of powerful and prosperous. He bred livestock, moving from place to place, wherever he could find water and grass.
>
> Further to the west of his territories were the lands of Yen-ch'i [Karashahr], and the lands of Ch'ao-hsien; in the north his realm occupied all the sandy desert and reached Hanhai [the upper reaches of the Amur], and in the south approached the Great Desert. He held all the small countries as if they were on a leash, and they were subject to him. Because of this, She-lun assumed the local title of *ch'iu-tou-fa kaghan*: in the language of the Wei dynasty, *ch'iu-tou-fa* means 'ruling and leading to expansion' and *kaghan* means 'emperor'.

Around 400 the Juan-juan established a powerful empire (402–555) in Mongolia.[10] From 402 onwards, Juan-juan forces made regular incursions on the frontier districts of northern China; in the ensuing wars, which lasted for several decades, sometimes the Juan-juan were victorious and sometimes the Northern Wei. At the beginning of the fifth century the Juan-juan repeatedly attacked the Wu-sun state, situated in Semirechye, driving the local tribes of herdsmen out to the Pamir mountains.

According to the Chinese chronicles, the Juan-juan:

> graze their livestock, going from place to place in search of water and grass. They live in dome-shaped huts. They plait their hair. They wear narrow-sleeved silk robes with woven patterns, tight trousers and high waterproof boots. In their land they suffer from cold, and as early as the seventh moon ice-floes float on the rivers, blocking their course.
>
> In their realm they use sorcery to offer sacrifices to heaven and call up a wind that brings snow. [As a result], ahead of them the sun shines brightly and behind them there are streams of muddy water. Because of this, when they are defeated it is impossible to catch up with them.

Another chronicle reports:

> They do not have towns surrounded with inner and outer walls, but herd livestock, going from place to place in search of water and grass. Their homes are felt tents, which they take to the place where they stop. There is no green grass in the steppes,

---

10. Sinor, 1969, pp. 97–9.

the climate is cold, the horses and cattle chew dry grass and lick the snow, but are naturally fat and strong. The administration of the state is simple. There are no official written documents, and they keep records by making notches in wood.

The Juan-juan *kaghans* and nobles were well acquainted with Buddhist teachings and were probably Buddhists as early as the beginning of the sixth century. It is known that in 511 they sent a Buddhist monk and preacher to China with the gift of an image of the Buddha ornamented with pearls for the emperor.

It was at this time that the Juan-juan are reported to have first built a town: they surrounded it with inner and outer walls and called it Mumo-chen. They also gradually learnt to write, and by now there were many learned people among them.

It may be assumed that by then some of the Juan-juan already lived a settled life and practised agriculture. The original sources repeatedly mention that their *kaghans* obtained 'seed millet' from China (some 10,000 *shi* each time). This shows that the Juan-juan society and state had gradually developed from nomadic herding to a settled agricultural way of life, from yurts to the building of houses and monumental architecture, from the nomadic district to towns. They had invented their own system of writing and developed their own local culture and Buddhist learning flourished.

The Juan-juan state was undoubtedly multi-ethnic, but there is no definite evidence as to their language. As the ancient sources regard the Juan-juan as a separate branch of the Hsiung-nu, it may be assumed that the Juan-juan language belonged to the same linguistic family as that of the Hsiung-nu (whose language is also unknown). Some scholars link the Central Asian Juan-juan with the Avars (see also page 323) who came to Europe from the east in the mid-sixth century. According to a widespread but unproven and probably unjustified opinion, the Avars spoke a language of the Turkic group.

During the late years of their rule in Central Asia, the Juan-juan contracted to guard the frontiers of northern China, with whose court they were allied by marriage. In 538 the daughter of the Juan-juan *kaghan* A-na-kui became empress of the Western Wei kingdom (535–556). In 535 a princess from the Eastern Wei kingdom (534–550) married A-na-kui, and in 545 the real ruler of the Eastern Wei married another of A-na-kui's daughters. A relative peace was thus established on the frontiers of northern China. The previous constant wars with China had exhausted the human and economic resources of the *kaghanate* and led to internal revolts and risings of the peoples subjugated by it.

The Türks

Among these peoples the Türks, who lived on the Altai and supplied the Juan-juan with ferrous metal products such as iron blooms, tools and weapons, became particularly powerful in the 530s. The rising of the Türks, who at about that time were joined by the T'ieh-le nomads (with up to 50,000 wagons), was crowned with success. In 552 the Juan-juan *kaghan* A-na-kui was routed by the Türks and committed suicide.[11] In the period before 555 the Türks and the Chinese had killed large numbers of Juan-juan who were fleeing to China and westward towards the Aral Sea. A new state, the Türk *Kaghanate* (552–630, 683–745), was established in Mongolia (see Chapter 14).

It was precisely at this time that the first information about the Avars being pursued by the Türks appears in Western chronicles. In *c*. 562, for example, the Byzantine historian Menander Protector[12] wrote that Silziboulos, the ruler of the Türks, having learnt of the Avars' retreat after an attack on the Türks, sent the following message to Byzantium:

> The Avars are not birds, to escape Türk swords by flying through the air; they are not fish, to dive into the water and disappear in the depths of the sea; they wander over the surface of the earth. When I finish the war with the Hephthalites I shall attack the Avars, and they will not escape my forces.

According to Menander, in 568 the emperor Justin II asked a Türk who was visiting Constantinople: 'Tell us how many Avars have cast off Türk rule, and whether you still have any Avars.' He was told that: 'There are Avars who are still faithful to us; we suppose that up to 20,000 have fled from us.' The Türks also called the Avars 'Ouarchonites' and regarded them as their subjects. As mentioned previously, from these facts some scholars conclude that the Avars, sometimes known as Ouar, Koun or Ouarchonites, are the same people as the Juan-juan.

The T'ieh-le and Kao-chü

The T'ieh-le group was the strongest and largest of the various tribes subject to the Juan-juan *Kaghanate*. According to the Chinese chronicles, of the 15 tribes belonging to the T'ieh-le, some were the descendants of the Hsiung-nu. Those tribes whom the Chinese called Kao-chü (High Chariot) were regarded as the closest to the T'ieh-le in terms of ethnic composition. The Chinese sources provide a fairly detailed picture of the Kao-chü, who were apparently the last surviving branch of the ancient Chidi. Originally known as the Ting-ling, in

11. Taskin, 1984, pp. 267–95.
12. Blockley, 1985.

the north they were called the Chi-lei, and in China the Kao-chü Ting-ling (High Chariot Ting-ling).

The Kao-chü were constantly at war with the Juan-juan and also frequently attacked and plundered the borders of the Wei state. In 397 the Kao-chü, together with the Juan-juan, became subject to T'o-pa Kui, who founded the Northern Wei dynasty. When T'o-pa Kui declared himself emperor the following year, the Kao-chü confirmed their subjection to him. At the end of the fourth century their territories situated to the north of the 'sandy steppe' (i.e. the Gobi) were seized by the first Juan-juan *kaghan*, She-lun (402–410).

From the end of the fourth to the beginning of the fifth century the Northern Wei launched 9 successive campaigns against the Kao-chü, taking prisoners and reportedly seizing over 200,000 head of horses, cattle and sheep. Finding themselves between two fires, the Kao-chü were later forced to surrender to the Northern Wei forces. Several hundred thousand yurts, with more than a million head of horses, cattle and sheep, were resettled to the south of the desert.

The Kao-chü later tried to exploit the disagreements between the Juan-juan and the Northern Wei kingdom to gain their independence. In 487 the Kao-chü leader A-fu-chi-lo raised a revolt against the Juan-juan and migrated westwards at the head of 100,000 warriors. He established a kingdom (487–541) to the north-west of the present-day Turfan and there he declared himself a *wang* (prince). In his message to the Northern Wei court, A-fu-chi-lo describes the situation in these terms:

> The Juan-juan rob the Son of Heaven. I exhorted them, but they would not listen to me, and therefore I stirred up a revolt, travelled to the territory I now occupy, and declared myself ruler. In the interests of the Son of Heaven I must punish and annihilate the Juan-juan.

The Kao-chü state lasted for 55 years and won a number of victories over the Juan-juan forces, but quarrels broke out among the Kao-chü nobles. A-fu-chi-lo was killed and Mieh-tu was made ruler. On his accession to the throne, Mieh-tu began to send tribute to the court of the Wei dynasty again.

War then broke out with the Juan-juan, in which the latter were victorious and killed Mieh-tu. The Juan-juan *kaghan* Ch'ou-nu covered Mieh-tu's skull with black lacquer and made it into a drinking goblet. During the reign of the new rulers of the Kao-chü, I-fu, Yüeh-ch'u and Pi-shih, war between the Kao-chü and the Juan-juan continued from 520 to 542, with success now on one side, now on the other.

Despite all these failures, the Kao-chü, who are known as the T'ieh-le in later Chinese chronicles (see the *T'ang shu*, for example), did not give up the idea of founding their own state. In 536 the first Türk *kaghan*, Bumin, attacked the T'ieh-le and captured as many as 50,000 wagons. Even after the incorporation of the T'ieh-le into the Türk state, they continued their struggle for freedom. They waged war with the Türks from 602 to 605, and in 618 were subjugated by the Türk ruler, T'ung *yabghu*. The chronicles state that 'the Türks performed feats of valour with their forces in the deserts of the north'.[13]

The T'ieh-le tribes were numerous. The best known among them at a later stage were the Hsieh-yen-to, the Qurigan and the Uighurs, who created their own states. Although they spoke Turkic languages, their origins and culture differed from all the other Turkic-speaking peoples of the Middle Ages. During the early sixth century the entire Eurasian steppe zone came under the power of the Türk *Kaghanate*. Turkic gradually took the place of several Iranian languages, some of which ceased to be used.

Archaeological evidence

The archaeological remains of the ethnic groups which inhabited the steppe zones in the first five centuries A.D. such as the Hsien-pi, Yüeh-pan, Juan-juan and Kao-chü or T'ieh-le have not yet been studied in depth. However, remains from the first to the fifth century, presumably connected with the Western and White Huns, are partially known to archaeologists. It appears that their nobility wore richly adorned garments in what is called the polychrome style, made of gold and decorated with many inset semi-precious stones and patterns in *cloisonné* enamel. Examples of richly decorated weapons, harness, 'Hun-type' cast bronze cauldrons and other articles have been found far to the west.

The tombs of nobles, containing articles in the above-mentioned style, have been discovered over a wide area reaching from the T'ien Shan and the Altai in the east to Pannonia and the sources of the Danube in the west. The most thoroughly studied antiquities are those of Hungary, the Danube area and the steppes adjoining the Black Sea to the west of the Volga. As for the northern region of the steppes, we have some knowledge of the antiquities of the areas around the lower Volga, the Aral Sea and the lower reaches of the Syr Darya, where the Alans and White Huns lived.

The wide steppes of Kazakstan, Mongolia and Dzungaria, however, are still blank spaces in the archaeological map of the first five centuries. Much further investigation of both archaeological and written sources will be required before we know where the various northern semi-nomadic peoples lived and understand their economy, way of life and culture.

---

13. Bichurin, 1950, Vol. 1, pp. 228, 243, 279, 283, 301; Taskin, 1984, pp. 278–9, 401–6.

THE TÜRK EMPIRE*

D. Sinor and S. G. Klyashtorny

Part One

THE FIRST TÜRK EMPIRE (553–682)

(D. Sinor)

The two centuries during which the Türks were the dominant power in Inner Asia would seem to mark a turning point since, for the first time in recorded history, an essentially nomad empire bordered simultaneously on three major sedentary civilizations: those of China, Iran, and the Western world as represented by Byzantium. A more or less permanent link was established between these three civilizations, allowing the free flow of trade and with it, one must presume, a range of ideas and information.

There are other reasons for attaching great importance to the emergence of the Türks: not only were they the first Altaic people to leave behind indigenous historical documents; they were also the first Altaic people to leave behind documents written in an Altaic language, namely Turkic – these constitute the earliest textual evidence of any Altaic language. It follows from these two points that the Türks were the first people to form a major nomad empire centred on present-day Mongolia whose language can be established with absolute certainty. The attribution of a given language to any of the earlier great nomad empires (such as, for instance, that of the Hsiung-nu or the Juan-juan) remains highly speculative. Finally, the Türks became the eponymous people of all the Turks who followed them throughout history. We are particularly fortunate in that the history and civilization of the Türks can be studied through a variety of written sources, including Chinese, Persian, Armenian, Greek and Latin texts, in addition to the indigenous Türk or Sogdian inscriptions.

Ethnogenesis

In terms of political history, the Türks entered the scene in 552 with the revolt of the Türk *kaghan* (chief) Bumin, who overthrew the Juan-juan Empire of

* See Map 7.

which his people had, up to then, formed an integral part. For the period preceding this fateful event, we must rely on the (often self-contradictory) testimony of Chinese sources.

According to the *Chou shu*, 'No doubt the Türks are a detached branch of the Hsiung-nu,' an opinion taken over verbatim by the *Pei-shih*. But the *Chou shu* also relates 'another tradition' according to which the Türks 'originated in the country of So, located north of the Hsiung-nu'. Since the location of So cannot be established, the information is of little use and simply shows that, according to this 'other tradition', the Türks were not a part of the Hsiung-nu confederation. Moreover, Chinese sources are wont to attribute Hsiung-nu origin to any people belonging to the vast group of Northern or Western Barbarians. Indeed, such an indication may almost be considered a simple stylistic device, just as Greek sources would attribute Scythian origins to any nomad people appearing on the steppe.

More importantly, Chinese sources record at least three different legends concerning the origin of the Türks. The first of these, which we may call that of 'The Abandoned Child Brought up by a Wolf', is related with slight variations by both the *Chou shu* and the *Pei-shih*. It tells the story of a young boy mutilated by the enemy and thrown into a marsh where he has intercourse with a she-wolf. The wolf and the boy subsequently take refuge in a cavern, where the wolf gives birth to ten boys. Several generations later the Türks emerge from the cavern and become the blacksmiths of the Juan-juan. There is another legend, also related in the *Chou shu*, which, in the words of this source, 'differs from the other [legend], nevertheless it shows that [the Türks] descended from a wolf'.

A third legend is preserved only in a collection of anecdotes, curious and miraculous histories probably compiled in 860 and entitled the *Yu-yang tsa-tsu*. According to this legend, which we may call that of 'The Spirit of the Lake', the ancestor of the Türks, who is called Shê-mo-shê-li and lives in a cavern, has a liaison with the daughter of the lake spirit. One day, as the Türks are preparing for a great hunt, the girl says to Shê-mo: 'Tomorrow during the hunt a white deer with golden horns will come out from *the cavern where your ancestors were born* [author's emphasis]. If your arrow hits the deer we will keep in touch as long as you live, but if you miss it our relationship will end.' In the course of the hunt, a follower of Shê-mo kills the deer. Shê-mo angrily decapitates the culprit and orders that a human sacrifice be established in which a man of that follower's tribe be beheaded. According to the *Yu-yang tsa-tsu*, the sacrifice remained in practice 'to this day'.

There is no reason to impugn the authenticity of these legendary traditions, which clearly reveal the composite ethnic character of the Türks. The three legends differ in so many essential points (which cannot be examined here in detail) that they cannot possibly represent a single tradition.

The theme of the 'wolf' in two of the three Türk legends is shared with the Wu-sun, who preceded the Türk Empire by many centuries. Also shared with the Wu-sun is the theme of the mutilated child abandoned in the wilderness by the enemy. According to the *Shih-chi*, the Wu-sun ruler K'un-mo was cast out to die when still a baby, but was nourished by birds that brought him meat and by a wolf that suckled him. The story is also related in the *Han shu* and its close relationship with one of the Türk origin myths is obvious. There is, however, the significant difference that, whereas in the Wu-sun myth the wolf saves the ancestor of the tribe, it is not – as in the case of the Türks – the ancestor of the people. (The connections with Mongol myths, though undeniable, should not concern us here.)

The theme of the 'cavern' that appears in two of the three Türk ancestral legends has its parallels in later Mongol mythology. More importantly, it establishes a link between the Türks and the Kyrgyz, whose ancestor, according to the *Yu-yang tsa-tsu*, 'lived in a cavern to the north of the Kögmän mountain'. According to the same source, however, 'the Kyrgyz do not belong to the race of the wolf'.

There is convincing evidence to show that Türk ceremonial practices took into account the existence of these two themes, namely those of the cavern and the wolf. For example, the *Pei-shih* clearly states that, 'In front of the gate to the camp [the Türks] placed a standard with a wolf's head on it, so as to show that they had not forgotten their origins.' This is confirmed by the *Chou shu*: '[The Türks] put golden wolves' head on their standards . . . The Türks descended from a wolf and did not want to forget their origin.' A bas-relief on the Sogdian Bugut inscription (see pages 342 and 343) erected by Türk rulers represents a she-wolf with a small human figure under her belly and thus supports the evidence of written sources. The present author ventures the hypothesis that the 'wolf theme' represents an Indo-European, perhaps Iranian, element in the Türk system of beliefs linking at least some sections of the Türk ruling class to the Sogdians and, beyond them, to the Wu-sun who – for all we know – may have been Iranians. At the same time, it must be emphatically stated that the widely accepted view according to which the Wu-sun had blue eyes and blond hair rests on a textual misunderstanding, as was shown by Otto Franke as early as 1904.

Nor is the theme of the cavern a literary invention: it was a belief actively held by the Türks. The *Yu-yang tsa-tsu* even gives the name of the cavern (A-shih-tê), which is that of a Türk clan of great importance, a perennial antagonist of the A-shih-na clan, whose claim to rule the Türks is clearly implied by the other two legends. The legend of 'The Spirit of the Lake' speaks of a 'birth cavern' and the existence of such an 'ancestral cavern' is demonstrated by the *Chou shu*'s statement that every year the Türk *kaghan* leads the notables of his people 'to the ancestral cavern to offer a sacrifice'. The *Tung tien* (193, 14a) cites from a work (now, alas, lost) entitled *On the Origin and Development of the Türks* in which the caverns of the Türks were also mentioned.

Of the various themes which can be identified in the Türk ancestral legends, those of the wolf and the cavern appear together only in one, namely, 'The Abandoned Child Brought up by a Wolf', which justifies the rule of the A-shih-na clan. The theme of the cavern also appears in 'The Spirit of the Lake', though this story differs so fundamentally from the other two legends that it cannot be ascribed to the same clan. It is just possible – and the suggestion is made with the utmost caution – that this theme indicates some links with the Kyrgyz.

The composite character of the Türk nation, as revealed by an examination of their ancestral legends, is supported by evidence of a different nature. Türk civilization as we know it from the written sources contained a number of specific elements which are atypical for Turkic peoples. Among them were, first, a system of orientation facing east; and, second, an unusual system of numerals where, in double-digit numbers, the tens are indicated by the next highest multiple of ten, e.g. *bir otuz* '21' (= one thirty), and which cannot be of Turkic origin.

It has been established beyond doubt that the population of the Türk Empire was multilingual – the existence of the Bugut inscription, written in Sogdian, would in itself prove this point. It has also been shown that Türk – as used in the inscriptions of the Orkhon – contains a number of Samoyed or Ugric loan words which are specific to this language and form no part of the common Turkic vocabulary. Even in the solemn, funerary style of these inscriptions, Ugric or Samoyed words appear, expressing concepts as common as 'word' (*ay*, *sab*) or, indeed, 'horse' (*yunt*). Their occurrence in Türk indicates the presence of Ugric or Samoyed elements in that stratum of Türk society which had some cultural influence on the ruling class. It can be taken for granted that the language of the funerary inscriptions (be it Sogdian as in Bugut, or Turkic as on the Orkhon) was that of the contemporary ruling class. Reference in the Orkhon inscriptions to a feminine deity, Umay, of clearly Mongol origin, attests to the presence of some Mongol element within the fabric of early Türk civilization.

Türk personal names appear in a great variety of sources and scripts which, apart from Türk itself, include Chinese, Sogdian and Greek. No methodical, comprehensive study of these names has been undertaken, but even a cursory examination of Türk anthroponyms reveals a substantial number which cannot be explained from Turkic. It is seldom easy to reconstruct the original form of a proper name that is attested only in Chinese transcription. Nevertheless there have been several successful attempts, particularly in instances where the language to which the name belongs is known – as, for example, with Chinese transcriptions of Buddhist technical terms. However, the original Turkic forms of many Türk proper names have not yet been established. Such is the case, for example, of the clan names A-shih-na or A-shih-tê (attempts to see in the former a Mongol (?) word meaning 'wolf' lack proper phonetic foundations). Nor has a satisfactory Turkic form been established for the Türk personal name that is written as Silziboulos in Greek characters.

In several instances (for example, Nivar *kaghan*; see page 333) the personal names of Türk dignitaries are clearly non-Turkic – with the exception of a few, clearly specified cases, the initial *n-* does not occur in Old Turkic. It is well known that a Turkic word cannot begin with a consonant cluster, yet the names of two Türk chiefs appear in Greek sources as Spartseugoun and Stembis. The latter name is known also in Chinese transcription and occurs in the Orkhon inscriptions either with or without the initial *i-*: *shtmi* or *ishtmi*, to be read Ishtemi. There is no reason why the Greek transcription would have ignored an initial *i-* had the name had one in its original form. There are, however, very good linguistic reasons for the Türks to attach a prosthetic *i-* to an initial *st-* consonant cluster. Clearly, the name Ishtemi, though borne by a Türk ruler (see page 332), was not Turkic. Although a detailed examination of Türk proper names is beyond the scope of the present chapter, it is clear that many of the personal and tribal names and dignitary titles used by the Türks are neither Turkic, nor Mongol, nor Iranian.

The economy

In 552, as previously mentioned, a successful Türk uprising overthrew the Juan-juan ruler A-na-kui and effectively ended the Juan-juan Empire which, for the previous century and a half, had been the dominant power on the eastern steppe. Bumin, the leader of the coup, is said to have been angered by A-na-kui's refusal to grant him the hand of one of his daughters on the grounds that the suitor was merely a 'blacksmith slave' and thus unworthy of such an honour. There is overwhelming evidence that the Türks – the people of Bumin – were originally a group of metallurgists engaged in the mining or processing of iron, or possibly both. The above-mentioned 'caverns' of the Türks were, in fact, underground mines where they laboured for the principal benefit of the Juan-juan.

Thus the overthrow of Juan-juan rule was not the result of an invasion by an external enemy but was brought about by an internal upheaval, the revolt of a discontented faction which, ethnically or linguistically, may not have been different from the dominant group. (There is as yet no conclusive evidence as to the language of the Juan-juan – it might even have been Turkic.) The only distinction between the Juan-juan and the Türks which can be established with any degree of certainty relates to occupation. To put it in simple terms, through Bumin's action the reins of power were seized by the metallurgists of the Juan-juan Empire.

Although (if for no other reason than military necessity) pastoral nomadism was the dominant economic activity of the ruling stratum of the newly created Türk state, it did not involve the whole population. Besides metallurgy – which, at some time, the Türks seem to have left to the Kyrgyz – important sections of the population must have continued to provide for themselves through hunting and fishing, the traditional economic activities of the forest region where pastoral nomadism could not be practised and where many Türks continued to live. That the leaders were preoccupied with the necessities of daily life is evident from the words on Bilge *kaghan*'s funeral stele: 'I [Bilge] did not reign over a people that was rich; I reigned over a people weak and frightened, a people that had no food in their bellies and no cloth on their backs.' In some campaigns the Türks were even short of horses. The inscription of Tonyuquq (see below) reveals that at least on one occasion 'two parts [of the Türk army] were mounted, one part was on foot'. The very precariousness of their existence made the Türks, or at least their leaders, vulnerable to the lure of those 'Chinese riches' mentioned in the inscriptions.

Political history

Bumin died shortly after he had deposed A-na-kui. He was followed by his son Kuo-lo (Qara?), who ruled for only a few months. On his death, the government of the newly created Türk Empire was divided between Bumin's other son Muhan (553–572) and Ishtemi (553– ?), Muhan's uncle, and brother of the late Bumin. Muhan ruled over the eastern part of the empire, centred on Mongolia, while Ishtemi was in charge of the western areas. The heart of the empire – where the 'ancestral cavern' and Mount Ötükän, the sacred forest of the Türks, were located – was the eastern part. Thus it can be said that almost from the moment of its inception, the Türk Empire was bicephalous.

Uncle and nephew embarked on a series of military campaigns. In the east, this brought victory over the Kitans and the incorporation of the Kyrgyz into the Türk state. In the west, between 557 and 561, the Hephthalite Empire was crushed through a joint action of the Türks (probably led by Ishtemi) and the Sasanian king, Khusrau I Anushirvan, resulting in the establishment of a common border between the two empires. Through their conquests the Türks now controlled large sections of the trade routes to the West and, edged by their Sogdian subjects, they wished to take advantage of the lucrative silk trade formerly dominated by the Hephthalites. After their attempts to establish commercial footholds in Persia met with failure, they aimed to bypass Persia altogether and establish direct links with Byzantium, the principal consumer of silk.

The first Türk delegation known to us arrived in Constantinople in 563. It had been sent by Askel, head of the first tribe of the Nu-shih-pi tribal federation of the Western Türks. It was followed five years later by a more substantial trade delegation headed by a Sogdian called Maniakh. He was received by Emperor Justin II, who was more interested in securing an ally to the rear of the Sasanians (with whom, since 527, Byzantium had been in almost permanent conflict) than in the importation of silk. According to the Byzantine historian Menander, the Türk ruler on whose behalf Maniakh negotiated was Silziboulos (who is usually wrongly identified with Ishtemi, even though this name is rendered Stembis in Greek sources; see above). Silziboulos and his son Turxath were minor rulers in the westernmost parts of the Türk Empire, perhaps on the same level of authority as the previously mentioned Askel. Menander clearly states that Turxath was but one of the eight chiefs among whom rule over the Türks was divided.

On his return journey, Maniakh was accompanied by a Byzantine counter-embassy led by the *strategos* Zemarkhos, who was, in his turn, very well received by Silziboulos. Other diplomatic exchanges followed until 572 when, on his second mission to the Türks, the Byzantine envoy Valentine was received by Turxath (perhaps Türk *shad*), son of the just deceased Silziboulos. In sign of mourning, members of the Byzantine delegation were not only requested to lacerate their faces, but were given a bitterly hostile reception by Turxath, who accused the Byzantine emperor of treason for having given asylum to the Avars (considered by him to be fugitive subjects of the Türks: see Chapter 13). At that time the principal ruler of the Western Frontier Region of the Türk Empire was Tardu, a son of Ishtemi, whose year of accession is unknown, although it cannot have been later than 572 since it was to him that the irate Turxath sent Valentine.

The principal Türk ruler Muhan (553–572) was followed on the throne by his younger brother Taghpar (572–581).[1] Having converted to Buddhism, Taghpar embarked on an ambitious programme of building monasteries and sponsoring the translation of Buddhist canonical works, presumably from Chinese into Sogdian and Turkic. These activities continued under Taghpar's brother, Nivar (581–587) (his name is read Jibü by Harmatta), whose court became an important centre of Buddhist learning. It was at the time of Nivar that the rift separating Eastern and Western Türks occurred, an event which has long been thought to have taken place immediately following the death of Bumin.

At Taghpar's death Muhan's son, Apa *kaghan* (known as Ta-lo-pien in Chinese sources), had not taken kindly to his uncle Nivar occupying the throne. He enlisted the help of Tardu but failed to oust Nivar, who received support from his father-in-law, the Sui emperor Kao-tsu. Obsessed with the desire to have a state of his own, Apa *kaghan* then turned against his former ally Tardu, chased him from his domain and established the state of the Western Türks opposed to that of the eastern parts controlled by Nivar. In 585 Tardu fled to the Sui court; nothing further is known of his activities until 594, when he

---

1. Harmatta's reading instead of the currently used Taspar.

reappeared in a conflict with the Eastern Türk *kaghan*, Yung-yü-lü (588–599). It seems likely that the Türk *kaghan* who, in 598, wrote a letter to the Byzantine emperor Maurice describing himself as 'lord of the seven races, master of the seven climes' was Tardu, once again riding high, ruling over an ill-determined part of Türk territory. The destiny of this extraordinary man remains unknown; chased by a revolt in 603, he fled and we lose his traces for ever.

Apa *kaghan* did not live to enjoy the fruits of his treacherous victory over Tardu. After being taken prisoner by Nivar's successor Ch'u-lo-hu (587–588), he disappeared from the stage of history. His place was taken by Ni-li (587–604?), a somewhat shadowy figure; he may have been the 'Great King of the Türks' who, according to the Armenian historian Sebeos, was killed in battle in 589 by the Sasanian general, Bahram Chobin, while fighting Hormizd IV in Persia. Türk involvement in Iranian affairs continued under T'ung *yabghu* (619–630), *kaghan* of the Western Türks, an ally of Emperor Heraclius against Khusrau II. T'ung *yabghu* received the Chinese pilgrim Hsüan-tsang, who was duly impressed by the magnificence of the Türk court. However, pride and unbridled ambition caused T'ung *yabghu*'s downfall. In the words of the *T'ang shu*, he was no longer 'good to his people and the tribes hated him' and he fell victim to a revolt led by the Karluks.

The Chinese, past masters in the art of fighting Barbarians with Barbarians, exploited the Türks' endemic internal dissensions to the full. In the words of the *Sui shu*, 'The Türks prefer to destroy each other rather than to live side-by-side. They have 1,000, nay 10,000 clans who are hostile and kill one another.' Because, owing to their location, the Eastern Türks presented the greater danger, the short-lived Chinese dynasties of the period attempted to keep them at bay with trade concessions which were tantamount to the paying of tribute. Thus, for example, both Muhan and Taghpar received 100,000 pieces of silk per year from the Northern Chou, a gift barely compensated for by the horses sent to China by Taghpar.

Both Kao-tsu, founder of the T'ang dynasty, and his son T'ai-tsung skilfully played off one Türk ruler against another. Constant attempts were made to persuade T'ung *yabghu* and other Western Türk rulers to keep the Eastern Türk *kaghan*s Shih-pi (609–619) and Hsieh-li (619–634) at bay, but final defeat came through direct Chinese victory. T'ai-tsung's troops routed those of Hsieh-li who, taken prisoner, died in China. With his death, darkness would descend on the Eastern Türk Empire for half a century.

The Western Türk Empire, which was less bothersome for the Chinese, was left to its own devices of self-destruction. Always a confederation of tribes acting more or less independently, the Western Türk state was swiftly falling apart. The Ten Arrows (*On oq*) or, as the Chinese called them, the Ten Clans were rent by the murderous conflicts of their leaders. The Orkhon inscriptions give the reasons for the internal decay:

Because of discord between the nobles and the commoners, because of the cunning and deceitfulness of the Chinese who set against each other younger and elder brothers, nobles and commoners, the Türk people caused the disintegration of the empire that had been their own, [and] caused the ruin of the *kaghan* who had been their *kaghan*.

Ho-lu, the last *de facto* ruler of the Western Türks, was captured by the Chinese in 657 and died two years later, to be buried beside Hsieh-li. Thus the two rulers of the fratricidal Türk empires were put to rest, side-by-side and in Chinese soil.

Part Two

THE SECOND TÜRK EMPIRE (682–745)

(S. G. Klyashtorny)

Resurgence of the Türk Empire

After the First Türk Empire had been defeated by the emperor T'ai-tsung in 630, the Eastern Türk tribes were resettled north of the Ordos and Shansi. T'ai-tsung drafted his new subjects into the service of the T'ang Empire, but the existing tribal and administrative system was not altered and measures were taken to attract the Türk aristocracy to the imperial service. The author of the ancient Türk inscriptions in honour of Kül-tegin (732) notes with disapproval, when speaking of those times, that 'The Türk *begs* abandoned their Türk titles. The *begs* who went to China held Chinese titles, obeyed the Chinese emperor; they served him for fifty years' (KT, E 7–8). For most of the Türk people, forcibly resettled in strictly defined regions, life was hard. The Türk historian recalls those five decades as a time of shame, degradation and humiliation; the heaviest burden was the 'blood tribute', the obligation to fight in the imperial wars: 'Your blood flowed like a river; your bones were heaped up like a mountain; your *beg*-like sons became slaves; your lady-like daughters became servants' (KT, E 23).

The Türk uprising in 679–681 was at first unsuccessful, although it led, in 682, to the withdrawal of Kutlug-chor, one of the Türk leaders of the *kaghan* tribe of the A-shih-na, into the Gobi desert. Once they had established themselves in the Yin Shan mountains (*Čuğay quzï* in ancient Turkic), Kutlug-chor and his closest comrade-in-arms, Tonyuquq, succeeded in winning the support of most of the Türks and conducted successful military operations against the imperial forces in Shansi between 682 and 687. Kutlug-chor

335

proclaimed himself Ilterish *kaghan*, and in so doing ushered in the resurgent Türk Empire.

In 687 Ilterish *kaghan* left the Yin Shan mountains and turned his united and battle-hardened army to the conquest of the Türk heartlands in central and northern Mongolia. Between 687 and 691 the Tokuz-Oghuz tribes and the Uighurs, who had occupied these territories, were routed and subjugated; their chief, Abuz *kaghan*, fell in battle. The centre of the Second Türk Empire shifted to the Ötükän mountains (now called the Khangai mountains), on the rivers Orkhon, Selenga and Tola. Having united two powerful tribal groups under his command – the Türks and the Tokuz-Oghuz – Ilterish *kaghan* was now a dangerous menace to the T'ang Empire.[2]

Political and social structure

Under Ilterish *kaghan* the traditional structure of the Türk state was restored. The empire created by Ilterish and his successors was a territorial union of ethnically related and hierarchically co-ordinated tribes and tribal groups; they were ideologically linked by common beliefs and accepted genealogies, and politically united by a single military and administrative organization (*el*) and by general legal norms (*törüs*). The tribal organization (*bodun*) and the political structure (*el*) complemented one another, defining the strength and durability of social ties; in the words of the Türk inscriptions, the *khan* (*kaghan*) '*el tutup bodunïm bašladïm*' (controlled the state and was head of the tribal group).

The principal group in the empire was composed of twelve Türk tribes headed by the dynastic tribe of the Ashina.[3] Next in political importance was the Tokuz-Oghuz tribal group of 'nine Oghuz [tribes]'.[4] The Tokuz-Oghuz were more numerous than the Türk tribes themselves, but were politically less united; however, at the beginning of the seventh century, they were united under the Uighurs, themselves a group of ten tribes led by the dynastic tribe of the Yaghlakar. Two further confederations of tribes played an active role in the political life of the empire – the Karluks and the Basmils. Each individual tribe had its leader, the *irkin*, and each tribal group was headed by an *elteber*. Türk monuments frequently mention these important representatives of the tribal aristocracy – the *elteber* of the Uighurs, the great *irkin* of the Bayirku, and others.

The administrative structure of the empire, which incorporated the tribal leaders, was more complex. At the head of the administration stood the *kaghan*

2. Klyashtorny, 1964, pp. 25–32.
3. Czeglédy, 1972, pp. 275–81.
4. Czeglédy, 1982, pp. 89–93.

and his closest kinsmen, who held the titles of *shad* and *yabghu*. The *kaghan* was surrounded by his counsellors (*buyur*), who discharged military, administrative, diplomatic and legal functions and bore titles such as *tarkhan*, *chor* and *tudun*. In order to facilitate the administration, the tribes were divided into two territorial groups, the Tardush (western) and the Tölish (eastern). The soldiery of these two groups composed the right and left wings of the army's battle order, and they were led by the close kinsmen of the *kaghan* (the *shad*s) and the most influential tribal leaders of each wing.

With its dual system of tribal and political principles, the administrative structure was a natural reflection of the social structure of the ancient Türk community. Its highest stratum consisted of *begs* (*begler* in Türk), a hereditary aristocracy; it was composed of members of families whose special status in the management of the affairs of the tribe was considered unchallengeable and hallowed by tradition. The dynastic families and tribes (the A-shih-na, the A-shih-tê and the Yaghlakar) formed the élite of this hereditary aristocracy. Another stratum of that same community was the *igil qara bodun* (the 'common people'). Any deterioration of relations between strata or tribes represented a grave threat to the political organization of the empire. The *kaghan*, who personified the unity of the community and exploited its military and economic potential to the full, clearly had a vested interest in minimizing all opposition. As the manifestos recorded in inscriptions dating from the *kaghanate* show, there were frequent appeals for unity between the *begs* and the people and for obedience to the *kaghan*.

Whereas the *kaghan* was the personification and supreme power of the community, its base was the fraternity of full male members of the family and tribe, who were designated *er* (man-warrior). Any youth could become an *er* when he reached a certain age and had accomplished an initiation rite (some exploit in battle or the hunt), receiving his *er aty* (man's or hero's name) whether he was one of the hundreds of common soldiers or a prince of the royal line. In practice, however, the situation of an *er* in the tribe and in the state depended on his rank and riches.

Epigraphic and archaeological records show that there was a considerable degree of social and material discrimination within the Türk tribes. Wealth became a subject of pride and praise for the Türk aristocracy. Rich men (*bays*) are contrasted in Türk inscriptions with the poor (*čyǧay*), who are described as 'pitiful, insignificant and base'. Far from arousing sympathy, poverty was despised. A real *er* would obtain riches by force of arms. The inscriptions often list the spoils of war – gold, silver and slaves, both male and female. The Türks' principal wealth and most coveted booty, however, was livestock, especially herds of horses. 'The Türk people were hungry. I took the cattle and fed them,' says Bilge *kaghan* in his account of one of his campaigns (BK, E 38).

The burial mounds of the common soldiers, where the saddled warhorse lay next to its fully armed master, pale into insignificance when compared to the burial chambers of the higher aristocracy. In the graves of the poorest peasants, however, neither costly weapons nor horses were to be found. Impoverished nomads who had lost their livestock were settled in winter quarters and in small, permanent settlements (*balïqs*), where they engaged in a primitive form of agriculture. They mainly sowed millet and built small forts (*qurgans* or kurgans) in which to store their grain.

Some impoverished members of a tribe would maintain their nomadic way of life with the help of rich relations. Free *ers* of slender means inevitably became dependent on the *begs*, whose bodyguard and servants were drawn from their ranks. But no matter what quarrels soured relations between poor and rich *ers*, and between *begs* and the 'common people', the community as a whole was quite distinct from another sector of the population – the slaves (*qul kün*, male and female slaves), who were entirely dependent on the *ers*, enjoyed no rights and formed the periphery of ancient Türk society.

The basis of the economy of the Türk tribes was nomadic cattle-raising. The organized hunt in the steppes and mountains was of military as well as economic significance: it was during such hunts that warriors were trained and the various detachments were co-ordinated. A Chinese chronicler describes the economy and way of life of the Türks thus: 'They live in felt tents and wander following the water and the grass.' Horses were of vital importance to the Türks. Although the economy rested on cattle-raising, winter feed for livestock was not stored. The advantage of the horse was that it could be at grass all the year round, feeding even under a light cover of snow. Sheep and goats followed the horses, eating the grass that they themselves would have been unable to clear of snow. Bulls, yaks and camels are also frequently mentioned in Türk texts as valuable items of livestock.

Relations with China

In 691 Ilterish *kaghan* died and was succeeded by his younger brother, who assumed the title Kapagan *kaghan* ('Conquering *kaghan*'; Mo-ch'o in Chinese sources). His reign (691–716) marked the apogee of the military and political might of the Second Türk Empire – and the beginning of its decline.

Between 693 and 706 Kapagan's army forced a crossing of the Huang He (Yellow River) six times and made deep inroads into northern China against which the Chinese forces could offer no effective resistance. The empress Wu paid vast indemnities to Kapagan and sent him gifts, which were in effect thinly disguised tributes. In 696–697 Kapagan subjugated the Kitan tribes and sealed an alliance with the Khi (*tataby* in Turkic texts), which stemmed the advance of the Chinese armies to the north-east, into the foot-hills of the Khingan, and secured the empire's eastern frontier. Between 698 and 701 the northern and western frontiers of Kapagan's state were defined by the Tannu Ola, Altai and

Tarbagatai mountain ranges. After defeating the Bayirku tribe in 706–707, the Türks occupied lands extending from the upper reaches of the Kerulen to Lake Baikal. In 709–710 the Türk forces subjugated the Az and the Chik (tribes living in Tannu Tuva), crossed the Sayan mountains (the *Kögmen yiš* in Turkic texts), and inflicted a crushing defeat on the Yenisey Kyrgyz. The Kyrgyz ruler, Bars *beg*, fell in battle; his descendants were to remain vassals of the 'kaghan of the Ötükän mountains' for several generations.

In 711 the Türk forces, led by Tonyuquq, crossed the Mongolian Altai, clashed with the Türgesh army in Dzungaria, on the River Boluchu, and won an outright victory. Tonyuquq forced a crossing over the Syr Darya in pursuit of the retreating Türgesh, leading his troops to the border of Tokharistan. However, in battles with the Arabs near Samarkand the Türk forces were cut off from their rear services and suffered considerable losses; they had difficulty in returning to the Altai in 713–714. There they reinforced the army that was preparing to besiege Beshbalyk (Pei-t'ing). The siege was unsuccessful and, after losing in six skirmishes, the Türks raised it.[5]

The empire in crisis

These military defeats changed the situation drastically, serving as a signal for formerly submissive tribes to revolt. The Kitans and the Khi seceded; and first the Karluks then all the Tokuz-Oghuz tribes revolted, the latter representing a particularly serious threat to the Türk Empire. The Toguz-Oghuz were defeated in five battles in 715, but the revolt was not crushed. The following year, the great *irkin* of the Bayirku tribes fell on Kapagan's headquarters on the Tola river. Although the attack was repulsed, Kapagan himself was ambushed and killed.

Kapagan had tried to change the existing order of succession, according to which he would be succeeded by the elder son of Ilterish, known as 'the *shad* of the Tardush' since 698, who in turn would be followed by his younger brother Kül-tegin. At the time of Kapagan's death, both were renowned generals. Nevertheless, with the help of Kapagan's retainers, his son Bögü came to power. After this flagrant breaking of the law, Kül-tegin, who was the hero of many battles and very popular with the forces, and enjoyed the support of all the influential Türk families, attacked the headquarters. He killed Bögü *kaghan* and many of Kapagan's retainers, and then set on the throne his elder brother, known as Bilge *kaghan* ('Wise *kaghan*'), who ruled from 716 to 734.

Bilge *kaghan* mounted the throne at a time when the empire founded by his father was on the verge of collapse. The western lands seceded for good; and immediately after the death of Kapagan, the Türgesh leader Suluk

5. Klyashtorny, 1964, pp. 35–40.

proclaimed himself *kaghan*. The Kitan and Tatabi tribes refused to pay tribute; the Oghuz revolt continued; and the Türk tribes themselves began to rebel. Feeling unable to control the situation, Bilge *kaghan* offered the throne to his brother, Kül-tegin. The latter, however, would not go against the legal order of succession. Then, at last, Bilge decided to act. Kül-tegin was put at the head of the army, and the septuagenarian Tonyuquq, who enjoyed great authority among the tribes, became the *kaghan*'s closest adviser. Bilge and Kül-tegin now attacked the Uighurs; the rout of the Uighurs broke the resistance of the Tokuz-Oghuz tribes and the rich spoils heartened the Türk forces. In the summer of 718 Bilge crushed the Tatabi and the Kitans and regained possession of the Khingan. The detachment led by Tudun Yamtar, one of Bilge's captains, attacked the Karluk tribes, forced them to submit and took vast herds of horses, which were distributed among the tribes loyal to Bilge.

In 718 those Türk and Oghuz tribes which had fled to China during the time of internecine strife in 716 returned to Bilge's empire. The *kaghan*'s army became so strong that he decided to resume the war with China, his southern neighbour, which had offered help and protection to his adversaries. In the face of determined opposition from his chief counsellor, Tonyuquq, however, Bilge sent an embassy to Ch'ang-an instead, proposing a peace treaty. The emperor Hsüan-tsung, who had pacified his border with Tibet, refused to negotiate with the Türks in the hope of destroying their state, which had nevertheless been weakened by the internecine strife.

The last war with T'ang China

In 720 the Chinese army, whose main attacking force was the cavalry of its confederates – the Basmil, Kitan and Tatabi tribes – advanced on the Ötükän mountains in two directions. Tonyuquq's army met the Basmils and defeated them, taking Beshbalyk as they pursued the defeated tribe. The Türks then swiftly invaded Gansu and annihilated the Chinese garrison in the vicinity of Liang chou. The army of Bilge *kaghan*, which had participated in the victory over the Basmils and in the Gansu campaign, wheeled east and inflicted further severe defeats on the Kitans and Tatabi. In 721 Hsüan-tsung immediately accepted the new peace proposals.

The war of 720–721 was the last between the Second Türk Empire and China. The Chinese emperor no longer dared to disturb the peace, and Bilge *kaghan* broke with the policy of his predecessor, Kapagan. He strove consistently to expand trade with China and to establish family ties with the imperial House of Li, conserving the territorial status quo and the policy of non-interference in each other's internal affairs. It should be noted that Hsüan-tsung paid dearly for peace on his northern frontier, a fact that Bilge *kaghan* does not fail to mention in Kül-tegin's epitaph: 'I made peace with the Chinese people;

they gave us gold, silver and silk in abundance' (KT, S 4–5). In the year 727 alone, the Chinese emperor gave Bilge *kaghan* a 'present' of 100,000 pieces of silk in return for a symbolic 'tribute' of 30 horses. And it was not until 734 that the Chinese participated in a war between the Kitans and the Tatabi, siding with the latter; Bilge *kaghan*, fearing for his eastern frontier, fought against the Tatabi and defeated them. There were no direct confrontations between Chinese and Türk forces.

The winter of 723–724 was a hard one for the Türks: they lost most of their cattle because of the icy conditions. In spring the war with the Oghuz and the Tatars broke out afresh, imperilling the gains of previous years. It took a supreme effort to defeat the rebels and ensure political stability within the *kaghanate*. In 727 Bilge *kaghan* refused to ally himself with the Tibetans against China; he was rewarded with concessions from the imperial government in Ch'ang-an, allowing an expansion of the frontier trade between the nomads and Chinese merchants. From then on, gifts of huge amounts of silk arrived annually.

In 732 Bilge *kaghan* entered the sixteenth year of his reign. 'By the grace of Heaven and because of good fortune and propitious circumstances, I brought back to life the dying people, the naked people I clothed, and I made the few many' (KT, E 29).[6]

The final decade

Kül-tegin died in 731. Bilge *kaghan* did not long outlive his brother – in 734 he was poisoned by one of his retainers. Near the River Orkhon, in the Koshotsaidam basin between the mountains, monuments were erected to both brothers with inscriptions that chronicled the turbulent history of the Second Türk Empire (see below).

Bilge's successors, his short-lived sons Izhan *kaghan* (734–739) and Tengri *kaghan* (740–741), did not depart from their father's policies, but with Tengri *kaghan*'s death, in 741, the empire began to disintegrate. Apanaged rulers of the *kaghan*'s House of Ashina were less and less able to cope with central power. The young Tengri *kaghan* was killed by his uncle, Kutlug *yabghu*, who seized power. War broke out with the tribal groups of the Uighurs, the Basmils and the Karluks, and Kutlug *yabghu* and his followers perished in the fighting. In 745 the Second Türk Empire ceased to exist. The Türk tribes, who retained part of their lands, played no significant role in succeeding events. The last reference to them in Chinese sources relates to the year 941.[7]

---

6. English translation: Sinor, 1990, p. 313.
7. Klyashtorny, 1964, pp. 41–3.

FIG. 1. Mongolia.
Stele with the Bugut inscription.
(Photo: © S. G. Klyashtorny.)

FIG. 2. Mongolia.
Stele with the Bugut inscription.
(Photo: © S. G. Klyashtorny.)

FIG. 3. Mongolia. Bulgan *aimak*. Obverse of the stele.
(Photo: © S. G. Klyashtorny.)

FIG. 4. Mongolia. Bulgan *aimak*. Reverse of the stele.
(Photo: © S. G. Klyashtorny.)

Epigraphic memorials of the Türks

Türk stone inscriptions date back to the second half of the sixth century, when a
stele in honour of the Türk *kaghan* Taspar (Taghpar in Harmatta's reading) was
erected, with inscriptions in Sogdian and Sanskrit (the Bugut inscription, 582)
(Figs. 1 and 2).[8] However, the heyday of ancient Türk epigraphy – in the original
runic script, which was invented no later than the middle of the seventh century,
and in the Türk language – was the era of the Second Türk Empire. The earliest
example appears to be the memorial from Choiren, which dates from between
687 and 691; the inscription tells of the Türks' return to their lands in northern
Mongolia and of their victory over the Tokuz-Oghuz. The largest and most
significant memorials are the Koshotsaidam steles (monuments in honour of
Kül-tegin and Bilge *kaghan*, who died in 731 and 734 respectively), written on
behalf of Bilge *kaghan* by his nephew Yollyg-tegin; and the memorial written by
Tonyuquq after 716 and subsequently incorporated in his burial mound.

Further inscriptions of this kind are known to us; these historical and
biographical texts are memorials or eulogies for the living, and they tell of the
deeds of Türk *kaghan*s and their retainers. They combine descriptions of events
that involved the hero of the inscription (or his ancestors) with an exposition
of the political beliefs and ideas of the author of the text; they may be seen as
'declarations of intent' and to some extent were used as propaganda (Figs. 3
and 4). Even more common were memorial inscriptions on rock faces, some of

8. Klyashtorny and Livshits, 1972, pp. 69–102.

FIG. 5. Mongolia. Gobi-Altai *aimak*.
(Photo: © S. G. Klyashtorny.)

which proclaimed the author's right to use the adjacent pasture or site (Figs. 5 and 6).[9]

The Türgesh state

At the end of the seventh century Wu-chih-lê (699–706), leader of the Türgesh tribes that lived in the western T'ien Shan mountains, had driven the T'ang protégé Böri-*shad* out of Semirechye and established his own power over the

9. Klyashtorny, 1975, pp. 119–28.

FIG. 6. Mongolia. Gobi-Altai *aimak*.
(Photo: © S. G. Klyashtorny.)

territory from Chach (present-day Tashkent) to Dzungaria. 'Major' and 'minor' headquarters for the *kaghan* were established in Nevaket on the rivers Chu and Ili, and the country was divided into 20 districts ruled by the *kaghan*'s stewards (*tutuk*), each of whom was able to muster between 5,000 and 7,000 warriors. Wu-chih-lê assumed the traditional title of the Western Türk states, '*kaghan* of the People of Ten Arrows'; and also the new title, 'Türgesh *kaghan*' – copper coins were now minted in Nevaket bearing this legend in Sogdian. Wu-chih-lê's successor, Sakal *kaghan* (706–711), met with opposition from tribal leaders who supported his younger brother's claim to the throne. The Eastern Türk leader, Kapagan *kaghan*, intervened in the civil unrest, and after the defeat

345

of the Türgesh forces in a battle on the River Boluchu in 711 both brothers were killed. What was left of the Türgesh army was rallied by the commander, Suluk Chabish-chor (Su-lu in Chinese sources), and retreated beyond the Syr Darya into Tokharistan. It was not until 715 that Suluk, having proclaimed himself Türgesh *kaghan*, was able to return and restore the independence of his state.

Throughout his reign (715–738) Suluk Chabish-chor had to fight on two fronts. From East Turkestan he was threatened by pretenders to the throne who belonged to the family of the Western Türk *kaghan*s and were supported by Chinese troops. Suluk obviated this danger by means of diplomacy (marriage to the daughter of one of the pretenders) and military action (laying siege to the capital of the T'ang governor of Kucha in 726–727). By marrying the daughters of the Eastern Türk leader Bilge *kaghan* and the king of Tibet, the Türgesh *kaghan* firmly consolidated his eastern flank.

From the west the Türgesh were threatened by the conquering Arab armies, who crossed the Syr Darya (Jaxartes) several times in 714–715. This compelled Suluk to join battle with the Arabs, along with other Central Asian states striving to retain their independence. In 720–721 Suluk's general, Küli-chor (Kursul in Arab sources), led successful military actions against the Arabs in Sogdiana. In 728–729 Suluk supported the anti-Arab revolts of the citizenry of Samarkand and Bukhara, and drove the Arabs from Sogdiana. It was not until 732 that the Arab governor defeated the Türgesh, near Tavavis, and entered Bukhara. In 737 the Türgesh crushed the Arabs in Tokharistan, but were subsequently defeated. When Suluk returned to Nevaket the following year, he was killed by one of his retainers; and in 739 the Arabs captured and executed Küli-chor.

The death of Suluk and the brief reign of his son, Kut-chor *kaghan* (T'u-ho-hsien in Chinese sources) (738–739), marked the beginning of a 20-year struggle for power between the leading members of the 'yellow' and 'black' tribes, which polarized the Türgesh tribal group. Taking advantage of the internecine strife in 748, the T'ang governor of Kucha led an invasion force into Semirechye, capturing Suyab, one of its most important towns. In 751, however, the Chinese forces were defeated by the Arabs and the Türks near Talas, and they fled Semirechye. The *kaghan*s of the 'black' Türgesh seized power (749–753) but they were unable to end the internal conflicts. In 766 the Karluks, who had consolidated their hold on Semirechye after being driven from Mongolia in 746–747 by the Uighurs, killed the warring Türgesh *kaghan*s, and the Karluk *yabghu* became the founder of a new state in the T'ien Shan mountains.[10]

10. Chavannes, 1903, pp. 279–303.

The Uighurs and the Karluks

The fall of the Second Türk Empire and the revolt of the Uighur, Basmil and Karluk tribes had created a political vacuum in the steppe. The struggle to obtain power and the title of *kaghan*, and to set up a new state, intensified between the Basmils (whose leader was proclaimed *khan*) and the Uighurs. The Uighurs emerged victorious. Their allies, the Karluks, who had gained no advantage from their participation in the war with the Türks, then allied themselves with the Türgesh, but, failing to defeat the Uighurs in battle, fled to the T'ien Shan mountains in 746. The following year, the Karluks, with the support of the Tatar tribes living in eastern Mongolia, attacked the Uighurs once again, but without success. In 744, with the Uighur tribes' proclamation of Kül-bilge *kaghan* as their leader, the Yaghlakar dynasty came to power in the steppe. Meanwhile in Central Asia a powerful state of Turkic-speaking nomads – that of the Uighurs – came into being.[11]

11. Klyashtorny, 1982, pp. 335–66.

The Western Regions (Hsi-yü) under the T'ang Empire and the kingdom of Tibet*

Mu Shun-ying and Wang Yao

Three great empires

The seventh century is of particular significance for the political history of Central Asia. In its first quarter it witnessed the rise of three great powers, each of which was to have a major impact on the course of events in the two succeeding centuries. In the east, China came under one of its most powerful and prosperous dynasties, the T'ang (618–907). At the foot of the towering peaks of the Himalayas, the ancient Tibetan people, the Bod (known as the Tu-po or more commonly as the Tu-fan in Chinese records, and as Tüpüt in Sogdian and Turkic), emerged victorious from their age-old inter-tribal rivalry and were quick to establish a unified monarchy of the Yar-klung-spu-rgyal family. In the west a series of historical events led to the sudden rise of the Arabs.

By a curious coincidence, all three empires were founded almost simultaneously. In the 640s the T'ang came to dominate the oasis states of the Tarim. From the 660s onwards, Tibet, having established itself firmly in the Koko Nor area (now Qinghai province in China), began to dispute supremacy over the Gansu corridor and the Tarim with the T'ang. This rivalry, which lasted more than two centuries, brought several other peoples in this area into the conflict. Thus, a multilateral relationship between the T'ang, the Tibetans and many Türk confederations evolved in the Western Regions (Hsi-yü), which reflected a motley combination of interests. At the same time, the Arabs accomplished their conquest of the Sasanian Empire in 651 and continued to push eastwards.

One hundred years later, in 751, the Arabs under the command of Ziyad b. Salih, in alliance with the Karluks and other Turkic peoples, defeated the Chinese forces under the military governor Kao Hsien-chih near the Talas river.

---

* See Map 6.

In itself this battle was not of great importance, but the outbreak of the An Lu-shan rebellion (755–763) in China proper, and the consequent withdrawal of the Chinese armies from the Western Regions, left the Arabs in a strong position to extend their influence in Central Asia. However, according to the evidence of both Chinese and Tibetan sources, any further Arab advance seems to have been temporarily checked by the Tibetans.[1]

The Western Regions under the Early T'ang

Before the establishment of the T'ang dynasty in 618, the Eastern and Western Türks dominated the vast expanse of the Central Asian hinterland. The Eastern Türk *kaghan* Hsieh-li (619–634) made repeated incursions into China and even reached the vicinity of Ch'ang-an, the T'ang capital, in 626; but the tide of events then began to turn in favour of the T'ang. In 630 Hsieh-li was taken prisoner by the T'ang expeditionary forces, thus ending the power of the Eastern Türk *Kaghanate* for over half a century. In the same year, the Western Türk *kaghan*, T'ung *yabghu* (619–630), was murdered. His death triggered off a series of quarrels and bitter rivalries among the Western Türks. Most of the nomadic tribes on the steppe, together with the oasis city-states of the Tarim basin, were caught in the conflict between the T'ang and the Western Türks, changing their allegiance as the situation required.

It is no accident that the first oasis city-state that the emperor T'ai-tsung (627–649), the real founder of the T'ang dynasty, intended to conquer was Kocho: located in the Turfan depression, a strategic location on the Silk Route, this oasis was the closest to Ch'ang-an as well as the largest of the Western Regions. Ever since the first century B.C., it had been more influenced by Chinese culture than other oasis states. From 502 to 640, it was even ruled by the royal House of Ch'ü, of Chinese origin. In 638 the king of Kocho, an ally of the Western Türks, was encouraged by them to defy the T'ang. The emperor T'ai-tsung dispatched an expeditionary army against the king. The Western Türks, whose troops were stationed at Beshbalyk (present-day Jimsa in Xinjiang), an important city to the north of Turfan, had promised to assist Kocho in case of attack, but fled upon the arrival of the Chinese. In 640 Kocho was forced to surrender. The occupation of Kocho not only inaugurated the Chinese penetration of the Western Regions, but also increased tension between the Chinese and the Western Türks. The T'ang set up Hsi-chou Prefecture in Kocho and T'ing-chou Prefecture in Beshbalyk in 640.

T'ang policy after the conquest of Kocho was aimed at dominating all the Western Regions. In spite of opposition by the Western Türks, the king of Karashahr acknowledged T'ang rule in 644. Two years later, Haripuspa, who

---

1. Beckwith, 1980, pp. 30–8; 1987; Bacot et al., 1940–46; Chang, 1959–60.

had succeeded Suvarnadeva (624–646) as ruler of Kucha, submitted to the Western Türk *Kaghanate*. In response, the T'ang army crossed the T'ien Shan and captured the city. Most of the other oasis states hastened to offer their submission. On the death of Emperor T'ai-tsung in 649, Ho-lu, *kaghan* of the Western Türks, sought to reassert his supremacy over the Western Regions. After a campaign lasting seven years (651–657), the T'ang defeated Ho-lu and the Western Türks ceased to exist as a political force.

ADMINISTRATIVE SYSTEM

To rule the newly conquered areas, the T'ang created a double administrative system, which took account of local conditions. Three oases in the eastern part of the region, where Chinese influence was most evident – Hami, Turfan and Jimsa – were incorporated into the Chinese civil administration. The discovery of many administrative documents bearing official seals has provided concrete evidence of T'ang rule in the Turfan district.[2] Nomadic tribes and city-states that had pledged allegiance to the T'ang court were allowed to maintain their privileged status in their localities in accordance with a system called *chi-mi*. This was an institution by which the conquered rulers were 'restrained' (*chi*), and 'won over' (*mi*) by the honour of being invested with a title and the conferment of an embroidered silk robe, together with the standard, drums and horns as the emblems of mandate.

The *chi-mi* system was an important means of resolving conflicts between the T'ang court and the various nationalities under their rule. The T'ang usually appointed representative members of those ruling clans, or hereditary royal families, who had pledged allegiance to government posts and bestowed on them honourable ranks or titles. In principle, all the original rulers within the *chi-mi* governorates or prefectures were allowed to continue to reside in and oversee the domestic affairs of their districts. For example, the T'ang set up for the nomadic Western Türks two *chi-mi* Protectorates-General – those of Meng-chih and K'un-ling – with the subordinate Türk chieftains appointed as *khan*s and protectors-general. Four *chi-mi* governorates were also established for the sedentary inhabitants of the oasis states.

The officials in charge of the various *chi-mi* administrations were all members of the local minority élites. For example, King Su-chi (son of Haripuspa) and King Fu-shih-hsiung were nominated governors-general of Kucha and of Pi-sha (Visha in Khotanese, Vijaya in Tibetan) in Khotan respectively. *Chi-mi* administrators had to pledge allegiance to the T'ang, accepting the patents issued to them by their Chinese overlords. Their task was to guarantee the security of the empire's borders, while the T'ang government stationed troops only in key locations, namely the 'Four Garrisons'. All *chi-mi*

2. *Tu-lu-fan chu-tu wen-shu*, 1985–92.

administrators regularly had to pay taxes to the T'ang court. The tribute included horses, sheep, camels, eagles, the skins of leopards and martens, rare birds, jade, agate, pearls, *shui-ching* ('germ of water' crystal), gold and silver wares and various kinds of woollen blankets. Of all the items of tribute, the horses from the Western Regions were the most important.

To control the *chi-mi* governorates the T'ang set up a combined civil and military administration, the Protectorate-General of An-hsi (i.e. 'Pacifying the West'). It was first established immediately after the conquest of Kocho in 640 and moved to Kucha after the suppression of the revolt of Ho-lu in 657. The Four Garrisons – Kucha, Su-le (Kashgar), Khotan and Yen-chih (Agni in Tokharian, Karashahr in Turkic) – came under the jurisdiction of this Protectorate-General. From 679 to 719 Suyab was listed among the Four Garrisons instead of Yen-chih. It should be noted that the An-hsi Protectorate-General, with its Four Garrisons, was in control of all the region's military and administrative affairs. In 702 the Protectorate-General of Pei-t'ing was established at Beshbalyk to strengthen the T'ang position to the north of the T'ien Shan (the Celestial Mountains).

THE TIBETAN CHALLENGE

After 659 the T'ang faced their most powerful opponent in the Tarim when the Tibetans appeared on the stage to challenge T'ang supremacy. Allying themselves with the revived Eastern Türks and various tribes of the resurgent Western Türks, the Tibetans invaded the Tarim and repeatedly occupied the oasis states. Under their attacks, after 663, the Chinese were more than once forced to withdraw and to abandon An-hsi with its Four Garrisons to the Tibetans. At the peak of its power, the territory controlled by Tibet ranged from the T'ien Shan in the north to T'ien-chu (the Chinese name for present-day India) in the south, and from the present western Gansu province and Sichuan in the east to eastern Central Asia. In 692 the T'ang finally defeated the Tibetans, restored the Protectorate-General of An-hsi in Kucha and recovered the Four Garrisons. At this time a Chinese force of some 30,000 men was stationed in the Western Regions. The presence of a permanent garrison indicates the threat posed by the Tibetans and the T'ang court's need to keep control of the Four Garrisons and the route by which they were supplied.

SOCIETY, RELIGION AND CULTURE

Under the Early T'ang, the Turkic tribes had a nomadic economy with the corresponding customs and way of life. Later they became semi-nomadic, transmigrating between winter quarters and seasonal pastures.

Under T'ang rule, the sedentary population in the area south of the T'ien Shan adopted new customs. In Kucha, for example, people had their hair cut short around the top of their heads – the only exception was the king, who, moreover, wore a hat and robe made of brocade, and a bejewelled belt. At the start of each year, there were games involving goats, horses and fighting camels. These festivities lasted for seven days, with predictions about the year's harvests based on the results of such fights. The 'sprinkling with cold water' was a winter solstice dance. In the tenth month of the year, participants had to wear masks, paint their faces to resemble animals or disguise themselves as ghosts, leaping about to the clamour of drums and other musical instruments. They splashed cold water on each other and over passers-by in order to drive out devils. The local population were adherents of Buddhism (see pages 364–5), especially the Hinayana school. Every year, on the occasion of certain Buddhist festivals, people would gather to hear the exposition of Buddhist doctrines; statues of the Buddha were taken from the monasteries and carried on a 'parade of Buddhas', often drawing thousands of participants.

Of all the cultural activities in Kucha, music and dance seem to have had the greatest importance and influence and to have enjoyed the greatest popularity among the people. The music and dance of Kucha were celebrated by many T'ang poets. 'Rainbow Skirt and Feathered Dress', a song and dance of Central Asian origin, was probably brought into Ch'ang-an, the T'ang capital, by way of Kucha. The best known of all was the popular music of Western Liang, a town of the Gansu corridor (now Wu-wei in Gansu province): it was actually an amalgam of the music of Kucha with traditional Chinese music. After being introduced into the two T'ang capitals, Ch'ang-an and Lo-yang, the songs and dances of the population of the Western Regions also became very popular. Even the so-called *Ta-yüeh* (Grand Music), played at the imperial court, was mixed with Kuchean music and used Kuchean musical instruments, as recorded in the *T'ang shu*. The Kuchean four-stringed bent-neck lute, the oboe, the flute and the drum were among the most popular instruments adopted by Kuchean musicians.

Under the influence of the musical styles of Kucha and that of Sogdiana, Chinese T'ang music began to sound like that of the city-states of Central Asia. Following the fashion, many members of the imperial family and of the aristocracy took to playing drums of the type widely used in musical performances in the Western Regions. During that time, almost all the famous musicians and dancers in the T'ang capital – for example, the Kuchean musician Po Ming-ta – were of Central Asian origin. As for the dancing girls, with their long hair, fluttering sleeves and gauzy scarves, they excelled in beautiful dances with whirling gyrations 'as swift as the wind'.

In the kingdom of Khotan, the people were pious and enthusiastic Buddhists and it seems likely that Khotan had already adopted Buddhism some time before the first century. Hundreds of *saṅghārāmas* (monasteries), studying the Mahayana doctrine, were active centres of religious and literary life, engaged in copying Buddhist Sanskrit and Khotanese Saka manuscripts, translating and adapting Indian poetry and religious literature, and so on. Khotan was always attractive to Chinese pilgrims seeking Buddhist scripts.

The Khotanese paid particular attention to etiquette. Whenever they sent a letter, they would hold it over their heads to show respect for the recipient. They used wood to make pens, and jade to make seals. The people of Khotan excelled in woollen rugs and carpets and silk tapestries of fine workmanship, with figurative and floral motifs. They were also, like the people of Kucha, devoted to singing and dancing.

Many areas of Central Asia maintained their own distinctive styles and considerably influenced the development of T'ang culture. The Barbarian (*Hu*) styles constituted a prominent element in T'ang culture and art; and Barbarian and Turkic costumes became fashionable in Ch'ang-an and Lo-yang, with even the imperial family and the aristocracy adopting the fashion. Many well-known painters came from the Western Regions. Among the painters of the seventh century, a father and son from the Yü-chi family – Yü-chi Pa-chih-na and Yü-ch'ih I-sen (Visha Irasangä in Khotanese) – were the best known. Famous as 'Yü-chi the Elder' and 'Yü-chi the Younger, they were members of the Khotan royal family. Yü-chi the Younger specialized in painting Buddhas and foreigners; a painting of a *devaraja* by this master has survived.[3]

ARCHAEOLOGICAL EVIDENCE

The frequent passage of caravans along the Silk Route had not only stimulated trade, but also promoted the exchange between East and West of scientific, artistic and cultural achievements, as documented by abundant archaeological evidence. The most important material remains found in the tombs at Astana and Karakhoja (two cemeteries in the suburbs of Kocho) are Chinese documents, silk fabrics, clay sculptures, wooden figures (Fig. 1), paintings (Fig. 2), pottery and woodwork, building equipment, dried fruit and dried foods, Byzantine gold and Persian silver coins, as well as T'ang copper coins. Although most of these relics are damaged and incomplete, they are authentic products of the T'ang period. In the paintings on silk, for example, the 'plump women' are typical of the peak period of T'ang art. Many of the Confucian classics were found in the tombs around Kocho.

Archaeological evidence shows that elaborate funerals were held for the dead. The tombs of the period usually had one or more chambers, doors and paved approaches. In the case of government officials and persons of importance, the funerary objects included wooden models of chambers and pavilions, clay figurines representing male and female attendants, and men and women riding horses or playing polo. The same group of graves (i.e. tombs at

3. Liu, 1969; Samolin, 1964; Tikhvinskiy and Litvinsky, 1988; Litvinsky (ed.), 1992.

FIG. 1. Kocho. Seated Buddha. Wood.
(Photo: © Staatliche Museen zu Berlin.)

Astana and Karakhoja) also yielded painted clay tomb-guardians or guardian
genii, and figures showing the fabulous creatures of composite monsters with
both human and animal features. A T'ang copper coin, a Persian silver coin or
a Byzantine gold coin was frequently placed in the mouth of the deceased and
the face was covered with a special type of brocade called *fu-mien*.

355

Fig. 2. Kocho. Head of Buddha. Wall painting.
(Photo: © Staatliche Museen zu Berlin.)

From both the archaeological evidence and the literary sources, it is clear that there were workshops in the oasis states specializing in the production and manufacture of textiles, paper, wine, pottery, wooden objects, utensils, coaches and horse trappings. There were also grain-depots, firewood merchants and jewellers' shops. In the markets, people traded in silks, cattle, horses, camels and slaves. A new wine-making grape, the famous 'mare teat' or 'horse-nipple' grape, was introduced from Kocho to China, and with it, knowledge of the art of making grape wine in 'eight colours' of this highly aromatic beverage. Another novelty was cotton cloth (*tie-pu*), spun and woven by the natives of Turfan.

Silk had long been China's traditional export. Chinese documents unearthed from ancient tombs in Turfan show that Chinese silk was then available in all Central Asian markets. Under the T'ang, the silk industry made important progress and textile centres began to appear in the Western Regions. There were special brocades from Kucha, Kashgar and Kocho and Persian *dibādj*-brocade was also on sale.[4] A batch of T'ang silk products, discovered in tombs at Turfan, includes brocade, damask, lute-strings, silk gauze, and printed and embroidered silk fabrics. The bright colours and unique designs of this superb collection are very impressive. Advanced Chinese techniques in textile-production, paper-making and printing were transferred to Western Asia and eventually reached Europe.

The art of paper manufacture was first introduced from China to Kocho (Turfan), and Chinese paper was imported to Samarkand as early as 650. Among the T'ang soldiers captured by the Arabs at the battle of Talas in 751 were craftsmen skilled in the manufacture of paper, textiles, and gold and silver ornaments.[5] According to the Arabic sources, the paper-makers among the Chinese prisoners were taken to Samarkand to start a local production. Samarkand became a centre for paper-making after the eighth century and thence the paper industry passed to Baghdad.[6]

BUDDHISM

The dominant religion of the period was Buddhism. From the third to the ninth century, a vigorous Buddhist civilization developed in all the ancient oasis kingdoms, such as Khotan, Kucha, Agni and Kocho. Buddhist monasteries and temples were built with donations from members of the local royal family, aristocrats, government officials and other rich people. The kings of the various oasis states became ardent patrons of Buddhism (see Chapter 18).

During the 630s and 640s, the Chinese Buddhist pilgrim Hsüan-tsang made the round trip to India by way of the Western Regions. In the account of his travels, he notes that in the areas south of the T'ien Shan, some places have 'a dozen or so *chia-lan*s and about 2,000 monks', while other places have 'more than 100 *chia-lan*s and over 5,000 monks'.[7] (*Chia-lan* is a Chinese transliteration of the Sanskrit word *saṅghārāma*, meaning 'Buddhist monastery'.) Hsüan-

4. *Tu-lu-fan chu-tu wen-shu*, 1985–90, Vol. 1, pp. 181, 187; Vol. 2, pp. 18, 60.
5. Du Huan, 'Travels', in Tu Yu, 1988, chapter on the Frontier Defence. On this work, see Rotours, des, 1932, pp. 84, 99, 149.
6. Maillard, 1973; 1983; Litvinsky (ed.), 1992; Yaldiz, 1987.
7. Hsüan-tsang, 1985, Ch. 1, pp. 48, 54. See also Litvinsky (ed.), 1992.

tsang also remarks that Hinayana Buddhism is prevalent in Kucha, while the Mahayana is represented principally in Yarkand and Khotan.

Buddhism was also widespread among the Türks. The Western Türk *kaghan*, T'ung *yabghu*, was converted by an Indian monk called Prabhakaramitra. Several other minor Türk rulers also showed respect for, and devotion to, Buddhism.

Most Buddhist monasteries and temples in the Western Regions were built along streams in mountain valleys, or in cave-temples. The best-known of these are the Kyzyl in present-day Bay, the Kumtura, the Kyzyl-kargha and Simsim cave-temples in the Kucha area and the Bezeklyk and Toyoq cave-temples in Turfan. In addition, there are large Buddhist temples and stupas built on flat

FIG. 3. Kyzyl. Wall painting. (Photo: © R.M.N. Paris.)

FIG. 4. Kumtura. Bodhisattva. Musée Guimet, Paris.
(Photo: © R.M.N. Paris.)

ground, such as the ruins of the Su-bashi monastery in Kucha, the large monastery of Miran, and Ming-oi at Karashahr, and monasteries at Kocho and Yar in the Turfan area. More than 1,000 Buddhist caves have been located in present-day Xinjiang region, most of them with painted murals. For example, the walls and ceilings of every cave in the Kyzyl cave-temple have murals illustrating Buddhist legends and representing the finest expression of Graeco-Irano-Gandharan art (Fig. 3). There are also styles typical of T'ang painting in the murals of the Kumtura and Bezeklyk cave-temples. Some temples had clay figures of Buddhas and Bodhisattvas (Fig. 4), but most are badly damaged.

The kingdom of Tibet

As mentioned above, a Tibetan royal line sprang up in the Yarklung valley in the first quarter of the seventh century. The power of this family – the Yar-klung-spu-rgyal – spread rapidly to the north-west and the constant disputes between the numerous warlike clans, fragmented throughout the rugged valleys of southern and central Tibet, were quickly ended. The Sumpa (Supi), the Greater and Lesser Yang-t'ung (Upper and Lower Zhangzhung), the Bailan, the A-zha (T'u-yü-hun) and other peoples of Chiang stock were annexed in quick succession. The great reserve of energy of the Tibetan people, tempered by an austere life in the wilderness, was set free and directed to politico-military expansion. This extended over the vast space of the Koko Nor–Tibetan plateau and lasted for some two and a half centuries.

Early in the seventh century, gNam-ri-srong-brtsan (c. 570–620), *btsan-po* (chief) of the Yar-klung-spu-rgyal clan, had already laid the foundations of the new monarchy by bringing more than a dozen clans under his rule.[8] But the feudal customs of the tribal chieftains and the noble clans remained semi-autonomous, although incorporated into the comparatively centralized state under the *btsan-po*. The death of gNam-ri-srong-brtsan provoked a rebellion. The brilliant new era in Tibetan history was ushered in with the enthronement of Srong-brtsan sgam-po (c. 620–649 or 650), gNam-ri's son, as *btsan-po*. The new ruler quickly unmasked all intrigues and quelled all signs of open revolt. In 633 Srong-brtsan sgam-po moved the royal residence from Lho-kha to Lhasa ('place of the god'), a step of great strategic importance for the rapid expansion that followed.

According to Tibetan and Chinese records, Srong-brtsan sgam-po under-took sweeping legislative reforms with the assistance of his chief minister, sTong-brtsan yul-bzung of the mGar clan (Lu-dong-zang in Chinese literature, ?–667). sTong-brtsan served the *btsan-po* until the latter's death, and his office of Great Minister (*blon-chen-bo*) was filled by his descendants for decades. The *btsan-po*, fully aware of the presence of four powers in the monarchy – majesty (*nMga-thang*); magic (*dBu-ring*; literally, the 'helmet' worn by the *btsan-po* at sacred functions); religious law (*chos*), which originated with the Bon-po; and political authority (*chab-srid*), which the ruler exercised through his officials[9] – set up new political institutions. Many of them were modelled on the T'ang adminis-trative system and regulations: the ministers had, for example, credentials and emblems of rank. The Great Minister and the vice-Great Minister (*blon-chen-vog-ma*) were followed by the 'inner' (*nang-blon*) and 'outer' (*phyi-blon*) min-isters and a supreme judge (*shal-ce-pa chen-po*), each of whom had the insignia

8. There seem to have been 18 noble clans. A list of them is found in *Bka' thang sde lnga*, c. 1285, Vol. 5, fol. 7. See Tucci, 1949, pp. 737–8; Chang Kun, 1959–60, pp. 130–1, 153, note 10.
9. Hoffman, 1975, p. 389.

accorded to his position in the hierarchy. The 'inner' minister handled the internal affairs of the court while the 'outer' minister was in charge of relations between subordinate clans, external reconnaissance and the launching of punitive expeditions. The supreme judge oversaw the administration of justice; his position was similar to that of the 'minister of punishment' under the T'ang dynasty. In addition, there was an official (*mngan-pon*) who was responsible for the budget and a chief accountant (*rtsis-pa-chen-po*) in charge of book-keeping. Laws were drawn up, some of which were designed for the half-cultivator/half-herdsman activities of the population, as evidenced by the fragmentary Tibetan scrolls of legal documents found in Dunhuang.[10]

One of the most important reforms seems to have been the integration of the entire Tibetan territory, setting up 5 *ru* (*dbu-ru, g'yo-ru, g'yas-ru, ru-lag* and *sum-pa-ru*) and 61 *stong-sde* as unified military and administrative units.[11] This institution was supplemented by the oath-of-alliance, a characteristic practice among the Tibetans when subordinates pledged their loyalty to the nobles, and the nobles in their turn swore allegiance to the monarch.

The king had subjects who were 'near to his heart' and others who were 'distant from his heart'.[12] They regularly exchanged oaths of fealty, accompanied by a ceremony of sacrifice, a minor one every year and a major one every three years. The words of the oaths, apart from expressing a feeling of awe for the deities called as witnesses, stipulated the rights and obligations of all the allied parties. This system – forming alliances by oaths and even concluding treaties – brought great advantages to the newly founded Tibetan regime. Such oath-taking rituals between the *btsan-po* and his ministers appear to have become a fixed procedure in the political life of Tibetan society. In addition, when the *btsan-po* proclaimed some important policy, the oath-taking ceremonies were often used as the form for such proclamations. For example, Khri-srong lde-brtsan (755–797) held such ceremonies twice during his reign to make public the royal edict on advocating Buddhism. The ceremonies were also staged when establishing relations with the T'ang or with neighbouring clans.

Judging from the lists of names attending several large-scale alliance ceremonies, and found in the Tibetan chronicle discovered in Dunhuang, the system seems to have been instrumental in realizing the dynastic aspirations of Srong-brtsan sgam-po and his successors. The essence of these alliances was their military strength: by joining the alliance, every clan inevitably became a military unit. The *stong-sde* and *ru* were in effect the designations for different clans under the command of the 'Supreme Commander of all Troops under Heaven'.

---

10. For example, 'Compensation Law on Hunters who Injure a Third Party', a Tibetan manuscript in the collection of the Bibliothèque Nationale of Paris, Fond Pelliot tibétain, PT 1,071.
11. See Bacot et al., 1940–46; Uray, 1962, pp. 353–60.
12. Stein, 1972, p. 132.

RELATIONS WITH T'ANG CHINA

In 634 the Tibetans established diplomatic relations with the T'ang court, sending envoys and tribute. Soon afterwards, Srong-brtsan sgam-po was granted a marriage with a Chinese princess, Weng-cheng Kung-chu, known to the Tibetans as Mun-chhang Kong-cho; she was sent to Tibet in 641. Then followed a period of friendship lasting two decades between the Tibetans and the Chinese. Young people of the Tibetan nobility were sent to Ch'ang-an to study the Chinese classics, Chinese books were brought to Lhasa and there were constant attempts to translate and adapt Chinese classics and literary works into Tibetan. Some of these translated texts can be found in the Tibetan manuscript hoard of Dunhuang. At the same time other clans, including the Yangtong, Türgesh, Bolor and Nepal, also built up relations with Tibet by marriage.

Within half a century the power of the Tibetan state had expanded westward towards the Pamirs, eastward towards Su-chuan, Yun-nan (Nan-chao) and northward to impinge upon the Koko Nor area and the Gansu corridor. After 663 Tibetan military incursions, especially those led by the ministers and commanders of the mGar clan (sometimes in alliance with the Western Türks), posed a direct threat to, and exerted pressure on, the Chinese western and southwestern frontier. With the deliberate aim of counterbalancing Tibetan influence over the Western Regions, the T'ang court organized successive expeditions against the Tibetans both in the Gansu corridor and in the Tarim (670, 675–679, 692). In 692 the T'ang decided to station some 30,000 'protective' soldiers permanently at the Four Garrisons of the An-hsi Protectorate-General to defend the Tarim area and the communication route against the Tibetans in the south and their Türk ally in the north.

In 710 another Chinese princess, Chin-ch'eng (Kyim-sheng Kong-cho), was granted to a Tibetan king. According to some sources, in 742 she gave birth to a son who was destined to become king: this was Khri-srong lde-brtsan. Under his reign, the Tibetans once again ruled over Gilgit (Drusha). The possession of Gilgit and its neighbour Baltistan was of great strategic importance: it allowed the Tibetans to control the main route from Kashgar through the Mintaka pass to Kashmir and the Indus valley, and made it possible for Tibet to establish direct contact with the Turkic tribes of the Tarim area and the Arabs of Central Asia. At the same time, tribute was paid twice by the Pala kings of Magadha and Bengal to Tibet, in 755 and in 756. According to some records, the Tibetans may also have invaded India in search of relics of the Buddha in Magadha and set up an iron column on the Ganges.[13]

In the reverse direction, the Tibetans took the opportunity of the An Lushan rebellion (755–763) to invade China proper and even captured Ch'ang-an, placing a boy-emperor on the T'ang throne for 15 days (in the eleventh

13. Stein, 1972, p. 64.

month of 763). Then, availing themselves of the withdrawal of the Chinese garrison, they succeeded in occupying the Gansu corridor and the Four Garrisons of the An-hsi Protectorate-General (from 763 onwards). Thus the Tibetans attained their long-desired objective: complete control of the route through the Gansu corridor and the Tarim to Central Asia, Kashmir and northern India; and through modern Afghanistan to Transoxania and Iran. Their military presence in these vast areas also allowed them, from 791 onwards, steadfastly to oppose the challenge posed by the Arabs in Central Asia.

AGRICULTURE, ANIMAL HUSBANDRY AND CRAFTS

Tibet's high-altitude environment, with a diversity of local conditions, gave its economic life a two-fold structure of cereal culture and animal husbandry, with people frequently alternating between the two modes of life according to the environment and the season. All political and cultural centres were located in regions of intensive cultivation. The rise of the first Tibetan monarchy was mainly due to its control of the most fertile cultivated regions, where highland barley, wheat, buckwheat and beans were grown. Two yoked oxen were used for ploughing, and irrigation and drainage techniques were known.

Tibetan pastoral stockbreeding was more advanced than agriculture. Domesticated animals comprised yaks, a yak-and-cow hybrid, goats, sheep, horses and a few pigs and dogs. The yak played (and continues to play) an important role – indeed, one could go so far as to say that without the yak, there would be no Tibetan culture. These animals roved around during spring and summer in search of pasture and water, and during autumn and winter they stayed on pastureland. Stories of levying 'taxes for oxen legs' reveal one aspect of the development of animal husbandry.

Tibetan metallurgical techniques (in iron-working) had reached a very high level, suggesting a development over several centuries, and the skills of quench-hardening and grinding had already been mastered. Needless to say, these techniques ensured an ample supply of suits of armour and sharp swords for the troops. Even today, in their religious rituals, Tibetans still use large bells and elaborate golden utensils cast during the time of the ancient Tibetan monarchy.

In the mid-seventh century, in response to an earnest request from Srong-brtsan sgam-po and his Chinese bride, Chinese craftsmen and artisans trained in the manufacture of rice alcohol, mill-stones, paper, ink and glass were sent to Tibet. Silk-worms and tea were also introduced. Simultaneously, Tibet fell under the influence of its western and southern neighbours: from India, for example, came astrological calculations and medical science.

A Tibetan script and grammar

The most outstanding attainments during the reign of Srong-brtsan sgam-po were the creation of a Tibetan script and the introduction of Buddhism. According to Tibetan tradition, Srong-brtsan sgam-po sent a young minister named Thon-mi-sambhota, *sambhota* of the Thon-mi clan, with other youngsters to the Kashmir area to study languages. After many vicissitudes, the minister succeeded in learning Sanskrit and several other languages of ancient India; he then made comparative studies of them before creating an alphabetic system for the writing of documents. Thon-mi-sambhota is also credited with compiling a Tibetan grammar on the Indian pattern.

Introduction of Buddhism

Before the introduction of Buddhism the religion of the Tibetans was Bon-po, which had many similarities with other primitive religions. Some scholars believe that Bon-po is a variant of Shamanism, while others insist on seeing the country of Zhang-zhung as the home of the Bon-po religion. Since most of Tibet's neighbours were Buddhist, the influence of Buddhism was strong. The introduction of Buddhism was marked especially by the occasion when Princess Weng-cheng of the T'ang dynasty and Princess Khri-brtsun, daughter of the king of Nepal, each brought a figure of the Buddha into Lhasa. Both princesses were married to Srong-brtsan sgam-po and propagated Buddhism among the Tibetans. After several generations, the aboriginal religions in the Tibetan area were either gradually displaced or became integrated into the more systematic and better-knit philosophical system of Buddhism.

A decisive event in the history of Tibetan Buddhism was the adoption in 791 by King Khri-srong lde-brtsan of Indian Buddhism as the state religion. It was the culmination of a process in which Indian Buddhism replaced not only the Bon-po religion but also counteracted the influence in Tibet of the Chinese Ch'an tradition of Buddhism. The main task was the translation of Buddhist writings into Tibetan and the unification of Buddhist terms (the drafting of the *Mahāvyut-patti* in 814), an activity vigorously supported by the king. He was greatly helped by one Shang-shi, who brought Buddhist books to Tibet from China, and by gSal-snang, governor of a Tibetan province bordering Nepal who not only brought in Indian books but also persuaded the great Mahayana teacher Santiraksita to spend some time in Tibet. He ordained seven young men as 'the chosen ones' (*sad-mi*) to continue his work. On Santiraksita's departure, his place was taken by the towering figure of Padmasambhava from Uddiyana. During the same period, the great Buddhist temple of bSsam-yas was completed (755?). Important though the advance of Buddhism was, it did not go unhindered. Nor did it eliminate Bon-po beliefs, which were vigorously supported by some factions of the feudal nobility.

THE FINAL YEARS

Since 789 the Tibetan troops had been pushing towards Beshbalyk and were in fierce confrontation with the Uighurs. As the two sides plunged into an even-handed war, their relations deteriorated irretrievably. The protracted warfare constantly forced the Tibetan regime to enlist Nanshao troops from the Yunnan to fight on the frontier. The Tibetans found themselves increasingly isolated, however, and the domestic situation reached a crisis. Although the army remained powerful, it could not avert the regime's final defeat. The palace coup of 846 revealed the serious corruption in the Tibetan ruling class, and frequent factional conflicts and religious strife sapped the morale of its troops and caused the collapse of the once powerful alliance of clans. Under the pressure of uprisings by the nobles and the common people in various areas, as well as in their own territory, Tibet's glorious early history of more than two centuries came to an end.

Tokharistan and Gandhara under Western Türk rule (650–750)*

J. Harmatta and B. A. Litvinsky

Part One

History of the regions

(J. Harmatta)

Trade, and above all the silk trade, played a major role in the economic life of the states of Central Asia in the sixth and seventh centuries. Political and military events, for both the sedentary and the nomadic peoples of the time, were largely determined by the struggle for control of the Silk Route. About the middle of the sixth century, the Hephthalite kingdom controlled (and derived considerable economic benefit from) the most important sections of the route, which led across Central Asia together with its branches from the Tarim basin to the Aral Sea in the west and to Barygaza-Broach in the south.

At that very time, however, a powerful rival appeared in Central Asia, the Türk tribal confederation (see Chapter 14). The Türks first came to the Chinese frontier fortresses to barter their products for silk in *c.* 545 but they were refused. After their military victory over the T'ieh-le and the Juan-juan, however, they received great quantities of silk from the Chinese states. From 569 the Chou court supplied the Türks with 100,000 bales of silk a year.[1] As the Türks accumulated great stores of the precious material, their efforts to develop the silk trade and to gain control over the Silk Route became ever more aggressive. As a consequence of their economic interests, and in alliance with the Sasanians (who shared these interests in many respects), the Türks overthrew the Hephthalite kingdom, but could only take possession of the territory of Sogdiana. The Sasanians secured Chaganiyan, Sind, Bust, Rukhkhaj, Zabulistan, Tokharistan, Turistan and Balistan as vassal kingdoms and principalities.[2]

Thus, the Türks took possession of great sections of the Silk Route in Central Asia. In spite of their military success, the Türks and their Sogdian merchants could only sell their silk stocks to the Sasanians, who refused, however, to establish trading relations with them. At first, the Türks tried to estab-

---

* See Map 7.
1. Ecsedy, 1968, pp. 131–80.
2. Harmatta, 1969, p. 401 and note 71.

lish trading relations with the Byzantines and to sell their silk stocks directly to them. But the steppe route – starting from Sogdiana and crossing the deserts to the north of the Caspian Sea and the Volga to reach Byzantine territory on the south-eastern shores of the Black Sea, and thence by ship to Constantinople – proved too difficult for the nomads. It was also unsafe because, from their fortresses on the *limes Sasanicus* in the Caucasus, the Sasanians controlled the land to the north up to the Kuban valley. Thus the Türks soon reverted to military force. In 569–570 they launched a great military expedition against Sasanian Iran in which they conquered the territory of the former Hephthalite kingdom belonging to Iran in the form of vassal kingdoms and principalities. (The Sasanians were powerless to resist because they were also engaged in war against Byzantium.) Although there is no source that gives the details of the war waged by the Türks against Iran in 569–570, it is clear from the phrase '*Turkun wa Kābulu*' (The Türks and [the people of] Kabul), in a poem written between 575 and 580 by the Arab poet al-ʿAsha, that the Türk army was operating in the Kabul–Gandhara area in 570.[3]

Later historical events show that the successor principalities of the Hephthalite kingdom, formerly annexed to Iran, accepted Türk supremacy and became vassals of the Western Türk *kaghan*. Thus, the southern section of the Silk Route was opened to the Türks and the Sogdian silk merchants, who were able to transport their merchandise to the harbours on the western shores of India. The taking of the city of Bosporus by the Türk army in the Crimea in these years was also designed to ensure control of the steppe Silk Route up to the Black Sea.

The former Hephthalite territories were probably not yet under permanent military occupation at this time. Since the Türk army consisted of tribal military forces, the permanent garrisoning of troops would only have been possible through the transfer of entire tribal groups and their livestock, providing them with an economic base. Thus, the Hephthalite principalities continued to exist as vassals of the Western Türk *kaghan*s, while the Xingil dynasty ruled in Kabul and Gandhara.

However, the Sasanians did not renounce their claim to eastern Iran nor did the Hephthalites abandon their aspirations for independence. According to the *Pei-shih* (Chapter XLIV, p. 4), both the Sasanians and the Hephthalites revolted against Tardu (Ta-t'ou) *kaghan* in 581 or 582.[4] Some years later, in 588–589, in a further war with the Hephthalites, the Sasanian army, under their commander-in-chief Bahram Chobin, took Balkh and crossed the Amu Darya. In the battle against the Türk army coming to the aid of the Hephthalites,

---

3. Harmatta, 1962, p. 133, note 5.
4. Chavannes, 1903, p. 50.

Bahram Chobin killed Ch'u-lo (**Čor*), the Türk *kaghan*, with an arrow and obtained great booty.[5]

Bahram Chobin's military successes were to have no lasting consequences, however, because shortly after his victory he revolted against the Sasanian emperor, Hormizd IV (579–590). Nevertheless, Vistahm, who was appointed governor of Khurasan by Khusrau II (590–628) after Bahram Chobin had been defeated, compelled the Hephthalite rulers Shaug and Pariowk to acknowledge his supremacy. Later, in 595 or 596, however, Vistahm was treacherously murdered by Pariowk.

The troubled years between 591 and 596 led to the Western Türk *kaghans'* decision to change the system of vassal Hephthalite principalities in eastern Iran and to submit the territory of the former Hephthalite kingdom to direct Türk rule. The realization of this plan was delayed, however, because of internecine wars between the Northern and the Western Türks. The accession of Jig (Shih-kuei) *kaghan* in 611 stabilized the internal situation of the Western Türk Empire. When war broke out between the Sasanians and the Hephthalites in 616–617, the Türk *kaghan* sent an army to the aid of the Hephthalites, won a great victory over the Sasanians and advanced as far as Ray and Isfahan.[6]

Two interesting material relics connected with the Türk invasion of Iran have recently become known. The Foroughi Collection of Sasanian seals includes a remarkable specimen with Middle Persian and Türk runic inscriptions. The Middle Persian legend runs as follows: (1) *zyk*, (2) *ḫḫn*, (3) *GDH* (Zig *kaghan*, glory!), while the Turkic text runs: (1) *b(a)q (e)š eb*, (2) *qïy (ü)g (o)ŋkü* (Take care for companions, house, settlement; make a good name for yourself!). This is clearly a seal of Jig *kaghan*, destined for the administration of the conquered territories. The Middle Persian legend was probably prepared with the help of Sogdian scribes because the spelling *ḫḫn* of the word 'kaghan' reflects Sogdian orthography (Sogdian *γ'γ'n* versus Middle Persian *ḫ'k'n*). The runic text gives the norms of royal behaviour for the Türk *kaghans* in concise form. The other noteworthy material relic of the Türk invasion of Iran is a medal representing Jig *kaghan* in profile with the legend: (1) *GDH 'pzwn zyk*, (2) *MLK' 'n MLK'* (Glory, growth! Zig King of Kings),[7] which was probably minted to commemorate his victory.

It is clear from the inscriptions that the Western Türk *kaghans* intended to annex the eastern Iranian territories to their realm. In spite of their military success, however, they failed to realize their plans. For unknown reasons, the

---

5. Marquart, 1901, p. 65; Markwart, 1938, pp. 138 et seq., 141 et seq., 153 et seq.; Czeglédy, 1958, p. 24.
6. Nöldeke, Tabari, 1973, pp. 435, 478 et seq.
7. It was published by Göbl, 1987, pp. 276 et seq., Pl. 39, Fig. 2, who could not, however, read the name of the king and erroneously dated the medal (anonymous in his opinion) from Islamic times.

Türk army was recalled by Jig *kaghan*. Thus Smbat Bagratuni, the Persian commander of Armenian origin, was again able to defeat the Hephthalites, killing their king in single combat.

The definitive annexation of Tokharistan and Gandhara to the Western Türk Empire was to take place some years later, in *c.* 625, when Sasanian Iran became involved in the war against Byzantium that ultimately led to its eclipse.[8] The Western Türk army of T'ung Yabghu *kaghan* advanced to the River Indus, took possession of the most important cities and replaced the Hephthalite dynasties with Türk rulers. This event was commemorated by a medal minted probably by Tardu *shad*, the new Türk ruler of Tokharistan, in honour of T'ung Yabghu *kaghan*, with the legend *GDH 'pzwt' yyp MLK' 'n MLK'* (The glory increased, ǰeb (= Yabghu) King of Kings!)[9]

Of the territories annexed in *c.* 625 by the Western Türk Empire, Khuttal and Kapisa–Gandhara were independent kingdoms after the disintegration of the Hephthalite kingdom. The Hephthalite kings bearing the title *xingil* of Kapisa–Gandhara continued the coinage of the Hephthalite kings of Tokharistan. The names of the kings Khingila II, Purvaditya, Triloka, Narana, Narendra I and Narendra II are attested by the legends of their coins. All the coin legends are written in the Brāhmī alphabet and all kings (with the exception of Khingila) bear Indian names. This is clear evidence of the slow Indianization of the Hephthalite royal dynasty during the sixth century. The same is true of the Hephthalite princes of Khuttal, who also minted coins with Indian legends: *jayatu Baysāra Khotalaka* (Be victorious Baysara, [Lord] of Khuttal!), *jayatu Baysāra* (Be victorious Baysara!) and *śri Vasyāra* (His Highness Vasyara!).[10]

The last Hephthalite king of Kapisa–Gandhara, Narendra II, bears on his coin (Cabinet des Médailles 1974.443) a crown decorated with a bull's head. Since the bull's head also appears on the coins of the Türk *yabghu*s of Tokharistan, this symbol clearly implies the recognition of Türk sovereignty. The appearance of the bull's head among the royal symbols of the Western Türk *kaghan*s probably goes back to the title *buqa* (bull) adopted by Tardu *kaghan* after becoming the sole ruler of the entire Türk Empire in 599.[11]

---

8. For the connection of this war with the struggle for the Silk Route and the events in Central Asia, see Harmatta, 1974, pp. 95–106.
9. Harmatta, 1982, pp. 167–80.
10. Humbach, 1966, pp. 31, 58.
11. Chavannes, 1903, p. 51.

Tokharistan

Compared with Kapisa–Gandhara, Tokharistan (with its capital, Balkh) lost much of its former importance. Although the Hephthalite ruler of Balkh bore the Bactrian title *šāva* (king), the name of his son, Pariowk (in Armenian, clerical error for *Parmowk) or Barmuda, Parmuda (in Arabic and Persian, clerical error for *Barmuka, *Parmuka) which goes back to the Buddhist title *pramukha*, shows that he was the lord and head of the great Buddhist centre Naubahar at Balkh. His dignity and power were thus more of an ecclesiastic than a secular nature. The famous Barmakid family of Islamic times were apparently the descendants of the Hephthalite *pramukha*s of the Naubahar at Balkh.

After the Türk conquest, all the principalities of the former Hephthalite kingdom came under the rule of the Türk *yabghu* of Tokharistan residing in Qunduz. The Chinese encyclopedia the *Chih-fu-yüan-kuei*[12] lists the kingdoms subject to the Türk *yabghu* of Tokharistan: Hsieh-yü (Zabulistan), Chi-pin (Kapisa–Gandhara), Ku-t'u (Khuttal), Shih-han-na (Chaganiyan), Chieh-su (Shuman), Shih-ni (Shignan), I-ta (Badhghis), Hu-mi (Wakhan), Hu-shih-chien (Gozgan), Fan-yen (Bamiyan), Chiu-yüeh-to-chien (Kobadian) and Pu-t'o-shan (Badakhshan). The Chinese pilgrim Huei-ch'ao, who travelled in these lands between 723 and 729, asserts that in Gandhara, Kapisa and Zabulistan the kings and military forces were T'u-chüeh (Türks).[13] This evidence clearly shows the immigration of a Turkic population into these territories. The settlement of the Karluks is attested by the Chinese sources and the immigration of both the Karluks and the Kalach is shown by the Arabic and Persian sources.[14]

The first Türk ruler of Tokharistan and the subjugated petty kingdoms was Tardu *shad*, the son of the Western Türk T'ung Yabghu *kaghan*. When Tardu was poisoned by his wife a few years later, he was succeeded by his son Ishbara *yabghu*, who, as first among the Türk rulers, began to mint coins. His coin effigy represents him bearing a crown decorated with two wings and a bull's head. The legend on one of his coins (Cabinet des Médailles 1970/755) runs as follows: obverse: *šb'lk' yyp MLK'* (*Išbara J̌eb* [= *yabghu*] *šāh*); reverse: *pnčdḥ ḥwsp'* ([minted in his] 15th [regnal year at] Khusp). If Ishbara *yabghu* ascended the throne in *c.* 630, the coin would have been minted in 645 at Khusp, a town in Kuhistan. Another issue[15] was struck in the 13th year of Ishbara at Herat (Harē) and a third one in his 20th year at Shuburgan. This shows that Ishbara's reign lasted to 650 and that at least three mints (at Khusp, Herat and Shuburgan) were working in the western part of Tokharistan during this period. In *c.* 650, however, Western Türk power declined and its fragmented parts

---

12. Chavannes, 1903, pp. 250 et seq.
13. Fuchs, 1938, pp. 444, 447, 448.
14. Minorsky, 1937, pp. 347 et seq.; Czeglédy, 1984, p. 216.
15. Göbl, 1967, Vol. 3, issues 265/2, 265/1.

became, at least nominally, vassal kingdoms and principalities of the T'ang Empire.

The first Türk *yabghu* (king) of Tokharistan, confirmed by the Chinese emperor, was Wu-shih-po of the A-shih-na dynasty. By this time, however (653), the Arab advance towards Central Asia had already begun. In 652–653 al-Dahhak b. Qais (al-Ahnaf), the commander of the advance guard of Amir ⁽Abdallah b. ⁽Amir, took Merv-i rud, conquered the whole of Tokharistan and agreed with the inhabitants of Balkh on the terms of their capitulation. Under the rule of the Umayyad caliph ⁽Ali (656–661), however, the Arabs were driven from eastern Iran (even from Nishapur) and the rule of Peroz III, son of Yazdgird III, was reestablished by the *yabghu* of Tokharistan in Seistan.[16] Under the reign of the caliph Mu⁽awiya (661–680), Balkh and Kabul were retaken by ⁽Abd al-Rahman b. Samura, but Arab rule did not last long.

As a consequence of the Arab invasions, the power of the Türk *yabghu* of Tokharistan was considerably weakened. After Ishbara *yabghu*, relations with China also seem to have been interrupted because of the Tibetan conquest of the Tarim basin (see Chapter 15). It was not until 705, under P'an-tu-ni-li, the *yabghu* of Tokharistan, that another mission was sent to the Chinese court. By that time, the *yabghu* had moved to Badakhshan because his capital, Balkh, and the central territories of his kingdom were occupied by the Arabs. Thus, Shuburgan, Khusp and Herat (where the mints had worked for the *yabghus* of Tokharistan) were lost and their coinage ceased to exist at the beginning of the eighth century.

Accordingly, the two issues known besides that of Ishbara *yabghu* can only be dated to the second half of the seventh century. One of them (Cabinet des Médailles 1965.1915), which bears the legend *sym yyp MLK'* (*Sēm J̌eb* [= *yabghu*] *šāh*) on the obverse and *ḫpt špwlg'n'* ([minted in his] 7th [regnal year at] Shuburgan) on the reverse, is evidence that Shuburgan was still among the possessions of the *yabghu* of Tokharistan. Another specimen of the same issue[17] indicates *ḫwsp'* (Khusp) as the minting place on the reverse. Sem *yabghu* may be identified with Wu-shih-po, the first Türk king of Tokharistan. The Chinese spelling (taking the Chinese character *po* as a clerical error for *mu*) and its North-Western T'ang form ·ᵘo- śi(ß)-m(uγ) may well reflect a foreign prototype *Āsēm ~ *Āsīm. Counting the reign of Sem Wu-shih-mu as starting in 653, his 7th regnal year would be 659–660, i.e. a year before the repeated Arab invasions under Mu⁽awiya.

The third issue (Cabinet des Médailles 1970.749),[18] which bears the legend *gwn špr' yyb MLK'* (*Gün Išpara J̌eb* [= *yabghu*] *šāh*) on the obverse, does not indicate either the regnal years or the mint. This striking phenomenon can

16. Marquart, 1901, pp. 67 et seq.; Harmatta, 1971, pp. 140 et seq.; Daffina, 1983, p. 133.
17. Göbl, 1967, Vol. 3, issue 266.
18. Ibid., Vol. 3, issues 267–71.

probably be explained by historical events, in the course of which (as mentioned previously), the *yabghu* of Tokharistan withdrew to Badakhshan, while his central territories and mints came under Arab rule. After Gün Ishpara *yabghu*, whose reign may be dated to the last decades of the seventh century, the coinage of the *yabghus* of Tokharistan came to an end and the region lost its political and military importance.

It appears that even the rule of the Türk A-shih-na dynasty ceased at that time. P'an-tu-ni-li was succeeded as *yabghu* of Tokharistan by Ti-shê, king of Chaganiyan, in 719. The later *yabghus* are only mentioned by the Chinese sources on the occasion of their missions to the T'ang court: in 729 Ku-tu-lu Tun Ta-tu (*Qutluɣ Ton Tardu*) asked for aid against the Arabs; 20 years later, Shih-li-mang-kia-lo asked for and received military aid against the Tibetans; and in 758 Wu-na-to came personally to the T'ang court and took part in the fight against the rebel An Lu-shan.[19]

Kapisa–Gandhara

As mentioned above, the Hephthalite kingdom of Kapisa–Gandhara managed to preserve its independence even after the annexation of the western territories of the Hephthalite kingdom, first by the Sasanians and subsequently by the Western Türks. At the time of the Western Türk conquest in *c.* 625, the last ruler of the Xingil dynasty in Gandhara, Narendra II, recognized the supremacy of T'ung *yabghu kaghan* and thus maintained his throne.

According to the report of Hsüan-tsang, the Chinese Buddhist pilgrim, the royal dynasty of Gandhara was extinct by the time of his visit in 630 and the land had come under the rule of Kapisa.[20] From Hsüan-tsang's account it becomes clear that prior to his arrival, the authority of the Xingil dynasty had been confined to Gandhara, while in Kapisa another prince, probably of Western Türk origin, was ruling and only united the two kingdoms under his rule after the death of Narendra II. There is no other evidence for the separation of Kapisa from Gandhara prior to the Western Türk conquest. At the time that the Western Türks advanced to the Indus, in *c.* 625, Kapisa was probably separated from Gandhara and entrusted to a Western Türk prince who also became ruler of Gandhara after the extinction of the Xingil dynasty.

According to the *T'ang shu*, the king of Kapisa and Gandhara in 658 was Ho-hsieh-chih,[21] whose name (North-Western T'ang *xâɹ-ɣiɹ-tśi* < Türk **Qarɣilaci*) clearly points to Turkic origin. At first, he may have been appointed king of Kapisa, then, after some years (but before 630) he succeeded Narendra II

---

19. Chavannes, 1903, pp. 155–8; Chavannes, n.d., p. 95.
20. Chavannes, 1903, p. 130.
21. Ibid., p. 131 and note 4.

even in Gandhara, where his accession may have been facilitated by a marriage alliance. The new Türk dynasty adopted the Hephthalite royal title *xingil* and regarded themselves as the heirs to the Xingil dynasty.[22]

In spite of the emphasis on continuity, the new Türk dynasty of Kapisa–Gandhara began to strike a new coin type[23] on which the king is represented with a crown similar to that of Ishbara *yabghu* but decorated with only one moon sickle instead of two; the Brāhmī legend is replaced by a Pahlavi one, running as follows: *nyčky MLK'* (King Niza/i/uk). The minting of this coin type lasted for almost a century (*c.* 630 – *c.* 720). The same effigy was maintained by the subsequent issues although minor modifications in the form of the crown and the ear-pendant can be observed and the legend gradually became deformed.[24] In view of the long period of minting and the fact that the first ruler of the Türk dynasty of Gandhara bore the name **Qaryilacï*, the legend *nyčky MLK'* cannot represent a proper name; it can only be interpreted as a title or a dynastic name. The reading *nyčky MLK'*[25] is firmly supported by the report of the *Chih-fu-yüan-kuei* according to which Na-sai, king of Ko-p'i-shih, sent a delegate to the Chinese court.[26] Without doubt Ko-p'i-shih (Ancient Chinese *kâ-b'ji-śie*) is the Chinese transcription of Kapisi (the kingdom of Kapisa–Gandhara) while Na-sai (Ancient Chinese *nâ-sək*) may well reflect the Bactrian variant **Nazuk* of the name **Nizük*. The reading *nyčky* had previously been identified with the name of Tarkhan Nizak, the ruler of Badhghis. A thorough revision of the palaeographic and historical evidence, however, has revealed the true form of the latter to be Tirek,[27] a name of Türgesh origin.

When the supposed connection between *nyčky MLK'* and Tarkhan Nizak is dropped, the relation of the Nizük dynasty with the tribal aristocracy of the Western Türk tribe A-hsi-chieh Ni-shu Szu-kin (**Äskil Nizük Jïgin*) becomes evident. The heads and nobles of this tribe bore the name Ni-shu (**Nizük*, cf. *Ni-shu Mo-ho shad, Ni-shu kaghan, Ni-shu Szŭ-kin, Ni-shu ch'o*). At the time of the Western Türk conquest, the royal powers and princely ranks in the successor states of the Hephthalite kingdom appear to have been distributed among the Western Türk tribal heads and nobles. Thus, the kingdom of Kapisa was entrusted to a member of the aristocracy of the Äskil Nizük Jigin tribe. The element Nizük (going back to a Saka form **näjsuka-*, meaning 'fighter, warrior', from the Saka *näjs-*, 'to fight') in the tribal name became the dynastic

---

22. Harmatta, 1969, pp. 404–5.
23. Göbl, 1967, Vol. 3, issues 198–205, 217–24.
24. Göbl, 1967, Vol. 3, issues 198 (*nyčky MLK'*), 200 (*yčky MLK'*), 219 (*čky MLK'*).
25. Besides, the readings *npky* and *nypky* are also possible, while *nspky* is impossible from a palaeographic viewpoint.
26. Chavannes, n.d., p. 40.
27. Esin, 1977, pp. 323 et seq.

name of the kings of Kapisa–Gandhara, while their family name may have been Ho-hsieh-chih (*Qaryilaci*), which was borne by the first Western Türk *yabghu* of Kapisa–Gandhara.

The Nizük dynasty of Kapisa–Gandhara separated into two branches in *c.* 670. Following a conflict between the king and his brother, the latter escaped to the Arab governor of Seistan, who permitted him to take up residence in the town of Zabul. The Arabs had already conquered Seistan in *c.* 650, but under the caliph ʿAli both Seistan and Khurasan were lost. Under Muʿawiya, however, Seistan, Tokharistan and Kabul again came under Arab rule for a decade. After the death of the Arab governor ʿAbd al-Rahman b. Samura in 670 or 671, the king of Kabul (Kapisa–Gandhara) expelled the Arabs from his territories. At the same time, his brother (by now the ruler of Zabul) conquered Zabulistan and Rukhkhaj. Although he was then defeated by the new Arab governor al-Rabiʿ b. Ziyad, the Arab sub-governor of Seistan, Yazid b. Ziyad, later suffered a heavy defeat and fell in battle at Ganza (modern Ghazni). This clearly points to the strengthening of the kingdom of Zabul. Its ruler assumed the title *zibil* (earlier misreadings include *zanbil*, *zunbil* and *rutbil*), going back to the ancient Hephthalite title *zaßolo* which was still borne by the kings of Zabul as late as the ninth century.

The relationship between the two branches of the Western Türk Ho-hsieh-chih (*Qaryilaci*) royal family, ruling in Kapisa and Zabul respectively, was far from peaceful. According to the *T'ang shu*, Zabul (i.e. the branch of the family ruling in Zabul) extended its power over Kapisa–Gandhara after 711. This event is probably the basis of the legend concerning the origin of the Türk Shahi dynasty of Kabul, as told by al-Biruni in his *India* three centuries later. According to this legend, the founder of the dynasty (Barhatakin) hid in a cavern and then unexpectedly appeared before the people as a miraculous being, thus coming to power.

It is clear that the story of Barhatakin, with its cavern motif, represents a late echo of the legend of origin of the Türks (see Chapter 14, Part One) according to which their ancestors lived in a cavern. The real historical event, however, was quite different. According to the Chinese pilgrim Huei-ch'ao, who visited Gandhara between 723 and 729 (i.e. a decade after the event), when Wu-san T'ê-chin Shai was ruling there:

> the father of the T'u-chüeh [Türk] king surrendered to the king of Chi-pin [Kapisa–Gandhara] together with all sections of his people, with his soldiers and his horses. When the military force of the T'u-chüeh strengthened later, he killed the king of Chi-pin and made himself lord of the country.[28]

---

28. Fuchs, 1938, p. 445. Fuchs did not realize that at the time of Huei-ch'ao's visit, it was Wu-san T'ê-chin Shai and not Barhatakin who was king in Kien-to-lo (Gandhara). For the origins of the Türk Shahi dynasty of Kabul, see Stein, Sir Aurel, 1893, pp. 1 et seq.

Accordingly, power in both Zabul and Kapisa–Gandhara was concentrated in the hands of the same line of the Qaryïlacï royal family. Indeed, Huei-ch'ao explicitly states that the king of Zabul was the nephew of the ruler of Kapisa–Gandhara. In spite of his legendary garb, the founder of the new dynasty, Barhatakin, must have been a real person. His name, Barha, is a hyperSanskritism for *Baha*, going back to Turkic *Baγa*, while *takin* represents the Turkic title *tegin*. The name *Baγa* is well attested among the Western Türks (in Chinese transcription *Mo-ho*; North-Western T'ang *mbâγ-γâ* < Türk *Baγa*) and the title *tegin* (in Chinese transcription *t'ê-ch'in*) was also widely used by them. Thus, the name *Baγa tegin* in the legendary tradition may in fact be authentic.

It follows from Huei-ch'ao's report that Barhatakin had two sons: one who ruled after him in Kapisa–Gandhara, and another whose son became king of Zabul. According to the *T'ang shu*, the king of Kapisa–Gandhara between 719 and 739 was Wu-san T'ê-ch'in Shai. It is clear from the historical context that he was the son of Barhatakin. The Chinese transcription (Ancient Chinese *·uo-sân d'ǝk-g'iǝn ṣai*) reflects the Iranian title *Horsān tegin šāhi*. The Chinese form of the name follows the Chinese word order, however, and may be interpreted as 'Tegin *šāhi* of Horsan'. The word *Horsān* may be the Hephthalite development of *Xvārāsān* (Khurasan) and the whole title obviously means 'Tegin, king of Khurasan'.

The coming to power of the new dynasty of Barhatakin was reflected in the coinage. The characteristic effigy of the Nizük kings was replaced by a new royal portrait. The king bears a new crown decorated with three moon sickles, or tridents, which indicates a return to Hephthalite traditions[29] and is a clear declaration of independence from the Türk *yabghu* of Tokharistan. In the first issues, the meaningless remnants of the legend *nyčky MLK'* were retained,[30] although they later came to have a purely decorative function.[31] At last, a new legend written in the Bactrian alphabet appears on the coins: σριο ραυο (His Highness the King).[32] Seemingly, the name of the king does not appear in the legend. According to al-Biruni, Barhatakin assumed the title 'šāhiya of Kabul' on coming to power. He could therefore be identified simply as 'the šāhi' in the coin legend. Perhaps simultaneously, he also minted coins with the Brāhmī legend *śri ṣāhi* (His Highness the *šāhi* [King]).[33]

Barhatakin was followed by his son Tegin *shah,* who was ruler of Kapisa–Gandhara from 719. On his accession, Tegin assumed the high-ranking title *Khurāsān shah* (king of Khurasan): this was a return to Hephthalite traditions because the two most important Hephthalite kings, Lakhana and Jabula, had

---

29. Göbl, 1967, Vol. 1, p. 155.
30. Ibid., Vol. 3, issues 225–31.
31. Ibid., Vol. 3, issues 232–4.
32. Ibid., Vol. 3, issues 236–7.
33. Ibid., Vol. 3, issue 252.

both borne this title. Tegin *shah* continued the coinage of his father in so far as he retained the crown decorated with moon sickles to which he added two wings (the symbol of the *farn*, or royal splendour). He also took into account the various ethnic elements of his kingdom in the coin legends. His earliest issue (which can be dated to 721) has an exclusively Pahlavi legend to be read in the following way: obverse (10 h) *GDH 'pzwt* (2 h) 1. *tkyn' bgy* 2. *ḥwtyp* 3. *ḥwl's'n MLK'*; reverse (9 h) *TLYN* (2 h) *z'wlst'n* (The royal splendour is increased! Tegin, the Majestic Lord, King of Khurasan, [minted in his] second [regnal year in] Zāvulistān). The remarkable fact that the issue was minted in Zabulistan points to cordial relations between the kingdoms of Kapisa–Gandhara and Zabul.

The next issue was again struck in Gandhara. Its legend is written partly in Bactrian, partly in Pahlavi and partly in Brāhmī alphabets and in Bactrian (or Hephthalite), Middle Persian and Sanskrit languages. It runs as follows: obverse (2 h) σρι ταγινο ραυο; reverse (3 h) *w'y* (9 h) *TLT'*, on both sides of the fire altar 1. *śrīla devī* 2. *Pinaśrī* (His Highness Tegin, the King, [minted at] Way<hind> [in his] 3rd [regnal year]. The beautiful Queen Pinaśrī). The peculiarity of this issue lies in its mentioning the name of the queen. This was obviously a gesture towards the Indian population of Gandhara since the queen was of Indian origin and she enjoyed high status in Indian society. This is clearly shown by the Gilgit birch-bark manuscripts, which mention the name of the queen besides that of the king. Another interesting feature of this issue is that it was minted in Way<hind> (ancient Udabhandapura, and subsequently Hund), the capital of the *šāhi* kings of Kabul. Its name occurs in its Middle Indian form here for the first time.

The third coin type of Tegin *shah* was also minted in Gandhara. The style of the king's crown differs from those of the former issues. The legend is written exclusively in the Bactrian script and language: obverse (2 h) ταγινο υωρσανο ραυο; reverse (2 h) χρονο υφδ, (10 h) πορραοορο (Tegin, king of Hōrsāno [Khurasan], [minted in] era-year 494, [at] Purṣavur [Purushapura]). The development *Purṣavur* of Purushapura almost exactly coincides with the medieval form of the name in Arabic literature, viz. *Puršāwar* and *Puršor*.[34] No less noteworthy is the dating of the issue. The date is given in the Late Kushan era, which began in 231–232.[35] Accordingly, the issue was minted in 725–726.

The fourth coin type of Tegin *shah* represents the king again bearing a new crown decorated with three moon sickles, two wings and an animal head. The legend on the obverse is written partly in Bactrian and partly in Brāhmī; the reverse is in Pahlavi script. It runs as follows: obverse, in Bactrian: οςι ραυο (His Highness the King); in Brāhmī: *śri hiḍibira kharalaca parameśvara śrī ṣahi tigina devākāritaṃ* (His Highness, the *hiḍibira*, the *Kharalaca*, the Supreme

34. Markwart, 1938, p. 109.
35. Harmatta, 1969, p. 425.

377

Lord, His Highness the *šahi* Tegin, the Majesty has [the coin] minted); reverse, in Pahlavi: (a) *tkyn' hwl's'n MLK'* (b) *hpt' hpt't'* (Tegin, king of Khurasan, [minted in the era-year] 77).

This coin legend presents some interesting problems. As concerns the date, the year 77 is apparently reckoned in the post-Yazdgird era,[36] which began in 652. Thus, the year 77 corresponds to 729. Another question is raised by the word *hidibira*. This may be the same term as the Turkic title *ilteber* or *elteber*, which also has the variants *iltber, ilber*, attested among others by the Chinese transcription *hsieh-li-fa* (North-Western T'ang *Xi(ɹ)-lji-pfvyɹ*), reflecting a foreign prototype: **ilber*.[37] The second problematic word of the coin legend is *kharalaca*, which must surely be a name or a title. It can be identified with the family name **Qarɣilaci* of the dynasty if we assume a development $r\gamma > r$ and $ï > a$ (**Qarɣilaci* > **Qaralača*) in it, which is abundantly attested in Old Turkic.[38]

This recognition may dispel the confusion in both the Chinese sources and the scholarly literature about the Chinese name Ko-ta-lo-chih or Ko-lo-ta-chih for Zabulistan. According to the *T'ang shu*, the original name of Zabulistan was Ts'ao-chü-cha (**Jaguḍa < Javula*); between 656 and 660 it was named Ho-ta-lo-chih; and then the empress Wu changed this name to Hsieh-yü (North-Western T'ang *Zi-i̯vyɹ < *Ziβil*). It is a notorious mistake of early scholarly research that, on the basis of a superficial phonetic resemblance, the quoted Chinese spellings were identified with the name Rukhkhaj, used in Arabic geographic literature to denote ancient Arachosia (Middle Persian *Raxvad*). However, this identification is impossible for several reasons.

First, Ho-ta-lo-chih was only used officially by the T'ang court from 656 to 660. It is, therefore, impossible for it to have been used instead of the official name Hsieh-yü in a document written in the imperial chancellery in 718–719. Second, the Arabic form Rukhkhaj is not attested before the tenth century. It developed as a guttural assimilation from Middle Iranian *Raxvad* > **Raxvag*, but simultaneously the original form Rakhwadh was still used by Ibn Rusta and Maqdisi as late as the tenth century. Moreover, the phonetic change $g > \check{j}$ had not yet taken place in Arabic in the seventh century, as is clearly proved by the Middle Persian transcriptions of Arabic names. Consequently, a form **Rukhkhaj* could not have existed in Arabic in the seventh century when the Chinese name Ko-ta-lo-chih came into being.

The Chinese initial *ko/ho* (Ancient Chinese *kât/ɣât*) clearly points to a foreign initial **q*. The North-Western T'ang form of the name was *kâɹ-d'â(ɹ)-lâ-tśi* and counting on $q - \gamma > q - d$ dissimilation, or on the confusion of the sign *hsia* with *ta* (which are very similar), one can regard the Chinese form

---

36. Göbl, 1967, Vol. 1, p. 144.
37. The resemblance of the form *hitivira* to the Turkic title *elteber* had already been noted by Humbach, 1966, p. 60.
38. Cf., for example, *qarɣuy* (sparrow hawk) > *qaruy*, *baliq* (fish) > *balaq*, Gabain, 1950, p. 49.

Kâi-d'â(ɹ)-lâ-tśi or *kâɹ-γa-lâ-tśi* as an exact transcription of the Türk royal family name Qarγïlacï, which became the name of the country. The case of Zabulistan shows the Chinese practice of naming a country after the name or title of its ruler. This may date back to nomadic usage and is attested up to the time of the Mongols. The first Chinese name for Zabulistan was Ts'ao-chü-cha < *Jaguḍa ~ Jagula*, the Hephthalite form of the royal title and name Javula. After the accession of the Qarγïlacï, the name of the country became *Ko-ho-lo-chih* (*Qarγïlacï*). Finally, after the separation of the two branches of the Qarγïlacï dynasty and the establishment of the Zibil kingdom at Ghazni, the Chinese named the country Hsieh-yü-kuo, or 'the country of the Hsieh-yü [*Zivil]*'. This name was retained during the eighth century because all kings of Zabulistan bore the royal title *zibil*. Consequently, in the coin legend of Tegin *shah*, the terms *hiḍibira Kharalaca* (just as the Chinese phrases *Ko-ta-lo-chih hsieh-li-fa* and *Ko-ta-lo-chih t'ê-ch'in*) do not mean 'the *elteber* of Arachosia' and 'the *tegin* of Arachosia', but simply indicate the family name (*Qarγïlacï ~ Qaralača*) and the titles (*elteber* and *tegin* respectively) of the kings.

The characteristic features of the coinage of Tegin *shah* can be seen as reflecting the historical situation, the rich cultural tradition and the ethnic composition of Kapisa–Gandhara at that time. The coin legends are written in all the important languages (Bactrian, Middle Persian, Sanskrit) and scripts (Pahlavi, Bactrian, Brāhmī) of the country and their contents refer equally to Persian, Hephthalite, Turkic and Indian traditions of royal ideology. The same syncretism is seen in Tegin *shah*'s dating of coins – in regnal years to stress his independence, in the Late Kushan era referring to local traditions, and in the post-Yazdgird era to indicate his distance from the Sasanian dynasty.

Zabulistan

As a contemporary of Tegin *shah*, his nephew Zibil ruled in Zabulistan from 720 to *c.* 738. His name was registered in the T'ang court in two different forms, Shih-yü and Shih-k'ü, but both spellings represent variants of the same title and name. Zibil Shih-yü (North-Western T'ang, *Zi-ivyɹ*) reflects the form *Zibil ~ Zivil*, also attested by the Arabic sources, while Shih-k'ü (North-Western T'ang *Zi-kivyɹ*) represents a form *Zigil*, being the Hephthalite development of *Zivil*.

The independence, importance and power of Zabulistan are well illustrated by its coinage at that time. In this respect too, Zibil was independent from his uncle, Tegin *shah*. He created an effigy based on Sasanian traditions and on the coinage of the Arab governors, a phenomenon which reflects the fact that his interests lay towards the west, while his Indian links are only represented by a short legend in Brāhmī. The legend of his coins runs as follows: obverse (1 h) *yypwl ḥwtyp'* (11 h) *GDH* (9 h) *'pzwt*; on the rim around (1 h)

PWN ŠM Y yzt' (3 h) *yypwl bgy ḥwtyp'* (6 h) *wḥm'n'n mlt'n* (9 h) *MLK'*; reverse (11 h) *śrī vākhudevaḥ* (1 h) *pncdḥ z'wlst'n* (3 h) *'pl plm'n yzd'n* (King Jibul, [his] glory increased! In the name of god, Jibul, the Majestic Lord [is] King of brave men – His Highness the Majestic Lord – [minted in his] 15th [regnal year in] Zāvulistān, by the order of the gods).

Coin issues of Jibul ~ Zibil are so far known from his 2nd, 9th, 10th and 15th regnal years. It is very likely that he died shortly after his 15th regnal year (corresponding to 735) because his son Ju-mo-fu-ta ascended the throne in 738.[39] In spite of the apparently entirely different form of his name in Chinese spelling, the new king of Zabulistan again bore the name or title Jibul. The North-Western T'ang form of Ju-mo-fu-ta was *Ji-mbui pfvyɹ-d'âɹ*, which clearly reflects a foreign prototype *jibul Pīrdar* (Elder Jibul), probably to be distinguished from a 'Junior Jibul'.

The fight for independence

One year later, in 739, Tegin *shah* abdicated the throne of Gandhara in favour of his son, Fu-lin-chi-p'o (also known as Fromo Kesaro, the Bactrian form of his name).[40] In this name, there is a confusion between the sign *p'o* and *so*; accordingly, the correct form is Fu-lin-chi-so (North-Western T'ang *pfvyr-ḷ̣um-k̠ie-sâ*) in which it is easy to recognize the Iranian name *Frōm Kēsar* (emperor of Rome [= Byzantium]). This name implies an anti-Arab programme and propaganda at the time, which might be explained by Fromo Kesaro's having entered into manhood as an *er at* (meaning 'man's name') in 719, the year in which a Byzantine delegation travelled through Tokharistan on their way to the Chinese emperor and informed the kingdoms of Central Asia of the great victory they had won over the Arabs the previous year.[41]

The coinage of Fromo Kesaro (Fig. 1)[42] is more closely connected with that of the Late Sasanians and of the Arab governors than with that of Tegin *shah*. The legends are written only in Bactrian and Pahlavi scripts and languages. They run as follows: obverse (11 h) (1) *GDH* (2) *'p<zwt>* (2 h) (1) *bg* (2) *ḥwtyp* (The glory increased! The Majestic Sovereign); on the rim around, *φρομο κησαρο βαγο χοαδηο* (Fromo Kesaro, the Majestic Sovereign); reverse (10 h) *ŠT'* (2 h) *ḥwndy* ([minted in his] 6th [regnal year at] Hund). This is the latest issue of Fromo Kesaro known so far to have been minted in Hund (ancient Udabhandapura).

---

39. Chavannes, 1903, p. 210 and note 1. As Chavannes noticed, the death of Shih-yü (*Zivil) and the accession of Ju-mo-fu-ta could also have taken place two to three years earlier.
40. Chavannes, 1903, p. 132.
41. Harmatta, 1969, p. 412.
42. Mochiri, 1987, Pl. XXI, 125.

FIG. 1. Coin of Fromo Kesaro
(obverse and reverse).
(Courtesy of M. I. Mochiri.)

The coinage of the kings of Zabulistan and Kapisa–Gandhara bears witness to the economic and political force and importance of both countries. They were able to preserve their ethnic and cultural identity and successfully fought for independence against the Arab conquerors. Arab rule was firmly established in Seistan, Badhghis, Gozgan, Tokharistan and Transoxania and even in Sind by the beginning of the eighth century. Nevertheless, and in spite of Qutaiba b. Muslim's tax-collecting expedition against Zabulistan in 710–711, both Zabulistan and Kapisa–Gandhara stood as islands in the sea of Arab predatory raids. It was only towards the end of the eighth century that both lands formally acknowledged the supremacy of the Umayyad caliph al-Mahdi and the true conquest of Kabul did not take place until the end of the ninth century.

An important recent discovery has provided a surprising insight into the events of this epoch. On the coins of some Arab governors, a Bactrian text overstruck on the rim has been discovered.[43] The reading of the text is as follows: φρομο κησαρο βαγο χοαδηο κιδο βο ταζικανο χοργο οδο σαο βο σαβαγο ατο ι μο βο γαινδο (Fromo Kesaro, the Majestic Sovereign [is] who defeated the Arabs and laid a tax [on them]. Thus they sent it.). These coins formed part of the tax paid by the Arabs to Fromo Kesaro and were overstruck with a legend telling of his victory over them. Obviously, this event occurred during the reign of Fromo Kesaro (739–746) and may have contributed to his transformation in later historical tradition[44] into the Tibetan national hero Phrom Ge-sar, whose figure still survives today in the folklore of the territory of ancient Gandhara.

The memory of the taxes paid by the Arabs has also been preserved in the Tibetan historical tradition according to which two Ta-zig (= Arab) kings, La-mer-mu and Hab-gdal, 'having taken kindly to Tibetan command, paid punctually without fail their gems and wealth'.[45] La-mer-mu may be an abridged form of the name ʿAmr b. Muslim, while Hab-gdal may have preserved the memory of ʿAbdallah b. al-Zubair. The latter evidence may also illustrate the successful resistance of the Gandharan population against the Arab conquest. However, the struggle was not decided here but in the far north at Talas, where the Arabs and Türks won a decisive victory over the Chinese army in 751.

Beside the most important successor states of the former Hephthalite kingdom (that is, Tokharistan, Kapisa–Gandhara and Zabulistan), some minor principalities also played a remarkable historical role during the time of the Arab conquest. Thus, Badhghis surrendered to the Arabs at an early date, but its energetic ruler, Tarkhan Tirek, continued the struggle until his death in 709. More successful was the resistance of Khuttal and Bamiyan, which disposed of greater military forces. The kings of Khuttal also struck coins, the land having had a tradition in this respect since the Late Hephthalite epoch. By the time of Huei-ch'ao's visit in the 720s, Khuttal already acknowledged Arab supremacy.

To the north of Gandhara were two small states of great strategic importance: Great Po-lü and Little Po-lü according to the Chinese sources. The routes leading through these countries were equally significant for T'ang China and Tibet, and as a consequence of the Arab conquest of Khurasan, the arduous Silk Route connecting India directly with the Tarim basin became of vital importance. The Chinese name *Polü* (North-Western T'ang *Bʌ\-lʲʌ*) reflects the local form, *Bolōr* (noticed later by al-Biruni), which goes back to the form

43. The discovery was made by Humbach, 1987, pp. 81 et seq.
44. Harmatta, 1969, pp. 409 et seq.
45. Thomas, 1935, Vol. 1, p. 273.

*Bhauṭṭapura (city of the Bhauṭṭas), the latter being a Sanskrit term used for the Tibetans.[46] The population of the two Bolor (Po-lü) states consisted, however, of different ethnic elements: Tibetans, Dards and Burushaskis. It is interesting to note that the name Gilgit occurs in the Chinese sources for the first time during this epoch, appearing in the form *Nieh-to* in one text and *Nieh-ho* in another. Since no confusion of the sign *to* with *ho* seems possible, one sign is obviously missing from both spellings here. The correct form is therefore *Nieh-ho-to* (North-Western T'ang *giɪ-ɣuâ-tâ*), which is a rather exact transcription (*Gilgat*) of the name Gilgit.

The conflicting Chinese and Tibetan interests led to China's military intervention in Gilgit in 747. Commanded by Kao Hsien-chih, a Chinese general of Korean origin, the Chinese forces won a decisive victory over the Tibetans and thus secured their routes to Khurasan and Gandhara.[47]

The period from 650 to 750 was a critical epoch in the history of Central Asia. The eclipse of Sasanian Iran, and the Western and Northern Türk empires, the crisis of the Byzantine Empire and the decline of T'ang China on the one hand, and the rise of the Arab caliphate and Tibet on the other hand, clearly indicate major historical changes. On the ruins of the ancient great empires, a new world was in the making. However, several centuries were to elapse before the emergence of significant new cultural achievements.

Part Two

LANGUAGES, LITERATURE, COINAGE, ARCHITECTURE AND ART

(B. A. Litvinsky)

Ethnic groups and languages

The kingdom of the Kabul Shahis was multiracial, inhabited by many different peoples. A considerable part of the population was composed of sedentary speakers of: (i) Middle and New East Iranian languages, Late Bactrian, and the New Iranian phase – the Afghan language; and (ii) West Iranian languages in the Middle Iranian and New Iranian phases – Tajik or Persian. Sanskrit and Prakrit were widespread. A large group of the population used Indo-Iranian

---

46. Chavannes, 1903, pp. 149 et seq.; Markwart, 1938, pp. 103 et seq.; Fuchs, 1938, pp. 452 et seq.: (Khuttal), p. 443 (Great Bolor), p. 444 (Little Bolor).
47. Stein, Sir Aurel, 1923, pp. 173–7.

Dardic languages as their mother tongues. Of the aboriginal languages of the east of the region, the linguistically isolated Burushaski should be mentioned. Of particular importance are the Türks (see Chapter 14), who brought their language from the depths of Central Asia. Information is given below about those ethnic groups and languages not discussed in previous chapters.

The origins of the Tajiks and of their language lie in remotest antiquity. According to the eminent Iranologist Lazard:

> The language known as New Persian, which may usually be called at this period by the name of *dari* or *parsi-i dari*, can be classified linguistically as a continuation of Middle Persian, the official, religious and literary language of Sasanian Iran . . .

New Persian belongs to the West Iranian group. In its phonetic and even its grammatical structure, New Persian had changed little from Middle Persian. Its vocabulary had changed, however, because New Persian drew heavily on the East Iranian languages, especially Sogdian, and also on the Turkic languages and Arabic.[48] Middle Persian was widespread in Khurasan and some parts of Middle Asia, partly promoted by the Manichaean movement. At the time of the Arab conquest, New Persian had already appeared in Tokharistan. According to Huei-ch'ao (writing in 726), the language of Khuttal – one of the most important domains of Tokharistan, located in the south of modern Tajikistan – was partly Tokharian, partly Turkic and partly indigenous.[49]

In connection with the events of the first third of the eighth century, the Arab historian al-Tabari relates that the inhabitants of Balkh used to sing in the New Persian (Tajik) language. It is quite possible, therefore, that a third ('indigenous', according to Huei-ch'ao) language was current in Tokharistan in addition to Tokharian and Turkic. If that is the case, Parsi-i Dari would appear to have been in use in Tokharistan as early as the sixth and seventh centuries. After the Arab conquest, the Dari language also spread to other parts of Middle Asia and Afghanistan. Much later it divided into separate Persian and Tajik branches, and a third branch is sometimes identified too – the Dari that is the contemporary New Persian language of Afghanistan. Some 30 million people speak these languages today. Like its close relatives Persian and Dari, Tajik has a rich history documented by literary sources. The wealth of literary and scientific writings created in the Middle Ages in Parsi, the literary language that is common to both the Tajiks and the Persians, is a cultural asset of the peoples of Iran, Afghanistan and Tajikistan.[50]

The Tajiks emerged as a people in the ninth and tenth (or perhaps the tenth and eleventh) centuries, but it was not until the first third of the eleventh century that the term 'Tajik' began to be applied to them. That too was when

48. Lazard, 1971; 1975, pp. 595–7.
49. Fuchs, 1938, p. 452.
50. Oransky, 1988, p. 298.

Tajik (Persian) literature was founded, and its first great representatives lived and worked in Middle Asia.

Although the origins of the Afghans lie in very ancient times,[51] the first mentions of the Afghan people appear only in the sixth and seventh centuries. The *Bṛhat-saṃhitā* (XVI, 38 and XI, 61) speaks of the *pahlava* (Pahlavis), the *svetahūṇa* (White Huns or Hephthalites), the *avagāṇa* (Afghans) and other peoples. On his return journey from India, the Chinese pilgrim Hsüan-tsang travelled from Varnu (possibly modern Wana) to Jaguda in Ghazni, crossing the land of A-p'o-k'ien,[52] a word derived from *Avakān* or *Avagān*, meaning Afghans. In Islamic sources, the first reliable mention of the Afghans is found in the *Hudūd al-ʿālam*, which says of a settlement on the borders of India and the Ghazni district that 'there are Afghans there too'. Mention is also made of a local ruler some of whose wives were Afghan women.[53] The Afghan language, or Pashto, is one of the East Iranian groups. Among its characteristics, it contains a stratum of Indian words and its phonetic system has been influenced by Indian phonetic systems, which is not the case of other Iranian languages. There are approximately 23 million Pashto-speakers in Afghanistan and Pakistan today.[54]

The mountains in the east of modern Afghanistan and the north of modern Pakistan were settled by Dards. They were known to the ancient Greek authors, who used several distorted names for them: Derbioi, Durbaioi, Daidala, Dadikai and Derdaios.[55] In their descriptions of India, the *Purāṇa*s speak of the Darada in the same breath as the inhabitants of Kashmir and Gandhara. They are repeatedly mentioned in the *Rāmayana* and the *Saddharmasmṛtyupasthāna*, together with the Odra (the Uddiyana). In Tibetan sources, the Darada are known as the Darta.[56]

There are two groups of languages that are now generally known as Dardic. The first are the languages of Nuristan (a region of Afghanistan): they form an 'individual branch of the Indo-Iranian family belonging neither to the Indo-Aryan, nor to the Iranian group'. The second group of languages (particularly the Dardic) are 'part of the Indo-Aryan [group], though far departed in their development from the latter'. The two groups, however, have much in common in their 'structural and material features [phonetical, grammatical and lexical]'.[57] The Nuristani languages include Kati, Waigali, Ashkun and Prasun (or Paruni) and are chiefly spoken in Nuristan. The Dardic languages proper include Dameli, which is the link between the Nuristani languages and the

51. Morgenstierne, 1940; Grantovskiy, 1963.
52. Hui-li, 1959, p. 188.
53. *Hudūd al-ʿālam*, 1930, p. 16-a.
54. Morgenstierne, 1942; Gryunberg, 1987.
55. Francfort, 1985, Vol. 1, pp. 397–8.
56. Tucci, 1977, pp. 11–12.
57. Edelman, 1983, pp. 14–15, 35–6.

Central Dardic. According to one classification, the Central Dardic languages comprise Pashai, Shumashti, Glangali, Kalarkalai, Gawar, Tirahi, Kalasha and Khowar. The Eastern Dardic group is divided into three sub-groups containing the Bashkarik, Torwali, Maiyan, Shina, Phalura and Kashmiri languages. In the early 1980s Dardic languages were spoken by 3.5 million people in Pakistan, India and Afghanistan, of whom 2.8 million spoke Kashmiri, some 165,000 spoke Khowar and some 120,000 spoke Pashai. The Nuristani languages were spoken by around 120,000 people.[58]

Burushaski is a completely distinct language: it stands at the confluence of three great families – the Indo-European, the Sino-Tibetan and the Altaic – but belongs to none of them. Its speakers live in northern Pakistan, in the region of the Hunza and Vershikum rivers, and number around 40,000. The language's morphological structure is very rich and the verb has a particularly extensive system of accidence. Burushaski is one of the oldest tongues, but its place in the system of ancient and modern languages remains obscure. Although a literary tradition may well have existed in the early Middle Ages, when Buddhism was widespread, no literary records have been found, which hampers attempts to reconstruct the language's past. There have been repeated attempts to trace its affiliations, and links with the Caucasian, Dravidian, Munda, Basque and other languages have been suggested, but from the standpoint of contemporary linguistics the case is not conclusive. Burushaski was unquestionably more current in ancient times and occupied a number of regions where Dardic languages are now spoken and where Burushaski acted as a substratal or adstratal foundation. Grierson has even postulated that speakers of Burushaski or related languages once inhabited all or almost all the lands now held by Dardic-speaking tribes.[59]

Writing systems and literature

We have considerable information about the literature and writing systems of the period. Hsüan-tsang reports of the writing system of Tokharistan:

> In the composition of its language [Tokharistan] differs somewhat from the remaining realms. The number of letters in its script is 25, they combine to form various combinations and with their help all may be reproduced. The script is read horizontally, from left to right. Literary works are composed in great quantity and exceed the Sogdian in volume.[60]

---

58. Morgenstierne, 1944; 1967; 1973; Fussman, 1972: Gryunberg, 1980; Edelman, 1983.
59. Grierson, 1919; Zarubin, 1927; Lorimer, 1935, Vol. 1; 1938, Vol. 2; Klimov and Edelman, 1970.
60. Pelliot, 1934, p. 50.

This refers to the Late Bactrian writing system (for its development and writing, see Chapter 6), which persisted in some parts of Tokharistan as late as the twelfth century. With time, changes obviously occurred in the Bactrian language and its various written records may reflect different dialects.[61] The script became increasingly cursive, some characters were identical in shape and some had several meanings (this is particularly true of the ligatures), making the script difficult to decipher.

Among the more famous written records of Late Bactrian (sometimes called Hephthalite) writing, mention should be made of two cursive inscriptions carved on rocks in Uruzgan (north-west of Kandahar in Afghanistan). According to Bivar, who published them, one speaks of a king of Zabul called Mihira(kula) and dates from around 500,[62] although other scholars (Henning and Livshits) suggest a far later date in the eighth or ninth century. The Bactrian inscriptions in the Tochi valley of north-western Pakistan are very badly preserved. The Tochi valley also has Arabic and Sanskrit inscriptions from the first half of the ninth century. The text of the Bactrian inscription, which is very cursive, cannot be read with confidence: Humbach's proposed reading is completely rejected by other scholars.[63]

Inscriptions have also been found on sherds and walls in Middle Asia (at Afrasiab, Zang-tepe and Kafyr-kala among others). Hsüan-tsang's account suggests that many more manuscripts existed than have yet been discovered. Nevertheless some have been preserved in East Turkestan, in the Turfan oasis.

Brāhmī manuscripts are known from Sir Aurel Stein's discovery of the Gilgit birch-bark manuscripts, which were immured in a stupa some time between the fifth and the seventh century. They include a *Prātimokṣa-sūtra*, a *Prajñāpāramitā* and others. A mathematical manuscript found near Peshawar, the Bakhshali manuscript (see below), may date from the end of this period.[64] Other birch-bark manuscripts have been found in Zang-tepe, 30 km north of Termez, where fragments of at least 12 manuscripts have been found. One of them bears a Buddhist text from the *Vinaya-vibhanga*. A fragment of birch-bark manuscript bearing a text of apparently Buddhist content has been found at Kafyr-kala in the Vakhsh valley. Mention should also be made of the Buddhist birch-bark manuscripts found at Merv and nearby at Bairam-Ali. The latter find consists of 150 sheets, both sides of which bear a synopsis of various Buddhist works, written in Indian ink. It was compiled for his own use by a Buddhist priest of the Sarvastivada school.[65] Sanskrit manuscripts of varied

61. Gershevitch, 1985, p. 113.
62. Bivar, 1954.
63. Humbach, 1966, pp. 110–17; see Gershevitch, 1985, p. 93; Harmatta, 1969, p. 345.
64. Kaye, 1927; *Gilgit Buddhist Manuscripts*, 1959–60, Parts 1–2; and others.
65. Vorobyova-Desyatovskaya, 1983, pp. 63–8.

content, including medical materials, and dating from different periods have been found in the Bamiyan valley (see also Chapter 18).[66]

It was during the late eighth and early ninth centuries that the Śāradā script was developed on the basis of Brāhmī. In Afghanistan, two marble sculptures have been found with inscriptions which 'represent transition scripts from Brāhmī to Śāradā'[67] and which date from the eighth century. The origin and chronology of the 'proto-Śāradā script [are] far from being certain and [are] still open to speculation'.[68] In this regard, some materials from Bamiyan are of interest.

The Bakhshali manuscript is written in Śāradā script and was copied by five scribes, the chief of whom was Ganakaraja. It appears to have been a commentary on an earlier mathematical work and contains rules and techniques for solving problems, chiefly in arithmetic but also in geometry and algebra. The standard of knowledge in this field is indicated by the fact that the work treats square roots, geometric and arithmetic progressions and so on. Grammars are also known. 'The oldest work of this school of grammar known to us is by Durga Siṁha who flourished in about 800 A.D. and has written a commentary entitled *Durgavṛitti* and a *Tīkā* of it.'[69]

The provinces and their rule

According to Hsüan-tsang, in the year 629 Tokharistan (Tou-ho-lo) measured approximately 1,000 *li* from south to north and some 3,000 *li* from east to west. He reports:

> For many centuries past the royal race has been extinct. The several chieftains have by force depended for the security of their possessions upon the natural divisions of the country, and each held their own independently, only relying upon the natural divisions of the country. Thus they have constituted twenty-seven states divided by natural boundaries, yet as a whole dependent on the T'u-chüeh tribes [Türks].[70]

Later reports paint a somewhat different picture. From the year 718 we have another Chinese report (see page 371 above). The *yabghu*'s younger brother ruled over Po-lü (probably Baltistan but possibly Gilgit). The capital of the 'dominion of the *yabghu* of Tou-ho-lo [Tokharistan]' was in the vicinity of modern Qunduz.[71] T'ang chronicles report that the state of Tokharistan had a

66. Levi, 1932; Pauly, 1967.
67. *The Archaeology of Afghanistan*, 1978, p. 244.
68. Sander, 1989, pp. 108–12.
69. Pandey, 1973, p. 240.
70. Beal, 1969, pp. 37–8.
71. Enoki, 1977, p. 88.

'select host of 100,000, all expert in battle'.[72] In Khuttal alone, there were reportedly 50,000 troops.[73] The rulers (*mulūk*, pl. of *mālik*, in Arabic sources) of some provinces bore specific titles. In the state of Uddiyana (valley of Swat), 'by custom people are not killed. Serious crimes are punished by exile, while trivial offences are pardoned. There are no tributes or taxes.'[74] There were reportedly 5 cities in this state and the ruler lived in the city of Chu-meng-yeh-li.[75] Use was made of trial by ordeal. The ruler took decisions only after consulting the priests.[76] In 745 the ruler of Kapisa was also the ruler of Uddiyana.[77] Earlier, in 726, a kinsman of the ruler of Kapisa was the ruler of Zabulistan.[78] Earlier still, in the time of Hsüan-tsang, 10 provinces were under his rule.[79] Thus, in the seventh century, Kapisa was a very powerful state.

In the state of Bamiyan, 'the literature, customary rules and money used in commerce are the same as those of the Tukhāra country [Tokharistan]. Their language is a little different.'[80] The ruler of Bamiyan had a large and powerful army[81] and bore the title '*sher-i* Bamiyan', while the ruler of Kabul province bore that of *ratbil shah*.[82] The capital of the state, or so al-Biruni bluntly asserts, was Kabul. Against this must be set the account of the Chinese Buddhist pilgrim Wu-k'ung, who visited these parts in the 750s and reported that 'Kāpiśī country had its eastern capital in Gandhara. [The] king resided in winter here and in summer in Kāpiśī.'[83]

Coinage

The coinage not only differed considerably from region to region, but was different in each of the provinces of Tokharistan. In what is now southern Tajikistan three variations of cast copper coins with central holes circulated: (i) coins of Tokharistan with legends in late cursive Bactrian (Hephthalite) script; (ii) coins with Sogdian legends; and (iii) coins without legends. Particularly noteworthy

72. Malyavkin, 1989, p. 68.
73. Chavannes, 1903, p. 200.
74. Malyavkin, 1989, p. 70.
75. Ibid., p. 245.
76. Bichurin, 1950, Vol. 2, p. 270; Chavannes, 1903, pp. 128–9.
77. Enoki, 1977, p. 91.
78. Fuchs, 1938, p. 448.
79. Hui-li, 1959, p. 55.
80. Beal, 1969, p. 50.
81. Fuchs, 1938, p. 448.
82. There is also a view that 'ratbil is the result of the corrupt scribe of the word Zabul' (Pandey, 1973, pp. 73–4). In the edition of the *Tārīkh-i Sistān*, the editor reports that the manuscript gives the word *ZNBYL*, supporting the reading *Zunbil*. See also Ibn Khordadbeh, 1889, p. 39; Kohzad, 1950.
83. Levi and Chavannes, 1895, pp. 349–57.

are the local imitations of Peroz drachms, some countermarked with Sogdian legends, which remained current as late as the mid-eighth century.[84]

In the part of northern Tokharistan that is now the Surkhan Darya region of Uzbekistan, different varieties of coins circulated. In Chaganiyan, silver coins of the Sasanian *shahanshah* Khusrau I (531–579) were common because Khusrau's conquests had extended to this region. Subsequently, imitations began to be struck. Interestingly, both genuine coins and imitations were countermarked, some with a cursive Bactrian legend of the ruler's name, others with a miniature portrait and others again with a symbol (*tamgha*). Sometimes the same coin was countermarked several times, with one impression on top of the other. Later, copper coins of the local *Chaghān khudāt* dynasty began to be issued. On the obverse was a portrait copying Khusrau I, in the margin three portraits of the *Chaghān khudāt* and on the reverse a fire altar. On some coins the obverse bore a Bactrian legend; sometimes it merely carried the title *khidev* (ruler) or 'Khnar (or Enar) the *khidev*'. There were also copper coins bearing the likeness of the ruler and his consort. These are the characteristic coins of the Sogdian and Turkic states. Unlike similar coins from Chach (modern Tashkent) and Sogdiana, they bore a non-Sogdian inscription and another symbol.

In Termez, copper coins were struck bearing a portrait of the ruler on the obverse, and a symbol of a different shape from that used in Chaganiyan on the reverse. This coinage was probably issued by the local dynasty of Termez-*shahs*.[85]

Although the coinage of Afghanistan and Pakistan has not been studied in such detail, issues of Vrahitigin (or Vahitigina) should be noted. These were silver coins (probably struck in the late seventh century) bearing the bust of the ruler and inscriptions in Bactrian and proto-Śāradā, the meaning of which was: 'Caused to be made by Śrī Hitivira Kharalāva, the Supreme Lord Śrī Vahitigīna the God'. On the reverse is a divinity crowned with a flame and a Pahlavi inscription. The ruler's crown comprises a wolf's head, indicating Turkic affiliations, while the divinity replicates the images on coinage of Khusrau II (590–628). Coins of this kind are found in the Indus valley, in northern Pakistan and in Afghanistan, including Kabul. Humbach[86] has suggested that Vahitigina is the same as Barhatakin, the founder of the Kabul Türk dynasty, of which al-Biruni reports, 'The Hindus had kings residing in Kabul, Türks who were said to be of Tibetan origin.' Sachau[87] suggested that this name derived from the Hindu Brhatkina or Brhatketu (for linguistics, see pages 375–6 above).

84. Davidovich and Zeimal, 1980, p. 74.
85. Rtveladze, 1987, pp. 120–9.
86. Humbach, 1966.
87. Sachau, 1888.

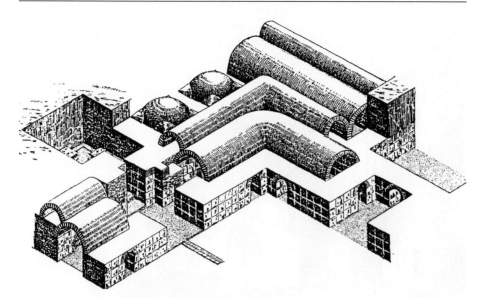

FIG. 2. Ajina-tepe. Reconstruction of the south-eastern part of the complex.

Cities, architecture and art

The capital of the state of Kapisa–Gandhara (possibly, its winter capital) was Udabhandapura, now the settlement of Hund, situated on the right bank of the Kabul river. Most of the city was surrounded by a defensive rampart. Later, in the Islamic period, it formed a square and its total length measured 1.3 km. Each side had a central gate fortified with bastions. Traces of older fortifications have been discovered and there is also a well-preserved section of the old wall some 20 m long. Around the fortified portion, the remains of buildings have been found, indicating the great extent of the town.[88]

Although Balkh remained the capital of Tokharistan, there were many other large towns that acted as provincial centres. One of them, the Vakhsh valley centre now known as Kafyr-kala, has already been described (see Chapter 6). In this period, the city was characterized by a radical restructuring of the palace and residential quarters.

Individual structures, including palaces (Kafyr-kala), castles (Balalyk-tepe, Zang-tepe, etc.), houses (Kala-i Kafirnigan) and, of course, Buddhist buildings, have been studied in considerable detail. Here we shall concentrate on Ajina-tepe (Fig. 2). This fully excavated Buddhist monastery consists of two halves that made up a single complex of religious and residential buildings, each half occupying an area of 50 × 100 m. The south-eastern half, which

88. Another identification is possible: see Caroe, 1962, pp. 97–8.

FIG. 3. Ajina-tepe. Axonometric projection
of locations XXIV and XXV. Reconstruction.

formed the monastery proper, consists of a quadrangle of buildings around a
square courtyard. In the centre of each side is an *aiwān* (hall) and behind it a
cella. The cella on the south-eastern side contained sculptures, including a
4-m-high statue of the Buddha, placed on figured pedestals. The other cellas
were large halls, which served both as assembly rooms for the *saṅgha* (monastic community) and as refectories. The *aiwān*s were linked by winding,
vaulted corridors from which passages led off into tiny cells. Some or all of
the complex was two-storied.

The second part could be called the temple. Its overall layout was identical, but there were no cells for the monks. In the central shrine there was a vast
quantity of Buddhist sculptures on pedestals, or on the floor between. In each
wall of the long, winding corridors there were three or four deep-set niches
(Fig. 3), in which large statues of the Buddha sat in varied poses. At the end of
the final corridor was a gigantic pedestal taking up almost an entire section, on
which was a 12-m-high statue of a recumbent Buddha in Nirvana (Fig. 4). The
vaulted ceilings of the corridors, and their walls, were covered in paintings and
there were also paintings in the shrines (Fig. 5).

The entire centre of the courtyard was occupied by the main stupa,
which was star-shaped in plan and accessed by four staircases, one in the

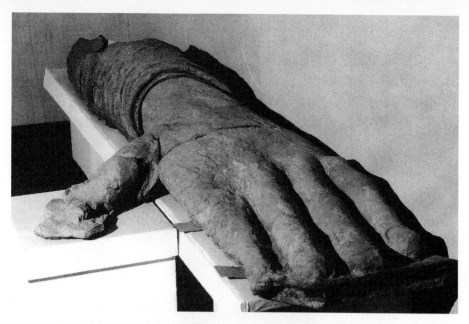

FIG. 4. Ajina-tepe. Hand of the 12-m statue of the Buddha in Nirvana.
(Photo: © Vladimir Terebenin.)

FIG. 5. Ajina-tepe. Mural painting. (Photo: © Vladimir Terebenin.)

FIG. 6. Ajina-tepe. Torso of a Bodhisattva. Painted clay.
(Photo: © Vladimir Terebenin.)

centre of each side. In the corners of the yard were miniature stupas of the
same type, some ornamented with reliefs depicting small human figures
(Figs. 6-10).[89] Buddhist temples have also been found in Kala-i Kafirnigan
(where some excellent paintings and sculptures have been preserved) and in
the palace complex at Kafyr-kala. Overall, there are grounds for speaking of

89. Litvinsky and Zeimal, 1971.

FIG. 7. Ajina-tepe. Head of a Buddha. Painted clay.
(Photo: © Vladimir Terebenin.)

Fɪɢ. 8. Ajina-tepe. Head of a brahman. Painted clay.
(Photo: © Vladimir Terebenin.)

FIG. 9. Ajina-tepe. Head of a noblewoman. Painted clay.
(Photo: © Vladimir Terebenin.)

FIG. 10. Ajina-tepe. Head of a monk. Painted clay.
(Photo: © Vladimir Terebenin.)

FIG. 11. Fundukistan. Two *naga* kings (seventh century). Musée Guimet, Paris.
(Photo: © UNESCO/Lore Hammerschmid.)

a Tokharistan school of art, related to, but not identical with, the art of central Afghanistan.[90]

Bamiyan has already been described in Chapter 6. Here we shall say a few words about the Fundukistan complex, which has been ascribed to the seventh century.[91] The part that has been excavated includes a shrine and, linked to it by a vaulted passageway, another area consisting of several monastic cells, an assembly hall and other communal rooms. The shrine is in the form of a square hall with three deep vaulted niches along each side: it appears that there were originally just two on the entrance side. Between the niches are pilasters with Corinthian-style capitals. In the centre of the shrine there was a slender stupa with an arcade on each side of its pedestal. The building material consisted of large-sized blocks of *pakhsa*. Clay statues stood in the niches, whose surface was lined with murals. The art of Fundukistan is characterized by vivid colours, bold foreshortening and elegance: although it betrays a powerful Indian influence, there is also a certain similarity with the art of Ajina-tepe and Kala-i Kafirnigan (Figs. 11 and 12).

90. Litvinsky, 1981.
91. Carl and Hackin, 1959.

Buildings of the late period at Tepe Sardar, near Ghazni, are of similar date. In this large Buddhist monastery complex, the main stupa is surrounded by many miniature stupas and shrines, ornamented with clay bas-reliefs. There were several colossal statues of the Buddha, including one seated and one of the Buddha in Nirvana. In one shrine, which is in the Hindu style, a clay sculpture of Mahishasuramardini (a form of the Hindu goddess Durga) was found. Thus a Hindu element was inserted within the Buddhist context. It is thought that this shrine is linked with the upper classes of society.[92] The remains of a Hindu shrine have also been found in Chigha Saray (or Chaghan Sarai) in the Kunar valley, dating from the eighth or ninth century.[93]

Hindu art is also represented by finds of marble sculpture such as a Shiva and Parvati (Umamaheshvara) from Tepe Skandar 30: 'It is carved from one block of white marble and represents the four-armed, three-eyed Shiva seated on Nandi, flanked by his consort Parvati and Skanda standing at the left side of his mother.'[94] The group stands on a pedestal with two steps. On the upper step there is a three-line inscription in a transitional script between Brāhmī and Śāradā. It cites Shiva as Maheshvara.[95] Another fine example of Hindu art is a marble statue of Surya from Khair Khanah:

> The piece can be divided into upper, middle and lower parts. In the centre of the upper part is Sūrya, flanked by Danda and Pingala. In the middle part is the driver Aruna holding the reins of two horses whose backs are shown as they veer upwards to the right and left. The lower part is the pedestal.[96]

A whole series of other marble Hindu sculptures dating from this period has been discovered.[97] Taken together, they indicate a powerful Indian influence and the spread of non-Buddhist Indian religions.[98]

92. Taddei, 1972; 1973; 1974.
93. Van Lohuizen, 1959.
94. Kuwayama, 1976.
95. Ibid., pp. 381–3.
96. Hackin and Carl, 1936; Kuwayama, 1976, pp. 375–6.
97. For the latest analytical review, see Kuwayama, 1976, pp. 375–407.
98. *The Archaeology of Afghanistan*, 1978, pp. 291–2.

FIG. 12. Fundukistan. Dressed Buddha (seventh century).
Musée Guimet, Paris.
(Photo: © UNESCO/Lore Hammerschmid.)

RELIGIONS AND RELIGIOUS MOVEMENTS – I*

Ph. Gignoux and B. A. Litvinsky

Part One

ZOROASTRIANISM

(Ph. Gignoux)

Nothing would be known about Zoroastrianism (Mazdaism) under the Sasanians had not one of its most outstanding religious leaders, the *mōbad* (high priest) Kartir (Kirder), left four inscriptions carved in rock at various places in Fars: near Persepolis, at Naqsh-i Rustam (KKZ and KNRm) and Naqsh-i Rajab (KNRb), and to the south of Kazerun at Sar Mashhad (KSM) (Figs. 1 and 2). In them, the magus begins by describing his own career. A mere *ehrpat* (theologian) under Shapur I (241–272), he was appointed by Shapur's successor, Hormizd I (272–273), as '*Magupat* of Ohrmazd [Ahura Mazda]' (a title that refers to the supreme god, not the king himself), and eventually by Bahram II (276–293) as '*Magupat* of the Blessed Bahram [i.e. referring back to Bahram I (272–276)] and of Ohrmazd'.[1] It was under Bahram II that Kartir obtained his most important offices, including judicial appointments. He benefited from the great favour of the king, who not only authorized him to have inscriptions carved and decorated with his bust but even had him included among the royal family and court officials on several reliefs.

The work of the magus was essentially, as he tells us in the inscriptions, to encourage the foundation of fire temples and increase the number of their attendants, and to combat religions other than Mazdaism: Manichaeism (see Part Two of the present chapter), which was beginning to spread under the vigorous leadership of its founder Mani, in whose death Kartir doubtless played a significant role; Christianity (see Chapter 18, Part One), which was gaining a foothold in Mesopotamia and Iran as early as the second century; and also Judaism and Buddhism (see Chapter 18, Part Two). However, Kartir also combated deviations from Zoroastrianism, which had been open to the influence of Greek philosophy and Babylonian astrology during the Hellenistic period. There is therefore no doubt that he contributed to the rise of a more orthodox

---

* See Map 1.
1. Grenet, 1990; Gignoux, 1991.

FIG. 1. Sar Mashhad. Inscription. General view.
(Photo: R. Ghirshman. Courtesy of Ph. Gignoux.)

FIG. 2. Sar Mashhad. Inscription. Detail.
(Photo: R. Ghirshman. Courtesy of Ph. Gignoux.)

Zoroastrianism, to establishing its supremacy over the other religions and, it is thought, to turning it into a 'state religion' linked to the power of the throne, though it is not certain that he succeeded in the last objective.

The Persians had no temples, but worshipped at fire altars on which the symbol of the supreme god burned. In the third century, only two types of fire appear to have existed: the *ādurān*, a lower category established in small localities; and the *Vahrām* fires, which served a province (*shahr*)[2] and were probably named after the king, as is suggested by coins and inscriptions – especially the great trilingual inscription of Shapur I at Naqsh-i Rustam (which mentions the fire of Shapur and fires named after members of the royal family) – rather than after the god of victory, *Vərəthraghna*.[3] There was also a temple to the goddess Anahita, for which Kartir became responsible.

The *Vahrām* fires remained the most important type during the post-Sasanian period, but at some moment that is impossible to identify, there came into being three major fires associated with social groups and bearing names that point more to a founder than to a deity. *Ādur-Farrbay* was the fire of the priests; *Ādur-Gušnasp*, the fire of the warriors; and *Ādur-Burzēn-Mihr*, the fire of the farmers. The second of these is the best known to us through German archaeological excavations[4] which discovered the exact site at Takht-i Sulaiman in Azerbaijan and a large collection of administrative documents, including the temple's official seal. The original location of the temple, however, is said to have been Media. The location of the other two major fires is also thought to have shifted westwards over the centuries, though archaeological research has failed to confirm what may be conjectured from some late texts, i.e. that the first of the fires, founded in Khwarizm, is thought to have been transferred to Kariyan, in Fars.[5] The site has not been found, but as its name was related to the *Xvarənah* (royal glory), it was also called *Ādur-Khvarreh*. The third great fire was established in Parthia, on Mount Revand (*Bundahišn* 9, 21), but its site has not been identified. It appears to have been the most venerated fire during the Arsacid dynasty. According to Boyce,[6] this triad of fires reflected the division of Iran between the Parthians, the Persians and the Medes.

Very little is known about the architecture of the fire temples since the only ones to have been properly excavated are the large Takht-i Sulaiman complex, the temple of Kuh-i Khwaja and the little temple of Tureng-tepe.[7] The monument at Bishapur, identified as a fire temple by Ghirshman,[8] is probably

---

2. Harmatta, 1964, p. 226.
3. Boyce, 1975–78, pp. 222–3.
4. Osten, von der, and Naumann, 1961; Vanden Berghe, 1979.
5. *Encyclopaedia Iranica*, Vol. 1, p. 474.
6. Boyce, 1975–78, p. 473.
7. Boucharlat, 1987, pp. 51–71.
8. See Schippmann, 1971, pp. 142–53.

not one since it is an underground construction. The most common type is the domed *chahār-tāq*, of which some 50 are known (many discovered by Vanden Berghe), consisting of 4 quadrangular pillars connected by 4 arches supporting a cupola. They are small monuments with sides less than 10 m long, a few of them surrounded by a narrow corridor and some with subsidiary buildings (called *aiwān*s) added. This type of monument has often been equated with the Sasanian fire temple but it is impossible to say whether the *chahār-tāq* was a location for public ceremonies, a temple reserved for the priesthood or the place where the fire was kept. In addition, it may date back to the Parthian period and is certainly attested at the beginning of the Islamic era.[9] Some of these monuments are hard to distinguish from signal fires that were located at the tops of hills or mountains to guide travellers while also serving as places of worship. The existence of *open* temples, however, is highly improbable.

Although the worship of fire, which had to burn eternally, appears to have constituted the central ritual of Zoroastrianism, as is also attested by the *Nebenüberlieferung* (Acts of the Syriac martyrs, Graeco-Latin sources), the sacrifice of animals accompanied by various libations continued under the Sasanians. We learn this from the great Naqsh-i Rustam inscription of Shapur, who built up stocks of sheep, wine and bread, in particular for the maintenance of pious endowments established for the souls of dead and living members of the royal family, an institution which testifies to the importance of individual eschatology among the Mazdeans. The sacrificial victim was probably smoth-ered or strangled, but not bled as among the Semites.[10]

The doctrine expounded by Kartir, which did not even refer to Zoroaster, was also essentially eschatological and could be summed up in a few simple ideas, such as the existence of a paradise for the righteous and a hell for the wicked. The need is stressed for justice and for obedience to the kings and the gods. Among the latter, explicit mention is made of Ohrmazd. In the account of a vision vouchsafed to Kartir by the gods, several deities with an eschatological function appear; though not named, they may be Rashn, Mihr or Vahman. This kind of journey into the other world, although presented for the purpose of moral edification and as a warning for the faithful, has several points in com-mon with the journey of Arda Viraz,[11] a descent into hell suggesting a shaman-istic experience.

Kartir appears to distinguish between two different rituals, that of Yasna, defined by the word *yašt*, and other rituals called *kirdagān*.[12] It should be noted that liturgical texts had not yet been written down: the Avestan alphabet had not been invented and a canon was not constituted until the fifth century at the

---

9. Boucharlat, 1985, pp. 461–72.
10. Gignoux, 1988, pp. 11–12.
11. Gignoux, 1984*a*.
12. Back, 1978.

earliest. Until that time, the only written language available was Pahlavi, but no written work from before the Islamic period has come down to us.

The *Gatha*s [Hymns] attributed to Zoroaster, and the so-called 'Recent *Avesta*' texts, were not written down until some ten to fifteen centuries later. This came after the invention of an alphabet derived from the cursive script of Book Pahlavi, supplemented by extra signs and admirably adapted to the phonetics of a language whose geographical home (Khurasan, Margiana, Bactria or even Seistan) is still a matter of discussion. Such a precise system may even not have been perfected until the Middle Ages by Zoroastrians who had taken refuge in India after the Islamization of Iran and who were familiar with the structures of Sanskrit, since the Avestan language can be correctly analysed only through comparison with that language. Indeed, it is through the Parsees of India that the *Avesta* manuscript tradition – and that of the Late Pahlavi texts – have come down to us.

The Avestan alphabet[13] comprises over 50 signs, many of them borrowed from Book Pahlavi, which serves to represent various phonemes or historical pronunciations. Old Avestan is the language of the *Gathas* (*c.* 1000 B.C.; divided into 5 sections in verse) and of the *Yasna Haptanhāiti* (in prose), but this arrangement remains rather artificial. The Sasanian collection of the *Avesta* (most of which is lost) and its commentary (called the *Zand*) is described in Book VIII of the *Dēnkard* (see page 411). It was composed of 21 *nask*s (chapters), divided into 3 sections called *gathic*s (commentaries on the *Gathas* and the legend of Zoroaster), ritual (liturgy, cosmogony, etc.) and law (primarily juridical texts). The extant *Avesta* contains, besides *Yasna* 28–53 (= *Gathas*), various prayers, invocations and professions of faith. The *yašts* (hymns to deities) constitute, together with the *Small Avesta* and the *Vendīdād* (laws relating to purification; comparable to the Book of Leviticus in the Bible), the main texts of the 'Recent *Avesta*'.[14]

In establishing itself, orthodox Zoroastrianism not only had to vie with Manichaeism, which rapidly constituted a body of doctrines presented in a great variety of writings and languages and was thus able to claim universality; it also had to struggle against internal deviations, the importance of which has occasionally been exaggerated. Among these deviations, Zurvanism was probably more a matter of popular belief than of heresy in the strict sense.[15] It expressed a more radical dualism than the Mazdean doctrine by making Zurvan, the god of time, the father of the two twin gods, Ohrmazd and Ahriman, in this way conferring equality on Good and Evil, both of which were thus created by God. This doctrine, which is described in particular in the *Nebenüberlieferung*, has been given too much weight by some authors, who either con-

---

13. Hoffmann, 1971, pp. 64–73.
14. *Encyclopaedia Iranica*, Vol. 3, Fasc. 1, pp. 36–44.
15. See Shaked, 1969.

sider it the normal form of Sasanian Mazdaism[16] or attempt to expose this heresy in the Pahlavi literature. Zaehner,[17] for instance, believed he had detected three strands of Zurvanism, a claim that was rightly rejected by Molé.[18]

Mazdakism, which was as much a social as a religious movement, enjoyed a certain success because it was supported by the monarchy under Kavad I (488–531). The movement was not initiated by Mazdak but by one Zardusht. Thanks to the famous polygraph al-Shahrastani, who included a brief analysis of it in his *Kitāb al-milal wa 'l-niḥal*,[19] and to a few allusions in the *Dēnkard*, its doctrine is quite well known: in some ways reminiscent of communism, the movement impressed people by its teaching that possessions and women should be held in common. Shaki[20] has noted its limits, showing how such a system of marriage in common or in a group could only have evolved in a very closed society that practised incest or consanguineous marriage (*xwēdōdah*). In his view, too, the cosmogony of Mazdak hardly differed from that of Mazdaism.[21] Recently, however, Sundermann[22] has emphasized the Mazdakite community's sense of solidarity in times of famine, and pointed out that the consequences of holding women in common would tend to create a matrilinear society, which could only offend the Zoroastrians, attached as they were to male predominance. The fact that a few women (Boran, Azarmigdukht) attained supreme royal power at the beginning of the seventh century may reflect a certain change in attitudes.

The esoteric or mystical character of Mazdakism, which was welcomed by Arabo-Persian authors, who related it to the *bāṭiniyya*, enables us to define it as a gnosis, the principal traits of which have been defined by al-Shahrastani. Salvation was achieved through faith and justice, not through observance. There was no longer any religious obligation for those in whom the 4, 7 and 12 powers (an obvious reference to the planets and the signs of the zodiac) were united. Shaki recognizes that it was, like any gnosis, a syncretic movement in which doctrines deriving from the Graeco-Jewish writer Philo, neo-Platonism and neo-Pythagorism may also be detected, but that it had little in common with Manichaeism. Mazdak is said to have been put to death by Khusrau I (531–579), who brought the movement to an end.

Al-Shahrastani believes that there were a large number of sects or heresies in Sasanian Iran. Indeed, as Shaked[23] has shown, a pluralist attitude to faith may have predominated. He points to great tolerance over differences in

16. Christensen, 1944, p. 150.
17. Zaehner, 1955.
18. Molé, 1963.
19. Shahrastani, 1986.
20. Shaki, 1978.
21. *Papers in Honor of Professor Mary Boyce*, 1985.
22. Sundermann, 1988.
23. Shaked, 1987.

the formulation of doctrines, though such deviations from religious orthodoxy did not necessarily entail the constitution of separate ecclesiastical structures – it was simply that Sasanian Zoroastrianism was not monolithic.

The presence and expansion of Zoroastrianism in the eastern provinces of Sasanian and Kushano-Sasanian Iran, and further east through Central Asia and as far as China, remain obscure, despite large numbers of excavations in regions governed by the former Soviet Union. These have so far yielded little evidence apart from archaeological monuments and objects relating to the religious or material culture. There are almost no texts apart from those found at the famous sites of Turfan and Dunhuang. These do not concern Zoroastrianism but are essentially related to Manichaeism, Nestorianism and Buddhism, which cohabited or succeeded one another in East Turkestan. They are fundamental for the history of those religions and even more so for our knowledge of Middle Iranian (Sogdian, Middle Parthian and Middle Persian) and Turkic.

Using the literature published in Russian over the last few decades and as a result of his own studies, Grenet has shown that the northern regions, Sughd and Khwarizm, provide evidence of funeral practices and eschatological doctrines that accord with what we learn from the works in Pahlavi (see below) on sixth- and seventh-century ossuaries. For several of these, Grenet[24] has identified scenes of Mazdean liturgy, the representation of the six *Amesha Spentas* (Abstract Entities), or even the judgment of the soul, in accordance with the doctrine of the Pahlavi texts, even though lamentation rites (as on the Panjikent frescoes) were normally prohibited.

In Bactria, Kushan coins attest to a whole series of Zoroastrian deities but to only two of the *Amesha Spentas*, Shahrewar and Wahman, whose relationship to Greek and Indian gods provides evidence of a clear tendency to syncretism.[25] The cult of water, concentrated on the deified Oxus (Amu Darya), which is represented on these coins as a bearded man with a fish, is also found at Panjikent. On the Kushano-Sasanian seals, it is Mithra who invests the king (further west this falls mainly to Ohrmazd) and plays an important role together with the river god.

Central Asia seems to have been unaffected by the development of the fire cult as the only legal form of Zoroastrianism, the type found in western Iran. This is shown by the Kushano-Sasanian coins and by the name of the temple in Sughd (*vaγn* < **bagina*: 'dwelling-place of god'), where there appear to be signs of the worship of statues of Iranian deities. Of the temples excavated, only Temple B of Surkh Kotal may be regarded as a genuine fire temple. Those at Toprak-kala (Khwarizm, fourth–fifth century), Er-kurgan (Sogdiana, second–seventh century, and where a *dakhma* for exposing the dead has, it

24. Grenet, 1986.
25. Grenet, 1988.

seems, also been identified), Kurgan-tepe (Samarkand, third–fourth century), Panjikent (fifth–eighth century) and Kayragach (Ferghana, fifth–sixth century), among others, are not fire temples, although their functions as places of worship are well established. The temple of the god Oxus at Takht-i Sangin merely has two 'chapels' reserved for the worship of fire. The cassolettes for incense or for the burning of offerings, found in connection with a deity in Kushan Bactria, in Sogdiana and as far as Gandhara, should not be confused with the receptacles for fire in the fire temples. The lack of texts rules out a detailed overview but the essential fact that emerges is that the cult of images was not, in eastern Iran, subject to the iconoclastic taboo of Sasanian Zoroastrianism.

In Margiana and Bactria, Sasanian Zoroastrianism had to compete with Buddhism, and also with Hinduism and the worship of Shiva, but the Buddhist complex at Kara-tepe was abandoned in the fourth century (?), probably because of the Zoroastrians. Merv had a Nestorian community in the fourth century and there was a bishopric at Samarkand, where Jews and Manichaeans also lived, in the sixth century. To the north in Khwarizm and Sogdiana, on the other hand, Buddhism made little headway.

As far as is known, relations between Iran and China did not really start until the end of the fourth century when, with the decline of the Kushan Empire, the Sasanians were able to gain control over the first portion of the Silk Route, the rest of it being in the hands of Sogdian and Indian merchants and later, after the fall of the Hephthalite Empire, of Persians. These last did not really establish themselves in China until some time during the sixth century, as attested by the discovery of several hoards of Sasanian coins. There was at that time a considerable penetration of Iranian culture into China from Central Asia. One eloquent, albeit rather late (784) piece of evidence is the Pahlavi-Chinese tomb inscription of Xian.[26]

Although we are unable to determine the nature of Zoroastrianism in China itself, the works in Pahlavi, though not written until the ninth and tenth centuries, are a rich source of information concerning the religion as it was practised in the east. This collection includes translations of Avestan texts (the *Yasna*, the *Vendīdād*, etc.) and compendiums covering a wide range of subjects. For example, the cosmogonic myths about the creation of the world, together with eschatological doctrines concerning the destiny of the individual soul and the events of the last days leading to the restoration of a world identical to that of the beginning of time, are found chiefly in the *Bundahišn* [The Primal Creation] and in the *Vizīdagīhā-i Zādsparam*. The latter is an 'anthology' which includes a large section on the hagiography of Zoroaster, describing the attacks starting in childhood and from which he escaped, and his miraculous powers. The same stories appear in the *Dēnkard* (Books V and VII). Another topic concerns the rules of legal purity, dealt

---

26. Humbach and Wang, 1988.

with at length in the *Vendīdād* or *Šāyist-nē-šāyist* (what is permitted and what is prohibited, with a list of the fines to be paid as reparation for transgressions) or the *Dādestān-i dēnig*. The *Mādayān-i hazār dādestān*, a document of a more strictly legal nature, provides specific information on family law, the law of property and judicial procedures. Other texts concerned with correct ritual are the *Nērangestān*, which deals with liturgical expressions and headings, and the *Hērbadestān*, which is chiefly a manual for the use of Mazdean priests.

Manushcihr, the brother of the ninth-century priest Zadsparam, left three long letters in which he protests against the tendency to simplify the ritual, necessitated by the difficult conditions in which the community found itself after the Islamization of Iran. These conditions are described in numerous texts – though the Muslims are almost never mentioned – in particular, in the *Dēnkard*, an enormous compilation divided into nine books (the first two of which are lost) and intended to encompass all the knowledge of the Zoroastrians. This work makes much greater use of philosophical argumentation than do the other books, frequently using concepts borrowed from Greek or Indian science, in order to refute the tenets of Islamic philosophy, as de Menasce[27] has clearly shown, and hence belongs to the literature of apology. Faced with Muslim attacks concerning the problems of divine attributes and of divine causality with regard to evil, the Mazdeans wanted to defend their dualism and reject the patent determinism of certain schools of Islamic thought. The *Škand gumānig wizār*[28] is even more of an apologia for Mazdaism, not only against Islam but also against Manichaeans, Jews and Christians.

The *andarz* (wisdom literature), later highly valued by the Persians, is represented in the *Dēnkard* (Book VI)[29] and in a few other scattered texts. The Mazdean *Apocalypse* was probably a late work,[30] and the events it predicts may be related to the troubles arising from the rebellion of Bahram Chobin (sixth century) and even more closely to the revolt of Mazyar (between 823 and 840), reported in the *Zand-ī Vahman yašt* (a so-called translation of an Avestan *yašt* which never existed).

The royal ideology – immortalized by Sasanian sculpture as its sole artistic expression, and associated with the glory of the ancient mythical Kayanian kings – occurs in numerous texts. It must have been the basis for the *Khwadāy-nāmag* [The Book of Lords], now unfortunately lost, which linked the history of legendary kings with that of historical kings and inspired the authors of epics, the most famous of whom is Firdausi. The alliance between royalty and religion, presented as two sisters or two twins unable to live without each other,

27. Menasce, de, 1958; 1973.
28. Menasce, de, 1945.
29. Shaked, 1979.
30. Gignoux, 1986.

is a recurring theme which, however, must not be taken literally. It seems to have represented an ideal which impressed Arabo-Persian writers and provided the inspiration for a literary theme.[31]

The palace revolutions which led to a whole succession of kings after the reign of Khusrau II (591–628), and the conquest of the empire by the Arab armies, must have rapidly disrupted the Mazdean Church. Wealthy supporters of the temples probably preferred to support the new power and Islam in order not to be ruined by the heavy taxes henceforth imposed on minorities, since the Mazdeans were held in even lower esteem than the Jews or Christians. The priests, as can be seen from certain chapters of the *Dādestān-i dēnig*,[32] faced serious financial difficulties in celebrating their offices. Many Zoroastrians later emigrated to India, where they are known as Parsees. Here they established flourishing communities and were able to safeguard the texts of the Sacred Canon which can still be read today.

Part Two

MANICHAEISM

(B. A. Litvinsky)

The founder of the Manichaean religion, Mani (216–274 or 277), was able to propagate his teaching without let or hindrance in Iran during the reign of Shapur I. After Shapur's death in 272, however, the opposition of the Zoroastrian priesthood became increasingly active. Finally, the prophet of the new religion was imprisoned and tortured to death and Manichaeism became a persecuted religion in its birthplace, the Sasanian Empire.

Mani, who was acquainted with many religions, especially Zoroastrianism, Christianity, Mandaeism and Buddhism, proclaimed the foundation of a world religion to replace all existing religions. He borrowed much from their doctrines and practices, and therefore, for all its idiosyncrasies, Manichaeism is a syncretic religion. In consequence, it was partly familiar to Zoroastrians, Christians and Buddhists and the prophets of these religions were adopted by Manichaeism as its precursors. This encouraged the spread of Manichaeism and made it a universal religion, one that was easily propagated among the followers of other faiths.

The basic principle of the Manichaean religion was an all-embracing dualism, reflecting the dualism of the environment in an idealistic form. In working out his dualistic conception, Mani borrowed much from Iranian

31. Gignoux, 1984*b*.
32. Kreyenbroek, 1987.

religion and the Gnostics. According to the Manichaean religion, the 'two principles' (*dō-bun*), Good (= Light) and Evil (= Darkness), have existed from the beginning; they are uncreated and are the direct opposites of each other. The modern world as a whole, and man in particular, is a mixture of the two principles. At the same time, they are not equal – Good is the higher. In the world of light, the Father of Light (in Middle Persian, *pydr rwšn*) (also called the First Parent) sits enthroned. The Divinity of Light has a twelvefold Diadem of Light and is surrounded by twelve sons.

The good god is called the God of Light and acts more as an abstract principle than a personality. The God of Light has five 'light elements': Ether, Air, Light, Water and Fire. His kingdom reaches out limitlessly to the north, west and east.[33] In the south it borders on the kingdom of the Prince of Darkness (in Middle Persian, Ahriman). This kingdom is divided into five worlds (or caves). The Kingdom of Darkness is the source of eternal disturbance and agitation. Incursions are made from it into the Kingdom of Light. In outward appearance, the Prince of Darkness is a mixture of a number of different beings.[34] The origin of the universe is the junction or merging of the forces of light and darkness.

When the forces of the Prince of Darkness invaded the Kingdom of Light, the King of Light offered resistance. For this purpose he evoked two spiritual principles, or rather he 'called up' the Mother of Life, who in her turn called up Primordial (or the First) Man, her son (in the Central Asian texts, Ohrmazd, or Ahura Mazda). He entered the struggle and suffered a fatal defeat. The second part of the cosmogonic act was the liberation of captive Primordial Man. Although he was liberated, he left five elements, his sons, in captivity when he returned to the heavens. Nevertheless particles of darkness penetrated into the light-bearing principle. With the aim of 'purifying' it, the Father of Light created the visible world: the earth, heaven and the heavenly bodies.

The earth and heaven were created from the bodies of the slain demons, 'from the generation [or line] of darkness' (Augustin, *Contra Faustin*, XX, 9), and the heavenly bodies from the liberated particles of light. In order that victory might be complete, a third messenger came into the world at the behest of the Father of Light – the Living Spirit. He had the attributes of the Iranian sun god Mithra (the name by which he is called in the Middle Persian work the *Shābuhragān*) and at the same time he prefigured Mani himself. The third messenger evoked the Maiden of Light (Twelve Maidens) and forced the demons of darkness to ejaculate the seed and embryos from which plants and animals were born. In answer to this, the forces of darkness gave birth to Adam and Eve in the form of gods, in an attempt to keep back particles of light so that the flesh would continue to absorb light elements. They passed on to the

33. *Fihrist*, 1970, pp. 786–7.
34. Ibid., p. 778.

first human couple the particles of light which had been absorbed by the forces of evil that gave birth to them, and formed the souls of this couple. This was a dark or material soul, made up of such things as lust, greed and envy. Jesus, evoked by the Father of Light, aroused this couple, and they became 'new' people instead of 'old', able to distinguish between good and evil.[35] At this time a constantly operating mechanism was set up for the liberation of the light particles, which finally rose up into the Kingdom of Light.[36]

The elements of light were separated from the elements of darkness with the coming of Mani. Their complete separation will occur when the Last Judgment takes place – the Great War, when the spirit is freed from the body, the particles of light rise up to heaven and the carriers of darkness are cast down.[37] It will be a sign of the end of the world when the forces of evil prevail and a considerable part of the light is driven out of the world. This will be followed by the second coming of Jesus, who will sit in judgment and separate the righteous from the sinners. Then heaven and earth will collapse, a Great Flame will arise and all the particles of light will be liberated. A new paradise will come into being and evil will be fettered and incarcerated in a great stone: the Kingdom of Light will have arrived.[38]

Thus man is destined to work for the liberation of the light particles in his own being and in the world around him, and for their union with the principle of light; he must support the principle of light. Man should not kill his fellow men, nor should he kill animals; he should lead a moral life. Nevertheless, evil and the forces of darkness are very active, and man, because of his origin, is predisposed to evil. Man, who has free will, should struggle resolutely with evil (darkness) and choose good.

These precepts were addressed to the Manichaean laity, the 'hearers', both men and women, who had to observe certain rules of conduct. For example, they were forbidden to kill animals, and they could eat only the flesh of animals that had died a natural death or been killed by others.[39] The main aim of their life was to do good and above all to provide food for the 'elect' and to serve them. The task of the 'elect' was to pray and to spread the doctrine. In addition, they ate vegetable food (especially melons and cucumbers, in which light was supposedly concentrated) and bread, and let these foods pass through them. Thus their bodies served as a 'filter' for the liberation of the particles of light contained in the plants, which then 'along the Column of Glory mount from Earth to Heaven'.[40] Although the 'elect' were allowed to eat only vegeta-

---

35. Boyce, 1975, p. 7.
36. *Fihrist*, 1970, p. 782.
37. Polotsky, 1935; Puech, 1949; Widengren, 1961; 1983; Klima, 1962.
38. Boyce, 1975, p. 8; for a detailed description in the *Shābuhragān*, see Mackenzie, 1979, p. 513.
39. Asmussen, 1975a, p. 27.
40. Gershevitch, 1980, p. 282.

ble food, they were forbidden to pick the plants and fruits themselves – this was the task of the 'hearers'. The preferred drink was fruit juice. All sexual life was forbidden.

The 'elect' who lived in the monasteries were required to journey on foot, spreading the doctrine. They ate once a day, after sunset, and were allowed to possess no more food than was necessary to feed them for one day and no more clothing than was needed for one year.

A pious layman 'hearer' could become an 'elect' and then attain paradise, but only after a cycle of reincarnations. (Mani's doctrine included a belief in the reincarnation of souls similar to the Indian concept of *saṃsāra*.) The practice of repentance and absolution was widespread. An adherent could acquire the chance of salvation by devoting his life to the service of the 'elect', in which case he could hope to be born again as one of the 'elect' and attain paradise. The impious would go to hell. The lowest rank in the Manichaean hierarchy was that of the 'hearers', then came the 'elect'; even higher were 360 Elders, then 72 Bishops and finally 12 Teachers. At the head stood Mani's successor, whose seat was in Babylon.[41]

Manichaeism contained a considerable element of social criticism, declaring the world to be the incarnation of evil. Manichaeans rejected everything in the world around them, including social institutions, and this could be regarded as a form of social protest. Nevertheless, since they held that evil was eternal, they did not believe it was possible to destroy evil on earth. This explains their characteristic pessimism, their feeling that there was no solution. According to this doctrine, the rich would inevitably go to the Kingdom of Darkness. The future of the adherents of the religion was seen as a liberation from all adversities – the Kingdom of Light. The element of social protest inherent in the Manichaean religion made it attractive to the oppressed masses.[42]

Manichaeism inspired a rich literature. Mani and his followers used a special 'Manichaean script' (supposedly invented by Mani himself), which was related to Syriac Estrangelo and even more closely to the Mandaean script. Mani used the East Aramaic language, for reasons which are clear: it was the language spoken over the widest area and could be used as a linguistic medium for the propagation of the new doctrine. All the earliest Manichaean religious works, with the sole exception of the *Shābuhragān*, were written in East Aramaic. Mani himself is said to have thought and spoken in Aramaic.[43]

For the study of the Manichaean doctrine, the Manichaean sources themselves are of the first importance, especially the seven canonical texts: the *Shābuhragān*, the *Living Gospel*, the *Treasure of Life*, the *Pragmateia*, the *Book*

41. Asmussen, 1975a, pp. 29–31; for a detailed analysis, see Schaeder, 1934, pp. 11–16; Van Tangerloo, 1982.
42. Kats, 1955; Sidorov, 1980.
43. Schaeder, 1934, p. 11.

of Mysteries, the *Book of Giants* and the *Letters*. Only the first of these, the earliest work, is written in Middle Persian; the others were compiled in Syriac. Among the other Manichaean sources, the *Kephalaia* is important. Mention should also be made of the *Homilies* and a collection of illustrations of the most important aspects of the doctrines, the *Ārdhang*.[44]

In addition, in Manichaean circles in Egypt and East Turkestan, canonical Manichaean works were translated and original works written in various languages. Many Manichaean works have been found in East Turkestan; they are written in Middle Persian, Parthian, Bactrian, Sogdian, Ancient Turkic and Chinese. For example, there was a translation of the canon into Parthian by Mar Ammo (see below), an associate of Mani. There was an extensive Manichaean religious literature in Parthian, consisting of two cycles of hymns, prose works about the life and activities of Mani and his death, expositions of the doctrine and liturgical texts.[45] The canon was also translated into Sogdian, as were prayers, precepts and Manichaean prose works, including the history of the spread of Manichaeism in the east, and the text of the confession for the use of the leaders of a Manichaean community. Even letters have survived, addressed to various people, including a certain Manichaean teacher.[46] Old Turkic works include the penitential prayer of the Manichaeans, the *Xᵘāstvanīft*.

Much information (some of it valuable) can be found in Christian polemic works such as the *Acts of Archelaus* (*Acta Archelai*), the works of St Augustin, the Syrian Christian chronicles, and the *Book of Commentaries* of the Syrian Theodor bar Konai. Especially valuable Islamic sources are the *Chronology* of al-Biruni and *al-Fihrist al-ʿUlum* by Ibn al-Nadim.[47]

Mani's teaching spread far and wide even during his lifetime and he himself undertook a missionary journey to Sind. In the course of his journey, he also visited the town (and region) of Turan in Baluchistan. Here Mani was received as a true Buddha, and as a result of his preaching many were converted, including the ruler Turanshah and the nobility.[48] Although Mani claimed that he 'converted the whole country of India to the doctrine', in fact he meant the north-west part of India.[49] It is possible that he made other journeys to the east – the sources mention 'the Parthian state', 'Kushan' and other lands,[50] but this may be a reference to missionary travels undertaken by his disciples. Manichaean missionaries engaged in polemics with other religions. According to one Middle

---

44. Boyce, 1968, p. 70.
45. Boyce, 1954; 1968; 1975; Asmussen, 1975*b*; Sundermann, 1973; 1979; 1981.
46. Asmussen, 1975*b*.
47. Flügel, 1862; Hegemonius, 1906; Alfaric, 1918–19; Polotsky, 1934; 1935; Säve-Söderbergh, 1948; Widengren, 1961, pp. 77–86; Klima, 1962, pp. 401–512; Abel, 1963; Rudolph, 1974; Adam, 1969; Heinrich and Koenen, 1975; Asmussen, 1975*a*, 1975*b*.
48. Henning, 1977, 1, p. 385; Sundermann, 1971*b*, pp. 375–6.
49. Sundermann, 1971*a*, pp. 88–91.
50. Henning, 1977, 1, p. 386.

Persian text, they were especially vehement in their opposition to 'idols, idol priests, altars and their gods'.[51]

Mar Ammo was one of the main preachers of Mani's teaching in the east. He had a good knowledge of the Parthian language and script. On Mani's instructions, and in the company of the Parthian prince Ardavan and several scribes, Mar Ammo travelled to Abarshahr (Nishapur), whence he continued to Merv. According to the *Missionary History*, 'he ordained numerous kings and rulers, grandees and noblemen, queens and ladies, princes and princesses . . . He completed and fulfilled all orders and injunctions that [had been given] him by [Mani].' He then travelled further east into the lands of the Kushan Empire, where he set up a Manichaean community in one of the towns.[52]

Merv became one of the main centres of Manichaean propaganda in the east. After the death of Mani, the head of the Manichaean hierarchy came to Merv, where he found that 'all the brothers and sisters lived in piety'. He sent one of them, called Zurvandad, with two sacred books to Mar Ammo, who was preaching in the town of Zamb (according to Arab geographers, this was Zamm on the Amu Darya). In his accompanying letter, he wrote that other copies of these books would be made in Merv.[53]

In the east, in Middle Asia and later in East Turkestan, a distinct Manichaean sect arose. According to Ibn al-Nadim, it was called 'Dinawariyya', from the Middle Persian *dēnāvar*, meaning 'giver [or carrier] of religion'. This sect – which constituted an independent church, having its own leader – came into being very early, either during Mani's lifetime or soon afterwards.[54]

The Eastern Manichaean Church used Middle Persian as its main sacred language. There were also Manichaean texts in Parthian; the Sogdians copied them, and added versions in Sogdian. Most of the Manichaean texts discovered in East Turkestan were the work of copyists in Sogdian Manichaean communities. Parthian was apparently supplanted as early as the fifth century, and was preserved in the Eastern Manichaean Church as a dead language. In the sixth century it was replaced by Sogdian in the region of Transoxania, although it remained in use in northern Khurasan. There were flourishing Manichaean communities in Merv and Balkh.

Buddhism and Manichaeism coexisted in Central Asia for a long time. Even the most ancient Parthian Manichaean texts (poems which can be attributed to Mar Ammo himself) contain some Indian Buddhist terms and the number of these increases in fourth-century Parthian texts. A Manichaean text on magic, which was probably written on the border of Iran and India, perhaps in Balkh, in the sixth century, indicates that there were very close

51. Asmussen, 1975*b*, p. 13.
52. Henning, 1977, 1, pp. 200–3; 2, pp. 225–30.
53. Ibid., 1, p. 285.
54. Ibid., 1, p. 202, footnote 1; Sundermann, 1974, pp. 12–128, 131.

contacts between Manichaeans and Buddhists. Sogdian Manichaean texts also include borrowed Buddhist terms and concepts connected with Buddhist tradition.[55]

Buddhism had a considerable influence on the pantheon, the terminology and even the concepts of Eastern Manichaeism, and also on its religious practice. For example, one of the central concepts of Eastern Manichaeism, that of the confession of sins, may have been borrowed from Buddhism or the reverse.[56] Under the influence of Buddhism, Manichaean monasteries (*mānistāns*) appeared in the east and later in the west. Information about them comes from documents found in East Turkestan, including one Old Turkic document of the tenth or eleventh century which mentions a monastery in Turkestan. The document even lists the provisions which were to be delivered: 'Every day 30 melons must be taken to a big monastery and 30 to a small monastery.'[57]

Manichaean worship included prayers, the singing of hymns, and preparations for the feast of the remission of sins. The 'elect' had to pray seven times a day and the 'hearers' four times. They prayed facing the sun during the daytime and facing the moon at night. Manichaeans had a religious ceremony which marked the imprisonment and death of Mani; it took place in spring and lasted the whole month. On the last day of this month (i.e. the thirtieth) there was the celebration of *Bema* ('the Throne'). An empty throne was set on a dais and a portrait of the prophet was placed on it.[58] The dais had five steps and was covered with rich draperies.

In the second half of the sixth century the Central Asian Manichaean community, then led by Shad-Ohrmazd (from Babylon), declared its independence. In the eighth century, however, the schism was healed, and during the period of office (710–740) of Mihr as head of the Babylonian community his jurisdiction was recognized also in Central Asia.[59]

Manichaeism played an important role in the ideological life of Central Asia right up to the time of the Arab conquest. In the year 719, for example, Tokharistan was among the countries that sent envoys to China. The embassy was headed by the Great Mu-shia, a Manichaean 'elect', and a man profoundly versed in the 'configurations of the heavens'. His name is a Chinese transcription of the Manichaean term *mōčag* (literally, 'the teacher'). The king of Chaganiyan (a region in Tokharistan) asked the Chinese emperor to confer

---

55. Henning, 1977, 1, p. 383; 2, pp. 227–30, 283–4; Asmussen, 1965, pp. 136–47; Sims-Williams, 1983, pp. 132–40. For general issues concerning the relationship between Manichaeism and Buddhism, see Ries, 1980.
56. Asmussen, 1965.
57. Zieme, 1975, pp. 332, 334, 336.
58. Boyce, 1975, p. 3.
59. Ibid.

with his envoy on the subject of the condition of the state and 'our religious teachings'.[60]

Following the Arab conquest, a more lenient attitude was adopted towards the Manichaeans and many of them returned to Iran and Mesopotamia. Under the ʿAbbasids, however, savage persecutions began again. The head of the Manichaean Church lived in Baghdad until the tenth century, when his residence was transferred to Samarkand.[61] According to Ibn al-Nadim, during this century there were Manichaeans in Samarkand, Sogdiana and especially Tunkat (in the Tashkent region).[62]

There were many conversions to Manichaeism in East Turkestan. Its advance was encouraged when the Uighur ruler Bögü *kaghan* adopted Manichaeism in 762, after which it became the established religion of the Uighur state. According to a Uighur text, the ruler decided to become a convert after an inner conflict. After two days and nights of unceasing preaching by Manichaean missionaries, Bögü *kaghan* appeared before the assembly of the Manichaean 'elects', and 'falling before them on his knees and bowing, begged them to absolve him of his sins'. Then he said, 'When your "elects" give the command, I shall move [act] according to your words and your advice.'[63] Under normal circumstances, however, as can be seen from the Chinese version of the Karabalgasun inscription,[64] conversion required a long time and the participation of the highest echelons of the Manichaean Church. It is possible that the stream of Manichaeans arriving from Mesopotamia, Iran and Central Asia as a result of the Arab conquest and the introduction of Islam contributed to Bögü *kaghan*'s conversion. As a result of his adoption of the new religion, the conflict between the two schools of Mesopotamian Manichaeism was transferred to East Turkestan, where their followers coexisted with members of the Eastern Manichaean Dinawariyya community.[65] The Patriarch and the upper hierarchy of the Eastern Manichaean Church resided in Kocho, the capital of the Uighur state of Turfan (850–1250).[66]

The importance of Manichaeism in the Uighur state gradually waned. As late as 983–984, however, the Chinese traveller Wang Yen-te remarked that, in addition to 50 Buddhist temples there were 'Manichaean temples', and that 'Persian monks pray according to their laws'. Manichaeism had also spread through East Turkestan to China as early as 672. Manichaean missionaries appeared at the T'ang court in 694; and in 732 an imperial edict allowed them to

---

60. Chavannes and Pelliot, 1913, pp. 152–3, 197; Belenitskiy, 1954, pp. 44–5; Schafer, 1963, p. 50.
61. Puech, 1949, pp. 64–5; Boyce, 1975, p. 3.
62. *Fihrist*, 1970, p. 803.
63. Bang and von Gabain, 1972, pp. 32–42. See also Marquart, 1912.
64. Chavannes and Pelliot, 1913, pp. 190–5.
65. On the subject of the two schools, see *Fihrist*, 1970, p. 393.
66. Sundermann, 1980.

preach[67] to co-religionists, although the same permission was not granted to proselytes. Later edicts were more tolerant, but then persecutions began again.[68]

Manichaeism played an important role in the development of art. Mani was very fond of music, to which his followers ascribed a divine origin (Augustin, *De moribus manichaeorum*, II, V, 16). Even in Mani's lifetime, religious works were adorned with ornaments and illustrations to heighten the effect of the text. Splendidly illuminated manuscripts were common in the Hellenistic circles with which Mani and his followers were in contact. Mani himself was an exceptionally skilled artist (*Kephalaia*, CLIV, 2). Later, during the Islamic era, the name of Mani in Persian literature came to signify an artist of the first order. Even Mani's contemporaries were impressed by the size and magnificence of Manichaean manuscripts and Arab authors were later to comment on this. The scribes formed a special class among the 'elect'.[69] Texts were usually written in ink on paper, or on silk or leather.[70] Manichaean scribes paid special attention to the beauty of their calligraphy and, as Boyce states, the manuscripts are written in a 'clear and elegant' script. The headings at the beginning of a work and of each section were filled in with vignettes and the text was frequently framed with intricate ornamentation. Miniatures, however, were the most striking ornament of the manuscripts. They portray all the ranks of Manichaean society – Mani, the 'elect' (dressed in white) and the laity – and depict religious feasts and symbolic images.[71]

The Manichaeans had the reputation of being initiated into magic lore and did, indeed, engage in magic. They were, however, also well versed in astronomy (astrology), geography and other sciences.[72] They also produced theologians and poets.[73]

67. Boyce, 1975, p. 3.
68. Asmussen, 1975*a*, p. 24.
69. Ibid., p. 62.
70. Boyce, 1975, p. 14; 1968, p. 67.
71. Le Coq, 1973; 1979, Pl. 2–6.
72. Asmussen, 1975*b*, pp. 44–5; Boyce, 1968, pp. 75–6.
73. *Fihrist*, 1970, p. 803.

RELIGIONS AND RELIGIOUS MOVEMENTS – II[*]

B. A. Litvinsky and M. I. Vorobyova-Desyatovskaya

Part One

CHRISTIANITY, INDIAN AND LOCAL RELIGIONS

(B. A. Litvinsky)

Christianity

According to al-Biruni, a Christian preacher appeared in Merv 200 years after the birth of Christ,[1] but Christian preachers must have been in Iran even earlier. In the western areas of the Parthian Empire, 'Christian communities existed . . . from the beginning of the second century, and during the century these communities consolidated themselves by some form of organization.'[2] Under the Parthians, religious minorities, including Christians, were tolerated. They gradually spread eastward and the list of bishops of the Syrian Church in 224 includes the bishop of Dailam, a province to the south of the Caspian Sea.[3]

During the Early Sasanian period the number of Christians increased, but at the same time persecutions began. They reached their peak under the *mōbad* Kartir (Kirder) (see Chapter 17, Part One), a champion of orthodox Zoroastrianism and of the power of the higher Zoroastrian priesthood. In his inscription at the Ka‘be of Zoroaster, Kartir records the persecution, in *c.* 280, of Nazarenes (*n'cl'y*) and Christians (*"klstyd'n*). During the war with the Roman Empire, large numbers of Greek- and Syriac-speaking Christians were taken prisoner. These communities, which used different languages, became increasingly influential. The head of the Eastern Church was the bishop of Ctesiphon (Seleukia), but the other bishops did not always recognize his jurisdiction.[4] At the synod of 410, the bishop of the diocese of Abarshahr (Nishapur) was mentioned.

It can be assumed that the large Christian community in Khurasan came into existence as early as 334 in Merv and 430 in Herat.[5] There is some

---

[*] See Map 1.
1. Biruni, 1957, p. 330.
2. Asmussen, 1983, p. 928.
3. Sachau, 1915, p. 20.
4. Asmussen, 1983, pp. 929–32.
5. Bartold, 1964, pp. 271–2; see also Asmussen, 1983, p. 932.

archaeological evidence that Christian communities existed in Merv and southern Turkmenistan in general from the third to the sixth and seventh centuries. The necropolis at Merv, which has several Christian tombs, dates back to this time; the ruins of a small Christian monastery and other religious buildings have also been found here. A treasure of early Christian gold medallions and plaques has been found in Geok-tepe, and impressions of seals bearing a Nestorian cross and other objects of a Christian character have been discovered in Ak-tepe (southern Turkmenistan).[6]

The history of Christianity in the Sasanian Empire, including Khurasan, was determined by three groups of interwoven and constantly interacting factors: the history of the Eastern Christian Church itself; the relationship between the Sasanians and the Roman Empire; and the political and religious situation within the Sasanian state. A schism took place at the oecumenical councils in Ephesus in 431 and in Chalcedon in 451, when the Dyophysites, who recognized a dual nature (the human and the divine) in Christ, separated from the main body of the Church. This belief came to be known as Nestorianism, after one of its apologists, Nestorius. The Monophysites (who held that Christ had a single, divine nature) prevailed and the Nestorians had to flee to the east, where they attained the leading position in the Eastern Church.

Throughout the Early Sasanian period, Christians lived under normal conditions and systematic persecutions occurred only when the Zoroastrian priesthood and the state took concerted action against them. Even the persecution under Bahram I and Bahram II (between 273 and 276), which was linked with the activities of Kartir, 'had no catastrophic consequences for the Christian communities, because Narseh (A.D. 293–302) altered the directions that had hitherto been followed, giving rise to cool relations with the Zoroastrian dignitaries'.[7] The position changed dramatically under Shapur II (309–379), when Christianity became the state religion of the Roman Empire under Constantine. This led to the long and systematic persecution (lasting almost 40 years) of their brethren in Sasanian Iran. Shapur II's heirs did not continue his religious policy, however, and under Yazdgird I (399–421), who was hostile to the Zoroastrian priesthood, circumstances again became favourable for the Christians.

The autonomy of the Iranian Church had been stressed at the third synod, in 424;[8] the number of Iranian Christians had increased considerably and included members of the nobility. Within the Iranian Church a serious struggle then broke out between Nestorianism and Monophysitism, the latter being more rigid and ascetic than the former. Iranian Christians, who had only recently converted from Zoroastrianism, were ideologically closer to

6. Nikitin, 1984, p. 123.
7. Asmussen, 1983, p. 936.
8. Ibid., p. 941.

FIG. 1. Sasanian Iran.
Bas-relief in stucco representing a cross.
(Photo: © Musée du Louvre/Antiquités
Orientales.)

Nestorianism, which recognized the human nature of Christ and rejected rigid monastic rules. As a result, the synods of 484 and 497 confirmed Nestorianism as the dominant Christian teaching in Iran. This did not mean that Monophysitism was completely ousted, however, and under Khusrau II (591–628) it enjoyed the strong support of Shirin, one of the *shahanshah*'s two Christian wives, and also of his court physician, Maruta of Tagrit (d. 649), who played a considerable role in strengthening Monophysitism. In general, Khusrau II showed great favour to the Christians. Shirin enjoyed wide-reaching influence and is said to have preached the Gospel in the palace; Khusrau had a church and a monastery built for her. There were several Christians among the higher nobility (Fig. 1). An imperial edict was issued permitting Christians to restore churches that had been destroyed. According to al-Tabari, anyone except the magi (members of the priestly caste) was allowed to convert to Christianity.[9] A rumour arose, which has survived in Persian tradition, that the *shahanshah* himself secretly became a Christian.[10]

9. Nöldeke, Tabari, 1973, p. 287.
10. Pigulevskaya, 1946, pp. 234–49.

Many remarkable people were involved in the work of the Eastern Christian Church. One of these was the Catholicos (Patriarch) Mar Aba, a Persian by origin and a former Zoroastrian. A man well versed in Zoroastrian lore, he studied extensively and spoke at disputations in the Academy of Nisibis (see Chapter 3, Part Two) (where he later taught) and in Alexandria, Constantinople and other Christian centres. As a result of the synod summoned by Mar Aba in 544, the organization of the Nestorian Church of Iran was more clearly defined and became more centralized.[11] The Arab conquest finally brought an end to the Sasanian Empire: the last *shahanshah*, Yazdgird III (632–651), was killed in Merv (a Christian outpost in the East and a base for Christian preaching in Central Asia). Interestingly, it was the Christian bishop of Merv who arranged Yazdgird's burial.

Although it is known that Christianity came to Bactria (Tokharistan) from Parthia, there is very little information about the Christian community there,[12] and it is unclear whether there was a Nestorian bishop in Balkh.[13] The Syrian *Book of the Laws of the Lands*, from the school of Bardaishan (d. 222), gives information about Christian women in the 'Kushan country' which, according to Marquart, means Bactria. The statement by the fifth-century Armenian author Elishe Vardapet that Christianity had spread to the land of 'K'ušankʿ' and from there southwards to India refers to the reign of Shapur II, that is, to the fourth century. In his *Christian Topography*, Cosmas Indicopleustes writes that the Bactrians, 'Huns', Persians and 'other Indians' had many churches.[14] In 549, at the request of the Hephthalites, the Catholicos Mar Aba appointed a bishop for all the Christians in Hephthalite domains. The *History of Mar Aba* tells us that later, at the request of the king of the Hephthalites and of those Hephthalites who were Christians (*Krestyāne haptarāyē*), the Catholicos appointed one of their priests as bishop of the kingdom of the Hephthalites.[15]

Christianity was widespread among the Turkic peoples of Central Asia. It is known that in 644 Elijah, the Metropolitan of Merv, converted a large number of them – the Türk *kaghan* (king) with all his army 'beyond the river Oxus', that is, in Tokharistan.[16] In 719 several embassies from Tokharistan went to China. Information drawn from one of them shows that Nestorianism existed in Tokharistan, and it is also suggested that there was a link between the Nestorian Church and the ruling circles there.[17] An inscription in Si-an-fu (781) mentions a priest named Miles from Balkh.[18] It is known that there were

11. Pigulevskaya, 1979, pp. 204–6.
12. Sachau, 1919, p. 67.
13. Spuler, 1961, p. 140.
14. Bartold, 1964, p. 278, note 88; Mingana, 1925, p. 302; Marquart, 1961, p. 283.
15. Mingana, 1925, pp. 304–5; Altheim, 1961, pp. 104–5.
16. Mingana, 1925, pp. 305–6.
17. Enoki, 1964, p. 72, note 114.
18. Sachau, 1919, p. 68.

differences in dogma and liturgical practice in the eastern regions, including Central Asia.[19]

Christian preachers went from Bactria to Sogdiana, and Syrian sources from 410–415 provide information about the founding of a Metropolitan See in Samarkand. Even if this see was in fact established later, it is still indirect evidence that there were numbers of Christians in this region at an early date. Narshakhi reports the existence of a Christian church in pre-Arab Bukhara,[20] and according to Ibn al-Nadim there were 'dualists' (i.e. Nestorians) and Christians in Sogdiana in ancient times. Archaeological work has confirmed these reports. As one example, a potsherd bearing a fragment of a psalm in Syriac has been found in the course of excavations in Panjikent. This was a school text, written as a dictation, and judging from the nature of the errors the writer was a Sogdian. It dates from the first half of the eighth century, no later than 740. Nestorian burial-grounds have also been found in Panjikent.[21]

The Christian mission went from Sogdiana to Semirechye, where archaeological and epigraphic evidence reveals the spread of Christianity. A Christian necropolis dating back to the sixth or seventh century and an eighth-century Christian church have been found at the site of Ak-Beshim. Christian inscriptions in Syriac and Sogdian have also been found in Semirechye; and when the Türk tribes came to Semirechye they found Christians there. From the epistle of the Nestorian Catholicos Timothy I, it appears that certain Turkic peoples, probably the Karluks (among whom Christianity was particularly widespread), were converted at the end of the eighth or the beginning of the ninth century. One of the most famous missionaries of the Nestorian Church at that time was Shubkhalisho, who preached in Central Asia.[22] In 893, when Ismail Samani seized the town of Taraz, there was a large church there.[23]

Christianity penetrated even further east and reached the Kyrgyz tribes. A runic inscription in Sudzhi mentions the 'instructor in the faith' of the Kyrgyz chief and uses the Syriac title *mar*, which denotes a Christian clergyman. Other Kyrgyz steles with runic inscriptions are marked with crosses.

Christianity penetrated to East Turkestan even before the formation of the Uighur kingdom of Turfan. As East Turkestan had very close links with Central Asia, Christian missionaries (apparently including many Sogdians) made their way there in the fourth and fifth centuries. They were to play an even greater role in the fifth and sixth centuries, the period during which it appears (according to the earliest Christian texts found in East Turkestan) that the first Christian

---

19. Mingana, 1925, p. 321. For more information about Christianity in Bactria (Tokharistan), see Litvinsky, 1971, pp. 122–3.
20. Narshakhi, 1954, p. 53.
21. Paykova and Marshak, 1976; Paykova, 1979.
22. Nikitin, 1984, pp. 126–7.
23. Narshakhi, 1954, pp. 86–7.

communities appeared there.[24] The translation of Christian works into Middle Persian in Iran and into Sogdian in Sogdiana had already begun. Many remains of Christian texts have been discovered in the sites of East Turkestan, including the library of the ruined Nestorian monastery in the oasis of Turfan. They were written in Syriac, Middle Persian, Parthian, Khotanese Saka, Sogdian and Turkic. Sogdian texts predominate, however, and Sogdian became the second most important language (after Syriac) in the Nestorian Church in Central Asia.[25]

According to the *Chin-shih* (Chapter 124), the family of Ma Si-ling-tsi-sa (i.e. Mar Sargis) settled in Lintau (in what is now the province of Gansu) in 578. Christian missionaries clearly penetrated even further east and in 635 Bishop Aloben (A-lo-pen in the Chinese sources) reached the T'ang court, bringing with him sacred books and images. The emperor treated him favourably and a Christian monastery was built, marking the beginning of Christianity in China itself.[26]

Indian religions (except Buddhism)

As an important source of religious teachings, India had a major influence on the peoples of neighbouring countries. This was true of both Buddhism and Hinduism. During the period of the Graeco-Bactrian kingdom in northern India and Pakistan, and apparently in Afghanistan as well, the worhip of Vishnu was widespread. Vishnu was regarded by his worshippers as the basis of creation and the source of all that exists.[27] Judging from certain Indo-Greek coins bearing the image of a humped bull, the worship of Shiva was also widespread[28] – he was a fierce god, combining the characteristics of the Vedic Rudra and some non-Aryan fertility god. Shiva rode on the humped bull, Nandi, and was frequently accompanied by his wife, the beautiful Parvati. The linga, a phallic pillar, was often used as a symbol of Shiva.

There is much evidence that the worship of Shiva flourished in north-western India immediately before the coming of the Kushans. For example, a group of coins of the Indian Saka ruler Maues bears the image of Shiva. In Sirkap (Taxila), in a stratum corresponding to approximately the first century A.D., a bronze seal has been discovered bearing the image of Shiva with an inscription in Brāhmī and Kharoṣṭhī: *Śivarakṣita* (protected by Shiva).

The worship of Shiva was also widespread in the Kushan Empire, as can be seen from Kushan coins: those of Vima Kadphises, Kanishka, Huvishka and

24. Hansen, 1968, p. 93.
25. Nikitin, 1984, pp. 128–30, including a detailed bibliography.
26. Kychanov, 1978, pp. 76–8.
27. Tarn, 1951, pp. 137, 172, 381, 391, 406; Agravala, 1970; Majumdar, 1970, pp. 30–2.
28. Tarn, 1951, pp. 135–6, 163, 172–3, 213.

Vasudeva bear a figure of Shiva or of Shiva with his vehicle, the bull Nandi. The inscription *Oēšo* on coins refers to Shiva. It used to be believed that this legend reflected the Prakrit word *haveśa* (in Sanskrit, *bhaveśa*), an epithet of Shiva meaning 'Lord of Being', or the Prakrit development *veṣa* of the Sanskrit *vṛṣa* (bull).[29] The theory has now been advanced that this name is in fact an East Iranian development of the name of the Zoroastrian wind god Vayu, who took on the iconographic appearance of Shiva.[30] A stele has been discovered in Mathura with the image of two Kushans worshipping the Shiva linga.

The worship of Shiva also spread to those areas of the Kushan state that are now in Afghanistan, and reached the Amu Darya (Oxus). In Airtam, near Termez, a stone slab has been found with a Bactrian inscription and a carved image of Shiva. In Soazma-kala, near Balkh, a stone slab was discovered bearing the image of a three-headed standing Shiva with a trident and other attributes, which strongly resembles Hercules.[31] A wall-painting still to be seen in the temple of Dilberjin has a central group depicting Shiva and Parvati mounted on the recumbent bull Nandi,[32] which cannot be earlier than the fifth century. Many works of Shivaite art and of Hindu art in general, dating back to between the fifth and the eighth century, have been discovered in Afghanistan. These include some 25 marble sculptures and other works of art.[33] Recent excavations in Panjikent have yielded a large sculptural group of Shiva–Parvati.

Brahmanism played an important role in the religious life of Afghanistan in early medieval times; individual brahmanic images even penetrated into Buddhist circles and can be found in Buddhist sites such as Tepe Sardar. 'Indianization' also affected Bamiyan.

All these influences must have affected the religion and (to a greater degree) the fine arts of Central Asia. The wall-paintings of Panjikent include images directly related to the iconography of Shiva worship, in particular a standing three-headed god. Yet in many details they are quite unlike the Indian prototypes. The clothing of the three-headed deity bears the inscription *wšprkr* (or *wyšprkr*). Linguists suggest that this name links the Sogdian *Vyšprkr* with the name *Oēšo* on Kushan coins, which in turn comes from the Zoroastrian wind god Vayu. *Vēš-parkar* (Veshparkar) is believed to come from the Avestan *Vaiiuš Uparō Kairitiō* ('the wind whose action spreads in the upper region'). In Sogdian translations of Buddhist texts, he corresponds to Shiva (Mahadeva) and is described as having three faces. Thus this god with a Sogdian name and found in the art of Panjikent appears in a form connected with the worship of Shiva, which is in keeping with the Sogdian written tradition.[34]

29. Rosenfield, 1967, pp. 22 et seq., 93–4, 111, etc.
30. Humbach, 1975, pp. 404–5.
31. Fischer, 1957.
32. Kruglikova, 1976, pp. 93–4, figs. 54, 55.
33. Kuwayama, 1976.
34. Humbach, 1975, p. 404; Belenitskiy and Marshak, 1976, pp. 78–9.

Local religions

Despite the fact that Nestorianism, Manichaeism and Buddhism spread in the non-nomadic areas of Central Asia such as Tokharistan, Sogdiana and Khwarizm, most of the population continued to profess the local Iranian religion. This could be described as a Central Asian version of Zoroastrianism, which differed substantially from the orthodox Iranian form.

In Sogdiana, according to Chinese sources, 'they honour the Buddhist religion; they sacrifice to the god of heaven', which Chavannes takes as referring to Mazdaism.[35] The texts report that believers worshipped a golden image and sacrificed animals to it. Thousands of worshippers came every day to offer sacrifice. According to other information, in Samarkand 'the king and the people did not follow Buddhism, but worshipped fire'.[36] There was a temple for ancestor worship in the palace of the Sogdian ruler. The feasts and customs of the Sogdians are also described (in the eleventh century) by al-Biruni. He mentions that the Sogdians celebrated the coming of the New Year, which was connected with ideas about the death and revival of nature. Once a year, the people of Sogdiana mourned the dead. When doing this they lacerated their faces and offered food and drink to those who had died.[37]

The worship of Siyavush was connected with the worship of the dead. On the first day of the New Year a cock was sacrificed to him. It was believed that the divine youth had died and his bones had been lost. On a particular day, the believers, dressed in black and bare-footed, looked for them in the fields. The custom of burial in ossuaries (ceramic receptacles for bones) was widespread in Sogdiana, Khwarizm, the oasis of Tashkent and Semirechye. When the flesh had fallen away from the bones, these were gathered into the ossuaries, which were placed in a special chamber. Some ossuaries were richly decorated with magnificent reliefs.

Sources relating the Arab conquest mention 'fire temples' and 'idol temples'. They were richly decorated and contained many precious objects for use in worship – for example, a pearl the size of a hen's egg is mentioned. The imagination of the Arab conquerors was fired by the size of the gold and silver idols in these temples.[38] Firdausi's *Shāh-nāme* also mentions 'fire temples' in Bukhara and Paikent. The ninth-century Pahlavi geographical treatise *Šahrīhā-i Ērān* mentions the establishment of a 'miraculous fire' in Samarkand by Siyavush's son and the placing there for safe-keeping of gold (or gilded) plates inscribed with the text of the *Avesta*. The treatise also mentions the destruction, by Sokandar (Alexander of Macedon), of these plates, after which the

---

35. Chavannes, 1903, p. 135.
36. Hui-li, 1959, p. 46.
37. Biruni, 1957, p. 258; see also pp. 236, 255.
38. Belenitskiy, 1954; Gafurov, 1972, pp. 285–7.

Turanian Frasiak (Afrasiab) 'made the dwelling of the gods into temples of the *daevas*'. In Kushaniya stood a temple on whose walls were depicted the ancient kings of various nations.

Sogdian texts mention various divinities. First there is *zrw* (Zurvan). In translations of Buddhist texts this name is used in place of the Indian Brahma. He is called 'King Zurvan' and given the epithet of 'great' and 'king of gods'. His particular iconographic feature was the beard. *Xwrmzt'βγ* (Ahura Mazda, or Orhmazd), the supreme god of Zoroastrianism, is very rarely mentioned. There is more frequent mention of *Āδβaγ*, who held the second place in the divine hierarchy and was worshipped by *Zrwšc* (Zoroaster). Clearly Ohrmazd (Ahura Mazda) was also referred to as *Āδβaγ*. The deity Veshparkar (*wšprkr*) has already been mentioned. All this is evidence of the Zurvanite tendency of Sogdian Zoroastrianism and of certain links with Indian religions. There is also mention of *Vṛθraγna* (*wšγn*), *Druvāspa* (*δrw'sp*), *Haoma* (*γwm*), *Xᵛarənah* (*prn*) and other gods, among whom one of the most important was the female divinity Nanai. It is significant that the *Amesha Spenta*s (see Chapter 17, Part One) occur in personal names. Henning has described the Sogdian religion as 'the impact of Zoroaster's teachings on the native paganism of Sogdiana'[39] – perhaps it would be more accurate to say 'the native Iranian paganism'.

Religious iconography and architecture, as well as burial customs, are proof that the local religions of Sogdiana, Khwarizm and Tokharistan were closely related. The principles of the ancient Iranian religion, which was dualistic, served as the unifying factor and idiosyncratic variations of these principles continued to develop right up to the conversion to Islam. At the same time, there were considerable changes in their pantheon and principles, which assimilated many new subjects, elements and figures that did not appear in the west Iranian religion. Some of these inclusions were due to interaction with religious systems of foreign origin (see also Chapter 17). The religion of the Central Asian nomadic Iranian peoples was even more idiosyncratic. From the fourth to the eighth century they continued the practice of burying the dead in tumuli. Both inhumation and cremation were practised.

The beliefs of the ancient Turkic and Mongol peoples belong to a completely different religious and mythological system. Their cosmogonic ideas are known from runic inscriptions in honour of Kül-*tegin* and Bilge *kaghan*:

> When high above the blue sky was created and down below the brown earth had been created, between the two were created the sons of men. When this took place, the heaven rose up like a roof above the earth.

The rising sun was also worshipped and the east was considered the most important direction: the doors of the *kaghan*'s tent faced east. The earth was seen as square; the *kaghan*'s headquarters was in its centre, where the Türk people

39. Henning, 1965, p. 250.

lived, while their enemies lived around the periphery. There are hints of a myth concerning a cosmic catastrophy which was part of a cosmogonic myth.

The Turkic peoples, and those belonging to the Siberian Central Asian religious system in general, saw the universe as divided into three parts: an Upper (= Heaven), a Middle (= Earth) and a Lower World. The Lord of the Lower World (the Underworld) was Erklig (in Mongolian, Erlik *kaghan*). One member of his retinue was Bürt, the spirit of sudden death; he was opposed by Tengri (Heaven), the supreme deity of the pantheon. Tengri determined the order that prevailed in the world and also the destinies of people. The West Turkic people of the Khazar conceived of Tengri as a hero of gigantic size; tall trees were dedicated, and horses sacrificed, to him. According to al-Kashgari, the Türks used the word 'Tengri' to mean 'high mountains' and 'big trees'. According to Chinese sources, it was on high mountains that the Eastern Türk *kaghan*s and 'nation' offered prayers to the 'spirit of heaven'. Tengri's divine consort was Umai, the goddess of fertility, protectress of the new-born. Prayers and sacrifices were offered to the sacred 'Earth-Water', belonging to the Middle World.[40]

In the mythology of the ancient Mongol nomads of the steppe (the Hsien-pi, Kitans and others), there were two main cosmic principles, Heaven and Earth (cf. the ancient Türk mythology). The Hsiung-nu and Wu-huan worshipped the spirits of their ancestors, heaven, earth, the sun, the moon and the stars. The legends of the Hsien-pi tribes included zoomorphic elements that had their origins in clan totems: a horse, a bull, a deer (elk). The Kitans worshipped abstract gods – which they personified – such as war and fire (sometimes in the form of totemic animals – a white horse or a deer) and also the spirits of their ancestors. They believed that the Initial Order, mounted on a white stallion, had met a celestial maiden in a cart drawn by a cow near the mountain of Mu-ye. Eight sons, the forefathers of the Kitan tribes, were born from the marriage of Initial Order and the celestial virgin.

The Mongols themselves had a dualistic system. Their supreme deity was Tengri (Heaven), the creator of all that exists, who determined the fates of men and affairs of state. He was called blue and eternal, and was viewed as the male principle. His counterpart was Ütügen, the goddess of Earth, who was associated with notions of fertility and the rebirth of nature. Ütügen was the feminine principle just as Umai was in ancient Türk mythology. The Mongols also worshipped the sun, which was regarded as the mother of the moon. There were distinctly totemic ideas in their legends.[41] Ancient Altaic religious and mythological systems and religious practices were shamanistic.

The religions of Central Asia not only co-existed, but also interacted, and competed for adherents. The religions which penetrated into Central Asia,

---

40. Roux, 1956–57; 1962; Potapov, 1978; Klyashtorny, 1981.
41. Wittfogel and Fêng, 1949; Rintchen, 1959; 1961; 1975; Tucci and Heissig, 1970; Zhukovskaya, 1977; Neklyudov, 1981.

such as Zoroastrianism, Buddhism, Manichaeism and Christianity, had to establish themselves in an environment where other beliefs existed, whether
Tokharian, Iranian (the Khotanese Sakas, Sogdians, Bactrians, Khwarizmians,
etc.) or Altaic (ancient Turkic and Mongol). Even the spread of the ideas embodied in Zoroaster's teaching did not have the same consequences among the
eastern Iranians as in western Iran, because a substratum of local beliefs and
rituals survived. There were considerable differences between Central Asian
and Persian Zoroastrianism. In other cases, several religious systems were superimposed, for example in the case of the spread of Buddhism, Manichaeism and
Christianity among the Türks and Uighurs, whose shamanistic beliefs remained,
to a greater or lesser degree, the substratum of their spiritual concepts.

As this process continued over many centuries, only a few traces were
left of the local religion. This was, for example, the case with the Khotanese
Sakas, whose conversion to Buddhism was so complete that almost nothing
remained of their original, ancient Iranian religion; the same is true of the
Tokharians. The Sogdians, who kept many elements of their original religion,
were in an intermediate position. There was also interaction between the various new religions, both local and imported, which had a developed written
tradition. This led to borrowings, the transference of religious concepts and
ideas, and syncretism.[42]

Part Two

BUDDHISM

(M. I. Vorobyova-Desyatovskaya)

Written sources

As mentioned in previous chapters, the enormous territory encompassing
Central Asia and East Turkestan constituted a single region in the final centuries B.C. and during the greater part of the first millennium A.D. This is explained by its common ethnic character, its shared historical fortunes, the similar geographic and economic circumstances that conditioned the character and
pace of its socio-economic development, and the region's cultural similarity. A
basic factor determining this cultural similarity was Buddhism, which was accepted over the entire territory as a doctrine of moral ethics, an ideology and a
religion.

42. Asmussen, 1965.

The spread of Buddhism beyond the boundaries of India took place at the time of the Mauryan emperor Ashoka (c. 268 B.C.), and found expression in his edicts engraved on pillars and rocks at various points throughout the empire. In the propagation of Buddhism and Indian culture in Central Asia and East Turkestan (of which Ashoka Maurya was the initiator), an important role was played by the Parthian, Saka and Kushan rulers of north-western India. A major influx of Buddhist missionaries into these territories occurred among the Kushans. The principal route of Buddhist expansion lay through Bactria and the western possessions of the Kushan Empire. Part of this territory (northern Bactria on the right bank of the Amu Darya, or Oxus – later Tokharistan) now forms part of Middle Asia (southern Uzbekistan and Tajikistan). Recent archaeological findings have shown that Buddhism and Indian culture permeated every area of Central Asia, leaving direct evidence in the form of inscriptions and religious structures, as well as profound traces in the cultural substrata of the local peoples. Buddhism only ceased to play an important role in the region from the end of the eighth century, after the arrival of Islam, and in the northern region of Central Asia (in Semirechye) Buddhist religious centres were evidently still functioning as late as the tenth century.

In the Kushan period, Buddhism also began to be actively propagated in East Turkestan. Buddhist penetration followed two paths: from Bactria, the centre of the Kushan possessions, to Kashgar and further east; and from north-western India and Kashmir to Khotan and the southern oases of East Turkestan (see Chapter 15). Although no precise information is available about the time when Buddhism penetrated to the northern oases of Turfan and Kucha, it probably became established there at the beginning of the Christian era. In 300 Chinese sources report the presence in Kucha of 1,000 Buddhist temples and sanctuaries; and in the fourth century Kucha became an important centre of Buddhist education, where translators were trained for China. It was from here that Kumarajiva, the celebrated translator of Buddhist texts, whose school was considered one of the most authoritative in China, was invited to that country. Judging by the borrowing of some Prakrit Buddhist terms from the Khotanese Saka language into the Tokharian languages, Buddhism came to the Tokharians from the south, in other words, from Khotan (Fig. 2).

One of the most important results of India's cultural influence on East Turkestan was the dissemination of ancient forms of Indian writing – Brāhmī and Kharoṣṭhī – which were adopted by the local peoples (who had no script) to set down their languages. From the adaptation of Indian Brāhmī to the writing of the Tokharian A and B languages in the northern oases of East Turkestan (Turfan and Kucha), a version of Brāhmī known as Central Asiatic slanting Brāhmī emerged.

In Khotan and Kashgar, Indian Brāhmī was adapted to the writing of the Saka language (one of the East Iranian languages current in the area), which was the tongue of the original population. From this adaptation another version

FIG. 2. Fragment of a manuscript on paper from the collection
of N. F. Petrovskiy (no. SI P/7). Text in Sanskrit *Saddharma-puṇḍarīka*.
On the lower level an inscription in Khotanese Saka.
Script in South Turkestan Brāhmī. Coloured illustration: Buddha receiving offerings.

of Brāhmī emerged – Central Asiatic upright Brāhmī, the writing of the southern oases. These processes had evidently been concluded by the fifth century. Palaeography is today used as one of the criteria for dating manuscripts in the Brāhmī script and for determining where they were copied.

Another form of ancient Indian writing which found its way into East Turkestan and Central Asia was Kharoṣṭhī, long thought to be a chancery hand which had spread to north-western India from the Achaemenid chancery. The Kushans promoted it to the rank of official state script and it was employed in Bactrian territory alongside the local Bactrian writing system. Besides two versions of the Bactrian script, other forms of writing which gained currency in Central Asia included Parthian, Sogdian, Khwarizmian and Pahlavi (Middle Persian). This is evidently the reason why the Indian scripts, Kharoṣṭhī and Brāhmī, did not develop local versions here; and in the following centuries their use was confined to a Buddhist context, where they appeared in inscriptions on monastic ceramic ware and similar articles, on reliquaries and in Buddhist manuscripts (Fig. 3).

In East Turkestan, no inscriptions on monastic ware have been discovered, but in the first and second centuries, local coins with a 'Sino-Kharoṣṭhī'

FIG. 3. Clay pot with an inscription in Brāhmī.
Found in Afrasiab near Samarkand.

legend were being minted in Khotan. The largest find of written monuments in Kharoṣṭhī characters is an archive of official documents on wooden strips, dating from the mid-third to the mid-fourth century and found in the southern oases of Niya and Kroraina in the territory of the small, independent, ancient state of Kroraina in the oases of the Taklamakan desert.

The inscriptions on monastic ceramic ware and reliquaries (deposited in Buddhist religious buildings) and Buddhist manuscripts are the main written sources that have enabled modern research to determine the territorial spread of Buddhism, the time when this propagation took place, and the principal Buddhist schools and centres which have influenced the region's history and culture. The Buddhist manuscripts found in East Turkestan and Central Asia remain the only original texts of the Buddhist canon known anywhere in the world. Even in India, virtually none of these texts has been preserved. Some of the Buddhist writings, and commentaries on them, found in India are merely in the form of late copies. Questions as to how the doctrinal, philosophical, dogmatic and religious tenets of Buddhism came to be established in the territories of India and beyond, and what transformation these aspects of Buddhism underwent in the new cultural milieu, can be answered only on the basis of the information obtained from the manuscripts of East Turkestan and Central Asia.

A large group of Buddhist texts, found in the territory of East Turkestan and in the ideologically, religiously, culturally and (for almost a century) administratively associated Dunhuang, were written (or copied) in these areas in Chinese, Tibetan and Uighur. For copying the Buddhist texts, the Türks, among whom Buddhism started to be professed as early as the sixth century, used the Uighur (Sogdian in origin), Brāhmī (seventh–eighth centuries) and Tibetan (eighth-century) scripts. Turkic Buddhist manuscripts and xylographs have been found in Turfan, Dunhuang, Miran (south-west of Lake Lop Nor) and Suzhou. The territories in which Buddhist texts in Indian scripts have so far been found are listed below, together with a brief description of the texts themselves.

EAST TURKESTAN

(a) Manuscripts written in Brāhmī characters (Indian and slanting), in Sanskrit and in Tokharian A and B, have been found in the northern oases – Turfan and Kucha – as well as in Dunhuang (for details of the manuscripts, see below).

(b) Manuscripts written in Brāhmī characters (Indian and upright), in the Khotanese, Tumshuq Saka and Sanskrit languages, have been found in Khotan and Kashgar.

(c) Manuscripts written in Kharoṣṭhī characters in Gandhārī, in which a local non-Indian substratum is traceable, have been found in the oases of Niya and Kroraina to the south of Lake Lop Nor (around 800 official documents on wooden strips, including many texts concerned with the activities of the local Buddhist community and the performance of religious rituals).

(d) A manuscript in the Kharoṣṭhī script in Gandhārī, on birch bark, containing the text of the Buddhist Hinayana sutra, the *Dharmapada* (Fig. 4), has been discovered in Khotan.

(e) A small fragment of palm leaf bearing a text in the Kharoṣṭhī script in Gandhārī, and evidently an excerpt from the Hinayana version of the *Mahāparinirvāṇa* sutra, has been discovered although the location of the find is unknown. The fragment, which has not been published, forms part of the S. F. Oldenburg Collection in the Institute of Oriental Studies of the Russian Academy of Sciences in St Petersburg. The fragment shows that the Kharoṣṭhī script was used for making manuscript copies of Buddhist canonical texts, and that the *Dharmapada* find is not an exception.

(f) The only known dedicatory inscription to a Buddhist community, in Gandhārī and written in Kharoṣṭhī characters, was found in Lo-yang.

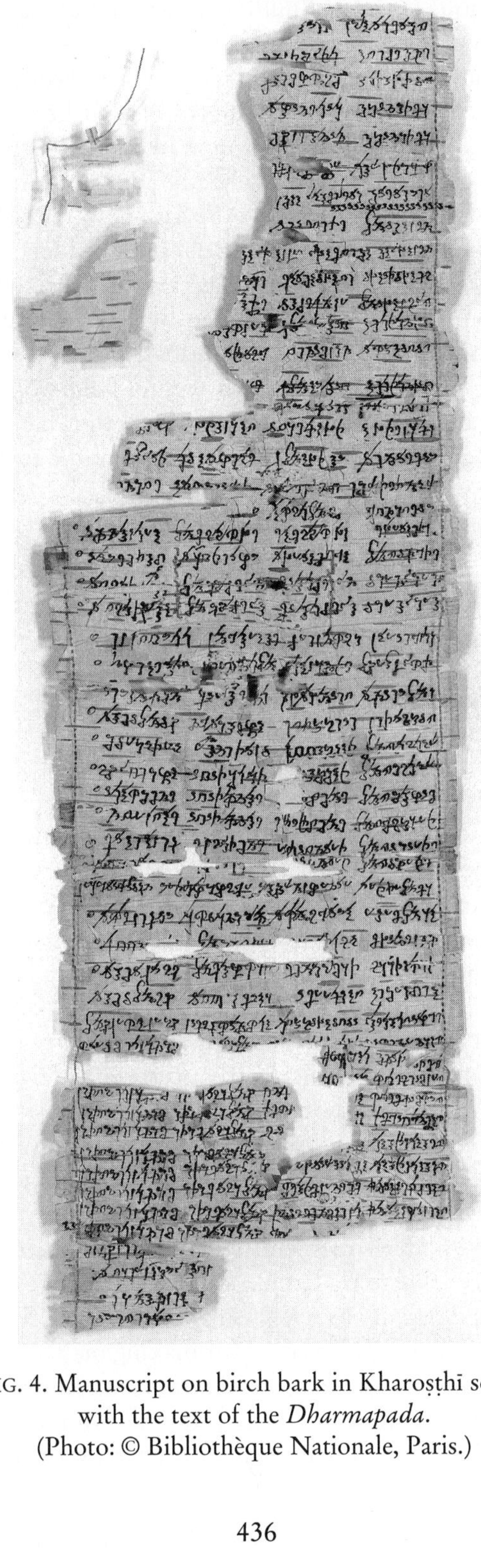

FIG. 4. Manuscript on birch bark in Kharoṣṭhī script
with the text of the *Dharmapada*.
(Photo: © Bibliothèque Nationale, Paris.)

BACTRIA (TOKHARISTAN)

(a) In the Kushan period, Old Termez was a prominent Central Asian Buddhist centre and many remnants of religious buildings have been found in the region, including the Buddhist monastery of Kara-tepe and the Fayaz-tepe monastic site. The Old Termez area has provided a large quantity of ceramic inscriptions written in Kharoṣṭhī and Brāhmī script connected with the activity of the Buddhist community of Mahasamghika. Dedicatory inscriptions on reliquaries and other objects have also been found.

(b) The castle of Zang-tepe, 30 km to the north of Termez, probably had a Buddhist stupa. Fragments of various Sanskrit manuscripts written in Brāhmī script on birch bark have been recovered.

(c) Round the demolished Buddhist stupa at the palace of Kafyr-kala (in the town of Kolkhozabad in the Vakhsh valley), scorched remains of manuscripts in Brāhmī script, written on birch bark, have been recovered from the débris.

(d) At Balkh, excavations of the Buddhist complex have brought to light a broken piece of pottery with a Buddhist dedicatory inscription written in Kharoṣṭhī characters.

(e) In southern Bactria, a copper vessel has been found with a dedicatory inscription, in which mention is made of the Buddhist school of Dharmaguptaka.

MERV OASIS (TURKMENISTAN)

In Merv, archaeologists have discovered an important Buddhist centre, with temples and a number of stupas. In one of the stupas in Merv, and in another stupa opened by chance in Bairam-Ali, immured vessels with two Buddhist manuscripts have been found: both were written in Sanskrit in Brāhmī characters and inscribed on birch bark. One of them has been restored and is preserved at the Institute of Oriental Studies in St Petersburg; the other is undergoing restoration in Moscow.

SEMIRECHYE (KYRGYZSTAN)

In the Krasnorechensk site, in the Chu valley, excavations have been in progress for many years on the site of the Buddhist temple. In 1985, in the passageway not far from the 11-m-high statue of Buddha in Nirvana, manuscript fragments in Sanskrit, written in Brāhmī characters on birch bark, have been found.

KAPISA REGION (AFGHANISTAN)

As regards contacts between Iranian and Indian cultures,[43] the numerous finds of Buddhist relics – monasteries, stupas and rock inscriptions – show that Buddhism flourished in the Kushan period. Ceramic, reliquary, vase, wall and rock inscriptions in Kharoṣṭhī script have been discovered in the following areas: Wardak, Begram and Gul Dara (all near Kabul); Tor Dheri (in Pakistani Baluchistan); and Dasht-i Nawur (a trilingual rock inscription in Bactrian, Kharoṣṭhī and an undeciphered script similar to Kharoṣṭhī). Manuscripts in Brāhmī and Kharoṣṭhī characters have also been found in the Bamiyan monastery (Afghanistan).

MOUNTAIN AREAS NORTH OF GANDHARA

The diffusion of Buddhism in this territory over a lengthy time span, from the Kushan period to the Muslim conquest, is attested by the many rock inscriptions left by Buddhist pilgrims and by reliquary inscriptions from Bajaur, Tirah, Swat, Gilgit and Hunza written in Kharoṣṭhī and Brāhmī scripts. In the first millennium B.C., the Gilgit and Hunza areas were crossed by Buddhist pilgrims, merchants and traders travelling between Central Asia, India and East Turkestan. It was in Gilgit, in the early 1930s, that Sir Aurel Stein made one of the most outstanding discoveries of the century – a Buddhist library of the seventh century, immured in a stupa and comprising Buddhist manuscripts, on birch bark and paper, written in Sanskrit in Brāhmī characters. Most of the manuscripts relate to the canon of the Mulasarvastivada Hinayana school.

NAGARAHARA (HADDA/JALALABAD AREA)

This area is rich in Buddhist monuments of the Kushan period. Many inscriptions written in Kharoṣṭhī script have been found on Buddhist reliquaries, vessels and walls in the monasteries of Bimaran, Hadda, Jalalabad and Basawal.

Inscriptions in Buddhist complexes

The contents of the inscriptions listed above provide information about the geographic spread of Buddhism and its various schools; about the chronological sequence of the diffusion process; and about the names of those who professed the religion. In some cases, this information can help to establish the

---

43. Identified by Fussman, 1989, p. 445. Thanks to Fussman's brilliant work, devoted to the palaeography of inscriptions in Indian scripts and to the Gandhārī language, the study of Indian inscriptions can, for the first time, be placed on a scientific basis.

ethnic group or native language of the donor or proprietor of the object, or the social status and occupations of the followers of Buddhism.

Chronologically speaking, Buddhist inscriptions in Kharoṣṭhī characters encompass the period from the first century B.C. to the second century A.D. (the earliest attested dating is 58 B.C. and the latest A.D. 129). Inscriptions in Brāhmī characters, on the other hand, bear no dates. Through palaeography and an analysis of the accompanying material, they may be dated approximately to the fourth–fifth centuries A.D.

It is legitimate to regard the oldest groups of inscriptional finds as the most representative. To judge from the finds made in Buddhist monasteries and temples, dedicatory inscriptions were usually made on earthenware that was donated to the Buddhist community. Another type of earthenware inscription is found on articles belonging to people living in the monasteries. In the area of Middle Asia (Uzbekistan, Tajikistan, Turkmenistan, Kyrgyzstan, etc.) where a number of monastic complexes have been excavated – Kara-tepe, Fayaz-tepe, Ajina-tepe, Merv, Dalverzin-tepe, Ak-Beshim, Kuva, Krasnorechensk urban region, and many others[44] – over 100 inscriptions have been found, both on whole pottery vessels and on shards. The majority of these relate to the Kara-tepe monastery and have been published in the works of Grek, Vertogradova, Harmatta and Vorobyova-Desyatovskaya.[45]

An important historical and cultural inference can be drawn from a study of the inscriptions on ceramic ware and other articles: it is that followers of the Mahasamghika Hinayana school settled in the Old Termez region. This is the only written evidence to show that, in the Kushan period, the doctrine of this school permeated to the extreme westerly point of the Kushan Empire. It is known that Mahasamghika was one of the most ancient Buddhist schools which broke away after the schism within early Buddhism in *c.* 350 B.C. According to the written sources, the language in which this school started to codify its doctrine was Prakrit. The inscriptions found show that, in the west, this Prakrit was Gandhārī, written in Kharoṣṭhī script.

Another Buddhist school which, judging by inscriptions, permeated beyond the frontiers of India was Dharmaguptaka. A third school, the name of which is attested in Buddhist manuscripts found in Central Asia, was Sarvastivada. Its establishment belongs to the period of Kanishka's rule, and evidently took place in Kashmir. The language employed by the adherents of the Sarvastivada school, and in which, according to Buddhist tradition, they codified their canon at the time of the Kashmir Council in the early second century, was Sanskrit. The findings of written sources have confirmed the information derived from Buddhist sources. The adherents of the Dharmaguptaka

---

44. Staviskiy, 1963, pp. 171–6; Litvinsky, 1971, pp. 110–33.
45. Grek, 1964, 1972; Vertogradova, 1983, p. 87; Harmatta, 1969, pp. 32–9; Vorobyova-Desyatovskaya, 1983.

and Sarvastivada schools used the Brāhmī script and the Sanskrit language. It is possible that the Kara-tepe ceramic inscriptions in Brāhmī characters were made by followers of the Sarvastivada school.

The written sources from Central Asia do not yet enable us to discuss the dissemination of Mahayana in this area. The local inhabitants evidently continued their traditional adherence to Hinayana, which, to judge from the paintings and sculptures found in Buddhist temples and monasteries, broadly represented early Buddhism in all its aspects. The division of Buddhism into two main systems – Hinayana and Mahayana – took place in Indian territory only at the beginning of the Christian era. Starting from religious dogma (the sutras), it then made the transition to philosophical doctrine and the methods and functions of the mental techniques of yoga practice. The Buddhist texts found in manuscripts in East Turkestan have enabled us to follow how this division took place, and how, in the core of Hinduism and early Buddhism, the foundations of the three main systems (Hinayana, Mahayana and Vajrayana) emerged, systems which have persisted to the present day.

The names of personal donors show that they included several Buddhist pilgrims from India, chiefly from the north-west. It is probable that the monasteries were founded by missionaries from that area, and the scribal schools that existed in the Kara-tepe monastery were linked to the scribal traditions of Kashmir and north-western India. The bulk of the donations were made by local inhabitants with Iranian names or names whose origin is unknown. People came to the monasteries with their relatives and probably lived there for some time. Among the donors were monks and lay people, and persons who performed economic functions within the monasteries. All of them made a 'gift of faith' (*deya-dharma* or *dana-mukha*) for the sake of their health and the health of those close to them, in order to ensure eternal life, to increase their religious merit and for favourable rebirths.

Manuscripts from East Turkestan and Central Asia

The manuscripts found in the oases of East Turkestan, Gilgit and Central Asia represent the canonical literature of a number of Hinayana and Mahayana schools, together with tantras and a quantity of writings of the Vajrayana school, which was established in Central Asia at the end of the first millennium. The establishment of Buddhist doctrines in this area took place simultaneously in a variety of cultural traditions, between which there were close contacts and much interaction. Without recourse to Chinese and Tibetan translations of Buddhist sutras, it is impossible to follow the history of Buddhist texts in other languages.

Collections of Sanskrit Buddhist manuscripts, copied in East Turkestan, are at present preserved in Europe, Japan and India. Manuscripts found in Middle Asia are preserved in St Petersburg, Ashgabat, Tashkent, Bishkek and

Delhi. The total number of Sanskrit manuscripts probably amounts to some 5,000 preserved items (around 100,000 sheets and fragments).

The earliest manuscripts in Brāhmī characters known to science date from the Kushan period. They comprise three manuscripts from the German Turfan collection, one manuscript from Bamiyan, numerous small manuscript fragments on palm leaves from the collections of Petrovsky and Berezovsky (probably of the second–third centuries) and some sheets of a manuscript found in Bairam-Ali (probably dating from the third–fourth centuries).

The manuscripts confirm that, during the Kushan period, the Buddhist doctrine had already acquired a fairly large number of adherents throughout the territories of East Turkestan and Central Asia, and that their contents encompass excerpts from different parts of the Buddhist canon and passages from various Buddhist authors. The Turfan manuscripts, for example, include excerpts from the writings of the Indian scholar Ashvaghosha, one of the first authors of Buddhist drama and poetry. Indian tradition holds that Ashvaghosha was a contemporary of Kanishka, who was his mentor and patron. After Kanishka's death, Ashvaghosha set down his actions in poetry. The creative heritage of Ashvaghosha in Central Asia is represented by passages from all his main works: the poems known as the *Buddhacarita*, which describe the life of Buddha Shakyamuni; the poems entitled the *Saundaranandakāvya*; and the Buddhist drama the *Śāriputraprakaraṇa*, a biography of Shariputra, one of the Buddha's pupils. Ashvaghosha's drama was unknown to Indian literature prior to the discovery of the early manuscripts in East Turkestan.

The presence of Buddhist literary texts in Sanskrit of the Kushan period goes hand in hand with the codification of the Sanskrit canon of the Sarvastivada school in Kashmir at the Buddhist council in the time of Kanishka. Although there is no doubt that sutras already existed in Sanskrit at this time, the question as to which type of Sanskrit was represented in these early sutras has not finally been resolved, despite much research. Investigation into the language of Buddhist texts started at the beginning of the twentieth century with the works of Lüders. The designation of this language as 'Hybrid Sanskrit' was introduced following the appearance in 1953 of Edgerton's grammar and dictionary.[46] In the view of modern scholars, the term 'hybrid language' arises from the 'transposition' of Prakrit texts into Sanskrit, as a transitional stage to literary Sanskrit. As investigations have shown, grammatical and orthographic peculiarities depend not only on the degree of grammatical competence and education of the communicator, but also on the special features of the mother tongue. It seems more neutral to refer to this Sanskrit as 'Buddhist', which also designates the sphere in which it was used.

It is clear that, in the fifth century, Sanskrit canonical texts started to be copied on a regular basis in local Buddhist centres in East Turkestan, chiefly in

46. Edgerton, 1953.

Khotan. At the same time, the translation of Buddhist texts into the Khotanese Saka language was also undertaken in Khotan. No information is available concerning the starting point for translations of Buddhist texts into the Tokharian languages. The earliest Tokharian manuscripts, copied in the northern oases of East Turkestan, date from the seventh century.

The gradual transformation of East Turkestan into an international Buddhist centre, in which great numbers of manuscripts were copied, translated into various languages, transmitted to both East and West and preserved in monastic libraries and the houses of local inhabitants, is attested by the discovery here of a large number of copies of these texts in various languages and several scripts. The earliest Tibetan Buddhist manuscripts (dating from the mid-eighth century) have been found in East Turkestan, and it was here that the Tibetans began to translate Mahayana canonical texts into their language.

In the northern oases, Tokharian, Uighur and Chinese translators worked on translations of Buddhist texts throughout the second half of the first millennium. The monasteries of Dunhuang maintained close cultural contacts with Turfan and Kucha. The earliest Chinese manuscripts from the Dunhuang library belong to the third–fourth centuries. Buddhist translation and literary activity in the Turkic languages started at a fairly early date but, with a few exceptions, the written texts of the seventh–ninth centuries are modest. The colophons of some manuscripts also mention translations from Tokharian A ('the language of Karashahr') and Tokharian B ('the language of Kucha'). A number of translations from Sanskrit and (probably) Sogdian are known.

It is important to note that the majority of Sanskrit Buddhist texts found in East Turkestan are not complete works, but merely excerpts and fragments, without headings or colophons. Due, however, to the unbroken tradition, from the manuscripts found in East Turkestan and Dunhuang, the Buddhist Hinayana canon and the principal Mahayana schools are the most fully represented in translations. This has allowed researchers to assess the structure of the canons of the various Hinayana schools, and the scope of the canonical literature of Mahayana.

HINAYANA, MAHAYANA AND VAJRAYANA

In the first millennium, the Hinayana, Mahayana and Vajrayana systems of Buddhism were represented in the region. No details are known about the sharp contradictions and hostilities that existed between the advocates of these systems, although it seems that the masses followed those who were victorious in open dispute. Between the northern and southern oases, however, there was a traditional doctrinal divergence connected with the cultural milieux defined by the Tokharian and Saka languages. Basically, Hinayana texts were popular in Turfan, Kucha and Karashahr and a huge body of Buddhist Hinayana literature was preserved in translation. Malov has suggested that virtually the entire

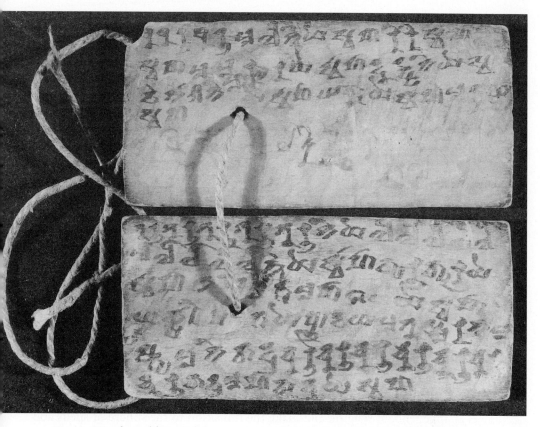

FIG. 5. Wooden tablets with incantational *dhāraṇi*. Script in North Turkestan Brāhmī. Found in Kucha by the archaeological mission of M. M. Berezovskiy.

Hinayana canon was translated by the Uighurs into their language and kept in monastic libraries.[47]

In the southern oases – Khotan and Kashgar – the findings have mainly been of Mahayana texts since only the texts of this school were translated into Khotanese and Tibetan. The great majority of Chinese manuscripts from Dunhuang contain Mahayana writings, with an insignificant number of Hinayana texts. In Middle Asia, on the other hand, only Hinayana writings have so far been found and we have no information concerning the dissemination of Mahayana in the region.

Towards the end of the first millennium, Vajrayana writings, sutras with a large number of incantational *dhāraṇi*s (formulae), collections of *dhāraṇi*s, magical formulized mantras, and so on, appeared throughout the territory of East Turkestan: they were in the Sanskrit, Tibetan, Khotanese, Chinese and Uighur languages (Fig. 5). A rupture in the fundamental doctrines of Buddhism

47. Malov, 1951, p. 142; Laufer, 1907, p. 302.

is apparent from this material. Mahayana, with its basic concept of Nirvana and its attainment by the path of the 'great wisdom' (*mahāprajñā*), gave way to more attractive and quicker methods, realizable in a single life-span, of achieving salvation in 'Sukhavati, the world of bliss', the 'pure land of Bodhisattva'. In difficult situations in life, recourse was had to the reading of *dhāraṇī*s and mantras, which explains their great popularity. Many magical texts were inserted into the Mahayana texts, thus achieving canonical status. As a result, Mahayana sutras began to be used for the attainment of practical blessings in life.

Among the Hinayana sutras, those which included *jātaka*s and *avadāna*s (stories in which Buddhas or Bodhisattvas were reborn in human or animal form) continued to spread. Moral and ethical exhortations in verse form (of the *Dharmapada* type) were exceptionally popular. These not infrequently served as models for poetic imitations: Buddhist poetry in the Turkic languages, for example, includes 1,500 verses of this kind, in which the customary and favourite forms of folk poetry were used. Collections of *jātaka*s and *avadāna*s appeared that had been borrowed from the Buddhist canon. A synopsis of one such collection, compiled for Buddhist homilies, was found in Bairam-Ali in manuscripts of the third–fourth centuries. Analogous collections have been preserved in Chinese and Tibetan translations.

The pragmatic character assumed by Buddhist doctrine towards the end of the first millennium was evidence of its incipient decline. With the loss of political backing by local rulers, Buddhism was forced to relinquish its status as an independent religion and make the transition to the sphere of spells and magic cults.

THE HINAYANA SCHOOLS

A second conclusion that can be drawn from the manuscripts found in East Turkestan and Central Asia is the existence of Sanskrit canons for most of the Hinayana schools. The 1982 Göttingen symposium established the existence of at least seven different versions of the *Sūtrapiṭaka*, relating to different schools. Fragments have been found of the *Vinayapiṭaka* of three schools, represented by the adherents of Sarvastivada, Mulasarvastivada and Dharmaguptaka. Research has shown that the majority of the Hinayana texts from East Turkestan belong to the Sarvastivada and Mulasarvastivada schools.

The structure of the Hinayana canons, and the distribution of the sutras over the various *āgama*s (sections), has not yet been precisely established. Sutras have been found which relate to four *āgama*s: *Dīrghāgama*, *Madhyamāgama*, *Saṃyuktāgama* and *Anguttarāgama*. The proper arrangement of the *āgama*s within canons of the various schools has not been settled. A number of sutras were particularly popular, and were used independently of their relationships to the *āgama*s. The finding in Bairam-Ali of a manuscript in which the colophon has been preserved enabled the structure of the *Vinayapiṭaka* of the adherents of Sarvastivada to be determined precisely (Fig. 6). Besides the general compositions for all schools (the *Prātimokṣa* sutra and comments on it), the canon was found to include special writings of the *karma-vācana* type, i.e. collections of rules for the performance of rites by monks and nuns.

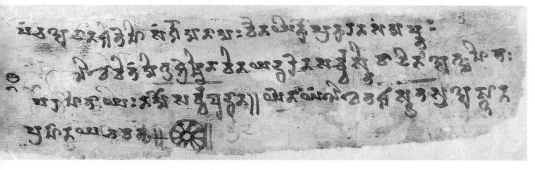

FIG. 6. Manuscript on birch bark from Bairam-Ali (Merv oasis).
Script in Indian Brāhmī. Text from Buddhist canon of Sarvastivada.

THE MAHAYANA SUTRAS

The range of Mahayana writings discovered in manuscripts in East Turkestan does not enable us to assert that this school of Buddhism possessed its own canon in India, constructed on the same principle as the Hinayana canon, the *Tripitaka*. In Sanskrit, as in the other languages, only sutras have been preserved. Fragments of 25 Mahayana sutras have, for example, been preserved in the Khotanese Saka language.[48] Khotan maintained permanent links with Kashmir and the monasteries of northern India. The range of literature in circulation in Khotan has been found to be identical to that discovered in the Gilgit library.[49]

Central Asia has yielded a large quantity of Mahayana texts, allowing a picture to be drawn up of the Buddhist schools and cults that held sway in the various cultural traditions. Among the schools, that of the *Prajñāpāramitā* held the foremost position. Significant quantities of its manuscripts have been found in all languages (except the Tokharian languages). The *Prajñāpāramitā* literature has been well researched, thanks to the work of Conze.[50]

The cult of the Buddha Amitabha, the lord of the west in Sukhavati (the world of bliss) was particularly popular among the peoples of Central Asia. In

48. Emmerick, 1992.
49. Hinüber, 1979.
50. Conze, 1977.

East Turkestan, the cult underwent further development and in the second half of the eighth century a special, apocryphal version known as the *Aparamitāyur* sutra arose, which was disseminated in all the local languages. The manuscripts found in Gilgit show that in India, too, the doctrine of 'Sukhavati, the world of bliss', became, in the second half of the first millennium, one of the chief Mahayana concepts.

In East Turkestan, yet another Mahayana school – that of the *Saddharma-puṇḍarikā*, or 'Lotus sutra' – experienced an important transformation. From this, the cult of the Bodhisattva Avalokiteshvara separated out and underwent further, independent development. In East Turkestan, the 25th chapter of the 'Lotus sutra' was translated into every language, and the Bodhisattva Avalokiteshvara, who was eulogized in it, was transformed into a major deity, providing a shield against all earthly ills and gaining the status of protector of Tibet.

The sutra of 'Golden Radiance' – the *Suvarṇaprabhāsa* sutra – underwent an analogous development in Central Asia. In the transformation of its text, preserved in a variety of versions and editions in many languages, it is possible to follow the growth of basic Mahayana doctrine into Vajrayana. The *dhāraṇi*s from the sutra of 'Golden Radiance' were also disseminated as a means of protection, and the reading of its text – thanks to a special preface added to it in East Turkestan that was in harmony with Buddhist tradition – afforded protection against being reborn in hell.

Besides the sutras existing in the popular milieu, important philosophical Mahayana sutras have been found in East Turkestan. These bear witness to the dissemination of the doctrines of two philosophical schools: Madhyamaka, which was established in India by Nagarjuna (150–250), and Yogacara, which derived its tradition from Asanga (310–390). An almost complete Sanskrit text of the sutra which provides the fundamentals of both schools (the *Mahāratnakūṭa-dharmaparyaya* or *Kāśyapaparivarta* sutra) has been discovered in East Turkestan.

East Turkestan – a major Buddhist centre

The pinpointing by archaeologists of the sites where manuscripts have been found, their palaeography, and the linguistic peculiarities preserved in their texts show that Buddhist centres were active in the territory of East Turkestan in the first millennium. In these centres (Turfan in the north and Khotan in the south), Buddhist texts were translated from Sanskrit and then Prakrit languages into the local idioms, and were then disseminated by copying and printing from wooden blocks (xylography). The centres' activities encompassed areas in which two local cultural traditions – the Tokharian and the Khotanese – were diffused. Both Turfan and Khotan experienced the powerful influence of the Indian and Iranian cultures, while in the north the cultural influence of China, and in the south that of Tibet, was felt.

The high level of literacy of the population of East Turkestan and Dunhuang was undoubtedly linked to the presence of a large number of Buddhist monasteries. In Tokharian manuscripts, the most frequently mentioned monastery is that of Yurpishka in Shorchuk, in the Kucha district, which was a major centre for the copying of manuscripts during the period of Hsüan-tsang's visit to Kucha in the first half of the seventh century. From 650, the role of Karashahr probably started to grow (Kucha was devastated by the Chinese and the Türks) and in the eighth–ninth centuries Turfan assumed the leading position. In the middle of the ninth century, after the disintegration of the Uighur *Kaghanate*, one Uighur branch established a small state in the Turfan oasis with its centre at Beshbalyk – later to be known as the Kocho state. The Buddhist centre moved there and, by the middle of the thirteenth century, Kocho was the single small island of Buddhist culture in the ocean of Islam, which engulfed the whole territory of East Turkestan.[51]

In the south, at the end of the seventh century, Khotan was gradually becoming an international Buddhist centre, encouraged by the tense political situation in the neighbouring countries. A period of wars and internal disorders had radically altered the situation in Central Asia and India. Among the inauspicious events for Buddhism, the following should be mentioned: the seizure of Central Asia by the Arabs in the eighth–ninth centuries; the persecution of Buddhism in T'ang China; the attempt to eradicate Buddhism from Tibet during the reign of gLang-dar-ma (836–842); the decline of Buddhism in India and the schism within the Buddhist community there; and, finally, the Muslim conquest of India. It is evident from the documents that regal power in Khotan continued to be strong, and afforded protection to Buddhism. The increase in the number of Buddhists is attested by the growing number of Buddhist centres referred to in the written sources in Tibetan, and of copies of Buddhist writings dating from the eighth and ninth centuries.

It is probable that this period saw an influx into Khotan of Buddhists from neighbouring regions. Vajrayana texts circulated in Khotan at this time and Tibetans, too, participated in the creation of Vajrayana cults. It was perhaps in Khotan that the features of Tibetan tantrism developed that were to determine the fortunes of Buddhism in Tibet. The active and creative role of the Khotanese Buddhist centres is clear from the part they played in formulating the Buddhist canon and perfecting its structure. For example, at least three collections of sutras were compiled in East Turkestan that were not in

---

51. Gabain, 1973. In 1986, Hamilton published 36 Uighur fragments of the ninth and tenth centuries from the P. Pelliot Collection and the British Library. These include many unidentified Buddhist fragments. The manuscripts relate to the period of existence of the Kocho state (see Hamilton, 1986).

circulation in India: the *Mahāratnakūṭa*, the *Mahāvataṃsaka* and the *Mahāsannipāta*. The assimilation of Buddhist doctrine and Indian culture evidently proceeded more vigorously in Khotan than in the northern oases.

Translations from Sanskrit and the Prakrit languages, and the compilation of collections of sutras and didactic, narrative writings, took place not only in Khotanese Saka, but also in the Tibetan and Chinese languages. It was in Khotan that the earlier, unaltered versions of many Mahayana sutras were preserved, and Chinese pilgrims in quest of Buddhist works started to travel not to India, but to Khotan. Finally, Khotan was the site of the creation of apocryphal works, on the basis of which the cults of individual Buddhas, patron Bodhisattvas and protectors evolved, as well as a number of abstract Buddhist categories of evil personified as demons and evil spirits, such as the *kleshas*.

The foregoing justifies the assertion that, towards the end of the first millennium, Khotan was transformed into an international Buddhist centre of the East. This was the region in which Sanskrit versions of the Buddhist sutras were in circulation; these versions were then adopted as the basis of Chinese, Tibetan, Tangut, Uighur and Mongol Buddhism.

The Buddhist centre in Khotan ceased to exist at the beginning of the eleventh century after its seizure by the Türks. As mentioned above, the sole Buddhist centre that continued to function in this region was Kocho, where the basic translations of Buddhist literature into the Uighur language were codified in written form. However, this lies outside the period covered by the present volume.[52]

---

52 . We express our deep gratitude to S. G. Klyashtorny for giving us access to his work before it was published (Klyashtorny, 1992). See also Litvinsky, 1992.

THE ARAB CONQUEST*

B. A. Litvinsky, A. H. Jalilov and A. I. Kolesnikov

Part One

THE ARAB CONQUEST OF IRAN

(B. A. Litvinsky)

The first Arab invasion of Iran

A new religion – Islam – was founded by Muhammad (d. 632) in Arabia at the beginning of the seventh century. In the ensuing conquests, the Arabs subjugated the peoples of the Near and Middle East and of North Africa, and a vast territory – extending from Spain to Sind at the time of maximum expansion and including the western part of Central Asia – came under Arab rule. The historical destiny of the peoples of Central Asia was to be profoundly influenced by the Arab conquest and the spread of Islam.

The Arabs advanced into Central Asia through Iran and so it is with Iran that the present account begins.[1] Arab tribes had settled in Mesopotamia even before the Sasanian era and the Sasanian Empire was therefore obliged to have dealings with them from the outset. According to al-Tabari, the Sasanian emperor Shapur I (241–271) actually settled one of the Arab tribes within Iran in Kerman.[2] Shapur II (309–379) subjugated the entire western part of the Persian Gulf. Islands were also incorporated in the Sasanian Empire and the Arab sea trade, linking the Mediterranean with India, was controlled by the Sasanians. Moreover, under Khusrau I (531–579) Iran intervened in the affairs of Yemen in an attempt to assist the Arabs against Byzantium.

Sasanian Iran also controlled the semi-independent Arab kingdom of al-Hira (located to the north of the great swamp of lower Iraq) under the Lakhmid dynasty. Under the reign of Nuʿman III (580–602), al-Hira had become increasingly independent. In spite of Nuʿman's attempts to pursue an independent policy that was inconsistent with or even contrary to Sasanian interests,

---

* See Map 5.
1. This account mainly follows the ideas and materials set out in the monograph written on the Arab conquest of Iran by Kolesnikov, 1982.
2. Nöldeke, Tabari, 1973, pp. 16–17.

however, the small kingdom was incapable of holding its own against its giant neighbour and was subdued. Al-Hira and its neighbouring Arab tribes nevertheless continued to be a thorn in the side of the Sasanian authorities (in 604–605, for example, they inflicted a defeat on the Sasanian forces).[3] Raids by individual Arab tribes inside the boundaries of the Sasanian Empire also continued.

In the 630s, the 16-year-old *shahanshah* Yazdgird III (632–651) came to power in Iran; a group of dignitaries acted as his guardians and a regent governed on his behalf. The rule of the first caliph, Abu Bakr (632–634), began at almost exactly the same time. In the spring of 633 the caliphate's forces under Khalid b. al-Walid embarked on their first campaign within Sasanian territory. They were opposed by the troops of one of the most powerful Iranian grandees, the governor of the border zone. The Iranian soldiers were fastened together by a chain to prevent them from fleeing. In the preliminary single combat, Khalid b. al-Walid slew his Iranian adversary and the Arabs were victorious in the subsequent attack, gaining possession of the *shahanshah*'s crown valued at 100,000 drachms. Whereas 'The Persians had probably regarded the Muslim advance on al-Hira as another annoying raid of the bedouins,'[4] the battle of Kadhima opened up the route to Iraq for the Arabs.[5]

The conquest of Iraq

The Arabs then set out to conquer Iraq, one army moving northwards from the Tigris-Euphrates delta and another moving across from the west. At a place near the harbour of ʿUbulla, the Arabs first joined battle with an Iranian army sent against them from the capital, Ctesiphon: the Arabs were again victorious. They next launched an attack against al-Hira, hitherto the main Sasanian stronghold west of the Euphrates and the key to the inner regions of Iraq. Although the Sasanian army was defeated, the local population continued to offer resistance for a time before eventually surrendering and paying tribute.

All these events occurred prior to the accession to the caliphate of ʿUmar b. al-Khattab (634–644), under whom the forces of Islam enjoyed further successes. During his rule the Arab army in Iraq came under a new military leader, Abu ʿUbaida. The Iranians also appointed a new commander-in-chief, the governor of Khurasan, Rustam b. Farrukhzad. Armour-clad war elephants helped the Iranians win one of the battles and Abu ʿUbaida himself was crushed to death by an elephant.[6] In subsequent battles, however, the Arabs regained the

3. Kolesnikov, 1970, pp. 74–6.
4. Frye, 1975, p. 56.
5. Al-Tabari, 1879–89, Vol. 1, pp. 2023–5; Ibn al-Athir, 1851–76, Vol. 2, p. 295.
6. Al-Tabari, 1879–89, Vol. 1, pp. 2175–6; Ibn al-Athir, 1851–76, Vol. 2, p. 388; al-Dinawari, 1888, p. 119; al-Baladhuri, 1866, p. 404.

upper hand and their territorial expansion continued. Their victory in the second battle of Yarmuk in August 636 completed the conquest of Syria and the caliph sent part of the Syrian army to the Mesopotamian front, their ranks swelled by large numbers of fresh volunteers. ʿUmar himself had intended to command these forces, but he subsequently assigned the task to one of the Prophet's first companions, Saʿd b. Abu Waqqas. Altogether, the Arab troops in Mesopotamia numbered some 30,000, the largest Muslim military force ever assembled in that country.

Saʿd b. Abu Waqqas then sent an embassy of 14 men to the Iranian capital; they demanded land concessions beyond the Euphrates, a trading corridor and the right to trade in Mesopotamia, together with the payment of taxes and tribute. The *shahanshah* rejected these demands out of hand. Arab sources give grossly exaggerated accounts of the size of the Iranian army that was subsequently raised. These estimates range from 60,000 to 120,000, some sources even maintaining that the figure of 60,000 refers only to the so-called 'professional' soldiers of the regular army, who were accompanied by 'assistants and slaves'. According to modern researchers, however, the Iranian forces probably did not greatly outnumber the Arabs.

THE BATTLE OF AL-QADISIYYA

The Iranians moved southwards until they were close to al-Qadisiyya, a small fortified town some 30 km from Kufa, and subsequent events took place on the bank of the ʿAtiq channel. To begin with, the Iranian general, Rustam b. Farrukhzad, again engaged in negotiations that were as protracted as they were futile. Then his men forced their way over the channel by a specially constructed crossing. They were drawn up in line along the channel, with the centre reinforced by a group of 18 war elephants, and smaller numbers defending the 2 flanks. The elephants' attack proved highly effective and the Arabs were terrified. As a result, the Iranians initially had the upper hand, but the Arabs soon recovered and began to strike the elephants' trunks with their spears while the archers shot down their Persian counterparts. The Iranians were forced to retreat to their original positions.

On the second day, the Arabs were more frequently on the offensive. The Iranians' war elephants were severely wounded and their opponents mounted palanquin-like structures on camels, causing panic among the Iranian horses. The Arabs were also reinforced with a 10,000-strong detachment from Syria. On the third day, both sides fought even more doggedly. The Iranians introduced new war elephants but without success: the wounded animals merely retreated into their own lines, sowing panic and confusion. The fighting was so fierce that it continued even after nightfall. Although the Arabs succeeded in breaking through the centre of the Iranian lines, both flanks stood firm. Nature itself was against the Iranians, who were lashed by winds of hurricane force.

One of the Arab units fought its way through to Rustam b. Farrukhzad's head-quarters and the general was killed in flight (according to another version, he died in single combat with Sa'd b. Abu Waqqas).

The Iranian troops retreated in panic to the eastern bank of the channel. Although individual contingents continued to offer staunch resistance, the main group was annihilated and the rest fell back. There were extremely heavy casualties. The Arabs seized the Sasanian imperial flag ornamented with precious stones.[7] The sources disagree on the date of the battle of al-Qadisiyya; according to Kolesnikov,[8] it took place at the end of September 636.

The Arab forces proceeded to capture the Iranian strongholds one by one, gradually drawing nearer to Ctesiphon. Yazdgird III himself fled the capital with his relatives and entourage and it surrendered without putting up any resistance. An enormously rich booty fell to the Arabs, including some of the contents of the state treasury that the fugitives had left behind in their haste. By 637 the whole of Mesopotamia had come under Arab control. According to Zarrinkub:

> On entering the palace of Khusrau, Sa'd had performed an eight rak'at prayer for his victory and, because of its appropriateness in recalling the fate of those who reject God, recited the Qur'ānic verse (44, 25–27) which begins with 'How many gardens and springs have they left'. He made a mosque in the citadel and the four-hundred-year-old capital of the Sāsānians became for a time the camping ground of this Muslim general.[9]

The conquest of Khuzistan

The conquest of Khuzistan then began. The Arabs were led by Abu Musa Ash'ari, the future governor of Basra. He first captured two border strong-holds, the outcome being determined by victory on the battlefield. In the meantime, Yazdgird had moved to Nihavend in central Media. One after another, the towns and strongholds of Khuzistan fell to the Arabs, including the provincial capital of Ahvaz. Then began the battle for Shushtar, which was of great strategic importance. A seventh-century Syriac chronicle describes the town as follows: 'Shushtar covers a wide area and is strongly fortified by large and deep channels, surrounding it on all sides like moats.' The sources disagree on the duration of the battle, mentioning periods ranging from a few months to two years. The action began on the outer defence lines, where the Iranian troops occupied trenches. Having crushed the outer defences (the defenders retreated into the town, reinforcing its own defences), the Arabs stormed the

---

7. Yusuf, 1945.
8. Kolesnikov, 1982.
9. Zarrinkub, 1975, pp. 12–13.

fortifications but their attacks were repulsed. However, they were assisted by a traitor called Siya, who led an Arab detachment through a secret entrance by night. They killed the guards and threw open the gates. The remainder of the garrison sought refuge in the citadel, where the treasure was deposited. Their commander was Hurmuzan (or Hurmuzdan), the *marzbān* (governor) of Khuzistan. Although the garrison put up fierce resistance, beating off the Arab attacks, the defenders' strength dwindled and the citadel eventually fell. According to some sources, the *marzbān* sued for peace and his life was spared following his conversion to Islam; the majority of his companions, however, were put to death.[10]

The battle of Nihavend

Finally realizing what a formidable adversary he was dealing with, Yazdgird III issued a decree for the mobilization of troops, especially from the neighbouring provinces. They were to assemble in Nihavend. The forces that gathered there came from Media itself, from Persia, the Caspian provinces, Khurasan, Seistan (modern Sistan) and other regions. A huge army was formed, estimated by the sources to number between 60,000 and 150,000 men. The caliph ʿUmar also mobilized an impressive number of troops, some of whom came from Syria; Nuʿman b. ʿAmr b. Muqarrin was appointed commander-in-chief.

The Iranians drew up their troops close to Nihavend, firmly resolved to fight a defensive battle. Iron spikes were strewn in front of the lines to hinder the attacks of the Arab cavalry. Once again, the Iranian infantry were chained together in groups of five to ten men to prevent them retreating. After initial fruitless parleying, the Arabs spread the rumour that the caliph was dead and they were about to retreat, even going through some of the motions of withdrawal. The ruse worked and part of the Iranian army advanced into the open field. During the fierce fighting that resulted, both sides incurred heavy losses, but the scales eventually tipped in the Arabs' favour. Although their commander-in-chief was killed, the Arabs continued to attack and the Iranian army was routed, part of it seeking refuge in the town and the neighbouring fortress. The Iranians then abandoned the fortress, emerged on to the battlefield and continued fighting. They were utterly defeated. The ruler of Nihavend managed to conclude a charter of immunity for the population of the town, but the Arabs seized great quantities of booty, including the treasures of the fire temple. It is believed that these events occurred in 642.[11]

According to Frye, 'this was the most difficult battle of all those which

10. Al-Kufi, 1968–75, Vol. 2, pp. 23–5; al-Baladhuri, 1866, pp. 380–1; al-Tabari, 1879–89, Vol. 1, pp. 2554–5; Qummi, 1934, p. 300.
11. Kolesnikov, 1982, p. 111.

the Arabs had to fight against imperial Sasanian forces'.[12] Described as the 'battle of battles', its role was extremely important since it took place on the Iranian plateau. After the battle of Nihavend, the organized resistance of the Sasanian authorities came to an end. According to al-Tabari, 'from that day on, there was no further unity among them [the Persians] and the people of the individual provinces fought their own enemies on their own territory'. After the fall of Nihavend, Yazdgird III is reported to have moved to Istakhr and from there to Kerman and finally Khurasan. Following their victory in Nihavend, the Arabs captured Hamadan, which had to be subdued on two occasions. The whole of Media was now under their control.

The sources do not give a clear-cut chronological account of the remainder of the conquest. This confusion is frequently due to the fact that many towns and even provinces had to be conquered two or more times. Isfahan was taken in 643 and 644, for example, and Ray was captured at around the same time. The Arabs' next step was to subjugate Iran's northern provinces. They also took possession of Persia and Kerman.

The conquest of Seistan

We shall now consider in greater detail the Arab conquest of Seistan and Khurasan, regions that form part of Central Asia. Seistan (in ancient times, Drangiana) was one of the remote eastern provinces of the Sasanian Empire. The Arab conquest of Seistan began in the middle period of the caliph ʿUthman's rule (644–656), although the first raids had taken place under the previous caliph. ʿUthman appointed his fellow tribesman, ʿAbdallah b. Amir, future governor of Basra, with instructions to complete the conquest. Having fortified his position in Kerman, ʿAbdallah b. Amir planned to advance on Seistan. An attack was possible from the west, but this would have meant crossing the vast desert of Dasht-i Lut, which extended for a distance of some 450 km. The other approach was from the north-west via Kuhistan and Herat: it was a much easier route but those regions would first have to be conquered.

It was nevertheless decided to take the route through the desert and the first offensive took place in 650–651. ʿAbdallah b. Amir placed the attacking forces under the command of Mujashi b. Masʿud. Many Arabs were slain in the fighting and their forces had to retreat. The following year, ʿAbdallah b. Amir himself took part in the campaign: he proceeded with the main body of the army to Khurasan, while Rabiʿ b. Ziyad was sent to Seistan, where he succeeded in reaching the town of Zaliq, some 30 km from the capital Zarang. The ruler of Zaliq preferred a peace treaty to the battlefield. The Arabs then subjugated the towns of Karkuya, Haisun and Nashrudh before arriving in the

12. Frye, 1975, p. 60.

vicinity of Zarang. They crossed the Huk, a channel or tributary of the River Helmand, and came to the walls of the capital. A fierce battle ensued and during the first attack many Muslims were killed. The second attack resulted in an Arab victory. But the town's fortifications, especially its citadel, were exceptionally strong – according to local tradition, they had been constructed by order of Kai Khusrau, Alexander the Great and Ardashir I Papakan, the co-founder of the Sasanian Empire.

Iran b. Rustam, the *marzbān* or *ispahbad* (local governor) of Zarang, then assembled the élite of the nobility and the Zoroastrian clergy, who agreed that hostilities should end even if the military commanders wished to continue fighting. A 'justification' was even found: the 'divine mission' of the Arab aliens was supposed to have been foretold in the Zoroastrian sacred books. Rabiᶜ b. Ziyad agreed to make peace on condition that Seistan paid an annual tribute of 1 million dirhams, to be handed over by 1,000 boy slaves (other sources say girls), each bearing a golden bowl. The entire region of Seistan was then subjugated and the conqueror, Rabiᶜ b. Ziyad, was appointed Arab governor. Arab-Sasanian coins minted in Seistan in 651–652 and 652–653 are known. When Rabiᶜ b. Ziyad was recalled to Basra some 18 months later, he was replaced by Abu Saᶜid ᶜAbd al-Rahman b. Samura. In the meantime, however, the local inhabitants had risen up against the Arabs and overthrown them, and the new governor had to resume military action. Zarang was subdued and this time the conquest was final. The Arab forces had extended the territory under the caliph's rule as far as India.[13]

The conquest of Khurasan

The conquest of Khurasan was bound up with the fate of the last Sasanian *shahanshah*. Abandoning Kerman, Yazdgird III had gone, according to most of the sources, straight to Khurasan (other versions say Seistan), halting in Nishapur (or, in another source, Bust). He then moved on to Merv because it was ruled by the *kanarang* (the east Iranian counterpart of *marzbān*) Mahoe, who was personally indebted to Yazdgird for his ascent to high office.[14] The *shahanshah* apparently hoped to enlist the aid of the Türks and Chinese and raise a new army.

In the meantime Yazdgird had no army. He travelled with a suite of several thousand relatives, courtiers and servants, accompanied (as far as Merv) by only a small military detachment. Friction then arose between Yazdgird and his vassal Mahoe. The sources offer different explanations for this conflict: some maintain that Mahoe had already come to an agreement with the Türk *kaghan*,

13. Bosworth, 1968, pp. 13–25.
14. For Khurasan on the eve of the Arab conquest, see Shaban, n.d.

hoping to secede from the Sasanian Empire; according to others, Yazdgird ordered Mahoe to pay a large tax; a third group claims that the *shahanshah* wished to remove Mahoe and appoint a military leader in his place, and when this plan failed sought to replace Mahoe by his nephew. According to one account, the people of Merv had also been turned against Yazdgird and refused him entry to the town. The Türk *kaghan*, whatever his role in the affair, can hardly have been well-disposed towards the *shahanshah*.

What is certain is that a conspiracy had been hatched against Yazdgird. Having no troops at his disposal, he secretly abandoned his residence and took flight, hiding in a mill on the River Murghab with a Christian miller. The fugitive's costly apparel, jewellery and performance of the Zoroastrian rites made it easy for his pursuers to track him down. According to some sources, the miller himself murdered his illustrious guest. The funeral was organized by Merv's Christian community, who buried him in the garden of the Metropolitan of Merv. (According to another report, however, his body was taken to Istakhr.) The sources also give divergent accounts of Mahoe's fate: according to some, he sought refuge from the approaching Arabs with the Türk *kaghan*; another source claims that the people of Merv themselves delivered their *marzbān* to an agonizing death.

Yazdgird's death in 651 finally brought an end to the Sasanian Empire, but it did not halt the Arab advance. Under ʿAbdallah b. Amir, the Arabs captured Nishapur, routing Hephthalite forces from Herat province in the process. Following a siege of several months, Nishapur was finally betrayed by a member of the Iranian aristocracy and its citadel captured. Towns such as Tus, Abivard, Nisa, Sarakhs, Herat and Merv then fell to forces commanded by the Arab general Ahnaf b. Qais. Continuing eastwards, he reached and captured Balkh. Khurasan was subdued but the local population persistently rebelled against the Arabs. A long struggle still lay ahead.

Part Two

THE ARAB CONQUEST OF TRANSOXANIA

(A. H. Jalilov)

The first Arab incursions into Transoxania

Under the Umayyads, the conquest began in the 680s of parts of the right bank of the Amu Darya (an area known to the Arabs as *Mā warā ʾl-nahr*: literally, 'that which is beyond the river', i.e. Transoxania). The forces came from Khurasan, where an Arab governorship had been set up with the town of Merv as its centre. At first the campaigns took the form of predatory raids. The first major raid into Transoxania was carried out by the governor of Khurasan, ʿUbaidallah b. Ziyad. In 673 he crossed the Amu Darya and reached Bukhara, which at that time was ruled by the *khatun* (queen), the mother of the young *Bukhār khudāt* (ruler of Bukhara), Tughshada. After the very first skirmish she made peace with ʿUbaidallah b. Ziyad, who obtained a ransom from her and returned to Merv.

In 676 the Arabs repeated their raid on Bukhara under the leadership of the new governor of Khurasan, Saʿid b. ʿUthman. The *khatun* made peace with him too and he went on to Samarkand, having taken 80 hostages.[15] All the attempts by Saʿid b. ʿUthman to capture the town proved unsuccessful: he was forced to make peace with the inhabitants and to leave the territory of Transoxania, taking 50 Sogdian hostages with him. On his return to Medina he made slaves of them, but they killed him and then committed suicide, preferring death to slavery.[16]

The Arabs next raided Khwarizm, Khujand and Samarkand in 680 under the leadership of the new governor of Khurasan, Salm b. Ziyad. Their rulers also made peace with him and, after obtaining a ransom from them, he withdrew from Transoxania. Similar raids were conducted by the next-but-one governor, al-Muhallab b. Abi Sufra, and his successors up to the year 705.[17] In spite of these raids, the local rulers still did not realize the seriousness of the Arab threat. Instead of uniting to repulse the foreign invaders, some rulers even invited their enemies into their country so that, with their help, they could settle accounts with neighbouring rulers.[18]

The beginning of the conquest of Transoxania

At the end of the seventh/beginning of the eighth century, Arab policy towards Central Asia underwent a fundamental change. The internecine strife among the Arabs subsided somewhat towards the end of the reign of the caliph ʿAbd al-Malik b. Marwan (685–705), and the Umayyads were able to begin the systematic conquest of Transoxania.

In the year 705, the task of conquering Transoxania was entrusted to the governor of Khurasan, Qutaiba b. Muslim (705–715), who ushered in a new and decisive stage in the conquest of Transoxania by the Umayyads. Qutaiba skilfully exploited the internal quarrels between the rulers of Central Asia. During his first campaign in Transoxania, his forces included the ruler of Balkh,

15. Narshakhi, 1897, p. 52.
16. Al-Baladhuri, 1866, p. 412; Gibb, 1923, pp. 18–19.
17. For these raids, see *Istoriya Tajikskogo naroda*, 1964, pp. 96–7.
18. Al-Tabari, 1879–89, Vol. 2, p. 994.

and the *Chagān khudāt* (ruler of Chaganiyan) invited Qutaiba into his country to participate in a joint struggle against the ruler of the neighbouring territories of Akharun and Shuman.[19] Such treason provided Qutaiba with the information he required about Transoxania and in 706 he undertook a bold campaign in the area of Bukhara.

One of the closest towns to the Amu Darya in the Bukhara oasis was the small trading centre of Paikent. This was the first place in which Qutaiba encountered stubborn resistance from the population of Transoxania. The Arabs were forced to take Paikent twice, killing all of its defenders and razing the town to the ground. In 707 and 708 Qutaiba attempted to seize the oasis of Bukhara, but was vigorously repulsed by the combined forces of Bukhara, Sughd and the Türks, and returned to Merv. It was only after making peace with the Sogdian *ikhshid* (king), Tarkhun, and driving a wedge between the allies that Qutaiba managed to capture Bukhara in 709, and Shuman, Kish and Nakhshab the following year. Tarkhun's policy of compliance with the invaders greatly displeased the Sogdians: in 710 they dethroned him and elected Ghurak in his place.[20] This was a convenient pretext for Qutaiba to begin the conquest of Sughd and Khwarizm. (For the conquest of Khwarizm, see Chapter 9.)

In 712 the Arab commander set out against Samarkand, after incorporating military detachments from Khwarizm and Bukhara in his own main forces. The Sogdians first gave battle to the Arabs at Arbinjan; this was followed by the siege of Samarkand, which lasted a month. Although the rulers of Chach (Tashkent) and Ferghana sent a small detachment to assist the people of Samarkand, the Arabs managed to destroy the force before it arrived.[21] Exhausted by the month-long siege, the Sogdians had no option other than to surrender and to make peace on the worst possible terms. In 713 and 714, Qutaiba conducted two major campaigns against Chach and Ferghana[22] and almost reached the territory of Kashgar.

The following year, Sulaiman (715–717) succeeded to the caliphate. Qutaiba b. Muslim, aware of Sulaiman's hostility to him, moved with his family to Ferghana in order to break away from the caliphate. But the Arab troops, wearied by the continuous bloody wars which had lasted for a decade, would no longer obey Qutaiba, and he and his family were killed. For several years after his death, there were no more Arab conquests in Central Asia. With the exception of a raid on Kashgar and the conquest of Dihistan (on the shores of the Caspian Sea), the Arabs launched no major campaigns to extend their dominions during the period 715–720, concentrating instead on consolidating their hold on the regions they had already conquered.

19. Al-Baladhuri, 1866, pp. 419–20.
20. Al-Tabari, 1879–89, Vol. 2, pp. 1229–30.
21. Ibid., Vol. 2, pp. 1242–3.
22. Ibid., Vol. 2, p. 1256.

From the first stages of the conquest, the nomadic Arab nobility had attempted to colonize the conquered areas of Transoxania. This policy was widely pursued by the Arabs, particularly under Qutaiba b. Muslim, who consolidated his military victories by settling Arabs among the population and through them conducting large-scale propaganda campaigns on behalf of Islam.[23]

The struggle of the peoples of Central Asia against the Umayyads

In order to attract the people to Islam, the Arabs initially offered certain privileges to converts as well as applying methods of coercion. Those who accepted Islam, for example, were exempted from payment of the *jizya* (poll-tax). But when mass conversions began and tax receipts declined, the governor of Khurasan, al-Jarrah b. ʿAbdallah al-Hakami (717–719), decreed that only converts who accepted circumcision and were acquainted with the Qurʿan would be exempted from payment of the *jizya*. This gave rise to the large-scale anti-Umayyad movement of the Sogdians in the years 720–722.

There were two stages in this movement. During the first stage (720–721), the Sogdians, with the aid of the Türks, destroyed the Samarkand garrison and expelled the Arabs from the town. All the attempts by the governor of Khurasan, Saʿid b. ʿAbd al-ʿAziz b. al-Hakam (720–721), to restore Arab power in Samarkand proved unsuccessful. In the autumn of 721 he was replaced as governor by Saʿid b. ʿAmr al-Harashi.

On his arrival in Khurasan, al-Harashi organized a major punitive expedition against the Sogdians. However, their *ikhshid*, Ghurak, instead of leading the rising, tried to persuade his subjects to offer allegiance to al-Harashi.[24] For these reasons, the anti-Umayyad movement among the Sogdians then entered a second stage (721–722), moving from an active to a passive struggle. Realizing that their forces were inadequate, the Sogdian rebels left their homeland and moved to regions which offered greater protection from their foes. The rebels from the western part of Sughd, led by Karzanj, the ruler of Pai (present-day Katta-kurgan), set out for Ferghana, whose king, at-Tar, promised them protection and refuge. The rebels from the eastern part of Sughd, led by Divashtich, the ruler of Panjikent, travelled east to the upper reaches of the Zerafshan. But at-Tar proved perfidious; when the Sogdians arrived he held them in Khujand and secretly informed al-Harashi of their whereabouts.[25] The Arab governor swiftly dispatched a large detachment and dealt brutally with

23. Narshakhi, 1897, p. 63.
24. Al-Tabari, 1879–89, Vol. 2, p. 1,439; Ibn al-Athir, 1851–76, Vol. 5, p. 78.
25. Al-Tabari, 1879–89, Vol. 2, pp. 1440–2; Ibn al-Athir, 1851–76, Vol. 5, pp. 78–9.

the Sogdian emigrants. He also killed over 3,000 farmers in the Khujand neighbourhood because of their solidarity with the Sogdians.[26]

After brutally annihilating the group led by Karzanj, al-Harashi rapidly dispatched a detachment against the Sogdians under Divashtich; they were occupying the fort of Abargar (now known as 'the castle on Mount Mug'), located on the left bank of the Zerafshan, some 120 km to the east of Panjikent.[27] At the approach of the Arabs, the Sogdians sortied and gave battle to the enemy at a distance of 6-7 km from the fort in a gorge near the village of Kum. The Arabs won and laid siege to the castle. Realizing that further resistance was useless, Divashtich gave himself up to the Arabs, who then seized and pillaged the fort. In the autumn of the same year (722), al-Harashi had Divashtich killed on the road from Kish to Arbinjan.[28] The defeat of this second group of rebels sealed the fate of the anti-Umayyad movement among the Sogdians in the years 720–722.[29]

Although the Arabs dealt harshly with the movement of 720–722 and re-established their authority over Sughd, the people of Transoxania continued their resistance, this time with the aid of the Türks. In 728, in an attempt to reduce popular discontent and consolidate Arab power in Transoxania, the governor of Khurasan, Ashras b. ʿAbdallah al-Sulami, decreed that anyone accepting Islam would be exempt from the *jizya*. So many people responded by becoming 'Muslims' that there was hardly anyone left to pay the *jizya*. But the abandoning of the tax conflicted with the interests of both the Arabs and the local élite. Al-Sulami therefore revoked his decision in the same year and again began to levy the *jizya* on all non-Muslims and on Muslims who had not yet been circumcized and were not familiar with the Qurʿan. This led to a major rebellion which extended to almost the whole of Transoxania.

The oasis of Bukhara became the centre of the rising, attracting rebels from Sughd and the Türks, led by their *kaghan*. The Arabs were practically driven out of Transoxania by a broad popular rising in 728: only Samarkand and Dabusiyya remained in their hands, and that was due to the indecisiveness of the *ikhshid*, Ghurak.[30] Al-Sulami only managed to recapture Bukhara in the summer of 729, after several months of hard fighting. In the spring of 730 a new governor of Khurasan, Junaid b. ʿAbd al-Rahman al-Murri, arrived in

---

26. Al-Tabari, 1879–89, Vol. 2, pp. 1445–6; Ibn al-Athir, 1851–76, Vol. 5, p. 81.
27. In 1933 various artifacts, including over 80 manuscripts, were discovered in the ruins of the fort that had once stood on Mount Mug (see *Sogdiyskie documenty s gory Mug*, 1962, Vol. 1; 1962, Vol. 2; 1963, Vol. 3). The excavation of ancient Panjikent, whose last ruler was Divashtich, was begun in 1947 and is still under way. The ruins of this ancient town, which ceased to exist after being conquered by the Arabs, are located to the south-east of the modern town of the same name (Jalilov and Negmatov, 1969; Belenitskiy and Raspopova, 1971; Isakov, 1982).
28. Al-Tabari, 1879–89, Vol. 2, p. 1447.
29. For a detailed account of this movement, see Jalilov, 1961, pp. 134–46.
30. *Istoriya Uzbekskoy SSR*, 1955, p. 147.

Bukhara to assist al-Sulami. Their joint forces reached Samarkand with great difficulty and, after consolidating the garrison there, Junaid returned to Khurasan the same year.

From that time the Arab position became more difficult in Transoxania and also in Khurasan itself. In 733–734 there was a drought and famine broke out.[31] One cause of the famine in Khurasan was the Arabs' loss of the Zerafshan valley, which supplied them with large quantities of grain. In 734 an anti-government movement led by Harith b. Suraij broke out in Khurasan among the Arabs themselves, but it was rapidly crushed by the new governor, Asad b. ꜤAbdallah.

Taking advantage of the troubles and disturbances among the Arabs, the people of Transoxania intensified their struggle against the invaders in the years 736–737. In response, Asad b. ꜤAbdallah transferred his capital from Merv to Balkh and in 737 led an expedition to Khuttal. Armed forces from Sughd and Chach and numbers of Türks arrived to support the population of Khuttal. The Türk *kaghan*, Sulu, emerged as their overall leader and the first blow was struck against the *Chagān khudāt*, who had previously supported the Arabs.[32] Asad b. ꜤAbdallah fled, leaving behind his baggage train containing the plunder from Khuttal. Sulu pursued Asad and on the left bank of the Amu Darya split his forces into small detachments, which then took to looting the countryside. On hearing this news, Asad, who was preparing to abandon Balkh for Merv, rapidly went over to the attack and won a resounding victory over the allies not far from Kharistan. With the subsequent appointment of Nasr b. Sayyar (738–748) as governor of Khurasan and the collapse of the anti-caliphate coalition, the Arabs succeeded in consolidating their position in Transoxania.

Having taken part in the Arab conquests in the time of Qutaiba b. Muslim, Nasr b. Sayyar knew Transoxania well and he realized that it would be impossible to subdue the country by military action alone. He therefore attempted to normalize relations with the local population by peaceful means. He introduced a fixed procedure for the levying of taxes and attempted to establish close relations with the local élite, even marrying the daughter of the *Bukhār khudāt*. Through several such measures, Nasr and his comrades managed to win influential groups of the local élite over to their side and began the process whereby the Arab aristocracy merged with the local élite. Nevertheless Nasr failed to restore order in Transoxania and discontent with Umayyad policies continued to grow, not only among the people of Transoxania and the other countries conquered by the Arabs but also among the Arab population itself.

The power of the Umayyads rested on the aristocratic élite and protected its interests alone; as a result, the broad masses of the Arab population were

---

31. Al-Tabari, 1879–89, Vol. 2, p. 1563.
32. Ibid., pp. 1600–1.

dissatisfied with Umayyad rule. This hostility was particularly strong in Khurasan and Transoxania. In those areas, not only the lower sections of the population (who had to meet obligations such as the *kharaj*, or land tax, and the *jizya*) but even the local aristocracy harboured resentment; although the aristocracy had established close relations with the conquering élite, they did not enjoy the same rights.

This general discontent was skilfully exploited by the ʿAbbasids (the descendants of ʿAbbas, the uncle of the Prophet Muhammad), who in the 740s secretly began to conduct a vigorous propaganda campaign against the Umayyads. At a crucial stage, the ʿAbbasids sent Abu Muslim, a man loyal to them, to Khurasan as leader of the movement. He enjoyed great success in Khurasan and Transoxania in 747–748: when the rebellion was raised, people flocked to join him under the black banners of the ʿAbbasids. Although Nasr b. Sayyar vainly attempted to rally the Arabs, his forces were destroyed and the rebels seized Merv and then the whole of Khurasan. Taking advantage of his success, Abu Muslim occupied Damascus, the seat of the caliphate, in the year 750. The power of the Umayyad caliphs collapsed, to be followed by a new Arab dynasty, the ʿAbbasids, with its first capital at Kufa (and, subsequently, its permanent capital at Baghdad). In the battle at the Talas river (751), the Arabs defeated the Chinese.

The struggle of the peoples of Central Asia against the ʿAbbasids and the local nobility

The fall of the Umayyads and the rise to power of the ʿAbbasids did little to alter the wretched conditions of the mass of the population. Like their predecessors, the ʿAbbasids were jealous defenders of Arab dominion over other conquered countries. Not one of the promises made to the people by the ʿAbbasids and the leader of the movement, Abu Muslim (appointed governor of Khurasan after the victory over the Umayyads), was fulfilled. The people still laboured under a host of burdensome obligations, provoking popular risings from the earliest years of ʿAbbasid rule.

In 750 a rebellion erupted in Bukhara, directed not only against the ʿAbbasids but also against the local aristocracy which had sided with them. The rising was led by Sharik b. Shaikh, who encouraged his followers by saying that they had not fought the Umayyads merely in order to submit to the ʿAbbasids. Abu Muslim dispatched a force of 10,000 against them, led by Ziyad b. Salih, but in the 37 days' fighting in Bukhara that ensued, the rebels were victorious in every battle.[33] The *Bukhār khudāt*, Qutaiba, then came to the aid of Ziyad b. Salih with a force of 10,000. With the help of these soldiers

---

33. Narshakhi, 1897, p. 82.

(together with the fact that the rebels were suffering from a severe shortage of food), Ziyad seized the town and dealt harshly with its population. Sharik b. Shaikh was killed in one of the battles. There was a similar rising in Samarkand, which was also brutally suppressed by the same Ziyad b. Salih. Although Abu Muslim fought the rebels and jealously defended ʿAbbasid power in Khurasan and Transoxania, the ʿAbbasid rulers did not trust him and they had him murdered in 755.

The murder of Abu Muslim gave rise to a number of rebellions against the ʿAbbasids. Although Abu Muslim had not been a true popular leader, the people saw in him the man who had freed them from the Umayyad yoke and had promised to improve their lot. In 755 a rebellion broke out in Nishapur which spread to almost the whole of Khurasan and Tabaristan: it was led by Sumbad, who declared himself a follower of Abu Muslim. Although this rising too was brutally repressed by the ʿAbbasids, it provided a powerful stimulus for a larger-scale rebellion which broke out in the territory of Transoxania during the 770s and was this time headed by a genuine popular leader, Hashim b. Hakim, known by the nickname al-Muqannaʿ.

Al-Muqannaʿ was born in one of the villages of Merv. In the years of the anti-Umayyad campaigns of the ʿAbbasids, he had been one of Abu Muslim's military commanders. In 776, aware that the people of Transoxania were hostile to the policies of the ʿAbbasids, al-Muqannaʿ dispatched his emissaries to call the people to rise in open revolt against the foreign yoke and the inequality of their property status. A number of towns and villages in the Zerafshan valley and the Kashka Darya immediately announced their readiness to support al-Muqannaʿ, the inhabitants of 60 villages rallying to him on a single day.[34] Convinced that the number of his supporters in Transoxania was growing quickly, al-Muqannaʿ travelled to Kish with 36 followers. By the time he arrived, the Kashka Darya valley and the villages around Bukhara were already in the hands of his followers, 'the people in white clothes' (al-Muqannaʿ's followers were distinguished by their white clothes and banners, whereas the ʿAbbasid colour was black).

The caliph, al-Mahdi (775–785), sent a large force under Jibra'il b. Yahya to crush the rising. On arrival in Bukhara, Jibra'il, along with the ruler, Hussain b. Muʿaz, attacked the village of Narshakh (a rebel strongpoint in the Bukhara area) and took it after a four-month siege. Jibra'il killed two of the rebel leaders, Hakim b. Ahmad and his comrade-in-arms, Khashvi. A new battle flared up by the walls of the settlement, but the superior Muslim forces once again emerged victorious over the defenders of Narshakh. Another rebel, Hakim Baga, was killed during this battle. The rebels' greatest success came in 777, when they controlled the entire Zerafshan valley (above the oasis of Bukhara), almost all the Kashka Darya valley and an area further south near

34. Al-Tabari, 1879–89, Vol. 2, p. 1952.

Termez. After the fall of Narshakh, Sughd became the centre of the rebellion. The Sogdian rebels and the Türks fought Jibra'il b. Yahya at Samarkand and dealt him a series of crushing blows. In 778 a new governor of Khurasan, Muʿaz b. Muslim, advanced against the rebels with a larger force.

After the fall of Samarkand, the main forces of 'the people in white clothes' began to assemble at Kish, in the mountain fortress of Sanam, where al-Muqannaʿ was based. The above-mentioned Saʿid b. ʿAmr al-Harashi set out to take the fortress and crush the rising in the Kashka Darya valley.[35] The third and decisive stage in the rebellion now began. The defenders of the fortress put up a stubborn resistance and al-Harashi managed to seize it only after a siege in the summer of 780. All the defenders of the fortress found alive were put to death, while al-Muqannaʿ, not wanting to surrender to his enemies, committed suicide.[36]

In spite of its defeat, the rising of 'the people in white clothes' was of great significance in the history of Central Asia, as it shattered the foundations of the dominion of the Arab caliphate in Transoxania. The rebellion was directed not only against the foreign invaders but also against local oppressors. Its main motive force was provided by the ordinary people, above all the peasantry.[37] Although the rising was suppressed, al-Muqannaʿ's ideas survived for a long time: 'the people in white clothes' were active until the twelfth century, organizing outbreaks of rebellion in various parts of Central Asia.

In 806 a major new uprising broke out in Sughd, led by Rafiʿ b. Laith. In ideological terms it was the continuation of the rising by 'the people in white clothes' and it was to have repercussions in Nasaf, Chach, Ferghana, Khujand, Ustrushana, Bukhara and several other areas of Central Asia. Because of the treachery of Rafiʿ b. Laith, the caliphate managed to put down this rising in 810.[38] Nevertheless the peoples of Central Asia did not give up the struggle until they had thrown off the rule of the ʿAbbasids and set up their own independent state, which was finally established under the Samanids.

The Arab conquest, like all other conquests, was responsible for many deaths and destroyed urban life. As a result of military action and fierce battles, the irrigation systems, which were left unattended, fell into ruin and became blocked, while beautiful works of calligraphy, architecture and art were destroyed. Islam replaced the former local beliefs and cults as the official religion of Transoxania. The population paid the *kharaj*, the *jizya* and other taxes to the Arabs and carried out various types of forced labour. Naturally, this impeded the further development of productive forces and of culture for

---

35. Al-Tabari, 1879–89, Vol. 3, p. 484.
36. For details of al-Muqannaʿ's movement, see Aini, 1944; Bolshakov, 1976; Kadyrova, 1965; Sadighi, 1938; Yakubovskiy, 1948.
37. Gafurov, 1972, p. 331.
38. For details of this rising, see Kadyrova, 1965, pp. 139 et seq.

a considerable period. At the same time, the Arab conquest brought large parts of the East into contact with each other, enabling them to develop economic and cultural exchanges, and this paved the way for the subsequent development of the culture of the peoples of Central Asia under different conditions and an absolutely new religious ideology, which influenced and determined private, public and state life.[39]

Part Three

SOCIAL AND POLITICAL CONSEQUENCES OF THE ARAB CONQUEST

(A. I. Kolesnikov)

The Arab conquest of the Sasanian Empire, except for its extreme northern and eastern provinces, was completed in the middle of the seventh century. Although pockets of resistance were still encountered, politically the whole of Mesopotamia and the Iranian uplands fell to the Eastern caliphate, which was ruled by the caliph's governors in Basra and Kufa.[40]

Reasons for the fall of the Sasanian Empire

Among the factors that hastened the fall of Sasanian Iran, the most important were: the reverses suffered in the protracted war with Byzantium (604–628); five years of civil war in Iran; and the economic collapse within the Sasanian Empire. Nevertheless, the military aspect of the conquest should not be overlooked. In military terms the Arabs proved formidable opponents; they were masters of weaponry, tactics and military strategy. In the great battles of the period of conquest, the Sasanian and Arab forces were practically on a par.[41]

The great ethnic and religious diversity within the population contributed to the Arab success in Mesopotamia. The area had been settled by Arabs, Syrians and Jews (professing Christianity and Judaism) who were persecuted by the official Zoroastrian Church. By no means all of them welcomed the Muslim forces, although if conditions were favourable they were willing to collaborate.

39. Gibb, 1923; Jalilov, 1961; Kolesnikov, 1982.
40. Most of the information about events in Iran at the time of the conquest is taken from a monograph on this period by Kolesnikov, 1982.
41. Al-Tabari, 1879–89, Vol. 1, pp. 2265–6.

A major factor in the Arab victory was the founding of garrison towns, which acted as springboards for the eastward military expansion of Islam. Basra and Kufa became the residences of the caliph's governors, who ruled the eastern part of the caliphate. They appointed Arab military leaders as their provincial deputies.

Relations between Muslims and non-Muslims in the first century A.H.

Relations between the Muslims and the subject population of the Sasanian Empire were regulated by peace treaties that established the parties' mutual obligations. The conquered were obliged to pay an indemnity and/or the *jizya* (poll-tax), as well as other dues. If the conditions of the agreement were respected, the victors guaranteed their subjects security of person and of property, defence from external enemies and the right to practise their various religions and follow their own way of life.

The conditions of the treaty for non-Muslims and the scale of the indemnity levied on them partly depended on the way in which the territory had been subjugated – whether 'by force of arms' (*anwatan*) or 'by peaceful means' *ṣulḥan*) – and on the resources of the population. In the historical tradition of early Islam (the works of al-Baladhuri, al-Tabari, al-Kufi and others) and in the legal works written between the eighth and the tenth century, the term *anwatan* is always opposed to *ṣulḥan*. The former means either that the local population did not accept the terms of the treaty proposed by the Arabs, or that the Arabs did not accept the conditions of their adversary, so that the matter was decided by force. If an area was subjugated 'by force of arms', part of the population was put to death or enslaved; those who escaped such a fate were constrained to pay heavy taxes, or were forced to emigrate, or had to conclude an agreement with the victors at great disadvantage to themselves. Subjugation 'by peaceful means' did not exclude military action, as long as it ended with the signing of a peace treaty by both sides.

Treaties on Iranian territory in the years of conquest were signed on the Arab side by the military commander, and on behalf of the local population by the governor of the town, district or province; in areas with a Christian population, treaties were signed by the bishop or the elders of the town. One copy of the treaty was retained by the Arabs and the other by the local governor.

People of 'other religions' who signed a treaty with the Muslims became *dhimmi*s (*ahl al-dhimma*), or people who enjoyed the protection of the Muslim community. Although Zoroastrians, Christians and Jews were not always accorded the same treatment, the conditions of the treaties did not vary greatly according to the religion of the subjugated group. Whereas the surviving texts of treaties contain no indication of the period of validity, historical sources show that it was determined by the extent to which the parties observed the treaty's provisions. The treaties were valid either until 'the Day of Judgment' (in practical terms, until a change was deemed necessary) or until they were violated by one side and abrogated by the other.

The lands of those who had been subjugated 'by peaceful means' and who had signed a treaty with the Muslims were retained by their former owners. The amount of land tax payable, which depended on the conditions of the treaty and on tradition, was often set at the level determined by the reforms of the Sasanian *shahanshah* Khusrau I (531–578), but could be lower or higher. The high rate of taxation provoked several local uprisings against the conquerors.

First steps towards Islamization

As the military expansion of Islam continued eastwards, the ranks of the Muslim armies were increased by *mawālī* (pl. of *mawlā*, new converts to Islam from Zoroastrianism and other religions). In the early period, conversion to Islam tended to mean recruitment into the conquering army rather than an acceptance of the new religion. Most of the Muslim sources mention examples of active collaboration with the Arab armies by part of the Zoroastrian and Christian communities.

At the battle of al-Qadisiyya in 636 (see above), the Arab armies were joined by the local nobility and local Arabs, 'allies' from Babylonia; there was also a detachment of Dailamites who had accepted Islam. Some Iranian soldiers taken captive at al-Qadisiyya also embraced Islam and supported the Arabs. Historical sources contain a list of the *dihqāns* of small districts of Babylonia who accepted Islam under the caliph ʿUmar (634–644). There were instances of collaboration with the Arabs even before the storming of Ctesiphon, when some of the inhabitants of the Sasanian capital showed the Arab leader where to ford the River Tigris. At the siege of Shushtar in Khuzistan, no fewer than 100 Iranian Muslim horsemen – an entire military unit – fought on the Arab side.[42]

Towards the end of the period of conquest, there were substantial numbers of *mawālī* of Iranian descent in the Muslim armies: the 5,000-strong army of Ahnaf b. Qais, which fought on the north-eastern frontiers of the former Sasanian Empire, for example, included 1,000 Persian Muslims,[43] and the local contingent in the army of Qutaiba b. Muslim, the conqueror of Middle Asia, accounted for at least a sixth of the entire force.[44]

---

42. Al-Tabari, 1879–89, Vol. 1, pp. 2562–3.
43. Al-Baladhuri, 1866, p. 407.
44. Gibb, 1923, p. 40.

Although the Muslim administration hardly ever resorted to forcible Islamization of the non-Arab population, the number of *mawālī* in Iran rose steadily. Some of the Iranian nobles were attracted to Islam as a means of avoiding the *jizya* that placed them on the level of the ordinary tax-payer. Professional soldiers who took up the new religion hoped to become rich on the spoils of war. For enslaved prisoners of war, conversion to Islam meant an opportunity to regain their freedom.

The acceptance of Islam conferred certain privileges on converts, and in theory it gave them equal rights with Muslim Arabs. This was encapsulated in the formula 'rights and obligations in equal measure'. The military nobles who accepted Islam received sums of money or wages from the caliph's coffers; they had the right to choose where they wished to live and held important posts in the caliphate. Iranian Muslim neophytes in the Arab army received their share of booty and land. An additional stimulus to the process of Islamization in Iran was the practice of returning lands taken 'by force of arms' on condition that the land-owner accepted Islam.

The Islamization of Iran during the conquest and in the years following the final collapse of the Sasanian Empire was nevertheless a very slow process and most of the population remained faithful to their old religion and customs. Changes in the ruling ideology had a more appreciable effect in the financial and clerical sectors.

Iranian regional administration in the conquered territories

Many of the nobles in the conquered regions retained their privileges not by accepting Islam, but by acknowledging their political dependence on the Muslim state and paying taxes to the conquerors. Where these conditions were satisfied, the Arab governors allowed the loyal local nobility to retain their lands and did not interfere in their internal affairs. One example is the Arabs' treatment of the Median governor Dinar, of the family of Karen, whose principal duty was to collect taxes for the Arabs from the subject territories. The same task was carried out by the *marzbān* of Azerbaijan and a number of other representatives of the Iranian administration who retained their former posts: Mahak in Istakhr, Kasmud or Kashmur in Herat and Pushang, Mahoe in Sarakhs, Bahiyeh in Nisa and Abivard, Dadoeh in Faryab and Taliqan, and Guraz in Balkh.[45]

The written sources reveal that the local administrations enjoyed a considerable degree of autonomy. The farther a province was from Basra or Kufa,

45. Al-Kufi, 1969, Vol. 2, pp. 102, 104, 107.

the seats of the caliph's governors, the greater its independence. The local nobility occasionally rebelled against Arab domination – one such revolt was led by Khurrazad, a noble from Khuzistan, who refused to acknowledge the sovereignty of the caliph ʿAbd al-Malik b. Marwan (685–705).[46]

From the beginning of the reign of the Umayyads (in 661) until the end of the seventh century, Iranian mints issued what are known as Arab-Sasanian drachms. They are distinguished from purely Sasanian coinage by the presence of an Arabic religious inscription on the obverse, and by the fact that the name of the Arab governor or the caliph replaces that of the *shahanshah*. Most of these Arab-Sasanian coins were dated according to the Islamic calendar.

Until the end of the seventh century and the beginning of the eighth – a period marked by the standardization of coinage in the caliphate – it was the local Iranian governors who issued this coinage. Evidence of this is found in the Iranian proper names on various issues of drachms minted in central Iran and in Balkh: Baffarnag in Kerman from the years 62–71 A.H.; Bundad in Ardashir-Khvarreh in 66 and 73; Farrukhzad in Ardashir-Khvarreh in 76 and in Bishapur in 79; Yuvan in Istakhr in 70; and Izdanbud or Gavbud in Balkh in 77. The reform of the caliph ʿAbd al-Malik at the end of the seventh century and the beginning of the eighth accomplished the transition to purely Muslim dirhams, and Arabic became the official language of the administration.[47]

The fact that the names of Iranian governors continued to appear on coins for 30 years after the official date of the Arab conquest of Iran is explained by the growing political unrest within the caliphate, which increased the power of the local administrations. In this unstable situation, both the Umayyads and their opponents sought recognition of their right to supreme power and needed the support of local nobles, who were responsible for the mints. The name of Bundad appears first on the drachms of ʿAbdallah b. al-Zubair, the enemy of the Umayyads, and after his death, on the drachms of the caliph ʿAbd al-Malik.

Tabaristan and Dailam

Before the Arab conquest, the southern Caspian provinces (Gilan, Dailam and Tabaristan) were vassals of the Sasanians. At the time of the conquest, Tabaristan embraced all the territory around the southern Caspian. The first Arab incursions into this almost inaccessible region date from the 640s. Until the mid-eighth century, however, all the Muslims' attempts to establish themselves there met with fierce resistance from the local population. The Tabaristan campaign under the caliph Muʿawiya I (661–680) ended in the rout and almost complete annihilation of the Muslim expeditionary force. The Arabs' later attempt at

46. Al-Baladhuri, 1866, p. 383.
47. Gaube, 1973, pp. 2–7.

taking the province in 716 compelled the *ispahbad* (local governor) to sign a peace treaty involving the annual payment of a sum of dirhams as well as a tribute of goods and troops. Power, however, remained in the hands of the *ispahbads* and Tabaristan subsequently refused to pay the tribute. Around 760 Tabaristan was conquered by the Muslims, as was the mountainous land of Dailam. The *ispahbad* Khurshid was replaced by governors appointed by the ʿAbbasids. Under the caliph al-Maʾmun (813–833), the Arabs, with the assistance of a Tabaristan military leader, took control of the mountainous land of Sharvin. A revolt there in 838 was put down. Tabaristan was finally subjugated in the middle of the ninth century, when the *ispahbad* Karen, son of Shahriyar, accepted Islam.[48]

Zabul, Kabul, Gandhara and Ghur

Arab military action against Zabulistan and other principalities in what is now Afghanistan commenced during the conquest of Seistan. Operating from Seistan, which served as a forward base for their eastern campaigns, the Arabs managed for a time to gain control of Zabul, to the north-east of Seistan; but as soon as the army returned to Zarang (the administrative centre of Seistan), the population ceased to obey their conquerors. Under the caliph Muʿawiya, the military commander ʿAbd al-Rahman b. Samura restored the power of the Arab governor in Seistan and moved east, taking Zabul once again and gaining Rukhkhaj; he reached Kabul, whose ruler was obliged to pay tribute to the Arabs. This state of affairs did not last long, for the king of Kabul soon drove the Arabs from his lands. Another Arab expedition against Kabul in 697–698 was repulsed.

A century later, the Muslims successfully invaded Zabul (in 795) and went on to Kabul. In the subsequent eastern campaign, under the caliph al-Maʾmun, the ruler of Kabul was captured and he then converted to Islam. The Arabs succeeded in gaining a firm hold of the region only in 870, when the founder of the Seistan dynasty of the Saffarids invaded Kabul through Balkh and Bamiyan.[49]

Until the second half of the ninth century the main obstacle encountered by Arab forces in the east was Rukhkhaj, whose rulers (called by the title *zunbil*) waged protracted wars against the army of the Arab governor of Seistan. The tide of these wars waxed and waned, and the Arabs more than once lost all their territorial gains to the east of Bust; but during periods when anti-Arab resistance weakened, the local population temporarily accepted vassalage to

48. Walker, 1941, pp. lxix–lxxx.
49. Bosworth, 1974, p. 356.

the caliphate, paying tribute to the governor. The rise of the powerful Saffarid state put an end to the Zunbil dynasty and their power.[50]

The remote region of Ghur, on the upper reaches of the rivers Farah-rud, Hari-rud and Murghab, remained beyond the reach of the Muslims for many decades, during which they were obliged to skirt around it. They only succeeded in establishing themselves there in the tenth century, by which time most of the inhabitants of Ghur had converted to Islam.

The Arabs in Sind

Sind, a principality on the shores of the Arabian Sea and the lower reaches of the Indus, was invaded from the sea by the Muslims in 711. The sea port of Daibul fell first, then several towns on the banks of the Indus, including Arur, the capital. Finally, in 713, the Arabs took Multan and the conquest was complete. The fall of Sind opened the way to the markets of Central Asia.[51]

The survival of pre-Islamic civilization

The Arab conquests brought an end to the Sasanian Empire as a political force and yet to some extent they preserved the pre-Islamic Iranian civilization: it underwent no radical change until several centuries later, with the process of Islamization and the emergence of new social and economic conditions. This pattern was repeated in the farflung corners of the former Sasanian Empire and in the neighbouring vassal and independent principalities, which were conquered much later.

Tabaristan, which was separated from Iran by the chain of the Elburz mountains, retained its independence for more than a century after the fall of the Sasanian Empire. It was ruled by the local dynasty, the *ispahbad*s, who issued their own coins (a smaller version of Sasanian coinage), remained faithful to Zoroastrianism and wrote in Pahlavi script. The year following the death of Yazdgird III (i.e. 652) marked a new era in the calendar in Tabaristan, which demonstrates the region's loyalty to Sasanian tradition and the continuity of royal succession. The local reckoning of years was used for over 160 years in the mints both of the rulers of Tabaristan and of the ʿAbbasid governors who replaced them. The continuance of local tradition was encouraged by the fact that Arab garrisons were stationed in the main towns of Tabaristan – Amol and Sari – and not in the countryside.[52]

50. Bosworth, 1976, p. 559.
51. Haig, 1934, pp. 433–4.
52. Walker, 1941, pp. lxix–lxxx.

In central Afghanistan and in areas to the north of the Hindu Kush, ancient Kushan culture continued and the principal religion was Buddhism.[53] In Seistan and neighbouring regions, elements of Sasanian culture and the Zoroastrian cult flourished, as is revealed by archaeological data such as the ruins of fortresses and watchtowers, ceramics and coins.[54] In Bamiyan in the seventh century there were more than 10 Buddhist monasteries and over 1,000 monks (see Chapter 6). The main Buddhist monastery there was destroyed by the Saffarids in the second half of the ninth century.[55] Kabul and its surrounding areas also had many buildings devoted to Buddhist and Hindu cults. Further evidence of the strength of pre-Islamic civilizations in the east in the seventh and eighth centuries is afforded by the issues of so-called Arab-Hephthalite coins with legends in Pahlavi, Kufic and Bactrian scripts.[56]

Most of the Arab-Sasanian coins that circulated in the eastern principalities bore local counterstamps with images of simurgs (a monstrous bird of Persian myth, with the power of reasoning and speech), camels, elephants, *tamghas* and other symbols that were typical of east Iranian culture. Some of the coins bore legends in Bactrian script.[57] Evidence of religious syncretism in the regions to the north of the Hindu Kush is to be found in the silver coinage of the *kaghan* of the Western Türks, whose iconography combines elements of Iranian Zoroastrianism and Indian Shivaism.[58] The leaders of the autonomous and semi-autonomous eastern principalities retained names in the local toponymy that were known to Arab geographers as late as the tenth to the twelfth century.

53. Ball and Gardin, 1982, Vol. 1, Nos. 99, 100 et seq.; Vol. 2, p. 483.
54. Ibid., Vol. 1, Nos. 145, 206, 270, 369, 900 et seq.; Vol. 2, pp. 484–5.
55. Barthold and Allchin, 1960, pp. 1009–10.
56. Walker, 1941, pp. lxv–lxix, 127–9, Pl. xxii, 6–10, xxviii, 1–4.
57. Göbl, 1967, Vol. 2, pp. 112–202.
58. Harmatta, 1982, pp. 167–80.

CENTRAL ASIA, THE CROSSROADS OF CIVILIZATIONS[*]

B. A. Litvinsky and Zhang Guang-da

This concluding chapter aims to give an overview of the interactions and multilateral cultural exchanges between all the great civilizations standing at the crossroads of Central Asia during the period from the third to the eighth century. For most of this time, the reign of the Sasanian Empire (224–651) remained stable in Iran. China, however, went through a cycle of rapid dynastic changes until, at the close of the sixth century, the long era of disunity and invasions by alien tribes that had plagued the country for four centuries finally ended. A new unified and flourishing empire was established under the Sui (589–618) and T'ang (618–907) dynasties. From 640 to 792 the eastern part of Central Asia was under T'ang domination.

On the vast expanse of the steppes, many powerful nomadic confederations emerged, particularly those of the Huns: Alans, Juan-juan, Chionites and Hephthalites, Türks, Türgesh, Karluks, Uighurs and other Turkic tribes in the east, the Khazars (the only Turkic-speaking people ever to have converted to Judaism) and Pechenegs in the west. These nomadic peoples dwelled in tents, organized in clans and tribes, and moved about in search of water and pasture. The formation of one or other such confederation usually indicated a shift of the ruling clan from one ethnic group to another, with the population assimilated into the new confederation. Byzantium, Sasanian Iran, China and the nomad *kaghanates* were not the only powers with influence in the region, however. There was a flourishing Tokharian-speaking culture with its centres at Kucha, Agni and Turfan; a blossoming Saka-speaking culture centred on Khotan, Kashgar and Tumshuq (all these oasis city kingdoms were located within the Tarim basin in modern Xinjiang); and the highly developed and widespread Sogdian culture in Transoxania.

Towards the end of the period covered by this volume, other major powers took the stage. In the eastern part of Central Asia, the ancient Tibetan people,

---

[*] See Map 1.

the Bod, emerged victorious from their age-old inter-tribal struggles and were quick to establish a unified monarchy on the Tibetan plateau at the beginning of the seventh century. Constantly expanding far into the territories of its neighbours, this new power challenged first the T'ang and then the Arabs for supremacy over Central Asia.

In the west a series of historical events led to the sudden rise of the Arabs. By a curious coincidence, the T'ang, the Tibetans and the Arabs arose as major powers at almost the same time and embarked almost simultaneously on the road of expansion and conquest. The seventh and eighth centuries are of special significance for the cultural history of the region. The rivalry between the three major powers and several Turkic tribal confederations had a profound influence on the course of cultural developments in the succeeding centuries. In the conflict between the Arabs and the Chinese, for example, the former won an easy victory over the latter at the battle of Talas in 751, paving the way for the later Islamization of the whole area. Another example is the start of a process by which Turkic languages came to predominate in Central Asia.

There was also much reciprocal political influence. Since the south-western part of Central Asia belonged to the Sasanian Empire, for example, there were similarities in their social structures. By the fifth century, society in Iran was divided into four orders (*rešaq*): the priests (*āsrōn*), the warriors (*artēštārān*), the scribes (*dibīrān*) and the cultivators (*vāstrōšān*). Each order had its own subdivisions. Thus the first order also included judges; the fourth comprised not only peasants, but also craftsmen and merchants; while the numerous representatives of the central and local bureaucracy belonged to the third. A similar social classification apparently existed in Central Asian society.

As wave upon wave of nomadic migration swept Central Asia, nomadic peoples settled in the area, inevitably influencing the local institutions. In many regions of Sogdiana and Tokharistan, the higher administrative echelons were filled for a certain time by *tudun*s, supervisers set up by the Türks, besides local *khudāt*, *afshin*, *khatun* and great *dihqān*s.

The period from the third to the eighth century also saw momentous social changes which were to determine the development of Central Asian society for almost 1,500 years. Feudal relationships began to form in the settled areas of the region and an early form of feudal society arose; this led to the emergence of nomadic societies such as that of the Türks.

The productive sector was based on free peasant producers belonging to village communes, which were often agnatic. The members of the commune were known as *hamdūdagān* ('people of the same smoke', from the word *dūdag*: literally, 'smoke'). The leader of the agnatic commune was the *kadag-khvaday*, who later became the head of the village commune and was invested with certain administrative functions. The Sasanian Law Book, the *Mādigān-i hazār dādestān*, made a distinction between the concepts of 'privately owned' and 'common' land. If a private individual dug a subterranean canal (*kahrīz*) on common land, it would belong to him and the members of the commune would have to pay him for the use of the water. This led to the break-up of the commune. Syrian sources mention free peasants (known as *gabra*, meaning 'man') and dependent producers (*pabāḥa*) among the peasantry of the Mesopotamian part of the Sasanian Empire. There were some serfs on church land. The free peasants, including the *marē kuriē* (country gentlemen), were also divided into social strata. According to the Babylonian Talmud, slaves were used in agricultural work and land was sold together with the slaves. The same type of system probably prevailed throughout Iran. In practice, the partially freed slaves mentioned in the *Mādīgān-i hazār dādestān* (18, 9–10; 38, 13–17, etc.) were much the same as serfs.

The total number of slaves (known as *bandak*, *anšahrīk*, etc.) was considerable. In Iranian law a slave was regarded as an object (*khvāstag*) and was part of his master's property. Thus a slave employed in agriculture and living on his master's land (*dastagird*) was part of the inventory of living things, together with the draught animals and beasts of burden, and could be alienated together with the property. The higher social class was represented by the nobles (*āzād*). The highest position was occupied by the *shahanshah* (king of kings). Many of the nobles had thousands of slaves and owned whole villages, huge orchards or other land. It is evident, therefore, that Sasanian society was marked by wide economic and social disparities.

At the head of the military administration stood the *hazārbed*, while the civil administration was directed by the *vuzurg-framadār*. A highly developed bureaucratic system linked central, regional and local administrative organs. Similarly, the Zoroastrian priesthood had its own complex hierarchy.

The Sasanian authorities strove for the centralization of the empire and opposed the decentralizing tendencies of the great nobles and the rulers of the outlying provinces. During the Late Sasanian period the state was divided into 4 parts, known as 'sides' (*pādgōs*), which were administered by the greatest of the nobles. These 'sides' were divided into 37 districts. In addition, certain provinces (usually the outlying ones) enjoyed a degree of autonomy, and their rulers bore the title of *shah* (king).

The productive strata of society laboured under an oppressive burden of taxation – land tax, poll tax and taxes on goods, in addition to customs and various other duties. In the event of crop failure, the peasants were ruined and abandoned their villages. When Bahram V acceded to the throne in 420, arrears of land tax alone reached 70 million drachms.[1] At the end of the fifth century and the beginning of the sixth, Iran saw the rise of the powerful Mazdakite movement, which tried to alleviate the burdensome economic and social conditions of the majority of the population. Although the Mazdakites

---

1. Nöldeke, Tabari, 1973, p. 105.

suffered defeat and Mazdak was executed in 529, the movement succeeded in reducing the power of the great nobles and the Zoroastrian priesthood. Many heresies and anti-feudal movements of the Middle Ages were ideologically linked to that of the Mazdakites.[2]

Certain similarities can be detected between the social conditions of Central Asia and those of Sasanian Iran. However, Central Asia was not occupied by a single state; moreover its social development and institutions were considerably influenced by the nomadic peoples that inhabited it. It appears that there were various social classes in Central Asian society. One of the documents found on Mount Mug shows that Sogdian society consisted of three strata: the nobility (*"z'tk'r*), the merchants (*w'kry*) and the workers (*k'ryk'r*), i.e. the peasants and craftsmen.

There were also large numbers of slaves and other dependent groups living in Sogdiana and in East Turkestan in the seventh and eighth centuries. They belonged to various categories: purchased slaves, slaves taken captive in battle, slaves taken as hostages, and those who had entrusted themselves to a master's protection. Members of a family could be sold into slavery by its head. Arab historians' reports of the conquest of Middle Asia mention a considerable number of slaves. The 'property registers' from Toprak-kala, dating from the very beginning of the third century, show that every household had many patriarchal slaves (or dependent people). Document I, for example, lists the names of 21 men: 4 are freemen (the head of the household, 2 sons and a son-in-law) and 17 are slaves (dependants).

Peasants sent out to work are called 'people' in the documents from Mount Mug. Linguistic analysis of the name of one of the categories of peasants strongly suggests the original meaning 'forced labourer'. Some of the workers performed their duties for payment. There was also a class of agriculturalists, comprising farmers and ploughmen. The village commune appears to have coincided with the agnatic group.

The social hierarchy of the ruling class was complex. The highest rank was that of the rulers, the *afshīn* and the *ikhshid*, the supreme ruler in Sogdiana. Below them came the freemen and nobles (*āzād*), including *dihqān*s and great *dihqān*s. These were large-scale landowners (sometimes the owners of whole provinces) who enjoyed considerable power and had armed retinues at their command. The members of these retinues, the *chakir*s, were professional warriors and formed the core of the armed forces. They were distinguished by exceptional valour.

At the end of the seventh century and the beginning of the eighth, it was the custom of the *khatun* (queen) of Bukhara every day to:

2. Christensen, 1925; 1944; Pigulevskaya, 1940; Solodukho, 1956; Perikhanyan, 1973; 1983*a*; 1983*b*; Lukonin, 1983.

sit upon a throne, while before her stood slaves, masters of the seraglio, that is, the eunuchs, and the nobles. She had made it an obligation for the population that every day, from the dihqāns and princes, two hundred youths, girded with gold belts and swords carried [on the shoulder], should appear for service and stand at a distance. When the Khātūn came out, all made obeisance to her and stood in two rows while she inquired into the affairs of state. She issued orders and prohibitions, and gave a robe of honour to whomsoever she wished and punishment to whom she wished . . . When it was evening she came out in the same manner and sat on the throne. Some dihqāns and princes stood before her in two rows in attendance till the sun set.[3]

The above account by Narshakhi, the historian of Bukhara, gives a vivid picture of the relations between the rulers of large provinces and their vassals. The details have been confirmed by iconographic materials from Sogdiana. The ruling class owned vast riches and large numbers of dependent people. Thus, in Bukhara, 'the greater part' of the people 'were peasants and servants' of the ruler, whose title was *Bukhār khudāt*.[4]

Archaeological materials also provide proof of profound social and economic differentiation. In Kala-i Kafirnigan, for example, a luxurious mansion belonging to the local ruler has been discovered: next to it can be seen the poor dwellings of the ordinary citizens. The excavations at Panjikent have revealed the splendid two-storied houses, or rather palaces, of the nobles of the town, each of which could almost be said to be an art gallery. The wall-paintings of the castle of Balalyk-tepe show feasting *dihqāns*: richly dressed men and women sit or recline on rugs; the men wear gold belts, from which hang magnificent swords and daggers. In the background are servants: their rank is clearly indicated, for they are shown as approximately half the size of their master.

As in Iran, the administrative system was highly developed. In Sogdiana its highest level was represented by the *tudun* (perhaps the head of the civil service), the *farmandār* (in charge of all financial and economic affairs), the *š'ykn* (commander in chief of the armed forces), who enjoyed particular honour and influence, and the *dapirpat* (chief clerk). There were also tax-collectors. The local administration consisted of the rulers of settlements and rural districts, village headmen and other officials. The Sogdian administrative system worked efficiently and smoothly in the Early Middle Ages. All receipts and transfers of articles of value had to be recorded; records, registers and receipts were drawn up; all documents were copied, and when they were signed, seals were affixed.[5]

Society in Central Asia could be divided into three sectors – the towns and the urban population; the villages and the rural agricultural population;

3. *The History of Bukhara*, 1954, pp. 9–10.
4. Ibid., p. 8.
5. Mandel'shtam, 1954; Smirnova, 1957; 1960; Livshits, 1962, pp. 34–7, 62, 69, 134–5, 176–8; 1984, pp. 266–7; Gafurov, 1972, pp. 295–300.

and the steppes (and sometimes the mountains), with their nomadic population. Much can be learnt from the structure of settlements and the way of life of the rural population. In the oasis of Berkut-kala in Khwarizm, for example, the distribution of the population can still be clearly observed. The oasis lies in a narrow strip (approx. 40 × 4–5 km) along the main canal. Fortified farms, consisting of massively built houses with courtyards, stand a mere 200–300 m apart. The farms themselves were clustered in 8–13 'nests', each centred round a castle. Most of the farms were small, the areas of arable land they possessed being in proportion to their size. The largest castle in the oasis was Berkut-kala, at the foot of which lay a small town, the centre of craft production. It appears that the oasis was also home to several large rural communes with a total population of 7–8,000. Agnatic groups of varying size lived on the farms.[6]

The castle of Balalyk-tepe in Tokharistan gives an idea of the size and dimensions of the castles. It is an isolated structure, standing 10 m high, with a 6-m stylobate. On the upper platform there is a structure measuring 24 × 24.5 m. In the middle of the ground floor there is a large square courtyard with narrow, partially communicating corridors leading off it. The outer walls of the building had loopholes in them. Two buildings were erected in the courtyard at first-floor level. The north-west angle of the courtyard was occupied by a square building measuring 4.85 × 4.85 m, with *sufas* along the four sides. The entire surface of the walls was covered with remarkable murals depicting a banquet (perhaps this was a chamber for ritual feasts). Adjoining it was a rectangular reception hall measuring 5.3 × 9.3 m. Along its walls stood *sufas* and there was a fire altar on a pedestal in the centre. The roof was flat, with carved beams. Some of the buildings were two-storeyed.

Another type can be seen at Zang-tepe, also in Tokharistan. This is a square site measuring 150 × 150 m. In its north-east corner are the ruins of a castle: its upper platform measured 40 × 40 m while its height was 15 m.[7]

Castles were often erected on the banks of rivers and controlled the upper reaches of the main irrigation canals.[8] Found both on the plains and in the mountain areas of Central Asia, the lay-out of such castles differs considerably according to their social and economic functions. Their main characteristic, however, is that they always combine the functions of a dwelling for nobles with highly developed defensive functions. According to Gafurov:

> Like the *shahristan*s and citadels of the cities, the castles were inhabited by aristocrats, the nobles mentioned in the written sources. The structure of the town and the large number of castles, the style of art and the traditions of 'the life of chivalry', the armed retinues of the great aristocrats, political disunity and the signs of vassalage – these all mark profound changes in the social and economic life.

6. Nerazik, 1966; 1976.
7. Al'baum, 1966; Nilsen, 1966, pp. 140–75.
8. Davidovich and Litvinsky, 1955, pp. 165–7.

A feudal system was being formed:

> From the fifth to the eighth century, its institutions were still in their initial stage and not fully developed. Much about them can only be surmised from indirect evidence, but this does not change the basic fact that the non-nomadic areas of Middle Asia were entering the path of feudal development during the fifth to the eighth century.[9]

The same can be said of Central Asia as a whole.

It should be stressed that this social development was far from uniform throughout the region. The role of religion, for example, differed widely in the various areas: although it was very important in all parts of the region, theocratic states came into being only in Tibet and Khotan.

The development of nomadic society also was accompanied by a trend towards feudalism, although in less marked and more idiosyncratic forms. This trend was most pronounced in Türk society.

The economic complexity of Central Asia society only becomes apparent when this society is considered as a whole. Agriculture was fairly intensive and artificial irrigation was very widely practised, especially in the oasis-states. Simple but effective water-intake structures supplied water from the rivers to the main irrigation canals, which were tens and sometimes hundreds of kilometres in length. There were many such canals in Khwarizm (fed by the River Amu Darya), Sogdiana (fed by the River Zerafshan) and Tokharistan (fed mainly by the rivers Kunduz Darya, Vakhsh, Kafirnigan and Surkhan Darya) and also in the Tarim basin. Where necessary, aqueducts, dams and other hydraulic structures were built. Underground water-collecting galleries (*kahriz*) were constructed if demanded by the particular land configuration, as in parts of Khurasan and the west of Turkestan.

Other sources of irrigation, such as springs, were also used. Large canals branched off from the main ones, and from them the water passed to the irrigation network itself. In the Dunhuang district the cultivated areas were irrigated. During the T'ang period, there were 7 main canals in this area, and the names of over 100 smaller canals are known. There was a large service staff, which had to be properly administered.[10] In the more humid areas – on the mountains and foothills – the crops were watered by the rain, but the harvests were less plentiful.

Various types of iron-tipped wooden ploughs, iron spades and mattocks and large and small iron sickles came into use throughout the region. The variety of agricultural, horticultural and orchard produce approached that of the present day. More advanced tools and equipment came into use for processing agricultural produce, including wine presses. Besides hand presses, there were

9. Gafurov, 1972, p. 299.
10. Chuguevskiy, 1983, pp. 35, 251–2.

large presses turned by animals, and even larger ones (with millstones 1 m and more in diameter) turned by water.[11]

The rural population and agriculture were still largely based on a natural economy. At the same time, agriculture supplied both the urban population and the nomads with foodstuffs, indicating the existence of trading, mainly in the form of barter. Nevertheless a considerable proportion of the produce which came onto the market in the towns consisted basically of rent in kind paid to feudal lords by the peasants. Documents from Dunhuang, Turfan and other sites in East Turkestan show that such rents were paid not only by free peasants but also by various categories of dependent people. In the areas of Buddhist culture, monastery farms with their administration played an important role in agriculture.

The wide open spaces of the steppes and semi-deserts were populated by nomadic and semi-nomadic tribes, who practised a rudimentary form of farming. Their crafts were of a domestic nature, although some, such as toreutics, had developed to a considerable degree. The nomads, and especially their nobles, bartered surplus livestock for agricultural produce and, to an even greater degree, for works of urban craftsmanship.

In Central Asia, with its oases, urbanization was highly developed. Although there were far fewer towns than rural settlements (in Tokharistan, for example, the ratio was one urban settlement to seven or eight rural ones), they were the bases of the whole infrastructure, the focal points of the political, economic, cultural and religious life.

In the largest towns of Central Asia, early medieval structures are usually buried under many layers of medieval strata. Many medium-sized towns (which acted as regional centres) are much more accessible to investigation and historical interpretation. Of such towns, ancient Panjikent has been studied in the greatest detail. The town consists of a *shahristan* (the town proper), a citadel and suburbs. The area of the *shahristan* is 19 ha and its perimeter 1,750 m. It is surrounded by a strong system of fortifications, which joined it to the citadel situated to the west. The suburbs were all situated to the east and southeast of the *shahristan* except for one suburb which lay to the south.

The *shahristan* was interlaced by a network of streets which sometimes ran parallel to each other and sometimes merged. The width of the main streets was 3–5 m. Along the main streets there were housing areas, outbuildings, shops and workshops. Each residential block (they were 2-storeyed) included dozens of dwellings, comprising more than 100 rooms, and consisted of a front part and the living quarters proper. The ground-floor rooms were vaulted and ill lit and access could be gained from them to the lighter and better lit first floor. The principal architectural feature of the first floor was a large, square hall, the roof of which was supported on columns. Along the walls there were

11. Andrianov, 1969; Litvinsky, 1978.

high *sufas*; opposite the entrance, the *sufa* took the form of a wide projection. The walls were covered with several stripes of brightly coloured paintings, and the columns were ornamented with carvings and wooden sculptures. There were rooms for the owner and his family, separate accommodation for servants, and outhouses. This is what the homes of the urban nobility were like. In the house areas there were much more modest, even poor, dwellings belonging to the ordinary urban population.

On the sides of the residential blocks facing the streets stood separate (sometimes two-part) premises, used as workshops by the town's craftsmen. There were also several small markets.

In the northern half of the site, in a spacious square, stood two temple complexes surrounded by a ring of walls. Each of them consisted of the temple itself, which was raised on a stylobate and richly decorated with paintings around the perimeter of a group of auxiliary rooms.

A series of ceremonial buildings, including enormous halls, has been discovered in the citadel. The wooden parts of a pedestal for a throne have also been discovered. The walls were covered with beautiful paintings. These are probably the remains of the ruler's palace. Panjikent came into being in the fifth century and continued to exist, although it was rebuilt, until the eighth century.[12]

The capital cities of the smaller states were similar. The area of these towns spread over 10–20 ha. The capitals of the most important historical and cultural regions – Merv, Balkh and Samarkand – were somewhat larger. Thus, the area of Samarkand extended over 200 ha, and that of Merv over more than 300 ha. By contemporary estimates, the population of the largest towns, such as Merv, reached 60,000.[13] Very large towns, such as Kocho in Turfan, also flourished in East Turkestan. They were important and highly developed centres of urbanization, of political power, and of economic life, culture and religion. The processes of urbanization also gained ground, although not to such a marked degree in areas which had earlier been exclusively nomadic, such as the Uighur towns in Tuva and certain Mongol towns.

Building and architecture reached a very high level of development. There were marked differences in style in the various regions, with recognizable schools of architecture, such as the Sodgian, Khwarizmian and Tokharian schools. These local distinctions did not, however, present an obstacle to the establishment of a 'unity in diversity' throughout the territory of Central Asia. Many types of building were erected: palaces; Buddhist, Manichaean and Nestorian places of worship and monasteries, Buddhist stupas and buildings connected with local Iranian, Buddhist and other religions; the palaces of rulers and feudal castles; the houses of the urban aristocracy; the homes of the

12. Belenitskiy et al., 1973; Belenitskiy et al., 1980.
13. Belenitskiy et al., 1973.

urban middle classes and the poor; shops and workshops; burial chambers; barracks; and a whole range of fortifications and bulwarks.

In India, architectural handbooks were written, in particular the *Mānashāra*, compiled between 500 and 700, although the text includes later additions. It contains detailed instructions on building and architectural work, beginning with the preparation of the building site and marking out the plan into areas, right up to completion. A chief architect was to be in charge of construction, and his assistants included a 'planner'. According to the *Mānashāra* (II, pp. 36–7), 'In this work [the erection of a building] nobody can succeed without an architect and his guidance. Therefore it [the building work] should be conducted with the help of these architects.' In one Middle Persian text we read, 'Creation without a creator and decision without a decider are just as possible as writing without a writer or the erection of a house without an architect and builder.'

Analysis has shown that in the preparation of a plan, a module was used which took account, not only of the proportions between the various parts, but also of questions of symmetry and rhythm. One example is the Buddhist monastery of Ajina-tepe (Tokharistan), which was constructed according to the laws of mirror symmetry. The longitudinal axis of the monastery – the horizontal projection of the plan of symmetry – was marked by a path cutting across the monastery courtyard and by the two stairs of the central stupa in the temple. This mirror symmetry of the structure as a whole was combined with the axial (or congruent) symmetry of each half. The main stupa was similarly symmetrical. The clearly defined rhythmic order, with a contrasting rhythmic design, should be noted: the regular repetition of the cells; the alternation and contrast of the long corridors, their continuity interrupted by two-part sanctuaries at right-angles to them; and the smoothness of the walls, broken by the alcoves of the *aiwān*s. Combined with the single system of proportion, this creates harmonic balance and unity. The buildings (as in other centres) show a synthesis of tectonic, plastic and symbolic elements. Expressiveness was achieved by an organic synthesis between the architecture itself and its decorative features (murals, bas-relief and other sculpture).

The aesthetic perfection of the architecture was combined with a high quality of construction. The walls were built mainly of *pakhsa* (mud-brick) and compressed clay blocks. The roofs were mainly vaulted and domed or flat. The domes were supported on squinches which were often arched; the vaults were wedge-shaped and constructed by the method of slanting sections (as in Sasanian palaces), and they covered considerable spans. The outside space between the springing of the vaults of adjacent buildings was occupied by supplementary vaults. In other cases the roofs were supported on richly decorated wooden columns (Tokharistan, Sogdiana and East Turkestan). The development of the construction of wooden columns in East Turkestan and Middle Asia took place at the same time as the rise of stone construction in India, and their development was interrelated. One variant is represented by the lantern ceilings of buildings in Central Asia, which were richly decorated. Cave architecture (both individual caves and whole series of caves) also appeared. Its emergence in East Turkestan was connected with influences arriving through Bactria from India.[14]

Crafts were mainly centred in the towns, where the standard of craftsmanship was higher than in the country. There was a far wider range of crafts in the towns and more advanced techniques were used: thus pottery was made on the wheel and textiles of higher artistic quality were produced. Ceramic production developed in practically every town. At the Gyaur-kala site (Merv), 14 kilns have been discovered, showing evidence of very advanced construction. The pottery is also of a very high quality – the richly decorated vessels from Khotan are particularly magnificent. Central Asia also produced large quantities of glassware, some of a very high artistic quality. At the beginning of the seventh century, glassware sent from Tokharistan to China was greatly admired.

The number of smithies, bronze foundries and jewellery workshops grew enormously. They produced a wide range of articles: agricultural implements (the iron tips of primitive ploughs, and sickles); craft and household tools (axes, hammers, adzes and chisels); articles for everyday use (metal reinforcement plates, keys, scissors, mirrors, stirrups and buckles); and jewellery, including both serially produced and unique pieces. Weapons included magnificent daggers and swords for the nobles, decorated with gold and inlaid with precious stones. Toreutics (which showed evidence of various interacting cultural influences) should also be mentioned: vessels made of precious metals, for which Sogdiana was particularly famous.

Weaving was also an important craft. The textiles produced on the largest scale were cotton and wool, but the production of silk fabrics also increased. Silk-weaving was highly developed in the oasis of Turfan as early as the beginning of the fifth century. A Chinese document of 418 from the Karakhoja necropolis mentions baskets for the breeding of silk-worms, and a Chinese document of 456 describes the polychrome silk fabric produced in Gaochang. (This document shows that silk-weaving techniques were still at an early stage.) There is a vivid picture painted on a wooden panel discovered by M. A. Stein at Dandan-oïliq to illustrate the legend that silk-worms were smuggled out of China to Khotan by a Chinese princess.[15] In the fifth century silk fabrics were also produced in Kashgar, Kucha and Khotan. Later, silk-weaving reached Sogdiana. One of the main centres of production of such fabrics was Zandana near Bukhara. The Zandana fabrics were richly ornamented, depicting goats, horses, deer and other animals. Many of the motifs were influenced by Byzantine and Iranian textiles.

---

14. Nilsen, 1966; Litvinsky and Zeimal, 1971; Maillard, 1983; Litvinsky and Solov'ev, 1985.
15. Stein, 1975, Pl. LXIII, pp. 259–60.

Other crafts such as leatherwork and tailoring were also widespread and highly developed.[16] Some of the goods were sold locally in the towns where they were made, at town markets (those at Panjikent have been excavated) and at fairs; some went to rural areas; and some were traded between provinces or exported. The urban crafts thus served a commercial purpose: they provided revenue for the nobles of the town in the form of rent in cash and in kind. Country crafts were mainly of a domestic nature, and only some of these articles were sold in the town markets.

Written sources stress that there were intensive trade links between the towns of East Turkestan and Sogdiana. The Sogdians were renowned traders and famed for their commercial skills. In Bukhara one of the city gates was even called 'the market gate'. According to al-Biruni, some settlements held fairs every month – one even lasted for 7 days.[17] The Arabs called Paikent 'the city of merchants'. Enormous caravans were equipped for international trade – in 721 a caravan consisting of 400 merchants was detained in Khujand. The Silk Route continued to be used, as did the southern and northern routes around the Tarim basin in East Turkestan. The *Han shu* (96A, 5A) describes them as follows:

> The one which goes by way of Shan-shan [region near Lake Lop-Nor], skirting the northern edge of the southern mountains and proceeding west along the course of the River So-chü [Yarkand], is the Southern Route. To the west, the Southern Route crosses the Ts'ung-ling [Pamirs] and then leads to Ta-Yüeh-chih [Kushan state] and An-hsi [Parthia]. The one which starts from the royal court of Nearer Chü-shih [Turfan], running alongside the northern mountains and following the course of the river west to Su-le [Kashgar], is the Northern Route. To the west, the Northern Route crosses the Ts'ung-ling and leads to Ta-yüan [Ferghana], Kang-chü [region of the middle Syr Darya] and Yen-ts'ai [near the Aral Sea].

During the first centuries A.D., the directions (and also the network) of these routes changed considerably, and new ones appeared. Because life died out in some of the oases in the south, for example, the Southern Route moved even further southwards. When describing routes through East Turkestan, Chinese sources mention the 'Middle Route' (or the 'Direct Route'), and also the 'New Route'.

Starting from the western borders of China proper, these routes, as ancient sources bear witness, passed through Central Asia. The most southern route through Tashkurgan and the difficult passes of the Pamirs reached Vakhan and then Balkh. Another route from Kashgar, which went through the Terekdavan pass, the Alai valley and Karateghin, also came out at Balkh. The third route led through the valley of Ferghana to Samarkand and Bukhara, and between these towns one branch led to the south, to Balkh, and the other to

16. Schafer, 1963; Belenitskiy et al., 1973; Lubo-Lesnichenko, 1984; Litvinsky (ed.), 1995.
17. Biruni, 1957, pp. 254–5.

the south-west, to Merv. From the Vakhan section and from Balkh, routes led to India, to the area of Gandhara, as far as the mouth of the Indus, and from there into southern India. The sea route to the Mediterranean countries started from the sea ports of southern India.

Another route from Balkh went westwards as far as Merv, leading on through Iran to Mesopotamia and from there to Damascus.[18] It crossed Ferghana to the oasis of Tashkent, and from there to the area of the Aral Sea, passing through Khwarizm, the lower Volga, the northern Caucasus and the northern shore of the Black Sea.

Between the fifth and the seventh century the Northern Route moved further north. It passed through Qomul (Hami) and Beshbalyk, continuing past Lake Issyk-kül and the River Talas, then onwards to the lower reaches of the Amu Darya and the Volga, and from there to the northern Caucasus and then to Trebizond.

Needless to say, trading conditions varied over time in the different parts of these trade routes. The most active traders were the Sogdians, but the Chinese also travelled along these same routes. Material and numismatic evidence of intensive trade has been found over the entire network. The high level of trade was reflected in the intensive circulation of money. Bronze coins played a major role in domestic transactions and large numbers have been discovered in Panjikent and southern Tajikistan. Chinese bronze coins of the T'ang period circulated widely in East Turkestan. Different types of bronze coins were issued in Semirechye[19] (the so-called Türgesh coins), in the oasis of Tashkent, in Ustrushana, Khwarizm and elsewhere. Local coinages circulated mainly, although not exclusively, in their country of issue. Few coins from Vakhsh are found in neighbouring countries, and none in Chaganiyan, a territory which has been thoroughly studied. In Panjikent, however, although the coinage of Panjikent itself was predominant, copper coins from other centres of Sogdiana also circulated, especially those from Samarkand, Bukhara and Chach (the oasis of Tashkent).

The extensive bronze coinage was connected with the sale of grain and other agricultural produce in town markets, and probably represented the surplus value collected by feudal rulers as rent. In the Sogdian documents from Mug, however, with one exception the coins mentioned are not bronze but silver. They were mostly modelled on the drachms of the Sasanian king Bahram V (421–439) but were struck in Transoxania. They were mainly minted in Bukhara, and are usually called 'coins of the *Bukhār khudāts*', from the title of the ruler of Bukhara, but they were also struck in Samarkand. By the eighth century the original Pahlavi legend had become an illegible imitation.[20]

---

18. Hirth, 1885; Herrman, 1938; Shiratori, 1956*b*.
19. Smirnova, 1981.
20. Some of these coins were plated, with an inner core of copper and outer layers of silver.

Written sources give some idea of prices from the mid-eighth century: a slave cost 200 drachms (on average); a horse 200; brocade (a large piece) 100; brocade (a small piece) 60; silk (a roll) 28; a pair of oxen 12; a cow 11; *kafshi* (a type of footwear) 1–2; and a large earthenware jug 2 drachms.[21]

Trade on the Silk Route enabled great quantities of extremely valuable commodities to be distributed and exchanged between China, the states of Central Asia and the Mediterranean, especially Byzantium. Not only individual merchants or guilds (as in India) but also states participated in this trade; and rulers had an interest in the profits from it. Diplomatic relations were frequently determined by commercial and economic interests. This can best be illustrated by the conflict between the Sogdians and the Western Türks with Sasanian Iran over the transit of silk through Iranian territory; and the establishment of a military and political alliance between the Türks and Byzantium (against the Sasanians), who used routes through the northern Caucasus.[22] It should be noted that the Silk Route contributed to the exchange not only of goods but also of people, works of literature, works of art, ideas and concepts.

The period from the third to the eighth century was also a time when artistic and intellectual life were highly developed, in particular the fine arts – painting and sculpture. Important centres of art flourished in Central Asia. The earliest examples – at Fayaz-tepe, Toprak-kala and Miran – show clear signs of Hellenistic and Roman influence.

Several early medieval schools of painting developed simultaneously, but with wide distinctions in style and iconography, partly due to external links and influences. The art of various schools of East Turkestan is marked by very strong Indian, and at one stage (during the T'ang period) Chinese, influence; in Central Asia, especially in Sogdiana, local traditions and models prevailed; in Afghanistan there was a blend of local, Indian and Iranian traditions, particularly in the art of Bamiyan.

The interaction of schools and traditions, together with direct mutual influences, was revealed in and through the works of outstanding masters. The works of the great Khotanese artist Visha Irasangä and his influence on the artistic culture of China and also of Korea and Japan are of special interest.[23] The early medieval sculpture of Central Asia is magnificent. Its Gandharan sources, on which further layers of Gupta tradition were superimposed, can be clearly recognized. At the same time, the local element is also very strong. One of its typical features is the appearance of architectural colossi such as the 53 m and 35 m standing Buddhas in Bamiyan and the gigantic Buddhas in Nirvana

21. Smirnova, 1963; 1981; Vaynberg, 1977; Belenitskiy et al., 1980; Davidovich and Zeimal, 1980.
22. Moravcsik, 1958.
23. Schafer, 1963, p. 32.

from Ajina-tepe and Tepe Sardar. The Dunhuang caves are some of the richest and most magnificent in Buddhist painting and sculpture. The frescoes on the cave walls cover more than 45,000 sq. m and there are more than 2,000 sculptured statues. The gigantic Buddha of Dunhuang, a counterpart of Bamiyan, is 33 m tall. The elaborate compositions depicting many figures, the perfection of the technique and the polychrome colour scheme leave a very strong impression. In painting and sculpture, both secular and religious (Buddhist, Manichaean and Christian) art flourished. Both these branches developed as interrelated parts of a single art.[24]

Central Asia was also famed for the high level of its music, dance and theatrical art. Youths and maidens from Central Asia performed two types of dance: 'pliant' dances and vigorous dances. Large wooden statues of dancing girls have been preserved in Panjikent. Girls naked to the waist are depicted in an elaborate turn. The left hand is on the hip; the right leg is bent at the knee and crosses the straight left leg (see Fig. 13 in Chapter 10). Necklaces, strings of bells, the elaborate clothing of the lower part of the body – all this was in perfect harmony with the elegant, elongated figure. It brings to mind the Chinese descriptions of the 'Dance of Chach' (Tashkent), which was performed by two young girls:

> dressed in gauze caftans embroidered in many colours, with silver girdles. They wore the typical tight-sleeved blouses of the Far West, had peaked hats decorated with golden bells on their heads, and red brocaded shoes on their feet. They appeared first to the audience from the opening petals of two artificial lotuses, and danced to the rapid beating of drums. It was an amorous dance, the maidens ogled the spectators and, at the end, pulled down their blouses to reveal bare shoulders, and the delighted poet exclaimed: 'I watch – too soon the tune is done, they will not be detained; whirling in clouds, escorted by rain, they are off to the Terrace of the Sun.'[25]

The people of Central Asia were also known as excellent musicians. The names of 10 Bukharan musical instruments are known to us. There were melodies for songs and for dances. Some dances and songs were performed solo, others by a group. Music was also highly developed in Kucha, where the orchestra consisted of 20 musicians. A musical composition called 'The Great Reconciliation', with over 150 participants, was performed in Kucha during the T'ang period – a complicated magical drum-show. A performance of this type is depicted on a reliquary from Su-bashi. The musical culture of Kucha had a profound influence on that of China.[26]

---

24. Litvinsky and Zeimal, 1971; Belenitskiy, 1973; Rowland, 1974; Al'baum, 1975; Gaulier et al., 1976.
25. Schafer, 1963, p. 55.
26. Ibid., pp. 52, 54–5; Liu, 1969, Vol. 1, pp. 106–7, 206–7; Vol. 2, p. 268; Litvinsky, 1984, pp. 21–2.

The art of the theatre also reached a high level of development. Fragments of Buddhist dramas written in Sanskrit and archaic Prakrit, the most ancient Indian dramas, have been discovered in East Turkestan. It is known that they existed in Khotanese Saka, Tokharian and other languages. Performances of such religious dramas were often put on in monasteries.[27]

The culture of this period was a *written* culture. Sogdian children were taught reading, writing, arithmetic and so on. A school exercise book has been discovered in Panjikent, containing the Sogdian alphabet with an example for each letter. Large numbers of such educational textbooks and exercise books have been found in East Turkestan. Witnesses, especially the pilgrims Hsüan-tsang and Huei-chao, noted the high level of literacy and the existence of various literary works and whole literatures in East Turkestan, Sogdiana and Tokharistan. Thanks to the dry climate in East Turkestan, over 100,000 leaves of written documents have survived: they are in Sanskrit, Prakrit, Gandhārī, Tokharian, Khotanese Saka, Sogdian, Parthian, Middle Persian, Bactrian, New Persian, Syriac, Chinese, Tibetan, Old Turkic and other languages. Most of them are religious works, but there are other texts of various kinds – letters, travel diaries, scientific works, business documents and literature, including poetry. Many works, especially those of a religious character, are translations, and some are bilingual. This all adds up to a vast multilingual literature. The art of translation reached a high standard. Khotan was, for example, a major centre for scholars of the Imperial Court of T'ang China seeking authentic Buddhist records.

Monasteries were centres of learning and knowledge. In their scriptoria, books were copied and texts were carefully checked, for which purpose a whole staff was maintained. There was a large monastic library in one of the grottoes in Dunhuang. The copying of religious books was considered a work of piety, and every literate monk was eager to be engaged as a copyist, while the laity contributed money to the monasteries for the copying of sacred works.[28]

The translated literature includes all the basic works of Buddhism, Manichaeism and Christianity. Translators often inserted their own additions or reinterpreted the original text. If we bear in mind the original compositions in these languages, this gives us an idea of the local culture and ideology. Works which have survived nowhere else have come down to us in this literature, whether in their original language or in translation.

In this context we must emphasize the development of scientific literature. Indian treatises on medicine were studied and translated into the languages of Central Asia. Translations of Indian medical works into Khotanese Saka, Sogdian, Tokharian, Uighur, Tibetan and other languages have been preserved. There were also works on history and other branches of learning.

---

27. Lüders, 1911; Bailey, 1960, pp. 266–7; Emmerick, 1967, pp. 43, 45; Litvinsky, 1992.
28. Giles, 1935, pp. 810, 812, 815–17, 820–6.

Thus, another distinguishing feature of the culture of this period was that it was *syncretic*. Ideas, images and concepts were exchanged, and there was intensive cultural exchange and interpenetration in all fields of culture and intellectual activity and on all levels, from isolated phenomena to concepts. This produced remarkable results and led to striking achievements in art, architecture, literature and science. The same was true of religion.

Trade and other contacts between T'ang China and Central Asia introduced the people of Central Asia and the Arabs to paper as a writing material. Paper fragments of the third century have been found in Dunhuang, Lou-lan and Turfan and probably moved westwards to Central Asia before the seventh century. As early as 650, Chinese paper was imported to Samarkand. At the battle of Talas in 751, when the allied Arab-Türk forces routed the Chinese army, among the prisoners were craftsmen, including paper-makers. They were taken to start the manufacture of paper in Samarkand, from where the industry soon moved to Baghdad.[29]

This period ended with an event of importance for world history: the rise of Islam and the Arab caliphate and its extraordinarily rapid expansion to the north, east and west. A considerable part of Central Asia was incorporated into the caliphate. As seen both by contemporary observers and by later generations, one of the most important phenomena of the history of Central Asia from the eighth to the tenth century onwards was its gradual conversion to Islam and its incorporation into the sphere of 'Islamic' culture. Under this influence, a considerable – and in some ways fundamental – reorientation of the ideological sphere took place: the concepts of the Muslim religion and its ideology were widely disseminated and penetrated into various fields of intellectual life and also, to a certain degree, although indirectly, into the material environment. What, however, was the role and importance of pre-Islamic civilization in the new age?

The Arab conquest of the western part of Central Asia was completed towards the middle of the eighth century, but the adoption of Islam did not take place immediately. According to the information available, in the first half of the ninth century in Merv there was a library of Pahlavi manuscripts, which were freely available for reading and the copying of extracts.[30] Large numbers of works were translated. Pahlavi works were translated into Arabic, for example, and some of them, as well as the Pahlavi originals, including epics, were used in Persian-Tajik literature. Similar work went on in Central Asia.[31] The Sogdian language was still spoken and written for several centuries after the Arab conquest. On the other hand, Islam was superimposed on the Buddhist background. Buddhism had a certain influence on early Sufism, and individual

---

29. Needham (ed.), 1985, pp. 296–7.
30. Bartold, 1971*a*, p. 369.
31. Nöldeke, Tabari, 1973; Bartold, 1971*b*.

Buddhist images and ideas penetrated Tajik-Persian literature on a fairly wide scale.[32]

There is no doubt that during the first centuries of the dissemination of Islam, people's beliefs continued to be dominated by the old, pre-Islamic concepts, which were merely partially hidden beneath a thin layer of an Islamized amalgam. The situation was different only in the small group of the population directly involved in Muslim worship. Pre-Muslim and non-Muslim ideology formed the core of the people's ideology in the Middle Ages and – both directly and through folklore, and also through written tradition and reminiscences – had a profound influence on literature, philosophy and science, and on the intellectual climate of society. Indeed, this was the ideological breeding-ground from which many heresies and popular movements sprang.

The same continuity can be traced in art and architecture. Figurative art did not, as is frequently supposed, die out completely, but continued to exist side by side with decorative art. Murals dating from the Ghaznavid period in Lashkar-i Bazar (Afghanistan) and Khulbuk (Tajikistan) are in a direct line from the painting tradition of pre-Islamic Central Asia in Afghanistan. The four-*aiwān* composition – typical of the Islamic *madrasa* (school), mosque and caravanserai – was fully developed in Buddhist building (the Buddhist monastery of Ajina-tepe provides striking examples). There is every reason to assume the existence of a direct link between the Buddhist monastery and the Islamic *madrasa*; the plans and design of the centric Islamic mausoleum also have their roots in pre-Islamic architecture; and the traditions of pre-Islamic architecture were also continued in the building of dwellings, palaces, and so on. Last, it is important to note that there was no break with earlier traditions in the development of towns and urban life.[33]

Thus, in all aspects of its culture, Central Asian civilization from the third to the eighth century, or rather the structure of Central Asian civilization of that period, was the basis of many of the fundamental principles of Islamic civilization in later centuries.

32. Litvinsky, 1968; Gimaret, 1970; Melikian-Chirvani, 1974.
33. Grabar, 1973; Litvinsky, 1980.

MAPS

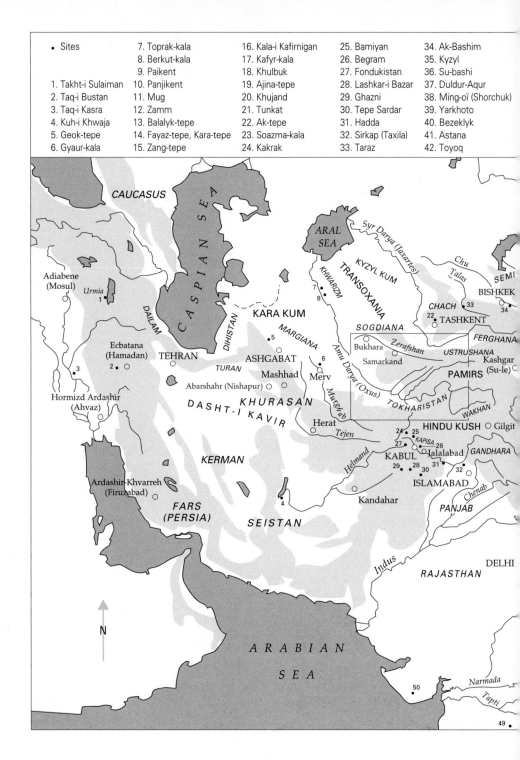

• Sites	

- Sites
- 7. Toprak-kala
- 8. Berkut-kala
- 9. Paikent
1. Takht-i Sulaiman
10. Panjikent
2. Taq-i Bustan
11. Mug
3. Taq-i Kasra
12. Zamm
4. Kuh-i Khwaja
13. Balalyk-tepe
5. Geok-tepe
14. Fayaz-tepe, Kara-tepe
6. Gyaur-kala
15. Zang-tepe
16. Kala-i Kafirnigan
17. Kafyr-kala
18. Khulbuk
19. Ajina-tepe
20. Khujand
21. Tunkat
22. Ak-tepe
23. Soazma-kala
24. Kakrak
25. Bamiyan
26. Begram
27. Fondukistan
28. Lashkar-i Bazar
29. Ghazni
30. Tepe Sardar
31. Hadda
32. Sirkap (Taxila)
33. Taraz
34. Ak-Bashim
35. Kyzyl
36. Su-bashi
37. Duldur-Aqur
38. Ming-oï (Shorchuk)
39. Yarkhoto
40. Bezeklyk
41. Astana
42. Toyoq

MAP 1. General map of Central Asia (fourth–eighth century).

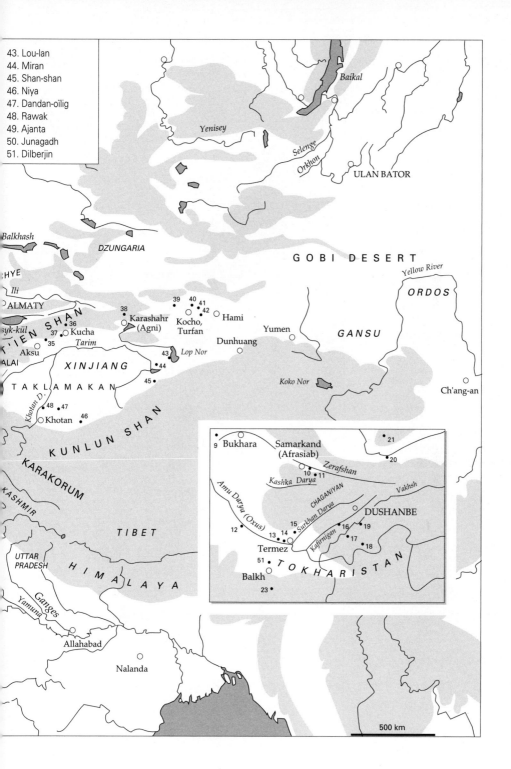

43. Lou-lan
44. Miran
45. Shan-shan
46. Niya
47. Dandan-oïlig
48. Rawak
49. Ajanta
50. Junagadh
51. Dilberjin

Baikal

Yenisey

Selenge
Orkhon
ULAN BATOR

Balkhash

DZUNGARIA

GOBI DESERT

Yellow River

ORDOS

HYE
Ili
ALMATY

T'IEN SHAN

39 40 41
38   42
Karashahr Hami
(Agni) Kocho,
Turfan
36
37 Kucha
35 Tarim
Aksu
ALAI

XINJIANG

Yumen

Dunhuang

GANSU

Lop Nor

43

44

45

TAKLAMAKAN

Koko Nor

Ch'ang-an

Khotan D.
48 47
Khotan 46

KUNLUN SHAN

KARAKORUM

KASHMIR

TIBET

HIMALAYA

UTTAR
PRADESH

Ganges
Yamuna

Allahabad

Nalanda

9 Bukhara
Samarkand
(Afrasiab)
21
20
10 11
Zerafshan
Kashka Darya
Amu Darya (Oxus)
CHAGANIYAN
Surkhan Darya
Vakhsh
DUSHANBE
15 16 19
12
13 14 17
Kafirnigan 18
Termez
51 TOKHARISTAN
Balkh
23

500 km

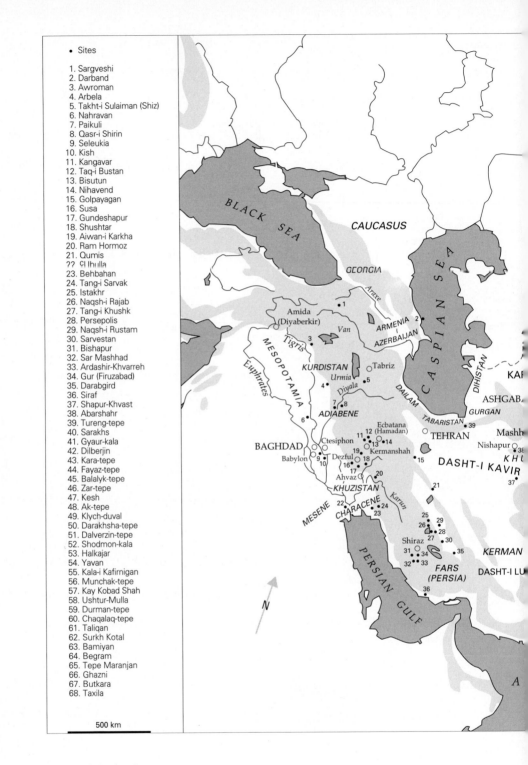

500 km

MAP 2. Sasanian Iran.

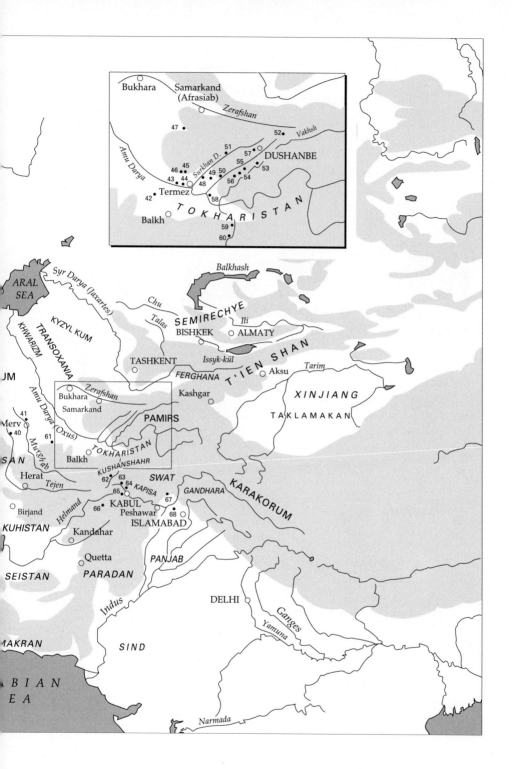

MAP 3. The Hephthalite Empire.

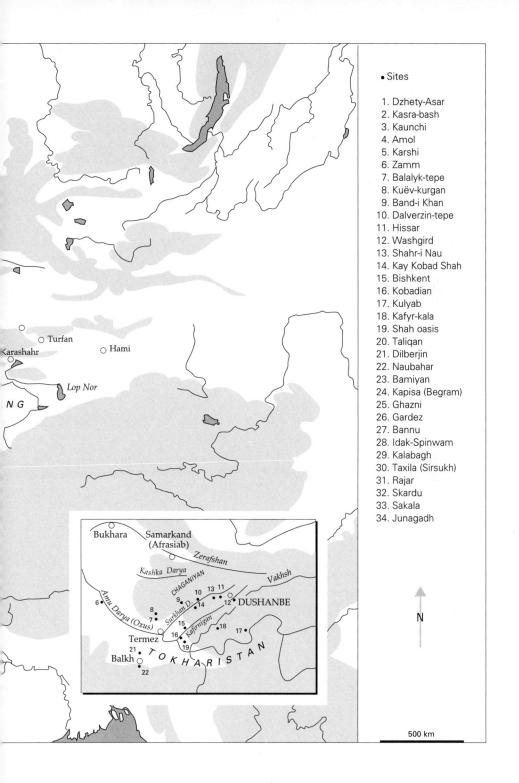

• Sites

1. Dzhety-Asar
2. Kasra-bash
3. Kaunchi
4. Amol
5. Karshi
6. Zamm
7. Balalyk-tepe
8. Kuëv-kurgan
9. Band-i Khan
10. Dalverzin-tepe
11. Hissar
12. Washgird
13. Shahr-i Nau
14. Kay Kobad Shah
15. Bishkent
16. Kobadian
17. Kulyab
18. Kafyr-kala
19. Shah oasis
20. Taliqan
21. Dilberjin
22. Naubahar
23. Bamiyan
24. Kapisa (Begram)
25. Ghazni
26. Gardez
27. Bannu
28. Idak-Spinwam
29. Kalabagh
30. Taxila (Sirsukh)
31. Rajar
32. Skardu
33. Sakala
34. Junagadh

500 km

MAP 4. The Gupta kingdom.

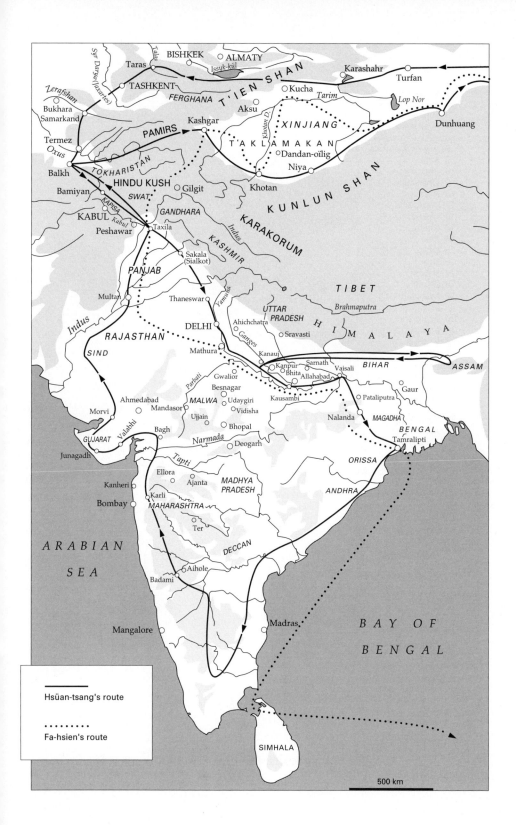

——————	Hsüan-tsang's route
• • • • • • •	Fa-hsien's route

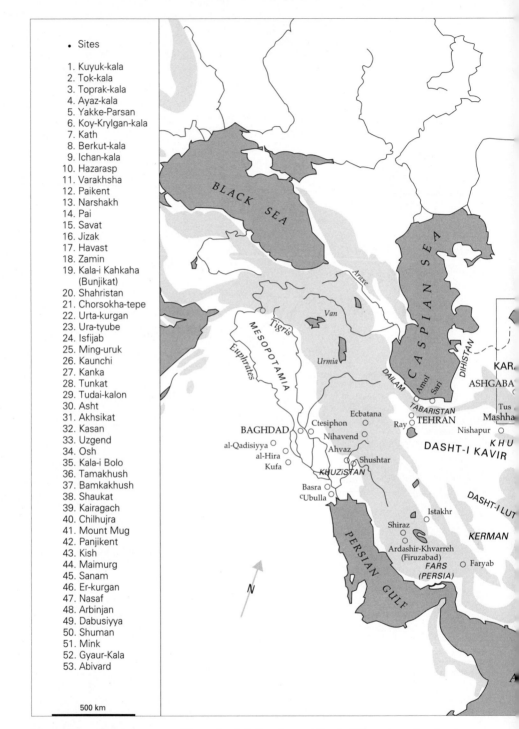

- Sites

1. Kuyuk-kala
2. Tok-kala
3. Toprak-kala
4. Ayaz-kala
5. Yakke-Parsan
6. Koy-Krylgan-kala
7. Kath
8. Berkut-kala
9. Ichan-kala
10. Hazarasp
11. Varakhsha
12. Paikent
13. Narshakh
14. Pai
15. Savat
16. Jizak
17. Havast
18. Zamin
19. Kala-i Kahkaha
    (Bunjikat)
20. Shahristan
21. Chorsokha-tepe
22. Urta-kurgan
23. Ura-tyube
24. Isfijab
25. Ming-uruk
26. Kaunchi
27. Kanka
28. Tunkat
29. Tudai-kalon
30. Asht
31. Akhsikat
32. Kasan
33. Uzgend
34. Osh
35. Kala-i Bolo
36. Tamakhush
37. Bamkakhush
38. Shaukat
39. Kairagach
40. Chilhujra
41. Mount Mug
42. Panjikent
43. Kish
44. Maimurg
45. Sanam
46. Er-kurgan
47. Nasaf
48. Arbinjan
49. Dabusiyya
50. Shuman
51. Mink
52. Gyaur-Kala
53. Abivard

500 km

MAP 5. The Arab conquest of Iran, Sughd, Ferghana, Chach, Khwarizm, Semirechye (fourth–eighth century).

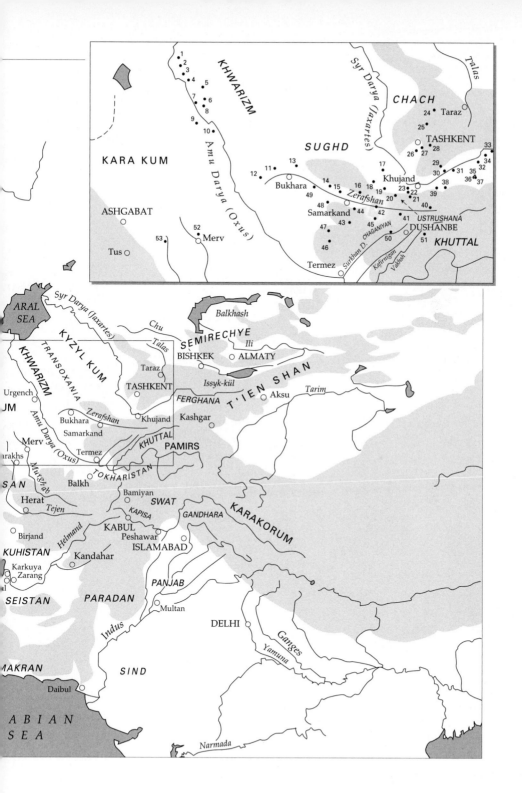

MAP 6. The Western Regions and Tibet (fourth–eighth century).

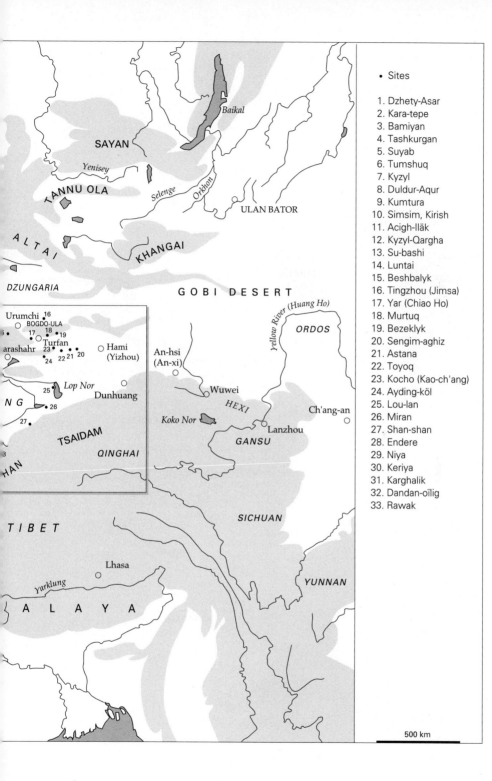

Baikal

SAYAN

Yenisey

Selenge

Orkhon

ULAN BATOR

TANNU OLA

ALTAI

KHANGAI

DZUNGARIA

GOBI DESERT

Yellow River (Huang Ho)

ORDOS

Urumchi 16
BOGDO-ULA
17   18   19
Turfan
arashahr 23   20
24 22 21

Hami
(Yizhou)

An-hsi
(An-xi)

Lop Nor
25
Dunhuang
26
N G
27

TSAIDAM

QINGHAI

HAN

Wuwei

HEXI

Koko Nor

Lanzhou

GANSU

Ch'ang-an

TIBET

SICHUAN

Lhasa

Yarklung

ALAYA

YUNNAN

500 km

- Sites

1. Dzhety-Asar
2. Kara-tepe
3. Bamiyan
4. Tashkurgan
5. Suyab
6. Tumshuq
7. Kyzyl
8. Duldur-Aqur
9. Kumtura
10. Simsim, Kirish
11. Acigh-Iläk
12. Kyzyl-Qargha
13. Su-bashi
14. Luntai
15. Beshbalyk
16. Tingzhou (Jimsa)
17. Yar (Chiao Ho)
18. Murtuq
19. Bezeklyk
20. Sengim-aghiz
21. Astana
22. Toyoq
23. Kocho (Kao-ch'ang)
24. Ayding-köl
25. Lou-lan
26. Miran
27. Shan-shan
28. Endere
29. Niya
30. Keriya
31. Karghalik
32. Dandan-oïlig
33. Rawak

MAP 7. The Türk Empire.

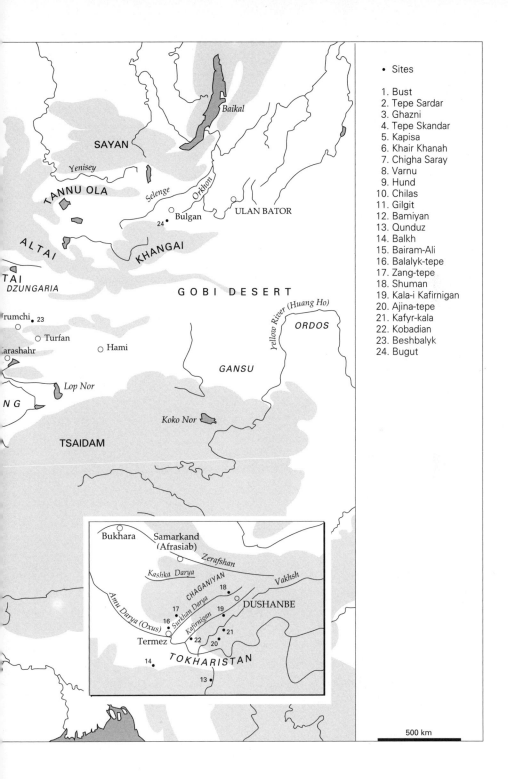

500 km

BIBLIOGRAPHY AND REFERENCES

ABBREVIATIONS OF PERIODICALS

AA = *Arts asiatiques*, Paris
Acta Ant. Hung. = *Acta Antiqua Academiae Scientiarum Hungaricae*, Budapest
AOH = *Acta Orientalia Academiae Scientiarum Hungaricae*, Budapest
BEFEO = *Bulletin de l'Ecole française d'Extrême-Orient*, Paris
BSOAS = *Bulletin of the School of Oriental and African Studies*, London
BSOS = *Bulletin of the School of Oriental Studies*, London
CII = *Corpus Inscriptionum Indicarum*, Calcutta
CRAI = *Comptes rendus de l'Académie des Inscriptions et Belles lettres*, Paris
EW = *East and West*, Rome
IIJ = *Indo-Iranian Journal*, The Hague
IsMEO = *Istituto italiano per il Medio ed Estremo Oriente. Reports and Memoirs*, Rome
JA = *Journal asiatique*, Paris
JAOS = *Journal of the American Oriental Society*, New Haven, Conn.
JCA = *Journal of Central Asia*, Islamabad
JNSI = *Journal of the Numismatic Society of India*, Varanasi
JRAS = *Journal of the Royal Asiatic Society*, London
MDAFA = *Mémoires de la Délégation archéologique française en Afghanistan*, Paris
NC = *Numismatic Chronicle*, London
SA = *Sovetskaya arkheologiya*, Moscow
TP = *T'oung-Pao*, Leiden

CHAPTER 1

The Age of Imperial Unity. 1951. *The History and Culture of Indian People*, Vol. 2. Bombay.
ALTEKAR, A.S.; MAJUMDAR, R.C. (eds.) 1946. The Vākāṭaka-Gupta Age (circa 200-550 A.D.). *New History of the Indian People*, Vol. 6. Reprint, 1954. Benares.
BAILEY, H.W. 1971. *Zoroastrian Problems in the Ninth-Century Books*, 2nd ed. Oxford.
BANERJI, R.D. 1933. *The Age of the Imperial Guptas*. Benares.

BARROU, J.; BONTÉ, P.; DIGARD, J.-P. 1973. *Etudes sur les sociétés de pasteurs nomades.* Vol. 1. Sur l'organisation technique et économique. Paris.

BONGARD-LEVIN, G.M.; IL'IN, G.F. 1969a. *Drevnyaya Indiya.* Moscow.

——. 1969b. In: *Vzaimodeystviye kochevykh kul'tur i drevnikh tsivilizatsii.* Alma-Ata.

——. 1985. In: *Indiya v drevnosti.* Moscow.

The Cambridge History of Iran. 1983. Vol. 3/1. Ed. E. Yarshater. Cambridge.

——. 1983. Vol. 3/2. Cambridge.

CHAVANNES, E. 1903. *Documents sur les Tou-kiue (Turcs) occidentaux. Recueillis et commentés, suivi de notes additionnelles. (Présenté à l'Académie Impériale des Sciences de St-Pétersbourg le 23 Août 1900.)* St Petersburg.

CHOKSY, J. 1988. Sacral Kingship in Sasanian Iran. *Bulletin of the Asia Institute*, new series, Vol. 2. Detroit.

CHRISTENSEN, A. 1944. *L'Iran sous les Sassanides*, 2nd ed. Copenhagen.

CHUGEVSKIY, A.I. 1971. Novye materialy k istorii sogdiskoy kolonii v rayone Dun'khuana. *Strany i narody Vostoka*, Vol. 10. Moscow.

The Classical Age. 1954. *The History and Culture of Indian People*, Vol. 3. Bombay.

DANDEKAR, N. 1941. *A History of the Guptas.* Poona.

DANI, A.H. 1983a. *Chilas - the City of Nanga Parvat. (Dyamar).* Islamabad.

——. 1983b. *Human Records on Karakorum Highway.* Islamabad.

FRANKE, O. 1936. *Geschichte des Chinesischen Reiches*, Vol. 2. Berlin/Leipzig.

FRYE, R.N. 1984. The Charisma of Kingship in Ancient Iran. *Iranica Antiqua*, Vol. 4. Gent.

GRENET, F.; SIMS-WILLIAMS, N. 1987. The Historical Context of the Sogdian Ancient Letters. In: *Transition Periods in Iranian History, Studia Iranica*, Cahier 5, pp. 101-22. Leuven.

HARMATTA, J. 1979. Sogdian Sources for the History of Pre-Islamic Central Asia. In: *Prolegomena to the Sources on the History of Pre-Islamic Central Asia*, pp. 153-65. Budapest.

HENNING, W.B. 1977. The Data of the Soghdian Ancient Letters. *Acta Iranica*, 2nd series, Vol. 6. Tehran/Liège.

HERRMANN, A. 1938. Das Land der Seide und Tibet im Lichte der Antike. *Quellen und Forschungen zur Geschichte der Geographie und Völkerkunde*, Vol. 1. Leipzig.

HULSEWÉ, A.F.P.; LOEWE, M.A.N. 1979. *China in Central Asia. The Early Stage: 125 B.C.-A.D. 23.* Leiden.

JETTMAR, K. (ed.). 1989. *Antiquities of Northern Pakistan. (Reports and Studies*, Vol. 1.) Mainz.

KHAZANOV, A.M. 1984. *Nomads and the Outside World.* Cambridge.

Khozyaystvo kazakhov na rubezhe XIX-XX vekov. 1980. Materialy k istoriko-etnograficheskomu atlasu. Alma-Ata.

KRYUKOV, M.V.; MALYAVIN, V.V.; SOFRONOV, M.V. 1979. *Kitayskiy etnos na poroge srednikh vekov.* Moscow.

——. 1984. *Kitayskiy etnos v srednie veka (VII-XIII vv).* Moscow.

LATTIMORE, O. 1974. *On Some Questions of Periodization in Nomadic History - Role of the Nomadic Peoples in the Civilization of Central Asia (A Record of Papers and Discussions of the International Unesco Symposium)*, pp. 171-173. Ed. S. Bira and A. Lutsandandev. Ulan Bator.

LEPPER, F.A. 1948. *Trajan's Parthian War*. London.

LITVINSKY, B.A. 1984. Istoricheskie sud'by Vostochnogo Turkestana i Sredney Azii: problemy etnokul'turnoy obshchnosti. In: *Vostoshchniy Turkestan i Srednyaya Aziya. Istorya. Kul'tura. Svyazi*. Moscow.

——. 1986. Drevnie svyazi Indii i Sredney Azii: do VII-VIII v.v. n.ê. In: *Rossiya i Indiya*. Moscow.

——. 1989. Gilgit Epigraphic-Petroglyphic Complex and its Significance. *IASCCA Information Bulletin*, No. 15. Moscow.

LIU MAU-TSAI. 1958. *Die chinesischen Nachrichten zur Geschichte der Ost-Türken (T'u-küe), 1-2 (Göttinger Asiatische Forschungen)*, No. 10. Wiesbaden.

LUKONIN, V.G. 1961. *Iran v epokhu pervykh Sasanidov. Ocherki kul'tury*. Leningrad.

MAENCHEN-HELFEN, O. 1973. *The World of the Huns. Studies in Their History and Culture*. Berkeley/Los Angeles/London.

MARKOV, G.E. 1976. *Kochevniki Azii*. Moscow.

Materialy po istorii kochevykh narodov v Kitae III-V v.v. 1989. Moscow.

MOOKERJI, R.K. 1952. *The Gupta Empire*. Bombay.

MORAVCSIK, G. 1958. *Byzantinoturcica. Die byzantinischen Quellen der Geschichte der Türkvölker*, Vols. 1-2. Berlin.

Pastoral Production and Society. 1979. Cambridge.

PIGULEVSKAYA, N.V. 1951. *Vizantya na putyakh v Indiyu. Iz istorii torgovli Vizantii s Vostokom v IV-VI v.v.* Moscow/Leningrad.

PULLEYBLANK, E. 1952. A Soghdian Colony in Inner Mongolia. *TP*, Vol. 41/4-5.

RADLOFF, W. 1893. *Aus Sibirien. Lose Blätter aus meinem Tagebuche*, Vols. 1-2. Leipzig.

RASCHKE, M. 1978. New Studies in Roman Commerce with the East. *Aufstieg und Niedergang der Römischen Welt*, Vol. 2. Berlin.

Rol' kochevykh narodov v tsivilizatsii Tsentral'noy Azii. 1974. Ulan Bator.

ROWLAND, B. 1970. *The Art and Architecture of India: Buddhist, Hindu, Jain*. Harmondsworth.

RUDENKO, S.I. 1961. K voprosu o formakh skotovodcheskogo khozyaystva i o kochevnikakh. *Materialy po etnografii*, Vol. 1. Leningrad.

SCHAFER, E.H. 1963. *The Golden Peaches of Samarkand. A Study of T'ang Exotics*. Berkeley/Los Angeles.

SHAKHMATOV, V.F. 1963. *Kazakhskaya pastbishno-kochevaya obshchina*. Alma-Ata.

TASKIN, 1968, 1973. *Materialy po istorii Syunnu: po kitayskim istochnikam*. Moscow.

TIKHVINSKIY, S.L.; LITVINSKY, B.A. (eds.). 1988. *Vostochniy Turkestan v drevnosti i rannem srednevekov'e. Ocherki istorii pod redaktsiey S.L. Tikhvinskogo i B.A. Litvinskogo*. Moscow.

TOLYBEKOV, S.E. 1971. *Kochevoe obshchestvo Kazakhov v VII -nachale XX v.v.* Alma-Ata.

VLADIMIRTSOV, B. 1948. *Le régime social des Mongols. Le féodalisme nomade*. Paris.

WIDENGREN, G. 1959. *The Sacral Kingship in Iran*. Leiden.

WRIGHT, A. 1959. *Buddhism in Chinese History*. Stanford.

ZHDANKO, T.A. 1968. Nomadizm v Sredney Azii i Kazakhstane: nekotorye istoricheskie i etnograficheskie problemy. In: *Istorya, arkheologiya i etnografiya Sredney Azii*. Moscow.

CHAPTER 2

ADAMS, R.M. 1961. Agriculture and Urban Life in Early Southern Iran. *Science*, Vol. 136, pp. 109-22.

——. 1965. *Land Behind Baghdad: A History of Settlement on the Diyala Plains.* Chicago.

AGATHIAS OF MYRINA. 1968. *Historiarum libri quinque.* Ed. Keydell. Berlin.

AMMIANUS MARCELLINUS. 1963-64. *Res Gestae* (LCL). Ed. and trans. J.C. Rolfe. Cambridge, Mass./London. 3 vols.

——. 1972. *The Surviving Books of the History.* With an English translation by John C. Rolfe. London.

BALᶜAMI. 1874. *Chronique de Abou Djafar Mohammed ben Djarir ben Yezid Tabari, traduite sur la version persane d'Abou-ᶜAli Mohammed Belᶜami par H. Zotenberg,* Vol. 4. Paris.

BIVAR, A.D.H. 1956. The Kushano-Sasanian Coins Series. *JNSI*, Vol. 18, pp. 13-42.

——. 1963. A Sasanian Hoard from Hilla. *NC*, pp. 157-78.

——. 1969*a*. Sasanians and Türks in Central Asia. In: G. Hambly (ed.), *Central Asia.* London-New York.

——. 1969*b*. *Catalogue of the Western Asiatic Seals in the British Museum. Sasanian Seals.* London.

——. 1970. Trade Between China and the Near East in the Sassanian and Early Muslim Period. *Colloquies on Art and Archaeology in Asia, No. 1, Pottery and Metalworks in T'ang China.* University of London.

——. 1972. Cavalry Equipment and Tactics on the Euphrates Frontier. *Dumbarton Oaks Papers,* pp. 276-91.

——. 1975. Hayatila. *Encyclopaedia of Islam,* pp. 312-13.

——. 1979. The Absolute Chronology of the Kushano-Sasanian Governors in Central Asia. In: J. Harmatta (ed.), *Prolegomena to the Sources on the History of Pre-Islamic Central Asia,* pp. 317-32. Budapest.

——. 1983. The History of Eastern Iran. *The Cambridge History of Iran,* Vol. 3/1.

BIVAR, A.D.H.; FEHREVARI, G. 1966. The Wall of Tammisha. *Iran,* Vol. 1, pp. 35-50.

BORISOV, A.Y.; LUKONIN, V.G. 1963. *Sasanidskie gemmy.* Leningrad.

CHRISTENSEN, A. 1944. *L'Iran sous les Sassanides,* 2nd edn. Copenhagen/Paris.

CURIEL, R. 1953. Le trésor de Tépé Maranjan. Une trouvaille de monnaies sassanides et kouchano-sassanides faite près de Kaboul. In: R. Curiel and D. Schlumberger, *Trésors monétaires d'Afghanistan. MDAFA,* Vol. 14.

DENNETT, D.C. Jr. 1950. *Conversion and the Poll Tax in Early Islamic Community.* Harvard University Press.

DESHAYES, J. 1973. Rapport préliminaire sur la neuvième campagne de fouilles à Tureng-tépé. *Iran,* Vol. 10. London.

ERDMANN, K. 1953. *Die Kunst Irans zur Zeit der Sasaniden.* Berlin.

ETTINGHAUSEN, R. 1938. Sasanian Pottery. In: *A Survey of Persian Art,* Vol. 1. London/New York/Oxford.

FRYE, R.N. 1961. Some Early Iranian Titles. *Oriens,* Vol. 15, pp. 353-55.

——. 1962. *The Heritage of Persia.* London.

——. 1975. The Rise of the Sasanians and the Uppsala School. *Acta Iranica,* Vol. 1, pp. 239-41.

——. 1977. The Sasanian System of Wall for Defense. In: M. Rosen-Ayalon (ed.), *Studies in Memory of Gaston Wiet.* Jerusalem.

——. 1983. The Political History of Iran under the Sasanians. *The Cambridge History of Iran*, Vol. 3/1.

——. 1984. *The History of Ancient Iran*, pp. 271-85. Munich.

FUKAI, S. 1977. *Persian Glass.* New York.

FUKAI, S.; HORIUCHI, K. 1972. *Taq-i Bustan. (The Tokyo University Iraq-Iran Archaeological Expedition Reports*, 10, 13). 2 vols. Tokyo, 1969 & 1972.

GHIRSHMAN, R. 1948. *Les Chionites-Hephthalites.* Cairo.

——. 1954. *Iran from the Earliest Times to the Islamic Period.* Harmondsworth.

——. 1956. *Bishapour II: Les mosaïques sassanides.* Paris.

——. 1962a. *Persian Art: the Parthian and Sasanian Dynasties.* New York.

——. 1962b. *Iran. Parthian and Sasanian.* London.

GIGNOUX, PH. 1978. Les sceaux et bulles inscrits. *Catalogue des sceaux, camées et bulles sassanides de la Bibliothèque Nationale et du Musée du Louvre*, Vol. 2. Paris.

GÖBL, R. 1971. *Sasanian Numismatics.* Brunswick.

——. 1976. *A Catalogue of Coins from Butkara (Swat, Pakistan).* Rome.

——. 1983. Sasanian Coins. *The Cambridge History of Iran*, Vol. 3/1, pp. 322-8.

HAMBLY, G. (ed.). 1969. *Central Asia.* London.

HANSMAN, J. 1978. Seleucia and the Three Dauraks. *Iran*, Vol. 16. London.

HENNING, W.B. 1937-39. The Great Inscription of Sapur I. *BSOS*, Vol. 9, pp. 823-49.

——. 1947-48. Two Manichaean Magical Texts. *BSOAS*, Vol. 12.

——. 1954. Notes on the Great Inscription of Sapur I. In: *Professor Jackson Memorial Volumes*, pp. 40-54. Bombay.

HERZFELD, E. 1924. *Paikuli: Monument and Inscription of the Early History of the Sassanian Empire.* 2 vols. Berlin.

——. 1930. *Kushano-Sasanian Coins (Memoirs of the Archaeological Survey of India*, Vol. 38).

——. 1947. Early Historical Contact Between the Old Iranian Empire and India. *India Antiqua.* Leiden.

HONIGMANN, E.; MARICQ, A. 1953. *Recherches sur les Res Gestae Divi Saporis.* Brussels.

HUFF, D. 1973. Firuzabad. A Survey of Excavations. *Iran*, Vol. 11. London.

——. 1978. Ausgrabungen auf Qal'a-ye Dukhtar bei Firuzabad. *Archäologische Mitteilungen aus Iran*, N.F., Vol. 2.

INOSTRANTSEV, C.A. 1926. The Sasanian Military Theory (in Russian translated into English by L. Bogdanov). *Journal of Cama Oriental Institute*, Vol. 7. Bombay.

KIANI, M.Y. 1982a. Excavations on the Defensive Wall of the Gurgan Plain, A Preliminary Report. *Iran*, Vol. 20, pp. 73-9. London.

——. 1982b. *Parthian Sites in Hyrcania. The Gurgan Plain.* Berlin.

KUDRYAVTSEV, A.A. 1982. *Drevniy Derbent.* Moscow.

LIVSHITS, V.A.; LUKONIN, V.G. 1964. Srednepersidskie i sogdyskie nadpisi na proizvedenyakh torevtiki. *Vestnik Drevney Istorii*, No. 3.

LUKONIN, V.G. 1969. *Kul'tura Sasanidskogo Irana.* Moscow.

——. 1977a. *Iskusstvo Drevnego Irana.* Moscow.

——. 1977b. Khram Anakhita v Kangavare. *Vestnik Drevney Istorii*, No. 4.

511

LUKONIN, V.G. 1979. *Iran v III veke.* Moscow.

——. 1983. Political, Social and Administrative Institutions, Taxes and Trade. *The Cambridge History of Iran*, Vol. 3/1.

MARICQ, A. 1958. Classica et Orientalia, 5, Res Gestae Divi Saporis. *Syria*, Vol. 35, pp. 295-360.

MARQUART, J.A. 1901. *Ērānšahr nach der Geographie des Ps. Moses Xorenacʿi (Abh. Göttingen N.F.*, Vol. 3, No. 2). Berlin.

——. 1931. In: G. Messina (ed.), *Catalogue of the Provincial Capitals of Eranshahr.* Rome.

MOCHIRI, M.I. 1972. *Etudes de numismatique iranienne sous les Sassanides*, Vol. 1. Tehran.

——. 1977. *Etude(s) de numismatique iranienne sous les Sassanides et Arabe-Sassanides*, Vol. 2. Tehran. Reprinted Louvain, 1983.

——. 1983. A Coin of Khusraw III's Third Year. *NC*, pp. 221-3.

NAUMANN, R. 1977. *Die Ruinen von Tacht-e Suleiman und Zendan-e Suleiman.* Berlin.

NÖLDEKE, T.; TABARI. 1973. *Geschichte der Perser und Araber zur Zeit der Sasaniden. Aus der arabischen Chronik des Tabari übersetzt und mit ausführlichen Erläuterungen und Ergänzungen versehn von T. Nöldeke.* Reprint. Leiden.

POLYBIUS. 1967-68. *Histories.* Trans. by W.R. Paton. London.

PORADA, E. 1965. *Ancient Iran: The Art of Pre-Islamic Times.* London.

PROCOPIUS. 1961. *History of the Wars.* Ed. and trans. by H.B. Dewing. London.

RAWLINSON, G. 1876. *The Seventh Great Oriental Monarchy*, I. New York.

REUTER, O. 1930. *Die Ausgrabungen der Deutschen Ktesiphon-Expedition im Winter 1928/29.* Wittenberg.

——. 1938. Sasanian Architecture. In: *A Survey of Persian Art*, Vol. 1. London/New York/Oxford.

RICCARDI, R.V. 1967. Pottery from Choche. *Mesopotamia*, Vol. 2. Turin.

SCHIPMANN, K. 1971. *Die Iranische Feuerheiligtümer.* Göttingen.

SELLWOOD, D. 1983. Minor States in Southern Iran, Persia. *The Cambridge History of Iran*, Vol. 3/1. *The Seleucid, Parthian and Sasanian Periods*, pp. 299-306.

SHEPHERD, D. 1983. Sasanian Art. *The Cambridge History of Iran*, Vol. 3/2. London.

SIMONETTA, B. 1956. A Note on Vologeses V, Artabanus V and Ardavadses. *NC*, 6th series, Vol. 16, pp. 77-82.

SPRENGLING, M. 1953. *Third Century Iran, Sapor and Kartir.* Chicago.

AL-TABARI. 1879-89. *Annales quos scripsit Abu Djafar Mohamed ibn Djarir al-Tabari, cum aliis.* Ed. by M.J. De Goeje. Prima Serie, Vols. 1 & 2. Leiden.

TREVER, K.V. 1937. *Novye sasanidskie blyuda Ermitazha.* Moscow-Leningrad.

TYLER-SMITH, S. 1983. Sasanian Mint Abbreviation. *NC*, pp. 240-7.

VANDEN BERGHE, L. 1961. Récentes découvertes de monuments sassanides dans le Fars. *Iranica Antiqua*, Vol. 1.

WEST, 1982. Sacred Books of the East, 37. *Pahlavi Texts*, 4.

WHITEHOUSE, D.; WILLIAMSON, A. 1973. Sasanian Maritime Trade. *Iran*, Vol. 11, pp. 29-49. London.

WIDENGREN, G. 1968. *Der Feudalismus im alten Iran.* Cologne.

——. 1971. The Establishment of the Sasanian Dynasty in the Light of New Evidence. *La Persia nel Medioevo.* Accademia Nazionale dei Lincei, Rome.

YARSHATER, E. (ed.). 1983. The Seleucid, Parthian and Sasanian Period. *The Cambridge History of Iran*, Vol. 3/1-2. See also Chs. 4, 5, 9, 17, 18, 19, 20 and 29.

CHAPTER 3

AFSHAR, I. 1964. Introduction. *Iskandar-nāma*. Tehran.

ʿAhd Ardašir. 1967. Ed. I. Abbas. Beirut.

ANKLESARIA, B.T. 1908. *The Bundahishn*. Bombay.

——. 1957. *Zand i Vohuman Yasn*. Bombay.

——. 1960. *The Pahlavi Rivāyat of Aturfarnbag and Farnbag Srōš*. Bombay.

——. 1964. *Vichitakihā-i Zātsparam*. Bombay.

ARBERRY, A.J. 1958. *Classical Persian Literature*. London.

BAHMAN, F. 1986. *Ardā Wirāz Nāmag*. London.

BAILEY, H.W. 1943. *Zoroastrian Problems*, pp. 149 et seq. Oxford.

BARR, K. 1936. Remarks on the Pahlavi Ligature. *BSOS*, Vol. 8, pp. 391-403.

BAUMSTARK, A. 1968. *Geschichte der Syrischen Literatur mit Ausschluß der christlich-palästinesischen Texte*. Bonn. (Photomechanical reprint Walter de Gruyter Co., Berlin.)

BAUSANI, A. 1965. *Die Perser: von den Anfängen bis zur Gegenwart*. Stuttgart.

BENVENISTE, E. 1932. Le mémorial de Zarēr. *JA*, Vol. 220, pp. 245-94.

BIVAR, A.D.H. 1970. The First Parthian Ostracon from Iran. *JRAS*, pp. 63-6.

——. 1972. Āpapāta. *JRAS*, pp. 119-24.

——. 1981. The Second Parthian Ostracon from Qūmis. *Iran*, Vol. 19, pp. 81-4.

BOYCE, M. 1957. The Parthian *gōsān* and Iranian Minstrel Tradition. *JRAS*, pp. 10-45.

——. 1968*a*. The Manichaean Literature in Middle Iranian. In: B. Spuler (ed.), *Handbuch der Orientalistik. 1. Abteilung, 4. Band, Iranistik, 2. Abschnitt, Literatur, Lieferung 1*, pp. 67-76. Leiden/Cologne.

——. 1968*b*. Middle Persian Literature. In: B. Spuler (ed.), *Handbuch der Orientalistik. 1. Abteilung, 4. Band, Iranistik, 2. Abschnitt, Literatur, Lieferung 1*, pp. 31-66. Leiden.

——. 1968*c*. *The Letter of Tansar*. Rome.

——. 1983*a*. Parthian Writings and Literature. In: E. Yarshater (ed.), *The Cambridge History of Iran*, Vol. 3/2, pp. 1,151-65.

——. 1983*b*. Manichaean Middle Persian Writings. In: E. Yarshater (ed.), *The Cambridge History of Iran*, Vol. 3/2, pp. 1,196-204.

BROCKELMANN, C. 1978. Kalila wa Dimna. *Encyclopaedia of Islam*, pp. 503-6. Leiden.

CHRISTENSEN, A. 1925. *Le règne du roi Kawadh I et le communisme mazdakite*. Copenhagen.

——. 1932. *Les Kayanides*. Copenhagen.

——. 1934. *Les types du premier homme et du premier roi dans l'histoire légendaire des iraniens*, Vol. 2. Leiden.

——. 1944. *L'Iran sous les Sassanides*. Copenhagen.

CHUKANOVA, O.M. 1987. *Kniga deyaniy Ardashira syna Papaka*. Transcription, translation from Middle Persian, foreword, commentaries and glossary by O.M. Chukanova. Moscow.

DHABHAR, B.N. 1912. *The Epistles of Manuschchihar*. Bombay.

——. 1913. *The Pahlavi Rivāyat*. Bombay.

DIAKONOFF, I.M.; LIVSHITS, V.A. 1976-79, Parthian Economic Documents from Nisa. Ed. by D.N. Mackenzie. *Corpus Inscriptionum Iranicarum*, Vols. 1-3. London.

DRESDEN, M. 1970. Middle Iranian. *Current Trends in Linguistics*, Vol. 6, pp. 26-63.

ENDRESS, G. 1987. Die wissenschaftliche Literatur. *Grundriss der Arabischen Philologie*, Vol. 2: Literaturwissenschaft, pp. 400-506. Wiesbaden.

FREIMAN, A. 1918. Andarz-i Kôtakân. In: *Dastur Hoshang Memorial Volume*, pp. 482-89. Bombay.

FÜCK, J. 1981. *Arabische Kultur und Islam im Mittelalter Ausgewählte Schriften*. Weimar.

GIGNOUX, PH. 1972. *Glossaire des inscriptions pahlavies et parthes*. London.

——. 1973. Etude des variantes textuelles des inscriptions de Kirdir. Genèse et datation. *Le Muséon*, 86, 1-2, pp. 193-216. Brussels.

——. 1984. *Le livre d'Ardā Virāz*. Paris.

——. 1991. Les quatre inscriptions du Mage Kırdır. Textes et concordances. *Studia Iranica*, Cahier No. 9. Paris.

——. 1992. Miscellanea Sasanidica. In: *Bulletin of the Asia Institute*, new series 4, pp. 234-6.

GIGNOUX, PH.; TAFAZZOLI, A. 1993. Anthologie de Zādspram. *Studia Iranica*, Cahier 13. Paris.

GIMARET, D. 1971. *Le livre de Bilauhar et Budāsaf*. Paris.

GRIGNASCHI, M. 1967. Quelques spécimens de la littérature Sassanide conservés dans les bibliothèques d'Istanbul. *JA*, t. 254, fasc. 1, pp. 1-142.

GROPP, G. 1969. Einige neuentdeckte Inschriften aus sassanidischer Zeit. In: W. Hinz (ed.), *Altiranische Funde und Forschungen*, pp. 229-60. Berlin.

——. 1970. Bericht über eine Reise in West-und Süd Iran. *Archaeologische Mitteilungen aus Iran*, N.F., Vol. 3, pp. 201-8.

——. 1975. Die Derbent-Inschriften und das Adur Gušnasp. *Acta Iranica*, Vol. 4.

GUTAS, D. 1981. Classical Arabic Wisdom Literature: Nature and Scope. *JAOS*, Vol. 101, No. 1, pp. 49-86.

HAMZA, AL-ISFAHANI. 1967. Ed. al-Yāsin. *Tanbīh*. Baghdad.

HARMATTA, J. 1958. Die partischen ostraka aus Dura-Europas. *Acta Ant. Hung.*, Vol. 6, pp. 87-175.

——. 1969. Byzantino-Iranica. *Acta Ant. Hung.*, Vol. 17, pp. 255-76.

——. 1971. Sino Iranica. *Acta Ant. Hung.*, Vol. 19.

——. 1973. Zu einem Buch von Walter Hinz. *Die Sprache*, Vol. 19, pp. 68-79.

HENNING, W.B. 1942. Mani's Last Journey. *BSOAS*, Vol. 10, pp. 948-53.

——. 1945. Soghdian Tales. *BSOAS*, Vol. 11, pp. 465-87.

——. 1947. Two Manichaean Magical Texts. *BSOAS*, Vol. 12, pp. 39-66.

——. 1958. Mitteliranisch. In: B. Spuler (ed.), *Handbuch der Orientalistik. 1. Abteilung, 4. Band, Iranistik. Abschnitt, Linguistik*, pp. 20-130. Leiden/Cologne.

——. 1962. Persian Poetical Manuscripts from the Time of Rūdakī. In: W.B. Henning (ed.), *A Locust's Leg*, pp. 85-104. London.

HUMBACH, H.; SKJAERVØ, P. 1978-83. *The Sassanian Inscription of Paikuli*, Vol. 1-3. Wiesbaden.

HUMBACH, H.; WANG SHIPING. 1988. Die pahlavi-chinesische Bilingue von Xi'an. *Acta Iranica*, Vol. 28, pp. 73-82.

IBN AL-NADIM. 1973. *Fihrist.* R. Tajaddud (ed.). Tehran.

INOSTRANTSEV, K. 1907. *Materialy iz arabskikh istochnikov dlya kulturnoy istorii Sasanidskoy Persii. Primety i poverya.* St Petersburg.

———. 1909. *Sasanidskie etyudy.* St Petersburg.

Istoriya Irana. 1977. Moscow University.

JAMASPASA, K.; HUMBACH, H. 1971. *Puršišnihā.* Wiesbaden.

JUNKER, H. 1912*a.* Ein mittelpersisches Schuhlgespräch. *Sitzungsberichte der Heidelberger Akademie der Wissenschaften,* Abh. 15, pp. 1-26.

———. 1912*b. Frahang i Pahlavik.* Heidelberg.

———. 1959. *Der Wissbegierige Sohn.* Leipzig.

KASUMOVA, S.Y. 1987. Novye srednepersidskie nadpisi iz Derbenta. In: *Etnokul'turnye protsessy v drevnem Dagestane,* pp. 102-5. Makhachkala.

KLIGENSCHMITT, G. 1968. *Frahang i Oīm* (inaugural dissertation). Erlangen.

KLIMA, O. 1957. *Mazdak. Geschichte einer sozialen Bewegung im Sassanidischen Persien.* Prague.

———. 1977. *Beiträge zur Geschichte des Mazdakismus.* Prague.

KNAUTH, W.; NADJMABADI, S. 1975. *Das altiranische Fürstenideal von Xenophon bis Firdousi.* Wiesbaden.

Kniga deyaniy Ardashira syna Papaka [The Book of Deeds of Ardashir]. 1987. (Transcription of text, translation from Middle Persian, introduction, commentary and glossary by O.M. Chunakovoy.) Moscow.

KOLESNIKOV, A.I. 1988. *Zoroastriytsy i khristiane v gosudarstve Sasanidov. Vzaimodeystvie i vzaimovlyanie tsivilizatsiy i Kul'tur na Vostoke.* Records of the Third All-Union Conference of Orientalists, Dushanbe, 16-18 May 1988. Moscow. (Vol. 1.)

KOTWAL, F. 1969. *The Supplementary Texts to the Šāyest nē-Šāyest.* Copenhagen.

KRYMSKIY, A. 1905. *Istoriya Sasanidov i zavoevanie Irana Arabami.* Moscow.

LUKONIN, V.G. 1969. *Kul'tura Sasanidkogo Irana.* Moscow.

MACUCH, M. 1981. *Das Sasanidische Rechtbuch.* Wiesbaden.

MARKWART, J. 1931. *A Catalogue of the Provincial Capitals of Eranshahr.* Ed. by G. Messina. Rome.

AL-MASᶜUDI. 1965. *Murūj,* I. Beirut.

MENASCE, J. DE. 1945. *Une apologétique mazdéenne, Škand-gumānīg-vičār.* Fribourg.

———. 1958. *Une encyclopédie mazdéenne, le Dēnkart.* Paris.

———. 1967. L'inscription funéraire pehlevie d'Istanbul. *Iranica Antiqua,* Vol. 7, pp. 59-76.

———. 1973. *Le troisième livre du Dēnkart.* Paris.

———. 1975. Zoroastrian Literature after the Muslim Conquest. In: R. Frye (ed.), *The Cambridge History of Iran,* Vol. 4, pp. 543-66.

———. 1983. Zoroastrian Pahlavi Writings. In: E. Yarshater (ed.), *The Cambridge History of Iran,* Vol. 3/2, pp. 1,166-95.

MESSINA, G. 1939. *Ayātkār i Žāmāspīk.* Rome.

MINORSKY, V. 1964. 'Vis-u-Ramin', A Parthian Romance. In: *Iranica,* pp. 151-99. London/Tehran.

MINOVI, M. 1968. *Pānzdah goftār*, pp. 169 et seq. Tehran.

——. 1975. *Nāme-ye Tansar*. Tehran.

MODI, J. 1903. *Jamaspi*. Bombay.

MOJTABAYI, F. 1984. Molāḥezāti dar bāre-ye a'lām-e Kalile va Demne. *Iranian Journal of Linguistics*, 1/2, pp. 33-63. Tehran.

MORANO, E. 1990. Contributi all'interpretazione della bilingue greco-partica dell'Eracle di Seleucia. In: *Proceedings of the First European Conference of Iranian Studies*, Part 1, pp. 229-38. Rome.

NÖLDEKE, T. 1920. *Das Iranische Nationalepos*, 2nd ed. Berlin/Leipzig.

NYBERG, H.S. 1970. Has, Hasēnag. In: *Henning Memorial Volume*. London.

——. 1988. *Frahan i Pahlavik*. B. Utas (ed.). Wiesbaden.

OL'DENBURG, S.F. 1907. Fablo vostochnogo proiskhozdeniya. 3. Constant du Hamel. *Zhurnal Ministerstva Narodnogo Prosveshcheniya*, Vol. 9/5/2, pp. 46-82.

ORANSKIY, I.M. 1977. *Les langues iraniennes*, pp. 62-108. Paris.

OSMANOV, M. 1975. *Jashn-nāme-ye Parvin Gonādi*. Tehran.

PERIKHANYAN, A. 1973. *Sasanidskiy sudebnik*. Erevan.

PIGULEVSKAYA, N.V. 1946. *Vizantya i Iran na rubeze VI i VII vekov*. Moscow.

——. 1979. *Kul'tura siriytsev v sredniye veka*. Moscow.

SAFA, Z. (ed.). 1965. *Dārāb-nāma*. Tehran.

SAFA-ISFEHANI, N. 1980. *Rivāyat-i Hēmēt i Ašawahištān*. Harvard.

SHAFIᶜ, M. (ed.). 1967. Introduction. *Vāmiq u ᶜAdhrā*. Lahore.

SHAKED, S. 1987. Andarz. In: E. Yarshater (ed.), *Encyclopaedia Iranica*, Vol. 2/1, pp. 11-16.

SIASSI, A.A. 1963. L'Université de Gond-i Shapur et l'étendue de son rayonnement. *Mélanges d'orientalisme offerts à Henri Massé*. Tehran.

Siyāsat-nāme. 1949. *Kniga o pravlenii vazira XI stoletiya Nizam al-Mul'ka*. Translation into Russian, introduction to study of the text and notes by Professor B.N. Zakhoder. Moscow/Leningrad.

STERNBACH, L. 1981. Indian Wisdom and its Spread beyond India. *JAOS*, Vol. 101, No. 1, pp. 97-131.

SUNDERMANN, W. 1971*a*. Zur frühen missionärischen Wirksamkeit Manis. *AOH*, Vol. 24, fasc. 1, pp. 79-125.

——. 1971*b*. Weiteres zur frühen missionärischen Wirksamkeit Manis. *AOH*, Vol. 24, fasc. 3, pp. 371-9.

——. 1974. Iranische Lebensbeschreibungen Manis. *AOH*, Vol. 36. pp. 125-49.

——. 1982. Die Bedeutung des Parthischen für die Verbreitung buddhistischer Wörten indischer Herkunft. *Altorientalische Forschungen*, Vol. 9, pp. 99-113.

TAFAZZOLI, A. 1968. Jawsān, jawāsāna. *Rāhnemā-ye Ketāb*, Vol. 11/7, pp. 410-11. Tehran.

——. 1974. Some Middle Persian Quotations in Classical Arabic and Persian Texts. In: Ph. Gignoux and A. Tafazzoli (eds.), *Mémorial Jean de Menasce*, pp. 337-49. Tehran/Louvain.

——. 1976. Ā'in-nāma. In: E. Yarshater (ed.), *Dānesh-nāma*, Vol. 1, p. 266. Tehran.

——. 1984. Observation sur le soi-disant Mazdak-nāmag. *Acta Iranica*, Vol. 23, pp. 507-10.

——. 1985. Abāliš, Ā'in-nāma. In: E. Yarshater (ed.), *Encyclopaedia Iranica*, Vol. 1.

——. 1991. L'inscription funéraire de Kāzerun II (Parišān). *Studia Iranica*, Vol. 20, pp. 197-202.

TAVADIA, J. 1930. *Šayast-nē-Šāyast.* Hamburg.

——. 1956. *Die mittelpersische Sprache und Literatur der Zarathustrier.* Leipzig.

UTAS, B. 1975. On the Composition of the Ayyātkār i Zarērān. *Acta Iranica*, Vol. 5, pp. 399-418.

VAHMAN, F. 1986. *Ardā Wirāz Nāmag.* London.

WEST, E.W. 1880. *Sacred Books of the East*, Vol. 5. Oxford.

——. 1882. *Sacred Books of the East*, Vol. 18. Oxford.

——. 1896-1904. Pahlavi Literature. In: W. Geiger and E. Kuhn (eds.), *Grundriss der iranischen Philologie,* Vol. 2, pp. 75-129.

WILLIAMS, A.V. 1990. *The Pahlavi Rivāyat Accompanying the Dādestān i Dēnīg.* Copenhagen.

YARSHATER, E. 1983*a*. Introduction. In: E. Yarshater (ed.), *The Cambridge History of Iran*, Vol. 3/1: *The Seleucid, Parthian and Sasanian Periods*, pp. xvii-lxxv. Cambridge.

——. 1983*b*. Iranian National History. *The Cambridge History of Iran*, Vol. 3/1, pp. 359-477.

CHAPTER 4

ALTEKAR, A.S.; MAJUMDAR, R.C. (eds.). 1946. The Vākātaka-Gupta Age (circa 200-550 A.D.). *New History of the Indian People*, Vol. 6. Reprint, 1954. Benares.

BALL, W.; GARDIN, J.-C. 1982. *Archaeological Gazetteer of Afghanistan*, Vols. 1-2. Paris.

BIVAR, A.D.H. 1956. The Kushano-Sasanian Coin Series. *JNSI*, Vol. 18.

——. 1979. The Absolute Chronology of the Kushano-Sassanian Governors in Central Asia. In: J. Harmatta (ed.), *Prolegomena to the Sources on the History of Pre-Islamic Central Asia*, pp. 317-32. Budapest.

——. 1983. The History of Eastern Iran. In: E. Yarshater (ed.), *The Cambridge History of Iran*, Vol. 3/1.

BLOCH, J. 1965. *Indo-Aryan from the Vedas to Modern Times.* Paris.

BURROW, T. 1955. *The Sanskrit Language.* London.

CHATTOPADHYAY, B. 1979. *The Age of the Kushanas.* Calcutta.

CRIBB, J. 1981. Gandharan Hoards of Kushano-Sasanian and Late Kushan Coppers. *Coin Hoards*, Vol. 6. London.

CUNNINGHAM, A. 1893. Later Indo-Scythians. *NC*, 3rd series, Vol. 13.

——. 1893-94. *Later Indo-Scythians.* Reprinted from the *NC*, Benares Reprint, 1962.

CURIEL, R. 1953. Le trésor de Tépé Maranjan. Une trouvaille de monnaies sassanides et kouchano-sassanides faite près de Kaboul. In: R. Curiel and D. Schlumberger (eds.), *Trésors monétaires d'Afghanistan. MDAFA*, Vol. 14.

DANI, A.H. 1963. *Indian Paleography.* Oxford.

Drevnyaya Bactriya. 1976. *Materialy Sovetsko-Afganskoy arkheologicheskoy ekspeditsii 1969-1973*, Vol. 1. Moscow.

——. 1979. *Materialy Sovetsko-Afganskoy arkheologicheskoy ekspeditsii*, Vol. 2. Moscow.

DYAKONOV, M.M. 1953. Arkheologitcheskie raboty v nizhnem techenii reki Kafirnigan (Kobadian) 1950-1951. *Materialy i issledovaniya po arkheologii SSSR*, Vol. 15. Moscow/Leningrad.

EDGERTON, F. 1953. *Buddhist Hybrid Sanskrit.* Vols. 1-2. New Haven.

ELIZARENKOVA, T. 1982. *Grammatika vediyskogo yazyka.* Moscow.

FRYE, R.N. 1963. *The Heritage of Persia.* Ohio.

——. 1979. Napki Malka and the Kushano-Sassanians. In: *Islamic Iran and Central Asia (7th-12th centuries).* London.

——. 1984. *The History of Ancient Iran.* Munich.

FUSSMAN, G. 1974. Documents épigraphiques kouchans. *BEFEO*, Vol. 61. Paris.

FUSSMAN, G.; LE BERRE, M. 1976. Monuments bouddhiques de la region de Caboul, 1. Le monastère de Gul Dara. *MDAFA*, Vol. 22.

GERSHEVITCH, I. 1967. Bactrian Inscriptions and Manuscripts. *Indo-Germanische Forschungen*, Vol. 72.

GHIRSHMAN, R. 1954. *Iran from the Earliest Times to the Islamic Period.* Harmondsworth.

GIGNOUX, Ph. 1972. *Glossaire des inscriptions Pehlevies et Parthes.* London.

GÖBL, R. 1984. *Münzprägung des Kušānreiches.* Vienna.

HACKIN, J. 1953. Le monastère bouddhique de Tépé Marandjan. *MDAFA*, Vol. 14.

HARMATTA, J. 1964. The Great Bactrian Inscriptions. *Acta Ant. Hung.*, Vol. 12/3. Budapest.

——. 1965. Minor Bactrian Inscriptions. *Acta. Ant. Hung.*, Vol. 13/1-2.

——. 1969. Late Bactrian Inscriptions. *Acta Ant. Hung.*, Vol. 18/3-4, pp. 297-432.

HENNING, W. 1958. Mitteliranisch. In: B. Spuler (ed.), *Handbuch der Orientalistik, 1. Abteilung, 4. Band, 1. Abschnitt.* Leiden-Cologne.

——. 1960. The Bactrian Inscription. *BSOAS*, Vol. 23, Part 1.

HERZFELD, E. 1930. Kushano-Sasanian Coins. *Memoirs of the Archaeological Survey of India*, Vol. 38.

HONIGMANN, E.; MARICQ, A. 1953. *Recherches sur les Res Gestae Divi Saporis.* Brussels.

HUMBACH, H. 1966-67. *Baktrische Sprachdenkmäler*, Vols. 1-2. Wiesbaden.

INGHOLT, H. 1971. *Gandhāran Art in Pakistan.* New Haven.

KRUGLIKOVA, I.T. 1974. *Dilberjin. Raskopki 1970-1972 gg*, Vol. 1. Moscow.

——. 1976. Nastennye rospisi Dilberjina. *Drevnyaya Baktriya. Materialy Sovetsko-Afganskoy ekspeditsii 1969-1973 gg*, Vol. 1. Moscow.

KRUGLIKOVA, I.T.; PUGACHENKOVA, G.A. 1979. *Dilberjin. Raskopki 1970-1973 gg*, Vol. 2. Moscow.

LAZARD, G.; GRENET, F.; LAMBERTERIE, C. 1984. Notes bactriennes. *Studia Iranica*, Vol. 13/2. Paris.

LITVINSKY, B.A. 1973. Arkheologicheskiye raboty v Yuzhnom Tajikistane v 1962-1970 gg. *Arkheologicheskiye raboty v Tajikistane (1970)*, Vol. 10. Dushanbe.

LITVINSKY, B.A.; SEDOV, A.V. 1984. *Kul'ty i ritualy Kushanskoy Baktrii. Pogrebal'niy obryad.* Moscow.

LIVSHITS, V. 1969. K otkrytiyu baktriyskikh nadpisey na Kara-Tepe. In: *Buddiyskie peshchery Kara-Tepe v Starom Termeze.* Moscow.

——. 1975. K interpretatsii baktriyskikh nadpisey iz Kara-Tepe. In: *Novye nakhodki na Kara-Tepe v Starom Termeze*. Moscow.

——. 1976. Nadpisi iz Dilberjina. In: *Drevnyaya Baktriya*, Vol.1.

LUKONIN, V.G. 1967. Kushano-Sasanidskie monety. *Epigrafica Vostoka*, Vol. 18. Leningrad.

——. 1969*a*. Zavoyevaniya Sasanidov na vostoke i problema Kushanskoy absolyutnoy khronologii. *Vestnik Drevney Istorii*, Vol. 2. Moscow.

——. 1969*b*. Srednepersidskie nadpisi iz Kara-Tepe. In: *Buddiyskie peshchery Kara-Tepe v Starom Termeze*. Moscow.

——. 1987. *Drevniy i rannesrednevekoviy Iran. Ocherki istorii kul'tury*. Moscow.

MACKENZIE, D.N. 1971. *A Concise Pahlavi Dictionary*. London.

MARICQ, A. 1958. La grande inscription de Kaniska et l'étéo-tokharien, l'ancienne langue de la Bactriane. *JA*, Vol. 246.

——. 1960. Bactrien ou étéo-tokharien. *JA*, Vol. 248.

MASSON, V.M. 1976. Kushanskie poseleniya i Kushanskaya arkheologiya. *Baktriyskie drevnosti*. Leningrad.

MIZUNO, S. (ed.). 1968. *Durman Tepe and Lalma. Buddhist Sites in Afghanistan Surveyed in 1963-1965*. Kyoto.

——. 1970. *Chaqalaq-Tepe. Fortified Village in North Afghanistan Excavated in 1964-1967*. Kyoto.

NÖLDEKE, T.; TABARI. 1973. *Geschichte der Perser und Araber zur Zeit der Sasaniden. Aus der arabischen Chronik des Tabari übersetzt und mit ausführlichen Erläuterungen und Ergänzungen versehn von T. Nöldeke*. Reprint. Leiden.

NYBERG, H.S. 1964, 1974. *A Manual of Pahlavi*, Vols. 1-2. Wiesbaden.

PARUCK, F.D.J. 1923. *Sasanian Coins*. Reprint, 1976, Delhi.

PUGACHENKOVA, G.A.; RTVELADZE, E.V. et al. 1978. *Dalverzin-Tepe. Kushanskiy gorod na yuge Uzbekistana*. Tashkent.

RASTORGUEVA, V.S. 1966. *Srednepersidskiy yazyk*. Moscow.

RASTORGUEVA, V.S.; MOLCHANOVA, E.K. 1981. Srednepersidskiy yazyk. In: *Osnovy iranskogo yazykoznaniya. Sredneiranskie yazyki*. Moscow.

SALEMAN, C. 1900. Mittelpersisch. In: *Grundriss der iranischen Philologie*, Vol. 1/1. Strasburg.

SASTRI, N.K.A. (ed.). 1957. *A Comprehensive History of India*, Vol. 2: *The Mauryas and Satavahanas, 35 B.C. - A.D. 300*. Bombay/Calcutta/Madras.

SEDOV, A. V. 1987. *Kobadian na poroge rannego srednevekov'a*. Moscow.

SPRENGLING, M. 1953. *Third Century Iran, Sapor and Kartir*. Chicago.

STAVISKIY, B. 1984. Kara-Tepe in Old Termez. In: J. Harmatta (ed.), *From Hecataeus to Al-Huwarizmi*. Budapest.

STEBLIN-KAMENSKIY, I.M. 1981. Baktriskiy yazyk. In: *Osnovy Iranskogo yazykoznaniya. Sredneiranskie yazyki*. Moscow.

TREVER, K.V.; LUKONIN, V.G. 1987. *Sasanidskoye serebro. Sobranie Gosudarstvennogo Ermitazha. Khudozhestvennaya kul'tura Irana III-VIII vekov*. Moscow.

VERTOGRADOVA, V.V. 1978. *Prakrity*. Moscow.

——. 1982. Indiyskie nadpisi na keramike iz raskopok 70-kh godov na Kara-Tepe. In: *Buddiyskie pamyatniki Kara-Tepe v Starom Termeze*. Moscow.

——. 1983. *Indian Inscriptions and Inscriptions in Unknown Lettering from Kara-Tepe in Old Termez*. Moscow.

VERTOGRADOVA, V.V. 1984. *Notes on the Indian Inscriptions from Kara-Tepe*. Summaries of papers presented by Soviet scholars to the VIth World Sanskrit Conference, 13-20 October 1984, Philadelphia, Pennsylvania, USA. Moscow.

VOROBYOVA-DESYATOVSKAYA, M.I. 1983. Pamyatniki pismom kharoshti i brakhmi iz Sovetskoy Sredney Azii. In: *Istoriya i kul'tura Tsentralnoy Azii*. Moscow.

WOOLNER, A.C. 1939. *Introduction to Prakrit*. Lahore.

ZAVYALOV, V.A. 1979. Raskopki kvartala pozdnekushanskogo vremeni na gorodishche Zar-Tepe v 1975-1976 gg. *Sovetskaya Arkheologiya*, No. 3.

ZEIMAL, E.V. 1968. *Kushanskaya khronologiya*. Dushanbe.

——. 1983. *Drevnye monety Tajikistana*. Dushanbe.

ZEIMAL, T.I. 1975. Pozdnekushanskie sloi v Yuzhnom Tajikistane. In: *Tsentralnaya Aziya v Kushanskuyu epokhu*, Vol. 2. Moscow.

——. 1987. Buddiyskaya stupa u Verblyuzhiey Gorki. *Proshloye Sredney Azii*. Dushanbe.

CHAPTER 5

ALLAN, J. 1914. *Catalogue of the Coins of the Gupta Dynasties and of Sasanka, King of Gauda*. London.

ALTEKAR, A.S. 1954. *Catalogue of the Gupta Gold Coins in the Bayana Hoard*. Bombay.

CRIBB, J. 1981. Gandharan Hoards of Kushano-Sassanian and Late Kushan Coppers. *Coin Hoards*, Vol. 6, pp. 84-108. London.

CUNNINGHAM, A. 1895. Later Indo-Scythians. *NC*, 1893, pp. 93-128, 166-202.

CURIEL, R. 1953. Le trésor de Tépé Maranjan. Une trouvaille de monnaies sassanides et kouchano-sassanides faite près de Kaboul. In: R. Curiel and D. Schlumberger (eds.), *Trésors monétaires d'Afghanistan*. *MDAFA*, Vol. 14.

ENOKI, K. 1969. On the Date of the Kidarites (1). *Memoirs of the Research Department of the Toyo Bunko, The Oriental Library*, No. 27, pp. 1-26. Tokyo.

——. 1970. On the Date of the Kidarites (2). *Memoirs of the Research Department of the Toyo Bunko, The Oriental Library*, No. 28, pp. 13-38. Tokyo.

FLEET, J.F. 1888. Inscriptions of the Early Gupta Kings and their Successors. *CII*, Vol. 3.

GHIRSHMAN, R. 1948. Les Chionites-Hephthalites. *MDAFA*, Vol. 13. Cairo.

GÖBL, R. 1967. *Dokumente zur Geschichte der iranischen Hunnen in Baktrien und Indien*, Vols. 1-4. Wiesbaden.

——. 1976. Catalogue of Coins from Butkara I (Swat, Pakistan). *IsMeo*.

——. 1984. *Münzprägung des Kuschanreiches. System und Chronologie der Münzprägung des Kuschanreiches*. Vienna.

HARMATTA, J. 1984. Kidara and the Kidarite Huns in Kašmir. In: J. Harmatta (ed.), *From Hecataeus to Al-Huwàrizmī*, series 1, Vol. 3. Budapest.

ISAMIDDINOV, M.H.; SULEIMANOV, R.H. 1984. *Erkurgan (stratigrafya i periodizatsiya)*. Tashkent.

KABANOV, S.K. 1953. K voprosu o stolitse Kidaritov. *Vestnik Drevney Istorii*, No. 2, pp. 201-206.

——. 1977. *Nakhseb na rubezhe drevnosti i srednevekov'ya (III-VII v.)*. Tashkent.

LITVINSKY, B.A.; SEDOV, A.V. 1983. *Tepai-Shakh. Kul'tura i svyazi kushanskoy Baktrii*. Moscow.

———. 1984. *Kul'ty i ritualy kushanskoy Baktrii.* Moscow.

LUKONIN, V.G. 1967. Kushano-sasanidskie monety. *Epigrafika Vostoka,* Vol. 18. Leningrad.

———. 1969*a. Kul'tura sasanidskogo Irana. Iran v III-V vv. Ocherki po istorii kul'tury.* Moscow.

———. 1969*b.* Zavoyevanya Sasanidov na Vostoke i problema kushanskoy absolyutnoy khronologii. *Vestnik Drevney Istorii,* No. 2, pp. 20-44.

MANDEL'SHTAM, A.M. 1958. K voprosu o kidaritakh. *Kratkie soobshcheniya Instituta etnografii AN SSSR,* Vol. 30, pp. 66-72. Moscow.

MARQUART, J. 1901. *Ērānšahr nach der Geographie des Ps. Moses Xorenac̣i.* Berlin.

MARSHAK, B.I. 1971. K voprosu o vostochnykh protivnikakh Irana v V v. *Strany i narody Vostoka.* Moscow.

MARTIN, M.F.C. 1937. Coins of Kidara and the Little Kushans. *Journal of the Asiatic Society of Bengal,* Vol. 3, pp. 23-50.

TER-MKRTICHYAN, L.K. 1979. *Armyanskie istochniki o Sredney Azii V-VII vv.* Moscow.

TREVER, K.V. 1954. Kushany, khionity i eftality po armyanskim istochnikam IV-VII vv. (K istorii narodov Sredney Azii.) *SA,* Vol. 21.

WILSON, H. 1841. *Ariana Antiqua.* London.

ZEIMAL, E.V. 1978. Politicheskaya istorya drevney Transoksiany po numizmaticheskim dannym. *Kul'tura Vostoka. Drevnost' i rannee srednevekov'e,* pp. 192-214. Leningrad.

———. 1983*a. Drevnie monety Tajikistana.* Dushanbe.

———. 1983*b.* The Political History of Transoxania. *The Cambridge History of Iran,* Vol. 3/1, pp. 232-262.

ZÜRCHER, E. 1968. The Yüeh-Chih and Kanishka in the Chinese Sources. In: A.I. Basham (ed.), *Papers on the Date of Kanishka,* submitted to the Conference on the Date of Kanishka, London, 20-22 April 1960 (Australian National University, Centre of Oriental Studies, Oriental Monograph Series, Vol. 4), pp. 346-90. Leiden.

CHAPTER 6

AL'BAUM, L.I. 1960. *Balalyk-tepe. K istorii materialnoy kultury i iskusstva Tokharistana.* Tashkent.

ALTEKAR, A.S.; MAJUMDAR, R.C. (eds.). 1954. The Vākāṭaka-Gupta Age (circa 200-550 A.D.). *New History of the Indian People,* Vol. 6. Reprint. Benares.

ALTHEIM, F. 1959-62. *Geschichte der Hunnen,* Vol. 1 (1959); Vol. 2 (1960); Vol. 3 (1961); Vols. 4, 5 (1962).

ANTONINI, C.S. 1972. Le pitture murali di Balalyk Tepe. *Annali dell'Istituto Orientale di Napoli,* Vol. 32 (N.S. 22).

BAILEY, H.W. 1931. To the Zamasp-Namak. *BSOS,* Vol. 6, No. 3.

———. 1932. Iranian Studies. *BSOS,* Vol. 6, No. 4.

———. 1954. L'Harahuna. In: *Asiatica, Festschrift Friedrich Weller,* pp. 13-21. Leipzig.

BALʿAMI. 1869. *Chronique de Abou Djafar Mohammed ben Djarir ben Yezid Tabari, traduite sur la version persane d'Abou-ʿAli Mohammed Belʿami par H. Zotenberg,* Vol. 2. Paris.

BALL W.; GARDIN, J.-C. 1982. *Archaeological Gazetteer of Afghanistan*, Vol. 1. Paris.

BEAL, S. 1969. *Si-yu-ki, Buddhist Records of the Western World. Translated from the Chinese of Hiuen Tsiang (A.D. 629)*, Vols. 1-2. London/Delhi. (First published in 1884.)

BELENITSKIY, A.M. 1950. Istoriko-geograficheskiy ocherk Khuttalya s drevneyshikh vremen do X v. n.ê. *Materialy i issledovanya po arkheologii SSSR*, Vol. 15. Moscow/Leningrad.

BELENITSKIY, A.M.; BENTOVICH, I.B.; BOLSHAKOV, O.G. 1973. *Srednevekoviy gorod Sredney Azii*. Leningrad.

BELENITSKIY, A.M.; MARSHAK, B.I. 1979. Voprosy khronologii zhivopisi rannesrednevekovogo Sogda. *Uspekhi sredneaziatskoy arkheologii*, Vol. 4. Leningrad.

BICHURIN, N.Y. 1950. *Sobranie svedeniy o narodakh obitavshich v Sredney Asii v drevnie vremena*, Vol. 2. Moscow.

BISWAS, A. 1973. *The Political History of the Hunas in India*. Delhi.

BIVAR, A. 1983. The History of Eastern Iran. *The Cambridge History of Iran*, Vol. 3/1.

BONGARD-LEVIN G.M.; IL'IN G.F. 1969. *Drevnyaya Indiya. Istoricheskiy ocherk*. Moscow.

BOSWORTH, C.E. 1981. The Rulers of Chaganian in Early Islamic Times. *Iran*, Vol. 19. London.

BURIY, V.P. 1979. Tekhnika rospisey pomeshchenya 16. In: *Drevnyaya Baktriya*, Vol. 2. Moscow.

CHAVANNES, E. 1903. *Documents sur les Tou-kiue (Turcs) occidentaux. Recueillis et commentés, suivi de notes additionnelles. (Présenté à l'Académie Impériale des Sciences de St-Pétersbourg le 23 Août 1900.)* St Petersburg.

CZEGLÉDY, K. 1980. Zur Geschichte der Hephtaliten. *Acta Ant. Hung.*, Vol. 28, fasc. 1-4.

DALTON, O.M. 1964. *The Treasure of the Oxus*, 3rd ed. London.

ENOKI, K. 1955. The Origin of the White Huns or Hephtalites. *EW*, N.S. 6, No. 3.

——. 1959. On the Nationality of the Ephtalites. *Memoirs of the Research Department of the Toyo Bunko*, Vol. 18.

FLEET, J.E. 1888. Inscriptions of the Early Gupta Kings and their Successors. *CII*, Vol. 3.

FRYE, R.N. 1984. The History of Ancient Iran. *Handbuch der Altertumwissenschaft*, 3. Abt., 7. Teil. Munich.

GAFUROV, B.G. 1972. *Tajiki. Drevneyshaya, drevnyaya i srednevekovaya istoriya*. Ed. by B.A. Litvinsky. Moscow.

GHIRSHMAN, R. 1948. Les Chionites-Hephtalites. *MDAFA*, Vol. 13. Cairo.

GÖBL, R. 1967. *Dokumente zur Geschichte der iranischen Hunnen in Baktrien und Indien*, Vols. 1-4. Wiesbaden.

——. 1971. *Sasanian Numismatics*. Brunswick.

GODARD, A.; HACKIN, J. 1928. *Les antiquités bouddhiques de Bamiyan. MDAFA*, Vol. 2.

GRIGNASCHI, M. 1980. Le chute de l'empire hephtalite. *Acta Ant. Hung.*, Vol. 28, fasc. 1-4.

GUPTA, P.L. 1974. *The Imperial Guptas*, Vol. 1. Benares.

HACKIN, J.; CARL, J. 1933. Nouvelles recherches archéologiques à Bamiyan. *MDAFA*, Vol. 3.

HARMATTA, J. 1969. Late Bactrian Inscriptions. *Acta Ant. Hung.*, Vol. 17.

HIGUCHI, T. 1983-84. *Bamiyan*, Vols. 1-3. Kyoto.

HUI-LI. 1959. *The Life of Hsuan-tsang*. Compiled by the monk Hui-li. Peking.

KLIMBURG, S.D. 1987. *The Kingdom of Bāmiyān. Buddhist Art and Culture of the Hindukush*. Naples/Rome.

KRUGLIKOVA, I.T. 1976. Nastennye rospisi Dilberjina. In: *Drevnyaya Baktriya*, Vol. 1. Moscow.

——. 1979. Nastennye rospisi v pomeshchenii 16 severovostochnogo kultovogo kompleksa Dilberjina. In: *Drevnyaya Baktriya*, Vol. 2. Moscow.

KUWAYAMA, S. 1987. Literary Evidence for Dating the Colosse in Bamiyan. Orientalia Josephi Tucci Memorial dicata. (*Serie Orientale Roma*, 61/2.) Rome.

LE BERRE, M.; SCHLUMBERGER, D. 1964. Remparts de Bactres. *MDAFA*, Vol. 19.

LITVINSKY, B.A. 1976. Problemy etnicheskoy istorii drevney i srednevekovoy Fergany. In: *Istoriya i kul'tura narodov Azii. Drevnost' i srednie veka*. Moscow.

——. 1981. Kalai-Kafirnigan. Problems in the Religion and Art of Early Mediaeval Tokharistan. *EW*, Vol. 30.

LITVINSKY, B.A.; SOLOV'EV, V.S. 1985. *Srednevekovaya kul'tura Tokharistana v svete raskopok v Vakhshskoy doline*. Moscow.

——. 1989. L'art du Toxaristan à l'époque du Haut Moyen Age (monuments non bouddhiques). *AA*, Vol. 11.

LIVSHITS V.A. 1969. K otkrytiyu baktriyskikh nadpisey na Kara-tepe. In: *Buddiyskie peshchery v Starom Termeze. Osnovnye itogi rabot 1963-1964 gg*. Moscow.

MAENCHEN-HELFEN, O.J. 1959. The Ethnic Name Hun. In: *Studia Serica Bernard Karlgren dedicata*. Copenhagen.

MAJUMDAR, R.S. 1954. The Expansion and Consolidation of the Empire. *The Classical Age. The History and Culture of the Indian People*, Vol. 3. Bombay.

MARQUART, J. 1901. *Ērānšahr nach der Geographie des Ps. Moses Xorenac̕i*. Berlin.

——. 1938. *Wehrot und Arang. Untersuchungen zur mythischen und geschichtlichen Landeskunde von Ostiran*. Leiden.

MARSHAK, B.I. 1971. K voprosu o vostochnykh protivnikakh Irana v V v. *Strany i narody Vostoka*, Vol. 10. Moscow.

——. 1986. *Silberschätze des Orients Metallkunst des 3-13. Jahrhunderts und ihre Kontinuität*. Leipzig.

MARSHALL, J. 1951. *Taxila*, Vol. 1. Oxford.

MILLER, R.A. 1959. *Accounts of the Western Nations in the History of the Northern Chou Dynasty*. Berkeley/Los Angeles.

MOHL, J. 1868. *Le livre des rois par Abou'l Kasim Firdousi. Publié, traduit et commenté*, Vol. 6. Paris.

MORAVCSIK, G. 1958. *Byzantinoturcica. Die byzantinischen Quellen der Geschichte der Türkvölker*, 2. Aufl. Berlin.

NÖLDEKE, T.; TABARI. 1973. *Geschichte der Perser und Araber zur Zeit der Sasaniden. Aus der arabischen Chronik des Tabari übersetzt und mit ausführlichen Erläuterungen und Ergänzungen versehn von T. Nöldeke*. Reprint. Leiden.

PATHAK, R.B. 1917. New Light on the Gupta Era and Mihirakula. In: *Commemorative Essays Presented to R.G. Bhandarkar*. Poona.

PIGULEVSKAYA, N.V. 1941. *Siriyskie istochniki po istorii narodov SSSR*. Moscow/ Leningrad.

PUGACHENKOVA, G.A. 1976. K poznaniyu antichnoy i rannesrednevekovoy arkhitektury Severnogo Afganistana. In: *Drevnyaya Baktriya*, Vol. 1. Moscow.

——. 1987. *Iz khudozhestvennoy sokrovishchnitsy Srednego Vostoka*. Tashkent.

ROWLAND, B. 1946. The Dating of the Sasanian Paintings at Bamiyan and Dukhtar-i-Nushirvan. *Bulletin of the Iranian Institute*, Vols. 6-7.

RTVELADZE, E.V. 1973. Novye arkheologicheskie dannye k istorii gorodishcha Budrach. *Istoria material'noy kul'tury Uzbekistana*, Vol. 18. Tashkent.

——. 1983. K istorii yuzhnogo Uzbekistana v eftalitskoe vremya. In: *Baktriya-Tokharistan na drevnem i srednevekovom Vostoke*. Moscow.

SAYILI, A. 1982. The Nationality of the Ephtalites. *Türk tarih-kurumu*. Ankara.

SCHWARZ, P. 1933. Bemerkungen zu den arabischen Nachrichten über Balkh. *Oriental Studies in Honour of C.E. Pavry*. London.

SEDOV, A.V. 1987. *Kobadian na poroge rannego srednevekov'ya*. Moscow.

SHARMA, T.R. 1978. *Personal and Geographical Names in the Gupta*. Delhi.

SHISHKIN, V.A. 1940. K istoricheskoy topografii Starogo Termeza. In: *Termezskaya arkheologicheskaya kompleksnaya ekspeditsiya 1936 g. (Trudy Uz FAN*, series 1, Vol. 2.)

SHMIDT, A.E. 1958. Materialy po istorii Sredney Azii i Irana. In: *Uchenye zapiski Instituta vostokovedeniya AN SSSR*, Vol. 10. Moscow/Leningrad.

SINGH, N.N.; BANNERJI, A.C. 1954. *Istoriya Indii*. Trans. from English. Moscow.

STEBLIN-KAMENSKIY, I.M. 1981. Baktriisky yazyk. In: *Osnovy iranskogo yazykoznania. Sredneiranskie yazyki*. Moscow.

TADDEI, M. 1968. Tapa Sardar. First preliminary report. *EW*, Vol. 18.

——. 1974. A Note on the Parinirvana Buddha at Tapa Sardar (Ghazni, Afghanistan). *South Asian Archaeology*. London.

TARZI, Z. 1977. *L'architecture et le décor rupestre des grottes de Bāmiyān*, Vols. 1-2. Paris.

TER-MKRTICHYAN L.K. 1979. *Armyanskie istochniki o Sredney Azii V-VII vv*. Moscow.

TREVER, K.V. 1954. Kushany, khionity i eftality po armyanskim istochnikam IV-VII vv. (K istorii narodov Sredney Azii.) *SA*, Vol. 21.

YAKUBOV, Y.Y. 1985. Serebrannaya chasha iz Lyakhsha. In: *Khudojestvennye pamyatniki i problemy kul'tury Vostoka*. Leningrad.

YANG HSÜAN-CHIH, 1984. *A Record of Buddhist Monasteries in Lo-Yang*. Translated by Yi-t'ung Wang. Princeton.

YOUNG, R.S. 1955. The South Wall of Balkh-Bactra. *American Journal of Archaeology*, Vol. 59.

ZAHARIAS OF MYTELENE 1891. Translated by F. Hamilton and R.W. Brooks. London.

CHAPTER 7

ALTEKAR, A.S.; MAJUMDAR, R.C. (eds.). 1946. The Vākātaka-Gupta Age (circa 200-550 A.D.). *New History of the Indian People*, Vol. 6. Reprint, 1954. Benares.

BAILEY, H.W. 1932. Iranian Studies. *BSOS*, Vol. 6.

——. 1954. L'Harahuna. In: *Asiatica, Festschrift Friedrich Weller*, pp. 13-21. Leipzig.

BANERJI, R.D. 1908. Notes on Indo-Scythian Coinage. *Journal of Asiatic Society of Bengal* (N.S.), Vol. 4.

BARTHOLD, W. 1928. *Turkestan Down to the Mongol Invasion*. Reprint, 1981. Karachi.

BATAILLE, G. 1928. Notes sur la numismatique des Koushans et des Koushan-Shahs Sassanides. *Arethuse*, Fasc. 18.

BEAL, S. 1969. *Si-yu-ki, Buddhist Records of the Western World. Translated from the Chinese of Hiuen Tsiang (A.D. 629)*, Vols. 1-2. London-Delhi. (First published in 1884.)

BELENITSKIY, A.M. 1950. Istoriko-geograficheskiy ocherk Khuttalya s drevneyshikh vremen do X v. n.ê. (*Materialy i issledovanya po arkheologii SSSR*, Vol. 15.) Moscow/Leningrad.

AL-BIRUNI. 1973. *Canon of the Mas'ūd*, Books 1-5. Introduction, translation and notes in Russian by P.G. Bulgakov and B.A. Rozenfeld with the collaboration of M.X. Rozhanskaya (translation and notes) and A. Akhmedov. Tashkent.

BISWAS, A. 1973. *The Political History of the Hunas in India*. New Delhi.

BIVAR, A.D.H. 1956. The Kushano-Sasanian Coin Series. *JNSI*, Vol. 18.

———. 1971. Hayāṭila. *The Encyclopaedia of Islam*, new ed., Vol. 3. Leiden-London.

BOSWORTH, C.E. 1981. The Rules of Chaghāniān in Early Islamic Times. *Iran*, Vol. 19. London.

BOSWORTH, C.E.; CLAUSON, G. 1965. Al-Xwārazmī on the Peoples of Central Asia. *JRAS*, Parts 1-2.

BOSWORTH, C.E.; DOERFER, G. 1978. *Khaladj. The Encyclopaedia of Islam*, new ed., Vol. 4. Leiden.

CHATTOPADHYAY, B. 1979. *The Age of the Kushanas*. Calcutta.

CHHABRA, B.; GAI, G.S. (eds.). 1981. Inscription of the Early Guptas. *CII*, Vol. 3. New Delhi.

CUNNINGHAM, A. 1893-94. *Later Indo-Scythians*. Reprinted from *NC*. Reprint, 1962. Benares.

DANI, A.H. 1964. Sibi – A Forgotten People of Sind. *Journal of Asiatic Society of Pakistan (now Bangladesh)*, Vol. 9, No. 1.

———. 1968-69. Excavation at Andandheri. *Ancient Pakistan*, Vol. 4. Peshawar.

———. 1986. *The Historic City of Taxila*. Tokyo.

DAVIDOVICH, E.A.; ZEIMAL, E.V. 1980. Denezhnoe khozyaystvo Sredney Azii v perekhodniy period ot drevnosti k srednevekov'yu (k tipologii feodalizma). In: *Blizhniy i Sredniy Vostok. Tovarno-denezhnye otnoshcheniya pri feodalizme*. Moscow.

FRYE, R.N. 1965. Ghalzay. *The Encyclopaedia of Islam*, new ed., Vol. 2. Leiden/London.

———. 1979. Napki Malka and the Kushano-Sasanians. In: *Islamic Iran and Central Asia (7th-12th centuries)*. London.

GHIRSHMAN, R. 1954. *Iran from the Earliest Times to the Islamic Period*. Harmondsworth.

GÖBL, R. 1967. *Dokumente zur Geschichte der iranischen Hunnen in Baktrien und Indien*, Vols. 1-4. Wiesbaden.

———. 1976. A Catalogue of Coins from Butkara I (Swat, Pakistan). *IsMEO*.

HARMATTA, J. 1969. Late Bactrian Inscriptions. *Acta Ant. Hung.*, Vol. 17.

———. 1984. Kidara and the Kidarite Huns in Kašmir. In: J. Harmatta (ed.), *From Hecataeus to Al-Huwàrizmī*, series 1, Vol. 3. Budapest.

HERZFELD, E. 1924. *Paikuli: Monument and Inscription of the Early History of the Sassanian Empire*. 2 vols. Berlin.

——. 1930. Kushano-Sassanian Coins. *Memoirs of the Archaeological Survey of India*, Vol. 38. Calcutta.

Hudūd al-ᶜālam. 1970. *The Regions of the World. A Persian Geography 372 A.H. - 982 A.D.* Translated and explained by V. Minorsky, 2nd ed. London.

LITVINSKY, B.A.; SOLOV'EV, V.S. 1985. *Srednevekovaya kul'tura Tokharistana v svete raskopok v Vakhshskoy doline*. Moscow.

MANDEL'SHTAM, A.M. 1964. Srednyaya Aziya v VI-VII vv. n.ê. In: *Istoriya tajikskogo naroda*, Vol. 2/1.

MARKWART, J. 1938. *Wehrot und Arang. Untersuchungen zur mytischen und geschichtlichen Landeskunde von Ostiran*. Leiden.

MARQUART, J. 1901. *Ērānšahr nach der Geographie des Ps. Moses Xorenaᶜi*. Berlin.

——. 1914. Über das Volkstum der Komanen. In: W. Bang and J. Marquart, *Osttürkische Dialekstudien*. Berlin.

MARSHALL, J. 1951. *Taxila*, Vols. 1-3. Cambridge.

MARTIN, M.F.C. 1937. Coins of the Kidara Kushanas. *Journal of Asiatic Society of Bengal, Numismatic Supplement*, Vol. 47, pp. 23-50.

McGOVERN, N.M. 1939. *The Early Empire of Central Asia*. New York.

MINORSKY, V. 1940. The Turkish Dialect of Khalaj. *BSOS*, Vol. 10. London.

MOHL, J. 1868. *Le Livre des Rois par Abou'l-Kasim Firdousi*. Published, translated and annotated by J. Mohl, Vol. 6. Paris.

NÖLDEKE, T.; TABARI. 1973. *Geschichte der Perser und Araber zur Zeit der Sasaniden. Aus der arabischen Chronik des Tabari übersetzt und mit ausführlichen Erläuterungen und Ergänzungen versehn von T. Nöldeke*. Reprint. Leiden.

PARGITER, F.E. 1913. *Dynasties of the Kali Age*. London.

RAHMAN, A. 1979. *The Last Two Dynasties of the Śahis*. Islamabad.

RAYCHAUDHURI, H.C. 1953. *Political History of Ancient India*, 6th ed. Calcutta.

RTVELADZE, E.V. 1983. K istorii Yuzhnogo Uzbekistana v eftalitskoe vremya. In: *Baktria-Tokharistan na drevnem i srednevekovom Vostoke*. Moscow.

SASTRI, N.K.A. (ed.). 1957. *A Comprehensive History of India*, Vol. 2: *The Mauryas and Satavahanas, 325 B.C. - A.D. 300*. Bombay/Calcutta/Madras.

SIRCAR, D.C. 1939. *Select Inscriptions Bearing on Indian History and Civilisation*, Vol. 1. University of Calcutta.

SMITH, V.A. 1906. *Catalogue of Coins in the Indian Museum, Calcutta*, Vol. 1. Oxford.

STEIN, A. 1900-1. *Kalhana's Rajatarangini*. English translation. Reprint, 1979. Delhi.

Tārikh-e Sistān. 1976. Translated by M. Gold. The Literary and Historical Texts from Iran, *Serie Orientale*, Vol. 48.

VOGEL, J.-P. 1921-22. Shorkot Inscription. In: *Epigraphia Indica*, Vol. 16.

WHITEHEAD, R.B. 1914. *Catalogue of Coins in the Punjab Museum, Lahore*, Vol. 1. Oxford.

ZEIMAL, E.V. 1983. *Drevnye monety Tajikistana*. Dushanbe.

CHAPTER 8

ALLAN, J. 1975. *Catalogue of the Coins of the Gupta Dynasty and of Śaśaṅka, King of Gauda*. New Delhi.

ALTEKAR, A.S. 1957. *The Coinage of the Gupta Empire*. Benares.

BASHAM, A.L. 1975. *The Wonder that was India*. Calcutta.

BROWN, P. 1942. *Indian Architecture, Buddhist and Hindu Periods*. Bombay.

CHATTOPADHYAYA, B.D. 1976. Origin of the Rajputs: The Political, Economic and Social Processes in Early Medieval Rajasthan. *The Indian Historical Review*, Vol. 3, No. 1.

DAS GUPTA, S.N. 1923-49. *History of Indian Philosophy*. 4 vols. Cambridge.

DEVAHUTI, D. 1983. *Harṣa: A Political Study*. Delhi.

ELIOT, C. 1922. *Hinduism and Buddhism*. 3 vols. London.

FLEET, J.F. 1970. *Inscriptions of the Early Gupta Kings and their Successors*. Benares.

GILES, H.A. 1959. *The Travels of Fa-hien*. London.

GOKHALE, B.G. *Samudra Gupta and his Times*. Bombay.

GOYAL, S.R. 1967. *A History of the Imperial Guptas*. Allahabad.

HAZRA, R.C. 1975. *Studies in the Purāṇic Records on Hindu Rites and Customs*. Delhi.

KEITH, A.B. 1928. *History of Sanskrit Literature*. Oxford.

MAITY, S.K. 1957. *The Economic Life of Northern India in the Gupta Period*. Calcutta.

MAJUMDAR, R.C. (ed.). 1970. *The Classical Age*. Bombay.

ROWLAND, B. 1970. *The Art and Architecture of India. Buddhist/Hindu/Jain*. Harmondsworth.

SHARMA, R.S. 1968. *Aspects of Political Ideas and Institutions in Ancient India*. Delhi.

SINHA, B.P. 1954. *The Decline of the Kingdom of Magadha*. Patna.

THAKUR, U. 1967. *Hūṇas in India*. Benares.

THAPAR, R. 1966. *A History of India*, Vol. 1. Harmondsworth.

WATTERS, T. 1961. *On Yuan Chwang's Travels in India*. Delhi.

CHAPTER 9

AL-BALADHURI. 1866. *Liber Expugnationis Regionum auctore Imâmo Ahmed ibn Jahjâ ibn Djâbir al-Belâdsorî*. Ed. M.J. de Goeje, Lugduni Batavorum.

——. 1924. *The Origin of the Islamic State, being a translation from the Arabic of the Kitab Futuh al-Buldan of Iman Abu-l-Abbas Ahmad ibn Jabir Balādhuri*. Translated by F.G. Murgotten. New York.

BALᶜAMI. 1874. *Chronique de Abou Djafar Mohammed ben Djarir ben Yezid Tabari, traduite sur la version persane d'Abou-ᶜAli Mohammed Belᶜami par H. Zotenberg*, Vol. 4. Paris.

——. MS 33, 4226, 6095, 7466, 11273 – Balᶜami, Abū ᶜAli Muḥammad, Tārīkh-i Tabarī. (These manuscripts are in the possession of the Institute of Oriental Studies of the Academy of Sciences of Uzbekistan.)

BARTOLD, V.V. 1965. Khorezm (Chorasmia). *Sochineniya*, Vol. 3. Moscow.

——. 1971. K istorii persidskogo eposa. *Sochineniya*, Vol. 7. Moscow.

BICHURIN, N.Y. 1950. *Sobranie svedeniy o narodakh, obitavshikh v Sredney Azii v drevnie vremena*, Vol. 2. Moscow.

BICKERMAN, E.J. 1967. The Zoroastrian Calendar. *Archiv Orientální*, Vol. 35. Prague.

BIRUNI, A. 1957. *Pamyatniki minuvshikh pokoleniy.* Translation and notes by M.A. Sal'e. Selected Works. Tashkent.

——. 1966. *Delimitation of Areas for Calculating Distances between Settlements (Geodesy).* Research, translation and notes in Russian by P.G. Bulgakov. Selected Works, Vol. 3. Tashkent.

——. 1973. *The Canon of Mas'ūd.* Books 1-5. Introduction, translation and notes in Russian by P.G. Bulgakov and B.A. Rozenfeld with the collaboration of M.X. Rozhanskaya (translation and notes) and A. Akhmedov. Selected Works, Vol. 5, Ch. 1. Tashkent.

BOLSHAKOV, O.G. 1973. Gorod v kontse VIII nachale XIII v. In: *Rannesrednevekoviy gorod Sredney Azii.* Leningrad.

D'YAKONOV, M.M. 1951. Obraz Siyavusha v sredneaziatskoy mifologii. *Kratkie soobshcheniya Instituta Istorii material'noy kul'tury*, Vol. 10. Moscow/Leningrad.

——. 1956. *Istorya Midii ot drevneshikh vremen do kontsa IV veka do n.ê.* Moscow/Leningrad.

——. 1961. *Ocherk istorii drevnego Irana.* Moscow.

GAFUROV, B.G. 1972. *Tajiki. Drevneyshaya, drevnyaya i srednevekovaya istoriya.* B.A. Litvinsky (ed.). Moscow.

GUDKOVA, A.V. 1964. *Tok-kala.* Tashkent.

GUDKOVA, A.V.; LIVSHITS, V.A. 1967. Novye Khorezmiyskie nadpisi iz nekropolya Tok-Kaly i problema 'Khorezmiyskoy ery'. *Vestnik Karakalpakskogo filiala Akademii Nauk Uzbekskoy SSR*, No. 1. Nukus.

HARMATTA, J. 1957. The Parthian Parchment from Dura-Europos. *Acta Ant. Hung.*, Vol. 5/2.

HENNING, W.B. 1965. The Choresmian Documents. *Asia Major*, new series, Vol. 9/2, pp. 166-79; Vol. 11, Part 2. London.

HERTEL, J. 1924. *Die Zeit Zoroasters.* Leipzig.

HERZFELD, E. 1935. *Archaeological History of Iran.* London.

——. 1941. *Iran in the Ancient East.* London/New York.

——. 1947. *Zoroaster and his World*, Vol. 1. Princeton.

IBN AL-ATHIR, M. 1301 A.H. (A.D. 1883-1884). *Ta'rikh 'al-Kāmil'*, Part 4. Cairo.

Istorya Turkmenskoy SSR. 1957. Part 1, Book 1. Ashkhabad.

'Koy-Krylgan-Kala – Pamyatnik kul'tury drevnego Khorezma'. 1967. *Trudy Khorezmskoy arkheologo-etnograficheskoy ekspeditsii*, Vol. 5. Moscow.

LIVSHITS, V.A. 1962. *Yuridicheskie dokumenty i pis'ma s gory Mug.* Moscow.

——. 1968. The Khwarezmian Calendar and the Eras of Ancient Chorasmia. *Acta Ant. Hung.*, Vol. 16/1-4.

——. 1970. Khorezmiyskiy kalendar' i ery drevnego Khorezma. *Palestinskiy Sbornik*, Vol. 21 (84). Leningrad.

——. 1984. Ch. 6. In: *Toprak-kala. Dvorets.* Moscow.

LUKONIN, V.G. 1961. *Iran v epokhu pervykh Sasanidov.* Leningrad.

——. 1969. *Kul'tura sasanidskogo Irana.* Moscow.

MASSON, V.M. 1966. Khorezm i kushany. *Epigrafika Vostoka*, Vol. 17. Moscow/Leningrad.

NERAZIK, E.E. 1966. *Sel'skie poselenya afrigidskogo Khorezma.* Moscow.

———. 1976. *Sel'skoe zhilishche v Khorezme (I-XIV vv.).* Moscow.

———. 1982. Chs. 1 and 6. In: *Gorodishche Toprak-kala.* Moscow.

NÖLDEKE, T.; TABARI. 1973. *Geschichte der Perser und Araber zur Zeit der Sasaniden. Aus der arabischen Chronik des Tabari übersetzt und mit ausführlichen Erläuterungen und Ergänzungen versehn von T. Nöldeke.* Reprint. Leiden.

NYBERG, H.S. 1938. *Die Religionen des alten Iran.* Leipzig.

PIGULEVSKAYA, N.V. 1956. *Goroda Irana v rannem srednvekov'ye.* Moscow/Leningrad.

RAPOPORT, Y.A. 1971. Iz istorii religii drevnego Khorezma. *Trudy Khorezmskoy arkheologo-etnograficheskoy ekspeditsii,* Vol. 6. Moscow.

———. 1984. Chs. 1, 3 and Conclusion. In: *Toprak-kala. Dvorets.* Moscow.

RTVELADZE, E.V. 1980. Po povodu dinasticheskikh svyazey Khorezma i Chaganiana v rannee srednevekov'ye. *Vestnik Karakalpakskogo filiala Akademii Nauk Uzbekskoy SSR,* No. 1. Nukus.

SMIRNOVA, O.I. 1963. *Katalog monet s gorodishcha Penjikent.* Moscow.

SPRENGLING, M. 1953. *Third Century Iran, Sapor and Kartir.* Chicago.

STRUVE, V.V. 1948. Rodina zoroastrizma. *Sovetskoe vostokovedenie,* Vol. 5. Moscow/Leningrad.

———. 1949. Vosstanie v Margiane pri Darii I. *Vetsnik Drevney istorii,* No. 2. Moscow.

AL-TABARI. 1879-89. *Annales quos scripsit Abu Djafar Mohamed ibn Djarir al-Tabari, cum aliis.* Ed. M.J. De Goeje. Series 2. Lugduni Batavorum.

TOLSTOV, S.P. 1948a. *Drevniy Khorezm. Opyt istoriko-arkheologicheskogo issledovaniya.* Moscow.

———. 1948b. *Po sledam drevnekhorezmiyskoy tsivilizatsii.* Moscow/Leningrad.

———. 1962. *Po drenim del'tam Oksa i Yaksarta.* Moscow.

VAYNBERG, B.I. 1977. *Monety drevnego Khorezma.* Moscow.

WIDENGREN, G. 1961. *Die Religionen Irans.* In: C.M. von Schröder (ed.), *Die Religionen der Menschheit,* Vol. 14. Stuttgart.

YAGODIN, V.N.; KHOJAIOV, T.K. 1970. *Nekropol' drevnego Mizdakhkana.* Tashkent.

CHAPTER 10

AL'BAUM, L.I. 1975. *Zhivopis' Afrasiaba.* Tashkent.

AZARPAY, G. 1981. *Sogdian Painting. The Pictorial Epic in Oriental Art.* Contributions by A.M. Belenitskiy, B.I. Marshak and M. J. Dresden. Berkeley/Los Angeles/London.

BELENITSKIY, A.M. 1980. *Mittelasien. Kunst der Sogden.* Leipzig.

BELENITSKIY, A.M.; MARSHAK, B.I.; RASPOPOVA, V.I. 1981. Sogdiyskiy gorod v nachale srednikh vekov. *SA,* No. 2.

BERNSHTAM, L.N. 1952. *Istoriko-arkheologicheskie ocherki Tsentral'nogo Tyan'Shanya i Pamiro-Alaya. Materialy i issledovaniya po arkheologii SSSR,* Vol. 26. Moscow/Leningrad.

BILALOV, A.I. 1980. *Iz istorii irrigatsii Ustrushany.* Dushanbe.

BRYKINA, G.A. 1971. Nekotorye voprosy ideologii i kul'turnye svyazi naseleniya yugozapadnykh predgoriy Fergany v V-VI vv, based on material from the Kaigarach estate. In: *Tezisy dokladov, posvyashchennykh itogam polevykh arkheologicheskikh issledovaniy v SSSR v 1970 gody/arkheologicheskie sektsii.* Tbilisi.

BULATOVA-LEVINA, V.A. 1961. Buddiyskiy khram v Kuve. *SA*, No. 3.

BURYAKOV, Y.F. 1975. *Istoricheskaya topografiya drevnikh gorodov Tashkentskogo oazisa – Istoriko-arkheologitseskiy ocherk Chacha i Ilaka.* Tashkent.

——. 1982. *Genezis i etapy razvitiya gorodskoy kul'tury Tashkentskogo oazisa.* Tashkent.

CZEGLÉDY, K. 1980. Zur Geschichte der Hephthaliten. *Acta Ant. Hung.*, Vol. 28.

DAVIDOVICH, E.A. 1958. Raskpoki zamka Kalai Bolo. In: *Materialy i issledovaniya po arkheologii SSSR*, Vol. 66. Moscow.

——. 1979. *Klady drevnikh i srednevekovykh monet Tajikistana.* Moscow.

ENOKI, K. 1955. Sogdiana and the Hsiung-nu. *Central Asiatic Journal*, Vol. 1/1.

——. 1959. On the Nationality of the Hephthalites. In: *Memoirs of the Research Department of the Toyo Bunka*, Vol. 18. Tokyo.

FILANOVICH, M.I. 1983. *Zarozhdenie i razvitie goroda i gorodskoy kul'tury.* Tashkent.

——. 1985. In: *Drevneyshie gosudarstva Kavkaza i Sredney Azii*. Moscow.

GAFUROV, B.G. 1972. *Tajiki. Drevneyshaya, drevnyaya i srednevekovaya istoriya.* B.A. Litvinsky (ed.). Moscow.

GERSHEVICH, I. 1969. Amber at Persepolis. *Studia Classica et Orientalia A. Pagliaro oblata*, Vol. 1. Rome.

——. 1976. Appendix (to Sims-Williams). *Indo-Iranian Journal*, Vol. 18.

GIBB, H.A.R. 1923. *The Arab Conquests in Central Asia.* New York.

GORBUNOVA, N.G. 1977. Poseleniya Fergany pervykh vekov nashey ery/nekotorye itogi issledovaniya. *SA*, No. 3, pp. 107-20.

——. 1979. Itogi issledovaniya arkheologicheskikh pamyatnikov Ferganskoy oblasti – k istorii kul'tury Fergany. *SA*, No. 3, pp. 16-31.

——. 1985. In: *Drevneyshie gosudarstva Kavkaza i Sredney Azii*, pp. 311-16. Moscow.

HARMATTA, J. 1971. Eine neue Quelle zur Geschichte der Seidenstrasse. *Jahrbuch für Wissenschaftsgeschichte*, Vol. 2.

HENNING, W.B. 1948. The Date of the Sogdian Ancient Letters. *BSOAS*, Vol. 12/3-4.

——. 1965. A Sogdian God. *BSOAS*, Vol. 28/2.

HUMBACH, H. 1975. Vayu, Śiva und der Spiritus Vivens im ost-iranischen Synkretismus. *Acta Iranica, Monumentum H.S. Nyberg.* Leiden.

——. 1980. Die sogdischen Inschriftenfunde vom oberen Indus (Pakistan). *Allgemeine und vergleichende Archäologie-Beitrage*, Vol. 2. Munich.

Istoriya Uzbekskoy SSR, Vol. 1. A967. Tashkent.

KLYASHTORNY, S.G. 1964. *Drevnetyurkskie runicheskie pamyatniki kak istochnik po istorii Sredney Azii.* Moscow.

KLYASHTORNY, S.G.; LIVSHITS, V.A. 1971. Sogdiyskaya nadpis' iz Buguta. *Strany i narody Vostoka*, Vol. 10. Moscow.

——. 1972. The Sogdian Inscription of Bugut Revised. *AOH*, Vol. 26/1.

LITVINSKY, B.A. 1960. Saki, kotorye za Sogdom. *Trudy AN Tajikskoy SSR*, Vol. 120. Stalinabad.

———. 1968. *Outline History of Buddhism in Central Asia*. Moscow.

———. 1976. Problemy etnicheskoy istorii drevney i rannesrednevekovoy Fergany. In: *Istorya i kul'tura narodov Sredney Azii – drevnost' i srednie veka*, pp. 49-65. Moscow.

LIVSHITS, V.A. 1968. Pis'mennost' drevney Fergany. *Narody Azii i Afriki*, No. 6.

———. 1981. Sogdiyskiy yazyk. Vvedenie. In: *Osnovy iranskogo yazykoznaniya. Sredneiranskie yazyki*. Moscow.

LIVSHITS, V.A.; KHROMOV, A.L. 1981. Sogdyskiy yazyk. In: *Osnovy iranskogo yazykoznanya. Sredneiranskie yazyki*. Moscow.

LIVSHITS, V.A.; LUKONIN, V.G. 1964. Srednepersidskie i sogdiyskie nadpisi na serebryanykh sosudakh. *Vetsnik Drevney Istorii*, No. 3. Moscow.

MARQUART, J. 1901. *Ērānšahr nach der Geographie des Ps. Moses Xorenacⁱi*. Berlin.

MARSHAK, B.I. 1971. *Sogdiyskoe serebro*. Moscow.

NEGMATOV, N.N. 1956. Geografy IX-XII vv. o Khojente i ego oblasti. *Izvestiya AN Tajikskoy SSR. Otdelenie obshchestvennykh nauk*, Vol. 8. Dushanbe.

———. 1957. *Ustrushana v drevnosti i rannem sredne-vekov'e*. Stalinabad.

———. 1977. Reznoe panno dvortsa afshinov Ustruschany. In: *Pamyatniki kul'tury. Novye otkrytiya. 1976*, pp. 353-62. Moscow.

———. 1984. Bozhestvenniy i demonicheskiy panteon Ustrushany i ikh indiyskie paralleli. In: *Drevnie kul'tury Sredney Azii i Indii*, pp. 146-64. Leningrad.

NEGMATOV, N.N.; KHMEL'NITSKIY, S.G. 1966. *Srednevekoviy Shakhristan*. Dushanbe.

NEGMATOV, N.N.; PULATOV, U.P.; KHMEL'NITSKIY, S.G. 1973. *Urtakurgan i Tirmizaktepa*. Dushanbe.

NEGMATOV, N.N.; SOKOLOVSKIY, V.M. 1975. 'Kapitalliyskaya volchitsa' v Tajikistane i legendy Evrazii. In: *Pamyatniki kul'tury. Novye otkrytiya. 1974*, pp. 438-58. Moscow.

———. 1977. Rekonstruktsiya i syuzhetnaya interpretatsiya rospisey malogo zala dvortsa afshinov Ustrushany. In: *Rannesrednevekovaya kul'tura Sredney Azii i Kazakhstana*. Dushanbe.

ORANSKIY, I.M. 1960. *Vvedenie v iranskuyu filologiyu*. Moscow.

———. 1979. *Iranskiye yazyki v istoricheskom osveshchenii*. Moscow.

PULATOV, U.P. 1975. *Chilkhujra*. Dushanbe.

SALTOVSKAYA, E.D. 1971. *Severo-Zapadnaya Fergana v drevnosti i rannem srednevekov'e*. Degree thesis abstract. Dushanbe.

SHISHKIN, V.A. 1963. *Varakhsha*. Moscow.

SIMS-WILLIAMS, N. 1976. The Sogdian Fragments of the British Library. *Indo-Iranian Journal*, Vol. 18.

SMIRNOVA, O.I. 1981. *Svodniy katalog sogdiyskikh monet. Bronza*. Moscow.

SNELLGROVE, D.; RICHARDSON, H. 1968. *A Cultural History of Tibet*. New York/ Washington.

Sogdiyskie dokumenty s gory Mug, 1-3. 1962-63. Moscow.

Sogdiyskie dokumenty s gory Mug. 1962. Legal documents and letters. Reading, translation and commentaries by V.A. Livshits. Moscow.

TOLSTOV, S.P. 1948. *Drevniy Khorezm*. Moscow.

VORONINA, V.L.; NEGMATOV, N.N. 1975. Otkrytie Ustruschany. In: *Nauka i chelovechestvo. Mezhdunarodniy ezhegodnik 1975*, pp. 50-71. Moscow.

YERUSALIMSKAYA, A.A. 1972. K slozheniyu shkoly khudozhestvennogo shelkotkachestva v Sogde. *Srednyaya Azya i Iran, Sbornik statey*. Leningrad.

ZEIMAL, E.V. 1983. *Drevnie monety Tajikistana*. Dushanbe.

CHAPTER 11

ASMUSSEN, J.P. 1965. X^uāstvānīft. Studies in Manichaeism. *Acta Theologica Danica*, Vol. 7. Copenhagen.

BACOT, J.; THOMAS, F.W.; TOUSSAINT, C. 1940-46. *Documents de Touen-houang relatifs à l'Histoire du Tibet*. Paris.

BAGCHI, P.C. 1981. *India and China*, new ed. Calcutta.

BAILEY, H.W. 1931. The Word 'But' in Iranian. *BSOS*, Vol. 6/2, pp. 282-3.

——. 1958. Language of the Saka. In: *Handbuch der Orientalistik. 1. Abteilung, 4. Band, Iranistik, 1. Abschnitt. Linguistik*. Leiden.

——. 1968. *Saka Documents*, text volume. London.

——. 1982. *The Culture of the Sakas in Ancient Iranian Khotan*. New York.

——. 1985. *Indo-Scythian Studies being Khotanese Texts*, Vol. 4/7. Cambridge.

BOYER, M.A; RAPSON, E.J.; SENART, E; NOBLE, P.S. 1920-29. *Kharoṣṭi Inscriptions, Discovered by Sir Aurel Stein in Chinese Turkestan*, Parts 1-3. Oxford.

BROUGH, J. 1962. *The Gandhāri Dharmapada*. London.

BURROW, T. 1937. *The Language of the Kharoṣṭi Documents from Chinese Turkestan*. Cambridge.

——. 1940. *A Translation of the Kharoṣṭi Documents from Chinese Turkestan*. London.

BUSSAGLI, M. 1963. *La peinture de l'Asie Centrale*. Geneva.

CHAVANNES, E. 1903. *Documents sur les Tou-kiue (Turcs) occidentaux. Recueillis et commentés, suivi de notes additionnelles. (Présenté à l'Académie Impériale des Sciences de St-Pétersbourg le 23 Août 1900.)* St Petersburg.

——. 1913. *Documents chinois découverts par Sir Aurel Stein*. Oxford.

DABBS, J.A. 1963. *History of the Discovery and Exploration of Chinese Turkestan*. The Hague.

EMMERICK, R.E. 1967. *Tibetan Texts Concerning Khotan*. London.

GAULIER, S.; JERA-BEZARD, R.; MAILLARD, M. 1976. Buddhism in Afghanistan and Central Asia, 1-3. *Iconography of Religions*, Vol. 13/14. Leiden.

GIBB, H.A.R. 1923. *The Arab Conquests in Central Asia*. New York.

GROPP, G. 1974. *Archäologische Funde aus Khotan*. Bremen.

GRÜNWEDEL, A. 1920. *Alt-Kutscha*. Berlin.

HENNING, W.B. 1977. *Selected Papers*, Vols. 1-2. (*Acta Iranica*, Vols. 14-15.) Leiden.

HOFFMANN, H. 1975. Tibet. A Handbook. *Indiana University Asian Studies Research Institute, Oriental Series*, Vol. 5. Bloomington.

——. 1990. Early and Medieval Tibet. In: D. Sinor (ed.), *The Cambridge History of Early Inner Asia*, pp. 371-99. Cambridge.

HSIA NAI. 1974. A Survey on the Persian Sassanid Silver Coins Found in China. *Kaogu Xuebao*, No. 1.

——. 1979. New Finds of Ancient Silk Fabrics in Sinkiang. In: *Essays on Archaeology of Sciences and Technology in China*, pp. 89-97. Peking.

HSÜAN-TSANG, 1985. *Records of the Western Regions*. Edited and annotated by Ji Xianlin et al. Peking.

HUANG, W.B. 1954. *Ta-li-mu Pen-di Kao-gu Ji*. Archaeological Report on the Tarim Basin. Peking.

HUNTINGTON, E. 1919. *The Pulse of Asia*, 2nd ed. Boston/New York.

JI XIANLIN; FO-TO; FO 1982. *Essays on the History of Sino-Indian Relations*. Peking.

LAUFER, B. 1919. *Sino-Iranica*. Chicago.

LE COQ, A. VON. 1922-33. *Die Buddhistische Spätantike in Mittel-Asien*. Berlin. 7 vols.

——. 1926. *Buried Treasures of Chinese Turkestan*. London.

LI, Y.H.; HSÜAN-TSANG. 1957. *A Record of the Buddhist Countries*. Peking.

LITVINSKY, B.A. (ed.) 1992. *Vostochniy Turkestan v drevnosti i rannem srednevekov'e. Etnos. Yazyki. Religii*. Moscow.

LIU, MAU-TSAI. 1958. *Die chinesischen Nachrichten zur Geschichte der Ost-Türken (T'u-küe), 1-2 (Göttinger Asiatische Forschungen)*, Vol. 10. Wiesbaden.

LÜDERS, H. 1911. *Bruchstücke Buddhistischer Dramen*. Berlin.

MAILLARD, M. 1983. *Grottes et monuments d'Asie centrale*. Paris.

MASPÉRO, H. 1953. *Les documents chinois de la troisième expédition de Sir Aurel Stein en Asie centrale*. London.

MATHER, R.B. 1959. *Biography of Lü Kuang*. Berkeley/Los Angeles.

MILLER, R.A. 1959. *Accounts of the Western Nations in the History of the Northern Chou Dynasty*. Berkeley/Los Angeles.

PELLIOT, P. 1959-73. *Notes on Marco Polo*. Vols. 1-3. Paris.

——. 1961-64. *Mission à Toumchouq*. Vols. 1-2. Bibliothèque Nationale, Paris.

——. 1967-88. *Mission à Koutcha*, Vol. 3, 4 and 8. Bibliothèque Nationale, Paris.

RAPSON E.J.; NOBLE P.S. 1929. Kings and Regnal Years. In: *Kharosthī Inscriptions*, Part 3, pp. 323-8. Oxford.

SAMOLIN, W. 1964. *East Turkestan to the Twelfth Century*. The Hague.

SIEG, E.; SIEGLING, W. 1921. *Tokharische Sprachreste*. Berlin.

SNELLGROVE, D.; RICHARDSON, H. 1968. *A Cultural History of Tibet*. New York/Washington.

STEIN, M.A. 1907. *Ancient Khotan*, Vols. 1-2. Oxford.

——. 1921. *Serindia*, Vols. 1-5. Oxford.

——. 1928. *Innermost Asia*, Vols. 1-4. Oxford.

TIKHVINSKY, S.L.; LITVINSKY, B.A. (eds.). 1988. *Vostochniy Turkestan v drevnosti i rannem srednevekov'e. Ocherki Istorii*. Moscow.

WINTER, W. 1984. *Studia Tocharica*. Poznan.

YAN WEN-RU. 1962. Grottoes in the South of the Tian-shan. *Wen-wu Journal*.

YERUSALIMSKAYA, A.A. 1972. Velikiy shelkoviy put' i Severniy Kavkaz. In: *Sokrovishcha iskusstva drevnego Irana, Kavkaza i Sredney Azii*. Leningrad.

ZÜRCHER, E. 1959. *The Buddhist Conquest of China. The Spread and Adaptation at Buddhism in Early Medieval China*, Vols. 1-2 (Sinica Leidensia, Vol. 11). Leiden.

CHAPTER 12

ASMUSSEN, J.P. 1965. X\u{u}āstvānīft. Studies in Manichaeism. *Acta Theologica Danica*, Vol. 7. Copenhagen.

ASMUSSEN, J.P. 1975. *Manichaean Literature. Representative Texts Chiefly from Middle Persian and Parthian Writings*. New York.

BAILEY, H.W. 1985. *Indo-Scythian Studies being Khotanese Texts*, Vol. 7. Cambridge.

BOYCE, M. 1968. The Manichaean Literature in Middle Iranian. *Handbuch der Orientalistik. 1. Abteilung, 4. Band, Iranistik, 2. Abschnitt, Literatur, Lieferung 1*, pp. 67-76. Leiden.

CHAVANNES, E. 1900. Les Pays d'occident d'après le Wei-lio. *TP*, series 2, Vol. 6, pp. 517-71.

——. 1907. Les pays d'occident d'après le Heou Han Chou. *TP*, series 2, Vol. 8, pp. 148-234.

——. 1913. *Documents chinois découverts par Sir Aurel Stein*. Oxford.

——. 1941. *Documents sur les Tou-kiue (Turcs) occidentaux recueillis et commentés, suivis de notes additionnelles*. Paris.

CHAVANNES, E.; PELLIOT, P. 1911. Un traité manichéen retrouvé en Chine. *JA*, Part 1, pp. 499-617; Part 2, 1913, pp. 99-199, 261-394.

DABBS, J.A. 1963. *History of the Discovery and Exploration of Chinese Turkestan*. The Hague.

FRANKE, O. 1907. *Eine Chinesische Tempelinschrift aus Idikutschari bei Turfan. (Abhandlungen der Königlischen Preussischen Akademie der Wissenschaften.)* Berlin.

——. 1909. Das Datum der Chinesische Tempelinschriften von Turfan. *TP*.

FUCHS, W. 1926. Das Turfan Gebiet. Seine ausseren Geschichte bis in die T'angzeit. *Ostasiatische Zeitschrift*, pp. 124-66.

GRÜNWEDEL, A. 1906. *Bericht über archäologische Arbeiten in Idikutschari und Umgebung im Winter 1902-1903*. Munich.

——. 1912. *Altbuddhistische Kultstatten in Chinesisch-Turkistan*. Berlin.

——. 1920. *Alt Kutscha*. Berlin.

HARTEL, H. 1956. Zwei unveröffentlichte Bruchstücke aus Turfan Fresken. *Baessler Archiv*, N.F., Vol. 3, pp. 169-74.

——. 1957. *Turfan und Gandhara. Frühmittelalterliche Kunst Zentralasiens*. Berlin.

HENNING, W.B. 1977. *Selected Papers*, Vols. 1-2. (*Acta Iranica*, Vols. 14-15.) Leiden.

HIRTH, F. 1917. The Story of Chang Kien, China's Pioneer in Western Asia. *JAOS*, Vol. 37.

HUI-LI. 1959. *The Life of Hsüan-tsang*. Compiled by the monk Hui-li. Peking.

HULSEWÉ, A.F.P.; LOEWE, M.A.N. 1979. *China in Central Asia. The Early Stage: 125 B.C.-A.D. 23*. Leiden.

KLEMENTZ, D. 1899. *Nachrichten über die von der Kaiserlichen Akademie der Wissenschaften zu St. Petersburg im Jahre 1898 ausgerustete Expedition nach Turfan*, Vol. 1: D. Klementz, *Turfan und seine Altertümer*, S. 1-53. St Petersburg.

LE COQ, A. VON. 1909. A Short Account of the Origin, Journey and Results of the First Royal Prussian (Second German) Expedition to Turfan. *JRAS*.

——. 1913. *Chotscho. Facsimile-Wiedergaben der wichtigeren Funde der ersten Königlich Preussischen Expedition nach Turfan in Ost-Turkistan*. Berlin.

——. 1923-24. *Die Buddhistische Spätantike in Mittel-Asien. Ergebnisse der Königlichten Preussischen Turfan Expedition*. Berlin. 7 vols.

——. 1925. *Bilderatlas zur Kunst und Kulturgeschichte Mittel-Asien*. Berlin.

——. 1926. *Auf Hellas Spuren in Ostturkistan. Berichte und Abenteuer der 2. und 3.*

Deutschen Turfan Expedition. Leipzig.

——. 1928. *Buried Treasures of Chinese Turkestan. An Account of the Activities and Adventures of the Second and Third Expedition*. London.

——. 1928. *Von Land und Leuten in Ost-Turkistan. Berichte und Abenteuer der 4. Deutschen Turfan expedition*. Leipzig.

LITVINSKY, B.A. (ed.) 1992. Buddizm. *Vostochniy Turkestan v drevnosti i rannem srednevekov'e. Etnos. Yazyki. Religii*. Moscow.

LITVINSKY, B.A. (ed.) 1995. *Vostochniy Turkestan v drevnosti i rannem srednevekov'e. Khozyaystvo. Material'naya kul'tura*. Moscow.

LÜDERS, H. 1922. Zur Geschichte und Geographie Ostturkestan. *Sitzungsberichte der Preussischen Akademie der Wissenschaften. Philosophisch-historische Klasse.*, pp. 243-61. Berlin.

——. 1930. Weitere Beiträge zur Geschichte und Geographie von Ostturkestan. *Sitzungsberichte der Preussischen Akademie der Wissenschaften*, pp. 7-64.

MAILLARD, M. 1973. Essai sur la vie matérielle dans l'oasis de Tourfan pendant le Haut Moyen Age. *AA*, Vol. 29.

MASPÉRO, H. 1953. *Les documents chinois de la troisième expédition de Sir Aurel Stein en Asie centrale*. London.

MIRSKY, J. 1977. *Sir Aurel Stein, Archaeological Explorer*. Chicago/London.

OTANI SHIN. 1937. *Saiiki ki*. Tokyo. In Japanese.

PELLIOT, P. 1912. Kao-Tchang, Qoco, Houo-tcheou et Qara-khodja. *JA*.

——. 1926. Compte rendu de O. Franke: Eine chinesische Templeinschrift aus Idikutshari bei Turfan. *TP*, Vol. 24, p. 247.

PULLEYBLANK, E.G. 1966. Chinese and Indo-Europeans. *JRAS*, pp. 9-39.

SAMOLIN, W. 1958. Ethnographic Aspects of the Archaeology of the Tarim Basin. *Central Asiatic Journal*, Vol. 4, pp. 45-67.

SHIMAZAKI, A. 1970. Ku-shih and the Anterior and Posterior Kingdoms of Ku-shih. *Memoirs of the Research Department of the Toyo Bunko*, Vol. 27.

STEIN, M.A. 1921. *Serindia, Detailed Report of Explorations in Central Asia and Westernmost China*. Oxford. 5 vols.

——. 1928. *Innermost Asia, Detailed Report of Explorations in Central Asia, Kansu and Eastern Iran*. Oxford. 3 vols.

WALDSCHMIDT, E. 1925. *Gandhāra, Kutscha, Turfan, Eine Einführung in die frühmittelalterliche Kunst Zentralasien*. Leipzig.

ZHANG GUANG-DA. 1988. The Political Situation of Si-chou after the T'ang's Conquest of the Kingdom of Qocho. *Tōyō Bunko*, Vol. 68, pp. 81-7.

Literature in Chinese

HOU TSAN. 1984. Qu-shi Gao-Chang wang-guo Guan-zhi yan-jiu. [A Study on the System of Governmental Organization of the Kingdom of Qočo, Ruled by the Qu Family]. *Wen-shih*, Vol. 22. Beijing.

HSIA NAI, 1966. Sin-kiang tu-lu-fan zui jin chu-tu di Po-si Sa-shan chao yin-bi [Sasanian Silver Coins, Recently Found in Turfan, Sin-kiang]. *Kao-gu*, Vol. 4.

HUANG WENG-BI. 1933. *Gao-Chang*.

——. 1934. Gao-chang zhuang ji [Collection of the Inscriptions on the Sepulchral Bricks Discovered in Turfan].

HUANG WENG-BI. 1954. Tu-lu-fan kao-gu ji [Archaeological Report on Turfan]. Shanghai.

———. 1959. Jiao-he cheng diao-cha Ji [A Survey of the Site of Ancient Yar]. *Kao-gu*, No. 5.

LIN WU-SHU. 1987. *Mo-ni jiao ji chi dong-jian.* [Manichaeism and its Diffusion Eastwards]. Beijing.

Xin Zhong Guo di Kao-gu fa-xian, ju yan-jiu [Recent Archaeological Discoveries and Studies in the New China]. 1984. Beijing.

TANG CHANG-RU, 1982. Xin chu tu-lu-fan wen-shu fa-jue zheng-li jing-guo ji wen-shu jian-jie [The Newly Found Turfan Documents, a Survey of the Process of Excavations and the Discovery of the Documents with a Preliminary Introduction on the Significance of these Manuscripts]. *Tōhō-kakuhō*, Vol. 54, pp. 83-100. Kyoto.

Texts of the Documents Found in Turfan. 1981-87. Vols. 1-8. Beijing.

YEN WEN-RU, 1962. Tu-lu-fan di Gao-chang gu-cheng. [The Ancient City of Kocho in Turfan]. *Wen-wu*, No. 7/8.

CHAPTER 13

BICHURIN, N.J. 1950. *Sobranie svedeniy o narodakh, obitavshchikh v Sredney Azii v drevnie vremena*, Vol. 2. Moscow/Leningrad.

BLOCKLEY, R.C. 1985. *The History of Menander the Guardsam.* Liverpool.

DOERFER, G. 1973. Zur Sprache der Hunnen. *Central Asiatic Journal*, Vol. 17, No. 1. Wiesbaden.

ENOKI, K. 1956. Sogdiana and the Hsiung-nu. *Central Asiatic Journal*, Vol. 1, No. 1.

GARDINER, K.H.J.; CRESPIGNY, R.R.C. DE. 1977. *T'an-shih-huai and the Hsien-pi tribes of the Second Century* B.C. Papers on Far Eastern History, No. 15. Canberra.

GROOT, Y.Y.M. DE. 1921. *Chinesische Urkunden zur Geschichte Asiens, II*. Berlin/Leipzig.

HULSEWÉ, A.F.P.; LOEWE, M.A.N. 1979. *China in Central Asia. The Early Stage: 125* B.C.-A.D. *23.* Leiden.

McGOVERN, N.M. 1939. *The Early Empires of Central Asia.* New York.

LIGETI, L. 1970. Le Tabgatch, un dialecte de la langue Sien-pi. In: L. Ligeti (ed.), *Mongolian Studies*, pp. 265-308. Budapest.

LITVINSKY, B.A. 1968. *Kangyuysko-Sarmatskiy Farn (k istoriko-kul'turnym svyazyam plemen yuzhnoy Rossii i Sredney Azii).* Dushanbe.

MAENCHEN-HELFEN, O. 1939. The Ting-ling. *Harvard Journal of Asiatic Studies*, Vol. 4. pp. 77-86.

———. 1944-45. Huns and Hsiung-nu. *Byzantium*, Vol. 17.

———. 1973. *The World of the Huns. Studies in their History and Culture.* Berkeley/Los Angeles/London.

MENANDER. 1861. In: *Vizantiyskie istoriki. Perevod s grecheskogo S. Destunisa.* St Petersburg.

PULLEYBLANK, E.G. 1966. Chinese and Indo-Europeans. *JRAS*.

ROLFE, J.C. 1939. *Ammianus Marcellinus.* With an English translation, Vol. 3. Loeb Classical Library.

SCHREIBER, G. 1947. Das Volk der Hsien-pi zur Han-Zeit. *Monumenta Serica*, Vol. 12, pp. 145-203.

SHAN YUE (ed.). 1959. *Ocherki po istorii Kitaya*. Moscow.

SHIRATORI, K.A. 1956. A New Attempt at the Solution of the Fu-lin Problem. Tokyo.

SINOR. D. 1969. *Inner Asia. History, Civilization, Languages. A Syllabus*. The Hague.

———. (ed.). 1990. *The Cambridge History of Early Inner Asia*. Cambridge.

TASKIN, V.S. 1984. *Materialy po istorii drevnikh kochevykh narodov gruppy dunkhu*. Moscow.

———. 1992. *Materialy po istorii kochevykh narodov v Kitae III-V vv*, Vol. 3. Moscow.

ZUEV, Y.A. 1957. K voprosu o vzaimootnosheniyakh usuney i kantszyuy vo vtoroy polovine I veka do n.ê. *Izvestiya AN Kazakhskoy SSR*, seriya istorii, philosofii, ekonomiki i prava, Vol. 2 (5). Alma-Ata.

CHAPTER 14

I. Inscriptions and comments on them (with the exception of Klyashtorny and Livshits, 1972, all these texts are in old Turkic.)

CLAUSON, Sir G. 1971. Some Notes on the Inscription of Toñuquq. Ed. L. Ligeti: *Studia Turcica*, pp. 125-32. Budapest.

HOVDHAUGEN, E. 1974. The Relationship between the Two Orkhon Inscriptions. *Acta Orientalia*, Vol. 36, pp. 55-82.

KLYASHTORNY, S.G. 1964. *Drevnetyurkskie runicheskie pamyatniki kak istochnik po istorii Sredney Azii*. Moscow.

———. 1971. Runicheskaya nadpis' iz vostochnoy Gobi. *Studia Turcica*, Ed. L. Ligeti, pp. 249-258. Budapest.

———. 1975. Einige Probleme der Geschichte der alttürkischen Kultur Zentralasiens, Schriften zur Geschichte und Kultur des Alten Orients. *Alt-Orientalische Forschungen*, Vol. 2, pp. 119-128.

———. 1977. Mifologicheskie syuzhety v drevnetyurkskikh pamyatnikakh. *Tyurkologicheskiy sbornik*, pp. 117-38.

———. 1982. The Terkhin Inscription. *AOH*, Vol. 36, pp. 335-66.

KLYASHTORNY, S.G.; LIVSHITS, V.A. 1972. The Sogdian Inscription of Bugut Revised. *AOH*, Vol. 26, pp. 69-102.

MALOV, S.E. 1951. *Pamyatniki drevnetyurkskoy pis'mennosti*. Moscow/Leningrad.

———. 1952. *Eniseyskaya pis'mennost' Tyurkov*. Moscow/Leningrad.

———. 1959. *Pamyatniki drevnetyurkskoy pis'mennosti Mongolii i Kirgizii*. Moscow/ Leningrad.

TEKIN, T. 1968. A Grammar of Orkhon Turkic. *Indiana University Uralic and Altaic Series*, Vol. 69, pp. 259-95 (translations of the inscriptions). Bloomington.

THOMSEN, V. 1896. Inscriptions de l'Orkhon déchiffrées. *Mémoires de la Société Finno-Ougrienne*, Vol. 5.

———. 1924. Alttürkische Inschriften der Mongolei. *Zeitschrift der Deutschen Morgenländischen Gesellschaft*, Vol. 78, pp. 121-175. Translated from Danish by H.H. Schader.

TRIJARSKIJ, E. 1981. Die alttürkischen Runen-Inschriften in den Arbeiten der letzten Jahre. Befunde und kritische Übersicht. *Altorientalische Forschungen*, Vol. 8, pp. 339-52.

II. Principal translations of Chinese sources

CHAVANNES, E. 1903. *Documents sur les Tou-kiue (Turcs) occidentaux. Recueillis et commentés, suivi de notes additionnelles. (Présenté à l'Académie Impériale des Sciences de St-Pétersbourg le 23 Août 1900.)* St Petersburg.

——. 1904. Notes additionnelles sur les Tou-kiue (Turcs) occidentaux. *TP*, Vol. 5, pp. 1-110. (Reprinted in the reprint of the *Documents*.)

LIU MAU-TSAI. 1958. Die chinesischen Nachrichten zur Geschichte der Ost-Türken (T'u-küe), 1-2. *Göttinger Asiatische Forschungen*, Vol. 10. Wiesbaden.

III. General

BARTHOLD, W. 1899. *Die alttürkischen Inschriften und die arabischen Quellen.* In: W. Radloff (ed), *Die alttürkischen Inschriften der Mongolei, Zweite Folge*. St. Petersburg.

——. 1935. *12 Vorlesungen über die Geschichte der Türken Mittelasiens*. Deutsche Bearbeitung von Theodor Menzel. Berlin.

BAZIN, L. 1974. *Les calendriers turcs anciens et médiévaux*. Lille.

BOMBACI, A. 1964-65. 'Qutluγ bolzun! A Contribution to the History of the Concept «Fortune» among the Turks'. *Ural-Altaische Jahrbücher*, Vol. 36, pp. 284-91; Vol. 38, pp. 13-14.

——. 1970*a*. Qui était jebu xak'an? *Studia Turcica*, Vol. 2, pp. 7-24.

——. 1970*b*. On the Ancient Turkic Title *eltäbär*. *Proceedings of the IXth Meeting of the Permanent International Altaistic Conference*, pp. 1-16. Naples.

——. 1971. The Husbands of Princess Hsien-li Bilgä. *Studia Turcica*. Ed. L. Ligeti, pp. 103-123. Budapest.

——. 1974. On the Ancient Turkish Title *'šaδ*. *Gururajamanjarika; Studi in onore di Giuseppe Tucci*, pp. 167-93. Naples.

——. 1976. On the Ancient Turkish Title *šadapit*. *Ural Altaische Jahrbücher*, Vol. 48, pp. 32-41.

CANNATA, P. 1981. *Profilo storico del I° impero turco, metà VI - metà VII secolo*. Istituto di Studi dell'India e dell'Asia Orientale. Rome. (Possibly the best modern presentation of the Türk Empire.)

CZEGLÉDY, K. 1972. On the Numerical Composition of the Ancient Turkish Tribal Confederation. *AOH,* Vol. 25, pp. 275-81.

——. 1973. Gardizi on the History of Central Asia 746-780 A.D. *AOH*, Vol. 27, pp. 257-67.

——. 1982. Zur Stammesorganisation der türkischen Völker. *AOH*, Vol. 36, pp. 89-93.

DOBLHOFER, E. 1955. *Byzantinische Diplomaten und östliche Barbaren. Aus den Excerpta de legationibus des Konstantinos Porphyrogennetos ausgewählte Abschnitte des Priskos und Menander Protektor*. Graz.

ECSEDY, H. 1965. Old Turkic Titles of Chinese Origin. *AOH*, Vol. 18, pp. 83-91.

——. 1972. Tribe and Tribal Society in the 6th Century Turk Empire. *AOH*, Vol. 25, pp. 245-62.

——. 1977. Tribe and Empire, Tribe and Society in the Turk Age. *AOH*, Vol. 31, pp. 3-15.

HANNESTAD, K. 1955-57. Les relations de Byzance avec la Transcaucasie et l'Asie Centrale aux 5e et 6e siècles. *Byzantion*, Vols. 25-7, pp. 421-56.

HARMATTA, J. 1962. Byzantinoturcica. *Acta Ant. Hung.*, Vol. 10, pp. 131-50.

——. 1972. Irano-Turcica. *AOH*, Vol. 25, pp. 263-73.

——. 1982. La médaille de Jeb Sahansah. *Iranica Antiqua*, Vol. 11, pp. 167-80.

LIGETI, L. 1971. A propos du 'Rapport sur les rois demeurant dans le nord'. In: *Etudes tibétaines dédiées à la mémoire de Marcelle Lalou*, pp. 166-89. Paris.

MALYAVKIN, A.G. 1981. *Istoricheskaya geografya Tsentral'noy Azii (Materialy i issledovaniya)*. Novosibirsk.

MARQUART, J. 1898. *Die Chronologie der alttürkischen Inschriften*. Leipzig.

——. 1901. *Ērānšahr nach der Geographie des Ps. Moses Xorenac'i*. N.F., Vol. 3/2.

NÖLDEKE, T.; TABARI. 1973. *Geschichte der Perser und Araber zur Zeit der Sasaniden. Aus der arabischen Chronik des Tabari übersetzt und mit ausführlichen Erläuterungen und Ergänzungen versehn von T. Nöldeke*. Reprint. Leiden.

PELLIOT, P. 1912. La fille de Mo-tch'o qaghan et ses rapports avec Kül-tegin. *TP*, Vol. 13, pp. 301-6.

——. 1929. Neuf notes sur des questions d'Asie Centrale. *TP*, Vol. 26, pp. 201-66.

ROUX, J.P. 1962. La religion des Turcs de l'Orkhon des VIIe et VIIIe siècles. *Revue de l'histoire des religions*, Vol. 161, pp. 1-24, 199-231.

SINOR, D. 1981. The Origin of Turkic *balïq* 'town'. *Central Asiatic Journal*, Vol. 25, pp. 95-102.

——. 1982. The Legendary Origin of the Türks. In: *Folklorica: Festschrift for Felix J. Oinas*. E.V. Žygas and P. Voorhies (eds.). Indiana University, Uralic and Altaic Series, Vol. 141, pp. 223-45. Bloomington.

——. 1985. Some Components of the Civilization of the Türks (6th to 8th Century) A.D. In: G. Jarring and S. Rosen (eds.), *Altaistic Studies. Papers Presented at the 25th Meeting of the Permanent International Altaistic Conference at Uppsala, 7-11 June, 1982 (Kungl. Vitterhets Historie och Antikvitets Akademien Konferenser, 12)*, pp. 145-59. Stockholm.

——. 1990. The Establishment and Dissolution of the Türk Empire. In: D. Sinor (ed.), *The Cambridge History of Early Inner Asia*, pp. 285-316, 478-83. Cambridge.

STEBLEVA, I.V. 1965. *Poêziya tyurkov VI-VIII vekov*. Moscow.

WANG HUAN. 1983. Apa Qaghan, Founder of the Western Turkish Khanate, the Splitting up of the Turkish Khanate and the Formation of the Western Turkish Khanate. *Social Sciences in China*, Vol. 2, pp. 124-54.

CHAPTER 15

BACOT J.; THOMAS F.W.; TOUSSAIN, C. 1940-46. *Documents de Touen-houang relatifs à l'histoire du Tibet*. Paris.

BECKWITH, C.I. 1980. The Tibetan Empire in the West. In: M. Aris and Aung San Suu Kyi (eds.), *Tibetan Studies in Honour of Hugh Richardson*. Warminster.

——. 1987. *The Tibetan Empire in Central Asia*. Princeton.

CHANG KUN, 1959-60. An Analysis of the Tun-huang Tibetan Annals. *Journal of Oriental Studies*, Vol. 5, pp. 130-1; 153, note 10. Hong Kong.

CHAVANNES, E. 1903. *Documents sur les Tou-kiue (Turcs) occidentaux. Recueillis et commentés, suivi de notes additionnelles. (Présenté à l'Académie Impériale des Sciences de St-Pétersbourg le 23 Août 1900.)* Vol. 6. St Petersburg.

GIBB, H.A.R. 1923. *The Arab Conquests in Central Asia*. New York.

HOFFMANN, H. 1975. *Tibet. A Handbook. (Indiana University Asian Studies Research Institute, Oriental Series)*, Vol. 5. Bloomington.

HSÜAN-TSANG, 1985. *Records of the Western Regions*. Ed. and annot. Ji Xian-lin et al. Peking.

LITVINSKY, B.A. (ed.) 1992. Buddizm. *Vostochniy Turkestan v drevnosti i rannem srednevekov'e. Etnos. Yazyki. Religii.* Moscow.

LITVINSKY, B.A. (ed.) 1995. *Vostochniy Turkestan v drevnosti i rannem srednevekov'e. Khozyaystvo. Material'naya kul'tura.* Moscow.

LIU MAU-TSAI. 1969. *Kutscha und seine Beziehungen zu China vom 2. Jahrhundert bis zum 6. Jahrhundert N. Chr*, Vols. 1-2. Wiesbaden.

MAILLARD, M. 1973. Essai sur la vie matérielle dans l'oasis de Tourfan pendant le Haut Moyen Age. *AA*, Vol. 29. Paris.

——. 1983. *Grottes et monuments d'Asie centrale, suivi d'un tableau de concordance des grottes de la région de Kutcha*. Paris.

PELLIOT, P. 1928. Des artisans chinois à la capitale sassanide en 761-762. *TP*, Vol. 26, pp. 110-12; 163.

——. 1961. *Histoire ancienne du Tibet*. Paris.

PULLEYBLANK, E. 1955. *The Background of the Rebellion of An Lu-shan*. London/New York/Toronto.

ROTOURS, R. DES. 1932. *Le traité des Examens*. Paris.

SAMOLIN, W. 1964. *East Turkestan to the Twelfth Century. A Brief Political Survey.* The Hague.

SNELLGROVE, D.; RICHARDSON, H. 1968. *A Cultural History of Tibet.* London.

STEIN, R. 1972. *La Civilisation Tibétaine*, 2nd ed. Paris. 1987. English trans. J.E.S. Driver. *Tibetan Civilization.* London.

THOMAS, F.W. 1936-63. *Tibetan Literary Texts and Documents concerning Chinese Turkestan*. London. 4 vols.

TIKHVINSKIY, S.L.; LITVINSKY, B.A. (eds.). 1988. *Vostochniy Turkestan v drevnosti i rannem srednevekov'e*. Moscow.

Tu-lu-fan chu-tu wen-shu. 1985-92.

TUCCI, G. 1949. *Tibetan Painted Scrolls*. Rome. 3 vols.

——. 1950. *The Tombs of the Tibetan Kings*. Rome.

TUCCI, G.; HEISSIG, W. 1973. *Les religions du Tibet et de la Mongolie*. Paris.

TU-YU. 1988 (new ed.).*T'ung tien*, Institutional History Encyclopedia. Completed and presented to the throne in 801 (735-812). Punctuated ed. Peking.

URAY, G. 1960. The Four Horns of Tibet according to the Royal Annals. *AOH*, Vol. 10/1.

——. 1962. The Offices of the Brun-pas and Great Mñans and the Territorial Division of Central Tibet in the Early 8th Century. *AOH*, Vol. 15, pp. 353-56.

——. 1975. L'annalistique et la pratique bureaucratique au Tibet ancien. *JA*.

——. 1979. The Old Tibetan Sources of the History of Central Asia up to 751 A.D. In: J. Harmatta (ed.), *Prolegomena to the Sources on the History of Pre-Islamic Central Aia*. Budapest.

VOSTRIKOV, A.I. 1970. *Tibetan Historical Literature*. Translated from Russian by H.C. Gupta. Calcutta.

YALDIZ, M. 1987. *Archäologie und Kunstgeschichte Chinesich-Zentralasiens (Xinjiang) (Handbuch der Orientalistik, 7. Abteilung, 3. Band, 2. Abschnitt)*. Leiden.

YUANG ZANG (HSÜANG-TSANG). 1969. = BEAL, S. 1884. *Si-yu-ki, Buddhist Records of the Western World. Translated from the Chinese of Hiuen Tsiang (A.D. 629)*, Vols. 1-2. London. (Reprint. Delhi, 1969.)

CHAPTER 16

The Archaeology of Afghanistan. 1978. *The Archaeology of Afghanistan from Early Times to the Timurid Period*. Ed. F.R. Allchin and N. Hammond. London/New York/San Francisco.

BEAL, S. 1969. *Si-yu-ki, Buddhist Records of the Western World. Translated from the Chinese of Hiuen Tsiang (A.D. 629)*, Vols. 1-2. Reprint. London. (First published in 1884.) Delhi.

BICHURIN, N.Y. 1950. *Sobranie svedenii o narodakh, obitavshikh v Sredney Azii v drevnie vremena*, Vol. 2. Moscow/Leningrad.

BIVAR, A.D.H. 1954. The Inscription of Uruzgan. *JRAS*, Parts 3-4.

CARL, J.; HACKIN, J. 1959. Le monastère bouddhique de Tépé Maranjān. *MDAFA*, Vol. 8.

CAROE, O. 1962. *The Pathans 550 B.C.-A.D. 1957*. London.

CHAVANNES, E. 1903. *Documents sur les Tou-kiue (Turcs) occidentaux. Recueillis et commentés, suivis de notes additionnelles. (Présenté à l'Académie Impériale des Sciences de St-Pétersbourg le 23 Août 1900.)* Vol. 6. St Petersburg.

——. n.d. *Notes additionnelles sur les Tou-kiue (Turcs) occidentaux*. Reprinted in the same volume as the '*Documents*'. Paris.

CZEGLÉDY, K. 1958. Bahrām Čōbīn and the Persian Apocalyptic Literature. *AOH*, Vol. 8, pp. 21-43.

——. 1984. Zur Geschichte der Hephthaliten. In: J. Harmatta (ed.), *From Hecataeus to Al-Huwārizmī*, pp. 213-17. Budapest.

DAFFINA, P. 1983. La Persia sassanide secondo le fonti cinesi. *Rivista degli Studi Orientali*, Vol. 57, pp. 121-70.

DAVIDOVICH, E.A.; ZEIMAL, E.V. 1980. Denezhnoye khozyaystvo Sredney Azii v perekhodniy period ot drevnosti k srednevekov'yu (k tipologii feodalizma). In: *Blizniy i Sredniy Vostok. Tovaro-denezhnye otnosheniya pri feodalizme*. Moscow.

ECSEDY, H. 1968. Trade-and-War Relations between the Turks and China in the Second Half of the 6th Century. *AOH*, Vol. 21, pp. 131-80.

EDELMAN, D.I. 1983. The Dardic and Nuristani Languages. Moscow.

ENOKI, K. 1977. Some Remarks on Chieh-shi. *EW*, Vol. 27, Nos. 1-4.

ESIN, E. 1972. 'Tös and Monucuk. *Central Asiatic Journal*, Vol. 16, No. 1. Wiesbaden.

———. 1977. Tarkhan Nīzak or Tarkhan Tirek? *JAOS*, Vol. 97, pp. 323-31.

FRANCFORT, H.-P. 1985. Notes sur la mort de Cyrus et les Dardes. In: *Orientalia Iosephi Tucci memoriae dicata*, Vol. 1. *Serie Orientale Roma*, 56/1. Rome.

FUCHS, W. 1938. Huei-ch'ao's Pilgerreise durch Nord-West Indien und Zentral-Asien um 726. *Sitzungsberichte der Preussischen Akademie der Wissenschaften, Jahrgang 1938. Philosophisch-historische Klasse.* Berlin.

FUSSMAN, G. 1972. *Atlas linguistique des parlers dardes et kafirs*, Vols. 1-2. Paris.

GERSHEVITCH, I. 1985. Philologia Iranica. *Beiträge zur Iranistik*, Vol. 12. Wiesbaden.

Gilgit Buddhist Manuscripts. 1959-60. Facsimile ed., Parts 1-2. New Delhi.

GÖBL, R. 1967. *Dokumente zur Geschichte der iranischen Hunnen in Baktrien und Indien*, Vols. 1-4. Wiesbaden.

———. 1987. Medaillen des islamischen Mittelalters und ihr Formenkreis. *Litterae Numismaticae Vindobonensis*, Vol. 3, pp. 265-87.

GRANTOVSKIY, E.A. 1963. Plemennoe ob'edinenie *Parçu-Parçava* y Panini. *Istorya i kul'tura drevney Indii*. Moscow.

GRIERSON, G.A. 1919. Specimens of the Dardic or Pischacha Languages. *Linguistic Survey of India*, Vol. 8/2. Calcutta.

GRYUNBERG, A.L. 1980. *Yazyk kati. Teksty. Grammaticheskiy ocherk.* Moscow.

———. 1987. *Ocherk grammatiki afganskogo yazyka (pashto)*. Leningrad.

HACKIN, C.; CARL, J. 1936. Recherches archéologiques au col de Khair Khaneh près de Kaboul. *MDAFA*, Vol. 7.

HARGREAVES, H. 1923-24. *Hund, the Ancient Udabhanda. (Annual report of the Archaeological Survey of India.)* New Delhi.

HARMATTA, J. 1962. Byzantinoturcica. *AOH*, Vol. 10, pp. 131-50.

———. 1969. Late Bactrian Inscriptions. *AOH*, Vol. 17, pp. 297-432.

———. 1971. Sino-Iranica. *AOH*, Vol. 19, pp. 113-43.

———. 1974. The Struggle for the Possession of South Arabia between Aksūm and the Sāsānians. *IV Congresso Internazionale di Studi Etiopici, Roma 10-15 aprile 1972*, pp. 95-106. Rome.

———. 1982. La médaille de Jeb Šāhānšāh. *Studia Iranica*, Vol. 11, pp. 167-80.

Hudūd al-ᶜĀlam. 1930. *Khudud al-alem. Rukopis' Tumanskogo*. With introduction and index by V. Bartol'd. Leningrad.

HUI-LI. 1959. *The Life of Hsuang-tsang*. Compiled by the monk Hui-li. Peking.

HUMBACH, H. 1966. *Baktrische Sprachdenkmäler*, Vols. 1-2. Wiesbaden.

———. 1987. New Coins of Fromo Kēsaro. In: *India and the Ancient World*, pp. 81-5. Leiden.

IBN KHORDADBEH. 1889. *Kitāb al-mazālik wa'l mamālik*, Vol. 6. Leiden.

KAYE, G.R. 1927. *The Bakhshali Manuscript*, Vol. 1. Calcutta.

KLIMOV, G.A.; EDELMAN, D.I. 1970. *Yazyk burushaski*. Moscow.

KOHZAD, A. 1950. Les ratbils shahs de Kaboul. *Afghanistan*, Vol. 2.

KUWAYAMA, S. 1976. The Turki Shahis and Relevant Brahmanical Sculptures in Afghanistan. *EW*, Vol. 26/34.

LAZARD, G. 1971. Pahlavi, pārsi, dari: les langues de l'Iran d'après Ibn al-Muqaffa. In: C.E. Bosworth (ed.), *Iran and Islam. In Memory of the Late V. Minorsky*. Edinburgh.

542

——. 1975. The Rise of the New Persian Language. *The Cambridge History of Iran*, Vol. 4.

LEVI, S. 1932. Notes sur les manuscrits sanskrits provenant de Bāmiyān (Afghanistan) et de Gilgit (Cachemire). *JA*, Vol. 220.

LEVI, S.; CHAVANNES, E. 1895. Voyages des pèlerins bouddhistes: l'itinéraire d'Ou-kong. *JA*, Vol. 6.

LITVINSKY, B.A. 1981. Kalai-Kafirnigan. Problems in the Religion and Art of Early Mediaeval Tokharistan. *EW*, Vol. 31/1-4.

LITVINSKY, B.A.; ZEIMAL, T.I. 1971. *Ajina-tepa. Arkhitektura. Zhivopis'. Skul'ptura.* Moscow.

LORIMER, C.L.R. 1935, 1938. *The Burushaski Language*, Vols. 1, 2. Oslo.

MACDOWALL, D.W. 1968. The Shahis of Kabul and Gandhara. *NC*, 7th Series, Vol. 8. London.

MACDOWALL, D.W.; TADDEI, M. 1978. The Pre-Muslim Period. In: R. Allchin and N. Hammond (eds), *The Archaeology of Afghanistan from Earliest Times to the Timurid Period*. London/New York/San Francisco.

MALYAVKIN, A.G. 1987. *Osnovy iranskogo yazykoznaniya. Novoiranskie yazyki: vostochnaya gruppa.* Moscow.

——. 1989. *Tanskie khroniki o gosudarstvakh Tsentral'noy Azii.* Novosibirsk.

MARQUART, J. 1901. *Ērānšahr nach der Geographie des Ps. Moses Xorenacʻi.* Berlin.

MARKWART, J. 1938. *Wehrot und Arang. Untersuchungen zur mythischen und geschichtlichen Landes kunde von Ostiran.* Leiden.

MINORSKY, V. 1937. *Hudūd al-ʿĀlam. The Regions of the World.* Translated and explained by V. Minorsky. London.

MOCHIRI, M.I., 1987. *Arab-Sasanian Civil War Coinage.* Leiden.

MORGENSTIERNE, G. 1940. Pashto, Pathan and the Treatment of r- Sibilant in Pashto. *AOH*, Vol. 18.

——. 1942. Archaisms and Innovations in Pashto Morphology. *Norsk tidsskrift for sprogvidenscap*, Vol. 12.

——. 1944; 1967; 1973. *Indo-Iranian Frontier Languages*, Vol. 3/2; Vol. 3/3; Vol. 4. Oslo.

NÖLDEKE, T.; TABARI. 1973. *Geschichte der Perser und Araber zur Zeit der Sasaniden. Aus der arabischen Chronik des Tabari übersetzt und mit ausführlichen Erläuterungen und Ergänzungen versehn von T. Nöldeke.* Reprint. Leiden.

ORANSKY, I.M. 1988. *Vvedeniye v iranskuyu filologiyu*, 2nd ed. Moscow.

PANDEY, D.B. 1973. The Shahis of Afghanistan and the Punjab. *Indo-Afghan Studies*, Vol. 3. Delhi.

PAULY, B. 1967. Fragments sanskrits d'Afghanistan. Fouilles de la Délégation Française en Afghanistan. *JA*, Vol. 255.

PELLIOT, P. 1934. Tokharien et Koutchéen. *JA*, Vol. 224.

RAHMAN, A. 1979. *The Last Two Dynasties of the Šāhis. An Analysis of their History, Archaeology, Coinage and Palaeography.* Islamabad.

RTVELADZE, Z.V. 1987. Denezhnoye obrashchenie v severo-zapadnom Tokharistane v rannem srednevekov'e. In: *Gorodskaya kul'tura Baktrii, Tokharistana i Sogda. Antichnost' rannee sredvevekov'e.* Tashkent.

SACHAU, E. 1888. *Alberuni's India. An Account of the Religion, Philosophy, Literature,*

Geography, Chronology, Astronomy, Customs, Laws and Astrology of India about 1030 A.D., Vols. 1-2. An English edition with notes and indices. London.

SANDER, L. 1989. Remarks on the Formal Brāhmī of Gilgit, Bāmiyan and Khotan. In: K. Jettmar (ed.), *Antiquities of Northern Pakistan. Reports and Studies*, Vol. 1. Mainz.

SCHAFER, E.H. 1963. *The Golden Peaches of Samarkand. A Study of T'ang Exotics.* Berkeley/Los Angeles.

STEIN, Sir Aurel. 1893. Zur Geschichte der Çâhis von Kâbul. *Festgruss an Rudolf von Roth*, 1-10. Stuttgart.

——. 1923. A Chinese Expedition across the Pamirs and Hindukush 747 A.D. *Indian Antiquary*, Vol. 52, pp. 98-103, 139-145, 173-177.

STEIN, M.A. 1973. A Contribution to the History of the Šāhis of Kabul. *EW*, Vol. 23/1-2. Rome.

TADDEI, M. 1972. IsMEO Activities: Archaeological Mission in Afghanistan. *EW*, Vol. 22.

——. 1973. The Mahisamardini Image from Tapa Sardar (Ghazni, Afghanistan). In: *South Asian Archaeology*. London.

——. 1974. A Note on the Parinirvana Buddha at Tapa Sardar (Ghazni, Afghanistan). In: *South Asian Archaeology*. Leiden.

THOMAS, F.W. 1935. *Tibetan Literary Texts and Documents concerning Chinese Turkestan*, Vol. 1; Vol. 2, 1951; Vol. 3, 1955. London.

TUCCI, G. 1977. On Swat. The Dards and Connected Problems. *EW*, Vol. 27/1-4.

VAN LOHUIZEN, DE LEEUW. 1959. An Ancient Hindu Temple in Eastern Afghanistan. *Oriental Art. N.S.*, Vol. 5. London.

VOROBYOVA-DESYATOVSKAYA, M.I. 1983. Pamyatniki pis'mom kharoshthi i brakhmi iz Sovetskoy Sredney Azii. In: B.A. Litvinsky (ed.), *Istoriya i kultura Tsentralnoy Azii*, pp. 22-96. Moscow.

ZARUBIN, I.I. 1927. Vershikskoe narechie kandshutskogo yazyka. *Zapiski Kollegii vostokovedov*, Vol, 2, No. 2. Leningrad.

CHAPTER 17

ABEL, A. 1963. Les sources arabes sur le manichéisme. (*Annuaire de l'Institut de Philologie et d'histoire orientales et slaves*, Vol. 16.) Brussels.

ADAM, A. 1969. *Texte zum Manichäismus*. Berlin.

ALFARIC, P. 1918-19. *Les écritures manichéennes*, Vols. 1-2. Paris.

ASMUSSEN, J.P. 1965. X^{u}āsvānīft. Studies in Manichaeism. *Acta Theologica Danica*, Vol. 7. Copenhagen.

——. 1975a. Der Manichäismus. *Handbuch der Religionsgeschichte*. Göttingen.

——. 1975b. *Manichaean Literature*. (*Persian Heritage Series*, Vol. 22.) New York.

BACK, M. 1978. Die sassanidischen Staatsinschriften. *Acta Iranica*, Vol. 18. Tehran/Liège.

——. 1988. Kirdegan. *A Green Leaf, Papers in Honour of Professor Jes P. Asmussen. (Acta Iranica*, Vol. 28), pp. 45-60. Tehran/Liège.

BANG, W.; GABAIN, A. VON. 1972. *Türkische Turfan-Texte, 2. (Sprachwissenschaftliche Ergebnisse der deutschen Turfan Forschung)*, Vol. 2. Leipzig.

BELENITSKIY, A.M. 1954. Voprosy ideologii i kul'tov Sogda po materialam pyanjikentskikh khramov. *Zhivopis' Drevnego Pyanjikenta*. Moscow.

BOUCHARLAT, R. 1985. Chahar Taq et temple du feu sasanide: quelques remarques. *De l'Indus aux Balkans. Recueil à la mémoire de J. Deshayes*. Paris.

——. 1987. *Fouilles de Tureng-Tepe, under the direction of J. Deshayes, 1: Les périodes sassanides et islamiques*. Paris.

BOYCE, M. 1954. *The Manichaean Hymn-cycles in Parthian*. London Oriental Series, Vol. 3. London.

——. 1960. *A Catalogue of the Iranian Manuscripts in Manichaean Script in the German Turfan Collection*. Institut für Orientforschung, Veröffentlichung, No. 45. Berlin.

——. 1968. *The Manichaean Literature in Middle Iranian*. Handbuch der Orientalistik, Part 1, Ed. 4, Section 2, Instalment 1. Leiden/Cologne.

——. 1975. A Reader in Manichaean, Middle Persian and Parthian Texts with Notes. *Acta Iranica*, Vol. 9. Tehran/Liège.

——. 1975-78. *A History of Zoroastrianism*. Handbuch der Orientalistik, Part 1. Ed. 8. Section 1, Instalment 2. Leiden/Cologne.

CHAVANNES, E.; PELLIOT, P. 1913. Un traité manichéen retrouvé en Chine, 2. *JA*, series 11, Vol. 1.

CHRISTENSEN, A. 1944. *L'Iran sous les Sassanides*. Copenhagen.

Encyclopaedia Iranica, Vol. 1, Part 5, pp. 472-6; Vol. 3, Part 1, pp. 36-44.

Fihrist. 1970. *The Fihrist of al-Nadim*, Vol. 2. Ed. and trans. B. Dodge. New York/London.

FLÜGEL, G. 1862. *Mani, seine Lehre und seine Schriften*. Leipzig.

GERSHEVITCH, I. 1980. Beauty as the Living Soul in Iranian Manichaeism. *Acta Ant. Hung.*, Vol. 28/1-4.

GIGNOUX, PH. 1984a. *Le Livre d'Ardā Virāz*. Transliteration, transcription and translation of the Pahlavi text. Paris.

——. 1984b. *Church-State Relations in the Sasanian Period. Monarchies and Socio-Religious Traditions in the Ancient Near East*. Ed. H.I.H. Prince Takahito Mikasa. Wiesbaden.

——. 1986. Nouveaux regards sur l'apocalyptique iranienne. *CRAI*.

——. 1988. Les interdits alimentaires de l'Iran sassanide et post-sassanide. *Revue de la Société Ernest Renan*. Orsay.

——. 1991. Les quatre inscriptions du mage Kirdir. Textes et concordances. *Studia Iranica*, Cahier No. 9. Paris.

GRENET, F. 1984. *Les pratiques funéraires dans l'Asie centrale sédentaire, de la conquête grecque à l'islamisation*. Paris.

——. 1986. L'art zoroastrien en Sogdiane, études d'iconographie funéraire. *Mesopotamia*, Vol. 21, pp. 97-130.

——. 1988. *Some Particular Features of Central Asian Zoroastrianism*. (Colloquium 'Religions of Central Asia'.) London.

——. 1990. Observations sur les titres de Kirdir. *Studia Iranica*, Vol. 19.

HARMATTA, J. 1964. Die sassanidischen Siegelinschriften als geschichtliche Quellen. *Acta Ant. Hung.*, Vol. 12/1-2.

——. 1971. Sino Iranica. *Acta Ant. Hung.*, Vol. 19/1-2.

HEGEMONIUS. 1906. *Acta Archelai*. Ed. C.H. Beeson. Leipzig.

HEINRICH, A.; KOENEN, L. 1975. Der Kölner Mani-Kodex. *Zeitschrift für Papyrologie und Epigraphik*, Vol. 19. Bonn.

HENNING, W.B. 1977. Selected Papers, 1-2. *Acta Iranica*, Vols. 14-15. Tehran/Liège.

HOFFMANN, K. 1971. *Zum Zeicheninventar der Avesta-Schrift*. (Festgabe deutscher Iranister zur 2500 Jahrfeier Irans.) Stuttgart.

HUMBACH, H. 1959. *Die Gathas des Zarathustra*. Heidelberg. 2 vols.

HUMBACH, H.; WANG SHIPING. 1988. Die Pahlavi-Chinesische Bilingue von Xi'an. A Green Leaf, Papers in Honour of Professor Jes P. Asmussen. *Acta Iranica*, Vol. 23, pp. 73-82. Tehran/Liège.

INSLER, S. 1975. The Gāthās of Zarathustra. *Acta Iranica*, Vol. 8. Tehran/Liège.

KATS, A.L. 1955. Manikheystvo Rimskoy imperii po dannym Acta Archelai. *Vestnik drevney istorii*, No. 3. Moscow.

KLIMA, O. 1957. *Mazdak, Geschichte einer sozialen Bewegung im sassanidischen Persien*. Prague.

——. 1962. *Manis Zeit und Leben*. Prague.

KREYENBROEK, G. 1987. The Dādestān ī Dēnīg on Priests. *IIJ*, Vol. 30, pp. 185-208.

LE COQ, A. VON. 1973. *Die buddhistische Spätantike in Mittelasien, 2: Die Manichäischen Miniaturen*. Reprint. Graz.

——. 1979. *Chotscho*. Reprint. Graz.

LITVINSKY, B.A. 1968. *Outline History of Buddhism in Central Asia*. Dushanbe.

MACKENZIE, D.N. 1979-80. Mani's Shabuhragān. *BSOAS*, Vol. 42/3 (1979); Vol. 43 (1980).

MACUCH, M. 1981. Das sasanidische Rechtsbuch 'Mātakdān ī hazār dātistān'. Teil 2. *Abhandlungen für die Kunde des Morgenlandes*, Vol. 45/1. Wiesbaden.

Manichäische Handschriften der Staatlichen Museen. 1940. Berlin. Kephalaia, Vol. 1. Stuttgart.

MARQUART, J. 1912. Ğuwainīs Bericht über Bekehrung der Uigur. *Sitzungsberichte der Preussischen Akademie der Wissenschaften. Philologische-Historische Klasse*. Berlin.

MENASCE, J. DE. 1945. *Une apologétique mazdéenne du IXe siècle, Skand Gumanik Vicar, La solution decisive des doutes*. Fribourg.

——. 1958. Une encyclopédie mazdéenne, le Denkart. *Bibliothèque de l'École des Hautes Études, Sciences Religieuses*, Vol. 69. Paris.

——. 1973. Le troisième livre du Denkart (translated from Pahlavi). *Travaux de l'Institut d'Etudes Iraniennes de l'Université de Paris III*, 5. Bibliothèque des Oeuvres Classiques persanes, 4. Paris.

MOLÉ, M. 1961. Une histoire du mazdéisme est-elle possible? *Revue de l'Histoire des Religions*, Vol. 436. Paris.

——. 1963. Culte, mythe et cosmologie dans l'Iran ancien. *Annals of the Musée Guimet*, Vol. 69. Paris.

——. 1967. La légende de Zoroastre selon les textes pehlevis. *Travaux de l'Institut d'Etudes Iraniennes de l'Université de Paris III*. Paris.

OSTEN, H. VON DER; NAUMANN, R. 1961. *Takht-i Suleiman. Vorläufiger Bericht über die Ausgrabungen*. 1959. Berlin.

Papers in Honor of Professor Mary Boyce. 1985. *Acta Iranica*, Vols. 24 & 25. Leiden.

PERIKHANYAN, A. 1973. *Sasanidskiy sudebnik (Mātakdān i hazār dātastān)*. Erevan.

POLOTSKY, H.J. 1934. *Manichäismus*, 1. Stuttgart.

——. 1935. Manichäismus, *RE*. Supplement 6. Stuttgart.

PUECH, H.-C. 1949. *Le manichéisme. Son fondateur, sa doctrine*. Paris.

RIES, L. 1980. *Bouddhisme et Manichéisme. Les étapes d'une recherche dans l'Indianisme et le Bouddhisme. (Mélanges offerts à Etienne Lamotte.)* Paris.

RUDOLPH, K. 1974. Die Bedeutung des Kölner Mani-Codex für die Manichäismus-forschung. *Mélanges d'histoire des religions offerts à H.-C. Puech*. Paris.

SÄVE-SÖDERBERGH, T. 1948. *Studies in the Coptic Manichaean Psalmbook*. Uppsala.

SCHÆDER, H.H. 1934. Iranica. *Abhandlungen der Gesellschaft der Wissenschaften zu Göttingen. Philologisch-historische Klasse*, series 3, No. 10. Berlin.

SCHAFER, E.H. 1963. *The Golden Peaches of Samarkand. A Study of T'ang Exotics*. Berkeley/Los Angeles.

SCHIPPMANN, K. 1971. *Die iranischen Feuerheiligtümer*. Berlin/New York.

SHAHRASTANI, 1986. *Livre des Religions et des Sectes*, 1. Trans. D. Gimaret and G. Monnot. Peeters/UNESCO.

SHAKED, S. 1969. *Esoteric Trends in Zoroastrianism. (Proceedings of the Israel Academy of Sciences and Humanities)*, Vol. 3/7. Jerusalem.

——. 1979. The Wisdom of the Sasanian Sages. *Dēnkard 6*. Boulder.

——. 1987. Notes on Some Islamic Reports Concerning Zoroastrianism. *Fourth Conference 'From Jahiliyya to Islam'*. Jerusalem.

SHAKI, M. 1978. The Social Doctrine of Mazdak in the Light of Middle Persian Evidence. *Archiv Orientalni*, Vol. 46/4.

——. 1985. The Cosmogonical and Cosmological Teachings of Mazdak. Papers in Honour of Professor Mary Boyce. *Acta Iranica*, Vol. 25. Tehran/Liège.

SIDOROV, A.I. 1980. Neoplatonizm i manikheystvo Aleksandr iz Likopolya Simplikii. *Vestnik drevney istorii*, No. 3. Moscow.

SIMS-WILLIAMS, N. 1983. *Indian Elements in Parthian and Sogdian. Sprachen des Buddhismus in Zentralasien*. Wiesbaden.

STAVISKIY, B.J. 1986. *La Bactriane sous les Kushans. Problèmes d'histoire et de culture*. Paris.

SUNDERMANN, W. 1971*a*. Zur frühen missionärischen Wirksamkeit Manis. *AOH*, Vol. 24/1. Budapest.

——. 1971*b*. Weiteres zur frühen missionärischen Wirksamkeit Manis. *AOH*, Vol. 24/3. Budapest.

——. 1973. Mittelpersische und parthische kosmogonische und Parabeltexte des Manichäer. *Schriften zur Geschichte und Kultur des alten Orients. Berliner Turfantexte*, Vol. 4. Berlin.

——. 1974. Iranische Lebensschreibungen Manis. *AOH*, Vol. 36.

——. 1979. Namen von Göttern, Dämonen und Menschen in iranische Versionen des manichäischen Mythos. *Altorientalische Forschungen*, Vol. 6. Berlin.

——. 1980. Probleme der Interpretation manichäische-soghdischer Briefe. *Acta Ant. Hung.*, Vol. 28/1-4. Budapest.

——. 1981. Mitteliranische Manichäische Texte Kirchen-geschichtlichen Inhalts. *Schriften zur Geschichte und Kultur des alten Orients. Berliner Turfantexte*, Vol. 11. Berlin.

SUNDERMANN, W. 1988. Neue Erkenntnisse über mazdakitische Soziallehre. *Das Altertum,* Vol. 34/3.

VANDEN BERGHE, L. 1979. *Bibliographie analytique de l'archéologie de l'Iran ancien.* Leiden.

VAN TANGERLOO, A. 1982. La structure de la communauté manichéenne dans le Turkestan chinois à la lumière des emprunts moyen-iraniens en Ouigour. *Central Asiatic Journal,* Vol. 26. Wiesbaden.

WIDENGREN, G. 1961. *Mani und der Manichäismus.* Stuttgart.

——. 1983. Manichaeism and its Iranian Background. *The Cambridge History of Iran,* Vol. 3/2.

ZAEHNER, R.C. 1955. *Zurvan. A Zoroastrian Dilemma.* Oxford.

ZIEME, P. 1975. *Ein uigurischer Text über die Wirtschaft manichäischer Klöster im uigurischen Reich.* (Researches in Altaic Languages.) Ed. L. Ligeti. Budapest.

CHAPTER 18

AGRAVALA, V.S. 1970. Bhakti Cult in Ancient India. In: D.R. Sircar (ed.), *The Bhakti Cult in Ancient Indian Geography.* Calcutta.

ALTHEIM, J.P. 1961. *Geschichte der Hunnen,* Vol. 3. Berlin.

ASMUSSEN, J.P. 1965. Xᵘāstvānīft. Studies in Manichaeism. *Acta Theologica Danica,* Vol. 7. Copenhagen.

——. 1983. Christians in Iran. *The Cambridge History of Iran,* Vol. 3/2.

BAREAU, A. 1955. Les sectes bouddhiques du petit véhicule. *Publications de l'Ecole française d'Extrême-orient,* Vol. 38. Reprint, Paris 1973. Saigon.

BARTOLD, V.V. 1964. O khristianstve v Turkestane v domongol'skiy period. *Sochineniya,* Vol. 2/2. Moscow.

BELENITSKIY, A.M. 1954. Voprosy ideologii i kul'tov Sogda po materialam pyanjikentskikh khramov. *Zhivopis' Drevnego Pyanjikenta.* Moscow.

BELENITSKIY, A.M.; MARSHAK, B.I. 1976. Cherty mirovozreniya sogdiytsev VII-VIII vv. v iskusstve Penjikenta. In: B. Gafurov and B.A Litvinsky (eds.), *Istorya i kul'tura narodov Sredney Azii (drevnost' i sredniye veka).* Moscow.

BIRUNI, A. 1957. *Izbrannye proizvedeniya,* Vol. 1. *Pamyatniki minuvschih pokoleniy.* Tashkent.

Buddiyskie pamyatniki Kara-tepe v Starom Termeze. 1982. Ed. B.J. Staviskiy. Moscow.

CHAVANNES, E. 1903. *Documents sur les Tou-kiue (Turcs) occidentaux. Recueillis et commentés, suivi de notes additionnelles. (Présenté à l'Accadémie Impériale dei Sciences de St-Pétersbourg le 23 Août 1900.)* St Petersburg.

CONZE, E. 1977. In: L. Lancaster (ed.), Prajñāpāmaritā and Related Systems: Studies in Honour of Edward Conze. *Berkeley Buddhist Studies Series,* Vol. 1.

EDGERTON, F. 1953. *Buddhist Hybrid Sanskrit Grammar and Dictionary,* Vol. 1 (grammar); Vol. 2 (dictionary). New Haven.

EMMERICK, R.E. 1992. *A Guide to the Literature of Khotan,* 2nd ed., thoroughly revised and enlarged. The International Institute for Buddhist Studies. Tokyo.

ENOKI, K. 1964. The Nestorian Christianism in China in Mediaeval Time According to Recent Historical and Archaeological Researches. *Accademia Nazionale dei Lincei,* Vol. 62. Rome.

FISCHER, K. 1957. Neue Funde und Forschungen zur indischen Kunst in Arachosien, Baktrien und Gandhara. *Archäologischer Anzeiger*. Berlin.

FUSSMAN, G. 1989. Dialectes dans les litératures indo-aryennes. *Publications de l'Institut de civilisation indienne*, 8th Series, fasc. 55, pp. 433-501.

GABAIN, A. VON. 1973. *Das Leben im uigurischen Königreich von Qočo (850-1250)*, Vols. I-II. Veröffentlichungen der Societas Uralo-Altaica Bd. 6. Wiesbaden.

GAFUROV, B.G. 1972. *Tajiki. Drevneyshaya, drevnyaya i srednevekovaya istoriya*. B.A. Litvinsky (ed.). Moscow.

GREK T.V. 1964. Indiyskie nadpisi na keramike iz Kara-tepe. In: B.Y. Staviskiy (ed.), *Kara-Tepe I*, pp. 62-81.

——. 1972. Novye indiyskie nadpisi iz raskopok Kara-tepe. In: B.Y. Staviskiy (ed.), *Kara-Tepe III*, pp. 114-17.

HAMILTON J. 1986. *Manuscrits ouïgours du IXe-Xe siècle de Touen-houang*, Vols. I-II. Paris.

HANSEN, O. 1968. Die buddhistische und christliche Literatur der Soghder. *Handbuch der Orientalistik*, 4/2. Leiden/Cologne.

HARMATTA J. 1969. Interpretatsii nadpisey na keramike iz Kara-tepe. In: B.Y. Staviskiy (ed.), *Kara-Tepe II*.

HENNING, W. A. 1965. Sogdian God. *BSOAS*, Vol. 28/2.

HERZFELD, E. 1932. Sakastān. *Archäologische Mitteilungen aus Iran*, Vol. 4. Berlin.

HINÜBER, O. 1979. Die Erforschung der Gilgit-Handschriften (Funde buddhistischer Sanskrit-Handschriften). *Nachrichten der Akademie der Wissenschaften in Göttingen, 1. Philologische-historische Klasse*, Nos. 3-34, pp. 338-50. Göttingen.

HUI-LI. 1959. *The Life of Hsuan-tsang*. Compiled by the monk Hui-li. Peking.

HUMBACH, H. 1975. Vayu, Śiva und der Spiritus Vivens in östiranischen Synkretismus. Monumentum H.S. Hyberg, I. *Acta Iranica*, Vol. 4.

Kara-tepe I. 1964. GREK, T.V.; STAVISKIY, B.Y.; PSHELINA, E.G. *Kara-tepe-buddiyskiy peshcherniy monastyr' v Starom Termeze*. Moscow.

Kara-tepe II. Buddiyskie peshchery Kara-tepe v Starom Termeze. 1969. B.Y. Staviskiy (ed.). Moscow.

Kara-tepe III. Buddiyskiy kul'toviy tsenter Kara-tepe v Starom Termeze. 1972. B.Y. Staviskiy (ed.). Moscow.

KLYASHTORNY, S.G. 1981. Mifologicheskie syuzhety v drevnetyurkskikh pamyatnikakh. *Tyurkologicheskiy Sbornik*, 1977. Moscow.

——. 1992. Pamyatniki drevnetyurkoy pis'mennosti. In: B.A. Litvinsky (ed.), *Vostochniy Turkestan v drevnosti i v rannem srednevekovye*, Vol. 2, pp. 326-69. Moscow.

KRUGLIKOVA, I.T. 1976. Nastennye rospisi Dilberjina. In: *Drevnyaya Baktriya*, Vol. 1. (*Materialy Sovetsko-Afganoskoy ekspeditsii 1969-1973 gg.*) Moscow.

KUWAYAMA, S. 1976. The Turki Śāhis and Relevant Brahmanical Sculptures in Afghanistan. *EW*, Vol. 26/3-4.

KYCHANOV, E.I. 1978. Siriyskoe nestorianstvo v Kitae i Tsentral'noy Azii. *Palestinskiy Sbornik*, Vol. 26 (89). Leningrad.

LAMOTTE, E. 1958. *Histoire du bouddhisme indien*. Louvain.

LANCASTER, L. (ed.). 1977. Prajñāpāramitā and Related Systems: Studies in Honour of Edward Conze. *Berkeley Buddhist Studies Series*, Vol. 1.

LAUFER, B. 1907. Zur buddhistischen Literatur der Uiguren. *TP*, 2nd Series, Vol. 8.

LITVINSKY, B.A. 1971. Ajina Tepa i istorya buddizma v Sredney Azii. In: B.A. Litvinsky and T.I. Zeimal, *Ajina Tepa, arkhitektura, zhivopis, skul'ptura.* Moscow.

——. 1992. Buddizm. In: B.A. Litvinsky (ed.), *Vostochniy Turkestan v drevnosti i rannem srednevekov'e. Etnos. Yazyki. Religii.* Moscow.

LITVINSKY, B.A.; SMAGINA, E.B. 1992. Manikheiystvo. In: B.A. Litvinsky (ed.), *Vostochiy Turkestan v drenosti i rannem sredeveko'e. Etnos. Yazyki. Religii.* Moscow.

MAJUMDAR, B.K. 1970. Emergence of the Bhakti Cult: Early History of Viṣṇavism in Bengal. In: D.C. Sircar (ed.), *The Bhakti Cult and Ancient Indian Geography.* Calcutta.

MALOV, S.E. 1951. *Pamyatniki drevnetyurkskoy pis'mennosti. Teksty i issledovaniya.* Moscow/Leningrad.

MARQUART, J. 1961. *Osteuropäische und ostasiatische Streifzüge.* Reprint. Darmstadt.

MINGANA, A. 1925. The Early Spread of Christianity in Central Asia and the Far East: A New Document. *Bulletin of the John Rylands Library*, Vol. 9/2. Manchester.

NARSHAKHI. 1954. *The History of Bukhara.* Translated by R. Frye. Cambridge, Mass.

NEKLYUDOV, S.Y. 1981. Mifologya tyurkskikh i mongol'skikh narodov. Problemy vzaimosvyazey. *Tyurkologicheskiy Sbornik.* Moscow.

NIKITIN, A.B. 1984. Khristianstvo v Tsentral'noy Azii (drevnost' i srednevekov'e). In: B.A. Litvinsky (ed.), *Vostochniy Turkestan i Srednyaya Aziya.* Moscow.

——. 1992. *Khristyanstvo.* In: B.A. Litvinsky (ed.), *Vostochniy Turkestan v drevnosti i rannem srednevekov'e. Etnos. Yazyki. Religii.* Moscow.

NÖLDEKE, T.; TABARI. 1973. *Geschichte der Perser und Araber zur Zeit der Sasaniden. Aus der arabischen Chronik des Tabari übersetzt und mit ausführlichen Erläuterungen und Ergänzungen versehn von T. Nöldeke.* Reprint. Leiden.

Novye nakhodki na Kara-tepe v Starom Termeze. 1975. Ed. B.Y. Staviskiy. Moscow.

PAYKOVA, A.V. 1979. The Syrian Ostracon from Panjikant. *Le Muséon*, Vol. 92/1-2.

PAYKOVA, A.V.; MARSHAK, B.I. 1976. Siriyskaya nadpis' iz Penjikenta. *Kratkie Soobshcheniya Institua Arkheologii*, Vol. 147. Moscow.

PIGULEVSKAYA, N.V. 1946. *Vizantya i Iran na rubezhe VI i VII vekov.* Moscow/Leningrad.

——. 1979. *Kul'tura siriytsev v srednie veka.* Moscow.

POTAPOV, L.P. 1978. K voprosu o drevnetyurkskoy osnove i datirovke altayskogo shamanstva. *Etnografya narodov Altaya i Zapadnoy Sibiri.* Novosibirsk.

RADLOFF, W. 1911. *Kuan-ši-im Pusar. Eine türkische Übersetzung des XXV Kapitels der chinesischen Ausgabe des Saddharmapuṇḍarikā.* St Petersburg.

RINTCHEN, B. 1959, 1961, 1975. *Les matériaux pour l'étude du chamanisme mongol*, Vols. 1-3. Wiesbaden.

ROSENFIELD, J. 1967. *The Dynastic Arts of the Kushans.* Berkeley/Los Angeles.

ROUX, J.-P. 1956-57. Tängri. Essai sur le Ciel-Dieu des peuples altaïques. *Revue de l'histoire des religions*, Vol. 161/1-2; Vol. 150/1-2.

——. 1962. La religion des turcs de l'Orkhon des VIIe et VIIIe siècles. *Revue de l'histoire des religions*, Vol. 161/1-2.

Rukopisnaya kniga v kulture narodov Vostoka. 1988. Book 2. Moscow.

SACHAU, E. 1915. *Die Chronik von Arbels.* Berlin.

——. 1919. *Zur Ausbreitung des Christentums in Asien.* Berlin.

SPULER, B. 1961. Die nestorianische Kirche. In: *Handbuch der Orientalistik*, 1, 8, 2. Leiden/Cologne.

STAVISKIY, B.J. 1963. Srednyaya Aziya, India, Rim (k voprosu mezhdunarodnykh svyazyakh v kushanskiy period. In: *India v drevnosti*. Moscow.

Symposien zur Buddhismusforschung II. 1980. Die Sprache der ältesten buddhistischen Überlieferung. *(Abhandlungen der Akademie der Wissenschaften in Göttingen, Philologisch-historische Klasse)*, Vol. 117. Göttingen.

Symposien zur Buddhismusforschung 3, 1, 2. 1987. Zur Schulzugehörigkeit von Sanskrit-Werken der Hīnayāna-Literatur. *(Abhandlungen der Akademie der Wissenschaften in Göttingen, Philologisch-historiche Klasse*, Vol. 149/2). Göttingen.

TARN, W.W. 1951. *The Greeks in Baktria and India*, 2nd ed. Cambridge.

TUCCI, G.; HEISSIG, W. 1970. *Die religionen Tibets und der Mongolei*. Stuttgart.

VERTOGRADOVA, V.V. 1983. *Indian Inscriptions and Inscriptions in Unknown Lettering from Kara-Tepe in Old Termez*. Moscow.

VOROBYOVA-DESYATOVSKAYA, M.I. 1983. Pamyatniki pis'mom kharoshthi i brakhmi iz Sovetskoy Sredney Azii. In: *Istoriya i kul'tura Tsentralnoy Azii*, pp. 22-96. Moscow, Nauka.

WINTER, W. 1984. *Studia Tocharica. Selected Writings*. Poznan.

WITTFOGEL, K.; FÊNG CHIA-SHÊNG. 1949. *History of Chinese Society, Liao (907-1125)*. Philadelphia.

ZHUKOVSKAYA, N.L. 1977. *Lamaism i rannie formy religii*. Moscow.

ZÜRCHER, E. 1959. *The Buddhist Conquest of China. The Spread and Adaptation of Buddhism in Early Medieval China*, Vol. 1 (text). (Sinica Leidensia, Vol. 11.) Leiden.

CHAPTER 19

AINI, S. 1944. *Is'ëni Mukanna'*. Stalinabad.

AL-BALADHURI. 1866. *Liber Expugnationis Regionum, auctore Imâmo Ahmed ibn Jahjâ ibn Djâbir al-Belâdsorî*, Vol. 8, pp. 228-539. Lugduni Batavorum.

BALL, W.; GARDIN, J.-C. 1982. *Archaeological Gazetteer of Afghanistan*, Vols. 1-2. Paris.

BARTHOLD, W.; ALLCHIN, F.R. 1960. Bāmiyān. *Encyclopaedia of Islam*, new ed., Vol. 1, pp. 1,009-10. Leiden/London.

BELENITSKIY, A.M.; RASPOPOVA, V.I. 1971. *Drevniy Penjikent*. Dushanbe.

BOLSHAKOV, O.G. 1976. Khronologiya vosstaniya Mukanny. In: B.G. Gafurov, B.A. Litvinsky (eds.), *Istoriya i kultura narodov Sredney Azii*. Moscow.

BOSWORTH, C.E. 1968. Sīstān under the Arabs: From the Islamic Conquest to the Rise of the Saffārids (30-250/651-864). *IsMEO*, Vol. 11.

——. 1974. Kābul. *Encyclopaedia of Islam*, new ed., Vol. 4, fasc. 65-6, pp. 356-7. Leiden.

——. 1976. Kandahār. *Encyclopaedia of Islam*, new ed., Vol. 4, fasc. 71-2, p. 559. Leiden.

AL-DINAWARI, H. 1888. *Kitāb al-Akhbār aṭ-ṭiwal*. Leiden.

FRYE, R.N. 1963. *The Heritage of Persia*. Cleveland/New York.

——. 1975. *The Golden Age of Persia. The Arabs in the East*. London.

GAFUROV, B.G. 1972. *Tajiki. Drevneyshaya, drevnyaya i srednevekovaya istoriya*. B.A. Litvinsky (ed.). Moscow.

GAUBE, H. 1973. *Arabosasanidische Numismatik*. Brunswick.

GIBB, H.A.R. 1923. *The Arab Conquests in Central Asia.* New York.

GÖBL, R. 1967. *Dokumente zur Geschichte des iranischen Hunnen in Baktrien und Indien,* Vol. 1/4. Wiesbaden.

HAIG, T.W. 1934. Sind. *Encyclopaedia of Islam,* Vol. 4, pp. 433-5. Leiden/London.

HARMATTA, J. 1982. La médaille de Jeb Šāhānšāh. *Studia Iranica,* Vol. 11, pp. 167-80. Leiden.

IBN AL-ATHIR. 1851-76. *Chronicon quod perfectissimum inscribitur.* Ed. C.J. Tornberg, Vols. 1-14. Lugduni Batavorum.

ISAKOV, A. 1982. *Panjakenti kadim.* Dushanbe.

Istoriya Tajikskogo naroda. 1964. Vol. 2, Book 1. Moscow.

Istorya Uzbekskoy SSR. 1955. Vol. 1, Book 1. (AN Uzbekskoy SSR.) Tashkent.

JALILOV, A. 1961. *Sogd nakanune arabskogo nashchestvya i bor'ba sogdiytsev protiv arabskih zavoevateley v pervoy polovine VIII v.* (AN Tajikskoy SSR). Stalinabad.

JALILOV, A.; NEGMATOV, N. 1969. *Kashfiëti Panjakenti kadim.* Dushanbe.

KADYROVA, T. 1965. *Iz istorii krest'yanskikh vosstaniy v Maverannakhre i Khorasane v VII-nachale IX vv.* Tashkent.

KOLESNIKOV, A.I. 1970. Iran v nachale VII veka. *Palestinskiy Sbornik,* Vol. 22, 85. Leningrad.

——. 1982. *Zavoevanie Irana arabami.* Moscow.

AL-KUFI, M. A. 1968-75. *Kitābu'l Futūh,* Vols. 1-8. Hyderabad.

NARSHAKHI, M. 1897. *Istoriya Bukhary.* Trans. N. Lykoshina. Tashkent.

NÖLDEKE, T.; TABARI. 1973. *Geschichte der Perser und Araber zur Zeit der Sasaniden. Aus der arabischen Chronik des Tabari übersetzt und mit ausführlichen Erläuterungen und Ergänzungen versehn von T. Nöldeke.* Reprint. Leiden.

QUMMI, H. M. 1934. *Tārikh-i Qumm.* Ed. J. Tihrani. Tehran.

SADIGHI, G. 1938. *Les mouvements religieux iraniens au IIe et IIIe siècles de l'Hégire.* Paris.

SHABAN, M.A. n.d. Khurāsān at the Time of the Arab Conquest. In: *Iran and Islam in Memory of the Late V. Minorsky.* Edinburgh.

Sogdiyskie dokumenty s gory Mug. 1962. Vol. 1. Reading, translation and commentaries by A.A. Freiman. Moscow.

——. 1962. Vol. 2. Reading, translation and commentaries by V.A. Livshits. Moscow.

——. 1963. Vol. 3. Reading, translation and commentaries by M.N. Bogolyubov and O.I. Smirnova. Moscow.

AL-TABARI. 1879-89. *Annales quos scripsit Abu Djafar Mohamed ibn Djarir al-Tabari, cum aliis.* Vols. 1-6. Lugduni Batavorum.

WALKER, J. 1941. *A Catalogue of the Arab-Sāsānian Coins.* London.

YAKUBOVSKIY, A. Y. 1948. *Vosstanie Mukanny – dvizhenie lyudey v 'belykh odezhdakh',* pp. 34-54. Moscow/Leningrad.

YUSUF, S.M. 1945. The Battle of Al-Qadisiyya. *Islamic Culture,* Vol. 19, pp. 1-28. Hyderabad.

ZARRINKUB, H. 1975. The Arab Conquest of Iran and its Aftermath. *The Cambridge History of Iran,* Vol. 4.

CHAPTER 20

AL'BAUM, L.I. 1966. *Balalyk-tepe. K istorii material'noy kul'tury i iskusstva Tokharistana.* Tashkent.

——. 1975. *Zhivopis' Afrasiaba.* Tashkent.

ANDRIANOV, B.V. 1969. *Drevnie orositel'nye sistemy Priaral'ya (v svyazi s istoriey vozniknovenya i razvitiya oroschaemogo zemledelya).* Moscow.

BAILEY, H.W. 1960. Māᶜhyāra. *Bulletin of the Deccan College Research Institute*, Vol. 20/1-4. Poona.

BARTOLD, V.V. 1971*a*. Persidskaya shchu'ubiya i sovremennaya nauka. In: V.V. Bartold, *Sochineniya*, Vol. 7. Moscow.

——. 1971*b*. K istorii persidskogo êposa. In: V.V. Bartold, *Sochineniya*, Vol. 7. Moscow.

BELENITSKIY, A.M. 1973. *Monumental'noe iskusstvo Penjikenta.* Moscow.

BELENITSKIY, A.M.; BENTOVICH, I.B.; BOLSHAKOV, O.G. 1973. *Srednevekoviy gorod Sredney Azii.* Leningrad.

BELENITSKIY, A.M.; MARSHAK, B.I.; RASPOPOVA, V.I. 1973. Sogdiyskiy gorod v nachale srednikh vekov. *SA*, Vol. 2.

——. 1980. K kharakteristike tovarno-denezhnykh otnoshcheniy v rannesrednevekovom Sogde. In: *Blizhniy i Sredniy Vostok. Tovarno-denezhnye otnosheniya pri feodalizme.* Moscow.

BIRUNI, A. 1957. *Pamyatniki minuvshikh pokoleniy.* Tashkent.

CHRISTENSEN, A. 1925. *Le règne du roi Kawadh I et le communisme mazdakite.* Copenhagen.

——. 1944. *L'Iran sous les Sassanides.* Copenhagen.

CHUGUEVSKIY, L.I. 1983. *Kitayskie dokumenty iz Dun'khuana*, Vol. 1. Moscow.

DAVIDOVICH, E.A.; LITVINSKY, B.A. 1955. *Arkhelogicheskiy ocherk Isfarinskogo rayona.* Stalinabad.

DAVIDOVICH, E.A.; ZEIMAL, E.V. 1980. Denezhnoe khozyaystvo Sredney Azii v perekhodniy period ot drevnosti k srednevekov'yu (k tipologii feodalizma). In: *Blizhniy i Sredniy Vostok. Tovarno-denezhnye otnoshcheniya pri feodalizme.* Moscow.

EMMERICK, R.E. 1967. Tibetan Texts Concerning Khotan. *London Oriental Series*, Vol. 19.

GAFUROV, B.G. 1972. *Tajiki. Drevneyshaya, drevnyaya i srednevekovaya istoriya.* Ed. B.A. Litvinsky. Moscow.

GAULIER, S.; JERA-BEZARD, R.; MAILLARD, M. 1976. Buddhism in Afghanistan and Central Asia, 1-2. *Iconography of Religions*, Vol. 13/14. Leiden.

GILES, L. 1935. Dated Chinese Manuscripts in the Stein Collections. *BSOAS*, Vol. 7, Part 4. London.

GIMARET, D. 1970. Bouddha et les bouddhistes dans la tradition musulmane, note 5. *JA*, Vol. 257/3-4, pp. 273-315.

GRABAR, O. 1973. *The Formation of Islamic Art.* New Haven/London.

HERRMAN, A. 1938. *Das Land der Seide und Tibet in Lichte der Antike.* Leipzig.

HIRTH, F. 1885. *China and the Roman Orient: Research into their Ancient and Mediaeval Relations as Represented in Old Chinese Records.* Leipzig/Munich/Shanghai/Hong Kong.

The History of Bukhara. 1954. Trans. from a Persian abridgement of the Arabic original by Narshakhi by R.N. Frye. Cambridge, Mass.

HUI-LI. 1959. *The Life of Hsuan-Tsang*. Compiled by the monk Hui-li. Peking.

HULSEWÉ, A.F.P.; LOEWE, M.A.N. 1979. *China in Central Asia. The Early Stage: 125 B.C. - 23 A.D.* Leiden.

LITVINSKY, B.A. 1968. *Outline History of Buddhism in Central Asia*. Moscow.

——. 1978. Orudya truda i utvar' iz mogil'nikov Zapadnoy Fergany. (Arkheologicheskie i etnograficheskie materialy po istorii kul'tury i religii Sredney Azii.) *Mogil'niki Zapadnoy Fergany*, Vol. 4. Moscow.

——. 1980. Domusul'manskie istoki sredneaziatskoy tsivilizatsii X-XI vv. In: *Istoriya i kul'tura êpokhi Abu Ali ibn Sino*. Dushanbe.

——. 1984. Istoricheskie sud'by Vostochnogo Turkestana i Sredney Azii (problemy etnokul'turnoy obshchnosti). In: B.A. Litvinsky (ed.), *Vostochniy Turkestan i Srednyaya Aziya. Istoriya, Kul'tura, Svyazi*. Moscow.

——. (ed.) 1992. Buddizm. *Vostochniy Turkestan v drevnosti i rannem srednevekov'e. Etnos. Yazyki. Religii*. Moscow.

——. (ed.) 1995. *Vostochniy Turkestan v drevnosti i rannem srednevekov'e. Khozyaystvo. Material'naya kul'tura*. Moscow.

LITVINSKY, B.A.; SOLOV'EV, V.S. 1985. *Problemy istorii i kul'tury srednevekovogo Tokharistana (v svete raskopok v Vakhshskoy doline)*. Moscow.

LITVINSKY, B.A.; ZEIMAL, T.I. 1971. *Ajina-Tepa. Arkhitektura. Zhivopis Skul'ptura*. Moscow.

LIU MAU-TSAI. 1969. *Kutscha und seine Beziehungen zu China vom 2. Jh. v. Chr. bis zum 6. Jh. u. Chr*, Vols. 1-2. Wiesbaden.

LIVSHITS, V.A. 1962. Yuridicheskie dokumenty i pis'ma. Reading, translation and commentaries by V.A. Livshits. *Sogdyskie dokumenty s gory Mug*, Vol. 2. Moscow.

——. 1984. Dokumenty. In: Toprak-kala. Dvorets. In: Y.A. Rapoport and E.E. Nerazik. *Trudy Khorezmskoy arkheologo-etnograficheskoy ekspeditsii*, Vol. 14. Moscow.

LUBO-LESNICHENKO, E.I. 1984. Mogil'nik Astana. In: B.A. Litvinsky (ed.), *Vostochniy Turkestan i Srednyaya Aziya. Istoriya, Kul'tura, Svyazi*. Moscow.

LÜDERS, H. 1911. Bruchstücke buddhistischer Dramen. *Koniglich-Preussische Turfan Expeditionen. Kleinere Sanskrittexte*, Vol. 1. Berlin.

LUKONIN, V.G. 1983. Political, Social, Administrative Institutions: Taxes and Trade. *The Cambridge History of Iran*, Vol. 3/2.

MAILLARD, M. 1983. *Grottes et monuments d'Asie centrale suivi d'un tableau de concordance des grottes de la région de Kutcha*. Paris.

MANDEL'SHTAM, A.M. 1954. K voprosu o znacheniy termina 'chakir'. *Izvestiya Otdeleniya obshchestvennykh nauk Akademii nauk Tajikskoy SSR*. Stalinabad.

MELIKIAN-CHIRVANI, A.S. 1974. L'évocation littéraire du bouddhisme dans l'Iran musulman. In: *Le monde iranien et l'Islam*, Vol. 2. Geneva.

MORAVCSIK, G. 1958. *Byzantinoturcica. Die byzantinischen Quellen der Geschichte des Türkvölker*, Vols. 1-2, 2nd edn. Berlin.

NEEDHAM, J. (ed.). 1985. *Science and Civilization in China*, Vol. 5, Part 1, pp. 296-7. Paper and Printing by Chian Tsun-hsung. Cambridge.

NERAZIK, E.E. 1966. *Sel'skie poseleniya afrigidskogo Khorezma*. Moscow.

——. 1976. Sel'skoe zhilishche v Khorezme (I-XIV vv). *Iz istorii zhilishcha i sem'i: Arkheologo-etnograficheskie ocherki.* Moscow.

NILSEN, E.A. 1966. *Stanovlenie feodal'noy arkhitektury Sredney Azii (V-VIII vv).* Tashkent.

NÖLDEKE, T. 1920. *Das iranische Nationalepos.* 2nd edn. Berlin/Leipzig.

NÖLDEKE, T.; TABARI. 1973. *Geschichte der Perser und Araber zur Zeit der Sasaniden. Aus der arabischen Chronik des Tabari übersetzt und mit ausführlichen Erläuterungen und Ergänzungen versehn von T. Nöldeke.* Note 6. Reprinted. Leiden.

PERIKHANYAN, A.G. 1973. *Sasanidskiy sudebnik. 'Kniga tysyachi sudebnykh reshcheniy' (Mātakdān i hazār dātastan).* Erevan.

——. 1983a. *Obschchestvo i pravo Irana v parfyanskiy i sasanidskiy periody.* Moscow.

——. 1983b. Iranian Society and Law. *The Cambridge History of Iran*, Vol. 3/2.

PIGULEVSKAYA, N.V. 1940. Mesopotamia na rubezhe V-VI vv. n.ê. *Trudy Instituta vostokovedeniya*, Vol. 31. Moscow/Leningrad.

ROWLAND, B. 1974. *The Art of Central Asia.* New York.

SCHAFER, E.H. 1963. *The Golden Peaches of Samarkand. A Study of T'ang Exotics.* Berkeley/Los Angeles.

SHIRATORI, K. 1956a. A New Attempt of the Solution of the Fu-lin Problem. *MRDTB*, Vol. 15.

——. 1956b. The Geography of the Western Region. *MRDTB*, Vol. 15.

SMIRNOVA, O.I. 1957. Iz istorii arabskikh zavoevaniy v Sredney Azii. *Sovetskoye vostokovedenie*, No. 2. Moscow.

——. 1960. K istorii samarkandskogo dogovora 712 g. *Kratkie soobshcheniya Instituta Vostokovedenyiya*, Vol. 38. Moscow/Leningrad.

——. 1963. *Katalog monet s gorodishcha Penjikent (materialy 1949-1956 gg).* Moscow.

——. 1981. *Svodniy katalog sogdiyskikh monet. Bronza.* Moscow.

SOLODUKHO, J.A. 1956. K voprosu o sotsial'noy strukture Iraka v III-V vv. n.ê. *Uchenye zapiski Instituta Vostokovedeniya AN SSSR*, Vol. 14, note 3.

STEIN, M.A. 1975. *Ancient Khotan.* New York.

TUCCI, J.; HEISSIG, W. 1970. *Die Religionen Tibets und der Mongolei.* Stuttgart.

VAYNBERG, B.I. 1977. *Monety Drevnego Khorezma.* Moscow.

WITTHOFEL, K; FÊNG CHIA-SHÊNG. 1949. *History of Chinese Society Liao (907-1125).* Philadelphia.

INDEX

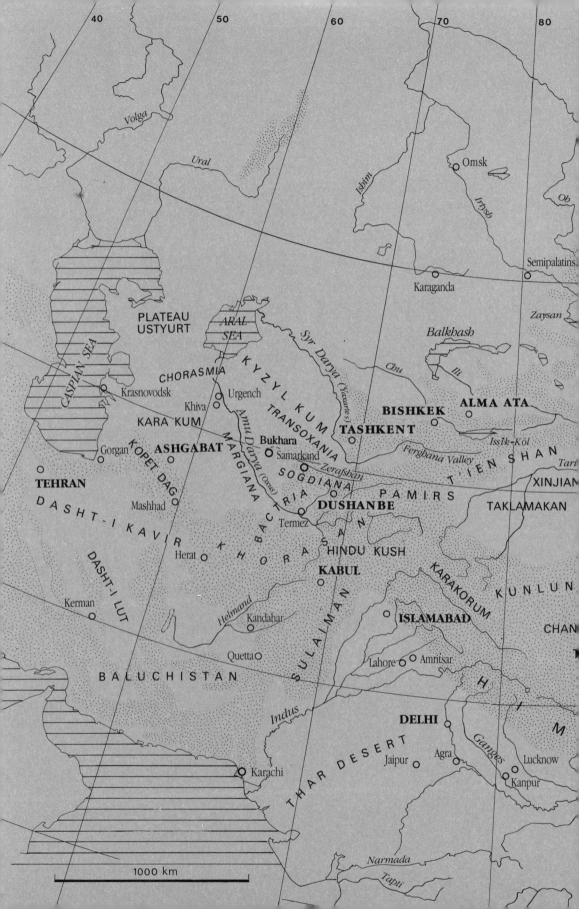